Praise for
The Last Days of the Incas

"This is a wonderful book about one of the most epic struggles of history, a conquest that transformed a continent."

—Wade Davis, Anthropologist and Explorer-in-Residence, National Geographic Society, and author of *One River*

"A colorful, superbly crafted historical narrative that masterfully demonstrates that when cultures collide, unforeseen and tragic consequences follow. . . . also a memorable adventure story, revealing the modern Indiana Jones–type characters that unearthed, and continue to discover, lost parts of the Inca Empire. *The Last Days of the Incas* is historical writing at its best."

—Broughton Coburn, author of *Everest: Mountain Without Mercy*

"*The Last Days of the Incas* surprises, delivers history, and reads like a great yarn. I've read yards of books on the Incas, but this one took me out of the classroom and into that long-lost world."

—Keith Bellows, Editor-in-Chief, *National Geographic Traveler*

"The story of the European conquest of the fascinating and fabulously rich empire of the Incas is one of history's most engaging and tragic episodes. . . . Thanks to *The Last Days of the Incas*, Kim MacQuarrie's superbly written new treatment of the subject, it is now accessible to the much broader audience it deserves."

—Vincent Lee, author of *Forgotten Vilcabamba*

"Thrillingly informative. . . . In addition to writing rousing and clear-eyed battle accounts and describing the Incas' early form of guerrilla warfare, MacQuarrie also manages to spin the oft-told story of the discovery of Machu Picchu into narrative gold. (A-)"

—Gilbert Cruz, *Entertainment Weekly*

"Lively and dramatic."

—Jonathan Yardley, *The Washington Post*

"Thoroughly and entertainingly recounted. . . . MacQuarrie excels in his depiction of this guerilla war, giving the lost city the honor it deserves."
—Jonathan Keats, *Forbes*

"With vivid and energetic prose, Emmy Award–winner and author MacQuarrie re-creates the 16th-century struggle for what would become modern-day Peru. . . . and the tale of digging up the empire is riveting."
—*Publishers Weekly* (starred review)

"A first-rate reference work of ambitious scope that will most likely stand as the definitive account of these people."
—*Booklist*

"Enthralling."
—Allen Pierleoni, *Sacramento Bee*

"A delightful, eminently readable account. . . . *The Last Days of the Incas* reads like a novel."
—Jules Wagman, *The St. Petersburg Times*

"Fascinating and enthralling. . . . the direct narrative brings alive people who existed 500 years ago. Truly a work worth Inca gold."
—*The History Magazine* (U.K.)

"Meticulous research and compelling storytelling."
—*National Geographic Traveler*

ALSO BY KIM MACQUARRIE

*Gold of the Andes: The Llamas, Alpacas, Vicuñas
and Guanacos of South America*

*Peru's Amazonian Eden: Manu National Park
and Biosphere Reserve*

Where the Andes Meet the Amazon

THE LAST DAYS
OF THE INCAS

Kim MacQuarrie

Simon & Schuster Paperbacks

NEW YORK LONDON TORONTO SYDNEY

SIMON & SCHUSTER PAPERBACKS
A Division of Simon & Schuster, Inc.
1230 Avenue of the Americas
New York, NY 10020

First Simon & Schuster trade paperback edition June 2008

SIMON & SCHUSTER PAPERBACKS and colophon are registered trademarks
of Simon & Schuster, Inc.

For information about special discounts for bulk purchases,
please contact Simon & Schuster Special Sales at
1-800-456-6798 or business@simonandschuster.com

Designed by Paul Dippolito

Manufactured in the United States of America

15 17 19 20 18 16

The Library of Congress has cataloged the hardcover edition as follows:
MacQuarrie, Kim
The last days of the Incas / Kim MacQuarrie.
p.   cm.
Includes bibliographical references and index.
1. Peru—History—Conquest, 1522–1548.   2. Vilcabamba Site (Peru).   I. Title.
F3442.M33 2007
985'.02—dc22   2007061700
ISBN-13: 978-0-7432-6049-7
ISBN-10: 0-7432-6049-X
ISBN-13: 978-0-7432-6050-3 (pbk)
ISBN-10: 0-7432-6050-3 (pbk)

To my parents, Ron and Joanne MacQuarrie

LIST OF MAPS

❖

CONTENTS

❖

The Four Suyus
of the Inca Empire
circa 1530

Caribbean Sea

Panama City

Quito .... Equator

CHINCHAYSUYU

Tumbez

Amazon Basin

Cajamarca

ANTISUYU

Lima
(founded
1535)

Cuzco

Lake Titicaca

La Paz

CUNTISUYU

COLLASUYU

*Pacific
Ocean*

*Atlantic
Ocean*

Santiago
(founded 1541)

Buenos Aires
(founded 1536)

Patagonia

N

W   E

S

0   500 miles

0   500 kilometers

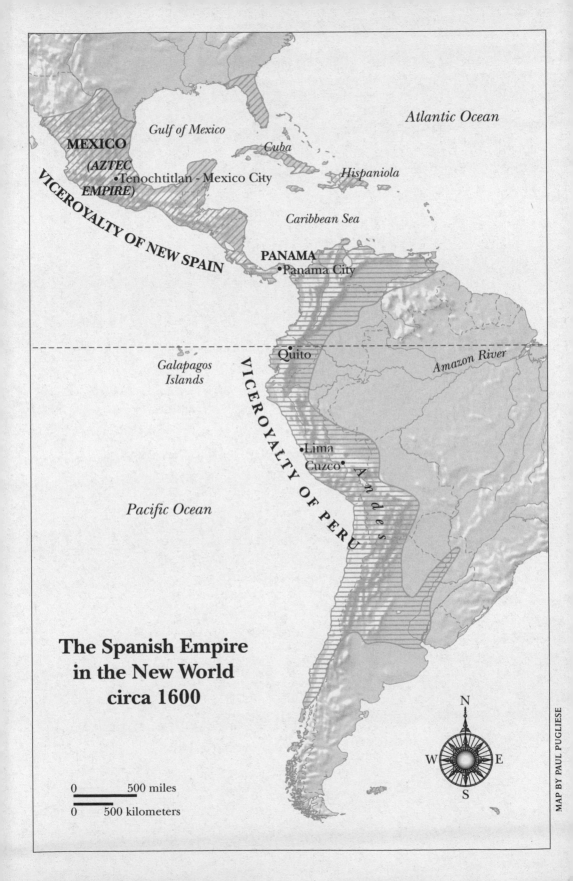

Atlantic Ocean

Gulf of Mexico

MEXICO
(AZTEC
•Tenochtitlan - Mexico City
EMPIRE)

Cuba

Hispaniola

VICEROYALTY OF NEW SPAIN

Caribbean Sea

PANAMA
•Panama City

•Quito

*Galapagos
Islands*

Amazon River

VICEROYALTY OF PERU

•Lima
Cuzco•

A n d e s

Pacific Ocean

**The Spanish Empire
in the New World
circa 1600**

N

W   E

S

MAP BY PAUL PUGLIESE

0   500 miles

0   500 kilometers

CHRONOLOGY OF EVENTS

❖

1492	Columbus lands in what is now called the Bahamas; this is the first of his four voyages to the New World.
1502	Francisco Pizarro arrives on the island of Hispaniola.
1502–1503	During his last voyage, Columbus explores the coasts of what will later be called Honduras, Nicaragua, Costa Rica, and Panama.
1513	Vasco Núñez de Balboa and Francisco Pizarro cross the Isthmus of Panama and discover the Pacific Ocean.
1516	The future Inca emperor Manco Inca is born.
1519–1521	Hernando Cortés conquers the Aztec Empire in Mexico.
1524–1525	Francisco Pizarro's first voyage heads south from Panama and explores along the coast of Colombia. The trip is a financial failure. Pizarro's colleague Diego de Almagro loses an eye in a battle with natives.
1526	Pizarro, Almagro, and Hernando de Luque form the Company of the Levant, a company dedicated to conquest.
1526–1527	Pizarro and Almagro's second voyage. Pizarro makes his first contact with the Inca Empire at Tumbez.
c. 1528	The Inca Emperor Huayna Capac dies from European-introduced smallpox. His death sets off a civil war between his sons Atahualpa and Huascar.
1528–1529	Pizarro journeys to Spain, where he is granted a license to conquer Peru by the queen.
1531–1532	Pizarro's third voyage to Peru. Pizarro captures Atahualpa.
1533	Atahualpa is executed; Almagro arrives; Pizarro captures Cuzco and installs seventeen-year-old Manco Inca as the new Inca emperor.
1535	Pizarro founds the city of Lima; Almagro leaves for Chile.
1536	Gonzalo Pizarro steals Manco Inca's wife, Cura Ocllo. Manco

rebels and surrounds Cuzco. Juan Pizarro is killed, and the Inca general Quizo Yupanqui attacks Lima.

1537   Almagro seizes Cuzco from Hernando and Gonzalo Pizarro. Rodrigo Orgóñez sacks Vitcos and captures Manco Inca's son, Titu Cusi. Manco escapes and flees to Vilcabamba, the new Inca capital.

1538   Hernando Pizarro executes Diego de Almagro.

1539   Gonzalo Pizarro invades and sacks Vilcabamba; Manco Inca escapes but Francisco Pizarro executes Manco's wife, Cura Ocllo.

1540   Hernando Pizarro begins a prison sentence of twenty years in Spain.

1541   Francisco Pizarro is murdered by supporters of Almagro. One of his assassins, Diego Méndez, flees to Vilcabamba.

1544   Manco Inca is murdered by Diego Méndez and six renegade Spaniards. Gonzalo Pizarro rebels against the king of Spain.

1548   Battle of Jaquijahuana; Gonzalo Pizarro is executed by representatives of the king.

1557   The Inca Emperor Sayri-Tupac leaves Vilcabamba and relocates near Cuzco.

1560   Sayri-Tupac dies. Titu Cusi becomes Inca emperor in Vilcabamba.

1570   The Augustinian friars García and Ortiz attempt to visit the capital of Vilcabamba; Titu Cusi refuses to allow them to enter. The friars burn the Inca shrine at Chuquipalta, and friar García is expelled.

1571   Titu Cusi dies; Tupac Amaru becomes emperor.

1572   The Viceroy of Peru, Francisco Toledo, declares war on Vilcabamba. Vilcabamba is sacked and Tupac Amaru—the final Inca emperor—is captured and executed in Cuzco.

1572   The Inca capital of Vilcabamba is abandoned; the Spaniards remove the inhabitants and relocate them to a new town they christen *San Francisco de la Victoria de Vilcabamba*.

1578   Hernando Pizarro dies in Spain at the age of 77.

1911   Hiram Bingham discovers ruins at Machu Picchu, Vitcos, and a place called Espíritu Pampa, which local Campa Indians refer to as "Vilcabamba." Bingham locates all three of these sites within four weeks.

1912   Bingham returns to Machu Picchu, this time with the sponsorship of the National Geographic Society—its first sponsored expedition.

1913   *National Geographic* dedicates an entire issue to Bingham's discovery of Machu Picchu.

1914–1915   Bingham's third and final trip to Machu Picchu. He discovers what is now called the "Inca Trail."

1920   Hiram Bingham publishes his book *Inca Land*, in which he states that Machu Picchu is actually the lost Inca city of Vilcabamba, the final refuge of the last Inca emperors.

1955   The American explorer/writer Victor von Hagen publishes *Highway of the Sun*, in which he argues that Machu Picchu cannot be Vilcabamba.

1957   Gene Savoy arrives in Peru.

1964–1965   Gene Savoy, Douglas Sharon, and Antonio Santander discover extensive ruins at Espíritu Pampa, which Savoy claims is the location of Vilcabamba the Old.

1970   Savoy publishes *Antisuyo*, an account of his explorations at Espíritu Pampa and elsewhere. Savoy leaves Peru and relocates to Reno, Nevada.

1982   Vincent Lee visits the Vilcabamba area while on a climbing trip.

1984   Vincent and Nancy Lee discover more than four hundred structures at Espíritu Pampa, confirming that it was the largest settlement in the Vilcabamba area and thus was undoubtedly the site of Manco Inca's capital of Vilcabamba—home of the last Inca emperors.

2002–2005   Peru's *Instituto Nacional de Cultura* (INC) conducts the first archaeological excavations at Vilcabamba.

THE LAST DAYS
OF THE INCAS

PREFACE

❖

NEARLY FIVE HUNDRED YEARS AGO, ROUGHLY ONE HUNDRED and sixty-eight Spaniards and a handful of their African and Indian slaves arrived in what is now Peru. They soon collided with an Inca empire ten million strong, smashing into it like a giant meteor and leaving remnants of that collision scattered all over the continent. The modern-day visitor to Peru, in fact, can still see the results of that collision almost everywhere: from the dark brown skins of the very poor to the generally lighter skins and aristocratic Spanish surnames of many of Peru's elite; from the spiked silhouettes of Catholic cathedrals and church spires to the presence of imported cattle and pigs and people of Spanish and African descent. The dominant language of Peru is also a forceful reminder. It is still referred to as *Castillano,* a name derived from the inhabitants of the ancient Spanish kingdom of Castile. The violent impact of the Spanish conquest, in fact—which nipped in the bud an empire that had existed for a mere ninety years—still reverberates through every layer of Peruvian society, whether that society exists on the coast, or in the high Andes, or even down among the handful of uncontacted indigenous tribes that still roam Peru's Upper Amazon.

Determining precisely what happened before and during the Spanish conquest, however, is not an easy task. Many of the people who actually witnessed the event were ultimately killed by it. Only a handful of those who survived actually left records of what occurred—and not surprisingly most of those were written by Spaniards. The literate Spaniards who arrived in Peru (only about 30 percent of Spaniards were literate in the sixteenth century) brought with them the alphabet, a powerful, carefully honed tool that had been invented over three thousand years earlier in Egypt. The Incas, by contrast, kept track of their histories via specialized oral histories, genealogies, and possibly via *quipus*—strings of carefully tied and colored knots that held abundant numerical data and that were also used as memory

I

prompts. In a relatively short period of time after the conquest, however, knowledge of how to read the *quipus* was lost, the historians died out or were killed, and Inca history gradually grew fainter with each passing generation.

"History is written by the victors," the adage goes, and indeed, this was as true for the Incas as it was for the Spaniards. The Incas had created an empire 2,500 miles long, after all, and had subjugated most of the people within it. Like many imperial powers, their histories tended to justify and glorify both their own conquests and their rulers, and to belittle those of their enemies. The Incas told the Spaniards that it was they, the Incas, who had brought civilization to the region, and that their conquests were inspired and sanctioned by the gods. The truth, however, was otherwise: the Incas had actually been preceded by more than a thousand years of various kingdoms and empires. Inca oral history was thus a combination of facts, myths, religion, and propaganda. Even within the Inca elite, divided as they often were by different and competitive lineages, histories could vary. As a result, early Spanish chroniclers recorded more than *fifty* different variations of Inca history, depending upon whom they interviewed.

The record of what actually occurred during the conquest is also skewed by the sheer disparity of what has come down to us; although we now have perhaps thirty contemporaneous Spanish reports of various events that occurred during and within fifty years of the initial conquest, we have only *three* major native or half-native reports during that same time period (Titu Cusi, Felipe Huamán Poma de Ayala, and Garcilaso de la Vega). None of these three chronicles, however, were written by native authors who had personally witnessed any of the events during the critical first five years of the conquest. One of the earliest of these sources, in fact—a report dictated by the Inca emperor Titu Cusi to visiting Spaniards—dates from 1570, nearly forty years *after* the capture of his great uncle, the Inca emperor Atahualpa. Thus, in trying to determine who did what and to whom, the modern writer encounters a historical record that is inevitably biased: on the one hand we have a pile of Spanish letters and reports and on the other we have only three indigenous chronicles, with perhaps the most famous of them (by Garcilaso de la Vega) written in Spain by a half-native writer who published his chronicle more than five decades after he had left Peru.

Of the Spanish records that have survived, there is a further barrier in try-

ing to determine what happened: the Spaniards wrote most of their early reports in the form of documents called *probanzas* or *relaciones,* which were
largely written in an attempt to try and impress the Spanish king. The authors of these documents, often humble notaries temporarily turned conquistadors, were well aware of the fact that if their own exploits somehow
stood out, then the king might grant them future favors, rewards, and perhaps even permanent pensions. The early writers of the Spanish conquest,
therefore, were not attempting necessarily to describe events as they actually occurred, but were more inclined to write justifications and adver-
tisements about themselves to the king. At the same time, they tended to
downplay the efforts of their Spanish comrades (the latter were, after all,
competitors for those self-same rewards). In addition, Spanish chroniclers
often misunderstood or misinterpreted much of the native culture they encountered, while they simultaneously ignored and/or downplayed the actions of the African and Central American slaves the Spaniards had brought
along with them, as well as the influence of their native mistresses. Francisco
Pizarro's younger brother Hernando, for example, wrote one of the first reports of the conquest—a sixteen-page letter to the Council of the Indies,
which represented the king. In his letter, Hernando mentioned his own accomplishments repeatedly while mentioning the exploits of only *one* other
Spaniard among the 167 who accompanied him—those of his elder brother
Francisco. Ironically, it was these first, often self-serving versions of what
had occurred in Peru that became instantaneous bestsellers in Europe when
they were published. It was also from these same documents that the first
Spanish historians fashioned their own epic histories, thus passing the dis-
tortions of one generation on to the next.

The modern writer—especially the writer of a historical narrative—must
therefore and by necessity often choose from among multiple and conflict-
ing accounts, must rely sometimes by default upon some authors not known
for their veracity, must translate from misspelled and often verbose manuscripts, and often must use third and fourth person sources, some of which
have come down to us as copies of copies of manuscripts. Did the Inca emperor Atahualpa really do such and such or say such and such to so and so?
No one can say with certainty. Many of the quotations in this manuscript
were actually "remembered" by writers who sometimes didn't commit their
memories to paper until decades after the events they described. Like quan-

tum physics, we can thus only *approximate* what actually happened in the past. The abundant quotations used in the book, therefore—the vast majority of them dating from the sixteenth century—have to be viewed for what they are: bits and fragments of colored glass, often beautifully polished, yet which afford only a partial and often distorted view onto an increasingly distant past.

All histories, of course, highlight some things, abbreviate others, and foreshadow, shorten, extend, and even omit certain events. Inevitably, all stories are told through the prism of one's own time and culture. The American historian William Prescott's 1847 tale of Pizarro and a handful of Spanish heroes defying the odds against hordes of barbaric native savages not coincidently mirrored the ideas and conceits of the Victorian Age and of American Manifest Destiny. No doubt this volume also reflects the prevailing attitudes of our time. All a historical writer can really do, to the best of one's ability and within one's own time, is to momentarily lift from the dusty shelves of centuries these well-worn figures—Pizarro, Almagro, Atahualpa, Manco Inca, and their contemporaries—clean them off, and then attempt to breathe life into them once again for a new audience so that the small figures can once again replay their brief moments on earth. Once finished, the writer must then lay them gently back down in the dust, until someone in the not-so-distant future attempts to fashion a new narrative and resuscitates them once again.

Some 400 years ago, Felipe Huamán Poma de Ayala, a native from a noble family that lived within the Inca Empire, spent much of his life writing a more than 1,000-page manuscript, accompanied by 400 hand-drawn illustrations. Poma de Ayala hoped that it would one day cause the Spanish king to rectify the abuses of the Spaniards in post-conquest Peru. Somehow, Poma de Ayala managed to carry his bulky manuscript about the country with him, wandering through the wreckage of the Inca Empire, interviewing people, carefully recording on his pages much of what he heard and saw, and all the while guarding his life's work from being stolen. At the age of eighty he finally finished his manuscript, sending the lone copy by ship for the long voyage to Spain. The manuscript apparently never arrived at its destination or, if it did, was never delivered to the king. More than likely it was filed away by some low-level bureaucrat and subsequently forgotten. Nearly three hundred years later, in 1908, a researcher accidentally discovered the manuscript in a library in Copenhagen and with it found a treasure trove of information. Some of its drawings have been used to illustrate the narrative in this book. In his accompanying letter to the king, an aged Poma de Ayala wrote the following:

> In weighing, cataloguing and in setting order [to] the various [historical] accounts I passed a great number of days, indeed many years, without coming to a decision. At last I overcame my timidity and began the task which I had aspired to for so long. I looked for illumination in the darkness of my understanding, in my very blindness and ignorance. For I am no doctor or Latin scholar, like some others in this country. But I make bold to think myself the first person of Indian race able to render such a service to Your Majesty. . . . In my work I have always tried to obtain the most truthful accounts, accepting those which seemed to be substantial and which were confirmed from various sources. I have only reported those facts which several people agreed upon as being true. . . . Your Majesty, for the benefit of both Indian and Spanish Christians in Peru I ask you to accept in your goodness of heart this trifling and humble service. Such acceptance will bring me happiness, relief, and a reward for all my work.

To which the present writer, having undergone a similar yet far less imposing challenge, can only ask for the same.

Kim MacQuarrie
Marina del Rey, California
Sept. 10, 2006

I ❖ THE DISCOVERY

July 24, 1911

THE GAUNT, THIRTY-FIVE-YEAR-OLD AMERICAN EXPLORER, Hiram Bingham, clambered up the steep slope of the cloud forest, on the eastern flank of the Andes, then paused beside his peasant guide before taking off his wide-brimmed fedora and wiping the sweat from his brow. Carrasco, the Peruvian army sergeant, soon climbed up the trail behind them, sweating in his dark, brass-buttoned uniform and hat, then leaned forward and placed his hands on his knees in order to catch his breath. Bingham had been told that ancient Inca ruins were located somewhere high up above them, nearly in the clouds, yet Bingham also knew that rumors about Inca ruins were as rampant in this little explored region of southeastern Peru as the flocks of small green parrots that often wheeled about, screeching through the air. The six-foot-four, 170-pound Bingham was fairly certain, however, that the lost Inca city he was searching for did not lie ahead. Bingham, in fact, had not even bothered to pack a lunch for this trek, hoping instead to make a quick journey up from the valley floor, to verify whatever scattered ruins might lie upon the jagged peak rising above, and then to hurry back down. As the lanky American with the close-cropped brown hair and the thin, almost ascetic face began to follow his guide up the trail again, he had no idea that within just a few hours he would make one of the most spectacular archaeological discoveries in history.

The air lay humid and warm upon them, and, looking up, they saw the ridgetop they were seeking stood another thousand feet above, obscured by sheer-sided slopes festooned with dripping vegetation. Above the ridge, swirling clouds alternately hid and then revealed the jungle-covered peak. Water glistened from freshly fallen rain, while an occasional mist brushed across the men's upturned faces. Alongside the steep path, orchids erupted

7

in bright splashes of violet, yellow, and ocher. For a few moments the men watched a tiny hummingbird—no more than a shimmer of fluorescent turquoise and blue—buzz and dart about a cluster of flowers, then disappear. Only a half hour earlier, all three had carefully stepped around a *vibora,* a poisonous snake, its head mashed in by a rock. Had it been killed by a local peasant? Their guide had only shrugged his shoulders when asked. The snake, Bingham knew, was one of many whose bite could cripple or kill.

An assistant professor of Latin American history and geography at Yale University, Bingham ran a hand down one of the heavy cloth leg wrappings that he had wound all the way up from his booted ankles to just below his knees. Might prevent a snakebite, Bingham no doubt thought. Sergeant Carrasco, the Peruvian military man who had been assigned to the expedition, meanwhile, undid the top buttons to his uniform. The guide trudging ahead of them—Melchor Arteaga—was a peasant who lived in a small house on the valley floor more than a thousand feet below. It was he who told the two men that on top of a high mountain ridge Inca ruins could be found. Arteaga wore long pants and an old jacket, and had the high cheek-bones, dark hair, and aquiline eyes of his ancestors—the inhabitants of the Inca Empire. Arteaga's left cheek bulged with a wad of coca leaves—a mild form of cocaine narcotic that once only the Inca royalty had enjoyed. He spoke Spanish but was more at home in Quechua, the Incas' ancient language. Bingham spoke heavily accented Spanish and no Quechua; Sergeant Carrasco spoke both.

"Picchu," Arteaga had said, when they had first visited him the day before. The words were difficult to make out, filtering as they did past the thick gruel of coca leaves. "Chu Picchu," it sounded like the second time. Finally, the short peasant had firmly grabbed the American's arm and, pointing up at a massive peak looming above them, he uttered two words: "Machu Picchu"—Quechua for "old peak." Arteaga turned and squinted into the intense brown eyes of the American explorer, then turned toward the mountain. "Up in the clouds, at Machu Picchu—*that* is where you will find the ruins."

For the price of a shiny new silver American dollar, Arteaga had agreed to guide Bingham up to the peak. Now, high on its flank, the three men looked back down at the valley floor, where far below them tumbled the Urubamba River, white and rapids-strewn in stretches, then almost turquoise in others, fed as it was by Andean glaciers. The river would eventually flatten out and coil its way down into the Amazon River, which stretched eastward for nearly another three thousand miles, across an entire continent. One hundred miles to the west lay the high Andean city of Cuzco, the ancient capital of the Incas—the "navel" or center of their once nearly 2,500-mile-long empire.

Almost four hundred years earlier, the Incas had abruptly abandoned Cuzco, after the Spaniards had murdered their emperor and installed a puppet emperor on the throne. A large number of them had then headed en masse down the eastern side of the Andes, eventually founding a new capital in the wild *Antisuyu*—the mostly jungle-choked eastern quarter of their empire. The Incas called their new capital Vilcabamba and for the next nearly four decades it would become the headquarters of a fierce guerrilla war they would carry out against the Spaniards. In Vilcabamba, Inca warriors learned to ride captured Spanish horses, to fire captured Spanish muskets, and often fought alongside their nearly naked Amazonian allies, who wielded deadly bows and arrows. Bingham had been told the remarkable story of the Incas' little known rebel kingdom a year earlier, while on a brief trip to Peru, and was amazed that no one seemed to know what had become of its capital. A year later, Bingham was back in Peru, hoping that *he* would become the person to discover it.

Thousands of miles from his Connecticut home and clinging to the side of a cloud forest peak, Bingham couldn't help but wonder if his current climb would result in a wild-goose chase. Two of his companions on the expedition, the Americans Harry Foote and William Erving, had remained on the valley floor in camp, preferring that Bingham go off in search of the ruins himself. Rumors of ruins often remained just that—rumors—they no doubt thought. One thing his companions knew well, however, was that no matter how tired *they* were, Bingham himself always seemed tireless. Not only was Bingham the leader of this expedition, but he had also planned it, had selected its seven members, and had raised the financing bit by difficult bit. The funds that now allowed Bingham to be hiking in search of a lost Inca city, in fact, had come from selling a last piece of inherited family real estate in Hawaii, from promises of a series of articles for *Harper's* magazine on his return, and from donations from the United Fruit Company, the Winchester Arms Company, and W. R. Grace and Company. Although he had

married an heir to the Tiffany fortune, Bingham himself had no money—
and never had.

The only son of a strict, fire-and-brimstone Protestant preacher, Hiram
Bingham III had grown up in near poverty in Honolulu, Hawaii. His impoverished youth was no doubt one of the motivations for why Bingham, even
as a boy, had always been determined to climb his way up the social and financial ladders of America or, as he put it, "to strive for magnificence." Perhaps one episode from Bingham's younger years best illustrates how he
presently came to be scrambling up a high Peruvian mountain: when Bingham was twelve years old, suffocating from what he considered the dreary,
strict life of a minister's son (where for the smallest infraction he was punished with a wooden rod), Bingham and a friend decided to run away from
home. Bingham had read plenty of Horatio Alger stories, and, torn between
his own dreams and possible eternal damnation in hell, he decided that he
might best escape by taking a ship to the mainland, and then begin his
climb toward fame and fortune.

That morning, with his heart no doubt pounding and trying hard to appear at ease, Bingham pretended he was going to school, left the house, and,
as soon as he was out of sight, went directly to the bank. There, he with-
drew $250, which Bingham's parents had insisted he save, penny by penny,
so that he could go to college on the mainland. Bingham quickly bought a
boat ticket and a new suit of clothes, packing everything into a suitcase he
had hidden in a woodpile near his home. Bingham's plan was to somehow
make his way to New York City, to find a job as a newsboy, and then—when
he had saved up enough money—eventually to go to Africa, where he
hoped to become an explorer.

"I believe that he got the fancy from the books he has read," the wife of a
neighbor later told his parents. Indeed, young Bingham was a voracious
reader. But his carefully laid plans soon began to unravel, although through
no fault of his own. For some reason, the ship on which he had booked passage did not depart that day and instead remained in port. Meanwhile,
Bingham's best friend and fellow escapee—whose very different and happy
home life hardly justified such a drastic undertaking—had lost his courage
and confessed everything to his father. Soon, the boy's father alerted the
Bingham household. Bingham's father found his son down at the port in
the late afternoon, standing determinedly with his valise in hand before the

ship that was to bear him across the seas and ultimately to his destiny. Amazingly, Bingham was not punished; instead, he was given more freedom and latitude. And, perhaps not surprisingly, twenty-three years later Hiram Bingham found himself scrambling up the eastern face of the Andes, on the cusp of making one of the most spectacular archaeological discoveries in the history of the world.

Shortly after noon, on July 24, 1911, Bingham and his two companions reached a long, wide ridgetop; on it sat a small hut, roofed with dried brown *ichu* grass, some 2,500 feet above the valley floor. The setting was magnificent—Bingham had a 360 degree view of the adjacent jungle-covered mountain peaks and of the clouds rimming the whole area. To the left, and connected to the ridge, a large peak—Machu Picchu—rose up and towered above. To the right, another peak—Huayna Picchu or "young peak"—did the same. As soon as the three sweaty men reached the hut, two Peruvian peasants, wearing sandals and typical alpaca-wool ponchos, welcomed them with dripping gourds of cool mountain water.

The two natives, it turned out, were farmers and had been cultivating the ancient terraces here for the last four years. Yes, there were ruins, they said, just ahead. They then offered their visitors some cooked potatoes—just one of an estimated *five thousand* varieties of potatoes that grow in the Andes, their place of origin. Three families lived there, Bingham discovered, growing corn, sweet and white potatoes, sugarcane, beans, peppers, tomatoes, and gooseberries. Bingham also learned that only two paths led to the outside world from atop this high mountain outpost: the path that they had just struggled up and another one, "even more difficult," the peasants said, that led down the other side. The peasants traveled to the valley floor only once a month, they said. Natural springs bubbled up here, and the area was blessed with rich soil. Eight thousand feet up in the Andes, with abundant sun, fertile soil, and water, the three peasant families had little need of the outside world. A good defensive site, Bingham no doubt thought, as he drank several gourdfuls of water, looking around at the surroundings. He later wrote,

> Through Sergeant Carrasco [translating from Quechua into Spanish], I learned that the ruins were "a little further along." In this country one can never tell whether such a report is worthy of credence. "He may

have been lying," is a good footnote to affix to all hearsay evidence. Accordingly, I was not unduly excited, nor in a great hurry to move. The heat was still great, the water from the Indian's spring was cool and delicious, and the rustic wooden bench, hospitably covered immediately after my arrival with a soft woolen poncho, seemed most comfortable. Furthermore, the view was simply enchanting. Tremendous green precipices fell away to the white rapids of the Urubamba [River] below. Immediately in front, on the north side of the valley, was a great granite cliff rising 2,000 feet sheer. To the left was the solitary peak of Huayna Picchu, surrounded by seemingly inaccessible precipices. On all sides were rocky cliffs. Beyond them cloud-capped, snow-covered mountains rose thousands of feet above us.

After resting awhile, Bingham finally stood up. A small boy had appeared—wearing torn pants, a brightly colored alpaca poncho, leather sandals, and a broad-rimmed hat with spangles; the two men instructed the boy in Quechua to take Bingham and Sergeant Carrasco to the "ruins." Melchor Arteaga, meanwhile—the peasant who had guided them here—decided to remain chatting with the two farmers. The three soon set off, the boy in front, the tall American behind, and Carrasco bringing up the rear. It didn't take long before Bingham's dream of one day discovering a lost city became a reality.

Hardly had we left the hut and rounded the promontory, than we were confronted by an unexpected sight, a great flight of beautifully constructed stone-faced terraces, perhaps a hundred of them, each hundreds of feet long and ten feet high. Suddenly, I found myself confronted with the walls of ruined houses built of the finest quality Inca stone work. It was hard to see them for they were partly covered with trees and moss, the growth of centuries, but in the dense shadow, hiding in bamboo thickets and tangled vines, appeared here and there walls of white granite carefully cut and exquisitely fitted together.

Bingham continued:

I climbed a marvelous great stairway of large granite blocks, walked along a pampa where the Indians had a small vegetable garden, and

came into a little clearing. Here were the ruins of two of the finest structures I have ever seen in Peru. Not only were they made of selected
blocks of beautifully grained white granite; their walls contained ashlars
of Cyclopean size, ten feet in length, and higher than a man. The sight
held me spellbound. . . . I could scarcely believe my senses as I examined the larger blocks in the lower course, and estimated that they must
weigh from ten to fifteen tons each. Would anyone believe what I had
found?

Bingham had had the foresight to bring a camera and a tripod, just in
case, and thus spent the rest of the afternoon photographing the ancient
buildings. Before a succession of splendid Inca walls, trapezoidal doorways,
and beautifully hewn blocks, Bingham placed either Sergeant Carrasco or
the small boy—and asked them to stand still while he squeezed the release
to his shutter. The thirty-one photos Bingham took on this day would become the first of thousands that Bingham would eventually snap over the
coming years, many of them ending up within the covers of *National Geographic* magazine, which would co-sponsor subsequent expeditions. Only a
week after having left Cuzco, Hiram Bingham had just made the major
achievement of his lifetime. For even though Bingham would live nearly another half century and would eventually become a U.S. senator, it was this
brief climb up to an unknown mountain ridge in Peru that would earn him
everlasting fame.

"My dearest love," Bingham wrote his wife the next morning from the
valley floor, "We reached here night before last and pitched the 7 x 9 tent in
a cozy corner described above. Yesterday [Harry] Foote spent collecting insects. [William] Erving did some [photographic] developing, and I climbed
a couple of thousand feet to a wonderful old Inca city called Machu Picchu."
Bingham continued: "The stone is as fine as any in Cuzco! It is unknown
and will make a fine story. I expect to return there shortly for a stay of a
week or more."

Over the next four years, Bingham would return to the ruins of Machu
Picchu two more times, clearing, mapping, and excavating the ruins while
comparing what he discovered with the old Spanish chronicles' descriptions
of the lost city of Vilcabamba. Although he at first had some doubts, Bingham was soon convinced that the ruins of Machu Picchu were none other

than those of the legendary rebel city of Vilcabamba, the final refuge of the Incas.

In the pages of his later books, Bingham would write that Machu Picchu was "the 'Lost City of the Incas,' favorite residence of the last Emperors, site of temples and palaces built of white granite in the most inaccessible part of the grand canyon of the Urubamba; a holy sanctuary to which only nobles, priests, and the Virgins of the Sun were admitted. It was once called Vilca-pampa [Vilcabamba] but is known today as Machu Picchu."

Not everyone was convinced that Bingham had discovered the Incas' rebel city, however. For the few scholars who had actually read the old Spanish chronicles, discrepancies seemed to exist between the Spaniards' description of the city of Vilcabamba and the admittedly stunning ruins that Bingham had found. Was the citadel of Machu Picchu *really* the last strong-hold of the Incas as described in the chronicles? Or could it be that Hiram Bingham—a man now feted and lionized around the world as an expert on the Incas—had made a colossal error, and the rebel city had yet to be found? For those scholars who had their doubts, there was only one way to find out—and that was to return to the sixteenth-century chronicles in order to learn more about how and why the Incas had created the largest capital of guerrilla fighters the New World had ever known.

2 ❖ A FEW HUNDRED WELL-ARMED ENTREPRENEURS

"In the last ages of the world there shall come a time when the ocean sea will loosen its bonds and a great land will appear and a navigator like him that guided Jason will discover a new world, and then the isle of Thule will no longer be the final limit of the earth."

THE ROMAN PHILOSOPHER SENECA, WRITING IN
HESPERIDIUM [SPAIN] IN THE FIRST CENTURY A.D.

ON APRIL 21, 1536, ON SATURDAY AT THE END OF EASTER week, few of the 196 Spaniards in the Inca capital of Cuzco realized that within the next few weeks they would either die or else would come so close to dying that every one of them would ask for absolution, the forgiveness of their sins, and would entrust their souls to their Maker. Just three years after Francisco Pizarro and his Spaniards had garroted the Inca emperor, Atahualpa (ah tah HUAL pa) and had seized a large portion of an empire 2,500 miles long and ten million strong, things were beginning to unravel for the Spanish conquistadors. For the last few years the Spaniards had consolidated their gains, installed a puppet Inca ruler, stolen the Incas' women, gained dominion over millions, and sent a massive amount of Inca gold and silver back to Spain. The original conquistadors were by now all incredibly wealthy men—the equivalent of multi-millionaires in our time— and those who had stayed on in Peru had already retired to fabulously large estates. The conquistadors were established seigneurial lords, the founders of family dynasties. Already they had shed their armor for fine linen clothes,

CONQVISTA
EVBARCAROSEALASÍDIAS

The conquistadors Francisco Pizarro and Diego de Almagro
voyaging toward the new world and Peru, by the sixteenth-century
native artist Felipe Huamán Poma de Ayala.

rakish hats spiked with gaudy feathers, ostentatious jewelry, and sleek linen tights. In Spain and other European kingdoms, and on scattered islands and possessions throughout the Spanish Caribbean, the conquerors of Peru were already legendary figures: young and old alike dreamed of nothing more than walking in these same conquistadors' now finely appointed shoes.

On this crisp spring morning, however, at an elevation of 11,300 feet in the Andes, church bells of bronze had begun to clang incessantly from a structure the Spaniards had hastily erected on top of the immaculately cut gray stones of the Qoricancha, the Incas' temple of the sun. Rumors now swirled along the streets of this bowl-like city, surrounded by green hills, that the puppet Inca emperor had escaped and in fact was about to return with a massive native army, hundreds of thousands strong.

As the Spaniards swarmed out of their dwellings, arming themselves with steel swords, daggers, twin-pointed morion helmets, twelve-foot lances and saddling up their horses, they bitterly swore that the Inca rebels were so many "dogs" and "traitors." The air was clear, sharp, and thin, and the iron-clad hooves of the horses clattered on the cut stones of the streets. A question that no doubt arose in at least some of the conquistadors' minds, however, was—where had it all gone wrong?

Indeed, thus far the Spaniards had enjoyed one stunning success after another. Four years earlier, in September 1532, led by the conquistador Francisco Pizarro, 168 of them had made their way up into the Andes—sixty-two on horseback and 106 on foot—leaving a cluster of lanteen-rigged ships moored in the deep blue waters of the Pacific Ocean, or the "Southern Sea." The Spaniards had eventually climbed eight thousand feet and then had walked directly into the lion's den—where the lord of the Inca Empire, Atahualpa, with an army of possibly eighty thousand warriors, was waiting for them.

Francisco Pizarro at this time was a fifty-four-year-old, moderately wealthy landowner who had been living in Panama and who had thirty years of Indian fighting experience behind him. Tall, sinewy, athletic, with hollow cheeks and a thin beard, Pizarro resembled Don Quixote, even though Don Quixote wouldn't be created for another seventy-three years. A poor cavalryman (until literally the last moments of his life, Pizarro preferred fighting on foot), Pizarro was also quiet, taciturn, brave, firm, ambitious, cunning, efficient, diplomatic, and—like most conquistadors—could be as brutal as the situation required.

For better or for worse, Pizarro had been molded by the region he hailed from in western Spain—Extremadura.* An impoverished, rural, backward area, Extremadura was covered in arid, Mediterranean scrub and lay marooned like a landlocked island in the midst of a relatively poor country just emerging from the feudal ages that had yet to become a nation. The region, it was well known, typically produced men who were both uncommunicative and parsimonious, men who showed little emotion and who were known to be as tough and unsympathetic as the landscape that had nurtured them.

Of such gritty material were made both Pizarro and a large number of his fellow conquistadors, many of whom had also come from the same region. Vasco Núñez de Balboa—the discoverer of the Pacific Ocean—for example, was from Extremadura. So was Juan Ponce de León, the discoverer of Florida. Hernando de Soto, the seasoned explorer who would later fight his way through what are now Florida, Alabama, Georgia, Arkansas, and Mississippi, was an *extremeño*. Even Hernando Cortés, the recent conqueror of the Aztec Empire in Mexico, had grown up within forty miles of his compatriot and second cousin Francisco Pizarro.† That the conquerors of the New World's two most powerful native empires grew up within forty miles of each other, however, is certainly one of the world's most extraordinary facts.

Pizarro's native city of Trujillo, which had a population while he was growing up of only about two thousand *vecinos,* or citizens who had full rights, was divided into three sections. Each corresponded to the social stratification of the city's inhabitants. The walled town, or *villa,* rested on top of a hill with a view of the countryside. Here rose the turreted houses of the knights and of the lower nobility, with their coats of arms, or lineages, prominently displayed over their doorways. It was here, too, that Francisco's father and his father's family lived. The second section of the city, formed

---

* Extremadura at the time of the Conquest was part of the Kingdom of Castile; the nation that would later be called Spain would be formed by the gradual amalgamation of the kingdoms of Castile and Aragon. The region of Extremadura, comprising the modern provinces of Badajoz and Cáceres, is still the poorest region of Spain today.

† Cortés was a second cousin of Francisco Pizarro through Cortés's mother, Catalina Pizarro Altamirano.

around the town's plaza, lay on flat land beside the hill. Here lived the merchants, notaries, and craftsmen, although, somewhat later, more and more of the hilltop nobility moved to homes occupying prominent positions on the plaza, including Francisco's father. The final section of the city lay along its outer periphery, along the roads that led off toward the fields. Referred to derogatorily as the *arrabales,* a connotation that combined both the notion of "outskirts" and "slums," it was here that the peasants and artisans lived in homes that were as far physically as they were socially from those at the town's center. It was amid the outer section of this rural yet highly stratified city, which mirrored Spanish society at large, that Francisco Pizarro grew up with his mother, a common maid. A person who grew up in an *arrabal* was called an *arrabalero.* The latter referred to a person who was "ill-bred," or, in modern parlance, a person who has grown up on "the wrong side of the tracks." Such was the social stigma that Francisco Pizarro labored to escape from long before departing for the New World.

Pizarro, however, was not only stigmatized by growing up in an *arrabal,* he was also stigmatized by the fact that his father had never married his mother. That meant that not only would he be unlikely to inherit any part of his father's estate (even though he was the eldest of four half-brothers), but that he was also illegitimate, meaning that he would forever be regarded as a second-class citizen. In addition, Pizarro had received little if any schooling and thus remained illiterate for his entire life.

Pizarro was only fifteen years old (and Cortés eight) when Columbus returned in 1493 from his first voyage across the unexplored ocean. In announcing his supposed discovery of a new route to India, Columbus wrote a letter to a high-ranking official describing his voyage that was quickly published and became a runaway bestseller for the age.

It is likely that Pizarro overheard Columbus's fantastic tale, either as part of an eager group of listeners to whom the story was read, or else as the story was passed along by word of mouth. In any event, it was an extraordinary account, a tale as rich as any fiction, one that told of the discovery of an exotic world where riches could literally be plucked like so much ripe fruit from a landscape similar to the Garden of Eden. And, like the popular novels that had started circulating since the printing press had been invented two decades earlier, Columbus's *Letter,* or *Carta,* hit Europe like a thunderbolt:

I found very many islands, filled with innumerable people, and I have taken possession of them all for their Highnesses [King Ferdinand and Queen Isabella], done by proclamation and with the royal standard unfurled, and no opposition was offered to me. . . . The people of this island [Hispaniola, the island that today Haiti and the Dominican Republic share] and of all the other islands that I have found and of which I have gotten information, all go naked, men and women, as their mothers bore them. . . . They refuse nothing that they possess, if it be asked of them; on the contrary, they invite any one to share it and display as much love as if they would give their hearts. They are content with whatever trifle of whatever kind that may be given them, whether it be of value or valueless. . . .

Their Highnesses can see that I will give . . . [the king and queen] as much gold as they may need. . . . I will give them spices and cotton . . . and mastic . . . and aloe . . . and slaves, as many as they shall order. . . . I also believe that I have found rhubarb and cinnamon, and I shall find a thousand other things of value. . . . And thus the eternal God, Our Lord, gives to all those who walk in His way triumph over things that appear to be impossible, and this was notably one . . . with many solemn prayers for the great exaltation which they shall have in the turning of so many peoples to our holy faith, and afterwards for the temporal benefits, because not only Spain but all Christendom will have hence comforts and profits.

Done [written] in the caravel [*Niña*], off the Canary Islands, on the fifteenth day of February, in the year one thousand four hundred and ninety-three. . . .

The Admiral

Columbus's enthusiastic report no doubt fired the imagination of the teenaged Francisco Pizarro. Pizarro, of course, was already well aware of the fact that his future on his native peninsula would probably be a bleak one. The world that Columbus described, by contrast, must have seemed to offer so many more possibilities than his own.

By the end of the fifteenth century, the class system in the kingdoms of Spain had been in place for centuries and was a very rigid one. Those at the top—the dukes, the lords, the marquis, and the earls—owned vast estates on which peasants worked. It was they who enjoyed all the privileges and so-cial prestige that the late fifteenth-century Spanish kingdoms had to offer. Those at the bottom—the peasants, artisans, and, generally speaking, all those who had to perform manual labor for a living—usually remained in the same class to which they were born. In the kingdoms of Spain, as else-where in Europe, there was little upward social mobility. If one were born poor, illiterate, and had no family pedigree, then one could read one's future as plainly as a geographer could read one of Columbus's finely drawn maps. There were only two ways to gain entrance to elite status: either through marriage to a member of the elite (which was exceedingly rare) or else by distinguishing oneself in a successful military campaign.

Thus, in the year 1502, at the age of twenty-four, the impoverished, illit-erate, illegitimate, and title-less Francisco Pizarro had perhaps not surpris-ingly found his way onto a ship that had set out from Spain for the Indies—the islands Columbus had declared were located in Asia (known at the time as the "Indies") and thus were inhabited by "Indians." The fleet was the largest yet to cross the Atlantic; it carried 2,500 men and a large number of horses, pigs, and other animals. Its destination, in fact, was the very same island that Columbus had described only nine years earlier: Hispaniola. As Pizarro's ship arrived and set anchor before the lush green island rising up from a turquoise sea, a small boatload of Spaniards came out to meet them, soon informing the excited passengers that "You have arrived at a good mo-ment [for] . . . there is to be a war against the Indians and we will be able to take many slaves." "This news," recalled one young passenger, Bartolomé de Las Casas, "produced a great joy in the ship." *

---

* At the time, no one could have known that ironically in this fleet rode two men—twenty-four-year-old Francisco Pizarro and eighteen-year-old Bartolomé de Las Casas—as dia-metrically opposed to each other as two men would ever be. The former would conquer an empire of ten million and would distribute its native inhabitants to his fellow Spaniards as another would distribute so many heads of cattle. The latter would later become a priest and the greatest champion the natives of the New World would have during the period of the Conquest. Las Casas's influence upon King Charles V would prove so great, in fact, that laws protecting the Indians would be introduced that would ultimately lead to the death of one of Pizarro's brothers, Gonzalo, and to the destruction of the Pizarros' power in Peru. Did the two men ever meet each other? It's difficult to say. But with a population of just over one thousand on the island, most of whom lived in its capital, Santo Domingo, it's probably safe to say that the two men whom fate and personality would soon pit against each other must have at least passed each other on the street.

Whether Pizarro participated in that particular war against the local natives is unknown. By 1509, however—some seven years after his arrival—
Pizarro had risen to become a lieutenant in the local military of the
governor, Nicolás de Ovando, a loosely knit force that was frequently used
to "pacify" native rebellions. While Pizarro's exact duties are unknown, he
was working for a governor who at one point had rounded up eighty-four
native chiefs and then had them massacred—simply to send an unmistakable message to the island's inhabitants to do as they were told.

With Hispaniola and other nearby islands becoming increasingly de-
pleted of natives due to slaving (already by 1510 the first African slaves
began to be imported into the Caribbean in order to replace the quickly disappearing native population), Pizarro made his way around 1509 to the
newly discovered mainland of Central America. Pizarro was again following in Columbus's footsteps, as the great Italian mariner himself had discovered the coasts of Honduras and Panama on his fourth and last voyage of
1502–1504.* By 1513, at the age of thirty-five, Pizarro had risen still further;
he was now second-in-command on an expedition led by Vasco Núñez de
Balboa that eventually crossed the jungles of the Isthmus of Panama and
discovered the Pacific Ocean. As Balboa waded into the waters of that vast
ocean, claiming it for the Spanish monarchs, Pizarro must have realized that
at last he was nearly in the same position that Columbus had been in years
earlier. Now he, too, was exploring lands that no European had ever seen.
And this was only the beginning.

The expedition cut short by stumbling upon a vast ocean was a far cry
from the later Baroque portraits of handsome, noble Spaniards in armor
wading out into the Pacific, unfurling colorful flags as a scattering of naked
Indians watched in admiration. From the beginning, the Isthmus expedition
had been one of pure brute economics. Balboa and Pizarro's discovery of
the Pacific Ocean, in fact, had occurred as a by-product of a military campaign, one that had been carried out in order to find a tribe of natives reput-
edly rich in gold. Elsewhere in that very same year, another Spaniard, Juan
Ponce de León, had discovered a land he called *Florida* while on a slaving

---

* Columbus would die at the age of fifty-four in Valladolid in 1506, four years after Pizarro
  arrived in the New World. He died in relative obscurity, still believing that he had discovered a new route to Asia.

expedition amid the islands of the Bahamas. It was through slaving and plundering expeditions that the Spaniards were discovering more and more of the New World.

Unsuccessful in their search for gold, Balboa and Pizarro became increasingly brutal as they trudged their way back empty-handed through the mosquito-infested jungles. Along the way, Balboa captured some local chiefs and demanded that they reveal to him the location of the rumored gold. When the chiefs replied that they were unaware of any, Balboa had them tortured. After the chiefs still failed to supply any useful information, Balboa had them killed. Six years later, in January 1519, and as the result of a struggle for power with the new Spanish governor, Balboa was himself arrested and subsequently beheaded. Pizarro, once Balboa's second-in-command, was the arresting officer.

By 1521, the now forty-four-year-old Francisco Pizarro was one of the most important landowners in the new city of Panama, living on the coast of the very same ocean that he and Balboa had discovered. A part owner of a gold mining company, Pizarro had also received an *encomienda,* or Indian grant, of 150 natives on the island of Taboga, just off the Pacific coast. As an *encomienda* holder, Pizarro received both labor and tribute from the Indians. The island also had fertile soil for crops and abundant gravel that Pizarro sold to newly constructed ships as ballast.

Still, Pizarro was not satisfied. What good was owning a tiny island and living off a mere 150 natives when another Spaniard, Hernán Cortés, from the same region of Extremadura in Spain, had just conquered an entire *empire* at the age of thirty-four? In Spanish culture in the sixteenth century, the ages between thirty and forty-five were considered the prime years for men, that is, those were the years in which a man was considered to be both mature and to have the most energy.

Pizarro, however, at forty-four, was already ten years older than Cortés had been when the latter had begun his conquest of the Aztec Empire, an enterprise that had taken three long and grueling years. Pizarro thus had only one prime year left. The question no doubt on Pizarro's mind then was: had Cortés found the only empire in what was now known to be a New World? Or could there be more? For Pizarro, time was running out. It was either now or never. And since everything of value seemed to have already been discovered to the north and east, and since the west was bounded by what appeared to be a vast ocean, the only logical direction to look for new empires was toward the unexplored regions to the south.

By 1524, three years after Cortés's conquest, Pizarro had formed a company with two partners, Diego de Almagro—a fellow *extremeño*—and a local financier, Hernando de Luque. The three men were following an economic model that had originated in Europe and that by now was spreading throughout the Spanish colonies in the Caribbean—that of the private corporation, or *compañía*.

By the early sixteenth century, Spain had gradually transitioned from the age of feudalism to the age of capitalism. Under feudalism, all economic activities centered upon the manorial estate, owned by a lord who had been given his land grant, or benefice, by a king, to whom the lord owed his allegiance. Other than the lord and his family, the parish priest, and perhaps a few administrative officials, the entire population of a feudal estate consisted of serfs—those who worked with their hands and created the surplus upon which the noble and his family lived. It was a system as rigid as it was simple: the lord and his family did no manual labor, living at the peak of the social pyramid, while the peasant masses scratched out a meager living below.

Eventually, however, with the advent of gunpowder, the lords' castle walls were no longer impregnable; thus, they could no longer offer protection to their retinue of serfs. Gradually, the serfs migrated to towns and cities where commerce, and the notion of working for a profit, had begun to flourish. Men now often joined forces, pooling their resources, setting up companies, and hiring workers who were paid a wage. All profits now flowed to the owners, or capitalists, and anyone with the requisite skills and the right connections could become an entrepreneur. The acquisition of wealth had now become a motive in itself. In sixteenth-century Spain, therefore, if an individual could somehow scrape together a substantial pile of wealth, he could then purchase the equivalent of a manorial estate, he could use some of that wealth in order to receive various titles and pedigrees that would increase his social status, and he could hire a stable of servants and perhaps even buy a few Moorish or African slaves. The individual could then retire to a life of luxury and could pass all his capital on to his heirs. A new world order had emerged.

Although the popular myth is that conquistadors were professional soldiers sent out and financed by the Spanish king in order to extend the emerging Spanish Empire, nothing could have been further from the truth. In reality, the Spaniards who bought passages on ships headed for the New World formed a representative sample of their compatriots back home. They were cobblers, tailors, notaries, carpenters, sailors, merchants, ironworkers, blacksmiths, masons, muleteers, barbers, pharmacists, horseshoers, and even professional musicians. Very few had ever been professional soldiers and, in fact, permanent professional armies had not yet even appeared in Europe.

The vast majority of Spaniards, therefore, traveled to the New World not in the employ of the king, but as private citizens hoping to acquire the wealth and status that had so eluded them at home. Men joined expeditions of conquest in the New World in the hopes of getting rich, which invariably meant that they hoped to find a large population of natives in order to strip them of their wealth and live off of their labor. Each band of conquistadors, usually led by an older conquistador who had the most experience, was composed of a disparate group of men trained in an assortment of professions. None received a payment or wage for participating, but all expected to share in the profits gained by conquest and pillage, according to what they themselves had invested in the expedition. If a potential conquistador showed up with only his own weapons and armor, then he would receive a certain amount of any future plunder. If that same man provided these things plus a horse, then he would receive a larger share, and so on. The more one invested, the larger the share that he was entitled to if the expedition enjoyed success.

The leaders of most conquest expeditions, beginning in the 1520s, actually formed a company that was normally drawn up as a contract and was duly notarized. The participants thus became partners in the company and were the equivalent of shareholders. Unlike companies dedicated to providing services or manufactured goods, however, it was understood from the outset that the conquest company's economic plan was predicated upon murder, torture, and plunder. Conquistadors thus were not paid soldier-emissaries of a distant Spanish king, but were actually autonomous participants in a new kind of capitalist venture; in short, they were armed entrepreneurs.

By 1524, forty-six-year-old Francisco Pizarro and his two partners had formed a conquest company called the Company of the Levant and were busy interviewing potential conquistadors to share in their first planned venture.

The two captains of the venture, Pizarro and Almagro, had participated in expeditions together since at least 1519, and had forged a solid business relationship. Both were from Extremadura and hence were countrymen. Pizarro had always had the leading role in the partnership and also had ten more years' experience in the Indies than did Almagro, who had been in the New World only since 1514. Almagro, as second-in-command, was nevertheless a talented organizer and thus was placed in charge of all matters regarding the provisioning of the upcoming expedition. Unlike his tall, lean compatriot, Almagro was short and squat. As one Spanish chronicler later put it, Almagro was

> a man of short stature, with ugly features, but with great courage and endurance. He was generous, but was conceited and was given to boasting, letting his tongue run on sometimes without stop. He was sensible and, above all, was greatly afraid of offending the King. . . . Ignoring the opinions that others may have of him . . . I will only say that he was . . . born of such humble parentage that one could say that his lineage began and ended with himself.

Like Pizarro, Almagro was both illiterate and a bastard. His unmarried mother had spirited him away not long after birth, refusing to allow his father to have any contact with their son. Eventually she disappeared, leaving Almagro with an uncle who routinely beat him and who at one point even chained the young boy by his legs and kept him in a cage. When Almagro eventually escaped, he traveled to Madrid where he at long last found his mother living with another man. Instead of taking him in as he had hoped, however, his mother had stared at him through the partially opened door, then whispered that it was impossible for him to stay. His mother then disappeared for a moment, returning briefly to give her son a piece of bread before permanently closing the door. Almagro was on his own.

The details of the future conquistador's life after this are sketchy but eventually Almagro made his way to Toledo where he stabbed someone, left that person badly wounded, and then fled south to Seville in order to escape the consequences. By 1514, having reached a dead end in his own country, thirty-nine-year-old Diego de Almagro embarked on a ship headed for the New World, twelve years after Pizarro's departure. He was bound for Castilla de Oro, or Golden Spain, as Panama was then called. There he would meet his future partner and by 1524, ten years after his arrival, he and Pizarro would finally find themselves traveling in two ships, with eighty men and four horses, heading south toward the unexplored regions along the Southern Sea. The Company of the Levant was at last striking out on its own.

For a number of years before their expedition, rumors of a fabled land of gold lying somewhere to the south had been circulating in Panama City. In 1522, two years before Pizarro and Almagro set sail, a conquistador named Pascual de Andagoya had sailed two hundred miles southward along the coast of what would later be called Colombia (after Columbus) and had ascended the San Juan River. Andagoya was seeking a wealthy tribe he understood to be called "Viru" or "Biru." Eventually, the name of this tribe would be transmogrified and would come to refer to a land much further south: Peru—home to the largest native empire the New World would ever know.

Andagoya, however, had discovered little, and had returned to Panama empty-handed. Pizarro and Almagro fared little better, succeeding only in retracing some of Andagoya's previous voyage while engaging in skirmishes with natives along the way. At a place the marauding Spaniards no doubt fittingly called "burned village," forty-nine-year-old Almagro had one of his eyes permanently blinded in a clash with local natives. Here, the inhabitants were hostile, the land barren, and Pizarro and his band of armed entrepreneurs eventually returned to Panama with no booty whatsoever to show for their efforts. The voyage had lasted for nearly a year.

It was during their second expedition south, however—a two-year voyage in two ships with 160 men that lasted from 1526 to 1528—that Pizarro and Almagro sensed for the first time that they might be on to something at last. At one point, Almagro and one of the ships returned to Panama for reinforcements while Pizarro camped alongside the San Juan River. The expedition's second ship, meanwhile, headed further south, to do some additional exploring. Soon, off what is now the coast of Ecuador, the crew was surprised to see a sail in the distance. As the Spaniards drew nearer they were astonished to find a giant, oceangoing balsawood raft, powered by finely woven cotton sails and manned by numerous native sailors. Eleven of the twenty-two natives on board immediately leapt into the sea; the Spaniards then captured the rest. After seizing the contents of the mysterious vessel, the delighted entrepreneurs later described their first haul of booty in a letter sent to King Charles V:

> They were carrying many pieces of silver and gold as personal ornaments . . . [and also] crowns and diadems, belts, bracelets, leg armor and breastplates, tweezers, rattles and strings and clusters of beads and rubies, mirrors adorned with silver and cups and other drinking vessels. They were carrying many wool and cotton mantles . . . and other pieces of clothing all richly made and colored with scarlet, crimson, blue, yellow, and all other colors, and worked with different types of ornate embroidery . . . [including] . . . figures of birds and animals and fish and trees. And they had some tiny weights to weigh gold in the Roman manner . . . and there were bead bags [full of] some small stones of emeralds and chalcedonies and other jewels and pieces of crystal and resin. They were taking all of this to trade for fish shells from which they make counters, coral-colored and white, and they were carrying almost a full ship load of these.*

The seagoing raft was the Spaniards' first real proof that somewhere nearby a native kingdom must surely exist. Soon, the Spanish ship, with its cargo of plundered goods stowed securely in the hold, rejoined Pizarro. Then, with Pizarro once again aboard, the expedition turned toward the south. Anchoring alongside a jungle-covered island they named Gallo, off what is now the southwestern tip of Colombia, Pizarro and the rest of the crew waited on the mosquito-ridden shore for Almagro and his badly needed supplies to arrive from Panama.

As the ship's stores dwindled, however, the Spaniards began to sicken;

---

* The fish shells were undoubtedly those of *Spondylus*. These were pink bivalve shells that were highly valued and were used as offerings throughout the Inca Empire, but which were only found in the tropical waters off Ecuador.

then, one by one, they began to die. By the time three or four Spaniards were dying a week, the expeditionaries' morale hit a low point. Not surprisingly, the men wanted to return to Panama. Pizarro, however, the co-CEO of an expedition that had just found evidence of a possibly wealthy kingdom, was undeterred. By now nearly fifty years old, it had taken Pizarro a quarter century of effort to command an expedition for which he stood to gain the lion's share of the profits. As many later chroniclers noted, Pizarro normally did very little talking, but was strong on action. When sufficiently motivated, however, Pizarro could be counted upon to deliver a stirring speech. Thus, when the relief ships finally did arrive and his men made ready to abandon the expedition and return to Panama, Pizarro is said to have taken out his sword in frustration, to have etched a long line in the sand with its sharpened point and then, in his ragged clothes, to have dramatically confronted the emaciated men:

> "Gentlemen! This line signifies labor, hunger, thirst, fatigue, wounds, sickness, and every other kind of danger that must be encountered in this conquest, until life is ended. Let those who have the courage to meet and overcome the dangers of this heroic achievement cross the line in token of their resolution and as a testimony that they will be my faithful companions. And let those who feel unworthy of such daring return to Panama; for I do not wish to . . . [use] force upon any man. I trust in God that, for his greater honor and glory, his eternal Majesty will help those who remain with me, though they be few, and that we shall not feel the want of those who forsake us."

Only thirteen men are said to have crossed over the line, choosing to risk their lives and fortunes with Pizarro; they would later be known as "the men of Gallo." The rest of the Spaniards, however, chose to return to Panama and to give up the quest for Biru.

With their one remaining ship, Pizarro and his small group of expeditionaries now continued down the coast, heading into territory that no European had ever before explored. The coast was tropical and flush with thick trees, mangrove swamps, occasional chattering monkeys, and impenetrable forests. Beneath them flowed the cold Humboldt Current, wending its way up the South American coast from the still undiscovered Antarctic.

Slowly, as the Spaniards sailed south, the forests and mosquitoes began to retreat until, at the very northern tip of what is now Peru, they finally sailed into view of what Pizarro and the one-eyed Almagro had been searching for and dreaming about for years—a native city, complete with more than a thousand buildings, broad streets, and what looked to be ships in the harbor. The year was 1528. And for the small band of bedraggled Spaniards who had been traveling for more than a year and many of whom were as gaunt as skeletons, they were now about to have their first real contact with the Inca Empire.

As the Spaniards moored offshore, they soon saw a dozen balsa rafts set out from shore. Pizarro knew that because his men were few in number, he couldn't possibly try to conquer such a large city. Instead, he would have to rely upon diplomacy in order to learn more about who and what they had stumbled upon. As the native rafts drew nearer, the Spaniards buckled on their armor and readied their swords for battle. Were the natives going to be hostile or friendly? Were there more cities? Did they have gold? Was this a simple city-state or part of a larger kingdom?

One can only imagine the Spaniards' relief to discover that not only were the natives on the rafts friendly, but that they arrived with gifts of food that included a peculiar kind of "lamb" (llama meat), exotic fruits, strange fish, jugs of water, and other jugs containing a tangy liquid now called *chicha* and which the Spaniards soon learned was a type of beer. One of the natives who climbed aboard the ship was a man who obviously commanded respect; the native was rather well dressed in a patterned cotton tunic and had elongated earlobes with large wooden plugs in them, something none of the other natives wore.

Unbeknownst to the Spaniards, this was either an ethnic Inca noble or a local native chief, both of which formed part of the ruling elite. The Spaniards would later call these nobles *orejones,* or "big ears," because of the large, symbolic discs worn in their earlobes that denoted their elite status. This particular *orejón* had come to discover what this strange ship was doing in their waters and who these strange, bearded men were (the inhabitants of the Inca Empire, like the vast majority of the indigenous peoples of the Americas, had little if any facial hair). Unable to communicate except with hand gestures, the *orejón* was nevertheless so inquisitive that he astonished the Spaniards, using gestures to ask "where they were from, what land they had come from, and what they were looking for." The Inca noble then carefully examined the ship, studying its equipment and, according to what the Spaniards could decipher, apparently preparing some kind of report for his lord, a great king called Huayna Capac (Why-na KAH-pak), who the *orejón* indicated lived somewhere in the interior. The veteran Pizarro, who had been capturing, enslaving, killing, and torturing native Amerindians ever since his arrival in the New World, did his best to hide the true nature of their mission and to see how much he could learn about these people through feigned friendliness and diplomacy. In return for the natives' gifts, Pizarro quickly presented the *orejón* with a male and female pig, four European hens and a rooster, and an iron axe, "which strangely pleased him, esteeming it more than if they had given him one hundred times more gold than it weighed." As the *orejón* prepared to return to shore, Pizarro ordered two men to accompany him—Alonso de Molina and a black slave—the first European and African ever to step ashore in the area now known as Peru.* No sooner had Molina and the slave arrived than they became instant celebrities. The excited inhabitants of the city, which the Spaniards later learned was called Tumbez, turned out in droves to marvel at the strange ship and at their two exotic visitors. They

> all came to see the sow and the boar and the hens, delighting in hearing the rooster crow. But all that was nothing compared to the commotion created by the Black man. Because they saw that he was black, they looked at him over and over again, and made him wash to see if his blackness was color or some kind of applied confection. But he laughed, showing his white teeth, as some came to see him and then others, so many that they did not even give him time to eat . . . [he] walked here and there wherever they wanted to see him, as something so new and by them never seen before.

* Four years earlier, in 1524, a Portuguese adventurer named Aleixo Garcia had actually led a group of two thousand marauding Guaraní Indians and penetrated the southeastern corner of the Inca Empire, sacking several Inca towns in what is now Bolivia. The Incas under Huayna Capac repelled the invaders and refortified the border with a chain of forts. Garcia was killed in 1525 on the Paraguay River, only a year after his raid on the Inca Empire and three years before Francisco Pizarro and his small band of men landed on the far northwestern corner of what is now Peru.

Meanwhile, the Spaniard, Alonso de Molina—apparently awestruck by coming face-to-face with an advanced native civilization—received similar treatment from the excited crowd. The two were, after all, the sixteenth-century equivalent of today's astronauts—emissaries from a distant and alien civilization.

> "They looked at how the Spaniard [Molina] had a beard and was white. They asked him many things, but he understood nothing. The children, the old, and the women all looked at them delightedly. Alonso de Molina saw many buildings and remarkable things in Tumbez . . . irrigation channels, many planted fields, and fruits and some sheep [llamas]. Many Indian women—very beautiful and well attired and dressed according to their customs—came to talk to him. They all gave him fruits and whatever they had in order for him to take to the ship. They used gestures to ask where [the Spaniards] were going and where they had come from. . . . Among those Indian women who were talking to him was a very beautiful lady, and she told him to stay with them and that they would give one of them to him as a wife, whichever one he wanted. . . . And when he [Alonso] arrived back at the ship, he was so overwhelmed by what he had seen that he did not say anything. He [finally] said that their houses were of stone, and that before he spoke to the lord [the local Inca governor], he passed through three gates where they had gatekeepers . . . and that they served him in cups of silver and gold."

A subsequent landing party, which Pizarro sent to verify what Molina and the black slave had reported, stated that they:

> saw silver vessels and many silversmiths working, and that on some walls of the temple there were gold and silver sheets, and that the women they called of the Sun were very beautiful. The Spaniards were ecstatic to hear so many things, hoping with God's help to enjoy their share of it.

With their ship now loaded with fresh food and water, Pizarro and his men continued their exploration of the coast. At a spot near what is now called Cabo Blanco, in northwestern Peru, Pizarro went ashore in a canoe. There, looking up and down the rugged coast and then at his gathering of men, Pizarro is said to have stated, "Be my witnesses as I take possession of this land with all else that has been discovered by us for the emperor, our lord, and for the royal crown of Castile!"

To the Spaniards who witnessed Pizarro's speech, *Biru*—which was soon corrupted into *Peru*—now belonged to a Spanish emperor living twelve thousand miles away. Thirty-five years earlier, in 1493, Pope Alexander VI— a Spaniard who had bribed his way into the papacy—had issued a papal bull that had eventually resulted in the Spanish crown being granted all lands 370 leagues west of the Cape Verde Islands. All undiscovered lands to the east of this longitudinal line would go to Portugal, the other European maritime power at the time, which gave Portugal Brazil. With one simple pronouncement from this pope, the Spanish crown had received a divine grant that bequeathed to it an enormous region of lands and peoples that had as yet to be discovered. The inhabitants of these new lands, according to the proclamation, were already subjects of the Spanish king—all that remained was that they be located and informed of this fact.

In 1501, Queen Isabella had ratified this arrangement: the "Indians" of the New World were her "subjects and vassals," she said. Thus, as soon as they were located, the Indians would have to be informed that they owed the Spanish monarchs their "tributes and rights." The corollary of this mind-set, of course, was that the inhabitants of the New World had no right to resist the pope's edict, which was clearly God's will. Anyone who refused to submit to what God himself had commanded was thus by definition a "rebel" or an "unlawful combatant." It was a theme and argument that was to crop up over and over again in the conquest of Peru, all of the way down to the last Inca emperor.

Pizarro's expedition had been a successful one, as far as he was concerned. On board they now carried never before seen creatures called llamas, which may have reminded some of the Spaniards of scenes of camels they had seen in woodcuts in the Bible. They also carried finely crafted native pottery and metal vessels, intricately woven clothing of cotton and of an unknown material the natives called *alpaca,* and even two native boys, whom they baptized Felipillo and Martinillo. The Spaniards had asked for and had been given the boys, whom they intended to train for later voyages as interpreters. Pizarro now had proof positive of a contact with what appeared to be the outskirts of a wealthy native empire.

Pizarro was worried, however, for as his ship drew nearer to Panama, word would soon get out about what they had seen. Other Spaniards might soon get the idea of heading south themselves and of stealing from him a potentially lucrative conquest. There was only one thing for Pizarro to do—he had to return to Spain. Only by petitioning the king and queen in person could he hope to obtain the exclusive rights to conquer and sack what appeared to be an untouched native kingdom. If not, then some other hastily thrown together corporation of plunder might beat him to it. Leaving Almagro behind in order to begin the preparations for their next voyage, Pizarro crossed the Isthmus, booked passage on a sailing ship, then set off for a land he hadn't seen in thirty years—Spain.

Fifty-one-year-old Francisco Pizarro arrived in the walled city of Seville in mid-1528. King Ferdinand and Queen Isabella, who had sponsored Columbus, had died more than a dozen years earlier; now their grandson, twenty-eight-year-old Charles V, was on the throne. Pizarro quickly made his way to Toledo, where he asked for an audience with the king. It had been nearly three decades since an impoverished, twenty-four-year-old Pizarro had set off to find his fortune in the New World. Pizarro now had three decades of experience in exploration and conquest, had helped to discover the Pacific Ocean, and had sailed further south than any other European along the unknown coast of the Southern Sea. Having carefully transported with him some of the llamas, jewelry, clothing, a small amount of gold, and the two native Amerindian boys, who were rapidly learning Spanish, Pizarro was now about to try to leverage what he hoped would be his trump card: that he had discovered a heretofore unknown native empire in a land he called Peru.

Pizarro, however, soon discovered that he wasn't the only conquistador who had come to lobby the king. Forty-three-year-old Hernando Cortés, who had conquered the Aztec Empire some seven years earlier, had just dazzled the royal court with a procession of treasures that would have rivaled those of Alexander the Great. An excellent showman, Cortés had brought forty native Amerindians with him, including three sons of Montezuma, the

Aztec lord whose empire he had conquered and who had lost his life in the struggle. Cortés had also brought native jugglers, dancers, acrobats, dwarfs, and hunchbacks, fabulous feather headdresses and cloaks, fans, shields, obsidian mirrors, turquoise, jade, silver, gold, and even an armadillo, an opossum, and a brace of snarling jaguars, none of which had ever before been seen.

The spectacular display had its desired effect. Although Cortés had risked conquering the Aztecs with no official permission, King Charles brushed that aside and marveled at everything he was shown, honoring the great conqueror by having Cortés sit beside him. The king then anointed Cortés with the title of marquis, named him Captain-General of Mexico, granted him an estate of 23,000 Aztec vassals, and also granted him 8 percent of all future profits derived from his conquests. At one stroke of the royal scepter, Cortés officially became one of the richest men in Europe as well as one of the most famous. Now, after having secured royal patronage, Cortés and his conquest would also be safe from the predations of other Spaniards.

With the visit of Cortés fresh in his mind, King Charles gave Pizarro a friendly reception. Although it had taken him thirty years, Pizarro had clearly moved up in the world, for now the former peasant from Extremadura was having an audience with one of the most powerful rulers in Europe. Soon to be crowned Holy Roman Emperor, King Charles V was not only the monarch of the kingdoms of Spain, but was also the ruler of the Netherlands, parts of what are now Austria and Germany, the kingdoms of the two Sicilies, an assortment of islands in the Caribbean, the Isthmus of Panama, and—with Cortés's recent conquest—Mexico. Before the king and his court, Pizarro brought out the llamas, the native clothing, vessels, pottery, and other goods and then described what he and his men had seen in this recently explored part of the world—the well-ordered city of Tumbez, its buildings, its inhabitants, the intricately cut stones, and especially the interior walls lined with glimmering sheets of gold. The normally taciturn conquistador apparently made a good sales pitch, for in July 1529, while the king was on his way to his coronation, Queen Isabella* signed a

---

* King Charles V married his cousin Isabella of Portugal on March 10, 1526. She was named after her maternal grandmother, Isabella I of Castile, who was Columbus's patron.

capitulación, or royal license, granting Pizarro the exclusive right to conquer the unexplored land of Peru. The queen, however, made it very clear exactly what was expected from him:

> As for you, Captain Francisco Pizarro, because of the desire that you have to serve us, you would like to continue the said conquest and settlement at your cost and upkeep so that at no time are we obligated to pay you or satisfy the expenses that you might have in it, except what was granted to you in this agreement. . . .
>
> First, I give permission and authority to you . . . that for us and in our name and in that of the royal crown of Castile, you may continue the said discovery and conquest and settlement of the province of Peru up to two hundred leagues [seven hundred miles] of land along the same coast. . . .
>
> [And] understanding that you are the executor in the service of God Our Lord and ours, and to honor your person and to benefit you and grant you favor, we promise to make you our governor and Captain General of all the province of Peru, land [and] villages that are at present and will later be within the entire two hundred leagues, for all the days of your life, with the salary of seven hundred twenty-five thousand maravedis each year, counted from the day that you set sail from these our kingdoms to continue the said settlement and conquest. This should be paid to you from the income and interests belonging to us in the said land that you would thus settle. . . .
>
> Further, we grant you the title of our Governor of the said province of Peru as well as the office of Marshal of the same, all this for the [rest of the] days of your life.

It was an excellent contract, as good as Pizarro could have hoped for, and was duly notarized, signed, sealed, and delivered. The queen had made it clear, however, that in terms of financing, Pizarro was for the most part completely on his own. Since Pizarro was the co-CEO of the Company of the Levant, it was up to him and his partners to raise the capital to buy the means of production with which to carry out their corporation's specialty: plunder. Ships, guns, knives, swords, daggers, lances, horses, gunpowder, provisions—all the accoutrements needed to bring a native empire to its knees—would have to be supplied by the conquistadors themselves, just as they had supplied them during previous expeditions.

Pizarro, having formed a company, having found what he hoped would be a native empire, and having secured a royal license, nevertheless needed further help. What was crucial at this point was finding a large group of young, stout, and well-armed entrepreneurs who would be willing to travel to the New World with him and who would follow his orders. There could be no better place to find them than in Extremadura; thus, after meeting with the king, Pizarro traveled to his native town of Trujillo in order to recruit a fresh batch of conquistadors.

Pizarro had little trouble finding them, for it seemed that every young Spaniard wanted to take part in what must have seemed at the time to be the modern equivalent of a hot, new IPO. Who in this impoverished region of dry land and thin crops wouldn't drop everything if he had a reasonable chance of acquiring instant wealth and of retiring to a great, New World estate—or of bringing that wealth home? In Trujillo, Pizarro gathered up his four half-brothers: twenty-nine-year-old Hernando, eighteen-year-old Juan, seventeen-year-old Gonzalo, and sixteen-year-old Francisco Martín. The five brothers would soon form the core of the enterprise; throughout the coming years they would remain a tight, loyal band of brothers, no matter how difficult and formidable the circumstances would become.

According to some accounts, not long after his presentation at court, rich now with titles and rewards, Hernando Cortés met with Pizarro. Thus, for a brief moment in time, the trajectories of the two men who would each conquer an empire intertwined. What was said between the two? No record of their conversation exists. But it is likely that the fabulously wealthy Cortés gave advice to his older and equally ambitious kinsman, and that after the meeting the latter was even more determined to repeat in Peru what Cortés had wrought in Mexico.

At last, in January of 1530 and with a flotilla of would-be conquistadors—none of whom had any experience in the New World—Pizarro set sail from Seville. Nearly three years would pass before in November of 1532 he and his four brothers would finally find themselves marching with 163 other Spaniards high up in the Andes, the air growing colder and sharper, on their way to a fateful meeting with Atahualpa, the great lord of Peru.

3 ❖ SUPERNOVA OF
THE ANDES

"Men do not rest content with parrying attacks of a superior, but often strike the first blow to prevent the attack being made. And we cannot fix the exact point at which our empire shall stop; we have reached a position in which we must not be content with retaining but must scheme to extend it, for, if we cease to rule others, we are in danger of being ruled ourselves."

THUCYDIDES, *THE HISTORY OF THE PELOPONNESIAN WAR*, 5TH CENTURY B.C.

"The Inca [emperor Pachacuti] then attacked the province of the Soras, forty leagues from Cuzco. The natives came forth to resist, asking why the invaders sought their lands, telling them to depart or they would be driven out by force. Over this question there was a battle, and two towns of the Soras were subdued. . . . They were taken prisoners to Cuzco, and there was a triumph over them."

PEDRO SARMIENTO DE GAMBOA, *HISTORY OF THE INCAS*, 1572

WHEN IN APRIL OF 1532 FRANCISCO PIZARRO ARRIVED within view of the Inca city of Tumbez, ready to begin his attempt to conquer the Kingdom of Peru, he was startled by how dramatically the city had changed since his last visit. Four years earlier, Tumbez had been an orderly city with a thousand dwellings and well-appointed buildings of finely cut stones. Now, however, the city lay in ruins. Walls had been pulled down, houses destroyed, and much of the population seemed to have disappeared. What in God's name had transpired?

CONQVISTA
DEFVNTOGVAINACAPAC
INGA. ILLAPA

The embalmed body of the emperor Huayna Capac,
killed by European-introduced smallpox,
being carried by native bearers to Cuzco in a royal litter.

As Pizarro wandered about the ruined city and asked questions of its dazed inhabitants, he relied on his interpreters, Felipillo and Martinillo, the native boys whom he had taught to speak Spanish. Through his interpreters he began to slowly piece together the story of what had happened, although many of the details would take years to uncover.

When Pizarro first arrived in Tumbez in 1528, the Inca Empire was ruled by a powerful emperor named Huayna Capac. At this particular moment in their history, the Incas had been carrying out a military campaign in the area that is now Ecuador, pacifying a local uprising against Inca rule.* The Incas themselves were a relatively small ethnic group that hailed from a region far to the south, in the valley of Cuzco. For a two-hundred-year period, roughly from A.D. 1200 to 1400, the Incas had gradually been consolidating their power in the Cuzco basin, conquering or intermarrying with their neighbors and slowly developing a small state. Then, beginning in the early 1400s, the Incas suddenly launched a series of protracted military adventures, conquering tribes across the Andes and on the coast. Their martial and organizational abilities were obviously exceptional, for within the space of some sixty years the Incas had—like a supernova exploding in the heart of the Andes—transformed their tiny kingdom originally measuring perhaps less than one hundred miles in diameter into an immense empire stretching for thousands of miles.

The empire stitched together by the Incas—who as an ethnic group never numbered more than one hundred thousand individuals—was, however, only the latest in a long series of kingdoms and empires that had risen and fallen in the Andes and on the coast for more than a thousand years. Sometime between 12,500 to 15,000 years ago, the first people had arrived in South America. Their ancestors presumably had crossed the Bering Strait land bridge and had worked their way down through North and Central America. The continent was still in the grips of the last ice age, and for the next three thousand years or so men and women made a living from hunting and gathering while using a variety of stone tools. As the ice age slowly retreated, the fauna and flora gradually changed and then, around 8,000 B.C., the first evidence of agriculture appeared—archaeologists have found

* Or at least certain Inca informants told the Spaniards that there had been an "uprising." Inca conquest ideology, however, often revolved around propaganda justifying their numerous military campaigns and conquests.

the remnants of cultivated potatoes in what is now northern Bolivia. Eventually, during a five-thousand-year period between 8,000 and 3,000 B.C., people in what is now Peru learned to domesticate both animals (llamas and alpacas) and food crops (potatoes, corn, quinoa, beans, peppers, squash, guava, etc.), abandoned the hunting and gathering lifestyle, and settled in permanent villages and towns. As more food was produced, local populations increased. And then something odd began occurring on the coast.

Peru's coastal plain is a narrow strip of land about 1,400 miles long and averaging less than fifty miles wide, hemmed in on the west by the Pacific Ocean and on the east by the Andes. It is extremely dry along most of its length, and in many areas rain doesn't fall for years at a time. The desert strip is penetrated, however, by more than thirty river valleys that carry water from the Andes down to the Pacific. In these valleys both fertile soil and water are abundant—prime real estate for the first agriculturalists. The Humboldt Current, meanwhile, which sweeps northward along the coast, is also one of the richest seas in the world for fish. Beginning in about 3200 B.C.—roughly during the same period when the Egyptians were building their first pyramids—people on Peru's northern coast began building terraced mounds alongside large plazas, ceremonial architecture, and large-scale settlements. The unusual thing about these people is that they farmed little and instead relied upon fish from the sea. In certain lowland coastal valleys, meanwhile, other groups who *did* farm began building their own large settlements and urban architecture.

Fast forward another three thousand years and the gradual process of population growth, competition for arable land, an erratic climate, advances in food production, and the conquest of adjacent river valleys led to the formation of the first state, or kingdom, that of the Moche (A.D. 100–800) on Peru's northern coast.* Life for the Moche kingdom's inhabitants was quite different from the lifestyle of the first farmers, who by now had existed for thousands of years in Peru. The latter, for example, had originally produced only enough seed for their own use as food and for planting the following growing season. In general, they paid no taxes and were beholden to no one. By the time the first kingdoms arose, however, farmers were now re-

---

* Western South America is one of only six locations in the world, after all, where the formation of a state-level society occurred. The other areas were MesoAmerica, China, Mesopotamia, the Indus Valley, Egypt, and northern China.

quired to produce a surplus of food or labor over and above their personal needs. They were then required to relinquish that surplus in order to support a ruler and an emerging upper class. Over thousands of years, on different parts of the coast and in different areas of the Andes, a growing number of Peru's inhabitants had gradually become peasants, or taxpayers, a new class of human being. "Civilization" had thus begun, which in its incipient form can be defined as the development of a complex social order based upon the division of labor between rulers and food-producing cultivators. Here, amid the barren deserts of Peru and high up in the Andes, a revolution had taken place, one that would form the basis of every subsequent Peruvian civilization to come. Small groups of people, or elites, had gained control over much larger masses of people.

Eventually a series of large, complex polities emerged, such as the Tiwanaku, Wari, and Chimu. By A.D. 900, in the region of Lake Titicaca, for example, the Tiwanaku civilization had already flourished for more than seven hundred years, had erected giant, perfectly cut stone monoliths and temples, had forged copper tools, and had created and maintained a capital of some 25,000 to 50,000 people, located high up on the altiplano at 12,600 feet in elevation (the population of London at the time, by comparison, was less than 30,000).

By A.D. 1400 the Kingdom of Tiwanaku had long since disappeared while, on the northwestern coast of Peru, the Chimu Empire had gradually conquered river valley after river valley, eventually extending its rule for nearly a thousand miles, from Tumbez in the north all of the way down the coast to where the modern capital of Lima now lies. Had the Spaniards arrived in Peru one hundred years earlier than they did, say in 1432 rather than in 1532, the Spanish chroniclers would no doubt have written excitedly about the great Chimu Empire and about its golden treasures—while the tiny Inca kingdom far to the south would have been largely ignored.

As Chimu lords administered their empire, built irrigation canals, and collected the taxes in the form of labor from the masses of peasants under their control, far to the south, however, the tiny Kingdom of the Incas suddenly began to explode. According to Inca legend, the Inca "Alexander the Great" who began this process was a man named Cusi Yupanqui. At the time of his ascension sometime in the early fifteenth century, the Kingdom of the Incas spread over a relatively minuscule area that was centered around the valley of Cuzco, located at 11,300 feet in the Andes. The Kingdom of the Incas was no different from other kingdoms that had existed in Peru, however, with peasants relinquishing their power to warrior kings who, in this particular case, maintained their exalted positions by claiming divine descent from the ultimate source of all life, the sun.

Because land and resources were finite, the lords of Peru's scattered highland kingdoms and smaller polities were constantly on guard against the attacks of others, or else were busy planning attacks themselves. Rulers had to protect both the fertile soil they had either inherited or seized as well as the peasants who supported and defended them, if their kingdoms were to survive. Only by maintaining the integrity of their realms could the rulers and their associated elites maintain themselves in power and thus retain their own privileged lifestyles. No matter what other characteristic a ruler might possess, the primordial one was that he be good at warfare. And since theirs was a competitive world in which a hostile and expanding kingdom beyond their borders could at any time prove lethal to their own, the elites realized that there was an obvious advantage in possessing as large a kingdom as possible. The larger the kingdom, the more warriors that could be assembled, and thus the less vulnerable the kingdom would be to attack.

According to Inca oral history, in the early fifteenth century, the Kingdom of the Chancas, which lay centered in the Andahuayllas region to the west of Cuzco, began coveting the fertile valleys controlled by the tiny Kingdom of the Incas. Marshaling an army, the Chancas began marching east, determined to annex the Incas' kingdom and thus expand their own. Victory seemed imminent, for the Incas were few in number and were both weak and politically divided.

The Inca king on the throne at the time, Viracocha Inca, was already quite elderly. Rather than fight, he chose to flee the capital, holing up in a fortress and basically abandoning his kingdom. One of his sons, however, Cusi Yupanqui, seized the initiative: he quickly made alliances with nearby ethnic groups, raised an army, and then marched out defiantly to meet the Chancas. In the fierce battle that ensued—one that included heavy wooden clubs tipped with stone or copper spikes—the Incas decisively defeated the Chancas. An event that had once loomed as an imminent disaster had been transformed into an overwhelming victory.

After deposing his father, Cusi Yupanqui then decided to adopt the name

Pachacuti (pah cha KOO tee), which means "earthshaker" or "cataclysm," or "he who turns the world upside down." The name was an appropriate one, for Pachacuti immediately began a major restructuring of the Inca kingdom, laying out new thoroughfares in its capital, Cuzco, and ordering the construction of buildings and palaces in what has since been called the imperial style of precisely cut stones. According to the chronicler Pedro Sarmiento de Gamboa, Pachacuti next

> turned his attention to the people. Seeing that there were not sufficient lands for sowing, so as to sustain them, he went round the city at a distance of four leagues from it, considering the valleys, situation, and villages. He depopulated all that were within two leagues of the city. The lands of depopulated villages were given to the city and its inhabitants, and the deprived people were settled in other parts. The citizens of Cuzco were well satisfied with the arrangement, for they were given what cost little, and thus he made friends by presents taken from others, and took the valley of Tambo as his own.*

Perhaps with the recent memory of the Chanca attack still on his mind and how close the Inca kingdom had come to being exterminated, Pachacuti soon turned his attention to his kingdom's borders, most of which could be reached within a couple days' walk. Inca kings in the past had occasionally plundered neighboring villages and sometimes had demanded tribute from them. Pachacuti, however, now became the first Inca king to begin seizing adjacent lands and occupying them on a massive scale. Plunder, Pachacuti no doubt realized, is usually a one-time event, whereas he who controls the means of production—the land and the peasants—by contrast, has a source of power that is virtually inexhaustible.

Soon, and with an army of conscripted peasant warriors, Pachacuti began a series of military adventures on a scale that no Inca king had ever before envisaged. Turning toward the south, Pachacuti led his army on a campaign that soon pushed the boundaries of his kingdom six hundred miles, marching past Lake Titicaca and then down through what is now Bolivia and northern Chile, conquering as he went. Directing his attention to the north-

---

* The Tambo Valley is now known as the Sacred, or Vilcanota, Valley.

west, Pachacuti began rapidly to conquer the amalgam of tribes, kingdoms, and city-states that lay strewn across the Andes. Pachacuti's bold forays and those of his son, Tupac Inca, eventually culminated in the toppling of the old Chimu Empire, located on the northwestern coast. Within a single lifetime, then, Pachacuti and his son had seized a 1,400-mile stretch of the Andes, from present-day Bolivia to northern Peru, plus much of the adjacent coast. No longer were the Incas a small, pregnable group exposed to the vagaries of other kingdoms' marauding armies. Pachacuti had become the first Inca king to fashion a veritable *empire*—a vast, multiethnic conglomeration that had been created through conquest and that Pachacuti now ruled over with a tiny band of Inca elite.

Pachacuti called his new empire Tawantinsuyu, or "the four parts united," as he divided it into four regions: Chinchaysuyu, Cuntisuyu, Collasuyu, and Antisuyu.* The capital, Cuzco, lay at the intersection where all four *suyus* came together. In a sense, Pachacuti and Tupac Inca had created a conquest enterprise. Through threat, negotiation, or actual bloody conquest, they subjugated new provinces, determined the number of tax-paying peasants, installed a local Inca governor, and then left an administration in place that was empowered to supervise and collect taxes before their armies moved on. If cooperative, the local elites were allowed to retain their privileged positions and were rewarded handsomely for their collaboration. If uncooperative, the Incas exterminated them and wiped out their supporters. Peasants were a crop, a crop that could be harvested through periodic taxation. Docile, obedient workers who created surpluses, in fact, were a crop more valuable than any of the five thousand varieties of potatoes the Incas cultivated in the Andes, more valuable even than the vast herds of llamas and alpacas that the Incas periodically used for their meat and wool. It was the peasants and their associated lands that the Incas coveted, and it was by taxing the peasants' labor that the Inca elite continued to increase their wealth, prestige, and power.

Tupac Inca, who had carried out successful campaigns in the north and on the coast, also succeeded in extending the Inca Empire farther east, marching from the high frigid plains of the Andes down into the sweltering

---

* *Tawantin* in the Inca language, Quechua, means a group of four things (*tawa* means four with the suffix -*ntin,* which names a group; and *suyu,* which means "part").

Amazon jungle. He then extended the empire's southern border another seven hundred miles deeper into Chile, past modern-day Santiago.

By the time Tupac Inca's son, Huayna Capac, took the throne, the supernova that was the Inca Empire had reached its zenith and its expansion was almost complete. The empire now stretched from what would later become southern Colombia all the way down to central Chile, and from the Pacific Ocean up over the broad, uplifted Andes with its twenty-thousand-foot peaks and down into the Amazon jungle. Amazingly, an elite of perhaps one hundred thousand ethnic Incas ultimately controlled a population of perhaps ten million individuals. Beyond the empire's frontiers, there were neither kingdoms nor peasantry left to conquer, rather only non-state peoples who were impossible to control. In these areas the Incas demarcated their borders and built forts to protect themselves from the incursions of the stateless "barbarians." The Incas' revolutionary seizure of the Andes had occurred in just two generations, during the reigns of Pachacuti and Tupac Inca. Pachacuti's grandson, Huayna Capac, therefore, limited his own military campaigns to securing the empire's borders and to pacifying the last rebellious tribes in the north.

Soon after subjugating much of what is now known as Ecuador, however, Huayna Capac began to hear strange reports of a new danger confronting his empire, one that would prove far deadlier than any provincial rebellion. Native runners, or *chaskis,* presumably arrived breathlessly at court one day to report that a sickness had appeared in the north, a terrible one that was devastating the inhabitants. The afflicted people first developed frightful skin eruptions all over their bodies, then sickened and died. Even worse, the messengers reported, it appeared that the sickness was now spreading toward Quito, where Huayna Capac and his royal retinue were living. The descriptions were gruesome enough to cause the emperor to seclude himself and to begin to fast, hoping to avoid contact with the mysterious plague. It was already too late, however, for according to the chronicler Juan de Betanzos, Huayna Capac soon

> fell ill and the illness took his reason and understanding and gave him a skin irritation like leprosy that greatly weakened him. When the nobles saw him so far gone they came to him; it seemed to them that he had

come a little to his senses and they asked him to name a lord since he
was at the end of his days.

The stricken emperor told his nobles that his son, Ninan Cuyoche, should
inherit the empire, if the omens were propitious in this regard and, if not,
that another son, Huascar (HUAS car), should ascend to the throne. The
Inca nobles soon slaughtered a llama, opened it up, removed its lungs, and
then looked carefully at the animal's veins for an omen. The pattern of veins
unfortunately appeared to foretell a bleak future for both Ninan Cuyoche
and for Huascar. By the time the nobles returned with the news, however,
the great Huayna Capac, ruler of the largest empire in the Americas, was already dead. As they had been instructed, the nobles dutifully went in search
of the young king, "but when they arrived at Tumi-pampa, they found that
. . . Ninan Cuyoche was [already] dead of the pestilence."

Ironically, as Huayna Capac had lay dying from the strange affliction, it
was apparently at precisely this moment that he is said to have received the
first reports of a strange ship, one that had arrived from the north and had
moored before the conquered Chimu city of Tumbez. In his delirious state,
the emperor was told of the passengers' light-colored skin, of their full
beards, and of the strange tools (harquebuses) they possessed, some of
which made smoke and spoke like thunder. This, of course, was the native
version of Francisco Pizarro's second expedition of 1526–1528, during
which he and a handful of men had anchored before Tumbez and an inquisitive Inca noble had climbed on board. Pizarro had no idea at the time that
a pestilence from the Old World had preceded him to Peru. Or that even as
he was marveling at the wealth and orderliness of Tumbez, that natives elsewhere in the Inca Empire were already being decimated—including the
empire's very ruler, Huayna Capac—by this disease.

Diseases from the Old World had arrived in the Caribbean, however, as
early as 1494, introduced by some of the passengers on Columbus's second
voyage. Columbus had not only begun to ferry people over from the Old
World to the New, after all, but he unwittingly had also begun to transport
microscopic pathogens that were as deadly as they were invisible. Eventually, smallpox, measles, bubonic and pneumonic plagues, typhus, cholera,
malaria, and yellow fever arrived, either one by one or in clusters. They

quickly spread among the native inhabitants, who, due to their isolation, had no natural immunities. A plague of smallpox even followed in the footsteps of Hernando Cortés's expedition against the Aztecs, who called the frightening affliction *huey zahuatl,* or "the big rash." Wrote the sixteenth-century historian Francisco López de Gómara:

> It was a dreadful illness and many people died of it. No one could walk; they could only lie stretched out on their beds. No one could move, not even able to turn their heads. One could not lie face down, or lie on the back, nor turn from one side to another. When they did move, they screamed in pain.

After devastating the Aztecs and inadvertently helping Cortés to conquer their empire, the smallpox plague began moving southward, like a slowly moving wave, disseminating death through Central America and then finally onto the South American continent. There it was transmitted, always ahead of the Spanish advance, by natives who infected others before they themselves died. Sometime around 1527, the germs carried across an ocean by Columbus finally arrived at the outskirts of the Inca Empire, taking the life of Huayna Capac and his heir.

Roughly two years later, as Pizarro journeyed to Spain in order to lobby for permission to conquer the land called Peru, the last thing he could have imagined was that the conquest he was hoping to lead had already begun. The smallpox virus introduced from Europe had not only killed the Inca emperor, but had set off a brutal war of succession that now threatened to destroy the very empire that Pizarro hoped one day to conquer.

As in the kingdoms of Europe, Inca government was basically a monarchy in which the power to rule passed from father to son. Where it differed from the European version, however, was that the Inca emperor had multiple wives and Inca custom did not include the notion of primogeniture, that is, the right of the eldest son to inherit the title and property of his parents, to the exclusion of all other children. Instead, and apparently from earliest times, after the death of each ruler the Incas anticipated a struggle to take place amongst the potential heirs.

Europeans, of course, were not immune to struggles of dynastic succession. They were common enough, in fact, to provide Shakespeare the raw material from which he fashioned many of his history plays and tragedies. The difference between European and Inca versions of monarchy, however, was that among the Incas bloody dynastic struggles were expected; they were the norm, not the exception. Apparently the thinking was that if a royal contender were cunning, bold, and aggressive enough to seize control of the throne, then he probably had what it took to successfully rule the empire. The formula for dynastic succession in the Inca Empire, therefore, was one that allowed for the most able candidate to rise to the top. Even if an emperor designated an heir, there was no guarantee of a smooth transition. To leave no heir or, in the case of Huayna Capac's death, to suddenly designate one, only meant that the normal free-for-all of Inca dynastic succession would be exacerbated. Which is precisely what began to occur in Peru beginning around 1527.

Most Inca accounts state that after Huayna Capac's death, his son Huascar was crowned as emperor in Cuzco, a thousand miles to the south. Another son, Atahualpa, remained in Quito, meanwhile, which Huayna Capac had made into an ancillary capital during his constant campaigns in what is now Ecuador. Born from different mothers, Atahualpa and Huascar were half-brothers. Both were in their mid-twenties at the time of their father's death, yet had completely opposite temperaments. Atahualpa had been born in Cuzco, had lived for many years in the far north with his father, had taken an avid interest in military pursuits, and was known for being extremely severe with anyone who differed with him. Huascar, on the other hand, had been born in a small village to the south of Cuzco, had little interest in military affairs, drank to excess, commonly slept with married women, and was known to murder their husbands if they complained.* If Atahualpa was the serious type, then Huascar was the party boy. Each, however, bore a sense of entitlement that made him ruthless if even the smallest portion of those entitlements was threatened.

Though Atahualpa and Huascar shared the same father, they belonged to completely different royal descent groups, or *panaqas*. Atahualpa belonged through his mother to the descent group known as the *Hatun ayllu,* while Huascar belonged through his mother to the group known as the *Qhapaq*

---

* This description of Huascar comes down to us from Juan de Betanzos, a Spaniard who married Atahualpa's sister. The description, therefore, is probably a biased one.

ayllu. Both of these descent groups were competitive with one another, having struggled for supremacy and power now over several generations. And, as royal successions often provided the spark that unleashed open political warfare, from the moment that Atahualpa did not show up in Cuzco for his father's massive funeral and for his brother's subsequent coronation, Huascar became suspicious. Huascar's paranoia—derived no doubt from an Inca history that was richly embroidered with tales of brutal palace coups— became so acute that he is even said to have murdered some of his relatives who had accompanied his father's corpse to Cuzco, having suspected them of plotting an insurrection.

Huascar's suspicions eventually got the better of him, suspicions that were presumably only accentuated by the inefficiency of the many messages and counter-messages that had to be carried between the two brothers over a thousand miles each way by relay runners. The newly crowned emperor finally decided to wage a military campaign in order to settle the question of succession once and for all. His decision to launch a war was not well thought out however, for it immediately put Huascar at a disadvantage. Since Huascar's father, Huayna Capac, had been carrying out extensive military campaigns in the north, his brother Atahualpa now had the advantage of being able to take command of the empire's most seasoned and battle-hardened troops. The troops were led by the empire's three finest generals, who immediately pledged their allegiance to Atahualpa. Huascar, by contrast, was forced to assemble an army of native conscripts who had little if any military experience. Where Huascar in the south led a largely untested army, Atahualpa commanded a seasoned imperial force. Nevertheless, Huascar quickly went on the offensive, sending an army north into what is now Ecuador, under the command of Atoq ("the Fox").

The two Inca armies met on the plains of Mochacaxa, to the south of Quito. There the northern army, supervised by Atahualpa, scored the first victory in what was now a full-fledged civil war. Even in victory, however, Atahualpa's severity with those who dared challenge him was evident when General Atoq was captured. Atoq was first tortured and eventually executed with darts and arrows. Atahualpa then ordered Atoq's skull to be fashioned into a gilded drinking cup, which the Spaniards would note that Atahualpa was still using four years later.

With the momentum now on Atahualpa's side, his generals began a long military advance down the spine of the Andes, gradually pushing Huascar's forces further and further south. After a long series of victories on the part of Atahualpa's forces and defeats on the part of Huascar's, a final climactic engagement was fought outside Cuzco during which the Inca emperor himself was captured, as described by the sixteenth-century chronicler Juan de Betanzos:

> Huascar was badly wounded and his clothing was ripped to shreds. Since the wounds were not life-threatening, [Atahualpa's General] Chalcuchima did not allow him to be treated. When daylight came and it was found that none of Huascar's men had escaped, Chalcuchima's troops enjoyed Huascar's loot. The tunic Huascar wore was removed and he was dressed in another from one of his Indians who was dead on the field. Huascar's tunic, his gold halberd [axe] and helmet, also gold, with the shield that had gold trappings, his feathers, and the war insignias he had were sent to Atahualpa. This was done in Huascar's presence, [as Generals] Chalcuchima and Quisquis wanted Atahualpa to have the honor, as their lord, of treading upon the things and ensigns of enemies who had been subjected.

Atahualpa's northern Inca army now marched triumphantly into Cuzco. It was led by two of Atahualpa's finest generals, Quisquis and Chalcuchima, who had successfully directed the four-year-long campaign. One can only imagine what the citizens of Cuzco thought, seeing their former emperor stripped of his insignias and royal clothing, wearing the bloodstained clothing of a mere commoner, bound and led down the streets on foot, while Atahualpa's generals rode majestically in their decorated litters, surrounded by their victorious troops.

The aftermath of the civil war to determine who would inherit the vast Inca Empire—and all the peasants and fertile lands within it—was as predictable as it was brutal. Within a short while, Inca troops rounded up Huascar's various wives and children and took them to a place called Quicpai, outside Cuzco. There the official in charge "ordered that each and every one learn the charges against him or her. Each and every one was told why they were to die." As Huascar's captors forced him to watch, native soldiers methodically began to slaughter his wives and daughters, one by one, leav-

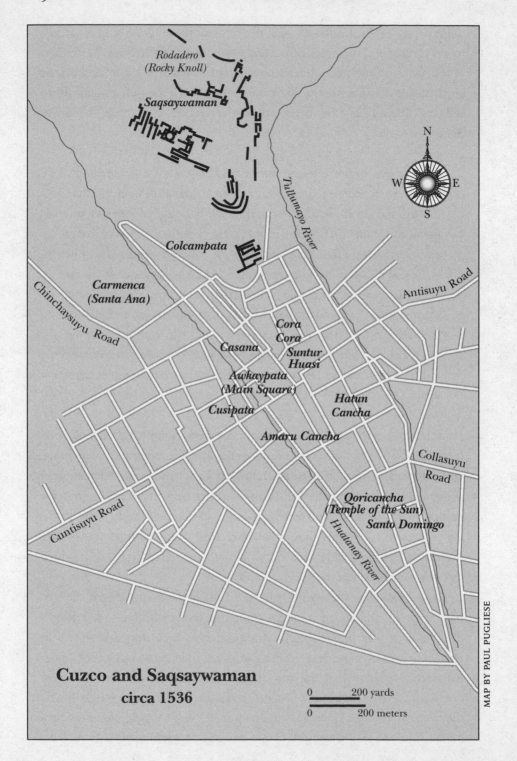

Rodadero
(Rocky Knoll)

Saqsaywaman

Tullumayo River

N
W   E
S

Colcampata

Carmenca
(Santa Ana)

Chinchaysuyu Road

Antisuyu Road

Cora
Cora
Casana   Suntur
          Huasi
Awkaypata
(Main Square)

Cusipata

Amaru Cancha

Hatun
Cancha

Collasuyu
Road

Cuntisuyu Road

Qoricancha
(Temple of the Sun)
Santo Domingo

Huatanay River

Cuzco and Saqsaywaman
circa 1536

0   200 yards

0   200 meters

MAP BY PAUL PUGLIESE

ing them to hang. Soldiers then ripped unborn babies from their mothers' wombs, hanging them by their umbilical cords from their mothers' legs. "The rest of the lords and ladies who were prisoners were tortured by a type of torture they call *chacnac* [whipping], before they were killed," wrote the chronicler Betanzos. "After being tormented, they were killed by smashing their heads to pieces with battle-axes they call *chambi,* which are used in battle."

Thus, in one final orgy of bloodletting, Atahualpa's generals exterminated nearly the entire germ seed of Huascar's familial line. Huascar was then forced to begin a long journey northward on foot to face the wrath of his brother.

Atahualpa, meanwhile, had traveled southward from Quito to the city of Cajamarca, located in what is now northern Peru, some six hundred miles to the north of Cuzco. There he waited for word of the outcome of his generals' attack on the capital. Even via the Incas' state-of-the-art messenger system, in which messages were carried by relay runners, or *chaskis,* news of the final battle and of Huascar's dramatic capture had to pass between more than three hundred different runners. It would take at least five days to arrive. Only then would Atahualpa receive word that he was now the unchallenged lord of the Inca Empire, emperor of the known civilized world.

With all of his attention concentrated upon the steady, though delayed, stream of successful battle reports sent by his generals, Atahualpa was already busy making preparations for the coronation he envisioned in Cuzco, the city of his youth. There, he would preside over the usual massive festivities—the processions, feastings, sacrifices, the debauched drinking and copious urinations—and finally, over the majestic coronation itself. Afterward—as his father, grandfather, and great-grandfather had done before him—Atahualpa would no doubt look forward to decades of uninterrupted rule, a monarch whose every action and pronouncement would be considered the divine acts of a god.

There was only one minor affair, however, that Atahualpa had yet to attend to before he began his triumphal march southward to claim his empire. *Chaski* reports of a relatively small band of unusual foreigners, who were now marching into the Andes in his direction, had been reaching him for the last several months. Some of the strangers, he was told, rode giant animals the Incas had no word for as none had ever before been seen. The men grew hair on their faces and had sticks from which issued thunder and clouds of smoke. Although few in number—the royal *quipu* knots carried by the messengers indicated that there were precisely 168—the foreigners behaved arrogantly and had already tortured and killed some provincial chiefs. Rather than immediately order their extermination, however, Atahualpa decided to allow the strangers to penetrate a short way further into his empire. Protected by his army, Atahualpa was curious to see these strange men and their even stranger beasts for himself.

It was November 1532, the season in which the Andes begins its slow transition into the Southern Hemisphere's summer. And, as news of the final victory in Cuzco continued to race northward on foot along the often lonely and fantastic contours of the Andes, Atahualpa no doubt pondered for a moment this strange intrusion from the west. Who were these people? Why would they dare intrude into an empire where his armies could crush them if he so much as raised his little finger? As Atahualpa listened to the latest report about the bold yet obviously foolish invaders, intermixed with the much more interesting news arriving each day from the south, he lifted up the gilded skull of his former enemy, Atoq, the Fox, took a long cool drink from its rim of gold and bone, then turned his attention to the more pressing matters at hand.

4 ❖ WHEN EMPIRES COLLIDE

> "For ourselves, we shall not trouble you with specious pretenses—
> either of how we have a right to our empire because we overthrew
> the Mede, or are now attacking you because of wrong that you
> have done us—and make a long speech that would not be be-
> lieved. . . . You know as well as we do that right, as the world
> goes, is only in question between equals in power, while the
> strong do what they can and the weak suffer what they must."
>
> THUCYDIDES, *THE HISTORY OF THE*
> *PELOPONNESIAN WAR*, 5TH CENTURY B.C.

AMID THE RUINS OF TUMBEZ, PIZARRO HAD LEARNED THE
general outlines of the current military situation in Peru. He had landed on
the outskirts of an empire, Pizarro was told, one that two royal brothers had
been fighting over. The ruler whom Pizarro had heard about during his last
voyage, Huayna Capac, was now dead. Tumbez lay in ruins because the inhabitants of that city—not ethnic Incas but citizens of the former Chimu
Empire that the Incas had conquered—had sided with one of the brothers,
Huascar. The city had thus been attacked and razed by the armies of
Huascar's brother, Atahualpa, who currently was with an army in the mountains only about two hundred miles, or about a two weeks' march, to the
southeast.

The grim news of native warfare, disease, and devastation could only have
excited the conquistadors. Twelve years earlier in Mexico, Hernando Cortés
had effectively exploited native political divisions to help bring down the
powerful Aztec Empire. Here, by the sounds of it, Pizarro had arrived at the
tail end of a full-fledged civil war. With any luck, he undoubtedly realized,
he might ally himself with one side or the other—either with the victor or

55

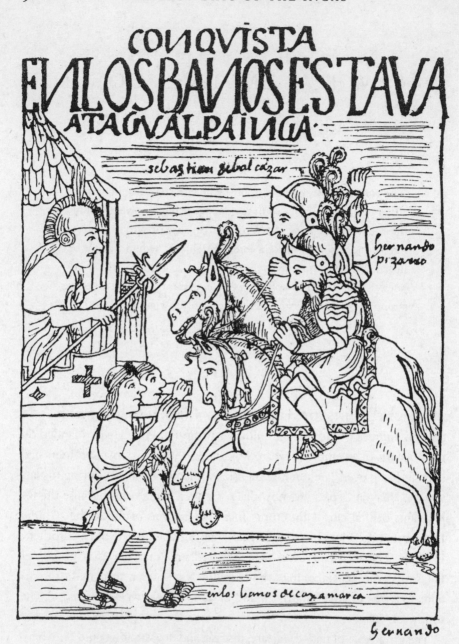

The first meeting between an Inca emperor and a Spaniard: Hernando
Pizarro and Atahualpa Inca. Atahualpa was actually seated on a small stool
on the ground for the encounter while Hernando Pizarro was accompanied
by Hernando de Soto, not by Sebastián de Benalcázar, as is depicted here.

with the vanquished—with the goal of destroying both sides in the end. But first he would have to make contact with one of the warring factions.

Pizarro and his men now became the first group of Europeans to climb into the Andes, a mountain chain more than four thousand miles in length and with dozens of peaks puncturing the heights at over twenty thousand feet.* Marching and riding along a well-maintained Inca road, the Spaniards found innumerable dead natives in one town, strung up and left to hang by their feet. Apparently these were citizens of a community loyal to Huascar that had been razed by his brother. Informed that Atahualpa was aware of their presence and worried about what forces he might bring to bear against them, the Spaniards seized and then tortured a reluctant informant, hoping to pry information out of him. The Inca emperor, the man finally blurted out, awaited them with hostile intentions; Atahualpa had said he would kill the bearded strangers.

Alarmed, yet not knowing whether to believe their informant or not, the conquistadors nevertheless continued to ascend higher and higher. At night, they "rested in the cotton tents they brought with them, making fires to protect themselves from the great cold of the mountains. For on the plains of Castile [in Spain] it is not colder than in these mountains, which are devoid of trees but are covered with a grass like a short *esparto*. There are a few stunted trees and the water is so cold that it cannot be drunk without first warming it."

The Spaniards numbered 168: 106 on foot and sixty-two on horse. They did not know how many warriors Atahualpa commanded. But the natives they questioned and tortured told them that Atahualpa commanded a large army. Pizarro by now was fifty-four years old. Alongside him traveled his four half-brothers: thirty-one-year-old Hernando, who was one of his captains; twenty-one-year-old Juan; twenty-year-old Gonzalo; and his nineteen-year-old half-brother from his mother's side, Francisco Martín. None of his four half-brothers had any previous experience in native conquests; what little they had had been gained on this trip.

Out in front of the group, on a handsome and energetic horse, rode one of the newest arrivals, the dashing Hernando de Soto, the future explorer of

---

* Aleixo Garcia, the Portuguese adventurer, was actually the first European to climb into the Andes.

Florida and discoverer of the Mississippi River. Thirty-two years old and given to wearing rakish clothes and an assortment of earrings, Soto had arrived on a separate ship just before Pizarro's departure from Tumbez. He had brought along his own, handpicked men and Pizarro had immediately made him a captain.

Also tagging along with the makeshift group of entrepreneurs—all armed, self-financed, and therefore entitled to a proportional slice of any future spoils—were a few black slaves, twelve notaries—four of whom would later write eyewitness accounts of the expedition—a Dominican friar, at least several *moriscas* (slave women of Muslim descent), native slaves from Nicaragua, and a handful of merchants. The latter had no interest in fighting but were there solely to sell their wares to the conquistadors on credit, hoping to be repaid if any gold or other treasure were found. The merchants, evidently, were banking on the old Spanish proverb, *"el dinero llama al dinero"* ("money attracts money"), hoping in the end to make large capital gains on their investments.

On Friday, November 15, the stage was finally set for the second major collision of two civilizations from completely different worlds. The first collision had been with the Aztecs, a fierce struggle that had lasted for three years, involved the capture of the Aztec emperor, and culminated with Hernando Cortés directing a mass slaughter and razing the Aztec capital. Now, as Pizarro and his fellow Spaniards climbed over a mountain pass and looked down for the first time upon the green valley of Cajamarca, located at an elevation of nine thousand feet, two empires were once again poised to collide. Here, just a few miles beyond the Inca town, Atahualpa and his army were encamped, spread out along a hillside beside a vast armada of tents. It was the Spaniards' first glimpse of an Inca army. The notary Miguel de Estete wrote:

> So many tents were visible that it truly frightened us. We never thought that Indians could maintain such a magnificent estate nor have so many tents. . . . Nothing like this had been seen in the Indies up till then. It filled all of us Spaniards with confusion and fear although it was not appropriate for us to show any fear nor to turn back. For had they sensed any weakness in us the very Indians [porters] we were bringing along would have killed us. Thus, with simulated good spirits and after having

thoroughly observed the town and the tents . . . we descended into the valley and entered the town of Cajamarca.

The Spaniards rode and marched into town, three abreast and in military formation, with the iron-shod hooves of their horses clacking against the stone-paved streets and with storm clouds gathering overhead. Like a scene from *High Noon,* the town appeared empty—most of the inhabitants had either hidden or fled. Described the notary Francisco de Xerez:

> This town, which is the principal town in the valley, is situated on the skirts of a mountain and there is a league of open plain [in front of it]. Two rivers flow through the valley, which is level and well populated and is surrounded by mountains. The town has two thousand inhabitants . . . the plaza is larger than any in Spain and is completely enclosed [by a wall], and has two doorways that open upon the streets of the town. The houses are more than two hundred paces in length and very well made; they are surrounded by strong walls some fifteen feet high. The roofs are covered with straw and wood which rest on the walls . . . their walls are of very well cut blocks of stone.

Pizarro led his men directly to the main square, where they could assemble together and decide what to do. Surrounded by a wall with only two entrances, the square seemed the safest place available while they waited for word from the Inca lord. Hail now began to fall, the tiny balls of ice bouncing upon the stone paving of the courtyard and striking the Spaniards' curved steel helmets and armor. The Spaniards took shelter in the buildings of cut stone flanking the plaza, which were built like a series of galleries with trapezoidal doors. When no messenger arrived from Atahualpa, the impatient Pizarro decided to send fifteen of his best horsemen, under the command of Captain Hernando de Soto, to invite the Inca emperor to a meeting.

The selection of Soto was a wise choice, for, other than Pizarro, he was perhaps the most experienced conquistador among them. Although small in size, Soto had arrived in Peru with an already well-established reputation. Impetuous, gallant, brave, and excellent with a lance, he was also a renowned rider, scout, and Indian fighter. Also an *extremeño,* Soto had arrived in the

New World while still a teenager in 1513, the same year that Balboa and Pizarro had discovered the Pacific. Despite his youth, Soto's rise had been meteoric. By the age of seventeen he and two partners had formed a corporation of plunder and by 1520, in his early twenties, he was already a captain.

By the time he was thirty, Hernando de Soto possessed large native estates in newly conquered Nicaragua and could have retired in comfort. Hugely ambitious, however, like Cortés and Pizarro, Soto wanted a governorship—a native realm to rule as his own. Thus in 1530 Soto and his partner—Hernan Ponce de León—negotiated an agreement with Pizarro: if Soto and his partner would provide two ships and a contingent of men, then Pizarro would give them partial command and some of the choicest fruits of the proposed conquest of Peru—whatever those fruits might prove to be. Two years later, and presently high up in Peru's northern Andes, the now thirty-two-year-old Soto was leading an advance party on horseback along the paved stone road connecting Cajamarca and the camp of the most powerful native lord in the Americas. According to Xerez,

> [The Incas' camp] was formed on the flank of a small hill with the tents, which were of cotton, extending for three and a half miles and with Atahualpa's in the center. All the warriors stood outside their tents with their weapons thrust into the ground, which are long lances that resemble pikes. There seemed to be more than thirty thousand warriors in the camp.

Soto and his men rode through the legions of motionless Inca infantry, who stared silently after them. The troops betrayed no emotion but no doubt must have been astonished to see bearded men, many of them wearing glinting metal and riding what looked to be some kind of giant llama. Avoiding a bridge, the Spaniards splashed their way on horses across a low river, sending up beads of water that glistened in the sunlight. At a second river Soto ordered most of his men to remain, taking only two along with him, as well as the interpreter Felipillo to meet the Inca emperor.

Not far ahead, a native pointed them in the direction of a building that proved to be a sort of bathhouse; inside lay a courtyard where an artificial pool of smooth stone had been constructed for bathing. Two stone pipes, one carrying hot thermal water and the other water that was icy cold, fed into the bath. There, on a grassy area before the entryway to the courtyard, sat a man on a low stool who wore a long tunic, abundant gold jewelry, and a scarlet sash that hung across his forehead. Although the man did not look up, both by his demeanor and by the obvious deference of those around him, Soto realized that this could be none other than Atahualpa, the great Inca emperor. After three expeditions, culminating in over four years of arduous travel, a vanguard of Pizarro's latest expedition had finally come face-to-face with "that great lord Atahualpa, about whom we had heard so many reports and had been told so many things. . . . He was seated on a small stool, very low on the ground, as the Turks and Moors are accustomed to sit. He projected such majesty and splendor as had never before been seen." Another eyewitness recounted, "He was seated [on a low stool] . . . with all the majesty in the world, surrounded by all of his women, and with many chiefs near him . . . each standing according to his rank."

Although all Inca nobles wore headbands and clothing with patterned symbols displaying both their rank and place of origin, the Inca ruler was the only individual in this empire of ten million souls who was allowed to wear the sacred royal fringe, or *mascaypacha*. Carefully woven by his female attendants, or *mamaconas*, the delicate fringe hung from a headband and was made of "a very fine scarlet wool, very evenly cut, and very cleverly bound in the middle by small golden tubes. This wool was corded, but below the tubes it was unwound and this was the part that fell upon the forehead. . . . This fringe fell to just above the eyebrows, was an inch thick, and covered his entire forehead."

Brash and impudent, having killed countless natives in hand-to-hand combat, Hernando de Soto rode his horse right up to the Inca emperor, approaching so close that the horse's breath caused the emperor's royal fringe to momentarily flutter. Atahualpa, however, confronted by a thousand-pound animal he had never seen before and by a strange foreigner who now looked down upon him from a height of nine feet, didn't so much as flinch. Instead, the Inca lord kept his eyes to the ground, neither looking up nor acknowledging the Spaniard's presence. With Felipillo interpreting, Soto launched into a prepared speech, the first one ever delivered by a European to an Inca emperor:

"Most serene Inca! You will know that there are in the world two princes more powerful than all the rest. One of them is the supreme pontiff who represents God. He administers and rules all those who keep his divine law, and teaches his holy word. The other is the emperor of the Romans, Charles V, king of Spain. These two monarchs, aware of the blindness of the inhabitants of these realms who disrespect the true God, maker of heaven and earth, and [who] adore . . . the very demon who deceives them, have sent our Governor and Captain General Don Francisco Pizarro and his companions and some priests, who are ministers of God, to teach Your Highness and all his vassals this divine truth and His holy law, for which reason they have come to this country. And having enjoyed the liberality of your royal hand on the way, they . . . entered Cajamarca, and have . . . sent us to Your Highness to lay the foundation of concord, brotherhood, and perpetual peace that should exist between us, so that you may receive us under your protection and hear the divine law from us and all your people may learn and receive it, for it will be the greatest honor, advantage, and salvation to them all.

In the midst of a vast army, and before the Incas' royal court, Soto and his small group waited for a response. Soto assumed that his words had been correctly translated and that the speech and the background information necessary to understand it were intelligible to the Inca emperor. At least one later chronicler, however, who was bilingual in Spanish and in the Incas' language of *runasimi,* or "people speech," questioned the ability of the young translator to accomplish such a daunting task.* The mestizo (mixed-blood) chronicler Garcilaso de la Vega wrote:

With regard to the version [of the speech] that reached Atahualpa, it is to be remarked that Felipe, the Indian translator who interpreted, was . . .

---

* The Incas more than likely called their language *runasimi,* from *runa,* which means "people," and *simi,* which means "speech." It wasn't until 1560 that the term *Quechua* first appeared in a Spanish document referring to the Incas' language. The name *Quechua* was probably derived from a misunderstanding by the conquistadors of the term *qheswa-simi. Qheswa* means "valley" and *simi* means speech. By 1560, the Spaniards were using the word *Quechua*—a garbled version of the Inca word *Qheswa,* or "valley," to refer to the official language of the Inca Empire.

a man of very plebeian origin, young . . . and as little versed in the general language of the Incas as in Spanish. He had in fact learned the language of the Incas not in Cuzco, but in Tumbez, from Indians who speak [it] barbarously and corruptly as foreigners . . . to all the Indians but the natives of Cuzco this [*runasimi*] is a foreign language. He had also learned Spanish without a teacher, but merely by hearing the Spaniards speak, and the words he heard most often were those used by the ordinary soldiers: "by heaven," or "I swear by heaven," and others like them or worse. He also knew the words necessary for fetching anything that was asked for, for he was a servant and slave to the Spaniards, and he spoke what he knew very corruptly as newly captured Negroes do. Though baptized, he had received no instruction in the Christian religion and knew nothing about Christ our Lord, and was totally ignorant of the Apostles' creed. Such were the merits of the first interpreter in Peru.

Whatever Felipillo's ability may have been, and whatever Atahualpa may or may not have understood of Soto's speech, the Inca emperor continued to gaze at the ground, completely ignoring the Spaniards. Atahualpa had been receiving regular reports about the mysterious group of strangers as soon as they had first arrived on the coast. And he had heard many remarkable things. According to the native chronicler Felipe Huamán Poma de Ayala:

Atahualpa and his nobles were amazed at what they heard of the Spaniards' way of life. Instead of sleeping, these strangers mounted guard at night. They and their horses were supposed to nourish themselves on gold and silver. They apparently wore silver on their feet and their weapons and their horses' bits and shoes were also reputed to be of silver, instead of the iron, which they were really made of. Above all, it was said that all day and all night the Spaniards talked to their books and papers.

After a long silence, one of the native chiefs in attendance finally informed Soto that Atahualpa was finishing the last day of a ceremonial fast and was indisposed; he was not receiving visitors. At precisely this moment, however, Hernando Pizarro came riding into camp, along with two of his men, having been sent by his brother Francisco, who was fearful that Soto's small party might be attacked. Hernando later wrote:

> When I arrived . . . I found the other horsemen near the camp of Atahualpa, and that Captain [Soto] had gone to speak with him. I left my men there and went ahead with two horsemen . . . and Captain [Soto] announced my approach and explained to him who I was. I then told Atahualpa that Governor [Francisco Pizarro] had sent me to invite him to come visit with him . . . and that he [the Governor] considered him a friend.

When Atahualpa understood that Hernando was the brother of the foreign leader, he finally looked up. And then, according to the notary Francisco de Xerez, he spoke—the first words ever recorded of an Inca emperor to a citizen of the Old World:

> "Maizabilica [a coastal chief], a Captain that I have on the river of Zuricara, sent to tell me that you mistreated the chiefs and put them in chains, and he sent me an iron collar [as proof] and he says that he killed three Christians and a horse."

Atahualpa appeared to be about thirty years old, Xerez said, and was "of good appearance . . . and somewhat thickset. He had a large face, handsome and fierce, and bloodshot eyes. He spoke with much gravity, as a great lord." Like most Incas, he had copper-brown skin, high cheekbones, dark eyes, and a prominent, aquiline nose. Not surprisingly, perhaps, the Inca lord's opening comment had been one about the Spaniards' behavior: there were rules and laws in the Inca Empire—and the various reports that the emperor had received indicated that the Spaniards had broken them. The visiting Spaniards, however, continued to ignore Inca protocol by their very behavior in camp. Normally, Inca lords and local chiefs—no matter how powerful—were not allowed to look directly at the emperor, had to arrive carrying a symbolic burden on their shoulders, and by their every move and gesture show great deference and obeisance. The Spaniards, by contrast, showed no humility whatsoever; they remained seated on their strange animals and spoke brashly and with insolence. In short, they ignored the Inca court's every rule, behaving in Atahualpa's eyes no differently than uncivilized barbarians.

Hernando Pizarro, meanwhile, knew very well that Atahualpa had spoken the truth. Three Spaniards *had* been killed by natives while crossing from the small island of Puna to the mainland of Peru, more than four months earlier. In addition, several of their horses had been wounded, although not killed. The Spaniards had exacted a punishing revenge, killing and wounding innumerable natives. Later, hearing rumors of a pending attack on the coast south of Tumbez, Francisco Pizarro had preemptively seized a local chief from a nearby village, along with the chief's "principal men." With no evidence other than these rumors, Pizarro had ordered that they all be burned alive, in a sort of primitive auto-da-fé, as the frightened villagers watched. It was a psychological ploy, a clear terror tactic, and obviously an effective one. Francisco de Xerez wrote:

> This punishment filled all the surrounding countryside with fear, so much so that a group of [native] leaders who were said to have been plotting with the local inhabitants to attack the Spaniards was dissolved; and from then on the Indians served better and with more fear than before.

Thirty-one-year-old Hernando—tall, heavily built, arrogant, and the least popular of the Pizarro brothers—decided to deny the Incas' report of Spanish casualties, insisting that the information Atahualpa had received was not true.

> "[Chief] Maizabilica is a scoundrel, [Hernando replied scornfully], and neither he nor all the Indians on that river could kill a single Christian. How could they kill Christians or a horse, since they are mere chickens?"

Hernando paused, waiting for Felipillo to finish translating, before continuing:

> "Neither Governor [Pizarro] nor the Christians mistreat the chiefs unless they are hostile towards him, while he treats those who are good and

wish to be friends very well. Those who want war are attacked until they are destroyed. When you see what the Christians do while helping you in your wars against your enemies, you will realize that Maizabilica lied to you."

While heavily outnumbered, the Spaniards clearly had the advantage in information control. Hernando knew very well that his older brother carried a signed license from the king and queen of Spain authorizing the plunder and subjugation of the very empire whose monarch he was addressing. Every member of the Spanish expedition knew about the recent history of the Aztecs. They themselves, in fact, were hoping to repeat in Peru what Cortés had accomplished in Mexico. None of them had any doubt whatsoever that their primary goal was to figure out a way to topple this newly discovered empire and in so doing to seize its inhabitants and its wealth for their own—before other Spaniards arrived and beat them to it.

Atahualpa, on the other hand, despite the previous reports of the Spaniards' marauding on the coast, didn't know where the Spaniards were from, knew nothing of their history, had heard of neither Cortés nor Mexico, had never seen the Spaniards fight, and was unsure of their intentions. Yet from the emperor's point of view, the Incas themselves clearly had an insurmountable advantage. Although the Spaniards were few in number, for some reason they had been brazen and foolish enough to come within striking distance of his own legions of warriors. If he so chose, Atahualpa knew that he could easily crush the entire group. Indeed, from Atahualpa's perspective, the Spaniards' fate now lay entirely in his hands. It had been more out of curiosity than anything else that he had even allowed the Spaniards to arrive in Cajamarca in the first place—and it was his decision that they were not now somewhere on the coast dangling lifelessly by their feet from a series of knotted cords.

Listening to Hernando's obvious boasting, Atahualpa now made the large, bearded man a pointed suggestion. "A [provincial] chief has refused to obey me. My troops will go with yours and you will make war on him." As Soto and the other four Spaniards watched the emperor carefully, Hernando gave a characteristic reply: "No matter how many men that chief has," he said, "you don't need to send any of your Indians. Ten Christians on horseback will be enough to destroy him."

Until now, Atahualpa's expression had been solemn and grave. At Hernando's reply, however, the emperor could not help but smile. What could be more absurd than ten foreigners thinking they could conquer a powerful chief with many hundreds of warriors? "He smiled like a man who did not think so much of us," Hernando wrote more than a year and a half later, apparently still smarting from the insult.

Hernando de Soto, seated on his horse as were the others, had meanwhile noticed something. Despite the Inca emperor's seeming nonchalance with the novelty of their presence, Atahualpa did seem keenly interested in their horses, which he had obviously never seen before. Soto therefore decided to perform a spontaneous demonstration, backing up his horse, rearing it up so that it stood on its hind legs and snorted, then putting it through some showy paces. Noticing the wide eyes on the faces of some nearby warriors, Soto now turned the animal around, dug in his spurs, then suddenly charged directly at them. Although Soto pulled up at the last moment, the charge sent a number of Atahualpa's elite guard running for cover, with several falling over themselves in a desperate effort to escape. Atahualpa remained seated throughout, watching yet showing no emotion during the entire display. Later that same day, however, he quietly ordered that the entire native battalion be executed. They had shown fear in front of the foreigners and had thus broken with Inca discipline. The sentence was carried out immediately.

The emperor now ordered drinks to be produced, and soon several women brought out golden goblets filled with *chicha*, or corn beer. None of the Spaniards wanted to drink, however, fearing that the mixture might contain poison, but when Atahualpa insisted they finally lifted the goblets and drank. With the sun now beginning to set, Hernando asked the emperor for permission to leave, and also asked what message he should take to his brother. Atahualpa replied that he would visit Cajamarca the next day, and that he would lodge in one of the three great chambers on the square. He would then meet with their leader, he said. With the valley of Cajamarca now bathed in shadows, the Spaniards turned their horses around and began to make their way back toward the city.

As they rode past the masses of native warriors, the Spaniards could not have known that Atahualpa had already made a decision. Tomorrow, Atahualpa had decided, he would capture the foreigners, kill most of them, and castrate the rest to use as eunuchs to guard his harem. Atahualpa would then seize the magnificent animals the foreigners rode in order to breed them in great numbers; the giant animals would surely make his empire even more powerful and would instill fear in his enemies. The strangers' arrogance and lack of respect had clearly angered him. Atahualpa had no doubt understood little of Soto's prepared speech, other than that they had been sent here by another king. Any king who had sent so few soldiers, however, Atahualpa no doubt was sure, could possess only a very small kingdom. As he drifted off to sleep that night, covered in the finest linens the empire could produce, Atahualpa presumably slept with the certainty that the foreigners' fates were as much as sealed.

When Hernando Pizarro and Soto arrived back in Cajamarca, the sun had already gone down and the stars were out. The air was crisp, clear, and very cold after the rain and the hail that had fallen, cleansing the courtyard and the cut Inca stones and raising the level of water that coursed through the culverts that ran along the centers of the streets. At the two entrances to the courtyard armed Spaniards stood watch, ready to warn the others in case of an attack. The two captains climbed down off their horses, then went directly to the governor's lodging, which was located in one of the great, cut-stone chambers fronting the square and was presumably illuminated from within by a fire. There, before the elder Pizarro and a large gathering of Spaniards, they described their meeting with the great Inca emperor.

The two told of Atahualpa's anger about the natives they had killed on the coast and of his accurate knowledge of the three Spaniards who had lost their lives; they also described in detail the massive, fully armed native legions and the air of power and majesty that the Inca lord had projected. Never before, the two said, had they met a native lord of such stature. If they had any doubt that they had penetrated an empire before today, then they were both certain that they had done so now. Soto explained how he had managed to scare a few of Atahualpa's warriors with his mock horse attack, even though the emperor himself had not so much as flinched. The two also said that they had been given goblets of gold to drink from and that they had seen many golden objects in Atahualpa's camp.

As the other men listened, they glanced at one another and their mood gradually turned gloomy. No matter how one looked at it, they had gotten themselves into a grim situation. Here they were, at least two weeks' march from Tumbez, where they had left their ships, isolated and cut off in the midst of mountainous terrain they scarcely knew. They could not retreat, as the high passes could be blocked and in the jagged canyons they could be easily trapped and killed. Besides, to attempt to flee would send an obvious signal of fear and would give the Incas the psychological advantage. Meanwhile, the Inca emperor was nearby, with legions of well-armed and obviously well-organized troops. Hernando Pizarro had stated that he had seen perhaps forty thousand warriors; privately he told his brother Francisco that the real number was closer to eighty thousand. That meant that the Spaniards were presently outnumbered by roughly four hundred to one. At the same time, if they chose to wait it out in the city, trying to feign friendship with the Incas, what could they possibly hope to achieve?

They could volunteer to fight with the emperor against the Incas' enemies, some of Pizarro's captains suggested, and perhaps could thus gain an advantage. They would then have to hope that eventually they might somehow wrest power from him at a later date. The Inca lord might decide to toy with them, however, as a cat does with a mouse, others said; at any time he might seize their weapons and horses and wipe them out. Trying to work with the Inca emperor seemed fraught with danger.

Another obvious possibility was to try to capture Atahualpa. Some of the Spanish captains argued that they should capture Atahualpa just as Cortés had captured the Aztec emperor, Montezuma. Besides, Pizarro and Soto had been capturing lesser chiefs with various degrees of success for decades, threatening to take their lives afterward unless the chiefs ordered their subjects to do as the Spaniards ordered. But others pointed out that that option, too, was risky, as they had no guarantee that they would ever actually be in a position to capture the Inca lord. It was also an all-or-nothing proposition: if they failed to capture the emperor on the first try, then the Incas would have no doubts about their hostile intentions and open warfare would inevitably ensue. Surely, with such large numbers arrayed against them, the Spaniards would be surrounded and overwhelmed.

On the other hand, if they were successful in capturing the Inca emperor, then they still didn't know what the Inca troops' reaction would be and whether Atahualpa's power might not immediately be transferred to another Inca lord. Just because Cortés's hostage strategy had worked well in Mexico, with Cortés controlling the Aztecs through their captured emperor, didn't mean that same strategy would work in Peru. No matter what option they could think of, all the strategies seemed to share one thing in common: each was highly risky and in every case the odds were stacked against them. For the moment, at least, it seemed as if they were trapped in the eye of a powerful hurricane—and that no matter what direction they might choose to head in, all hell was bound to break loose. The twenty-four-year-old notary, Miguel de Estete, wrote:

> [We were] very scared by what we had seen [and everyone] had many views and opinions about what should be done. Everyone was full of fear, for we were so few and were so deep in the land where we could not be reinforced. . . . That night, everybody gathered in the Governor's quarters to discuss what should be done the following day. . . . Few of us slept and we kept watch on the square, from which the campfires of the Indian army could be seen. It was a fearsome sight as most of . . . [the campfires] were on a hillside and close to one another . . . [making it] look like a brilliant, star-studded sky.

That night, Pedro de Candia, a giant Greek who was captain of the artillery, worked on preparing four small cannons they had brought on horseback, and also readied the fewer than a dozen harquebuses, primitive muskets, they had brought along. Some Spaniards sharpened their swords, using bits of pumice along the edges until they were so sharp they could easily slice through the strange ground fruits (potatoes) found in this region, which the Incas called *papa*. Many of the men met with the only religious representative who had traveled on this expedition, Friar Vincente de Valverde, who now listened to their confessions and prayed along with them. Pizarro, meanwhile, made the rounds, cheering up the men, rubbing his hands together against the cold, and urging everyone to place their faith in God, for, he said, "it is certain that everything that happens below and above heaven is arranged by His will."

Although their lives now hung in the balance, the stakes were probably highest at this particular moment for Francisco Pizarro. He'd labored thirty years to reach this position and had moved heaven and earth to assemble all the complex pieces that were currently in place—the ships, the supplies, the finances, the royal license, and his discovery of the native empire. He was also responsible for 167 conquistadors and for the entire male line of this branch of the Pizarro family. Only one massive obstacle remained: how to overcome an Inca army of perhaps eighty thousand warriors and seize an empire. As the lean commander with his thin, graying beard wandered through the Spaniards' camp that night, stopping to chat and occasionally looking off toward the twinkling lights that were the dying fires of the native warriors, Pizarro knew that everyone's lives—in addition to his own dream of one day ruling a native kingdom—depended upon whether he, the most seasoned of the conquistadors, would make the right decision on the morrow.

The next morning, Saturday, November 16, 1532, the sun began to rise in a nearly cloudless sky and slowly the night frost began to retreat. Water gurgled down the channels in the Inca streets while no roosters crowed, as the Spaniards had brought none with them; instead guinea pigs squeaked underfoot while scampering about on the floors of the houses—one of the few animals native South Americans had domesticated for food. On the far hillside, innumerable tendrils of smoke rose from the Incas' campfires while in the wide, walled plaza, the Spaniards were already awake and preparing themselves for war.

Pizarro had decided that since it was impossible to know if the Inca lord was going to arrive and, if so, how he was going to arrive and with how many warriors and where, that he would have to act spontaneously. When the time came, he told his men, he would make a last-minute decision on the precise strategy—whether to try to negotiate, be friendly, escape, or attack. The rest of them would have to follow his lead.

The town's plaza stretched some six hundred feet in length by six hundred feet in width. Three stone buildings, long and low, lined corresponding sides of the square and each was punctured by approximately twenty trapezoidally shaped doorways. Inside two of these buildings Pizarro had stationed the cavalry, in three groups of roughly twenty men, and commanded by Captains Hernando de Soto, Hernando Pizarro, and Sebastián de Benalcázar. Because of the numerous doorways, the Spaniards could charge out of the buildings simultaneously en masse, if and when needed. Pizarro and some twenty foot soldiers, meanwhile, were to wait in the third building, along with a few horsemen. It was their job—if the capture of the emperor became a possibility—to seize Atahualpa at all costs and to make sure that no harm came to him. A dead emperor would be useless to them and would probably unleash the immediate outbreak of war.

On the far side of the square squatted a fourth building, in which Pizarro stationed the Greek artilleryman, Pedro de Candia, with his four cannons and eight or nine harquebusiers plus the remainder of the infantry. Since most of the Spaniards would be hiding within the buildings and thus would be unable to observe what was happening, the firing of the artillery was the prearranged signal to attack. Candia would have to watch Pizarro at all times, he was told. If Pizarro gave the signal, then Candia would immediately order his men to fire. Every able-bodied person—save for the Dominican friar, the *morisca* women, and the merchants who had tagged along with the expedition—would then rush out through the doors onto the plaza and attack. The signal would be given, Pizarro told everyone, only if it appeared likely that they could capture Atahualpa, or if the Incas themselves decided to attack.

With so many variables at play, Pizarro was determined to hold out the option of parleying with the emperor and of coming to some kind of friendly agreement. That might buy his small force more time—time with which they might maneuver themselves into a more advantageous situation. If the emperor could be lured inside the walled plaza, however, and if Pizarro did make the decision to attack, at least his Spaniards would have the advantage of surprise and could launch their assault from all four directions. Only by sowing shock, surprise, and confusion, Pizarro knew, did they stand any chance of success.

While the Spaniards waited nervously in their positions, in the Inca camp the warriors were also ready, having woken at dawn and having been told by their captains to prepare themselves for travel. Atahualpa, however, hadn't even stirred yet and indeed did not wake until around ten o'clock. Only the day before, Atahualpa had been informed that his brother Huascar had been captured by his armies in the south, which meant that after the bit-

ter and divisive five-year struggle, Atahualpa would finally inherit his
father's empire. In an excellent mood, Atahualpa ordered food to be
brought to him as well as a golden vessel of *chicha* in order to celebrate.
Once he had taken care of this small band of renegade foreigners, Atahualpa
no doubt believed, then he and his army could begin their victorious march
toward Cuzco, some six hundred miles to the south. Determined to savor
the victory, Atahualpa lifted the golden goblet and took a drink of the sour-
flavored, alcoholic beer. He could now begin the task of reuniting the empire, of establishing his rule, and of never allowing any of his relatives to
challenge his authority again.

As the sun reached its zenith and then began to arc beyond it, the nervous
Spaniards finally saw the Inca camp begin to stir in the distance. They
watched as masses of warriors, like phalanxes of Roman legions, began to
assemble in their different formations. Then, in great order and ceremony,
the legions slowly began to wheel about and make their way across the
plain toward them. Remembered Pedro Pizarro, Francisco's eighteen-year-
old cousin and page:

> When his [Atahualpa's] squadrons were formed so that they covered the
> fields, and when he had seated himself on a litter, he began to proceed.
> Two thousand Indians marched before him, sweeping the [stone paved]
> road on which he traveled. Half of his troops marched on one side of the
> road and half on the other, with neither using the road itself. . . . So
> great was the amount of table service of gold and silver which they bore,
> that it was a marvel to observe how it all glittered beneath the sun. . . .
> In front of Atahualpa came many Indians singing and dancing.

As the sound of the approaching warriors grew louder, Pizarro moved
from one building to the next, ordering everyone to prepare themselves and
ordering the cavalrymen to mount their horses with their reins and metal-
tipped lances ready in their hands. Then, inexplicably, on the plains just
outside town, as many of the Spaniards literally sweated in fear and anticipation, the native procession suddenly ground to a halt. An hour went by,
agonizingly, yet the Spaniards couldn't tell what the Incas were doing. Were
they preparing for an attack? Were they receiving last-minute battle instructions? Was Atahualpa going to refuse to enter the square? Finally, however,
with only a few hours left before the sun would once more sink behind the

hills, it gradually appeared that Atahualpa and his giant entourage were simply going to make camp. At least for today, the Inca lord was going no further.

An exasperated Pizarro quickly sent a Spaniard by the name of Hernando de Aldana, who spoke a few words of *runasimi,* to ride out to Atahualpa's camp. Aldana was instructed to urge the emperor to continue on into the Spaniards' carefully prepared trap, which, with any more delay, might soon be discovered. Aldana dutifully galloped off, crossing the short distance to the camp, dismounting his horse in a cloud of dust, and then, via hand signs and his minute vocabulary, indicated to Atahualpa that he should proceed into town before the setting of the sun. Apparently the message was understood, for as Aldana raced back the Spaniards saw the Inca formations once again began to move. Soon, Atahualpa's bearers lifted the emperor, already seated in his litter, onto their shoulders, the litter itself consisting of an elegantly constructed wooden box mounted on two long poles with a seat and cushions and with a canopy to offer protection from the sun. The procession then slowly began to make its final approach toward the great square of Cajamarca, across which the sun's rays were already drawing long dark shadows.

With no more doubts that masses of native troops were about to arrive and with some of his men scarcely able to conceal their fear, Pizarro and his brother Hernando began visiting the different buildings in order to give their final encouragements to the men. Wrote the notary Francisco de Xerez:

> The Governor [Pizarro] and Captain-General [Hernando Pizarro] visited the quarters of the Spaniards, making sure that they were ready to rush forth when it was necessary and telling all of them that they must make fortresses of their hearts, for they had no others and no hope other than God, who would help those in greatest need who worked in His service. And he told them that although for every Christian there were five hundred Indians, that they must make the same effort that all good men are accustomed to make at such times, and that they must trust that God would fight on their side. He told them that when the time came to attack that they must rush out with desperate fury . . . and break through [the enemy ranks], taking care that the horses did not get in the way of each other. The Governor and the Captain-General spoke

these and similar words to the Christians in order to encourage them, and they wanted to go out [and fight] rather than to remain in their quarters.

Outside, as the sound of the approaching legions grew louder, the first warriors began to spill through one of the gateways onto the broad plaza. For those Spaniards who dared to steal a furtive look, they saw, in Xerez's account, that

> First came a squadron of Indians dressed in a colorful uniform that looked like a chess board. These marched [while] removing straws from the ground and sweeping the path. Behind these came three squadrons dressed in a different manner, all of them singing and dancing. Then came many men wearing armor, thin metal plates, and crowns of gold and silver. Among them traveled Atahualpa in a litter lined with multi-colored macaw feathers and adorned with plates of gold and silver.

Described Estete:

> Eighty lords carried . . . [the Inca lord] . . . on their shoulders, all wearing very rich blue uniforms. He himself was very richly dressed, with his crown on his head and a necklace of large emeralds around his neck. He was seated in the litter on a very small stool that bore a sumptuous cushion.

Concluded Xerez:

> Behind him came two other litters and two hammocks in which rode other important leaders, and lastly came squadrons of men with crowns of gold and silver. After the first [group] had entered the square, they parted to make room for the others. [Then] as Atahualpa reached the center of the square, he made the rest of them halt, [while] the litter in which he was traveling and the others were held up high. People continued to pour into the square without ceasing.

Soon, Atahualpa and some five to six thousand warriors crowded into the square, filling it up. The wide plaza was now like a packed theater, with only two small exits, and with Atahualpa borne aloft on a cumbersome litter, carried by some of the highest-ranking chiefs in the land. Because of the great number of troops and the relative lack of space, Atahualpa had ordered the rest of his legions to wait in the fields outside town.

As the Inca procession came to a stop not a single Spaniard was visible. Pedro Pizarro later reported that Atahualpa had sent spies earlier in the day to observe the Spaniards and that the spies had reported that the Spaniards were huddled in the stone houses out of fear. "And indeed the Indians told the truth," Pedro said, "for I heard that many Spaniards urinated on themselves without noticing it from sheer terror."

The crowd of nobles and warriors on the square had now become quiet and a light breeze blew. Visible in the building at the far end, four nondescript lumps of bronze with holes protruded from the doorways, looking like some kind of crude ornaments. They were actually four small cannons, primed, charged, and ready to be fired but here, too, no Spaniard was in sight. An Inca nobleman with distinctive golden plugs in his earlobes now walked toward the building as Pedro de Candia and the other artillerymen held their breath. Instead of going inside, however, the *orejón* suddenly stopped and thrust a lance he was carrying into the ground, then returned. From the lance flapped a cloth banner; this was Atahualpa's royal standard, a personal coat of arms that was always displayed wherever the emperor happened to be present.

As Atahualpa waited, wearing a soft vicuña-wool tunic and mantle and seated upon a small stool on his litter, the Spaniards pressed against the cold stone walls of the buildings, fingering their weapons and staying out of sight. Others sat on their horses, leaning forward and trying to keep their animals from whinnying or making other noise. At last, Atahualpa called out to them, ordering the Spaniards to emerge from their hiding places and show themselves. The square, however, remained completely silent, with only the sound of the royal standard flapping in the breeze. Finally, from one of the buildings, two figures emerged. One was a man dressed unlike any of the other foreigners Atahualpa had seen, wearing a long robe tied at the waist with a rope and carrying what appeared to be some gifts in his hand: a shiny ornament of silver that looked like a broken stick (a crucifix) and a black square-shaped object, perhaps a ceremonial cloth (a breviary, or prayer book). The other individual was Felipillo.

Vincente de Valverde, the Dominican friar, was now in his mid-thirties

and had traveled from Spain with Pizarro after receiving a royal appointment to accompany the present expedition. The only member of the group
known to have attended a university, Valverde had studied for five years at
the University of Valladolid and thus had been trained in both theology and
philosophy. Valverde's mission was not to participate in conquest or plunder
but rather to help fulfill that portion of Pizarro's contract that stipulated the
conversion to Christianity of any and all peoples who were conquered.

Because reports had filtered back soon after the discovery of the New
World of Spanish brutality toward the natives, in 1513 a document had been
drawn up that the Spanish king demanded be read from then on to all potential subjects before a conquest was carried out. The document, known as
the *Requerimiento,* or "Requirement," was both a justification and an ultima-
tum. In abbreviated form it explained to newly discovered peoples that since
(the Christian) God had created the world and had granted the divine right
to rule this world to his emissary on earth, the pope, and since the pope in
1493 had granted to the Spanish monarchs jurisdiction over all lands west of
the 46th meridian, which included the western part of South America, then
it was the duty of all newly discovered peoples in these regions to submit to
their rightful rulers, the Spanish monarchs.*

If upon hearing this information the natives refused to obey, then all necessary violence could and would be used against them to either force the natives to submit to the dictates of God, or else to eliminate them from the face
of his earth. The fact that the document was often read in Spanish to native
peoples who were unable to understand a word of that language didn't matter. The essential point was that the natives had been read their rights, so to
speak, and thus any violence that ensued had been legally sanctioned, ultimately, by God himself. In essence this was a ritual, a ritual symbolizing a
preapproved and highly flexible authorization, one that could be adapted to
a wide variety of situations. And now one of those situations was presently
unfolding nine thousand feet up in the Andes, amid the tightly packed main
square of the Inca city of Cajamarca.

Atahualpa watched as the robed foreigner and his interpreter picked their
way through the Inca warriors and approached his litter. Standing before

---

* The imaginary line designated by the pope in the Treaty of Tordesillas was located at 46
degrees, 37 minutes western longitude, or about 1,270 statute miles west of the Cape Verde
Islands off the African coast.

the Inca lord, who ruled with as much divine right as any European king, Friar Valverde began by inviting the emperor to dismount from his litter and enter one of the buildings. There he could meet with Governor Pizarro and could speak and dine with him. The friar knew, of course, that if Atahualpa did so that it would be easier for the Spaniards to capture him. Atahualpa, refused, however, stating "I will not leave this place until you return all that you have taken from my land. I know very well who you are, and what you have been doing."

Obviously, the time had come for the *Requerimiento*. In a loud voice, Friar Valverde began to paraphrase it, with the young interpreter Felipillo translating the often puzzling and no doubt largely unintelligible ideas as best he could:

> [In the name of the] high and mighty kings of Castile and Leon, conquerors of barbarian peoples, and being their messenger, I hereby notify and inform you . . . that God, Our Lord, One and Eternal, created Heaven and Earth and a man and a woman from whom you and I and all the people of the world are descended. . . . Because of the great multitude begotten from these over the past five thousand and some years since the world was made . . . God placed one called Saint Peter in charge over all these peoples.

Valverde paused as Felipillo translated, the feathers on Atahualpa's litter, plucked from brilliantly colored macaws in the jungle regions of the empire, fluttering in the breeze.

> And so I request and require you . . . to recognize the Church as your Mistress and as Governess of the World and Universe, and the High Priest, called the Pope, in Her name, and His Majesty in Her Place, as Ruler and Lord King. . . . And if you do not do this . . .

Valverde continued, his voice rising and the Spaniards in their hidden positions straining to hear,

> with the help of God we shall come mightily against you, and we shall make war on you everywhere and in every way that we can, and we shall subject you to the yoke and obedience of the Church and His Majesty,

and we shall seize your women and children, and we shall make them
slaves, to sell and dispose of as His Majesty commands. And we shall do
all the evil and damage to you that we are able. And I must insist that the
deaths and destruction that result from this will be [all] your fault!

After the interpreter finished delivering the speech, silence once again
gripped the square. For a moment, time seemed to freeze as two empires
stood watching each other. At stake for Atahualpa and the Inca elite were
their own vast fertile lands, their ten million tax-paying peasants with their
inexhaustible labor and crops, their own elite positions, and an empire that
had taken three generations and countless military campaigns to create. At
stake for the Spanish monarchy was a ragtag group of 168 expendable conquistadors, a handful of merchants, a few black slaves, a couple of *morisca*
women, and, much more importantly, the opportunity for the Spanish
monarchs to seize an empire with twice the population and size of the
Iberian peninsula itself. Whether any of the individual protagonists in the
present tableau understood the basic historical processes involved at this
particular moment is doubtful. The Spaniards, wearing armor and chain
mail and preparing themselves for attack, were certainly aware that their
own lives and fortunes lay in the balance, however, and, if in the moments
to come any of them were surrounded and overwhelmed by the native
hordes, that their personal destinies would certainly come to a violent and
sudden end.

Yet the Spaniards also knew that if somehow they were able to escape
from their present situation and were miraculously able to conquer this empire, that both their own fortunes and the king's dominions would be vastly
expanded. The friar, too, on a religious level, realized that success here
meant the expansion on earth of the Christian Church and hence an expansion of God's dominion. The reverse would be a victory for the forces of Lucifer and for the pagan barbarians of the world. It was precisely the
nonbelievers' refusal to accept the word of God, Friar Valverde believed,
that was delaying the reappearance of Christ on earth. A bold success here
meant that the Kingdom of God would surely arrive that much sooner.

Among the Incas, only Atahualpa's top military leaders apparently knew
of his plan—to capture and kill the Spaniards, to make eunuchs out of the
survivors, and to breed these powerful and majestic animals that the

Spaniards called *caballos*. Atahualpa could hardly have thought that this small group of foreigners—who presently appeared to be cowering from fear inside a few buildings—were any threat. Their successful capture would simply mean the elimination of the final small impediment preventing his march on Cuzco and the reunification of the Inca Empire. As soon as the Spaniards were disposed of, Atahualpa's coronation in Cuzco awaited him. An Inca emperor wielding control over a reunited empire would then once again rule the entire civilized world.

After listening to the inevitably mangled translation of the friar's speech, Atahualpa must have appeared puzzled, for Valverde next held up his breviary, or prayer book, and insisted that everything he had stated was contained within. Indeed, the Christian God's own voice was contained in this very book, the friar insisted. One can only wonder just what words the native interpreter used to convey the idea of objects for which the Incas had no known equivalents. Felipillo may have used the word *quipu*—the Inca word for their knotted string device on which they stored records—for *book,* as the Incas had neither books nor writing. Clearly intrigued, Atahualpa asked to see the strange object. He no doubt had already heard of the Spaniards' mysterious *quipus,* and that somehow the *quipus* themselves had the power of speech, but Atahualpa had yet to see or examine one.*

The friar dutifully held the breviary up toward Atahualpa's golden litter and the emperor took it. As Valverde watched Atahualpa fumble with the book, turning it over and upside down, however, he realized that Atahualpa didn't know how to open it. Valverde therefore stepped forward, reaching out his hand toward the book in order to show the emperor how it was done. Recounted Xerez:

> With great scorn, [Atahualpa] struck [the friar] on the arm, not wishing
> that it should be opened. Then stubbornly he opened it himself and,
> without any astonishment at the letters nor at the paper, as [had been

---

* *Quipus* were knotted cords that used a positional decimal system to keep track of quantities of things such as taxes, livestock, populations, and goods as well as serving as memory prompts for stories about history and other subjects. A type of primitive computer, *quipus* were created and deciphered by specialists called *quipucamayocs,* or "knot authorities." The intricately knotted *quipus* contained much of the vast quantity of information needed to help tie together the enormous and complex Inca Empire.

displayed by] other Indians, he threw it five or six paces away from him. And to the words that [the friar] had spoken to him through the interpreter he answered with much arrogance saying. "I know well how you have behaved on the road, how you have treated the chiefs, and have taken the [royal] cloth from the storehouses. . . . I will not leave this place until they return it all to me."

According to some eyewitnesses, Atahualpa now stood up on his litter and began shouting to his troops to prepare themselves for battle. As the interpreter Felipillo scrambled to retrieve the breviary from the ground, Friar Valverde rushed back to Pizarro's quarters, very agitated, and began shouting, "Come out! Come out, Christians! Come at these enemy dogs who reject the things of God!" Clutching his crucifix in one hand he shouted, "That chief has thrown the book of holy law to the ground!" Another eyewitness heard the apoplectic friar, the instrument of God's will, shout to Pizarro, "Didn't you see what happened? Why remain polite and servile toward this arrogant dog when the plains are full of Indians? Go and attack him, for I absolve you!"

With Atahualpa standing on his litter and the priest shouting for the Spaniards to attack, a decision had to be made. Pizarro hesitated for only a moment and then signaled to Pedro de Candia, waiting in the building on the far side of the square, who now ordered that the wicks of the assembled cannons be lit. With loud roars the cannons soon fired directly into the mass of warriors, spewing out smoke and metal shrapnel; simultaneously the nine harquebusiers also fired their guns, having carefully aimed them on tripods. The sudden explosions no doubt stunned the native warriors, as did the sight of bodies suddenly falling down among them and spurting blood. With plumes of smoke rising from one of the buildings they now heard coming from all directions the stark sounds of trumpets and multiple choruses of men shouting "Santiago!" as the Spaniards kicked their feet into their horses' sides and charged and ran out from their hiding places.* From every direction Atahualpa's warriors saw the metal-covered foreigners sud-

---

* "Santiago" is the Spanish translation of the patron saint, St. James (known in Galician language as Sant Iago), one of the twelve apostles of Christ. This was the traditional war cry Spanish troops had used since the twelfth century, while expelling the Islamic infidels, the Moors, from the Iberian peninsula.

denly rushing toward them, together with groups of seemingly ferocious, thousand-pound animals in padded armor, their hooves pounding the ground and each topped by a lance- or sword-wielding Spaniard, screaming hoarsely and with a crazed look in his eyes.

The Spaniards quickly began slashing, stabbing, impaling, hacking, and even beheading as many natives as they could, using their razor-sharp swords, knives, and lances. The native warriors, having confidently marched onto the square only moments earlier and thinking that they had trapped the cowering foreigners in a few buildings, now suddenly realized that *they* were in a trap, not the Spaniards. Attacking from all sides and suddenly crushing the warriors together, the Spaniards' surprise attack threw the natives into an immediate panic. The giant horses with mounted Spaniards had the same effect on Inca troops, in fact, that Hannibal's men on elephants must have had on Roman legions more than 1,500 years earlier. Terrified masses of warriors began surging toward the square's narrow exits, trampling those who got in the way and seized by an overpowering desire to save their lives. The Spaniards, meanwhile, mercilessly and methodically continued to cut off arms, hands, and heads, using their steel weapons like so many meat cleavers. "They were so filled with fear that they climbed on top of one another," wrote one eyewitness, "to such an extent that they formed mounds and suffocated one another." "The horsemen rode out on top of them, wounding and killing and pressing home the attack," wrote another.

Pizarro, meanwhile, with his twenty foot soldiers carrying swords and shields, had immediately begun slicing his way through the crowd in the direction of Atahualpa, who remained on his litter, attempting to rally his panic-stricken troops. Xerez recounted:

> The Governor [Pizarro] armed himself with a thick cotton coat of armor, took his sword and dagger and entered into the midst of the Indians with the Spaniards who were with him. With great bravery and with only four who could follow him, he reached Atahualpa's litter and fearlessly grabbed [the emperor's] left arm, shouting "Santiago." . . . But he could not pull him out of his litter, which was [still] held high. . . . All those who were carrying Atahualpa's litter appeared to be important

men and they all died, as did those who were traveling in the litters and hammocks.

Another eyewitness recounted: "Many Indians had their hands cut off [yet] continued to support their ruler's litter with their shoulders. But their efforts were of little benefit for they were all killed." As Pedro Pizarro described:

> Although [the Spaniards] killed the Indians who were carrying [the litter], other replacements immediately went to support it. They continued in this way for a long time, struggling with and killing the Indians until, becoming exhausted, one Spaniard tried to stab [Atahualpa] with his knife to kill him. But Francisco Pizarro parried the blow and in doing so the Spaniard trying to kill Atahualpa wounded the Governor on the hand.

Finally, as the desperate struggle to seize the emperor continued, seven or eight Spanish horsemen now turned and spurred their horses, slashing their way through the crowd toward Atahualpa's litter. Pushing against the bloodied nobles trying to steady it, the Spaniards then heaved up on one side, turning the litter over. Other Spaniards now pulled the emperor from his seat. Wielding his sword in one hand and fastening upon Atahualpa with the other, Pizarro and a group of Spaniards now rushed Atahualpa back to Pizarro's lodgings, thus imprisoning the Inca emperor.

Pandemonium coupled with slaughter, meanwhile, continued to reign on the square outside. As the hordes of trapped warriors continued to try to flee toward the overcrowded exits, those furthest from them, in complete desperation, now began to surge against the far wall, which was roughly six feet high and some six feet thick. Thousands lunged against it until finally a fifteen-foot section gave way. As the terrified natives scrambled over and through it, the Spaniards on horseback—like sixty deranged and screaming Horsemen of the Apocalypse—raced after them, spearing, lancing, cutting, and stabbing. Those eyewitnesses who recorded the event remembered the horsemen chasing the warriors out onto the plain, at first singling out the litters of the Inca nobles who were still being borne away by loyal retainers.

"All of them were shouting, 'After those in the uniforms! Don't let any escape! Spear them!' "

And so the slaughter continued, the Spaniards chasing after the fleeing natives, inflicting as much carnage as possible, and in the light and long shadows that photographers call the golden hour countless warriors now lay on the ground, many without limbs or with deep gashes and with pools of dark, maroon-colored blood growing quietly beneath them. Elsewhere hundreds lay trampled to death on the square, some crawling, others moaning, many dying and dead, and those who were gradually losing consciousness on this, their last day on earth, trying to understand the nightmare that had so quickly befallen them. Wrote the notary Xerez:

> [One of the men killed] in one of the litters was his [Atahualpa's] page and lord [the lord of Chincha], whom he regarded very highly. And the others were also lords over many people and were his advisors. The lord of Cajamarca also died. Other commanders died, but there were so many of them that they go unrecorded. For all those who came in Atahualpa's bodyguard were great lords. . . . It was a marvelous thing to see so great a ruler captured in so short a time, when he had come with such might.

Finally, as the sun sank behind the hills, the Spaniards could still be seen riding and lancing the last fleeing natives in the distance, looking for all the world like the small figures in Pieter Brueghel the Elder's painting *The Triumph of Death*. Eventually, however, a trumpet sounded and the Spaniards gradually began making their way back to the main square. Although the Spaniards had feared that Atahualpa's warriors had arrived bearing hidden weapons, not once that afternoon did a native warrior ever raise a weapon against a Spaniard. If the warriors *had* carried concealed weapons, then they had simply suffered too much shock to use them.

Miraculously, in the space of just a few hours, the Spaniards had killed or wounded perhaps six or seven thousand natives,* while they themselves hadn't lost a single man. Taking advantage of surprise, their artillery, and of their meat-cutting weapons, the Spaniards' Battle of Cajamarca had resulted

---

* Some of these, of course, had simply been trampled to death.

in a complete rout and slaughter. As darkness deepened around the city, the native emperor descended from the sun god—who had wielded total military, religious, and political control over an empire of ten million—suddenly found himself captive. In less than two hours, the Inca Empire had been beheaded, as neatly as one would sever the head of a llama or guinea pig. And now the emperor, no longer borne on a golden litter, his tunic stained with his nobles' blood, turned to face his exultant captors, one of whom was a tall, helmeted man, still wearing his bloodied and padded armor, and whom the others deferentially referred to as *El Gobernador*.

5 ❖ A ROOMFUL OF GOLD

" 'When I had a chief, the lord of an island, my prisoner, I set him free so that from then on he might be loyal. And I did the same with the chiefs who were lords of Tumbez and Chulimasa and others who, being in my power and deserving death, I pardoned.' "

FRANCISCO PIZARRO TO ATAHUALPA

"The promise given was a necessity of the past; the word broken is a necessity of the present."

NICCOLÒ MACHIAVELLI, *THE PRINCE*, 1511

AS THE TRUMPET SOUNDED, CALLING FOR THE SPANIARDS TO return to the square and the last Inca warriors were being skewered on the ends of lance points, Pizarro was already busy attending to his prisoner, Atahualpa, who after his capture had been taken to the temple of the sun at the edge of town and placed under a strong guard. Because the emperor's clothes had been ripped during his capture, Pizarro ordered that new ones be brought and waited while the emperor changed into them. He then ordered that a meal be prepared and had Atahualpa sit down beside him as they were served.

Atahualpa had never met Pizarro before that afternoon, and had only first laid eyes on him from the height of his litter, as the veteran conquistador had fought and slashed his way toward the emperor and then had reached out and seized him. That fateful, jerking grasp was both their mutual introduction and symbolic of their future relationship. For here, in Pizarro's des-

A native inspector in charge of one of Tawantinsuyu's numerous hanging bridges.

perate, clenched grip, the illiterate bastard from the lower classes of Spain had pulled the cream of Inca nobility abruptly from his throne.

On a more figurative level, Pizarro and his rugged band had climbed up the sheer sides of the Inca Empire's giant social pyramid, had reached the top, and now stood at its zenith, holding a proverbial knife to the throat of the emperor and daring anyone to throw them off. It was through Atahualpa that Pizarro hoped to manipulate the apparatus of the Inca state, believing that by remote control he could paralyze the movements of Inca armies, prevent counterattacks, and ultimately take command of the empire.

To be able to do so, however, Pizarro first had to establish a relationship with his hostage. The Inca emperor had to understand clearly what it was that he and the other Spaniards wanted. In exchange for prolonging Atahualpa's life, Pizarro wanted power and absolute control. If he could control the Inca elite at the top of the social pyramid, then he and his Spaniards could control everything that lay beneath—land, labor, gold, silver, women—everything that this obviously rich empire had to offer. If Pizarro's band of armed entrepreneurs could somehow maintain their new position, then, like parasites, they could feed off the Inca body politic—the labor of the masses—and could thus begin the lives of luxury that they had risked their very lives for.

In a sense, New World conquest was about men seeking a way around one of life's basic rules—that human beings have to work for a living, just like the rest of the animal world. In Peru, as elsewhere in the Americas, Spaniards were not looking for fertile land that they could farm, they were looking for *the cessation of their own need to perform manual labor.* To do so, they needed to find large enough groups of people they could force to carry out all the laborious tasks necessary to provide them with the essentials of life: food, shelter, clothing, and, ideally, liquid wealth. Conquest, then, had little to do with adventure, but rather had everything to do with groups of men willing to do just about anything in order to avoid working for a living. Stripped down to its barest bones, the conquest of Peru was all about finding a comfortable retirement.

Thus, as food was being served while native warriors still lay dying outside in the numbing cold of the Andean night, Pizarro sought to introduce Atahualpa to what he and his companions had in mind: "Don't take it as an insult that you have been defeated and taken prisoner," Pizarro began, presumably slicing off a hunk of llama meat and with one of his interpreters translating, "for with the Christians I have brought with me, though so few in number, I have conquered greater lands than yours and [I also] have defeated more powerful lords than you, placing them under the dominion of the Emperor, whose vassal I am, and who is King of Spain and of the universal world and under whose command we have come to conquer this land."

Pizarro was clearly exaggerating the rather minor skirmishes that he and his men had had prior to their arrival in Peru, while borrowing Cortés's capture of the distant Aztec Empire as his own personal accomplishment. But Pizarro's message was clear: the disaster that had befallen Atahualpa was as inevitable as were the movements of the stars in the heavens—and any future resistance would be as futile as it would be horrific. "You should consider it to be your good fortune that you have not been defeated by a cruel people such as yourselves," he continued, as his men outside cleaned blood off their daggers and swords. "We treat our prisoners and conquered enemies with mercy and only make war on those who make war on us. And, being able to destroy them, we refrain from doing so, but rather pardon them."

Pizarro was of course counting on the fact that Atahualpa knew nothing of the bloody atrocities the Spaniards had committed in the Caribbean, or in Mexico, or in Central America, and that he had never heard of Columbus, or the slave trade, or the assassination of Montezuma, the Aztec emperor. As Atahualpa listened in silence, Pizarro now began driving the main point of his message home: "When I had a chief, the lord of an island, my prisoner," Pizarro said, looking directly into Atahualpa's eyes, "I set him free so that from then on he might be loyal. And I did the same with the chiefs who were lords of Tumbez and Chulimasa and others who, being in my power and deserving death, I pardoned."

Pizarro paused to slice off more meat as the interpreter caught up. "If you were seized and your people attacked and killed, it was because you came with so great an army against us, [despite my] having begged you to come peacefully, and because you threw the book on the ground in which were written the words of God. For this reason our Lord allowed that your arrogance should be destroyed and that no Indian should be able to offend a Christian."

Atahualpa, widely reported to be a clever man, immediately understood the significance of Pizarro's offer. Wrote one eyewitness:

Atahualpa responded that he had been deceived by his captains, that they had told him to not take the Spaniards seriously. That he personally had desired to come in peace, but that they had prevented him and that all those who had advised him were now dead.

The Inca emperor, who only a few hours before had been absolute ruler of the greatest empire the Americas had ever known, now asked Pizarro for permission to confer with some of his men. According to another eyewitness:

> The Governor immediately ordered them to bring two important Indians who had been taken in the battle. The . . . [emperor Atahualpa] asked them whether many men were dead. They told him that the entire countryside was covered with them. He then sent word to the [native] troops who had remained not to flee but to come serve him, since he was not dead but was being held by the Christians.

As the two Inca nobles left to carry out Atahualpa's orders, the Spaniards who witnessed their departure must have breathed a collective sigh of relief. With their backs to the wall, they had taken a huge risk in trying to capture the emperor, a risk that had no guarantee of success. So many things could have gone wrong, not the least of which was the Incas' reaction to their attack. Had Atahualpa's warriors not panicked and instead of fleeing had charged directly at them, then it might have been the Spaniards who were massacred, and not the reverse. Pizarro had clearly understood, however, that even if he were successful in capturing the emperor, he couldn't predict the reaction of either the emperor or of his men. Would Atahualpa cooperate? And if so, would his subjects continue to obey him? Or would they ignore his capture and instead attack?

After the two lords had departed, Pizarro no doubt quietly made the sign of the cross, touching his forehead and then each side of his chest. Military leader, strategist, diplomat, CEO, terrorist, and now hostage taker, Pizarro was also a sincerely devout Christian. The fifty-four-year-old conquistador fully believed in divine providence. He also believed that God had intervened today on the side of the slashing, blood-splattered Christians on the square. The proof lay in Atahualpa's capture and in the fact that so many had been killed by so few. The Inca emperor and his subjects were nonbelievers, after all, whose souls, without conversion, were destined for hell. Though blood had been spilled, Pizarro was nevertheless convinced that in the end it would be he and his conquistadors and their bloody swords that would bring the great mass of nonbelievers into the sacred fold of the Lord.

Many of the Spaniards now sank into sleep, the first that some of them had had in more than forty-eight hours. Pizarro had appointed others to patrol the town that night. Soon, the town's inhabitants who had hidden in their houses that day heard the metallic footsteps of the strange giant animals the bearded invaders rode, the horse hooves clacking slowly on the deserted streets, while bodies still lay strewn about in darkened piles. Meanwhile, inside the temple of the sun, Pizarro ordered that a bed be prepared for Atahualpa in the same room where he himself slept. As the two leaders from different worlds lay down in their beds—Inca style, with a gathering of richly woven blankets on the ground underlain by a woven mat—each no doubt had entirely different thoughts as he drifted off to sleep. Here, within a stone chamber that Inca masons had assembled with painstaking care, long before any Inca had ever heard of a Spaniard, drifted off to sleep two men upon whom the fate of the entire empire now rested: Pizarro and Atahualpa—the conquistador and the native king.

The next morning, Pizarro sent Hernando de Soto with thirty horsemen to investigate Atahualpa's old camp, the same camp where Soto had had his first meeting with the emperor two days earlier. As they galloped along the now familiar road and then crossed the two rivers, Soto noticed that little seemed to have changed. The same great fleet of tents spread out before him in a vast tableau and here, too, stood what seemed to be the same vast ranks of native soldiers—as if the day before the Spaniards hadn't even made a dent in their numbers. While clearly tense, none of the warriors made a move against the Spaniards. At least for the time being, they were obviously obeying the orders of their commanders, who in turn were obeying the commands of their captured emperor. With free rein now to plunder all that he had seen only a few days before, Soto and his men ransacked the royal camp, gathering up all the gold, silver, and jewels they could find, then galloping their horses over the plains, where they collected even more golden objects. For it was on the plain that Atahualpa's frightened servants had dropped their serving pieces and ornaments as they themselves had fled. Before the sun had fully risen in the sky, Soto and his men

> returned to the camp . . . with a large quantity of [native] men, women, sheep [llamas], gold, silver, and cloth. Among these spoils were eighty thousand pesos of gold, seven thousand marks of silver, and fourteen emeralds. The gold and silver were in monstrous pieces, large and small dishes, pitchers, jugs, basins, and large drinking vessels and various other pieces. Atahualpa said that all this came from his table service and that his Indians who had fled had taken a great quantity more.

The Spaniards—most of whom were in their twenties and for many of whom this was their first expedition—couldn't believe their good luck. Almost overnight they seemed to have cracked open the hard outer shell of an empire and now, as if from a giant piñata, gold, silver, and jewels suddenly began to tumble to their feet. While his men admired the loot, Pizarro noted that the llamas—strange, flat-backed, camel-like creatures with large eyes and biting yellow teeth—were befouling the square, the same square that he had earlier ordered some of the captive natives to clean of dead bodies. Pizarro now insisted that the llamas be set free, as they might encumber troop movements if the Incas should decide to attack. Besides, there were so many of the animals that the Spaniards could easily kill as many as they needed for food. Pizarro next ordered the natives who had been captured to assemble on the square, choosing some to serve the Spaniards and ordering the rest to return to their homes. The governor then ordered Atahualpa to disband his army, overruling some of his captains who had suggested that first the right hand of each native soldier be cut off before sending them on their way. The bloody rout the day before, Pizarro no doubt felt, was sufficient to get his message across: that a new set of masters had arrived in Peru—and that those new masters were to be strictly obeyed.

The behavior of Pizarro and his entourage had thus far followed standard conquest procedure. First, evidence of a native empire had to be discovered, one civilized enough to include a mass of native peasants who were used to paying taxes to an elite. It was of no use to find "wild" Indians who didn't farm or had no experience with civilization. The Spaniards, after all, had come to create a feudal society over which to rule, and a feudal society, by definition, required a tax-paying peasantry.

Second, a few legalities had to be taken care of, which normally included the need for obtaining a royal license from the monarchs of Spain. Third came a legal pretext, which in the case of Atahualpa consisted of reading him the *Requerimiento* and thus his legal rights. Conveyed to him in probably a bad translation, the Requirement had informed Atahualpa that he had the right to accept the new power structure—and that if he or anyone else resisted they would quickly be put to the sword. According to the logic of sixteenth-century Spanish jurisprudence, by refusing to submit to the Spaniards and by throwing to the ground a black object with fine squiggles on its leaves that he had no way of understanding, Atahualpa had immediately forfeited his rights to the Inca Empire.

The fourth step in the normal process was to begin the conquest itself, one that was almost always accompanied by a massive display of terror in a typical "shock and awe," or "blitzkrieg," campaign. Savage attacks were purposely unleashed in order to crush native resistance and to terrorize the local inhabitants into obeying their new masters. Cortés had done this early on in Mexico, where in the town of Cholula he and his men had massacred an estimated three thousand natives in less than two hours. Spaniards throughout the Indies, in fact, had frequently cut off the arms or hands of any natives who resisted their demands, and had burned alive many native chieftains, using such spectacular displays to sow terror throughout the local population. Pizarro and his men, in their slaughter of perhaps seven thousand natives in less than a few hours, had obviously set a new benchmark for terror in the New World. Every Spanish leader, however, had to determine just how much terror was necessary in order to achieve the desired results. Pizarro's goal was not to exterminate the natives but to control them. Pizarro also knew that, if needed, additional terror could always be methodically applied.

One of the final protocols of the typical Spanish conquest was to capture alive the native leader, if at all possible. In most cases, the Spaniards could then leverage the bonds of loyalty the subjects had for their leader as a method of political control. The power gained by capturing one native leader, seized by a relatively small group of Spaniards, was similar to the effect of fielding a Spanish army of thousands, which no conquest expedition in the New World possessed.

In terms of standard operating procedures, then, the conquest of Peru was proceeding very well indeed. Pizarro had discovered a vast, wealthy civilization based upon tax-paying peasants, had acquired the proper licenses for its plunder, had informed the local ruler of the new power structure and of his obligation to submit, had successfully carried out a massive shock and awe campaign after the ruler's refusal, and now held that same ruler hostage, whom the rest of the empire's inhabitants appeared to be continuing to obey. The final steps in this process, Pizarro knew, were to consolidate and extend his already substantial gains, to carry out the empire's plunder, and then to begin diverting the vast stream of tax revenues away from the Inca elite and into the arms of Peru's new rulers.

Not long after Pizarro had ordered Atahualpa to disband his army, the giant Inca camp Soto had visited began to pack up and disperse. Abruptly decommissioned, Atahualpa's warriors now began fanning out in every direction as most headed off to the distant villages from where they had been conscripted. The planned triumphal march to Cuzco now canceled, confusion and rumors began to spread from Cajamarca to all parts of Peru, as the traveling warriors frequently paused on their return journeys to recount to groups of fascinated listeners the story of the recent massacre. In modern terms, their story was a simple one: a band of foreign terrorists had captured their leader and now held him prisoner. The inevitable questions in the shocked listeners' minds were: Who were these foreigners and what did they want? And, How long were they likely to stay?

As Atahualpa watched Pizarro's men marveling and shouting to one another excitedly about the golden plates and goblets from his camp, his observations of the invaders' behavior must have led him to an inescapable conclusion: obviously, these bearded foreigners were here merely to maraud and steal. Few in number, they were clearly not a conquering army and thus must have no intention of staying. Instead, their only interest appeared to be in plundering all they could. Once the foreigners had gathered all they could carry, Atahualpa reasoned, watching them with a slight frown, then surely they would take their booty and leave. The foreigners, after all, didn't even try to hide from view what seemed to excite them most. Anything made of gold, which the Incas called *qori,* or of silver, which they called *qullqi,* seemed to fascinate them more than anything else.

The Spaniards' behavior, in fact, no doubt reminded Atahualpa of the behavior of the barbarians the Incas had conquered in the Antisuyu, or eastern quarter, of their empire, those who inhabited the dark, dense, seemingly claustrophobic jungles and who seemed to have a fascination for almost anything the Incas produced. The Incas called the uncivilized peoples beyond their eastern borders the Antis.* Surely, Atahualpa no doubt believed, despite their strange animals and powerful weapons, these foreigners were no different. They, too, were like the Antis or other marauding tribes. Barbarians. The question no doubt foremost in Atahualpa's mind, therefore—as he observed the Spaniards excitedly fingering his dinnerware and babbling in an unintelligible tongue—was how could he hasten these savages' departure? And how could he, in the meantime, stay alive and regain his own freedom?

Having spent the last five years ruling as the de facto emperor of the northern half of the Inca Empire, making decisions on a daily basis and deciding which problems had to be addressed and how they might be overcome, Atahualpa not surprisingly now came up with a possible solution for his predicament. Motioning to one of the interpreters and to Pizarro, the emperor walked into one of the rooms of the temple of the sun, then with a piece of chalk drew a white line on the wall, reaching up well over his head to do so. Turning to Pizarro, Atahualpa told the grizzled conquistador, a quarter of a century older than himself, that he was well aware of why the Spaniards had come to Tawantinsuyu, and that he, Atahualpa, would present them with all the gold and silver objects they wished—if Pizarro would spare his life.† One eyewitness wrote:

* The Spanish corruption of the word *Antis*—a name given by the Incas to one of the ethnic groups (probably today's Machiguenga) in the eastern quarter of their empire, the Antisuyu, is thought to be where the name *Andes* derived from.

† The Spanish chronicles are not quite clear as to whether Atahualpa made his offer with the idea of offering Pizarro a large tribute, which was standard procedure for tribes conquered by the Incas, or whether he offered it as a ransom in return for his release, a concept the Spaniards were more familiar with. Even if Atahualpa offered the silver and gold to Pizarro as a tribute, however, because of the Incas' ingrained notion of reciprocity the emperor surely expected something in return.

The Governor asked him how much he would give and in what span of time. Atahualpa said that he would give a room full of gold that mea-sured twenty-two feet long by seventeen feet wide, filled to a white line half way up its height, which, from what he said, would be over eight feet high. He [also] said that he would fill the room to this height with various pieces of gold—jars, pots, plates and other objects and that he would fill that entire hut twice with silver, and that he would do all this within twelve months.

Most of the gold and silver objects were in Cuzco, Atahualpa explained, a city lying far to the south. Thus it would take him about a year to collect all that he had promised. If nothing else, Atahualpa no doubt thought, he would at least be increasing his own value to the Spaniards and therefore would be buying himself more time. With additional time, he would have more opportunities. For even though he was captive, Atahualpa still com-manded armies totaling perhaps 100,000 men. It was too dangerous, how-ever, to risk ordering his armies to attack, for he might be killed in the process. Yet if he could simply remain alive, and if the Spaniards were to let down their guard for even a moment, then he might still be in a position to do something about it.

Pizarro was clearly amazed by Atahualpa's sudden offer. In all of his thirty years in the Indies he had never heard of a native chief who had made such a proposition. Clearly, a roomful of gold would make this latest expe-dition an instant financial success. And, if such a quantity of gold were so easy to come by, then obviously he had stumbled upon an empire even richer than he had imagined. Was Atahualpa telling the truth, however? Or was he simply stalling for time? For even though the emperor had just dis-banded his army—how could he know for certain that Atahualpa hadn't simply ordered his army to reassemble nearby in order to prepare for an attack?

Pizarro still didn't understand the vast dimensions of the empire he had invaded, one that enclosed roughly three times the landmass of modern Spain, was five times its length, and had twice its population. If Atahualpa's offer, however, provided strong evidence that the empire must be vast, the emperor's next answer confirmed it. "How long will your messengers take to go to the city of Cuzco?" Pizarro asked, and then watched Atahualpa's expression intently as the translator converted Spanish into the Incas' *runasimi:*

> Atahualpa replied that when he needed a message to be delivered in a hurry, that [the messengers] run in relays from village to village and that the message arrives [in Cuzco] in five days. But if the men who start with the message go the whole way, though they be swift men, they will take fifteen days.

Upon further questioning, Atahualpa presumably stated that while Cuzco was quite distant, it was located perhaps only at the midway point in the length of his empire. Couriers racing in relays from one end of the empire to the other, from sunup to sundown, Atahualpa indicated, would take nearly twenty days, or forty days for a round-trip. For the first time since his arrival, Pizarro began to realize just how immense the empire was whose ruler he had seized.

Twelve notaries had traveled with Pizarro, men who were both literate and versed in verifying signatures and in drawing up basic legal contracts. Like their companions, they had volunteered to accompany the expedition, hoping to share in any of the plunder acquired. While notaries by profession, their current occupation was conquistador. Since sixteenth-century Spaniards lived in a litigious culture, lawsuits, writs, and legal documents were the stuff of everyday life.* A nicely produced document, handsomely signed with an elegant flourish of the pen, besides serving as a legal instrument also seemed to carry a certain cachet, especially for those who were either illiterate or only partly literate.

Pizarro, who never learned to read or write and thus for whom carefully penned Spanish texts could just as well have been written in Chinese, imme-

---

* Lawyers, no more popular in the sixteenth-century kingdoms of Spain than in modern times, were in fact banned by the crown from entering Peru in an agreement signed with Pizarro in 1529, even before the conquest of Peru began. The king apparently wished to avoid the perceived negative effects of Spanish litigation. With distances so great, however, the crown was unable to enforce the order; hence the first Spanish lawyers began to enter Peru by 1534. Lawsuits began to pour out of Spain's new colony soon afterward and continue to proliferate to this day.

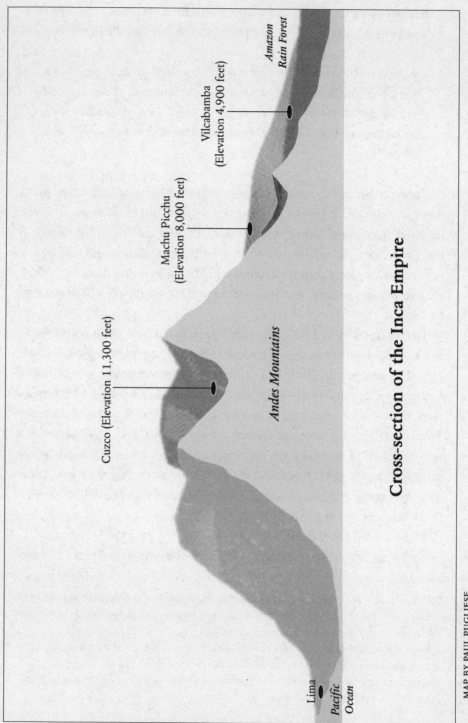

Cuzco (Elevation 11,300 feet)

Machu Picchu
(Elevation 8,000 feet)

Vilcabamba
(Elevation 4,900 feet)

*Amazon
Rain Forest*

Andes Mountains

Lima

*Pacific
Ocean*

Cross-section of the Inca Empire

MAP BY PAUL PUGLIESE

diately ordered one of the notaries to draw up a document outlining the basic points of Atahualpa's offer. While the notary busied himself, Pizarro promised Atahualpa that if the latter produced the gold he had promised, then he, Pizarro, would afterward allow him to return to Quito, where he could rule his own kingdom in the north.

It was a blatant lie, of course. Pizarro had no intention of ever letting Atahualpa go free, let alone of restoring him to a position of authority. First, he wanted Atahualpa to provide his part of the bargain—the roomfuls of gold and silver. If Atahualpa proved useful after that, then Pizarro might keep him alive. If not, then he would certainly have no qualms about killing him.

Just as Pizarro had understood little of the size of the Inca Empire and next to nothing about its culture or about how it functioned, Atahualpa equally failed to grasp that Spanish culture contained ideas that were utterly alien to him. The Inca emperor failed to understand that the Spaniards were not interested in his gold and silver tableware because they desired better drinking goblets or because they were dazzled by the tableware's shininess like other barbarians, but because the *materials* the cups and plates were made of coincidentally happened to consist of the exact same rare elements that formed the basis of money in the Old World. The only real requirement for a monetary system, after all, was that the material used be scarce and that everyone agree on the unit of exchange. In the emerging nations of sixteenth-century Europe, gold, silver, copper, and nickel were the widely used standards. Any Spaniard lucky enough to receive a pound of gold—whether as a payment or through plunder and conquest—could sell it to a merchant or banker with no questions asked and would receive roughly 120 golden ducat coins in return.

To get an idea of what this was worth, the average salary of a Spanish sailor in the 1530s, who risked his life at sea, was fifty or sixty ducats a year, equivalent to half a pound of gold. With four pounds of gold, one could buy an entire caravel ship in Spain. Ten pounds of gold could be converted into 1,200 ducats, the equivalent of twenty backbreaking years of labor at sea. It was no wonder then that the Spaniards' eyes widened so much when Soto and his men returned with their loot of gold and silver goblets, plates, and statues. If this was what Atahualpa possessed in a mere temporary camp, then what riches did the rest of the empire hold?

The Incas, too, were aware of the idea of monetary systems, even though their empire relied upon the bartering of goods, whose exchanges were nevertheless standardized. One ethnic group the Incas had conquered, the Chincha, who lived on the coast to the south of what is now Lima, were specialized traders possessing fleets of rafts they used to trade up and down the coast as far north as Ecuador. It was probably a Chincha trading vessel, in fact, that Pizarro's expedition had seized during their second expedition. Due to their constant business transactions, Chincha traders relied upon copper as a type of money, which they used to exchange for other goods. The standard unit of exchange was copper cast into the form of a blunt axe head.

But the Inca Empire never adopted a monetary system. Gold, the color of the sun, was considered by the Incas to be sacred, as the sun was the principal god in their religious pantheon. It was never, however, used as an item of exchange. Similarly, silver was considered to be the tears of the moon goddess, or *mama-kilya,* and was thus used in temples devoted to that god. Since it was from the sun god, Inti, that Atahualpa and his ancestors were descended, gold was inextricably linked with both the sun and with its incarnation on earth, the Inca emperor. Mined and sluiced from different regions of the empire, gold and silver were transported to the capital along the empire's arterial roads in a kind of one-way system: the sacred metals traveled to Cuzco and to the empire's other main cities and rarely did they leave. Instead, native artisans and jewelers fashioned the two metals into symbolic forms that reflected the divine nature of the moon, the sun, and the emperor, which is why Atahualpa dined from cups and plates made not of clay, but of the purest silver and gold.

The Inca economic system, meanwhile, was not a capitalist one, in which private individuals owned their own land, labor, and other resources and endeavored to make a profit. Instead, the Inca elite relied upon a redistributive economy. In it, a large part of the production of the countryside was controlled by the state, which in turn redistributed this wealth according to its own needs and the needs of the population. Nearly all land, for example, belonged to the state, which divided the land into church, state, and communal use. The Inca elite required peasant communities to sow and harvest both state and church lands, the produce of which went to support the teeming bureaucracies of the government and clergy and to fulfill a variety of other needs. Implicit in their social contract with the government was the peasants' right to work their own communal lands, which the state, however, continued to own.

The Inca elites also required that every inhabitant of the empire donate a specified sum of labor each year to the emperor. Called the *mit'a*, such labor was used by the emperor in any way he saw fit. Each male head of a family household thus had to supply up to three months of labor to the emperor per year, whether that be used in constructing roads, buildings, weaving, working as a *chaski* runner, carrying royal litters, fighting in wars, or some other useful activity. With millions of families annually harvesting the produce from church and state lands in addition to paying their labor taxes, the revenues of the empire were enormous. The surplus created by the taxed labor was stored in great warehouses located throughout the empire, repositories of goods so vast and richly stocked that they astonished all the Spaniards who encountered them. The gross domestic product of the Inca Empire was so great, in fact, that periodically the warehouses simply had to be emptied and their contents gifted to the inhabitants of nearby provinces, in order to make room for the constant production of goods. Wrote the conquistador Pedro Sancho de la Hoz:

> One can see . . . many . . . storehouses full of blankets, wool, weapons, metal [objects], and clothes, and of everything that is grown and made in this realm. . . . There are bucklers, shields, beams for supporting tents, knives, and other tools; sandals and armor for the warriors in such quantities that it is impossible to comprehend how they [the taxpayers] had been able to provide so much tribute of so many different things.

The emperor normally used the state-owned goods as gifts for his lords, chiefs, and other retainers, in order to secure their loyalty to the Inca state. The lords in turn gifted their own followers in a long descending chain that continued down to the peasants who had created all of the surplus in the first place. Through redistribution, the Inca elites—representing only a fraction of an ethnic group that made up less than one percent of the empire's total population—were able to maintain the loyalty of local rulers and hence were able to retain control of the vast empire they had created.

Just as Atahualpa periodically gifted his lords, why couldn't he gift

Pizarro and expect something from him in return? If the Spaniards wanted shiny tableware, then Atahualpa wanted his *life*. If he needed to exchange a roomful of gold in order to continue living, then he would gladly provide that and more. Atahualpa hadn't fought for the last five years to win an empire only to suddenly lose it to a small band of marauders. Perhaps reciprocity was the key.

Chaski runners now fanned out through the empire, carrying a desperate message from their ruler: send all available gold and silver objects to Cajamarca, including those from the temples of the sun and moon. Pizarro, meanwhile, sent his own message to the eighty Spaniards he had left behind in San Miguel, the new coastal town he had established to the south of the ruined city of Tumbez. Pizarro's message informed the Spaniards of the victory they had wrought and also urged them to send to Panama for reinforcements. Only with additional Spaniards, Pizarro realized, would he ever possess a sufficient force with which to subdue such an obviously large and populous empire. Pizarro's one-eyed partner, Diego de Almagro, in fact, had purposely stayed behind in Panama with the understanding that he would continue gathering more men, ships, and supplies and would join Pizarro at a later date. Pizarro could only hope that Almagro would arrive soon, before Atahualpa divined his true intent: that he and his men were here to stay and had no intention whatsoever of leaving.

Weeks passed before finally a slow trickle of gold and silver objects began to arrive, which each day continued to grow larger. Wrote the notary Francisco de Xerez:

> And thus, [on some days] twenty thousand, on others thirty thousand, fifty, or sixty thousand *pesos de oro* would arrive, [in the form of] large pitchers and jars of from two to three *arrobas* [fifty to seventy-five pounds] in size, and large silver pitchers and jars and many other vessels. The Governor ordered all of it to be placed in a building where Atahualpa had his guards. . . . To keep it more safely, the Governor placed Christians to guard it day and night, and as it was being placed in the building all of it was counted so that there would be no fraud.

The Spaniards carefully weighed each object and converted the weight into pesos, one of the Spaniards' standard units of measurement for gold.

Since one peso weighed a sixth of an ounce, thirty thousand to sixty thousand pesos meant that between three hundred and six hundred *pounds* of gold were arriving each day. For the rank-and-file conquistador, whether literate or illiterate, it didn't take a Renaissance mathematician to figure out that all of those present were about to become extremely wealthy men.

Not long after Atahualpa had sent out his first messengers—instructing his subordinates not only to help in the gathering and transport of the sacred objects but also that his generals not attempt to rescue him for fear that any such efforts might cost him his life—native chiefs and lords from throughout the empire began to arrive in Cajamarca. They came to pay their respects, both to their Inca lord and to the leader of the powerful bearded foreigners who had captured him.

"When the chiefs of this province heard of the arrival of the Governor and of the capture of Atahualpa, many of them came peacefully to see the Governor," wrote Xerez. The chronicler Estete recorded that "they came from each province to visit him and to see the Spaniards, and each one brought presents of what there was in their land such as gold, silver, and other things." Continued Xerez, "Some of these chiefs were lords of thirty thousand Indians, and all of them were subject to Atahualpa. When they arrived before him they paid homage to him, kissing his hands and feet. He received them without looking at them." According to Estete, "he behaved towards them in a most princely manner, showing no less dignity [despite being] defeated and imprisoned than he had before that had occurred."

The Spaniards, none of whom other than Pizarro had actually ever laid their eyes on a real emperor, had no real understanding of the reverence the Inca subjects had for their lord. Atahualpa was not the equivalent of a European king, as he was both secular *and* divine. In approaching Atahualpa, the natives in essence were entering the presence of a god, for Atahualpa was the equivalent of the king, the pope, and Jesus Christ all rolled into one. In this one, medium-sized native leader were concentrated all the legislative, judicial, executive, and religious powers of an empire ten million strong.

The Inca Empire was a theocratic monarchy; hence all dispensations emanated directly from its emperor—justice, divine intervention, wealth, titles, status, food, drink—even life and death itself. Just as Atahualpa had ordered the slaughter of the battalion of soldiers who had bolted from their ranks due to their fear of Soto's charging horse, so, too, could Atahualpa grant life.

While he was in captivity, Atahualpa was asked on one occasion by the lord of the province of Huaylas if that lord could go visit his native territory. Atahualpa granted him permission, but gave the lord a specific amount of time in which to go and return. "He delayed somewhat longer," Pizarro's cousin Pedro remembered, "and while I was present he returned and arrived with a present of fruit from his province. [Yet] once before the Inca Emperor, he began to tremble to such an extent that he could no longer remain standing. Atahualpa raised his head a little and, smiling, he made a gesture for him to leave."

The Inca emperor, however, was not nearly so magnanimous with his own brother, Huascar, as he was with the trembling native lord. Atahualpa still considered his captured brother to be his only competitor for the throne; thus, even though Huascar was now his prisoner, as long as he was alive, Huascar remained a threat. The Spaniards, Atahualpa no doubt believed, were going to leave, and hopefully would do so very soon. When they did, Atahualpa wanted to make sure that his position as emperor would remain unchallenged. Shortly after Atahualpa's capture by the Spaniards, messengers had informed him that his brother was only a few days' march away, having been brought there as a prisoner under an armed escort. By this time, almost all of Huascar's family line had been thoroughly exterminated. Having already witnessed the brutal murders of his wife, children, and relatives, Huascar must have realized that he was now being led to what could only be a grisly execution. According to one account, "Huascar, after being taken prisoner, was abominably maltreated. Rotten maize, bitter herbs and [llama] dung were given to him to eat. His cap was filled with llama's piss; [and] his natural desire was mocked by putting him to bed with a long stone dressed up as a woman."

Through his interpreters, Pizarro learned of the impending arrival of the rival Inca emperor and looked forward to having him, too, in captivity. The only pretender to the Inca throne, Huascar in captivity would mean that Pizarro would have *two* Inca emperors under his control, thus increasing his power over the central and southern portions of the empire. Atahualpa had begun his struggle while initially controlling only about 10 percent of the Inca Empire, in what is now northern Ecuador. Huascar, by contrast, had begun while controlling the other 90 percent. During the next five years, those percentages had gradually changed, until by the end of the civil war the area under Huascar's control had effectively shrunk to zero.

Unbeknownst to Pizarro, however, Atahualpa had sent secret messengers to intercept his brother's escort. About two hundred miles south of Cajamarca, Inca soldiers murdered Huascar and tossed his body into a river. Rather than release his brother and ask him to help organize a national resistance against the bearded invaders, Atahualpa had instead allowed traditional dynastic politics to take precedence. A captive Inca emperor had ironically decided that it was more important to protect his throne from his brother's aspirations than it was to protect that same throne from a group of foreign invaders. Confident that the Spaniards would soon leave, Atahualpa apparently believed that now that his brother was dead, his own control of the empire was finally complete.

Pizarro surprisingly accepted Atahualpa's explanation for Huascar's sudden death—that his brother's guards had murdered him without his orders. With only one Inca emperor left and with that one as securely in his possession as was an ever-increasing amount of gold, the important thing was that Pizarro was still able to control the empire through Atahualpa, whose lords and chiefs continued to obey their king.

The contrast between Atahualpa's behavior toward his subjects, meanwhile, and his behavior toward his captors fascinated the Spaniards. To those natives beneath him on the hierarchical scale—which included every citizen in the Inca Empire—Atahualpa's behavior remained aloof, stern, and magisterial. Usually the emperor received visitors while seated behind a screen, so that he himself could not be seen. Only with select individuals did Atahualpa grant them the privilege of viewing him in person. As a rule, the Inca style of governance was to treat one's underlings with disdain, thus reinforcing the divisions of power. In the presence of his subjects, therefore, Atahualpa behaved every bit the god descended to earth, projecting a culturally prescribed aura of power and divinity.

Toward the bearded invaders, however, who by their very seizure of him had trumped his own ranking in power, Atahualpa displayed a completely different side of his personality; in the Spaniards' presence, the imperial facade imposed by Inca culture disappeared. In its place, Atahualpa instead behaved more like an "emperor without clothes," perhaps revealing something closer to his true personality. Alone among the Spaniards, Atahualpa was convivial, friendly, even cheerful—a man in fact who bent over backward to please. The Spaniards, in the meantime, allowed Atahualpa to maintain his own servants, to continue the life of luxury to which he was accustomed, and to continue running his empire. But the Spaniards no longer allowed Atahualpa to wage war, to command armies, or to make any attempt to free himself.

During the many months of Atahualpa's captivity, a number of Spaniards grew fond of the native emperor, especially Hernando de Soto and Hernando Pizarro. The two Spanish captains even taught the Inca emperor how to play chess and spent hours with him enjoying a game originally invented in India. Atahualpa soon became proficient and gave chess the name of *taptana,* or "surprise attack," thoroughly enjoying the game's obvious parallels with military strategy.

Peppering his captors with questions, Atahualpa in fact amazed the Spaniards, who often marveled over the supposed barbarian's display of reason and logic. "After he was a prisoner," wrote the notary Francisco de Xerez, "the Spaniards who listened to him were astounded to find so much wisdom in a barbarian." "[The emperor] is the wisest and most capable [native] who has ever been seen," wrote Gaspar de Espinosa. "He likes to learn about the things we possess to such an extent that he plays chess very well. By having this man in . . . [our] power the entire land is calm."

The Spaniards, meanwhile, most of whom were from the lower classes and a third of whom were illiterate, were fascinated by their close proximity to royalty, even if this were only of the barbarian kind. Coming from an extremely hierarchical society themselves, the Spaniards couldn't help but be dazzled by Atahualpa's royal treatment, or by the fact that he was waited upon hand and foot by a covey of beautiful women, most of whom were his concubines. Remembered Pedro Pizarro, who was eighteen years old at the time:

> The ladies . . . brought him his meal and placed it before him on delicate green rushes. . . . They placed all the dishes of gold, silver, and earthenware [on these rushes] and he [Atahualpa] pointed at whatever appealed to him. It was then brought over, one of the ladies taking it and holding it in her hand while he ate. One day, while I was present and he

was eating in this manner, a slice of food was being lifted to his mouth when a drop fell onto the clothing he was wearing. Giving his hand to the Indian lady, he rose and went into his chamber to change his clothes, then returned wearing a tunic and a dark brown cloak. I approached him and felt the cloak, which was softer than silk, and said to him, "Inca, what is this robe made of that it is so soft?" He replied that it was from the skins of [vampire] bats that fly by night in Puerto Viejo and Tumbez and that bite the natives.

When asked how it had been possible to collect so many bats, Atahualpa paused and said that it was done by "'those [native] dogs from Tumbez and Puerto Viejo—what else did they have to do other than to catch bats and make clothes for my father?'"

On another day, Pizarro's young cousin accompanied a native to a royal storehouse filled with trunks made of dark leather.

I asked him what the trunks contained, and he showed me some in which they kept everything that Atahualpa had touched with his hands and the clothes he had thrown away. Some contained the rushes that they placed before his feet when he ate, in others the bones of the meat or birds he had eaten . . . in others the cores of the ears of corn he had held in his hands. . . . In short, everything that he had touched. I asked him why they kept all this there. They told me that it was in order to burn it because every year . . . what had been touched by the [Inca] lords, who were sons of the Sun, had to be burned, reduced to ashes, and thrown into the air, and that no one was allowed to touch it.

Perhaps the closest modern equivalent to such behavior is the reverence still shown by the Catholic faithful before the reliquaries of the saints, whose bones and bits of hair are kept as precious, sacred objects even today. Such was the adulation that Atahualpa, the Son of the Sun, received during his lifetime.

When November and December of 1532 and then January of 1533 rolled by, the pile of golden objects still had not reached the line that Atahualpa had drawn on the wall of the chamber. Both Pizarro and Atahualpa were by now restless. Pizarro was impatient to receive reinforcements, to complete the gathering of the treasure, then to journey south to Cuzco, the Incas' capital, and thus to finish the conquest. Atahualpa, meanwhile, was anxious to give the Spaniards what they coveted so that they would leave his empire forever. When one of Atahualpa's brothers arrived, supervising a caravan of treasure, he told Atahualpa that another treasure convoy had been delayed at Jauja, a city lying between Cajamarca and Cuzco, and that much more gold still remained in the capital and had yet to be removed from the temples.

Impatient for his release, Atahualpa suggested to Pizarro that the latter send some of his troops to Cuzco in order to supervise the collection of the ransom. Pizarro, however—knowing that Atahualpa had two armies in the south and another in the north—was reluctant to divide up his forces, for fear of an attack. Three of Pizarro's men—perhaps bored with so much waiting and having heard Atahualpa's glowing descriptions of the Inca capital—nevertheless quickly volunteered to make the journey south. Two of them—Martín Bueno and Pedro Martín de Moguer—were illiterate sailors from a seacoast town in southern Spain's Andalusia. The third was a Basque notary named Juan Zárate.

Pizarro agreed to send the three men yet just as quickly reminded Atahualpa of the nature of their relationship: if anything should happen to the three Spaniards, he warned, then he would have him killed. Atahualpa reassured Pizarro, offering to provide an Inca noble, a number of native soldiers, and also porters who could carry the three Spaniards on royal litters. Pizarro then met with the men, ordering them to take possession of the city of Cuzco in the name of the king and to do so in the presence of the notary, who was to draw up a legal document to that effect. He then gave the three orders to carefully behave themselves—to do nothing that the Inca *orejón* accompanying them did not wish, so that they would not be killed. Their mission was to reconnoiter the conditions and terrain to the south, to help with the collection of treasure in Cuzco, and to bring back a full and detailed report of everything they saw.

One can only imagine what a journey the three men had—the first Europeans to travel along the jagged crest of the Andes from Cajamarca to Cuzco—all seen from the height of their royal litters, as if the two rough sailors and the humble notary had suddenly been transformed into powerful Inca lords. The litters they traveled on were luxury vehicles consisting of two long poles, sheathed on their ends in silver in the form of animal heads, and with a floor built between them. On the floor was constructed a passenger seat which in turn was overlain with soft cushions. Low walls boxed in the sides of the seat for security while overhead a canopy of feathers interwoven with cloth protected the passenger from both sun and rain. Carried normally by members of the Rucana tribe, who were trained since their youth to provide the smoothest ride possible, litters were clearly a mark of power and prestige. Their use was restricted to only the highest Inca nobility.

The small procession soon headed south from Cajamarca, climbing the flanks of fantastic mountains, cutting past pale, blue-green glaciers, crossing through Inca cities and villages set beside rivers that sparkled in the sun, then traversing giant gorges on hanging Inca bridges while witnessing vast flocks of llamas and alpacas that seemed to extend for as far as the eye could see. Strangers in a strange land, these were the first Europeans to witness an untouched Andean world, one with a thriving civilization in all its color and scarcely understood complexity. Everything was new—plants, animals, people, villages, mountains, herds, languages, and cities. A trio of Marco Polos adrift in the New World, they were similarly off to seek riches in a distant and fabled city. Wrote the notary Pedro Sancho de la Hoz:

> All the steep mountains . . . [have] stairways of stone. One of the greatest works the conquistadors . . . [witnessed] in this land were these roads. . . . Most of the people on these mountain slopes live on hills and on high mountains. Their houses are of stone and earth [and] there are many houses in each village. Along the road every four to seven miles are found the houses built for the purpose of allowing the lords to rest while they were out visiting and inspecting their realm. And every seventy miles there are important cities, capitals of the provinces, to which the smaller cities brought the tributes they paid with corn, clothes, and other things. All these large cities have storehouses full of the things that are [harvested from] the land. Because it is very cold, little corn is harvested except in specially designated places. But [there are plenty of] vegetables and roots with which the people sustain themselves and also

good grass like that in Spain. There are also wild turnips [potatoes] that are bitter.* There are many herds of sheep [llamas and alpacas], which go about in flocks with their shepherds who watch over them and keep them away from the sown fields. They have a certain part of [each] province set apart for them [the herds] to winter in. The people, as I have said, are very polite and intelligent and always go about dressed and with footwear. They eat cooked and raw corn and drink a lot of *chicha,* which is a beverage made from corn that is much like beer. The people are very friendly and very obedient and [yet] warlike. They have many weapons of diverse sorts, as has been told.

Like Cortés's men gaining their first glimpse of Tenochtitlán—the capital of the Aztecs that his fellow Spaniards likened to a city more wondrous than Venice—when the three travelers finally arrived in Cuzco, after more than a month of being carried ever southward, they, too, were stunned by what they beheld. Nestled on a hillside that opened into a broad valley at 11,300 feet, the Incas' mountain capital appeared like some medieval town in the Swiss Alps, with smoke rising from the thatched roofs of its high-gabled houses and with green hillsides and snow-and-ice-covered mountains rising in the distance. "This city is the greatest and finest that has ever been seen in this realm or even in the Indies," the Spaniards later wrote the king. "And we can assure your Majesty that it is so beautiful and has such fine buildings that it would be very remarkable even in Spain." Wrote Sancho de la Hoz:

> [It is] full of the palaces of the lords. . . . The greater part of these houses are made of stone and others have half of the facade of stone . . . the streets are laid out at right angles. They are very straight and are paved with stones and down the middle runs a gutter for water and lined with stone. . . . The plaza is square and the greater part of it is flat and paved with small stones. Around it are four palaces of lords, which are the main

---

* All wild potatoes contain toxic glycoalkaloids, giving them a bitter taste. Those that grow at elevations of more than nine thousand feet and are frost-resistant have even higher concentrations of them. The Incas and their ancestors freeze-dried potatoes, a process of alternately freezing, crushing, and then drying potatoes that served to break down the glycoalkaloids and also made their storage easier. The Incas called the finished, freeze-dried product *chuño;* it was and still is an essential ingredient in traditional Andean stews.

ones in the city; they are painted and carved and are made of stone and the best of them is the house of Huayna Capac, a former chief, and the gateway is of red, white, and multi-colored marble. . . . There are . . . [also] many other buildings and grandeurs.

On the heights above the city, the Spaniards saw a fortress with three towers that resembled a European castle. When the three visitors presumably used sign language to point and ask, their hosts replied with a word that sounded like *Saq-say-wa-man,* which they eventually learned meant "(the fortress of) the satisfied falcon." Described Sancho de la Hoz:

Upon the hill, which . . . is rounded and very steep, there is a very beautiful fortress of earth and stone. Its large windows, which look over the city, make it appear even more beautiful. . . . And many Spaniards who have been in Lombardy and in other foreign kingdoms say that they have never seen another building like this fortress nor a more powerful castle. Five thousand Spaniards might fit within it. It cannot be given a broadside [with a cannon] nor can it be tunneled [beneath], because it is located on a rocky hill.

One side of the Inca fortress was protected by an immense stone wall composed of rocks of gargantuan size—thirty-ton behemoths that somehow the Incas had cut and carved and moved into place. Elsewhere in the city, as the Spaniards wandered about, they were stared at by the curious inhabitants, whose cotton or alpaca-wool tunics and headbands, as well as hairstyles, indicated both their rank and what part of the empire they hailed from. Everywhere they looked, the Spaniards saw finely constructed stone walls lining the streets, walls that exhibited the most remarkable craftsmanship the Spaniards had ever seen. According to Sancho de la Hoz:

The most beautiful thing that can be seen among the buildings of that land are these walls, because they are of stones so large that no one who sees them would say that they had been placed there by human hands, for they are as large as chunks of mountains. . . . These are not smooth stones but rather are very well fitted together and interlocked with one another.

Pedro Pizarro recounted: "[And they are] so close together and so well-fitted that the point of a pin could not have been inserted into any of the joints." Concluded de la Hoz: "The Spaniards who see them say that neither the bridge of Segovia nor any of the structures that Hercules or the Romans made are as worthy of being seen as this."

The capital of the New World's greatest empire was a clean, well-engineered, and obviously well-organized place. If the hallmark of civilization is the intensification of production of food and other goods and the corresponding increase of population and the stratification of society, then nowhere was this more apparent than in Cuzco, which in the Incas' language means "navel." It was in this very valley—where the four *suyus* met and formed their epicenter—that the Incas had begun their rise to power. Now the rest of the empire was connected to it via a webwork of umbilical-like roads—roads that, all combined, stretched for more than 25,000 miles, from the Inca capital to the furthest frontiers.

Here, in the polyglot navel, the ruling emperor normally lived, and also the lesser lords. It was here, too, that even chiefs from distant provinces had their homes. A sort of gated community for the elites, Cuzco was the royal hub of the empire, a city that was purposely meant to display the ostentation of state power. To serve the elites, peasants—the workhorses of the empire from which all the nation's power derived—visited the capital daily and kept it supplied with every conceivable kind of product the elites might require. Everywhere the Spaniards traveled in the city, in fact, they found warehouses stuffed to the ceiling with goods that millions of industrious citizens were constantly churning out, and that were then collected, tabulated by an army of accountants, and stored in massive, state-owned warehouses.

As they had been instructed, the three Spaniards "took possession of that city of Cuzco in the name of His Majesty." The Basque notary, Juan Zárate, dutifully drew up a document that he signed with a flourish and notarized with a seal, as puzzled natives no doubt watched over his shoulder. Neither the natives nor the two illiterate Spanish sailors who had accompanied him could read a word of what he had written.

What had really caught the trio's attention, however, from the moment they had looked down upon the capital after crossing the final crest of hills, were certain buildings that seemed to burn as brightly as the sun, as if the buildings themselves had been dipped into a golden fire. After some investigation, they discovered that, sure enough,

> These buildings were sheathed on the side where the sun rises with large plates of gold. . . . They said there was so much gold in all the buildings of the city that it was a marvelous thing . . . [and that] they would have brought much more of it if this would not have detained them longer, because they were alone and over 250 leagues from the other Christians.

Before the three conquistadors could begin collecting the gold, however, they first had to meet with the Inca general who was in command of the city. Cuzco, after all, was presently an occupied city, the former command post of the provinces that had fought against Atahualpa. Until very recently, Huascar had worn the royal fringe, or *mascapaicha,* and from here he had commanded his armies. It was here, too, that he had received reports about the battles raging to the north, which over the last few years had gradually moved closer and closer, until the final battle had finally crashed down upon him like a giant tsunami.

One of Atahualpa's finest commanders, General Quisquis, presently occupied the capital with thirty thousand troops—legions who were nearly as foreign to Cuzco's citizens as were the three men riding about on royal litters and speaking an unintelligible tongue. Like General Sherman's brutal march through Georgia during the American Civil War, Quisquis had fought an equally devastating campaign all the way down the spine of the Andes, had occupied Cuzco with his legions, had captured the emperor Huascar, and had exterminated almost all of Huascar's family including even the unborn children. Only after his successful campaign did the general receive surprising reports about the sudden attack of a marauding band of foreigners in the north, who had somehow managed to capture the emperor. And only later did he begin receiving the ominous and puzzling orders from Atahualpa to send all available gold and silver objects north to Cajamarca, sacred objects that apparently were needed in order to secure the emperor's release.

And now, sometime in March or April 1533, as the Andes were beginning to enter into winter, General Quisquis found himself gazing at the three foreign emissaries, seated comfortably on litters borne by native porters who stood with downcast eyes before him. The visitors wore strange clothes, the general saw, had hair growing from their faces—so unlike his own smooth-skinned people—and even though their skin had browned under the fierce Andean sun, Quisquis could see patches when they moved that were white in color, hidden beneath their ragged and dirty clothes. The foreigners also each wore a long piece of metal at their waist, which Quisquis no doubt presumed was some kind of mace or club, although it looked thin and flimsy. The visitors spoke a barbarian tongue, for they replied in an unintelligible manner when spoken to and understood nothing of the empire's lingua franca, *runasimi,* or apparently of any other native language. As such they were nearly impossible to communicate with. Wrote the native chronicler Felipe Huamán Poma de Ayala:

> To our Indian eyes, the Spaniards looked as if they were shrouded like corpses. Their faces were covered with wool, leaving only the eyes visible, and the caps that they wore resembled little red pots on top of their heads. Sometimes they also decorated their heads with plumes. Their swords appeared very long, since they had to be carried with the points turned in a backward direction. They were all dressed alike and talked together like brothers and ate at the same table.

The victorious Inca general himself was a spectacle that equally impressed the Spaniards: he wore resplendent clothing, consisting of a tunic, or *unqu,* decorated with black and white squares creating a chessboard-like effect, and he wore a mantle hanging from his shoulders made of the finest alpaca wool. The general's tunic reached to his knees and below it he wore colored knee and ankle fringes. Hanging from his neck Quisquis wore a golden disc, given to him by the emperor Atahualpa for bravery, while twin golden bracelets encircled his wrists. Sandals made from leather, cotton, and alpaca covered the general's feet, each overlain with a miniature golden mask.

General Quisquis's grave black eyes appeared quick and intelligent; he also had a proud face and possessed the long earlobes with inserted golden plugs of the Inca blood nobility, whom the Incas called *pakoyok.* The Spaniards undoubtedly noticed that not only was General Quisquis's voice commanding but that his attendants and lower officers obeyed him immediately. Not surprisingly, the proud Inca general gave the three Spaniards a cold reception. How does one behave, after all, toward foreign invaders who have just seized the leader of your country? Still, with direct orders from Atahualpa, there was little the veteran general could do.

"He didn't like the Christians, although he marveled greatly at them," wrote the notary Cristóbal de Mena. "This [Inca] captain told them not to ask him for much gold and that if they refused to release the chief [Atahualpa], then he himself would go to rescue him." General Quisquis, no doubt suppressing his own desire to immediately seize and kill the foreigners, was now forced to swallow his pride as he allowed the Spaniards to enter the Incas' most sacred temple—the Qoricancha, the temple of the sun. Doing so was akin to the cardinal secretary of state allowing three thieves to enter and sack St. Peter's Cathedral. The Qoricancha was the holiest temple in the Inca Empire. Not open to the public, it was visited only by specialized priests and by the reclusive temple virgins, or *mamacuna*. All who entered were required to remove their shoes and to perform numerous forms of religious observances and ablutions.

The two sailors and the notary, oblivious to Inca culture and concerned only with immediate plunder, entered the temple in their shabby leather boots and pushed past the stunned temple priests. They soon discovered that the Qoricancha was lined both inside and out with banded sheets of gold. Cristóbal de Mena described what happened next: "The Christians went to the buildings and with no aid from the Indians (who refused to help, saying that it was a temple of the sun and they would die) the Christians decided to strip the ornaments away . . . with some copper crowbars. And so they did." With native crowbars, much grunting, and no doubt planting their boots when necessary against the sacred walls, the three Spaniards began prying off the golden sheets, piling them up outside like so much scrap metal before a group of horrified onlookers and angry priests. "The greater part of this consisted of plates like the boards of a box, three or four *palmos* (two to two-and-a-half feet) in length," wrote the chronicler Xerez. "They had removed these from the walls of the buildings and they had holes in them as if they had been nailed." Each plate weighed about four and a half pounds, which meant that every plate in monetary terms was enough to buy a caravel, or was worth the equivalent of nine years of wages for either of the two sailors carrying them. Eventually, the Spaniards assembled a pile of some seven hundred golden plates, each rudely ripped from the empire's holiest of walls.

On May 13, 1533, after an absence of nearly three months and a journey of more than 1,200 miles, the first of the three Spaniards arrived back in Cajamarca, still carried on a royal litter. The two Spaniards left behind eventually shepherded a vast procession of 178 loads of gold and silver, each load carried on a type of stretcher borne by four native porters; in all, more than a thousand porters labored northward plus llamas carrying provisions.

Once they had arrived back in Cajamarca, the three travelers found Pizarro's camp much changed. Diego de Almagro—Pizarro's short, one-eyed, fifty-eight-year-old partner—had arrived a month earlier. Almagro had marched up into the Andes and had joined Pizarro with a force of 153 more men, including fifty new horses, leaving six ships behind.

Almagro's sudden arrival had apparently had the effect of crushing Atahualpa psychologically, as ever since his capture five months earlier the emperor had been waiting patiently for the Spaniards to depart. With the sudden near doubling of Pizarro's forces and the arrival of so many fresh horses and men, the message was now as clear to him as was the information spread across the colored knots of an Inca *quipu*. Watching the newly arrived Spaniards greedily eyeing the roomful of gold and excitedly chatting among themselves, Atahualpa no doubt realized that he had been fooled. Far from being a small party of marauders preparing to leave with their plunder, the Spaniards now appeared to be readying themselves for a full-scale invasion of his empire.

Trying to confirm Pizarro's true intentions, Atahualpa and one of his chiefs asked Pizarro at one point a leading question: how were the peasants in Tawantinsuyu going to be divided among the Spaniards, they asked. When Pizarro said without thinking that every Spaniard was going to be granted a native chief, which meant that every Spaniard was going to control an entire native community, Atahualpa's plans for assuming the Inca throne were suddenly dashed, just as unexpectedly as an unforeseen attack in a game of chess. One of the inherent challenges of chess, Atahualpa knew, was trying to divine the intentions of one's opponent while simultaneously trying to mask one's own. In this regard, Pizarro had clearly succeeded while Atahualpa had just as clearly failed.

Atahualpa no doubt also realized that if his present circumstances in Cajamarca were like one big game of chess, then this was probably his last game; he surely felt the sensation of being trapped in a sudden checkmate. Now, not only did Atahualpa not have even a proverbial pawn to protect him, but he was further hemmed in by forces more powerful than before the game had begun. Atahualpa must have also realized that all of the sacred gold and all of the sacred silver objects he had been so diligently collecting probably weren't going to amount to much more than a silver vase full of llama piss, for all the good they were going to do him. For the first time, Atahualpa must have realized that he was destined for precisely the same end as his brother Huascar.

"When Almagro and these men arrived," recalled Pedro Pizarro, "Atahualpa became anxious and . . . [feared] that he was going to die." Upon hearing Francisco Pizarro's reply, in fact—that the leader of the foreign invaders intended to divide up the empire among his followers—Atahualpa is said to have simply uttered, "[Then] I shall die."

6 ❖ REQUIEM FOR A KING

"In 1531 another great villain [Francisco Pizarro] journeyed with a number of men to the kingdoms of Peru. He set out with every intention of imitating the strategy and tactics of his fellow-adventurers in other parts of the New World . . . but, as time went on, his cruelty came to outstrip even that of his predecessors, as he criminally murdered and plundered his way through the region, razing towns and cities to the ground and slaughtering and otherwise tormenting in the most barbaric fashion imaginable the people who lived there. Throughout the territory, his wickedness was on such a scale that nobody will ever really learn the full extent of it until all is revealed on the Day of Judgment."

BARTOLOMÉ DE LAS CASAS,
THE DESTRUCTION OF THE INDIES, 1542

"When they reached the Governor [Pizarro], they found him grief stricken, with a large felt hat on his head for mourning, and his eyes wet with tears."

GONZALO FERNÁNDEZ DE OVIEDO Y VALDÉS,
HISTORY OF THE INDIES, 1547

"Politics have no relation to morals."

NICCOLÒ MACHIAVELLI, *THE PRINCE,* 1511

WHEN DIEGO DE ALMAGRO FINALLY ARRIVED WITH ADDItional men and supplies in Peru in 1533, like Pizarro he must have been surprised to have found the city of Tumbez lying in complete ruins. Traveling south along the coast, he and his men soon came upon the newly founded

The execution of Atahualpa Inca.

Spanish town of San Miguel, where Pizarro had left some eighty of the sick, young, or older conquistadors as citizens. Almagro learned from them that Pizarro was in the mountains and had somehow managed to capture the lord of what they believed was a powerful Indian empire. The natives were afraid to attack them, Almagro was told, because Pizarro held their lord prisoner. Almagro also learned that Pizarro was expecting his arrival and wanted Almagro to join him as quickly as possible.

By now, Almagro and Pizarro had been partners for at least fourteen years. Yet theirs had been a bumpy relationship as of late. When Pizarro had returned from Spain to Panama in 1529 with a royal license to conquer the Inca Empire—a realm that he was authorized to plunder for a distance of two hundred leagues, or seven hundred miles—he had also returned with the title of Governor of Peru. In addition, Pizarro had secured for himself the military title of Captain-General of Peru and had set in motion the process for being awarded the coveted Order of Santiago, a knighthood that would automatically pluck him from his lowly origins and deposit him securely among the elite of Spain.

In contrast to his own multiple titles, Pizarro had brought back just a single title for his loyal partner, Almagro—that of the Mayor of Tumbez, an area that, all told, covered a span of perhaps a few square miles and that now lay in ruins. This was despite the fact that, during their previous voyage, Almagro had rescued Pizarro and his starving followers on the island of Gallo, off the coast of Colombia, and despite the fact that it had been Almagro who had raised funds to send Pizarro to Spain in the first place. Not surprisingly, Pizarro's short, swarthy partner had been furious upon hearing the news that he had been completely shortchanged.

Pizarro, however, still needed Almagro. He needed his organizational skills, he needed his ability to find and enlist fresh recruits, he needed his partner's capacity to do the lion's share of all the thousand and one things that outfitting an expedition of conquest in the New World required. Almagro, on the other hand, had clearly been outmaneuvered: it was Pizarro who had been granted permission to conquer Peru, not he. And even if he refused now to participate, there was nothing he could do to prevent Pizarro from leaving for Peru without him.

After their long and intimate association, however, Pizarro knew his partner exceedingly well. He knew the man's strengths, weaknesses, and vanities. Like himself, Almagro was illegitimate. He therefore no doubt had a deep-rooted need to prove himself. Pizarro also knew that Almagro wanted a partnership of equality, that he didn't want to be treated as an inferior, and that he wanted respect. More than anything else, Almagro wanted a governorship, to be lord and master of his own realm.

In a deft negotiation, Pizarro ultimately succeeded in assuring his angry partner that, although the king had granted Pizarro the governorship of Peru, he would nevertheless do everything in his power to encourage the king to grant Almagro a governorship outside the territory of his own. With enough titles and promises now to go around, Almagro finally agreed to bury the hatchet and resumed preparations for their expedition.

Four years later, in April of 1533, when Diego de Almagro crested the final rise and rode with his men down into the city of Cajamarca, his partner, Francisco Pizarro, was there to meet them. The two leaders greeted each other warmly; it was easy, after all, to bury old animosities in light of the present exhilarating circumstances. Pizarro proudly introduced Almagro to a stunned Atahualpa, then led his old partner into the guarded chamber filled almost to Atahualpa's white line with countless glistening objects of gold. The two men no doubt clapped each other on the back. That night, Pizarro ordered that extra llamas be slaughtered to feed Almagro's men.

Underneath the outward display of comradeship, however, tensions between the two partners remained. Even before Almagro had arrived, Pizarro had heard rumors that his partner might attempt to conquer Peru on his own. Almagro showed no sign of making such a move, however, nor were such rumors ever discussed. In truth, Pizarro always had and always would consider Almagro his sidekick, a clear subordinate. Despite their legal partnership, to Pizarro, Peru and the titles that came with conquering Peru were his, and his alone. He was willing to share a certain amount of wealth and power with Almagro, but Pizarro would never consider his squat, one-eyed partner his equal.

With Almagro's arrival, there were now over three hundred Spaniards in Cajamarca and these belonged to two very obvious and distinct groups. Those who had participated in the capture of Atahualpa and in the slaughter on the square—168 of them—would forever more be known as the "Men of Cajamarca," the mythical founders of Spanish Peru. They had the right to share in Atahualpa's ransom and thus would soon become the equivalent of modern-day millionaires. The Spaniards who had just arrived with Almagro, on the other hand, even though they were now part of a force expected to subdue the rest of the empire, would receive only a token amount of Atahualpa's treasure. That was because they had not participated in the conquest's key event. According to Pedro Pizarro,

> Almagro . . . did not want . . . [the unequal division] to be that way, but rather that he and his companion [Pizarro] each take half [of every-thing], and that to the rest of the Spaniards they give a thousand or at most two thousand *pesos* each. In this [however] the Marquis behaved very Christianly, for he did not deprive anyone of what he merited. Since this distribution was made among all the Spaniards who entered Cajamarca [and who took part in] the capture of Atahualpa . . . nothing was given to those who came afterwards.

One of those who came "afterwards" and who was given next to nothing was Pizarro's own partner, Diego de Almagro.

As the newcomers eyed the roomful of gold and watched as more gold and silver continued to arrive each day, they were naturally both jealous and also impatient to finish the ransom process. Only once the ransom had been collected and they left Cajamarca would they have the chance of seizing plunder for themselves. Meanwhile, the disconsolate Atahualpa observed the Spaniards with growing desperation.

On June 13, 1533, two months after Almagro's arrival, the two Spanish scouts who had stayed behind in Cuzco finally arrived, escorting a convoy of 223 llama loads of gold and silver. If each llama were carrying an average load of fifty pounds, then that convoy alone would have added more than eleven thousand pounds of precious metals to Atahualpa's treasure.* One can only imagine how the second group of Spaniards must have reacted when they realized that not a bit of the newly arrived treasure would be

---

* Related to the camel, both alpacas and llamas were domesticated from wild guanacos at least five thousand years before the appearance of the Incas. Alpacas were used primarily for their fine wool, while llamas were used more as beasts of burden, as offerings to the gods, and for their meat, hides, and manure pellets, which were used as fuel. The average llama stands five to six feet in height, weighs around 250 to 450 pounds, and can carry pack loads of from fifty to eighty pounds.

theirs. Although they had traveled just as far as their companions and had endured their own assortment of dangers, they had arrived five months too late to partake in the ransom.

Four days later, with tensions growing among the Spaniards and a roomful of gold on his hands, Pizarro ordered that the job of melting and assaying the gold begin. He also ordered that the silver, which had already been melted down, now be distributed. Eventually, during a four-month period, from March to July 1533, the Spaniards fed more than forty thousand pounds of sacred Inca gold and silver into the furnaces. Roughly half of the Spaniards watched this process with mounting joy while the other half watched with mounting envy. Pound after pound of the finest objects created by the empire's craftsmen were fed into the fires—gold and silver statues, jewelry, platings, vessels, ornaments, and other works of art—all reduced to formless, red-hot puddles, then poured steaming into molds to make ingots. Today, Inca objects of gold and silver are a supreme rarity—the lion's share having disappeared nearly five hundred years ago into the furnaces of Cajamarca.

At long last, the moment Atahualpa's captors had been waiting for arrived. As notaries watched the careful weighing process and busily wrote everything down before signing and stamping the documents with a flourish, each horseman stepped forward and received 180 pounds of silver and ninety pounds of $22\frac{1}{2}$ karat gold—gold and silver pure enough to be melted down instantly into coins. If one calculates that a single pound of gold represented roughly two years of a common sailor's salary, then ninety pounds of the dense yellow metal represented 180 years' worth, not even counting the silver. And even though the foot soldiers received only half of this amount—ninety pounds of silver and forty-five pounds of gold—it was clear that all of the 168 Spaniards who had arrived with Pizarro in Cajamarca were now richer than they could ever have imagined. If expeditions of conquest were all about the search for an easy retirement, then Atahualpa's captors had just won the richest lottery in the world. They could, if they so wanted, now pack up their scanty belongings and return to Spain—and would never have to work another day in their lives.

Francisco Pizarro, however, had no thoughts whatsoever of retiring. Having just allotted himself seven times the amount of gold and silver of a horseman in addition to awarding himself as a present the golden throne that Atahualpa had been traveling on the day of his capture (which itself weighed 183 pounds), Pizarro had come to Peru not to retire but in order to create a feudal kingdom—a kingdom over which he himself would rule. To conquer, control, and administer such a kingdom, however, Pizarro desperately needed conquistadors who, like himself, were willing to become permanent residents. Although Pizarro allowed a few of the married conquistadors to leave immediately after the distribution of the treasure, he ordered the rest to remain in Peru, at least until the conquest was complete.

One of those slated to leave was Pizarro's thirty-two-year-old brother, Hernando, whom Pizarro now charged with the task of shepherding roughly half of the king's "royal fifth" back to Spain. Pizarro trusted no one else to transport the king's profits—the 20 percent standard cut that was the price all conquistadors paid if they wanted to carry out plunder in the New World with the blessing of a royal license. From this one massive gathering of precious metals in Cajamarca, and with little more effort on their part than signing a few royal documents, the king and queen of Spain received 5,200 pounds of Inca silver and 2,600 pounds of Inca gold.

As Hernando Pizarro and the small group of departing Spaniards prepared to leave, many of the conquistadors who were staying behind hurriedly wrote letters to send with them. The only surviving letter from that group was written by one of Francisco Pizarro's pages, Gaspar de Gárate, a young Basque in his early twenties from northern Spain. Like his compatriots, Gaspar was eager to relate to his family the surprising news of his recent good fortune.

> To my sorely missed father,
>
> It must be about three years ago that I got a letter from you, in which you asked me to send some money. God knows how sorry I was not to have anything to send you then, because if I had anything then there wouldn't have been any need for you to write; I've always tried to do the right thing, but there wasn't any possibility till now. . . .
>
> I'm sending you two-hundred-and-thirteen *pesos* [2.1 pounds] of good gold in a bar with an honorable man from San Sebastian; in Seville he'll have it turned into coin and then bring it to you. I'd send you more except he's taking money for other people too and couldn't take more. His name is

Pedro de Anadel, I know him, and he's the kind of person who will get the money to you, so that's why I asked him to do me a favor and take you the money. . . .

I'll tell you something of my life since I came to these parts; you must know how . . . we got news of how Governor Francisco Pizarro was coming to be governor of this Kingdom of New Castile [Peru] and so, hearing this news and having few prospects in Nicaragua, we came to this district, where there's more gold and silver than iron in Biscay and more sheep [llamas] than in [the province of] Soria, and great supplies of all kinds of provisions and fine clothing and lords among them; one of them rules over five hundred leagues [1,750 miles]. We have him [Atahualpa] in our power and, with him prisoner, a man can go by himself five hundred leagues without getting killed; instead they give you whatever you need and carry you on their shoulders in a litter.

We took this lord by a miracle of God because our forces wouldn't be enough to take him nor to do what we did, but God gave us the victory miraculously over him and his forces. You must know that we came here with Governor Francisco Pizarro to the land of this lord where he had sixty thousand warriors, and there were one-hundred-and-sixty [sic] Spaniards with the Governor, and we thought our lives were finished because there was such a horde of them, and even the [native] women were making fun of us and saying they were sorry for us because we were going to get killed; but afterward their bad thoughts turned out the opposite. . . .

Give my greetings to Catalina and my brothers and sisters and my uncle . . . and his daughters, especially the older one . . . and also to my cousins . . . and all the rest of my relatives . . . I really want you to tell them hello for me and to tell them that I greatly wish to see them, and pleasing God I'll be there soon . . . the only thing I want to ask you is to do good for the souls of my mother and all my relatives and, if God lets me get there, I'll do it very thoroughly myself. There is nothing more to write at present except that I'm praying to our Lord Jesus Christ to let me see you before I die.

From Cajamarca, in the Kingdom of New Castile, July 20, 1533.

Your son . . . ,
Gaspar. . . .

One can certainly imagine how this letter was read and reread by the writer's family, how it was passed around, unfolded and refolded carefully, circulating among the many family members, relatives, and friends, and how excerpts were undoubtedly also read aloud to interested visitors, eager as everyone was to learn of the miraculous adventures occurring on the distant fringes of the known world. This particular letter writer, however, who had left for the Indies in his teens, would never see his family or home again. Only four months after handing the bar of Inca gold and the letter to his friend, Gaspar would be killed in battle in Peru. It would take at least another year before the news of his misfortune would reach his family.

As the last gold and silver bars were being distributed, Atahualpa no doubt watched the unfolding events with a growing sense of despair. When he learned that Hernando Pizarro was departing for Spain, in fact, he had apparently sunk even further into his gloom. Hernando had been Atahualpa's best ally among the Spaniards, a man he had often played chess with and whom he had clearly befriended. The big, bearded, arrogant Pizarro brother was also a powerful influence in the camp, having served as Francisco's right-hand man thus far during the campaign.

When Hernando rode out of camp, therefore, leading a pack train of llamas that was carrying the king's treasure, Atahualpa "wept, saying that they would kill him since Hernando Pizarro was leaving." Years later, Hernando would tell the king that Atahualpa had actually begged Hernando to take him with him to Spain. If he didn't, Atahualpa had assured him, then "this fat man (meaning the [royal] treasurer [Alonso Riquelme]) and this one-eyed man (meaning Don Diego de Almagro) will kill me when you leave." If Atahualpa did indeed say this to Hernando, then it was a prescient thought. Obviously, the Inca emperor didn't like the hungry, penetrating look in Almagro's single eye. With the gold and silver already delivered as promised, yet with new Spaniards in town and his freedom nowhere to be seen, Atahualpa must have realized that Pizarro had lied to him. Pizarro, after all, had promised Atahualpa that he would restore him to power in Quito. Now, however, all Atahualpa saw were Spaniards readying their equipment and horses for a march south toward Cuzco. Clearly, Pizarro and his men were planning an expedition of conquest—a far cry from the triumphal march that Atahualpa had envisaged leading down the Andes in the wake of his brother Huascar's defeat.

Rumors now begin to swirl in the city that Atahualpa had actually sent secret orders to his northern army to rescue him, since it was now obvious to all that the Spaniards had no intention of fulfilling their side of the bargain. A local chief even told Pizarro that Atahualpa's northern army was already marching on its way south,

> and that all these men are marching under a great commander called Lluminabe [Rumiñavi] and are very close to here. They will come by night and will attack this camp, setting it entirely on fire. The first person they will attempt to kill will be you and they will release their lord Atahualpa from his prison. Two hundred thousand warriors are marching from Quito along with thirty thousand Caribs, who eat human flesh.

Pizarro immediately ordered that a permanent guard be mounted around the city and then went to confront Atahualpa with the incriminating information. "What kind of treason is this that you have prepared for me?" Pizarro angrily demanded. "After having treated you . . . like a brother, and having trusted in your words?" Pizarro had obviously missed the fact that it was hardly treasonous to want to escape from your kidnappers, especially if your kidnappers had agreed to a bargain that they now refused to honor.

"Are you joking?" Atahualpa had replied, trying at first to make light of Pizarro's accusation. "You're always telling me jokes. What reason would my men or I have of troubling men as brave as you? Stop telling me jokes!" When Pizarro replied that this was no joking matter and that if the rumors were true that Pizarro would kill him, Atahualpa attempted to reason with his captors, among whom paranoia was currently spreading as fast as an exploding contagion.

"It is true that if any warriors were coming they would be marching here from Quito on my orders," Atahualpa replied calmly. "Find out whether it is true. And if true, you have me in your power and can execute me!" Wrote one eyewitness:

> [He said] all of this without betraying any sign of anxiety. And he said many other brilliant things that a quick-witted man [would make] during the period after his capture. The Spaniards who heard them were amazed to see so much wisdom in a barbarian.

Atahualpa's arguments did him little good, however, for Pizarro, not wanting to take any chances, now ordered that a chain be fastened around Atahualpa's neck to prevent the emperor from escaping. Pizarro next called for a meeting of his top commanders to discuss Atahualpa's fate.

While the rank-and-file Spaniards waited nervously in the city, scanning the hills for signs of an approaching army, a handful of their leaders now debated what to do with the captive Inca king. The makeshift jury included the corpulent royal treasurer, Alonso Riquelme; the Dominican friar, Vincente de Valverde—whose mistreated breviary had set off the massacre eight months before; Almagro; Francisco Pizarro; and a few others. Almagro, Riquelme, and several other captains wanted to execute the Inca emperor immediately, believing that once Atahualpa was dead, it would be easier to pacify the country. Pizarro and another group of captains, on the other hand, were in favor of keeping Atahualpa alive. They had been able to rule the country through Atahualpa for eight months, after all—so why couldn't they continue? And who knew how the natives might react if their lord suddenly turned up dead? The entire country might rise up against them.

Like a hung jury, the Spaniards were unable to agree on whether Atahualpa had been sending out secret messages or had been telling the truth. They thus couldn't agree on whether they should execute the Inca lord or spare his life. In order to address their most immediate threat, Pizarro decided to send Hernando de Soto with four horsemen to ride north and investigate. If they found no native army, then it was possible that Atahualpa had been telling the truth. If, on the other hand, they found an army, then one thing was certain: before the Spaniards lost their lives, Atahualpa would surely lose his own.

After Soto and his men had galloped off, the rest of the Spaniards were forced to wait nervously. Some fingered their ingots of gold and dreamed of what they would do with them if they survived this adventure and made it back to Spain. Others no doubt read well-thumbed, contraband novels of chivalrous adventures, such as *Amadis of Gaul*.* A few scribbled or dictated

---

* At the time of the conquest, chivalric novels were all the vogue, one of the most popular being *Amadis de Gaula,* the story of a knight errant who dons armor and travels to the far ends of the earth. There he battles giants, monsters, and other fantastic creatures, all the while remaining faithful to his beautiful lady. Novels such as *Amadis* were considered so

letters to their friends or family, hoping to send them home one day. Pizarro and his captains, meanwhile, were unanimously agreed upon one point: their next step was to march south and then seize Cuzco, the capital of the empire and the wealthiest and grandest of its cities.

But with Cuzco lying some six hundred miles to the south and the Inca road leading there apparently crossing over some of the roughest terrain in the world, Pizarro and his captains worried that they would be unable to prevent Atahualpa from being rescued by Inca troops during their journey. Their isolated Spanish force would be much more vulnerable while traveling, and they would inevitably find themselves exposed amid unknown terrain. According to the three Spaniards who had helped to loot Cuzco, in fact, there were probably a thousand places where Pizarro's force could be successfully ambushed along the way. If Atahualpa were rescued by his troops, then surely the emperor would quickly galvanize the entire country to rise up against them.

That evening, after dinner, Pizarro and some of his captains began to play cards. The group of nouveaux riches undoubtedly bet quantities of gold and silver and generally enjoyed themselves. Suddenly, however, the door to the room burst violently open and a Spaniard rushed in, dragging a reluctant native behind him. The Spaniard, a Basque seaman named Pedro de Anadel, was one of the original conquerors of Nicaragua. The native accompanying him was one of his Nicaraguan servants, not a native from Peru. Nevertheless, Anadel rather breathlessly told the dinner party that his servant had recently journeyed outside Cajamarca and had seen a massive Inca army advancing toward the city, only eleven miles away.

Pizarro rose and began questioning the servant, who presumably spoke basic Spanish. After the servant described in great detail what he had seen, it soon became apparent that a native army was definitely on the move.

morally corrupting, however, that beginning in 1531—while Pizarro and his men were already headed south from Panama—the Spanish crown banned them from being transported to the New World; the Spanish authorities apparently feared that such suggestive literature might morally corrupt both the immigrants *and* the New World's impressionable natives. Contraband novels were smuggled into the New World anyway, and it is probable that every group of conquistadors carried at least one or two dog-eared copies of their favorite books, reading them by firelight in the midst of fantastic mountains and exotic scenery every bit as strange and wondrous as those depicted in their outlawed fiction.

Everyone in the room now became agitated, especially Almagro, who had been urging Pizarro to execute Atahualpa ever since the first rumors of the emperor's presumed treachery had surfaced. A chastened Pizarro quickly sent word to his men to prepare themselves for battle; he also ordered an immediate meeting to plan their strategy and to debate Atahualpa's fate anew. By now, however, the tide in support of Atahualpa had unmistakably turned. With the sudden and frightening threat of an impending attack, it didn't take long for those gathered to make a quick decision. "Insisting vehemently on his death, Captain Almagro . . . [gave] . . . many reasons why he should die," one eyewitness remembered. The obese royal treasurer, Riquelme, now sided with Almagro, urging that the emperor be quickly executed before the massing native forces could attack, thus fulfilling Atahualpa's own prophecy.

When a final vote was taken, all those in attendance voted that Atahualpa should die, the last one to do so being a reluctant Pizarro, who found himself no longer able to support his earlier view that they were better off with Atahualpa alive. An entire native army could not be marching against them without Atahualpa having ordered it, Pizarro no doubt reasoned. And since Atahualpa had thus committed treason—at least to the Spaniards' way of thinking—Pizarro finally gave the order that the Inca emperor "should die by burning unless he converted to Christianity."

The son of Huayna Capac—who had fought to gain the Inca throne for years before the Spaniards had arrived and who had had little compunction in killing his own brother to possess it—was quickly informed of the Spaniards' decision. Not surprisingly, Atahualpa was devastated by the news. "Atahualpa wept [openly] and said that they shouldn't kill him," recalled Pedro Pizarro, "for there wasn't one Indian in the country who would make trouble without his command. And since they had him prisoner," Atahualpa said, "what were they afraid of?" After trying with no success to convince his captors that his empire would devolve into chaos if he were executed, Atahualpa now tried a last-ditch effort to save his life. "If they were going to do it [kill him] for gold or silver," Atahualpa said, no doubt looking into his captors' eyes in order to gauge their reaction, "then he would give them twice what he had already commanded." The emperor's last-minute offer didn't even seem to register on the Spaniards this time, however, and Atahualpa noticed anxiously that Pizarro had difficulty even looking at him.

"I saw the Governor weep from sorrow at being unable to grant him [his] life," remembered Pedro Pizarro, "[but] . . . he feared the consequences and risks to the country if he were released." Pizarro, however, along with the rest of the Spanish leaders in camp, was now convinced about one thing: if a native army were less than eleven miles outside of town, then that army could launch an attack this very evening. Thus, in terms of keeping their hostage from falling into enemy hands, there was no time to lose. Atahualpa's life had to be ended immediately.

The sun was beginning to set on Saturday, July 26, 1533, as a group of Spaniards led the emperor of the four *suyus* to the main square, the same square where he had been captured the previous November. Always sticklers for formality, the Spaniards sounded the trumpet and began reading out loud the charges against the emperor. Atahualpa, meanwhile, was tied to a stake that had just been impaled into the ground. Apparently either because what was happening was so obvious or else because one or more of the interpreters had informed them, some of the local townspeople had gathered to watch. For the ordinary native inhabitant, watching the Spaniards prepare for the execution of their lord and god was as frightening as knowing that the sun was about to disappear—and that their world was about to be upended. For a Spaniard, the only thing similar would have been to witness Christ being led to the crucifixion at Golgotha.

The Incas, after all, believed that history was a succession of ages divided from one another by a cataclysmic event, a *pachacuti,* or an "overturning of the world." The first *pachacuti* had begun with the formation of the Inca Empire itself. Now, as the natives watched their lord Atahualpa being tied to a stake, many feared that a second grand *pachacuti* was about to begin. "When he [Atahualpa] was taken out to be killed," remembered Pedro Pizarro, "all the native people who were on the square, and there were many, prostrated themselves on the ground, letting themselves fall to the earth like drunken men."

Some of the Spaniards began gathering wood while others began stacking it in preparation for a fire around Atahualpa's feet. The Dominican friar, Valverde, meanwhile, spoke to the emperor through one of the interpreters.

"[He instructed him in] the things of our Christian faith, telling him that God had wished him to die for the sins that he had committed in the world and that he should repent of them, and that God would pardon him if he did."

It is impossible to know what Atahualpa actually understood of the friar's message. Did Atahualpa think that the god these Christians kept talking about would "pardon" him from being killed if Atahualpa agreed to worship him? Or did he fully understand that the "pardon" being offered was a very limited one that would only allow Atahualpa to select between two different forms of death? In any case, here he was, lord of the four *suyus,* now bound to a stake while bearded men babbling in an unintelligible tongue were obviously preparing to set him on fire. Atahualpa had done everything these invaders had asked for, and now an unfriendly man in a dark robe was threatening him with death by fire if he didn't accept the invaders' one and only god, whom the Spaniards called *Dios.*

The Spaniards, no doubt, were equally uncomprehending of the fact that there was nothing an Inca feared more than having his physical body destroyed—whether through burning or through some other physical process that made the body disappear. The Incas believed that access to the afterworld could only be guaranteed if, after death, the body were kept intact, with the Inca emperors actually going so far as to have their bodies mummified and carefully tended to by subsequent generations. The thought of being burned at the stake was thus a double threat: not only would one's last moments be very painful, but one would also forfeit the enjoyment of a pleasant afterlife.*

Atahualpa's chief concern for the moment seemed to be less about himself, however, and more about his two small sons. He had left them in Quito nearly a year earlier, when he had begun to make his way south in order to take over his brother's throne and thus to unify the empire. Friar Valverde,

---

* Like the Spaniards, the Incas believed in an afterlife. Virtuous individuals—those who were generous and hardworking—traveled off to live with the Sun God in the pleasant "upper world," or *hanac-paca,* where food and warmth abounded. Individuals without virtue, meanwhile—those who lied, stole, or were ungenerous or lazy—were sent off to the feared "interior world," *okho-paca,* a place of unending cold where the only food available was an assortment of inedible rocks.

prevented by his religion from marrying, impatiently told Atahualpa to for-get about his wives and children and to concentrate on accepting the Spaniards' Christian god instead. What was at stake here was the emperor's *soul,* the friar insisted, although exactly how the translator tried to convey this concept—or even how much the native translator understood of the friar's religion—is debatable. To Atahualpa, no doubt the Christians' god seemed to be a very jealous one. The friar, however, continued to insist that Atahualpa would burn for eternity if he did not reject his own gods and worship only theirs.

Atahualpa—dressed in a richly woven tunic and mantle—continued to plead the case of his small children, however. At one point he even re-quested that Francisco Pizarro take responsibility for them himself.

> Atahualpa said that he was entrusting his children to the Governor . . .
> [but] the friar . . . advised him to forget his wives and children and to die like a Christian, and that if he wanted to become one, that he [must] receive the holy baptismal water. But Atahualpa wept greatly and con-tinued to insist that his children be cared for, indicating their heights with his hand and making it clear through his gestures . . . that they were small and that he was leaving them [unprotected] in Quito. [Yet] the Father continued to try and induce him to convert to Christianity and to forget his children, [telling him] that Governor [Pizarro] would look after them and would treat them as his own.

Apparently reassured by the friar's promises, Atahualpa finally agreed to convert—whether to save his children, save himself from a fiery end, or to guarantee himself access to the Inca afterlife, is unknown. Friar Valverde—the same man who eight months earlier had commanded Atahualpa to obey the Spaniards' Christian god, or else face the Spaniards' wrath—quickly baptized the emperor with water.

As the sky began turning red from the setting sun, several Spaniards fas-tened around Atahualpa's neck a garrote—a loop of rope attached to a stick that could be turned like a wheel, thus tightening the loop until the blood supply through the carotid arteries was cut off to the brain. As the friar began intoning the last rites—*Yea, though I walk through the valley of the shadow of death*—one of the Spaniards began to twist the stick, the rope slowly tightening around Atahualpa's neck—*I will fear no evil, for thou art with me*—until the emperor's eyes began to bulge and the solitary vein on his forehead rose distended and illumed by the final rays of the sun—*and I will dwell in the house of the* LORD *forever*. Wrote the notary Pedro Sancho de la Hoz:

> With these last words, and with the Spaniards who surrounded him say-ing a credo for his soul, he [Atahualpa] was quickly strangled. May God receive him in heaven, for he died repenting of his sins and in the true faith of a Christian. After he had been strangled in this way and the sen-tence executed, some fire was thrown on to him to burn part of his clothing and flesh. That night (because he died late in the afternoon) his body was left in the square so that everyone could learn of his death.

"He died on Saturday," wrote another notary, "at the same hour that he was taken prisoner and defeated [eight months earlier]. Some said it was for his sins that he died on the [same] day [Saturday] and hour that he was seized."

So ended the life of Atahualpa, the thirty-one-year-old lord of the Incas, the first Inca emperor in over a hundred years who not only had failed to ex-pand his ancestors' empire, but had instead presided over the beginning of its collapse. For the second time in less than a decade, beginning with Huayna Capac's death by smallpox, the Inca Empire was suddenly without a ruler. Governors, administrators, generals, and accountants still busied themselves with their daily tasks—but there was now no one to give them orders. From this moment forward the Inca Empire was essentially para-lyzed, like an immense giant stumbling forward, incapable of defending it-self against the small band of invaders who, like parasites, had burrowed deeply into the Inca body politic and were continuing to wreak their havoc.

As Atahualpa's body lay crumpled and smoking and native onlookers prostrated themselves moaning on the ground, the Spaniards, meanwhile, prepared to defend themselves against the imminent onslaught of an attack. Pizarro ordered the entire Spanish camp to ready itself and ordered fifty horsemen to patrol the city. That night, neither Pizarro nor his captains slept, periodically visiting with the night watches and readying everyone for battle. As on the eve of Atahualpa's capture almost a year earlier, the bearded intruders were tense and on edge. Would dawn bring them face-to-face with hundreds of thousands of Inca warriors? And if so, how many of the Spaniards among them would live to finish the day?

Eventually, the dense star clusters overhead began to dim while in the east the first pale rim of dawn began to emerge. The Spaniards who were already awake now woke their comrades as all strained to listen, fully expecting to hear the dull thud and clank of the approaching native infantry. Slowly, with each minute stretching into what must have seemed like an eternity, the sky brightened until finally the first rays of the sun appeared, the long, shaftlike yellow fingers touching the thatched roofs of the houses and then flooding the green valley with light. As the sun rose further, however, still no attack came. Scouts sent out on horseback returned without having sighted an army, at least not in the vicinity. The question no doubt on everyone's mind was: what had become of the advancing native army? Why did it not appear and attack? Had the information they received been false—or had it been true?

Reprieved for the moment from the immediate necessity to fight, the Spaniards now found themselves confronted with a more mundane problem: what to do with Atahualpa's body. All agreed that they couldn't just leave an Inca emperor lying on the square as they had previously done with thousands of Atahualpa's slaughtered native soldiers. Atahualpa had been revered as a god, after all, and the natives continued to prostrate themselves on the square, greatly distraught over his death. Pizarro finally decided that the sooner they disposed of Atahualpa's corpse, the quicker the memory of him would fade. After a brief ceremony, Atahualpa's stiff, blackened body was interred in a hastily dug hole.

A few days after Atahualpa's burial, Spanish sentries sighted Hernando de Soto and his horsemen galloping toward camp. Unaware of what had transpired in their absence and assuming that Atahualpa was still alive, Soto rode back in a flourish and dismounted in the square. He immediately hurried off in search of Pizarro, no doubt glancing curiously at the stake impaled in the ground and at the charred wood nearby.

Soto must have wondered at the somber mood in the camp and at finding Pizarro wearing "a large felt hat on his head [as if] for mourning." Presumably looking about in vain for Atahualpa, Soto quickly informed Pizarro that he and his men had found "no native warriors in the countryside, but [rather that] everyone was at peace. . . . For that reason, seeing that it was a trick, an obvious lie and a palpable falsehood, they [had] returned to Cajamarca."

Pizarro's mournful reaction to the good news caught Soto completely by surprise. "I now see that I have been deceived," Pizarro quietly said. The normally taciturn Pizarro—tall, graying, with a sparse beard and looking like Don Quixote if Don Quixote were the kind of man who murdered other men for their gold—suddenly appeared shaken and had "eyes wet with tears." Pizarro told Soto that they had garroted Atahualpa a few days earlier, after new reports had arrived of an approaching Inca army. Obviously, Pizarro said, the information had been false.

Soto, who like Pizarro had killed countless natives in personal combat, was deeply disappointed by Atahualpa's death. Presumably this was both because of Atahualpa's exalted rank—which the Spaniards in general respected—and also for the obvious bond that he had made with the friendly emperor. Along with Hernando Pizarro, Atahualpa had counted the handsome, dashing Soto as a supporter, or at least as someone with whom he could relate on a personal level. An emotional Soto quickly told Pizarro that it would have been much better to have sent Atahualpa to Spain, and that he himself would have gladly escorted him there. They had killed the emperor for no reason, no justifiable reason at all, Soto said. He then turned and exited the room.

News of Atahualpa's death slowly began to make its way northward from Peru, across the Isthmus of Panama and eventually via square-rigger ship to Spain. Meanwhile Pizarro, Almagro, and their roughly three hundred Spaniards readied themselves for the second major military campaign of the expedition. Pizarro's plan was to begin a bold military thrust southward along the rugged spine of the Andes. No longer protected by a hostage emperor they could count upon to keep native armies at bay, however, they would now be forced to entrust their fates to their lances, to their swords, and to their solitary God. If capturing Atahualpa had been the equivalent of seizing the brain or command center of the empire, then Pizarro was now determined to fight his way southward in order to capture the empire's heart: the legendary city of Cuzco. Pizarro knew that two Inca armies stood between himself and his goal, however. He also knew that another Inca army lurked somewhere to his rear. How those native armies and how their commanding generals would behave, no one could predict.

With many of them no doubt making the sign of the cross, the cavalry-men with their long lances and the foot soldiers with their sheathed swords began to move out, leaving the town they had inhabited for nearly a year behind them, its wide square with its single forlorn stake slowly receding into the distance until, eventually, it was swallowed by their trail of dust.

7 ❖ THE PUPPET KING

"For a prince should have two fears: one, internal concerning his subjects; the other, external, concerning foreign powers."

NICCOLÒ MACHIAVELLI, *THE PRINCE*, 1511

FOR THE NEXT THREE MONTHS, PIZARRO AND HIS ROUGHLY three hundred conquistadors headed south, wending their way past snow-covered peaks, herds of llamas and alpacas tended by wide-eyed native boys wearing alpaca tunics, and occasionally clashing with local and mostly dis-organized native resistance. The Spaniards by now had a larger retinue trav-eling with them: in addition to some native slaves from Nicaragua and a sprinkling of black slaves from Africa, they also enlisted the aid of numerous local natives, who led their pack trains of llamas, the latter loaded with tents, food, weapons, and with Atahualpa's treasure of gold and silver.

Before he and his Spaniards had left Cajamarca, however, Pizarro had de-cided to crown the eldest surviving brother of the emperor Huayna Capac, a royal prince called Tupac Huallpa. Pizarro hoped that by doing so he would be able to continue controlling the Inca aristocracy and hence the empire, much as he had done with Atahualpa. The new Inca emperor's reign, however, was short-lived. Within two months, Tupac Huallpa sick-ened and died. A disappointed Pizarro had him buried in the town of Jauja, midway between Cajamarca and Cuzco. Once again, the Inca Empire was without a ruler.

Pizarro and his Spaniards had nevertheless been able to gain a rough idea of the Incas' current deployment of military forces before heading south. There were three Inca armies, Pizarro had been told: one in the north in what is now Ecuador with about thirty thousand soldiers and led by a gen-eral called Rumiñavi; another in what is now central Peru, with about

CONQVISTA
LEVĀTOSE·PO·REI·Ī
GA·MANGO   INGA

hono yaciento del ynga llama
do· usno·
enclcucio

mango ynga

The seventeen-year-old puppet emperor Manco Inca's coronation.

35,000 soldiers; and finally, General Quisquis's army of occupation in Cuzco with some thirty thousand troops. Pizarro, however—even before leaving Cajamarca—had decapitated the central army by luring its general, Chalcuchima, to visit the imprisoned Atahualpa. After seizing Chalcuchima, Pizarro had decided to bring the Inca general along on his journey. Pizarro had grown suspicious, however, that the general might be trying to incite local natives to attack and thus had burned Chalcuchima at the stake. That meant that now there was only General Quisquis's army standing between the Spaniards and their goal of capturing the capital of the Inca Empire.

In November 1533, as the Spaniards left the Inca town of Jaquijahuana, only a day's march from Cuzco, they encountered a seventeen-year-old, boyish-looking native who wore a yellow tunic and who was accompanied by a group of Inca nobles. Pizarro's interpreters soon learned that the young native was the son of the emperor Huayna Capac and thus was of royal descent. Pizarro also learned that the teenager's name was Manco Inca and that, although he was the brother of both Atahualpa and Huascar, he was also one of the very few survivors of Huascar's royal lineage. As Pizarro and his captains listened intently to their interpreter translating, the young prince explained how he had been living as a fugitive and had spent much of the previous year "fleeing constantly from Atahualpa's men so that they would not kill him. He came so alone and abandoned that he looked like a common Indian."

Pizarro quickly realized that not only was Manco Inca a possible heir to the throne, but that the royal prince also belonged to the Incas' Cuzco faction, precisely the faction that Pizarro wished to be perceived as allying himself with. Since Pizarro had already executed Atahualpa, nothing could be better than for him to arrive in Cuzco with a member of the same faction that had suffered under Atahualpa. Pizarro and his troops could thus position themselves as liberators, a perception that they hoped would forestall any native resistance from developing. The chronicler Pedro Sancho de la Hoz wrote:

> [Manco Inca] said to the Governor that he would help him all that he could in order to rid the land of all those from Quito [Atahualpa's occupying army], for they were his enemies and they hated him. . . . [Manco] was the man to whom, by law, came all that province and whose chiefs

all wanted for their lord. When he came to see Governor [Pizarro], he came by way of the mountains, avoiding the roads for fear of those from Quito. The Governor was happy to receive him and told him: "A lot of what you say pleases me, including your great desire to get rid of these men from Quito. You should know that I have come . . . for no other purpose than to prevent them from doing you harm and to free you from your slavery (to them). And you can be sure that I am not coming here for my own benefit . . . but knowing the injuries they were inflicting on you I wanted to come to rectify and undo them, as my lord the Emperor commanded me to do. You can thus be sure that I will do everything I can to help you and I will also (do the same to) liberate the people of Cuzco from this tyranny." The Governor made these big promises to him [Manco Inca] in order to please him and so that he [Pizarro] might get news of how things were going [elsewhere in the empire]. That chief [Manco Inca] was marvelously satisfied, as were those who had come with him.

Pizarro hoped that by allying himself with the young Inca prince he could fool the Cuzco faction into thinking that the Spaniards' only interest was to place those who had recently been oppressed by Atahualpa back in power. Pizarro was also quick to realize that the seemingly naive young son of Huayna Capac might serve perfectly as a puppet king—one that could easily be controlled by the Spaniards.

Before he could attempt to install Manco as the new emperor, however, Pizarro first had to capture Cuzco, which was still occupied by a large and hostile Inca army. General Quisquis intended to torch the city, Manco told the Spaniards, and to burn it to the ground rather than hand it over to the foreigners. In the distance, the Spaniards could already see smoke on the horizon: perhaps the destruction of Cuzco had already begun. Pizarro immediately ordered his twenty-three-year-old brother, Juan, and Hernando de Soto to lead forty horsemen to try to prevent the burning of the capital. While Pizarro and the rest of the horsemen, foot soldiers, auxiliary natives, and the supply train of llamas resumed their journey, Juan Pizarro, Soto, and their cavalry galloped off and disappeared over a rise.

After eighteen months of conquest and despite another potentially large battle looming, Pizarro and his Spaniards were by now, however, quite confident. The attrition rates of native and Spanish troops had thus far been decidedly in the Spaniards' favor. Beginning with the capture of Atahualpa, the Incas had lost more than eight thousand warriors, many high-ranking nobles, one of their three key generals, and of course their emperor. The Spaniards, by contrast, had thus far lost but a single African slave. Though relatively few in number, the Spaniards nevertheless possessed a number of advantages over the Incas in terms of military technology. Perhaps their greatest was their monopoly on horses—animals that could carry a fully armored Spaniard and still outrun the fastest native. The mobile tanks of the conquest, horses not only instilled fear in the natives but also provided a high platform from which the Spaniards could use their twelve-foot, metal-tipped lances or from which they could strike downward with their swords with brutal efficiency. Pizarro's conquistadors also possessed gunpowder, a limited number of cannons, and an assortment of harquebuses.

In terms of defense, the Spaniards often protected themselves with steel helmets, armor, and chain mail. In addition, Spanish footmen carried *escudos*—wooden shields about two feet in diameter—while horsemen carried *adargas*—larger shields made from doubled-up hides stretched over a wooden frame. Even the Spaniards' horses wore protection—thick cotton padding that made the powerful animals difficult to wound or kill. A mounted and armored Spanish knight, with a shield in one hand and a lance or a sword in the other, represented the height of European killing technology. Only a similarly armed knight, a soldier firing a harquebus at close range, or a knowledgeable European pike man on the ground stood a chance against a mounted attack.

Atahualpa's nephew Titu Cusi later described how he and his fellow natives viewed an attacking Spanish army, with their harquebuses firing invisible darts that miraculously killed their warriors at a distance, with their trumpets blaring, with the pounding of their horses' hooves, and with the glint of their steel blades:

> They seemed like *viracochas,* which is the name we gave in ancient times
> to the creator of all things. . . . And they [the Incas] named those people
> whom they had seen in this way, in part because they were very differ-
> ent in clothing and appearance and also because they rode . . . giant an-

imals, which had feet of silver, and they said this because of the shining of their horseshoes. . . . They called them *viracochas* because of their excellent appearance and because of the great differences there were among them: because some had black beards and others red ones, and because they saw them eat off of silver plates, and because they had *Illapas*—our name for thunder—and they said this to describe the harquebuses because they thought them to be thunder from heaven.

Besides their armaments, the Spaniards possessed other advantages: they could communicate much more efficiently through writing, thus being able to send and receive complex information between their often divided forces; they had ships and access to an international trade network through which they could resupply themselves periodically with more weapons, horses, and men from afar; and they had the experience of having successfully battled Moorish knights, armed like themselves, on the Iberian peninsula for centuries.

The Spaniards had also just spent more than thirty years conquering other native groups scattered throughout the Caribbean, Mexico, and different parts of the Americas, while Hernando Cortés had only recently conquered the Aztec Empire in Mexico. Pizarro had thus arrived knowing how, like Cortés, he might use native political divisions to his advantage and might incorporate native allies into his ranks. In addition, the Spaniards possessed two native interpreters they had trained in Spain and whom they could now rely upon to receive and transmit information.

Another potent weapon in the Spaniards' military arsenal was completely unpremeditated yet nevertheless was an extremely important one: a plague of what was probably European smallpox. The epidemic had arrived just prior to Pizarro's third and final voyage to Peru and had not only killed the ruler of the Inca Empire, Huayna Capac, but had also set off the brutal and devastating civil war that had fractured the empire in two. Only five years earlier, during Pizarro's second voyage, the Inca Empire had been united and strong. What Pizarro and his men found during their third voyage in 1532 was an empire that had been severely weakened both by disease and violent civil war.

In contrast to Spanish armaments, which were based upon the mixture of carbon and iron to make steel, Inca armaments were based upon bronze, copper, and stone. The Spaniards, therefore, found in Peru what was technologically speaking a Bronze Age culture, similar to what they would have found in Egypt a thousand years before Christ—if the Egyptians had been without horses. Although the Incas mined copper, tin, gold, silver, and mercury ores, iron ore within the realm of Tawantinsuyu was unknown (the first commercial iron ore was actually not discovered in Peru until 1915). Thus, even had the Incas been granted hundreds of more years of development, it is unlikely that they would have ever entered what the Old World knew as the Iron Age and, without iron, they could have never entered the Age of Steel. Confronted by steel-armored invaders from across the seas, the Incas' own stone and soft-metal weapons were simply no match.

For the most part, Inca weapons were designed for hand-to-hand combat with other similarly armed foot soldiers and consisted of an assortment of clubs. The largest, which required two hands to operate, the Spaniards called a *porra* and consisted of a long wooden handle with a ball of copper or stone that had five or six protruding points. Designed to crack open human skulls, the clubs, however, were incapable of penetrating a Spanish steel helmet. Only a direct blow to the face of a Spaniard not wearing a visor could inflict a fatal blow. The Incas also used battle-axes—with blades of copper, bronze, or stone—in a similar fashion, but none was sharp enough to dismember an enemy's limbs. While Spanish swords could slice through flesh and arteries like so much butter, Inca axes were designed to break bones and/or inflict contusions.

In addition to their clubs, Inca troops also used lances with tips of copper or bronze or sharpened wooden points. They also used darts with wooden or bone tips that could be propelled with a hand thrower. One of their most dangerous weapons, from the Spaniards' point of view, was the Inca sling— *warak'a*—made of wool or some other fiber. By twirling the sling rapidly with an egg-sized stone fitted in its center, a warrior could hurl a stone with such force and accuracy that it could snap a Spanish sword in two. Unless a Spaniard was not wearing a helmet, however, the hurled stones were almost never lethal.

Another weapon the Inca armies sometimes used, although sparingly, was the bow and arrow. Because only natives from the eastern jungles knew how to use such weapons, however, bows and arrows could only be used by incorporating into the Inca army natives from the Antisuyu, or Amazon region of the empire. Amazonian natives were few in comparison to the average peasant conscript from the highlands, however. Bows and arrows therefore had limited use—and were also unable to penetrate steel armor.

Despite their much greater number of troops, the Incas operated under a variety of other disadvantages: they possessed no writing, only their *quipus,* which allowed them to send less information back and forth than did the Spaniards. They also had little knowledge of the world beyond their frontiers; the Incas were thus unaware of the Spanish conquests of Mexico, Central America, and the Caribbean, nor did they know anything about the history of Europe or the rest of the world. Another disadvantage the Incas labored under was that while native warriors sometimes used copper breast or back plates, they generally wore only cotton armor, which protected them adequately against the weapons of other native armies but did little to protect them from the Spaniards' deadly lances and swords. Finally, of course, the Incas had no horses; they were thus constantly faced with having somehow to defend themselves against a charging group of massive, alien animals ridden by armored Spaniards who almost always had the advantage of striking downward from above.

Thus it was that on November 14, 1533, Captains Juan Pizarro and Hernando de Soto and their forty fully armored cavalry found themselves approaching the outskirts of the Incas' capital of Cuzco. The road to the city was blocked by the combined forces of the central and southern armies, however, which had somehow managed to join with each other. Completely outnumbered, the Spaniards nevertheless decided immediately to attack—a tactic that they by now relied upon almost instinctively. Whenever in danger, the Spaniards' natural reflex was to charge directly at whatever they perceived to be their largest threat. It was a strategy that thus far in the Andes had brought repeated success.

The native warriors, "in the greatest numbers . . . came out against us with an enormous shout and much determination," wrote Miguel de Estete. With their backs against the city and the experienced General Quisquis in charge, the northern army fought fiercely, driving the Spaniards back in an onslaught of sling-fired stones, arrows, and battering mace clubs. "They killed three of our horses, including my own, and that had cost me 1,600 *castellanos,*" wrote the notary Juan Ruiz de Arce, "and they wounded many Christians."*

Protected by their armor and fighting from their mobile platforms, however, the Spaniards exacted a tremendous toll; hundreds of natives fell that day in fighting that continued until late in the afternoon with human limbs and no doubt even heads lying on the ground after having been severed with sharpened steel. The Spaniards, by comparison, with stones and mace heads bouncing off their steel armor, no doubt received wounds, but they didn't suffer a single mortality; fighting on fairly level ground, they were able to rely alternately upon the battering ram effect of their horses and also upon their horses' greater speed. If one Spaniard were in trouble, others on horseback would charge toward him. If the Spaniards needed to escape a difficult situation, then they spurred their horses and were able to outrun even the fastest of native warriors. Late that day, Francisco Pizarro and the rest of his troops arrived, but only after the Spanish cavalry force and Quisquis's troops had ceased their fighting. With darkness now falling, the Inca and Spanish forces camped within sight of each other, the native campfires illuminating a nearby hillside. Wrote Sancho de la Hoz:

> [The Spaniards] set up their camp on a plain and the Indians stayed an harquebus-shot away on a slope until midnight, [continuously] shouting. The Spaniards spent all night with their horses saddled and bridled. The next day, at the crack of dawn, the Governor organized the foot soldiers and the cavalry, and he headed off on the road to Cuzco in good order ... having been warned and believing that the enemy would come to attack them on the road.

"We began marching towards the city," wrote Ruiz de Arce, now forced to walk after the loss of his horse, "with a lot of fear, thinking that the Indians

---

* Ruiz de Arce had good reason to be upset. With the loss of his horse he had now been automatically demoted to a foot soldier, was more apt to be wounded due to having to fight on the ground, would receive a smaller share of any future booty, and had just lost an irreplaceable military weapon. Due to the inflated prices in Peru, a horse now cost as much as an average house in Spain.

were waiting for us at its entrance. And so we . . . entered the city, which [no longer] had defenders." Apparently realizing that on level ground his native troops, although numerous, were no match for the mounted Spaniards, General Quisquis had decided to save his army to fight another day. Just after midnight, Quisquis had given the order for his troops to retreat and to give up the fight for Cuzco. They did so quietly, leaving their campfires lit behind them to fool the Spaniards into thinking that they were still there. The next day, at around noon, the Spaniards marched victoriously into the city. "The Governor and his troops entered that great city of Cuzco," wrote Sancho de la Hoz, "without any other resistance or battle on Friday, at the hour of high Mass, on the fifteenth day of the month of November of the year of the birth of our Savior and Redeemer, Jesus Christ, 1533."

As the Spaniards marched and rode cautiously in full battle order, the city's inhabitants turned out onto the stone paved streets to watch them. It had only been that morning that the surprised citizens had learned that the northern army from Quito, which had occupied the city for the last year, had suddenly melted away and was now nowhere to be found. The citizens already knew, of course, that Atahualpa—the emperor whose generals had seized the capital and had killed their ruler, Huascar—was dead and had been executed by the same group of foreigners who were now entering their city. More than a few of them were surprised, however, to see Manco Inca, the young prince who most of them had not seen in a year, walking with the strange bearded men and surrounded by giant animals that made guttural noises and that none of the city's inhabitants had ever seen before. Manco was obviously very much alive and through his behavior and speech the young prince made it known that the foreigners were friendly, not dangerous, and that they were to be treated as honored guests. For the weary inhabitants of Cuzco, the sudden disappearance of the hated northern army came as a relief. The question no doubt uppermost in their minds now, however, was—who were these strangers and why had they come?

For Pizarro and his men, their entry into the capital was a military triumph, the culmination of a long and difficult journey that had begun nearly three years earlier, when they had first set off from Panama. And although the Spaniards may not have been welcomed on this, their first day, with the Inca equivalent of rose petals, clearly their strategy of allying themselves with Huascar's faction and of presenting themselves as liberators, not as occupiers, was so far paying dividends. The city's inhabitants stood quietly in the streets, well dressed in colorfully patterned cotton or alpaca tunics and with sandals on their feet. None of them appeared to be carrying weapons. To their relief, the Spaniards found that not a single sword had to be unsheathed nor a single harquebus ball fired. For the rank-and-file conquistador, their unopposed march into the finest city any of them had ever seen in the New World seemed nothing short of miraculous. "The Spaniards who have taken part in this enterprise are amazed by what they have done," wrote Sancho de la Hoz. "When they begin to think about it, they can't imagine how they can still be alive or how they were able to survive such hardships and such long periods of hunger." "We entered [the city] without meeting resistance," wrote Miguel de Estete, "for the natives received us with goodwill."

In all, only six Spaniards had lost their lives on the six-hundred-mile, three-month-long journey from Cajamarca to Cuzco; by contrast, the Spaniards had probably killed several thousand native warriors.

Seventeen-year-old Manco Inca, too, was happy. Ever since Cuzco had been captured by Atahualpa's forces and Huascar seized and taken north as a prisoner, Manco had been in fear for his life. After most of his brothers, sisters, aunts, uncles, nieces, and the rest of his family had been rounded up and exterminated, Manco, a fugitive, must have known that he, too, would probably suffer a similar fate. No one, therefore, could have been more surprised than Manco that his brother Atahualpa had been killed, that the powerful Quitan army had been suddenly expelled from Cuzco, or that this small but powerful band of foreigners had arrived and wanted to place him on the throne. Now, with these fierce, light-skinned *viracochas* by his side, Manco suddenly found himself plucked from relative obscurity and placed alongside the Spaniards at the very pinnacle of power. To Manco, the long black period of the Quitan occupation appeared finally to be over.

Pizarro, meanwhile, was quick to consolidate his latest military triumph. Since General Quisquis's army could still mount a counterattack, Pizarro ordered his troops to quarter themselves in the larger of Cuzco's two main squares. He then commanded those with horses to keep their mounts ready at all times, day and night, in case of an Inca assault on the city. Not one to waste time, Pizarro also informed Manco the day after his arrival in Cuzco that the latter would soon become the new Inca emperor, for as Sancho de la Hoz described, he was a prudent and bright young man and was the most important [native] among those who were there at the time, and was the one to whom . . . by law belonged the kingdom. He [Pizarro] did this rapidly . . . so that the natives would not join the men of Quito, but would have a lord of their own to reverence and to obey and would not organize themselves into [rebellious] bands. And so he [Pizarro] commanded all the chiefs to obey him [Manco] as their lord and to do all that he should order them to do.

Pizarro instinctively understood both power and politics; he therefore tried to forestall any local resistance to the Spaniards' authority from developing by making it appear that he had granted full sovereignty to Manco, which of course Pizarro had no intention of doing. Well aware that the Spaniards were too few in number to control a vast empire and that they would need native allies, Pizarro urged Manco to quickly begin recruiting an army. With a native army they could control, the Spaniards would more easily be able to crush insurrections and would also be able to rid the country of Atahualpa's two remaining armies. Manco was only too happy to oblige, as raising an army would not only increase his own power but would also allow him to exact vengeance on the hated General Quisquis, who had exterminated nearly his entire family.

Manco soon departed from the capital in a campaign against General Quisquis, along with Hernando de Soto, fifty Spanish cavalry, and ten thousand native warriors. Together, the combined Spanish-Inca assault inflicted enough damage on Quisquis's forces that both the general's officers and peasant conscripts finally decided that they had had enough. Having been away from their homes now for nearly two years, the troops eventually forced their proud general to begin the long, thousand-mile retreat northward back to Quito.

With General Quisquis on the run, Manco wasted little time in preparing for his coronation, first retiring to the mountains for the traditional three-day fast, and then returning to Cuzco for his crowning as emperor.

Once the fast was over, he [Manco] emerged richly dressed and accompanied by a great crowd of people . . . and any place where he was to sit was decorated with very valuable cushions and with royal cloth [placed] beneath his feet. . . . On either side [sat] other chiefs, captains, provincial governors, and the lords of large realms. . . . No one was seated here who was not a person of quality.

According to Xerez: "They then received him as their lord with great respect and kissed his hand and cheek and, turning their faces to the Sun, they gave thanks to it, holding their hands together and saying that it had given them a natural lord. . . . They then placed a richly-woven fringe on him, tied around his head . . . which almost reached the eyes and that is the equivalent of a crown among them."*

Manco's coronation was unfurling in a city that not only had served as the capital of the ethnic group known as the Incas for hundreds of years, but that also housed its previous divine emperors, each carefully mummified and clothed and kept in his respective temple along with his attendants. Here dwelled the great Huayna Capac—the father of Manco, Atahualpa, and Huascar—felled presumably by smallpox after he had conquered the province of what is now Ecuador; here, too, rested Tupac Inca Yupanqui, whose legions had conquered a thousand miles of what is now Chile and who had pushed the already massive frontiers of the empire eastward into the Amazon; here resided the great Pachacuti, the Alexander the Great of Tawantinsuyu, the ruler whose grand vision had transformed a once small kingdom into a vast, polyglot empire. Here, too, dwelled a host of even earlier rulers who had governed the small, primordial Inca kingdom, long before their descendants had seized control of the resources of much of western South America.†

The presence at Manco's coronation of his ancestors' mummies—still venerated as gods by the empire's inhabitants—was the Spaniards' first real glimpse of the Incas' ancestor cult, a tradition common to native South

---

* The coronation quoted here was actually that of Tupac Huallpa, whom Pizarro and his men elevated to the position of Inca emperor the day after they had killed Atahualpa. Tupac Huallpa died two months later, however. Manco's coronation, which was described by a number of contemporary chroniclers, closely resembled that of Tupac Huallpa's, which had taken place just two months earlier.

† After his death in Quito of what was probably an introduced epidemic of smallpox, Huayna Capac had been embalmed and transported back to Cuzco, his dead body presumably still covered at the time with the contagious smallpox spores.

American cultures. The sight of the dead emperors' shriveled remains being consulted by the living must have horrified the Dominican friar, Vincente de Valverde, who undoubtedly perceived the Incas consorting with their dead as the work of the devil. Nevertheless, the Spaniards watched the ceremonies for Manco's coronation—attended by a retinue of dead Inca emperors—with what could only have been a mixture of both awe and disgust. In the words of the chronicler Miguel de Estete:

[They held] huge celebrations on the city square, [and] . . . such a vast number of people assembled . . . that only with great difficulty could they crowd into the square. Manco had all the deceased ancestors brought to the festivities in the following manner: after he had gone with a great entourage to the temple to make a prayer to the Sun, throughout the morning he went successively to the tombs where each [dead Inca emperor] was embalmed and was seated on his seat. With great veneration and respect, they were then removed in their order of precedence and were brought to the city, each one seated on his litter and with uniformed men to carry it [and with] all of his servants and adornments as if he were alive. The natives came down in such a manner, singing many songs and giving thanks to the Sun. . . . They arrived at the square accompanied by innumerable people and carrying the emperor [Manco Inca] in front of them in his litter and alongside him his father Huayna Capac. And the rest similarly in their litters, embalmed and with royal headbands on their heads.

For each of them a pavilion had been set up where each of the dead [Inca rulers] was placed in order, seated on their thrones and surrounded by pages and women with flywhisks in their hands, who treated them with the same respect as if they had been alive. Beside each one of them was a reliquary or small chest with insignia, in which were the fingernails, hair, teeth and other things that had been clipped from their limbs after they had become emperors. . . . Once they had been placed in order, they remained there from eight in the morning until nightfall without leaving the festivities. . . . There were so many people and so many men and women who were heavy drinkers and they poured so much into their skins—because what they do is drink and not eat . . . that two wide drains over half a *vara* [eighteen inches] wide that emptied into the river beneath the flagstones [of the square] . . . ran with urine throughout the day from those who had urinated into them, as abundantly as if they were flowing springs. This is not so astonishing given the amount they were drinking and the numbers drinking it, although it is . . . something that has never before been seen. . . . These festivities lasted for over thirty days without interruption.

The Spaniards were unaware that the Incas' heavy drinking was actually a ritualized form of worship, and instead interpreted their behavior as some sort of perverted, bacchanalian devil worship. Taking advantage, however, of the large audience of native chiefs and nobles who had arrived to honor their new Inca lord, Pizarro arranged to address the important gathering. The coronation ceremony was, after all, designed to herald the transmission of royal power. There would thus be no better moment for Pizarro to make it clear to the assembled elites that with this particular coronation there would be some fundamental changes made—and that the Spaniards intended to create a new power structure.

Using the Spaniards' now ritualized ceremony of conquest, Pizarro soon made it clear to all those gathered that they were now part of a larger world order than they had been used to and that henceforth they would be subservient to an empire even more powerful than their own. Wrote Pedro Sancho de la Hoz:

Once Mass had been said . . . he [Pizarro] came out onto the square with many men from his army and he gathered them together. And in the presence of the emperor [Manco Inca], the lords of the land, the native warriors who were seated together with his own Spaniards, with the Inca [emperor] seated on a small stool and with his men on the ground around him, the Governor made a speech as he is used to doing in similar situations. And I [Pedro Sancho], his secretary and the army notary, read out the demand and the Requirement that His Majesty had ordered to be done. And the contents were translated by an interpreter and they all understood them and replied [that they had].

The Requirement was the same document that Friar Valverde had paraphrased for Atahualpa that fateful afternoon in the square of Cajamarca a little more than a year ago. As Manco and his chiefs listened to Pizarro's interpreter—the mummies of the dead Inca emperors being fanned for flies and presumably listening along with all those assembled—Pizarro's notary read the final paragraph, pausing now and then for the words to be interpreted into the Incas' *runasimi*.

> And so I request and require you . . . to recognize the Church as your Mistress and as Governess of the World and Universe, and the High Priest, called the Pope, in Her name, and His Majesty in Her Place, as Ruler and Lord King. . . . And if you do not do this . . . [then] with the help of God we shall come mightily against you, and we shall make war on you everywhere and in every way that we can, and we shall subject you to the yoke and obedience of the Church and His Majesty, and we shall seize your women and children, and we shall make them slaves, to sell and dispose of as His Majesty commands, and we shall do all the evil and damage to you that we are able. And I must insist that the deaths and destruction that result from this will be your fault.

According to another notary in the group, Miguel de Estete, the message seemed to have been understood, for the natives "sang many songs and gave thanks to the Sun for having allowed their enemies to be driven from the land and for allowing the Christians to rule them. This was the substance of their songs, although I do not believe," Estete noted suspiciously, "that . . . [the songs] reflected their true intentions. They only wished to make us think that they were pleased with the words of the Spaniards."

Whatever the natives may actually have been thinking, each native chief was now made to come forward, was instructed to raise the Spanish standard two times, and then to embrace Francisco Pizarro to the sound of Spanish trumpets. Manco Inca then "stood up . . . and handed the Governor and the Spaniards a vase of gold to drink from and then all went off to eat, for it was already late." The coronation complete, the teenaged Manco Inca was now the new lord of the Inca Empire. He was the fifth Inca emperor in roughly six years, the last four having been his father, Huayna Capac; his two warring brothers, Atahualpa and Huascar; and, briefly, another brother, Tupac Huallpa, who had died three months earlier in Jauja.

Undeterred by the presence of a new Inca emperor, Pizarro and his

Spaniards continued plundering and looting the Inca capital and its environs, a process they had begun immediately after their arrival a month earlier. For Pizarro, this was the fulfillment of a dream he had harbored ever since he had first arrived in the Americas: to one day become the leader of an expedition that would sack and loot a wealthy, previously undiscovered native empire. This was one of the few times in the history of the world, in fact, that a small band of invaders was able to plunder the capital of a major empire literally at will.

Pizarro soon took over the royal palace of Pachacuti, located on the main square, as his own residence. Perhaps this was fitting, as Pachacuti was the Inca ruler who had envisioned and founded the Inca Empire, just as Pizarro had envisioned and carried out that same empire's conquest. Pizarro's younger brothers Juan and Gonzalo, meanwhile, quickly occupied residences alongside Francisco's palace that had belonged to Atahualpa's father, Huayna Capac. Diego de Almagro likewise took over a palace that Huascar had completed just before he was captured and executed by Atahualpa's men. Another palace was set aside for Hernando Pizarro, who was currently in Spain, and which was to be shared by Hernando de Soto. Having once belonged to Huayna Capac, it was the finest of the palaces and had a gateway of marble as well as two towers roughly thirty feet in height. Seventeen-year-old Manco Inca, meanwhile, began constructing a new palace for himself.

In March 1534—nearly two years after the Spaniards' arrival in Peru—Pizarro distributed the gold and silver looted from Cuzco. The haul was even larger than that of Cajamarca. Although less gold had been collected than for Atahualpa's ransom, the amount of silver was four times greater. Those Spaniards who had arrived late in Peru with Almagro—and who had missed the capture of Atahualpa and hence their chance of becoming instantly wealthy—now found that their patience had finally paid off. Those who had already become the equivalent of millionaires in Cajamarca were now doubly so. Pizarro also set aside individual shares "for himself and [his] two horses and the [two native] interpreters and for his page, Pedro Pizarro."

As each Spaniard walked away from Pizarro's palace, relying no doubt upon a combination of natives and llamas to help him carry away the fortune of a lifetime, all of the Spaniards assembled must have realized that a milestone had been reached in the conquest of Peru. The Company of the

Levant, which Pizarro and Almagro had created some ten years earlier, was now officially dissolved, as all of its accumulated profits had now been distributed. Its shareholder-participants—at least those who participated in the Cajamarca and/or Cuzco campaigns—had made such fantastic profits that they could all retire. Pizarro now presented his fellow Spaniards with two choices: they could either leave the country and return to Spain, where they could retire to lives of luxury, or else they could remain in Peru as that country's first Spanish citizens and thus could help found the new Spanish colony called the Kingdom of New Castile.

Pizarro, who had struggled and fought for more than thirty years to create precisely such a situation for himself—governor of a native empire—had no intention of leaving. Peru was the prize he had coveted and it was in Peru that he would stay. Since Pizarro couldn't rule an empire on his own, however, he needed as many Spaniards as possible to remain. There were, after all, currently fewer than five hundred Spaniards in an empire that contained ten million native inhabitants and that stretched for some two and a half thousand miles. To say that the Spaniards were stretched "thinly" would have been a gross understatement. Pizarro thus offered to any Spaniard who promised to remain in Peru an *encomienda*.

The Spanish verb, *encomendar,* means "to entrust." The basic idea of the *encomienda* was one derived from the medieval manorial system, in which a king granted a benefice—the right to tax the local peasantry—to various lords, who pledged their allegiance to the king in return. Just as European peasants had "entrusted" themselves to a manorial lord and had paid him a portion of their produce in return for protection, New World natives were now expected—upon threat of punishment or death—to labor for Spanish conquistadors who theoretically were charged with "protecting" and "Christianizing" them.

The conquistadors could thus settle down in native cities and live off the produce and other goods supplied by the native population in the countryside. Because in Spanish society both manual labor and trade were considered activities of the lower classes, by receiving the power to tax local peasants the conquistadors were immediately vaulted into the ranks of the Spanish aristocracy. In essence, a restructuring of the Inca Empire's social pyramid had begun, in which the Inca elite—exempt from manual labor due to their own elevated social status—was now being replaced by a ragtag group of largely uneducated, lower-class Spaniards, all of whom aspired to identical, laborless lives.

Whether the average conquistador realized it or not, this was one of the few times in Spanish history during which rank-and-file commoners were suddenly presented with the opportunity of becoming feudal lords, practically overnight. In the end, eighty-eight Spaniards chose to accept *encomiendas* and to take up permanent residence in Cuzco.

Unaware of the Spaniards' plans, the new Inca emperor, Manco Inca, nevertheless had a number of problems on his hands. He first had to take up the reins of an empire that had originally been ripped from the hands of his brother Huascar and then from the hands of his other brother, Atahualpa. Manco's immediate task was to try to reestablish the authority of the *Sapa Inca,* or "Unique Emperor," even while Atahualpa's two remaining generals—Rumiñavi and Quisquis—continued to maintain hostile armies in the north. While portions of Tawantinsuyu had continued to function on automatic, other areas had reverted to the rule of local warlords and chiefs. These had taken advantage of the civil wars and of Pizarro's campaign of conquest in order to throw off the yoke of Inca dominion. Seated on his royal stool, or *duho,* attended by his royal court, and with the scarlet sash of royalty hanging across his forehead, Manco now set about restoring the Incas' imperial authority as best he could. Soon, the young emperor began receiving visits from his provincial governors, began appointing new ones where they had gone missing, and slowly undertook the laborious task of reestablishing the intricate governing mechanism that his ancestors and thousands of years of cultural development in the Andes had produced.

The Spaniards, meanwhile, still had a very weak grasp of just how complex the empire that they had only partially conquered was. While they had immediately recognized the overall similarities with the Old World's culture of kings, nobles, priests, and commoners, they knew little of the actual mechanisms that enabled the Inca Empire to function. The Incas' genius—like that of the Romans—lay in their masterful organizational abilities. Amazingly, an ethnic group that probably never exceeded 100,000 individuals was able to regulate the activities of roughly ten million people. This was in spite of the fact that the empire's citizens spoke more than seven hundred local languages and were distributed among thousands of miles of some of the most rugged and diverse terrain on earth.

As with many of the world's earlier civilizations, the economy of the Inca Empire depended largely upon agriculture. Indeed, it was the Incas' skillful management of agriculture—with the building of canals, mountain terraces, and with the careful attention paid to the planting, harvesting, and the improvement of crops—that allowed them to maintain such dense populations of peasants in mountainous terrain that was generally inhospitable to cultivation. Because of good management and a vast campaign of building terraces, however, the amount of available agricultural land steadily increased during the Incas' reign. Even if crops did fail in one area, the network of state-controlled food storage systems and the ability to transport food from one part of the empire to another made famine virtually impossible. Whatever else may be said of life in the Inca Empire, every one of its citizens was guaranteed sufficient food, clothing, and shelter.

Unlike the Spaniards, however, the citizens of Tawantinsuyu owned no land privately and were not allowed to own luxury goods. While individual citizens did own their own homes, only the Inca rulers and some of the aristocracy owned their own private estates. The Inca Empire, in fact, was predicated upon one fundamental assumption, an assumption that was driven home, if necessary, by armies wielding bloody mace clubs: that all land and natural resources belonged to the state, which in turn was controlled by the Inca emperor. The latter's divine right to such resources derived directly from the sun. Just as a century later the French king Louis XIV would be said to proclaim *"L'etat, c'est moi,"* (I am the state), so, too, did the Inca emperor claim to be the empire's ultimate landlord and custodian.

The principle of state ownership, in fact, was a fundamental premise in the social contract that bound the empire's subjects together. Since the state owned all arable lands, by granting land rights to peasant communities for them to farm, the state by definition was owed something in return. That reciprocal obligation—the granting of land rights in return for the assumption of a debt—was the fundamental agreement upon which the empire was founded. Because the state had granted land rights, the state could demand taxes in return. The Incas, however, chose to collect their taxes not in units of goods, but in units of labor.

All male heads of households between the ages of roughly twenty-five to fifty were required to pay taxes. Since this group made up about 15 to 20 percent of the empire's total population, that meant that the Inca elite could siphon off the labor of roughly two million workers at any given time. Each year, the government required the heads of households to donate two or three months of work to the state and to the sun religion. The Incas called their labor tax the *mit'a,* a word meaning "to take a turn." If one considers that the average U.S. taxpayer pays a 30 percent tax on income received during a twelve-month period, then that same citizen actually "donates" roughly 3.6 months of work each year to keep the various federal, state, and local government bureaucracies functioning. The average U.S. citizen, therefore, ironically pays a greater amount of taxes in the twenty-first century than a typical sixteenth-century native did living in the Inca Empire. The head of an Inca household, however—unlike his U.S. counterpart—didn't necessarily have to work the entire two or three months himself; instead, he could distribute his tax burden among the members of his own family. The larger the family a native citizen had, the more easily his tax burden—the building of roads, the weaving of cloth, the making of pots, and so forth— could be paid.

To keep track of their citizens and of their respective births, deaths, marriages, ages, taxes paid and taxes owed, the government employed a virtual army of accountants and administrators. Specialists in each province stored on *quipus* census information such as the multiple categories of citizens and the numbers of citizens that belonged in each category. A centrally controlled group of inspectors, called the *tokoyrikoq*—meaning "he who sees all"—oversaw each of the provinces and reported to the inspector general, who was often a brother of the Inca emperor.

To better manage the vast empire they had created, the Inca elite invented a hierarchical system that organized the taxable heads of households into groups of 10, 50, 100, 500, 1,000, and 10,000. At the top of the Inca social pyramid, then, stood the emperor, who was the supreme commander of the state, of religion, and of the armed forces. Below him stood the four prefects, or *apus,* who formed the Incas' Supreme Council, each of whom represented one of the empire's four quarters, or *suyus.* Beneath these stood the imperial governors, or *tocrico apus,* who were selected from the Inca nobility. The governors resided in the roughly eighty-eight provincial capitals and carried out administrative and judicial functions. Death sentences, for example, could only be approved by a *tocrico apu,* not by a lower administrator. Beneath the governors operated several layers of local chiefs, called *curacas,* who in return for exemption from taxation and other perks were required to organize the collection of taxes from their own ethnic groups. The status of each *curaca* was directly proportional to the number of households he represented, which could range anywhere from 100 to 10,000 individuals and their families. Beneath this relatively thin veneer of governing elites, and making up more than 95 percent of the empire's social pyramid, labored the vast pool of commoners—the millions of working peasants, artisans, herders, and fishermen whose surplus labor was regularly siphoned off in order to keep the empire organized and functioning.

In return for land rights, protection from invasion, the maintenance of the state's religion, and guaranteed food, clothing, and shelter, Inca citizens were required to occasionally fight in wars, to donate two to three months of labor a year, and to obey the set of rules laid down by the Inca elite. Reciprocity was therefore the keystone, the master gear in the elaborate system of interrelationships that bound the Inca elite and the rest of the empire's inhabitants together. Remove those reciprocal relationships and—like a vast mechanical clock that had suddenly sprung a gear— the complex empire the Incas had devised would cease to function.

Such was the nature of imperial rule that Manco Inca began working to shore up in the latter half of 1534. His task was not an easy one. Already, the empire had been weakened by years of civil war. Although an Inca emperor once again ruled Tawantinsuyu, Manco had been placed there by a band of foreigners whose motivations began to be more and more suspect with each passing day. The Spaniards, for example, had already defiled the Incas' sacred temples and in so doing had humiliated the priesthood and a good portion of the local population. To at least some of the Inca elite—who were already beginning to believe that the Spaniards were usurpers, not liberators—the Spaniards' behavior began to make Manco Inca appear to be a collaborator rather than a sovereign Inca king.

Unlike his older brother Atahualpa, who toward the end of his captivity had finally grasped the Spaniards' truc intentions, Manco was still oblivious to the transformation occurring in Peru. For the moment, Manco didn't appear to understand that Francisco Pizarro was being friendly and attentive simply because he was stalling for time so reinforcements could arrive. From a military standpoint, the fledgling Spanish cities in Peru were like a tiny string of islands in the middle of an endless sea of potentially hostile natives. For the time being, that sea was relatively calm, yet conditions could easily change. The last thing Pizarro wanted to do therefore was to incite the natives to rise up against them.

At the same time, however, Pizarro was just beginning to realize that some of the Spanish reinforcements he had patiently been waiting for might prove more dangerous than a potential native attack. Back in March, Pizarro had learned the alarming news that Hernando Cortés's second-in-command, Pedro de Alvarado, had recently landed on the coast of Ecuador with 550 Spanish conquistadors. Alvarado was apparently determined to carve out his own governorship in the area, despite the fact that Pizarro was the only person who had a royal license to conquer any portion of the Inca Empire.

Pizarro's partner, Diego de Almagro, however, had hurried north as soon as he had learned the news. Unwilling to have their years of efforts derailed by competition, Almagro ultimately succeeded in negotiating a peaceful resolution. In return for 100,000 pesos (about one thousand pounds of gold), Alvarado agreed to cancel his plans of conquest and also to allow 340 of his conquistadors to join Pizarro and Almagro in completing the conquest of Peru. The negotiations had occurred just in time, it turned out. For no sooner had Almagro begun to head south again than he almost immediately ran into a large Inca army commanded by General Quisquis, who had been retreating gradually northward since having abandoned Cuzco more than six months earlier.

Quisquis and his troops, having been away from their homes now for more than two years, were dumbfounded to encounter a large Spanish army where they had least expected one. The Inca general had assumed that the northern part of the empire was still free of the hated foreigners. Soon a series of battles ensued. In one of them Quisquis's troops successfully ambushed a group of fourteen Spaniards and beheaded all of them. In another, they managed to wound twenty Spaniards and kill three of their horses. Still, after years of fighting and now suddenly confronted by a force of nearly five hundred Spaniards and a large number of horses, Quisquis's men became demoralized; the vast majority of them wanted simply to drop their weapons, muster themselves out of the army, and return to their homes.

Even more shocking to the proud Inca general, however, was the fact that his very own officer corps wanted to give up the struggle as well.

"His captains told Quisquis to sue the Spaniards for peace since they were invincible," wrote sixteenth-century historian Francisco López de Gómara. General Quisquis, however—the same commander who had led victorious armies down the length of the Andes, who had successfully fought and captured Huascar, and who had then occupied Cuzco—was insistent that his officers and troops remain and fight. An able tactician, Quisquis was gradually learning that by stationing his warriors on steep escarpments where the Spaniards' horses could not maneuver, he could neutralize the invaders' most powerful weapon. With his own officers now threatening to abandon the campaign, however, Atahualpa's former general found himself unable to hide his growing fury. "He [Quisquis] threatened them because of their cowardice and ordered them to follow him so that they could regroup [and fight again]." Quisquis's officers now rebelled, however, refusing to follow their general's commands.

Like any military group, the Inca army functioned on the basis of strict discipline. Atahualpa, after all, had executed a whole battalion of soldiers in Cajamarca simply for having shown fear of the Spaniards' horses. Insubordination was an even greater crime and was severely punished. Even in the chaos of the present situation, Quisquis's officers' behavior amounted to treason. "Quisquis heaped scorn upon them for this and swore to punish the mutineers," wrote López de Gómara. Suddenly, however, "Huaypalcon [one of Quisquis's officers] threw a lance that struck his chest. Many others then ran forward with their clubs and battle-axes and killed him."

So ended the life of one of the Inca Empire's finest generals, the man who had been forced to obey, although grudgingly, Atahualpa's orders to allow the first three Spaniards to ransack the Inca capital. Despite the execution of his emperor, Quisquis had valiantly led his men against the Spaniards, even as the chaos unleashed by the invasion had continued to turn the Incas' world upside down.

Not long after Quisquis's death, one of Pizarro's captains, Sebastián de Benalcázar, finally cornered the last of Atahualpa's three great military leaders, General Rumiñavi, in Ecuador. After a long, desperate campaign, a climactic battle finally took place in which Rumiñavi's troops surrendered yet he himself narrowly escaped. Spanish troops eventually caught up with the

Inca general, however, as he was attempting to cross a snow-covered mountain. Taken back to Quito, neither Rumiñavi nor a host of other captured nobles were shown any mercy by their captors. According to the chaplain Marcos de Niza, Captain Benalcázar

> summoned Luyes, a great lord of those that were in Quito and, burning his feet, he tortured him in many different ways in order to make him divulge the whereabouts of Atahualpa's [supposed] hidden treasure— which he knew nothing about. He [next] burned [chief] Chamba alive, another very important lord, who was innocent. He also burned Cozopanga, who had been the governor of the province of Quito and who had come in peace, because he did not give as much gold as [Captain Benalcázar] demanded, nor did he know anything about the buried treasure. [The captain] burned him along with many other chiefs and important men so that no native lords would remain in that land.

Finally, the Spaniards led General Rumiñavi out onto Quito's main square. There the great general was summarily executed for the "crime" of having resisted the occupation of his country by foreign invaders.

With Atahualpa's top three generals now dead, with Cortés's partner, Pedro de Alvarado, bought off, and with hundreds of new Spanish reinforcements currently headed south, control of the riches of Peru now seemed to be securely in the hands of the two original conquering partners, Francisco Pizarro and Diego de Almagro. Through their puppet emperor, Manco Inca, the two presently controlled the Incas' extensive governing apparatus, were able to collect taxes, and were in a position to suppress any potential native revolts that might develop. As long as they could maintain the peace, Pizarro and Almagro seemed set upon a course that would gradually transform Tawantinsuyu into a lucrative new colony of the rapidly expanding Spanish Empire.

Now, with the last military campaign against hostile Inca troops apparently over, Pizarro gradually began shifting his focus from his role of military leader to that of administrator. Pizarro was, after all, governor of the Kingdom of New Castile, a seven-hundred-mile-long section of the vast native realm the Spanish crown had authorized him to conquer. There remained only one small problem, however, a problem that had originally arisen when Pizarro had returned from Spain with titles only for himself and with virtually none for his partner. Almagro, of course, had been extremely angry at the time and had almost refused to proceed with the proposed conquest of Peru. Only by promising his partner partial control over whatever realm the two of them might conquer, had Pizarro finally been able to persuade Almagro to join him.

The question remained, therefore: What about Almagro? What about the partner he had counted upon to organize expeditions and who had loyally provided him with reinforcements and supplies for the last ten years? The one who had lost an eye on their very first expedition? What role would he play in Peru? While Pizarro had granted Almagro an *encomienda,* as he had to the other conquistadors who had chosen to remain in Peru, Pizarro nevertheless remained indisputably governor of Peru, the equivalent of a Spanish viceroy. In this area of the New World at least, Pizarro was second in power only to the Spanish king. The Inca Empire appeared to be thousands of miles long, however, much longer than the seven hundred miles the crown had granted to him. So what was Almagro's fair share?

In December 1534, Pizarro and Almagro met on the coast of Peru near the site of a new town Pizarro was busy founding: *La Ciudad de los Reyes,* the City of the Kings—or Lima, as it would later be called. As Pizarro busied himself with outlining his new city on barren sands in full view of the Pacific Ocean—where he no doubt envisioned future fleets of merchant ships onloading more gold and silver—Pizarro had every intention of living the remainder of his life peacefully while administering to his empire. Pizarro, therefore, no longer needed an ambitious ex-partner whose specialty was organizing, financing, and carrying out expeditions of conquest. Pizarro suggested to Almagro that the latter travel to Cuzco and take over the lieutenant governorship of that city, a position temporarily held by Almagro's friend Hernando de Soto. Maybe that would satisfy Almagro's ambitions. Surprisingly, Almagro accepted, but only because he was counting on receiving a grant of a governorship from the king, which he had already petitioned for. The two men no doubt embraced each other. Then Almagro climbed into his saddle, swung his horse around, and began the eleven-thousand-foot climb and four-hundred-mile journey to Cuzco.

Shortly after Almagro's departure, however, news arrived from Spain that King Charles had decided to split the Inca Empire in two. The king intended to award the "northern part" of the empire to Pizarro and the "southern part" to Almagro. The details of the arrangement and the precise delineations between the two kingdoms were to arrive by ship much later in the person of Hernando Pizarro, who was now on his way back to Peru and carried the king's orders with him.

As Pizarro continued tracing the outlines of his city's future plaza in the sand, he no doubt stopped long enough to watch a messenger hurry off on horseback to inform Almagro of the king's decision. Little did he or anyone else know, however, that the king's decision would soon drive a wedge between the two conquistadors that would alter the balance of power in Peru. For the time being, as the graying conquistador returned to surveying his new city, behind him in the distance, the horse with its messenger gradually disappeared in a fine plume of dust.

8 ❖ PRELUDE TO
A REBELLION

"As God and my conscience are my witnesses, it was evident to all concerned that it was only because of this maltreatment that the peoples of Peru were finally provoked into revolt and took up arms against the Spanish, as, indeed, they had every cause to do. For the Spanish never treated them squarely, never honored any of the undertakings they gave, but rather set about destroying the entire territory, for no good reason and without any justification, and eventually the people decided that they would rather die fighting than put up any longer with what was being done to them."

FRIAR MARCOS DE NIZA,
ORDER OF THE FRANCISCANS, 1535

"Men ought either to be indulged or utterly destroyed, for if you merely offend them they take vengeance, but if you injure them greatly they are unable to retaliate, so that the injury done to a man ought to be such that vengeance cannot be feared."

NICCOLÒ MACHIAVELLI, *THE PRINCE,* 1511

DIEGO DE ALMAGRO ARRIVED IN CUZCO IN LATE JANUARY OF 1535, having been appointed by Pizarro to take over the lieutenant governorship of the city. After nearly a year of military campaigns in the central and northern portions of the empire, Almagro had brought back with him more than three hundred of the new troops he had separated from Hernando Cortés's second-in-command, Pedro de Alvarado. Just before he

The Incas sometimes presented their women to the Spaniards as gifts; at other times, the Spaniards seized them as their own concubines.

reached the Inca capital, a messenger overtook Almagro with news that the king was going to grant him a governorship to the south of Pizarro's. In the year 1535, however, along the western coast of South America, only a ship's pilot could accurately measure geographical distances—and thus far none in Peru had attempted to demarcate the boundaries of Pizarro's territory. Exactly where Pizarro's governorship ended and Almagro's would begin, therefore, was anyone's guess.

As the new group of Spaniards rode and marched into the capital of the Incas, marveling at its setting and architecture, they soon realized that they had arrived too late to partake of its spoils or to be awarded *encomiendas* like the others. Undoubtedly, the conquistadors looked with envy at the eighty-eight *encomenderos* who had chosen to remain in the capital and who were now fabulously wealthy men. Many of the latter had already shed their armor and instead wore stockings, capes, and hats pierced by stylish feather plumes. By contrast, the newcomers wore patched and stitched clothing and scarcely had a coin to their names. This newest group of conquistadors had come to Peru in the belief that here they could instantly become rich. Abruptly disabused of this notion, they now realized that they had missed that opportunity by at least a year, if not longer; it was a realization that caused more than a few of them to become quite bitter.

With a minority of the Spaniards extremely wealthy and a majority extremely poor, political divisions between the two groups not surprisingly began to appear. Those Spaniards to whom Pizarro had granted *encomiendas* were naturally indebted to him; those who had arrived with Almagro, on the other hand, were hoping that loyalty to the aging, one-eyed conquistador who had brought them here would pay off for them in the long run. After all, if it turned out that Cuzco lay within Almagro's new realm, then the Spaniards who had already been awarded *encomiendas* might soon have those rescinded. Almagro would then surely distribute the *encomiendas* among his own followers.

The fact that no one currently knew which conquistador—Pizarro or Almagro—the city of Cuzco actually belonged to only exacerbated an already unstable political climate. In addition, the presence of two of the youngest and most impulsive of the Pizarro brothers—twenty-three-year-old Juan and twenty-two-year-old Gonzalo—only served to create further problems. With Juan and Gonzalo determined at any cost not to let Cuzco

fall into the hands of Almagro, it wasn't long before tensions began to sim-
mer and then finally to bubble and boil over. Wrote the sixteenth-century
chronicler Pedro de Cieza de León:

> Juan Pizarro and Gonzalo Pizarro were most resentful of Almagro be-
> cause they disliked him. . . . Almagro's friends coaxed him, telling him
> to look out for himself; the King had made him lord, so he should truly
> be one, and he should immediately send for those decrees that were
> coming and take possession of what the King had designated as his gov-
> ernance.

Concluded Cieza de León: "From then on there were two factions: one
bound to the Pizarros and another to the Almagros."

Disagreements over who would control Cuzco and its surrounding area
came to a head roughly a month after Almagro's arrival. One day in March
1535, fearing that Almagro might try to seize the capital as his own, the two
Pizarro brothers and their supporters carried several cannons into their
palace on the main square, barricaded it, and then "scandalously emerged
onto the plaza, ready to begin a great altercation." Their behavior so in-
censed Hernando de Soto—a longtime supporter of Almagro—that he and
Juan Pizarro quickly came to blows. According to Juan's cousin, Pedro,

> Juan Pizarro and Soto had words [while mounted on their horses] . . .
> whereupon Juan Pizarro seized a lance and thrust it at Soto who, had he
> not been on a fast horse, would have been brought down by the lance
> thrusts. Juan Pizarro chased after him until they reached the place where
> Almagro was staying [on Cuzco's square], and if Almagro's men had not
> saved him, he [Juan] would have slain him, for Juan Pizarro was a very
> brave and strong-willed man. . . . When Almagro and his men saw Soto
> enter [the square] fleeing and with Juan right behind him, they seized
> their weapons . . . and went after Juan Pizarro. Thus, men from both
> sides gathered on the square, brandishing their weapons.

Only through the intervention of a newly arrived royal official, Antonio
Téllez de Guzmán, were the two Spanish factions ultimately prevented
from killing each other. "Had the Christians fought one another the Indians

would have attacked those who survived," Guzmán later wrote the king. As Cieza de León described it: "All of them were so frenzied and full of envy of each other that it was a wonder that they did not all kill each other. . . . These were the first passions in this land between the Almagros and the Pizarros, or brought about on their behalf."

Two months later, after hearing reports of near civil war in the capital, Francisco Pizarro hurriedly went to Cuzco. Anxious to defuse the situation, yet with the precise details of the king's division of the Inca Empire still not having arrived, Pizarro decided to try to negotiate a solution with his former partner. Both Pizarro and Almagro were by now aware that they had conquered only perhaps two thirds of the Inca Empire. Sidestepping the incendiary issue of to whom Cuzco belonged, Pizarro soon agreed to help Almagro finance a massive expedition of exploration and conquest to the south. The southern portion of the Inca Empire would clearly lie within Almagro's future governorship. Pizarro therefore hoped that by helping to finance its conquest he would rid himself of his increasingly troublesome partner and would simultaneously defuse the current political crisis in Cuzco. With any luck, there would be enough gold, silver, and peasants in the south to satisfy both Almagro and also his hundreds of ambitious new conquistadors.

Anxious to begin exploring his future governorship, Almagro agreed to the proposal. It was certainly possible that wealthy Inca cities, peasants, and fertile lands existed to the south, yet the Spaniards knew little about the region. What Almagro now needed to do was select his own second-in-command, someone whom he could rely upon during the expedition and whose loyalty would be to Almagro—and not to Pizarro.

Thirty-four-year-old Hernando de Soto was quick to apply for the position, offering to pay Almagro a fantastic sum of gold and silver for the privilege. Such positions didn't grow on trees, after all, and although Soto was now very wealthy, he, too, was ambitious to govern a kingdom of his own. Perhaps he might find another native empire further to the south or to the east. Who knew? As second-in-command, Soto would be in an excellent position to petition the king for a governorship. Almagro declined Soto's offer, however, choosing instead a man named Rodrigo Orgóñez, who had proven his loyalty to Almagro during the last five years.

Manco Inca, meanwhile, faced his own set of problems, which had only been heightened by the struggle among the Spaniards for control of Cuzco. Because the Spaniards openly flaunted their control of the city, Manco's prestige was slowly being undermined. Even worse, within the Machiavellian world of Inca politics, rumors were now circulating in Cuzco that some of Manco's relatives coveted the young emperor's throne.

Manco's most likely challenger should theoretically have been his brother Paullu; the latter was about Manco's age and had somehow miraculously escaped being exterminated by General Quisquis during the northern army's occupation. From the moment that Pizarro had selected Manco to rule, however, Paullu had pledged complete loyalty to his brother. Manco had so few suspicions about Paullu, in fact, that while the young emperor had been off participating in military campaigns in the north, he had left Paullu in Cuzco as the de facto emperor. Paullu had immediately relinquished the position as soon as Manco had returned. Manco *was* suspicious, however, of his cousin, Pascac, and of another half-brother, Atoc-Sopa, the two of whom formed the nucleus of a potential group of rivals. As the days passed, rumors that Pascac was scheming to replace Manco with Atoc-Sopa continued to travel from cluster to cluster of Inca nobles in the streets and within the dark interiors of elite Inca homes. Not even a foreign occupation was enough to dampen the Incas' tradition of dynastic political intrigue.

Aware that the rivalries among the Inca elites might cause instability in his new realm, Pizarro attempted to end the power struggle by bringing the two Inca sides together to negotiate. The attempt was unsuccessful, however, so much so that Manco privately asked Almagro to help rid himself of the rival Inca faction. The year before, Manco and Almagro had spent considerable time together while on military campaigns and had become friendly. Although busy preparing for his expedition to the south, Almagro agreed to help the young emperor. The more he helped Manco, the more indebted to him the emperor would be.

One night, a small group of Spanish assassins crept along the frigid alleyways of the high Andean city, the moon causing slivers of steel to glimmer in their hands. Almagro had sent the men to exterminate Manco's half-brother Atoc-Sopa. Finding the latter's home in the dark and creeping into his bedroom, they located the potential Inca prince and murdered him in his bed. The assassination of Atoc-Sopa, however, only intensified the rupture within Manco's extended family, which now began to organize themselves along the same fault lines that divided the Spaniards. Manco and his brother Paullu allied themselves with Almagro; those of the Inca faction opposed to Manco, meanwhile, allied themselves with Pizarro.

Things continued to deteriorate to such an extent that one night Manco—fearing a reprisal for his brother's murder—fled his house and hurried to Almagro's palace, where he pleaded with the veteran conquistador to hide him in his bedroom. When the rival faction's Spanish supporters learned that Manco had essentially abandoned his home, "a noisy group of them went to rob and loot his house, causing a lot of damage, without anyone being able to stop or prevent it." Some said that Manco was so frightened of being assassinated that night that he literally crawled beneath Almagro's bed and hid.

On July 2, 1535, Diego de Almagro departed Cuzco with 570 Spanish cavalry and foot soldiers and with twelve thousand Inca porters. His goal was to explore and conquer the southern portion of the Inca Empire, of which he was soon to become governor. In a gesture of friendship, Manco had provided not only the porters for the expedition but had also sent Paullu and his high priest, Villac Umu, to accompany Almagro as well; both apparently enjoyed wide support among the southern native chiefs. Governor Francisco Pizarro and many of the Spanish *encomenderos* gathered to see the expedition off on what many felt was a permanent parting of the ways. While the *encomenderos* stood on the wide square wearing elegant stockings and plumed hats, Almagro's men wore pointed morion helmets, spare bits of armor, and carried carefully honed swords and lances. The two ex-partners wished each other well, then Almagro and his men marched out of the capital of the Incas, leaving behind the bowl-like city with the Inca fortress of Saqsaywaman squatting above it.

The departure of Almagro's expedition immediately emptied Cuzco of the majority of its impoverished Spaniards, leaving only the native inhabitants and the mostly wealthy Spanish *encomenderos.* Not long afterward, Pizarro departed from Cuzco as well, determined to continue his project of founding Spanish cities along the coast. Peru was connected to Spain by sea, after all, and if Pizarro's kingdom was going to continue exporting the raw materials of gold and silver in exchange for imported and manufactured goods from Spain, then it would need cities and ports. Besides, seaside settlements could be militarily reinforced by ship, if for some reason that should prove necessary. Cities located in the interior, on the other hand—such as Cuzco, Jauja, and Cajamarca—were both militarily and logistically isolated.

Cuzco's former lieutenant governor, Hernando de Soto, now prepared to depart from Peru as well. Unsuccessful in his attempt to accompany Almagro's expedition as second-in-command, Soto left Cuzco with a pack train carrying a fortune in gold and silver ingots, intent on finding passage on the next ship headed toward Spain. The dashing cavalry officer who had led the Spanish advance down the Andes would now leave Peru forever. Once in Spain, Soto would use his share of Inca treasure to win a royal license to conquer the little known land of Florida. Soto hoped to find and conquer an Indian empire there—similar to the ones Cortés and Pizarro had already discovered—and to rule over it as governor. Eight years later, however, after having wandered and fought his way for three years through what are now Florida, South Carolina, Tennessee, Alabama, Arkansas, Oklahoma, Georgia, and Mississippi, Soto would die destitute and delirious on the banks of the Mississippi River, which he was the first European to discover. The man who had befriended two Inca emperors—and who had lanced and ridden his way through Peru and had found wealth beyond his wildest dreams—was ultimately consigned to the same river, which carried his rag-covered and emaciated body gently downstream. He was forty-two years old at the time.

With Francisco Pizarro, Almagro, Soto, and most of the recently arrived Spaniards gone, the city of Cuzco was now left in the hands of Manco Inca and Pizarro's two younger brothers, Juan and Gonzalo. Although twenty-four-year-old Juan Pizarro had a reputation for being impetuous, he nevertheless was popular among the rank-and-file conquistadors. An excellent horseman, Juan had become a captain at the age of twenty-two and had ridden with Soto in the cavalry vanguard down the Andes. In the absence of Soto and Almagro, Francisco had appointed Juan as the new *corregidor,* or lieutenant governor, of the city.

One year younger than Juan and thirty-five years younger than his brother Francisco, Gonzalo Pizarro was tall, graceful, black-bearded, extremely handsome—and had a reputation as a womanizer. The twenty-three-year-old was also a "fine horseman and . . . a great shot with the harquebus," wrote sixteenth-century historian Agustín de Zárate. Though illiterate, "he expressed himself well although with great vulgarity." Gonzalo, however, suffered from a tendency to view other Spaniards either as good friends or bitter enemies. It was a decidedly negative characteristic that would ultimately deeply affect the history of both the Pizarros and Peru. Unlike Juan, who was the only Pizarro who had a reputation for being generous, Gonzalo was also known as the stingiest member of a family already infamous for its parsimony.

With Cuzco now in the hands of the two young Pizarro firebrands, and the ameliorating influence of Francisco Pizarro having disappeared, the relationship between the Spaniards in the city and its native inhabitants not surprisingly began to deteriorate. The Spanish citizens of Cuzco, well aware that Manco's brother, Atahualpa, had collected a stupendous amount of treasure, were convinced that Manco must know the location of more gold and silver. They soon began pressuring the young emperor to divulge its whereabouts. For a while, Manco did his best to give the Spaniards what they asked for, revealing cache after cache of gold and silver figurines, statues, and other objects. The more he revealed, however, the more the Spaniards clamored for more. "As the greed of men is so great," Manco's son Titu Cusi later commented, "it controlled them to such an extent that . . . one after the other they came to pester my father and to try and take from him [even] more silver and gold than had already been taken."

The Spaniards, however, weren't interested in only the power, the status, and the life of ease that gold and silver provided—they were interested in satisfying their sexual desires as well. From the moment of their arrival in Peru, in fact, the Spaniards had eagerly pursued native women. Since both the Inca and Spanish societies made a clear distinction between nobles and commoners, however, many of the Spanish leaders insisted on taking native mistresses only from the Inca royalty. Francisco Pizarro, for example, a fifty-six-year-old bachelor who had never married, soon took a daughter of the emperor Huayna Capac, whom he called Inés, as his mistress. Even the squat and ugly Almagro—fifty-nine years old and with one eye reduced to a pink pulp—began to sleep with a beautiful, royal-blooded sister of Manco Inca, called Marcachimbo,

> [who] was the daughter of Huayna Capac and of his sister, and who would have inherited the Inca Empire had she been a man. She gave Almagro a pit in which there was a quantity of gold and silver tableware,

which once melted down yielded eight bars or 27,000 silver marks. . . .
She also gave another captain 12,000 *castellanos* from the leftovers from
that pit. But the poor woman was not shown any greater respect or favor
by the Spaniards because of this. On the contrary, she was repeatedly
dishonored, for she was very pretty and had a gentle nature, and she
caught the pox. . . . Finally, however, she married a Spanish citizen and
in the end our Lord was well served when she died a Christian and was
a very good wife.

Since these particular Inca women were unmarried, their becoming the
mistresses of the Spaniards apparently did not unduly bother the Inca elite.
When Gonzalo Pizarro started taking an interest in Manco Inca's young and
beautiful wife, Cura Ocllo, however, the twenty-three-year-old Pizarro
quickly discovered that his advances completely scandalized Inca society.
Impetuous, arrogant, and with no existing law or authority in Peru to rein in
his more outlandish impulses, Gonzalo did as he pleased. More and more,
he treated Manco Inca and the rest of the native elite with contempt, insisting that the Inca emperor give him even more gold and silver *and* give up his
wife. When a high-ranking Inca general rebuked Gonzalo for coveting the
emperor's wife, Gonzalo turned on him, his face flushing, grabbed the hilt
of his sword, and threatened to kill the man on the spot.

> "Who gave you the authority to talk to the King's *corregidor* like that?
> Don't you know what kind of men we Spaniards are? By the King's life,
> if you don't shut up I'll seize you and play a game with you and your
> friends that you'll remember for the rest of your lives. I swear if you
> don't keep quiet I'll slit you open alive and will cut you into little
> pieces."

Although the Inca nobility, not the peasantry, was polygamous, every emperor, chief, or noble nevertheless had a "principal wife." The latter was a
woman with whom a ritual marriage ceremony had been performed and
who had a guaranteed and permanent status. Additional wives, by contrast,
were called "secondary wives," or concubines. In the case of certain emperors, such as Huayna Capac, the concubines numbered in the thousands.
Only children born of the principal wife had the "purest" blood and hence

were deemed legitimate. Those born of a concubine were considered illegitimate. While members of the Incas' high aristocracy were allowed to marry their half-sisters, only the emperor himself was allowed to marry his full sister. Once married, she became the *coya,* or queen, thus preserving the purity of the royal blood lineage. Cura Ocllo, therefore, was both Manco's principal wife *and* his full sister. It was thus inconceivable that anyone else in the empire, let alone a foreigner, should dare to ask the emperor to give up his queen. That twenty-three-year-old Gonzalo Pizarro did so shocked not only the Inca elite, but also Manco Inca.

Hoping to placate the brother of the powerful Francisco Pizarro, however, Manco ordered that a large quantity of gold and silver be gathered. He soon arranged for it to be delivered and personally accompanied it to Gonzalo's palace. "Come on, Mr. Manco Inca," Gonzalo is said to have exclaimed, examining the treasure with interest yet not forgetting his demand, "let's have the lady *coya.* All this silver is good, but [she] is what we really want."

Recognizing how serious Gonzalo was, Manco now became desperate. Having already had to suffer the humiliation of hiding in Almagro's bedroom to escape assassination, having had his palace ransacked, and presently being harassed on a daily basis for more gold and silver, Manco was now being ordered to hand over his very own wife and sister to an arrogant foreigner. Searching for a way out of his dilemma, Manco finally hit upon a seemingly reasonable solution: how about giving Gonzalo a beautiful woman other than his *coya*? An Inca woman even more beautiful than his queen? Recalled Manco's son Titu Cusi:

> My father, seeing with what insistence they were asking for the queen, and that he was unable to avoid [their request] in any other way, sent for a very beautiful woman, coiffed and very well dressed, in order to hand her over in place of the queen they were asking for. [But] when they saw her they said that she didn't seem to be the queen they were asking for but rather another woman . . . and that he [Manco] should give them the queen and stop wasting their time.

Not willing to give up, Manco assembled twenty more beautiful women, hoping that Gonzalo would choose one or more of them and would eventually forget about his wife. Gonzalo, however, showed no interest; he insisted even more vehemently on possessing only the Inca queen. With mounting desperation, Manco finally sent for another of his sisters, Inguill, who resembled his wife closely. Making sure that she was dressed and coiffed identically to his *coya,* Manco led his latest decoy out to the Spaniards. The emperor then pretended to be dismayed that he had finally been forced to relinquish his very own queen. "When the Spaniards saw her come out . . . so elegant and beautiful, they shouted with much enthusiasm and joy, 'Yes, she's the one, she's the one. She is the Lady *coya*—and not the others.'"

Gonzalo Pizarro, completely obsessed with having no other woman than the queen of the Incas, by this time could scarcely restrain himself. In Titu Cusi's recounting:

> "Mr. Manco Inca, if she is for me, give her to me right away because I can't stand it any longer." And my father, who had instructed her well, said "Many congratulations—do whatever you wish with her." So in front of everyone, and oblivious to all else, [Gonzalo] went and kissed and embraced her as if she were his legitimate wife. . . . Inguill, horrified and frightened at being embraced by someone she didn't know, screamed like a mad woman and said that she would rather run away than face people such as these. . . . And when my father saw her behaving so wildly and so strongly refusing to go with the Spaniards, he realized that his own freedom depended upon her complying. Completely furious, he ordered her to go with them and, seeing my father so angry, she did what he commanded her to do and went with them, more out of fear than for any other reason.

In the end, however, the deception didn't last. Gonzalo eventually realized that he had been deceived, then discarded the sister and seized Manco's wife as his own. "Gonzalo Pizarro . . . took my wife," Manco later said bitterly, "and [still] has her."

If Manco still had any doubts about the price he had to pay in order to become the emperor of the Incas, those doubts were soon accentuated when the high priest, Villac Umu, unexpectedly arrived back in Cuzco. Manco had sent Villac Umu to accompany his brother Paullu on Almagro's expedition to the south. Yet three months into that expedition Villac Umu had escaped; he now regaled Manco with horror stories of all that he had witnessed. Everywhere they had gone, Villac Umu recounted, the Spaniards had been consumed with finding objects of gold and silver. If the local chiefs didn't immediately produce what they demanded, then the Spaniards treated them with brutality. Even if gold and silver were produced, the Spaniards nevertheless demanded that the native villagers accompany the expedition as servants. "Those [natives] who did not want to go voluntarily with them [the Spaniards] were taken along bound in ropes and chains," wrote Cristóbal de Molina, a young priest who had accompanied the expedition.

> They carried off their wives and children, and the women who were attractive they took for their personal service, and for other things besides. . . . And when the mares of some Spaniards produced foals, they had the Indians carry these on hammocks and litters. And other Spaniards had themselves carried in litters as a pastime, leading the horses by their bridles so that they [the horses] would become very fat.

Even the native porters Manco had provided Almagro with, the high priest explained, were routinely treated in a violent fashion.

> [They] worked all day long without rest and without eating, except for a little roasted corn and water, and were barbarously imprisoned at night. There was one Spaniard on this expedition who locked twelve Indians in a chain and boasted that all twelve died in it, and that when one Indian died they cut off his head in order to terrify the others so that they didn't have to undo the padlock on the chain. If some poor Indian got sick or tired, then they routinely beat him until he died from it, because they said that if they were lenient with one, then the rest would become sick or tired.

Disgusted by what he had seen, Villac Umu had escaped from the expedition in what is now southern Bolivia, and then had hurried back to Cuzco. Not long afterward, all the remaining servants and porters Manco had sent along with Almagro abandoned the expedition as well, leaving the Spaniards to fend for themselves. Nevertheless, Almagro and his men would continue on into what is now Chile, pillaging native towns and killing any who resisted their demands. The Spaniards soon began suffering numerous deaths of their own, however, due to the freezing mountain passes they had to cross and also due to frequent attacks by increasingly hostile natives.

Coinciding with Villac Umu's graphic descriptions and with Manco's own recent humiliations, various reports began gradually filtering in from other areas of Tawantinsuyu of gross mistreatment by the Spaniards. Natives who had attractive sisters, daughters, or wives, it was said, now had to begin hiding them from the bearded foreigners, "for no woman who was good-looking was safe [even] with her husband [around and] it would be a miracle if she escaped from the Spaniards." Everywhere the Spaniards went, the anger of the natives "was smoldering and this was because the Spaniards were not satisfied with the service of the natives but tried to rob them in every town. In many areas the Indians would not put up with this and began to rise up and to organize themselves for their defense. The Spaniards certainly went too far in their abuse of them."

Not long after his arrival, Villac Umu and other high-ranking Incas began to organize secret meetings—making sure that they were not noticed by the Spaniards or by the Spaniards' native spies. Privately and together they began urging Manco to put an end to such abuses and to revolt. The bearded foreigners were not liberators, they argued, but occupiers. The Spaniards in Cuzco, in fact, had merely replaced the occupation of Atahualpa's army with an occupation of their own—and both occupations were intolerable. "We cannot spend our entire lives in such great misery and subjection [while being] treated even worse than the Spaniards' black slaves," they told Manco. "Let us rebel once and for all and die for our liberty, and for our children and wives, who every day they take from us and abuse."

By November 1535, a little over a year after the Spaniards had occupied Cuzco, Manco had reached a turning point. In the beginning, Manco had hoped to rule independently alongside the bearded *viracochas* and, being few in number, that they could easily be satisfied by giving them whatever they wanted. The problem was that the Spaniards' needs had no limits—up to and including Manco's own *coya,* or queen. With each passing day, in fact, it was more and more obvious who was really in control, not just of Cuzco but also of the rest of Tawantinsuyu. In the south, Almagro and his men were currently ravaging and pillaging the countryside, while on the coast, Manco was undoubtedly told, Francisco Pizarro was busy drawing lines on the sand where he expected new cities teeming with Spaniards to arise from the earth. In the far north, Pizarro's captain, Sebastián de Benalcázar, had conquered and was ravaging the area that Manco's brother Atahualpa had once controlled. Even in Cuzco, at the very heart of the empire, the *encomenderos* were clamoring each day for more and more produce to be delivered to them by way of tribute—yet they gave nothing to the natives in return.

The more Manco thought about it, the more he undoubtedly realized that he had been incredibly naive. All the words of Pizarro, Almagro, and Soto about restoring the Incas' liberty and about their brotherhood and friendship had obviously been lies. The *viracochas* had not come to restore Manco and Huascar's faction back to the throne—they had instead come to rule Tawantinsuyu. They had simply duped Manco into helping them do so.

Experiencing an epiphany that was no doubt magnified by the unforgettable image of Gonzalo Pizarro dragging away his tearful wife, Manco's situation had finally become as clear as the chilly waters that ran through the stone channels in the city, as clear as the view from the heights of the glistening, snow-covered mountains. At some point Manco must have also realized that if he chose to fight the Spaniards, he would essentially be resuming the war recently fought by Atahualpa's generals, Quisquis and Rumiñavi—at least one of whom he himself had helped to destroy. It was a grand awakening for the young emperor, and no doubt an unpleasant one. Along with his newfound perception, however, came a gradual decision that never again would he take the Spaniards at their word. The Christians' words were clearly designed only to distract and to deceive.

In early November of 1535, Manco Inca took his first concrete step in the direction of rebellion, calling for a secret meeting of his chiefs and governors from the four quarters of the empire—the Cuntisuyo, Antisuyu, Collasuyu, and Chinchasuyu. With his generals and the high priest, Villac Umu, in attendance, twenty-year-old Manco delivered a speech to what was essentially the cream of the Inca elite. It was a major turning point in the young emperor's career.

"I have sent for you in order to tell you in the presence of our relatives and attendants how I feel about what these foreigners intend to do with us,"

Manco said, no doubt wearing large golden ear spools, a soft vicuña tunic, and with the royal fringe hanging across his forehead,

> so that before more [Spaniards] join them we can arrange things in time so that in general everyone will benefit. Remember that the Incas, my fathers, who rest in the sky with the Sun, ruled from Quito to Chile, did so many things for those they received as vassals that it seemed they were children who had emerged from their own entrails. They neither robbed nor killed [anyone] except when it served justice, and they kept order and reason in the provinces that you [well] know. The rich did not succumb to pride and the poor were not destitute; [instead] they enjoyed tranquility and perpetual peace.
>
> Our sins made us unworthy of such lords and were the reason that these bearded ones entered our land, their own being so far away from here. They preach one thing and do another and [despite] all of the admonitions they give us, they do the opposite. They have no fear of [the Sun] God nor shame and, treating us like dogs, they can call us by no other names. Their greed has been so great that there is no temple or palace left that they have not pillaged. Furthermore, even if all the snow [on the mountains] were transformed into gold and silver, it would [still] not satisfy them.

Armed native guards peered from the doorways as Manco continued, the Inca leaders occasionally looking at one another, then back at the young emperor. None had presumably ever heard Manco speak with such intensity and clarity of purpose before. Manco continued:

> They keep the daughters of my father and other ladies, your sisters and relatives, as mistresses, desiring them bestially like this. They want to distribute, as they have [already] begun, all of the provinces, giving one to each of them so that as lords they can ravage them. They intend to keep us so subjugated and enslaved that we will have nothing to do other than to find them metals and to provide them with our women and livestock. Furthermore, they have taken for themselves the *yanaconas* and many *mitmaqkuna*. These [native] traitors didn't used to wear fine

clothing nor an opulent *llautu*.* Since they joined these foreigners, they act like Inca [lords]; it won't be long before they'll take my [royal] fringe. They do not honor me when they see me, and they speak boldly because they learn from the thieves they associate with.

The *yanaconas* of which Manco spoke were a separate class of natives who were lifelong servants of the Inca elite. *Yanaconas* tilled no land and in a sense were a rootless class, a kind of Inca proletariat; many were quick to attach themselves to the Spaniards, working for them as servants, auxiliary fighters, and spies. The *mitmaes* (or *mitmaqkuna*) that Manco was so bitter about were rebellious natives that the Incas had removed from their own provinces and had resettled in areas where they were surrounded by peasants loyal to the emperor. Not surprisingly, they, too, were quick to become collaborators of the Spaniards. Manco went on:

[What] justice and reason did they have to do these things and what [more] will these Christians do? Look, I ask you! Where did we meet them, what is it that we owe them or which one of them did we injure [in order] that with these horses and weapons of iron they have made such cruel war on us? They killed Atahualpa without cause. They did the same with his Captain General, Chalcuchima; they also killed Rumiñavi and Zope-Zopahua by burning them [to death] in Quito—so that their souls would burn with their bodies and couldn't go to enjoy [our Inca] heaven. It seems to me that it would be neither just nor honest that we put up with this. Rather, we should strive with the utmost determination to either die to the last man or [else] to kill our cruel enemies.

Instead of collaborators, they would become resistance leaders, Manco said. No longer would they obey the bearded foreigners from across the seas. Either they retook control of the realm their ancestors had built—or else they would all die fighting.

That same evening, no doubt realizing that the Spaniards were bound to

---

* The *llautu* was a headband created from many woven braids wrapped around the head. An opulent one would have been worn only by Inca nobles or royalty.

find out about the meeting, Manco slipped quietly out of the city. In the penetrating cold of the Andean night, Manco took with him some of his wives, personal servants, nobles, and chiefs. He was determined now to rebel, to wage war against the Spaniards, no matter what the cost. Behind him lay the soft yet increasingly unrewarding life of a puppet emperor; before him lay the far riskier life of an independent Inca lord, fighting to rid his empire of a brutal band of invaders. As Manco hurried out of the city, under the cover of night, he no doubt had already decided that the next time he entered Cuzco it would only be at the head of a conquering army, an army with which he was determined to exterminate the Spaniards.

"Manco Inca . . . sent messengers to every province, from Quito to Chile," wrote the Spanish chronicler Martín de Murúa, "commanding the Indians that on a certain day, within four months' time, everyone would rise up together against the Spaniards and that they would kill them all, pardoning no one, including the black [slaves] and the many Nicaraguan Indian [slaves] who had come to these parts in the company of the Spaniards . . . because in that way they would be able to achieve liberty from the oppression they were under."

Despite Manco's precautions, however, spies *had* been in attendance at the clandestine meeting and afterward had reported to Juan Pizarro the emperor's rebellious speech. The young lieutenant governor rushed off to search Manco's house and, not finding him, raised the general alarm. Soon, he and his brother Gonzalo and a group of Spanish horsemen saddled up and raced off into a night that was "wretched, dark, and fearful."

On the stone-flagged road that headed south toward the Collao—the region south of Cuzco and north of the vast, jewel-like expanse of Lake Titicaca—already miles outside the city, the Spaniards began to overtake some of Manco's entourage—dark figures standing motionless alongside the road and lit from overhead by the glittering *mayu,* or Milky Way. Although the Spaniards demanded that they tell them where their emperor was, the Inca nobles lied, indicating that Manco had gone in a certain direction when in reality he had gone in another. Racing ahead yet finding no sign of the emperor, Gonzalo soon captured another Inca noble and demanded that he divulge Manco's whereabouts. When the noble refused, Gonzalo "dismounted from his horse, and with help from the others they tied a rope to his genitals to torture him, which they indeed did so that the poor *orejón* screamed loudly, declaring that the Inca [emperor] was not traveling on that highway." The Spaniards quickly corrected their mistake and galloped off in the opposite direction.

Manco had until now been traveling on a royal litter, carried by native porters, but when he and his attendants eventually heard the unmistakable sound of horse hooves galloping in the distance, the young emperor realized that he had been betrayed.

> [Manco] feared the enemy and cursed a great deal those who had informed them that he had escaped. . . . With great fear he got out of it [the litter] and hid among some small rushes. The Spaniards [arrived and] loudly called out to him. [Soon] one of the horsemen approached the place where he was hiding and, believing that he had been discovered, he came out, saying that it was he and that they should not kill him. He told a great lie, which was that [Diego de] Almagro [had] sent him a messenger in order that he should follow him [to Chile].

The two Pizarro brothers, relieved to have found the emperor before he could organize an insurrection, didn't believe Manco's story for a minute. They quickly escorted him back to Cuzco and locked him in a room—just as they had imprisoned Atahualpa three years earlier. The same man who had stolen Manco's wife and who openly slept with her now supervised the removal of Manco's final outward vestiges of power. "Gonzalo Pizarro ordered [his men] to bring irons and a chain," recalled Titu Cusi, "with which they shackled my father as they pleased . . . and then all at once they threw a chain around his neck and irons on his feet."

With Manco now their prisoner, the Spanish inhabitants of Cuzco no longer made a pretense of showing the emperor any respect. Juan and Gonzalo Pizarro, in fact, were especially brutal, threatening Manco with even worse consequences if he didn't immediately reveal the location of more gold and silver. Manco was later quoted:

> I gave Juan Pizarro 1,300 gold bricks and 2,000 golden objects, bracelets, cups, and other smaller pieces. I also gave seven gold and silver pitchers. . . . They said to me: "Dog, give us gold. If not, you will be burned," and . . . they swore at me and said that they wanted me to

burn. . . . I am not lying [when I say that] I rebelled more on account of
the abuses they inflicted on me than because of the gold they took from
me, for they called me a dog and they struck my face, and they took my
wives and the lands that I used to farm.

Even with Manco's latest gifts, however, the Spaniards were still not satisfied; with little to restrain them, they became more and more abusive, both
to Manco and to the rest of the city's native inhabitants, whether aristocrats
or commoners. No longer did the Spaniards attempt to hide who was in
control, nor what kind of future lay in store for the native citizens of Tawantinsuyu. According to Titu Cusi, during his captivity Manco tried to reason
with the Spaniards, in an attempt to remind them of everything he had done
for them previously.

What have I done to you? Why do you treat me in this manner and tie
me up like a dog? Is this how you repay me for what I have done for you
and for helping you get established in my land? . . . And you are who
they say are *viracochas* sent by [the creator god] Tecsi Viracochan? It's
impossible that you're His sons since you treat those who have done you
so much good so badly. . . . Wasn't a great quantity of gold and silver
sent to you in Cajamarca? Didn't you take from my brother Atahualpa
all the treasure that my ancestors and I had there? Haven't I given you
everything in this town that you wanted? . . . Haven't I helped you and
your children and ordered my entire realm to pay you tribute? What
more do you want me to do? Judge for yourselves and see if I haven't the
right to complain. . . . I tell you that you are truly devils and not *viracochas* since for no reason at all you treat me this way.

The Spaniards, however, ignored Manco's complaints. Instead, they kept
him in chains, certain that if Manco were freed that he would immediately
try to stir the country into revolt against their rule. They told him:

"Look, [Manco] Inca, making excuses now is not going to help you . . .
We know without a doubt that you want to make this country rise up.
. . . They've told us that you want to kill us and for this reason we've im-

prisoned you. If it's not true that you want to rebel, then you can stop complaining and give us some gold and silver, which is what we came here to find. Give it to us and we'll set you free."

In the end, Manco no doubt realized, it didn't matter. No matter how much gold and silver he gave them, the Spaniards always wanted more. And whether he gave them treasure or not, or wives or not, or whatever they wanted or not—their treatment of him continued to worsen with each passing day. If Manco previously had had any illusions about his captors, they had by now completely disappeared. Manco undoubtedly saw the Spaniards for what they really were—false *viracochas,* foreigners whose only intent was to sack and plunder the empire that his very own family had created.

"They took and stole everything he [Manco] had, so that he had nothing," wrote the young Spanish priest Cristóbal de Molina. "And they kept him imprisoned this time for many days, guarding him day and night. They treated him very insultingly, urinating on him and sleeping with his wives. [And] he was very despondent over this."

While Manco was being humiliated and abused as a prisoner, the various Inca lords he had assembled for his clandestine meeting had nevertheless mostly escaped from Cuzco the night of his capture. Almost immediately, they had begun fanning out into the countryside to spread Manco's orders to begin preparing for a rebellion. In the Inca system of government, each provincial governor directed the local chiefs (*curacas*) below him, who in turn commanded households of commoners that numbered anywhere from a few hundred to ten thousand. As long as the Incas' chain of command continued to function—from emperor to governor to *curaca* to commoner—then Manco still wielded substantial control over the population. Like a massive piece of machinery that had not moved for years, the network of social gears that made up the Inca Empire now slowly began to creak into motion. And now, despite the confusion of recent events, many of the provinces began to respond to their emperor's simple yet weighty command: *Prepare yourselves—the time has come to wage war against the invaders.*

One of the more important men who had escaped the night of Manco's capture was General Tiso, Manco's uncle and the most formidable survivor of his grandfather Huayna Capac's generals. General Tiso had immediately traveled to the mountainous region of Jauja, lying some two hundred miles to the north, the same area where General Quisquis had fought Spanish troops before retreating to Ecuador. There, in the area of Tarma and Bombóm, Tiso began to organize a rebellion. Various chiefs who had attended Manco's meeting from the Collao, meanwhile, also returned to their provinces and similarly began fomenting revolt. The Inca leaders knew from experience by now that it was difficult to kill Spaniards who were well armed and who fought in large formations. It would be much easier to kill them if they attacked the Spaniards when they were isolated and alone and especially when the Spaniards traveled to their *encomiendas* in order to supervise the collection of their tributes.

Sometime in November or December of 1535, on isolated *encomiendas* in the southern Collao region, local natives overpowered and killed two *encomenderos*—Martín Domínguez and Pedro Martín de Moguer. The latter was an illiterate former sailor who had been present at the capture of Atahualpa in Cajamarca. He had also been one of the first three Europeans to enter Cuzco, having been sent there by Pizarro in order to help supervise the collection of Atahualpa's ransom. Moguer had later shared in the division of treasure of Cuzco and had been one of the eighty-eight conquistadors who had elected to stay on in that city, receiving an *encomienda* in the province of Collao. Three years after arriving in Peru and apparently unaware of the political sea change that was occurring in the countryside, the now wealthy *encomendero* had traveled out to inspect his holdings. There, natives more than likely cracked his head open with mace clubs tipped with bronze or stone. Moguer's New World journey—which included the undoubtedly fabulous voyage on a royal litter from Cajamarca to Cuzco—had come to an abrupt and bone-cracking end.

Following Moguer's and Domínguez's assassinations in the Collao, natives soon began killing other Spaniards in the same manner, waiting until the *encomenderos* were away from towns and cities and then ambushing them while they were traveling alone. In the region to the southwest of Cuzco known as the Cuntisuyu, an area studded with massive peaks of permanently frozen snow, local natives soon surprised and killed the conquistador Juan Becerril. The latter hadn't shared in the slaughter and spoils of Cajamarca but was still fabulously wealthy from his share of the gold and silver in Cuzco. Not long afterward, a provincial *curaca* informed the Spaniard Simón Suárez that the natives on his *encomienda* had collected his "tribute" and that Suárez should go there and pick it up from them. Suárez did—and was ambushed and killed.

In a relatively short period of time, in isolated regions from central to southern Peru, groups of rebellious natives continued implementing their strategy of waiting for or luring unsuspecting Spaniards away from the safety of the cities, then ambushing and killing them. Within a few months of Manco's first secret meeting, in fact, native rebels had killed more than thirty Spaniards—more than had been lost during the entire three years of the conquest.

In January 1536, while the two youngest Pizarro brothers were off trying to extinguish the now numerous sparks of native rebellion, thirty-four-year-old Hernando Pizarro arrived in Cuzco after an absence of more than two years. The second eldest of the Pizarro brothers, Hernando had accompanied the first consignment of the king's treasure from Cajamarca back to Spain. Tall, thickly bearded, heavily built, exceedingly selfish, and obsessed by power, Hernando had taken much of the family's share of Atahualpa's treasure and had gone on an investor's spree, purchasing royal treasury bonds, a variety of interest-bearing annuities, and a considerable amount of real estate in the form of land, buildings, and houses—especially in and around the Pizarros' hometown of Trujillo.

Visiting the royal court in Valladolid, Hernando had then conducted a deft negotiation with the king. As a result, King Charles had subsequently granted the Pizarros the right to transport two hundred tariff-free black slaves to work in Peru's mines, the right to import four white female slaves, the right to receive personal exemptions from taxation on goods imported into Peru, and the right for Francisco Pizarro to appoint three lifetime members to every town council in Peru, thus ensuring the Pizarro family's continued political control there. Hernando, not shy about advancing his own interests, also petitioned for and was ultimately anointed a Knight of the Order of Santiago. In addition, he attempted to prevent the king from granting a governorship to his brother's ex-partner, Diego de Almagro. In that, however, Hernando was unsuccessful.

The negotiations between Hernando and the king were a clear exercise in mutual reciprocity. The king wanted to guarantee himself a percentage of the profits he had been assured would continue streaming out of Peru. The Pizarros, meanwhile, craved social advancement and a guarantee that they would continue to control the exploitation of the vast empire they had just conquered. King Charles was only too happy to establish a legal framework that benefited both the Pizarros and the crown.

Once back in Peru, Hernando headed directly from the coast toward Cuzco. Hernando had never seen the Inca capital, since when he had left Peru two years earlier he had departed directly from Cajamarca to Spain; he had thus not participated in the subsequent military capture of the city. While having vastly improved his own situation and that of his elder brother in terms of overall political control, Hernando learned that he had missed out on the division of gold and silver in Cuzco, which had been every bit as profitable as that of Cajamarca. Hernando had also missed out on the distribution of *encomiendas* although, being the brother of the governor, he could be certain that he would eventually receive one. In the meantime, however, Hernando was determined to make up for his lost time in Peru, which basically meant amassing as much gold and silver as he could.

One of the first things Hernando did after arriving in Cuzco, therefore, was to visit Manco Inca, the ruler his brothers had imprisoned and had shackled in chains. Hernando immediately ordered that Manco be released, then apologized to the emperor for his mistreatment. Soon afterward, Hernando began inviting the young emperor to dine with him on a regular basis and doing everything possible to ingratiate himself with a ruler whom he was certain must know the location of more Inca treasure.

Although Hernando's friendly treatment of Manco was undoubtedly in large part motivated by his own personal greed, Hernando was nevertheless also complying with the king's wishes. King Charles had made it clear to him that Manco Inca was to be treated as a sovereign emperor, especially after the king had learned of Manco's recent help in pacifying the country. What the king desired more than anything else was that the conquest of Peru be quickly consolidated and that the country be stabilized; the efficient extraction of wealth from the new colony and its transmission to Spain could only occur under stable political conditions. If the new Inca emperor helped him to obtain that goal, then the king wanted that emperor to be amply rewarded. The king's orders, of course, were in direct contrast to the treatment Manco had already received at the hands of the younger Pizarro brothers and the rest of the Spaniards in Cuzco.

Not long after Hernando's arrival, Juan and Gonzalo arrived back in the city and greeted their elder brother effusively. They then reported to him the various disturbing signs of uprisings that had been cropping up in the countryside, the number of Spaniards who had been killed, and their efforts to punish those responsible. When they learned that Hernando had freed Manco Inca, however, they immediately became upset. Why had Hernando released a native emperor who had preached rebellion? An emperor who might any day escape from the city and lead a revolt?

Hernando brushed off his brothers' concerns. Manco had assured him that he would carry out no insurrection, Hernando explained; the Inca emperor had also sworn his loyalty and friendship to the Pizarros and had promised him even more silver and gold. Hernando saw no reason to distrust him.

The reality, of course, was otherwise. Ever since Hernando had set him free, Manco had been secretly receiving information about the progress that had been made for the eventual rebellion. While sporadic uprisings had occurred in the meantime, Manco still planned to raise a vast army and to coordinate it with a massive native rebellion. Even while Manco had been imprisoned, in fact, his high priest, Villac Umu, had been carrying out the mobilization of Inca troops in the provinces. Now that Manco was free, he and Villac Umu continued planning the rebellion while somehow keeping the entire mobilization process hidden from the eyes of the Spaniards. With native spies bringing Manco the news that Francisco Pizarro was preoccupied with supervising the construction of a new city on the coast, and with the knowledge that Diego de Almagro and his troops were far away to the south, Manco was now simply waiting for the cessation of the Andean rainy season before beginning a full-scale insurrection.

In the Inca language *runasimi*, February was known as *hatun pucuy*, or the "great ripening," as in this month the corn normally begins to ripen. March was known as *paca pucuy*, or "earth ripening," the time in which to sow new corn seed, and April was known as *ayrihua*—the month in which fifteen llamas were always sacrificed in honor of the first llama to appear on earth. As *hatun pucuy* turned to *paca pucuy* and *paca pucuy* turned to *ayrihua,* the sun crept daily northward and slowly the Andean rains began to end. Carefully keeping track of the sun deity's progress, Manco Inca often dined with Hernando Pizarro, all the while feigning his gratitude and friendship. By early April, however, even as the two men ate, masses of native warriors had begun filtering through mountain passes from all directions, heading toward the Inca capital. As Manco and Hernando toasted each other, native soldiers in high altiplano valleys stealthily gathered clubs, slings, dart throwers, shields, and even bows and arrows from the numerous state storehouses placed strategically throughout the empire. At times, whole valleys seemed to move as if their floors were covered with a vast carpet of ants, so numerous were the natives who were now answering the call of their Inca lord.

As the warriors drew nearer to the capital, the time had finally come for Manco to escape. Word would soon get out that native armies were approaching. It was thus time for Manco to take full and open control of the growing insurgency. Having already given Hernando Pizarro hidden caches of gold and silver, Manco now asked Hernando for a favor in return: could he and Villac Umu travel to the nearby Yucay Valley, about fifteen miles to the north? He and his high priest wanted to perform some important religious ceremonies there for his father, Huayna Capac, Manco explained, whose mummy was located in the nearby hills. If Hernando would allow him to go, then he promised that he would bring him back a life-sized gold and silver statue that belonged to his father. Hernando—ever eager to acquire more treasure—told Manco that, by all means, the two of them could go.

On April 18, 1536, the twenty-year-old lord of the Inca Empire and his high priest left Cuzco and headed for the Yucay Valley, carried aloft on royal litters. Not long after they had departed, some of the *yanaconas*—the Incas' landless proletariat—along with Juan and Gonzalo Pizarro and even some of Manco's own estranged kin, formed a delegation that visited Hernando Pizarro in his palace. Hernando had made a huge mistake, they informed him. The lieutenant governor must immediately send a force to recapture the Inca emperor. If not, then Manco Inca would return all right—but at the head of a large and hostile army. Hernando—the only Pizarro brother with formal military training, who had fought as a captain with his father in the Spanish-French wars of Navarre—dismissed their concerns. Manco would return, Hernando said confidently, just as Manco had promised he would. Scanning the group's anxious faces and shaking his head in derision, Hernando told them that they were all simply afraid of their own shadows. They should go home and stop worrying—Manco Inca would keep his word.

Two days later, a Spaniard arrived in Cuzco who had been surprised to meet Manco and Villac Umu heading into the hills above the Calca Valley and traveling in the direction of Lares, located some fifteen leagues, or fifty miles, from Cuzco. When the Spaniard had asked the emperor where they were going, Manco had replied that they were off to retrieve some gold. To Hernando, the information made perfect sense: Manco had promised that he would bring back a life-sized statue made of silver and gold. Once again, Hernando told his two brothers and the rest of Cuzco's citizenry to stop worrying. When more days went by with still no sign of the departed emperor, however, fears in the city continued to escalate; knots of worried Spaniards now gathered in the streets, often looking over their shoulder in the direction of the hills.

Finally, on the eve of Easter Sunday, news arrived that Manco Inca had been seen with a large group of native chiefs in the rugged, mountainous region of Lares. The Inca emperor had apparently convened a secret assembly of native chiefs and military leaders from all parts of the empire, the Spaniards were told. Various eyewitnesses, meanwhile, who had been traveling elsewhere in Peru, soon arrived and reported the disturbing sightings of vast numbers of armed warriors, moving from the provinces toward the capital. Manco Inca, it was now obvious to everyone—and that included a chastened Hernando Pizarro—had clearly rebelled. Recounted Pizarro's cousin Pedro:

> Manco Inca took refuge in the Andes, which is a land of enormous, rugged mountains with very bad passes and where it's impossible for horses to enter. And from there he sent many high-ranking captains all over the realm, in order to gather up all the natives who could fight and who could go with them to lay siege to Cuzco and to kill all of us Spaniards who were there.

After a little more than two years on the puppet throne, Manco Inca—son of the great Huayna Capac and great-great-grandson of the founder of the Inca Empire, Pachacuti—had formally declared war against the Spaniards. He was now free to devote himself, openly and without further subterfuge, to the extermination of the bearded foreigners who had arrived so brazenly from across the sea.

9 ❖ THE GREAT REBELLION

"The Spaniards in Peru should be made to refrain from arrogance and brutality towards the Indians. Just imagine that our people were to arrive in Spain and start confiscating property, sleeping with the women and girls, chastising the men and treating everybody like pigs! What would the Spaniards do then? Even if they tried to endure their lot with resignation, they would still be liable to be arrested, tied to a pillar and flogged. And if they rebelled and attempted to kill their persecutors, they would certainly go to their death on the gallows."

FELIPE HUAMÁN POMA DE AYALA, *LETTER TO A KING,* C.1616

"So numerous were the [rebel] troops who came here that they covered the fields, and by day it looked like they had spread a black cloth out over the ground for half a league around this city of Cuzco. At night there were so many campfires that it looked like nothing other than a cloudless sky full of stars."

PEDRO PIZARRO, *RELACIÓN,* 1571

"No enterprise is more likely to succeed than one concealed from the enemy until it is ripe for execution."

NICCOLÒ MACHIAVELLI, *THE ART OF WAR,* 1521

WHEN MANCO INCA AND VILLAC UMU, RIDING ON THEIR royal litters, arrived in the Inca town of Lares, Manco was gratified to find chiefs and nobles from across Tawantinsuyu already assembled, having responded to his call for the secret meeting. Each of the four quarters of the

Native warriors fighting Spaniards on horseback.

empire was represented and most in attendance wore large earplugs of gold or silver, as nearly all, save the servants, were nobles of the highest rank. A few individuals wore specially woven alpaca mantles filigreed with gold or silver—the equivalent of prestigious medals received from past emperors for their services. In this small town some thirty miles from Cuzco were now gathered much of the elite that ruled Peru, the high-status individuals who formed part of the governing apparatus the Incas had used to control some ten million commoners.

Those assembled were well aware, however, that representatives from certain areas of the empire—such as the Chachapoyas and the Cañari from the far northern provinces and many of the ethnic groups from the coast— were entirely missing; these had either sided with the Spaniards and were no longer part of the Inca federation, or else had decided to remain neutral and were unwilling to offer help. Nor were any representatives present from any of the native groups in the region that is now Ecuador, given the recent history of the Inca civil war and of the conquest there. For all practical purposes, the far northern region had been amputated from the Inca body politic. If the remaining empire were akin to a large, loosely stitched patchwork quilt of various ethnicities—with many patches now entirely missing—it was now Manco's job to use his power and prestige to stitch that quilt back together again as best he could. Manco then intended to utilize every ethnic group under his command to exterminate the Spaniards; he could visit punishment upon those ethnic groups that had sided with the Spaniards later.

As the various nobles chatted with one another and milled about, waited upon by attentive servants, Manco readied himself to inform them about his new strategy—a strategy that would reverse the commands he had been issuing for the last two years. Of great importance to Manco was the presence of the empire's finest remaining military leaders: Generals Tiso and Quizo Yupanqui, along with several high-ranking captains: his relative, Illa Tupac, and Puyu Vilca. Along with the high priest, Villac Umu, who shared with Manco the dual function of supreme military commander, the entire military staff of the Inca Empire was gathered before him. All would play key roles in the major campaigns to come.

Before the assembled crowd, and in full view of the sacred, white peaks of Canchacanchajasa and Huamanchoque, Manco rose from his low stool, or royal *duho*, to speak. Conversations died as the lean, bronze-colored faces of those assembled turned toward their young emperor and listened, their golden ear spools reflecting the brilliance of the sun god, Inti. For the first time since he had become emperor, Manco was now free to issue orders without the presence or control of the Spaniards. At twenty years of age, Manco had finally claimed his full birthright as the *Sapa Inca*—the "unique Inca," or divine king. Looking around at the crowd, Manco spoke:

> My beloved sons and brothers, I never thought that it would ever be necessary to do what I am now thinking of doing, because I always thought and felt certain that the bearded people, who you call *viracochas,* which is how I used to call them because I thought they had come from [the creator god] Viracocha, would not . . . give me grief in all things. . . . But now . . . I see . . . they are scheming once again to capture and kill me. . . . And you have also seen how poorly they have treated me and how ungratefully they have thanked me for what I have done for them, insulting me a thousand times over and then seizing me and tying me up by my feet and neck like a dog, and especially after they had given me their word that we had formed a partnership together based upon love and friendship. . . .
>
> I can't help but remind you of how many times you have asked me to do that which I am now intending to do, saying that I should rise up against them and asking me why I had allowed them in my land. I didn't think that what is happening now could ever have occurred. [Yet] that's what's happened—and because all they want is to persist in angering and tormenting me, I will be forced to do the same with them. . . . Since you have always shown me so much love and have endeavored to make me happy, let's all join together and unite as one and send our messengers throughout the land so that in twenty days' time everyone will arrive in this town, without the bearded ones knowing anything about it. I will send my Captain, Quizo Yupanqui, to Lima, so that the day we attack the Spaniards here he and his men will attack those [Francisco Pizarro and his men] who are there. And together, with [General Quizo] there and ourselves here, we will finish them off to the last man and thus we will end this nightmare that has been hanging over us.

Manco finished: "I am determined to leave no Christian alive in all this land . . . thus I first want to surround Cuzco. Those of you who want to serve me will have to stake their lives on this [effort]. Drink from these vases only [those of you who will join me] under this condition."

Immediately after Manco's speech, servants carried around two large golden jars of *chicha*. In full view of the sacred *apu* spirits associated with the nearby mountain peaks, each leader now stepped up, one by one, then drank from one of the jars before making an oath, reaffirming his allegiance to the Inca emperor and vowing to exterminate every bearded foreigner in the land. There were no abstentions. Those who had not already done so immediately sent *chaski* runners to their distant provinces, the latter carrying knotted *quipu* cords that bore a message to their sub-chiefs to begin mobilizing all available warriors. Manco Inca, the messages proclaimed, had ordered the extermination of the false *viracochas*. It was time now to prepare for a full-scale war.

In Cuzco, meanwhile, Hernando Pizarro had also called for a meeting. Hernando now finally admitted that Manco Inca had deceived him and was most likely organizing a rebellion. Reports had been coming in, Hernando told the assembled Spaniards, of large movements of native troops in the Yucay Valley, only fifteen miles to the north. The renegade emperor was said now to be headquartered in the town of Calca, overseeing the gathering of native forces. Obviously, Hernando said, he had made an error in judgment in allowing Manco and Villac Umu to leave. Yet there was no time to waste in recriminations, for their very lives were in danger. The most important thing they needed to do was to try to disperse the gathering forces and, if possible, to recapture the emperor. If Manco could be recaptured, Hernando said, then they could force him to end the rebellion. If Manco were not recaptured, however, then they could expect a large native army to attack the city at any time.

Wanting to find out if the reports of nearby troop movements were accurate, Hernando decided to send seventy cavalrymen, led by his twenty-five-year-old brother, Juan, to ride to the town of Calca in the Yucay Valley. Juan's orders were to scout the area, to search for and to try to recapture Manco Inca, and to disrupt any native forces they happened to find. As Juan's cavalrymen hurried out into the streets, arming themselves with steel swords, daggers, and twelve-foot lances, they soon began saddling up their horses, no doubt bitterly swearing that the Inca rebels were so many "dogs" and "traitors." Church bells of bronze began to clang incessantly in the newly finished church that the Spaniards had hastily erected on top of the dark, immaculately cut gray stones of the Qoricancha, the Incas' temple of the sun. The air was clear, sharp, and thin, and soon Juan Pizarro and the rest of the cavalry were off, riding their horses out of the city along the road that led northward toward the Yucay Valley, the hooves of their horses clattering on the stone paving as the rest of the worried Spanish citizens stood about, watching their finest forces ride off and thus leaving them unprotected.

Juan and his men quickly made their way up out of the city onto the lip of Cuzco's valley, then past the giant stone fortress of Saqsaywaman, with its gray cyclopean walls and three towers. It brooded over the city like some strange medieval castle. The men then turned and headed over the green hills that separated the valley of Cuzco from that of the adjacent Yucay Valley. After a ride of a dozen miles, they finally came to the edge of the plateau and looked out over the blue-green Yucay (Vilcanota) River, wending its way in the valley below. The Spaniards reined in their horses, looking down upon a scene they had often gazed at before, but now scarcely believing their eyes. The valley floor that was normally green had somehow turned a beige color—the color of Inca tunics. Masses of native soldiers had appeared seemingly from nowhere, gathering in the valley until they were so numerous that it looked like masses of tiny toy soldiers had been poured out upon the ground. If there had been any question in the Spaniards' minds that Manco Inca had indeed rebelled, the proof now lay directly before their eyes. Here, in this broad, sunlit valley, the rebellion that for the last few months had been undergoing sporadic outbursts in Peru had now concentrated itself into one massive Inca army. Even worse for the Spaniards was the fact that the army being assembled was presently only a four-hour march from Cuzco.

Despite his initial shock, Juan Pizarro soon led his cavalry boldly down into the valley, the snow-covered peaks of the Paucartambo range shining clearly in the distance, then headed toward the town of Calca, which lay on the other side of the Yucay River. It was here, native informants had told him, that Manco Inca was directing the rebellion. Manco had taken careful precautions, however; thus, even before the Spaniards had arrived, native troops had destroyed all bridges over the river. Now hordes of Manco's warriors stood yelling and taunting the Spaniards from the opposite bank, waving their axes and clubs and daring them to cross. With little choice other than to proceed, the Spaniards splashed their horses into the river and began to swim against the frigid, snow-and-glacier-fed current. Native warriors soon began swinging their woolen *warak'as,* or slings, and, as the horses struggled across, soon a hail of stone missiles either shot plumes of water into the air or else made metallic clanging sounds as they slammed into the Spaniards' armor.

Emerging on the opposite side, the Spaniards immediately spurred their mounts toward the sling throwers, who now began running, the Spaniards spearing them with their lances or slicing at them with their swords. The masses of native soldiers, meanwhile—newly conscripted peasants who had only just arrived—quickly retreated up the hillsides, having no doubt been instructed by their commanders that the steep terrain would prevent attacks by the Spaniards. After a series of charges and feints, Juan then suddenly broke off the attack and galloped with his men toward Calca, where they immediately began a door-to-door search for Manco Inca. Frightened native women and children stood outside their homes as the Spaniards searched the dark interiors, the latter no doubt cursing and swearing. Manco, however, had already escaped. Yet in his haste, the young emperor had left behind a hoard of gold and silver, many of his woman servants, or *aqllacuna,* and much of the native army's supplies.

For the next three days, the Spaniards remained in Calca, debating what to do, while the Inca army maintained its position on the hillsides, taunting the Spaniards continuously with insults and skirmishing with the Spanish sentries at night. Given the warriors' great numbers, the Spaniards were surprised that the natives didn't attack. The Inca commanders seemed strangely content to allow the Spaniards to remain virtually unmolested in Calca. Four days after their arrival, however, the Spaniards soon learned why no attack had occurred. A lone Spanish rider from Cuzco arrived in a great hurry and bearing a message from Hernando: Juan's forces were to return to Cuzco at once with all speed. Massive numbers of native troops had suddenly appeared on the hillsides surrounding the capital. If Juan and his cavalry didn't return at once, Hernando and his remaining Spaniards would be unable to hold the city.

Juan lost no time gathering up his men and galloping out of town. Some of the Spaniards carried with them various objects of gold or silver that they had pilfered; most, however, were forced to abandon what they had found. Riding out of the valley and up onto the plateau, the Spaniards noticed that the masses of natives were becoming even denser. Native sling throwers harassed them so much, in fact, that it was all they could do to fight their way back toward the city. As the Spaniards galloped past the fortress of Saqsaywaman and caught their first glimpse of the round, bowl-like valley of Cuzco again, many of them no doubt suddenly swore out loud. There, on the hills around the city, countless native troops had appeared, where before there had been none. So numerous were the natives, in fact, that there were scarcely any unencumbered paths back down into the capital.

The returning conquistadors now made a dash down into the city, rejoining the relieved Spanish citizens they had left behind along with a mere ten horses. Since Spaniards on foot were much less effective at inflicting damage on natives than were cavalrymen, Hernando and the 126 men who had remained in the capital would probably have been overwhelmed if Manco's troops had attacked. Even now, with a total cavalry force of eighty-six horsemen, however, the odds against them were still enormous. Pedro Pizarro, who had returned with Juan from Calca, recalled:

> When we returned we found many squadrons of warriors continuously arriving and camping on the steepest places around Cuzco to await the arrival of all [their men]. After they arrived, they camped on the plains as well as on the hills. So numerous were the [rebel] troops that came here that they covered the fields, and by day it looked like they had spread a black cloth out over the ground for half a league around this city of Cuzco. At night there were so many [rebel] campfires that it looked like nothing other than a cloudless sky full of stars.

In the days that followed, the Spaniards watched with growing anxiety as more and more native troops continued to gather, filling in the gaps on the hills around them. Clearly, the Spaniards had been caught off guard by the immense size and scope of the rebellion. Indeed, neither the Spaniards nor their native spies had even been aware that a massive rebellion had been brewing. That Manco Inca wielded enormous and unsuspected powers was evident by the vast numbers of troops he had assembled—and also by the fact that he had been able to keep the entire mobilization secret.

A headcount revealed that the Spanish force currently trapped in Cuzco was comprised of 196 Spaniards. According to Pedro Pizarro, of the 110 Spanish foot soldiers the "greater part [of the infantry] was thin and scrawny men." The Spaniards also counted upon a handful of African and *morisca* slaves, a number of native concubines, some five hundred native allies from the Chachapoya and Cañari tribes, and a certain number of *yanaconas,* who often acted as the Spaniards' spies but whose loyalty they could never be sure of. Amazingly, even despite the Spaniards' precarious position, some of Manco's family nevertheless decided to join them—most notably Manco's cousin Pascac, who in Manco's eyes now officially became a traitor.

On the hillsides around the city and pitted against the Spanish force were what appeared to be hundreds of thousands of Inca troops—too many to count, really. Even worse, the Spaniards had no idea how many more native troops were on their way. Trapped, isolated, and cut off from the outside world, nearly two hundred Spaniards—almost half of whom ranked as some of the wealthiest men in the New World—were now entirely on their own.

As Manco Inca continued to build his forces, Hernando led several cavalry sorties into the hills surrounding the city, in order to probe the strength of Manco's forces. Each time, however, the Spaniards were met by a virtual blizzard of stones, flung from slings by an enemy that showed increasing confidence and whose sheer numbers severely hampered the cavalry's movements. During one of their sorties, Hernando and a group of eight horsemen suddenly found themselves cut off and surrounded, pressed in on all sides by legions of emboldened warriors. As Hernando and the others tried to force a breach in the enemy's ranks, one of the men, Francisco Mejía, suddenly found himself surrounded by a sea of clubs and grasping hands. Swinging his sword in desperation, Mejía struggled to remain in his saddle, but "[they] pulled him off his horse with their hands," wrote one of the survivors, "and a stone's throw away from the Spaniards they cut off his head and also the head of his horse, which was white and very beautiful." Despite the natives now holding Mejía's head aloft, the rest of the Spaniards somehow managed to force an opening in the warriors' ranks and galloped back down to the city.

If Hernando Pizarro and his men were going to survive, they would have to rely upon their cavalry and also upon their roughly five hundred native allies, who, like the Spaniards, were now also trapped in the siege. To increase their mobility and to allow different forces to fend off attacks from different directions, Hernando decided to divide the cavalry into three groups. He appointed three captains to lead them: Gabriel de Rojas—a skillful horseman who had only recently arrived in Peru; Hernán Ponce de León—Hernando de Soto's partner, who had ridden with Soto in the vanguard down from Cajamarca; and Gonzalo Pizarro, who had stolen Manco's wife. Hernando himself, as lieutenant governor of the city, remained in overall charge, while designating his brother Juan as his second-in-command.

The military structure of the Inca forces arrayed against them was more complex than that of the Spaniards, mainly due to the greater number of troops. At the top of the Inca military pyramid stood Manco Inca, head of state, son of the sun god, and overall military commander. Alongside him stood Villac Umu, high priest and co-commander of the empire's military forces. In charge of the actual siege armies around Cuzco was General Inquill, who was aided by his lieutenant, Paucar Huaman. Various other commanders led their individual legions, each of which was ordered to occupy a specific location around Cuzco in order to strengthen what had now become a classic military encirclement. Recalled Titu Cusi:

> Coriatao, Cuillas, Taipi and many other [commanders] entered the city from the [northern] Carmenca side, and sealed one side with their men. Huaman-Quilcana and Curi-Huallpa and many others entered on the [western] Condesuyo [Cuntisuyu] side from the direction of Cachicachi . . . and closed a great gap of over half a league [two miles]. All were excellently equipped [and] in full battle array. Llicllic and many other commanders entered on the [southern] Collasuyo [Collasuyu] side with a great number of men, the largest group that took part in the siege. Anta-Aclla, Ronpa Yupanqui and many others entered on the [eastern] Antisuyo side to complete the encirclement of the Spaniards.

As overall military strategist, Manco Inca continued to remain in Calca, the same town that Juan Pizarro had recently seized and then been forced to abandon. From Calca, Manco could send and receive messages and could also continue to coordinate what was now a national mobilization. As native legions continued to arrive on the outskirts of Cuzco, however, another Inca general—Quizo Yupanqui—was currently leading a second army toward Lima. Manco's orders to Quizo were to prevent Francisco Pizarro from sending relief forces to Cuzco by pinning down Pizarro and his troops in Lima. In addition, Manco had sent messages by runners throughout the empire ordering that any Spaniards caught traveling outside the cities were to be exterminated and their weapons seized.

As Manco busied himself with coordinating the logistics of war, Villac Umu urged the young emperor to attack Cuzco immediately and not to wait for any more native troops to arrive. Manco, however, did not want to attack until every last possible contingent had been assembled into place. Manco had, after all, fought with Spanish troops against General Quisquis's army; thus he was well aware of the devastating effect the Spaniards' weaponry and especially their cavalry had. Following the classic Inca military principle of attacking one's enemies whenever possible with overwhelming force, Manco was determined to make his assault on the capital so overwhelming that neither the Spaniards' horses nor their obviously superior weapons would be able to save them. Once the Spanish forces in Cuzco had been wiped out, Manco would be in control of central Peru. He could then attack and smash Pizarro's forces in Lima, an objective that would break the backbone of the Spanish military occupation of Peru.

While the Spaniards' numbers remained fixed, as the weeks continued Manco gradually assembled a force of between 100,000 and 200,000 warriors—a stupendous feat of logistical organization. Soldiers in the Inca Empire were, after all, only temporary warriors—they were normally farmers or herders who were conscripted for martial duties as needed. For the most part, the warriors were married men between the ages of twenty-five and fifty and were conscripted from their native provinces in units of ten, one hundred, and one thousand. Younger unmarried men between the ages of eighteen and twenty-five served not as warriors but as messengers or porters. Called *awka kamayuq,* warriors from each province spoke their local language and were led by their own chiefs. The chiefs in turn operated under the command of the Inca military commanders. While *runasimi* was the lingua franca of the native commanders, the warriors from different regions could no more speak with one another than could an alliance of French, German, and Polish divisions. Thus the vast assemblage around Cuzco, like the Inca Empire itself, was a heterogeneous and polyglot affair.

Besides their standard cotton or alpaca tunics, native soldiers often wore helmets made of plaited cane or wood and wore thickly quilted cotton armor. Inca storehouses throughout the empire had remained well stocked with weaponry, uniforms, and the other accoutrements of war, despite the chaos of recent years. Pedro Pizarro recalled that many of the storehouses within the vast fortress of Saqsaywaman, overlooking Cuzco, for example, had been filled to the ceiling with native war materials when he had first arrived:

> All these rooms were occupied by and filled with arms, lances, arrows, darts, clubs, bucklers [small shields], and large oblong shields under which a hundred Indians could go, as though under a mantle, in order to capture forts. There were many morión [helmets] of certain canes very well woven together and so strong that no stone nor blow could penetrate them and harm the head which wore the morión.

Native artisans had created the vast supply of weapons as part of their yearly labor tax. And although most uniforms were standardized, soldiers from the different provinces wore additional finery in order for their commanders to be able to distinguish between the different agglomerations of troops. Wrote Father Bernabé Cobo:

> Over this defensive gear they would usually wear their most attractive and rich adornments and jewels; this included wearing fine plumes of many colors on their heads and large gold and silver plates on their chests and backs; however, the plates worn by the poorer soldiers were copper.

Depending on their specific battle formation, each native group carried weapons appropriate to their overall military function. Formations of jungle archers, sling throwers, or javelin hurlers, for example—each capable of striking the enemy from a distance—normally marched in front of the phalanxes of club-and-axe-wielding Inca shock troops, who marched behind.

Their principal weapon . . . [is] a sling . . . with which they can hurl a
big stone that will kill a horse and sometimes even its rider. . . . In truth,
its effect is almost equal to that of an harquebus. I have seen a stone
hurled from a sling break an old sword in two pieces, which was held in
a man's hand some thirty yards away.

As native troops from around the empire continued to arrive and reinforce the Incas' siege around the city, the individual formations on the hillsides grew to such an extent that soon the troops were camping right up
against the houses on the city's outskirts. Day and night, the warriors now
kept up a deafening roar, shouting taunts and insults in their various languages. The sound barrage was the equivalent of a modern psyops campaign
and had the same intended purpose: to keep the Spaniards off balance, unnerved, and afraid. "There was so much shouting and din of voices that all of
us were astonished," Pedro Pizarro said. In addition, the natives were continually mocking them, lifting their tunics up and "baring their legs at them
to show how much they despised them," as Titu Cusi described it. Baring
the leg was a grave Inca insult. Far from believing the Spaniards to be gods
from across the seas, the native warriors now clearly showed the Spaniards
their utter disdain and contempt.

Manco Inca, in the meantime—receiving constant updates of the situation at his headquarters in Calca—was determined not to overlook any aspect of the pending military assault. The young emperor was well aware that
the religious aspects of the impending struggle were as important to victory
as were the simply mechanical preparations of troops, weapons, food, and
supplies. Without the favor of their gods, the disproportionate number of
their troops versus those of their enemy really didn't matter. Manco thus
presided over a variety of feasts, fasts, and sacrifices—all in an effort to ensure divine intervention on their behalf.

It is likely that Manco even visited the famed oracle, named Apurímac
("great speaker"), located not far from Cuzco on the banks of the Apurímac
River. Inside the temple stood a wooden figure wearing a golden belt and
with golden breasts, dressed in finely woven woman's clothes and splattered
with the blood of numerous offerings. A temple priestess named Sarpay
served as both the guardian and the idol's interpreter. It was she who would
have instructed Manco in the kinds of sacrifices he had to make. Presumably,

the oracle of Apurímac informed the young emperor that the omens for the pending battle were good.

As the time of the final assault drew near, Manco now presided over the solemn Itu ceremony. For two days, the emperor and his troops fasted and refrained from all sex; priests, meanwhile, cut the throats of sacrificial llamas while ritual processions of boys—elegantly dressed in red tunics of delicate *qompi* cloth and wearing feathered crowns—paraded about. As priests scattered sacred coca leaves on the ground, the fasting period concluded with an enormous feast and with the consumption of vast quantities of *chicha*.

Finally, on what the Spaniards called Saturday, May 6, 1536, during the Catholic feast day of St. John-ante-Portam-Latinam, and with hundreds of thousands of native warriors shouting loudly, Manco Inca launched his all-out attack. As natives blew on single-note conch shells and clay trumpets, legions of javelin hurlers, sling throwers, and jungle archers suddenly began to unleash a violent barrage of stones, javelins, and arrows upon the city below. A giant "whoosh" sounded through the air and then turned into a crackling noise as the first missiles began to slam onto the stone flagging and walls. Those Spaniards caught outside on the streets ran for cover. Legions of native warriors, or shock troops, meanwhile, began to move slowly in unison down the hillsides, penetrating into the city and heading toward the capital's central square.

Manco's native infantry marched in close formation, carrying an assortment of three-foot-long clubs, battle-axes, and shields and all the while keeping up a deafening roar. Native military officers traveled with them, carried aloft in resplendent litters as sunlight glinted off the warriors' chest and back plates of copper, silver, or gold. Most of the natives wore wicker helmets, many of which were adorned with exotic plumes of scarlet, yellow, green, and cobalt blue bird feathers. Similar native legions had carved out and conquered the Incas' 2,500-mile-long empire. Now their descendants—having temporarily lost control of the very valley from which the Inca juggernaut had exploded—marched with the obvious determination of crushing the invaders who had so disturbed the equilibrium of their land. Manco and his generals' strategy was a simple one: first, they would force the Spaniards toward the center of the city, shrinking the area that the Spaniards currently occupied; then they would overwhelm and crush them with their vastly superior forces.

Francisco Pizarro (1478–1541). Peru was most likely his last chance to conquer an empire. (LIBRARY OF CONGRESS)

The execution of the Inca Emperor Atahualpa. (LIBRARY OF CONGRESS)

Spaniards with horses and harquebuses fighting native warriors in the jungle region of Antisuyu.
(LIBRARY OF CONGRESS)

Francisco Pizarro's assassination, at the age of sixty-three, in Lima.
(LIBRARY OF CONGRESS)

Street scene in Cuzco, Peru, in 1906, three years before Hiram Bingham's first visit. Note the massive stone blocks that date back to the Inca era. (LIBRARY OF CONGRESS)

Thirty-six-year-old Hiram Bingham during his second expedition to Machu Picchu, 1912. (NATIONAL GEOGRAPHIC, 1913)

View of the ruins of Machu Picchu. (PHOTO BY KIM MACQUARRIE)

The explorer Gene Savoy in front of the Chachapoyan ruins of Gran Pajatén, northern Peru, in 1965. (ANDEAN EXPLORERS FOUNDATION AND OCEAN SAILING CLUB)

Architect Vincent Lee's drawing of the Augustinian friar Diego Ortiz's mission at Guarancalla, based on the ruins Lee discovered at the site. According the Spanish chronicles, friar Ortiz said his last mass here before being martyred. The round structures behind the church were possibly the dwellings of Amazonian Indians. (VINCENT LEE)

SITE J. - Structure I.a.

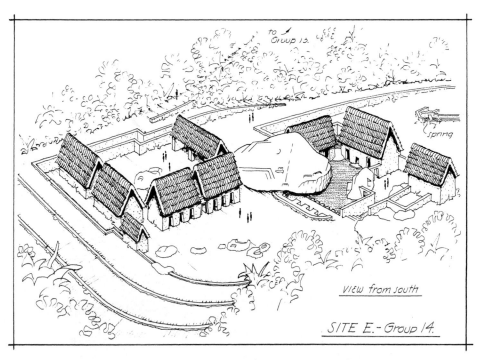

to Group 13.

spring

VIEW from south

SITE E. - Group 14.

Lee's drawing of the Inca sun temple at Chuquipalta, also known as Ñusta Ispanan. The Spanish friars Diego Ortiz and Marcos García burned and destroyed the temple complex in 1570. (VINCENT LEE)

The explorer/architect Vincent Lee, seen here before the remote ruins of Puncuyoc, has spent more than twenty years exploring and mapping the Inca ruins of Vilcabamba. Lee believes that somewhere in the region lies a "fifth Inca city," waiting to be found. (NANCY LEE)

An Inca doorway and stone walls at Vilcabamba el Viejo, Manco Inca's ancient capital.
(PHOTO BY PAUL GOLDRICK)

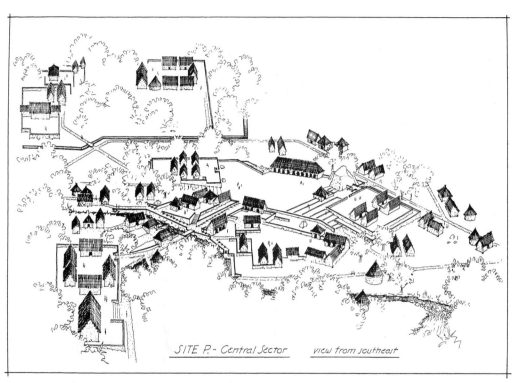

SITE P. - Central Sector   view from southeast

Lee's drawing of the central section of Vilcabamba. The round structures may have been the dwellings of the Incas' jungle allies—various tribes of Antisuyu Indians. (VINCENT LEE)

View of the Vilcabamba Valley. (PHOTO BY PAUL GOLDRICK)

The location of Manco Inca's rebel capital of Vilcabamba (more recently known as Espíritu Pampa). An entire Inca city remained hidden in the rain forest here for more than three hundred years. (PHOTO BY PAUL GOLDRICK)

With natives from every direction now entering the city, the conquistadors suddenly found themselves caught in the center of a rapidly tightening noose. Every one of them realized that if they couldn't find a way to stop Manco's onslaught, they would soon be squashed together and bludgeoned to death with clubs. The barrage of arrows and missiles had already forced the Spaniards into hiding. On the hillside just above the city, meanwhile, native troops seized and occupied the fortress of Saqsaywaman, along with its supply rooms of weapons. From here, Villac Umu and many of his commanders would oversee the battle and would send messages to Manco Inca in Calca, some two hours away by *chaski* runner. Other Inca forces soon captured the strategic enclosure of Cora Cora, which abutted the northern corner of the city's main square. Recalled Pedro Pizarro:

This [city of] Cuzco adjoins a hill on the side where the fortress [of Saqsaywaman] is, and on this side the Indians came down to some houses near the plaza that belonged to Gonzalo Pizarro and to his brother, Juan Pizarro, and from here they did us much harm, for with slings they hurled stones onto the plaza without our being able to prevent it. . . . This place . . . is steep and is between a narrow lane that the Indians had seized and thus it was not possible to go up it without all those who entered it being killed. . . . There was [also] incredible noise on account of the loud cries and howling that they made and the [conch shell] horns and gourds that they sounded, so that it seemed as if the very earth trembled.

Under a withering hail of stones and other projectiles, the Spaniards who had been caught elsewhere in the city retreated to the main square, which was lined with the Inca palaces the Spaniards had seized and occupied some two years earlier. If the Incas' strategy was to encircle, squeeze, and then crush their adversaries, the Spaniards' strategy was to hold on to, if at all possible, two massive stone buildings—Suntur Huasi and Hatun Cancha. The enclosures faced each other on the eastern side of the square and had high, gabled roofs of thatch that were supported by wooden beams. In desperation, the Spaniards converted them into bunkers, relying upon the roofs and walls to protect them from the relentless hail of stones.

Taking charge of one of the buildings, Hernando Pizarro placed the

other under the command of Hernán Ponce de León. So fierce was the native bombardment directed at them that the frightened Spaniards were now
unable even to venture out from either building. Within the dim interiors,
many now kneeled and prayed while, outside, rocks continued to thud
fiercely against the streets, walls, and roofs. "There were so many slingshot
stones coming in through the entryways of the doors," remembered one
survivor, "that it seemed like a dense hail at a time when the heavens are
hailing furiously." Forced now to relinquish control of the city, save for this
small portion of the main square, Pedro Pizarro recounted that:

> Hernando Pizarro and his captains assembled many times to discuss
> what should be done. Some said that we ought to desert the town and
> flee [while] others said that we should hole up in [the great hall of]
> Hatun Cancha, which was a great enclosure where we might all be, and
> which . . . had but one doorway and a very high wall of stone masonry.
> . . . [Yet] none of this advice was any good, for had we left Cuzco they
> would have killed us all in the many bad passes . . . that there are, and
> had we taken refuge in the enclosure, they would have imprisoned us
> with adobe bricks and stones due to the great number of [native] troops
> that there were.

Before Hernando Pizarro could even decide between the twin options of
being trapped in the two buildings and being clubbed like so many guinea
pigs or else trying to make a run for it and somehow breaking through the
encircling hordes, a new and even more frightening problem suddenly
reared its head: the roofs of many of the houses in the city had now abruptly
begun to burst into flames. The incredulous Spaniards, running to the doorways and peering from their buildings, looked out to see a virtual holocaust
of fire rising from building after building. Before they even understood how
it had happened, the Spaniards were trapped in a city that was rapidly being
incinerated.

Manco Inca and his war council, it turned out—faced with the Incas'
deadliest foe since the creation of their empire—had come up with an ingenious war plan: not only had they decided to surround their enemies, to unleash a withering barrage of stones, and, under the barrage's cover, to
gradually move in and crush their enemy—but they had also decided simul-

taneously to set fire to the city, hoping to smoke the Spaniards out of their hiding places or else to burn them to death. Manco's warriors had presumably lit a number of large fires on the city's outskirts and had then laid sling stones upon them, waiting patiently until the stones had turned the color of rubies. Removing them from the fires, the warriors wrapped the glowing stones in flammable cotton, loaded them into slings, then whirled them about, allowing centrifugal force to fire the stones at the city.

As the combination of superheated stone and the sudden blast of oxygen ignited the surrounding cotton midair, tiny versions of the Molotov cocktail began to rain down upon the rooftops of the city, setting the dry thatch of the houses on fire. Lending support to the sling throwers, jungle archers— no doubt decorated with face and body paint—let loose volley after volley of fire-tipped arrows into the city. Thus, within a relatively short time, a major conflagration now threatened to burn every last Spaniard alive.

It wasn't long, in fact, before tendrils of smoke began to curl downward from the ceiling of Hatun Cancha, where the Spaniards were trapped. As those inside gazed up in horror, all realized that their own rooftop had now caught on fire. Wrote one of the survivors:

> There happened to be a very strong wind that day, and, as the roofs of the houses were made of thatch, it seemed at one point as if the entire city were one great sheet of flame. The Indians were shouting so loudly and the smoke was so thick that the men could neither hear nor see one another.

Wrote Cristóbal de Molina: "There was so much smoke that the Spaniards almost choked to death. They suffered greatly because . . . the smoke and heat . . . were so intense."

Various sources now describe what happened next. According to some Spaniards, while the rest of Cuzco burned, the flames on the roof of Hatun Cancha somehow mysteriously went out. Later some of those present swore that the Virgin Mary herself had miraculously appeared, with flowing robe and hair, and extinguished the flames. Titu Cusi, however, who no doubt would have heard this story directly from his father, left a more prosaic version: the Spaniards owed their temporary reprieve to African slaves they had stationed on the roof. Despite being fired at with arrows by Amazonian warriors and despite the unceasing hail of sling stones, the Africans had been able to put out the fire.

With much of the city burning and realizing that if they stayed within the two buildings that they might soon be roasted to death, Hernando Pizarro decided that he and his men had no other choice but to leave the relative safety of the buildings and counterattack.

"It seemed to them that it would be better to go out than to perish there," wrote Cieza de León, "and as dense and continuous as the hail of rocks was they suddenly came out together with their Indian friends and they went charging into their enemies in the lower streets, destroying their entrenchment." The mestizo chronicler Garcilaso de la Vega added:

> When these [native warriors] saw the Spaniards all gathered together, they fell on them with great ferocity, hoping to overrun them . . . [during the first assault]. The cavalry attacked them and held them up valiantly, and both sides fought with great courage. . . . Arrows and stones shot from slings rained on the Spaniards in a remarkable way; but the horses and lances [and armor] were sufficient to cope with them and they made no . . . [attack] without leaving at least 150 or 200 Indians dead on the ground.

As flaming roofs began to collapse and crash throughout the city, native warriors were now able to run along the tops of the newly exposed walls, thus gaining the advantage of height over the Spaniards and also allowing the natives to protect themselves from cavalry charges. Other warriors fought on foot in the narrow alleyways, swinging their battle-axes and mace clubs and slinging stones at the Spanish foot soldiers, at the Spaniards' native allies and slaves, and at the metal-clad demons on horses. "The Indians were supporting one another so well," wrote one eyewitness, "that they charged through the streets with the greatest determination and fought hand-to-hand with the Spaniards."

All day, as smoke poured from the city, the battle raged fiercely; only with the greatest difficulty, in fact, were the Spaniards able to prevent the tiny portion of Cuzco that they presently held from being overrun. Lords of vast Indian estates—indeed of much of the Inca Empire only a month earlier— the Spaniards now saw their future prospects collapse as abruptly as the flaming roofs throughout the city. For all the Spaniards, however—rich and poor alike—the only thing that now mattered was preserving their lives.

As the seemingly endless day drew to a close, however, the Spaniards were granted a slight reprieve: the Incas were primarily day fighters and were reluctant to fight at night. Thus, as the sun god, Inti, finally began to sink behind the hills, the natives gradually ceased their attack. Manco's warriors seemed content to consolidate their advance into the city by building barricades across the streets and alleys they had captured. As the exhausted Spaniards watched the barricades rise, it was clear to all that Manco's noose around them was gradually cinching tight. That night, recalled Titu Cusi,

> As they [the Spaniards] knew of no solution, their principal help came in resorting to God, such that all that night in the [makeshift] church [of Hatun Cancha] they prayed for God to help them, on their knees and with their hands [clasped] near their mouths, which a lot of Indians saw and even those [Spaniards] who were on the plaza standing guard did the same, as well as many [Chachapoyan and Cañari] Indians who were [fighting] with them, who had come with them from Cajamarca.

Wrote the chronicler Huamán Poma de Ayala:

> On their knees, the Christians begged for God's mercy and called upon the Virgin Mary and all their Saints. With tears in their eyes they prayed aloud: "Bless us, St. James! Bless us, Holy Mary! God save us!" . . . They humbled themselves and with their weapons actually in their hands appealed to their Holy Mary.

That evening, Hernando Pizarro—who three years earlier had helped to buoy up the Spaniards' spirits the night before their desperate gamble to capture Atahualpa—called a general meeting. Outside and in the distance, roof beams continued to collapse, periodically sending up geysers of fresh sparks into the night air. On the square, the Spaniards' native auxiliaries stood guard, their tunics and faces illuminated by the city's eerie red glow. Although many of his fellow conquistadors disliked Hernando due to his arrogance, suspicious nature, and lack of generosity, he was nevertheless a natural leader who was extremely cool under pressure. For those gathered inside, waiting for Hernando to speak, all realized that their very lives now depended upon the decisions the heavyset, bearded man would make:

> "Gentlemen, I've asked you to meet here in order to speak to all of you together because it appears to me that . . . the Indians are shaming us more and more. I believe that the reason for this is because of the lack of forcefulness and timidity that some of you have shown. That is [why] we have abandoned [most of] the city.
>
> "I don't want it said of me that the land that Don Francisco Pizarro, my brother, conquered and populated, was lost in any way, shape, or form because of fear. . . . Because anyone who really knows the Indians knows that weakness [on our parts] only makes them stronger."

Pacing back and forth and no doubt gesticulating with his hands, Hernando continued.

> "In the name of God and our King, and defending our houses and our estates, we will die [if we must]. . . . Let's strengthen our resolve with the understanding of why we have to fight, and then we will not feel danger, because you already know that with courage one can achieve what appears to be impossible, and without it even that which is easy is made difficult. This is what I urge upon you—and I am asking that all of you agree to this, because divided we will be lost [even] without an enemy."

Unanimously, the trapped Spaniards pledged that they would fight fiercely with no thought of themselves for "with the men seeing their end, they prayed to our Lord and to our Lady [the Virgin Mary] saying that it would be better to go out . . . and die fighting than to die there like hogs." Outside, on the hills surrounding the city, a seemingly infinite number of campfires kept the native troops warm while they continued their campaign of unnerving the Spaniards by maintaining a continuous din of shouting and jeering. Beyond the ring of hills lay other native camps where tens of thousands of the warriors' wives busied themselves with cooking food and where even the soldiers' children slept. A traditional aspect of Inca military campaigns was to bring along an entourage of civilian camp followers. As many hundreds of native warriors had already been killed that day, the wails of grief-stricken women no doubt lifted up from the camps and drifted mournfully through the night air.

Villac Umu and his generals, meanwhile—looking down upon the city from their fortress of Saqsaywaman—were busy discussing their battle plans for the following day. Below them the city of Cuzco seemed to pulse and glow in the night, like some angry, fluorescent creature that had been suddenly hauled up from the ocean's dark depths. Fires continued to crackle, occasionally vomiting forth wreaths of sparks and flame while abrupt explosions relayed the constant, staccato-like collapse of roofs. As isolated and fervent Spaniards prayed on their knees to their lone God and the Incas made sacrifices to theirs, both sides nevertheless had to feel that they had been partially successful that day. The Spaniards because, despite the ferocious attack, no lives had thus far been lost and because they had prevented their positions from being overrun. The Incas because they had seized nearly the entire city and had tightened the noose around their enemies so severely that the latter were currently reduced to hiding within two buildings.

Before Manco Inca went to sleep in Calca that night—this, the first night of his assault—he sent word to his commanders that with renewed efforts the following day the last remaining pocket of Spanish resistance would surely be crushed. Lying upon a thick pile of blankets, Manco drifted off to sleep, no doubt dreaming of his warriors swarming into the Spaniards' final strongholds and then clubbing the frightened men to death.

The next day, soon after dawn, a great roar went up from the hundreds of thousands of native warriors on the hillsides as well as from the blasts of countless conch shells and clay trumpets. Once again, hordes of native troops descended upon the city, filling the streets and marching toward the main square, where they expected the Spaniards to make their final stand. In and around that same square the Spanish cavalry and foot soldiers waited, along with their African slaves and their native auxiliaries. Manco's troops soon began setting afire rooftops that had somehow escaped the conflagration the previous day; thus, as the city continued to smoke and burn, warriors ran along the tops of the house walls, hurling javelins and slinging stones down at their enemies. Fearing renewed attempts to set their two buildings on fire, the Spaniards had purposely posted men on both rooftops. The latter were now kept busy putting out fires as soon as the sling throwers or jungle warriors fired hot stones or flaming arrows at them. Meanwhile, in the narrow streets below, the two opposing forces met and grappled with each other in fierce mortal combat.

With their military options now severely reduced, the Spaniards relied upon a simple strategy: in order to prevent the small area they presently held from being overrun, their three cavalry units continually charged the native warriors in an effort to disrupt their attacks. It was better, all agreed, to meet one's end fighting on the open square or upon the narrow streets than to be caught cowering in one of their bunkers. No Spaniard wanted to be trapped inside either building and burned or clubbed to death. Thus, like the native warriors attacking them, the Spaniards fought savagely, stabbing and slicing at the enemy with their lances and swords, butchering native after native and leaving them on the ground in pools of blood and gore. Amid the cramped streets, however, choked as they now were with barricades, dead bodies, and with Manco's attacking troops, maneuverability for the cavalry had become difficult. The force of the cavalry was soon even further blunted by a number of native innovations.

When twenty-three-year-old Alonso de Toro led a cavalry charge down one of Cuzco's narrow streets, for example—which even in the best of circumstances were only wide enough for two horses to ride abreast—a group of Manco's warriors suddenly pushed a high wall over, which collapsed on top of Toro and his men. Knocked from their horses and stunned by the impact, Toro and his companions would have been annihilated if their own native auxiliaries had not now rushed forward, fought off their attackers, and pulled the Spaniards to safety.

Meanwhile, on the hillsides around the city, Manco's troops had been busy implementing additional strategies in an effort to neutralize the Spaniards' powerful horses. On the flat agricultural terraces that the Incas called *andenes,* and which they had used to transform the sloping hillsides in certain areas into a series of giant staggered platforms, native warriors now dug pits in the ground in order to prevent a cavalry charge. Elsewhere in the surrounding hills, other natives disrupted the aqueducts leading into the city, flooding the flatlands above the rim of the valley and making it impossible for horses to gallop on the marshy ground. Within Cuzco itself,

Manco's troops continued building more wicker barricades, using these to block off entire streets and thus to restrict their enemy's maneuverability.

As the cavalrymen wheeled on their horses and attempted to cope with so many new obstacles, Manco's warriors now unleashed another weapon against them, one that they had previously used only when hunting deer and other large game. Wrote one of the siege's survivors:

> They have many offensive weapons . . . [such as] lances, arrows, clubs, axes, halberds, darts, and slings, and another type of weapon that they call *ayllus,* which are made from three round stones placed and sewn up in leather bags and attached to a cord . . . a yard long. . . . They throw these at the horses and [thus] bind their legs together and sometimes they will hit the rider and will bind a man's arms to his body [in the same way]. These Indians are so good at this that they can bring down a deer in the countryside.

The Spaniards soon began calling the Incas' strange weapon *bolas,* or "balls."

In response to the Incas' latest tactics, the Spaniards were forced to quickly come up with counterstrategies of their own. Because of the *bolas,* the cavalrymen now needed foot soldiers to accompany them in order to cut them free when they became entangled. Parties of Spanish horsemen and infantry, meanwhile, worked on destroying the barricades in the streets, although they were often forced to do so under a withering hail of stones. Cañari and Chachapoyan natives, meanwhile, when not fighting alongside the Spaniards, worked on filling the anti-horse pits Manco's warriors had dug in the ground; they also worked on demolishing the stone terraces on the hillsides so that the cavalry and foot soldiers could more easily counterattack.

Although no Spaniards had yet been killed, many had nevertheless received wounds of varying severity on their arms, hands, legs, and faces; all of them realized that their desperate situation would have been even more so without the help of their native auxiliaries. Wrote Garcilaso de la Vega:

> The friendly Indians were of great help in curing their wounds and in ministering to all their other needs, bringing healing herbs and food to eat. . . . On seeing this, many of the Spaniards themselves said that they were in such straits that they did not know what would have happened

to them if it had not been for the help of those Indians who brought them corn, herbs, and everything they needed to eat and to cure their wounds, and went without food themselves so that their masters might eat, and served them as spies and watchmen, warning the Spaniards day and night of their enemies' intentions by secret signs.

Despite the Incas' best efforts, the Spaniards were still able to kill several hundred native warriors while suffering no fatalities themselves, although it is likely that many of their native auxiliaries did lose their lives. Manco's generals quickly learned that although their troops could apparently wound the Spaniards, it was nevertheless extremely difficult for their warriors to *kill* them. Only by surrounding a cavalryman and pulling him from his horse did they have a chance at killing an armored Spaniard in hand-to-hand combat. They soon noticed, however, that the Spanish horsemen were increasingly careful to remain together at all times, rode to each other's aid, and were careful to avoid obvious ambushes or traps.

The Spaniards, however, took little consolation from the fact that none of them had died yet. After two days of successive native attacks, their prospects still remained grim. The Spanish defenders continued to be hugely outnumbered; they remained isolated and cut off from the outside world and thus from reinforcements; they possessed dwindling supplies of food; and they were now also tired, wounded, and suffered from fierce, unrelenting onslaughts from a determined enemy. What had become increasingly clear to Hernando and his captains was that if they wished to survive this ordeal, they must somehow dislodge Manco's warriors from the nearby fortress of Saqsaywaman. Not only was the fortress the obvious command and control center of the Incas' military campaign, but from the heights around it Manco's warriors staged their most ferocious attacks. Native troops routinely descended the steep hillsides below the fortress and entered directly into the city, without having to worry about cavalry attacks. Elsewhere, in the open valley to the south, for example, flat ground made it difficult for Manco's generals to mount major assaults because their troops were exposed to cavalry charges. If the Spaniards could recapture the fortress, then they would be able to eliminate direct attacks on their most exposed flank and would also hold the most strategic military area on the surrounding heights.

After consultations with his captains, Hernando finally decided that seizing Saqsaywaman was the only means of reducing their vulnerability, despite the obvious dangers that a frontal attack on the heavily guarded fortress would entail. Recalled Pedro Pizarro:

> Hernando Pizarro agreed that we [should] go and [try to] capture the fortress, for it was from there that we were receiving the most damage. . . . Because at the very beginning an agreement was not reached to take it before the Indians laid siege, nor was the importance of holding it realized. This being agreed upon, we of the cavalry were given the job to ready our weapons and to go and take it, and Juan Pizarro was put in charge.

For twenty-five-year-old Juan, his appointment as the leader of such an important mission was evidence of his older brother's confidence in him. Unlike Hernando, Juan was popular among the Spaniards. Affable, approachable, generous, and an excellent horseman, he was also fearless. Juan's only weaknesses were impetuosity and, like many of the other Spaniards, a certain brutality in his relationships with the natives. Juan's and his brother Gonzalo's abysmal treatment of Manco Inca, after all, had served as one of the prime motivations for Manco's uprising in the first place.

Earlier that day, Juan had been fighting on horseback when another cavalryman, Pedro del Barco, was struck on his helmet with a large stone. Barco had fallen to the ground, unconscious. Spotting the danger, Juan had ridden over, leapt from his horse, and gone to Barco's aid. As Juan was dragging his fallen comrade to safety, a native sling thrower unleashed a stone that struck Juan squarely in his jaw.* Although stunned, Juan managed to pull his companion to safety. By evening, however, Juan's jaw had become so swollen that he was no longer able to wear a helmet. Nevertheless, the twenty-three-year-old was ready and willing to lead an attack on Saqsaywaman, as Hernando had asked. Helmet or no helmet, Juan realized, their lives no doubt depended upon the outcome.

The fortress Juan's cavalry was expected to storm was a formidable one.

---

* Although the Spaniards always wore helmets, few wore visors, as these tended to impede their vision.

Built upon a rocky hill on the northern edge of the city, Saqsaywaman was protected on three of its sides by steep slopes, which prevented a direct attack. On its northern side, and facing away from the city, the fortress fronted a grassy plain that the Incas frequently used for festivals and processions. Since the fortress was pregnable only from this direction, the Incas had built a series of giant walls there with which to defend it. As the notary Sancho de la Hoz wrote:

> On the . . . side [of the fortress] that is less steep there are three [walls], one above the other. . . . The most beautiful thing that can be seen among the buildings of that land are these walls, because they are of stones so large that no one who sees them would say that they had been placed there by human hands, for they are as large as chunks of mountains . . . and they have a height of thirty palms [twenty-one feet] and a length of as many more. . . . These walls twist [zigzag] in such a way that if they are bombarded (with cannons) it is impossible to do so from directly in front, but only obliquely. . . . The whole fortress was a warehouse of weapons, clubs, lances, bows, axes, shields, vests thickly padded with cotton, and other weapons of various sorts . . . gathered from every corner of the realm that was subject to the Inca lords.

Conferring with Manco's cousin Pascac, who had sided with the Spaniards, Juan and Hernando had decided that the only way to storm the fortress was to first break through the legions of warriors to the north of the city, gaining the road that led to Jauja, and then, if successful, to wheel about and ride east around the hills until they reached the grassy plain fronting the fortress. Once there, the Spaniards would have to somehow launch a frontal assault against the Incas' colossal walls. To many of those who listened to the plan, the mission seemed suicidal. Still, unless they were able to seize the initiative, all realized that they were doomed to remain in the city and gradually be worn down by attrition. With the grace of God, thought some, the desperate plan just might work.

Early in the morning on May 13, Juan Pizarro and about fifty horsemen

> emerged from the church [of Suntur Huasi] and mounted their horses as if they were going to fight and started to look from side to side. While

they were looking about in this way, they suddenly put spurs to their horses and at full gallop, despite the enemy, broke through the opening that had been sealed like a wall and charged off up the hillside at breakneck speed.

Juan's cousin, Pedro, recalled how he and the rest of the cavalry had to first break through the native contingents hurling stones at them and then how they had to zigzag up the steep hillside, stopping frequently while their native auxiliaries cleared the way.

> We went up through Carmenca, a very narrow road, bordered on one side by a hillside and on the other by a ravine, deep in some places, and from this ravine they inflicted much damage on us with stones and arrows, and they had [also] destroyed the road in some places and had made many holes in it. We went this way and with great effort and difficulty, because we kept stopping and waiting while the few friendly Indians we had with us—fewer than a hundred—filled up the holes and repaired the roads.

Assuming that the Spaniards were trying to flee the city, the Inca commanders sent runners racing to the distant Apurímac River, ordering that the great hanging bridge there be destroyed, thus cutting off that avenue of escape. The Spanish cavalry, however, once having broken through to the northwest, suddenly wheeled around to the east and then began riding rapidly through the country in the direction of the fortress. After much effort and having to breach earthen barricades that Manco's warriors had constructed, Juan and his cavalry finally succeeded in reaching the grassy plain that stretched before the fortress's massive northern walls.

Pausing to regroup, the Spaniards now contemplated their next step. Before them rose three, thousand-foot-long, staggered walls of gray, gargantuan-sized stones, the largest of which weighed more than 360 tons and rose more than twenty-eight feet in height. The Incas had filled in earth behind each stone wall to form a flat terrace at its top. Native defenders could thus stand upon both the terraces and the walls and from there could direct a withering volley of stones, darts, and arrows upon the exposed attackers below. If the attackers seized one of the walls, the defenders could retreat upward to the next wall and terrace, and then to the next. From the bottom of the first wall to the top of the third stretched a vertical distance of at least sixty feet. On the broad summit above the walls stood a labyrinth of buildings and from among their midst rose three stone towers. The central tower stood the tallest and was four to five stories in height, cone-shaped, and measured some seventy-five feet in diameter; the two flanking it on either side were nearly the same height and were rectangular. Beneath the towers ran a warren of secret tunnels that extended out at least as far as the defensive walls and perhaps even beyond.

Built during the previous century, Saqsaywaman—"the (fortress of the) satisfied falcon"—was so vast that the entire population of Cuzco, if necessary, could find refuge within its perimeter. With at least thirty thousand native warriors now defending it and with Villac Umu personally directing their efforts, the fifty Spanish cavalrymen and their perhaps one hundred native allies were now faced with a seemingly insurmountable task: they had to figure out a way to breach the massive walls and then to seize the fortress from its defenders.

Juan's brother Gonzalo and Hernán Ponce de León now led several frontal attacks. Charging across the grassy plain toward the fortress, the Spaniards immediately ran into a withering barrage of darts, arrows, and sling stones, propelled from above by shouting native warriors. The closer the Spanish horsemen approached the fortress's walls, the thicker the hail of missiles became. During their final charge, Manco's warriors managed to kill Juan Pizarro's page, who was felled by a single sling stone, presumably to the face, and also two of the Spaniards' African slaves, who more than likely owned no armor.* Many other Spaniards and their horses were wounded in the desperate assault.

Retreating to a rocky knoll that stood on the opposite side of the grassy plain, the Spaniards dismounted and deliberated about what to do. Below them in the city they could hear the sounds of iron-shod horse hooves pounding the streets and also the sounds of shouting and fighting. Their comrades were clearly engaged with attacking natives in the streets below.

---

* Armor imported from Spain was expensive. The wealthier a Spaniard was, the more protective armor he could afford. The corollary was that the poorer Spaniards were often exposed to the greatest danger. Slaves more than likely wore confiscated native cotton armor, which afforded far less protection than steel armor or chain mail.

High above the city and gathered together on the rocky knoll, the Spaniards felt isolated and exposed. As the sun began to set, Juan Pizarro decided to try a final attack; this time, however, he instructed his men to concentrate their forces on the main gate that created a break in the first wall. The gate was barricaded and had a defensive pit in front of it and two flanking walls on either side.

Not able to wear a helmet due to the head wound he had suffered the day before, and with the last rays of the sun illuminating the fortress walls and towers, Juan and his fellow cavalrymen, shouting traditional cries of "Santiago!," began galloping together across the grassy plain as stone missiles began to whiz down on top of them, bouncing back up from the ground like giant hailstones. Wheeling to a stop before the main gate and protecting themselves with their shields, the Spaniards leapt from their horses, then threw themselves against the wicker barrier that sealed the gateway. Somehow breaking through, the Spaniards now began to force their way up the stone stairway that led up to the first terrace.

As the native defenders rushed forward to close off the breach, an increasingly heavy volley of rocks and missiles rained down upon the Spaniards from above, loudly clanging off their armor. The warriors' fierce counterattack soon forced the Spaniards to retreat back down the stairway and out onto the plain. Shouting at his men to renew their efforts, Juan once again surged forward, however, swinging his sword fiercely and forcing his way ahead, literally hurling himself against a tide of native bodies. Juan's cousin Pedro remembered what happened next:

> From a terrace that is on one side of the courtyard they showered us with so many stones and arrows that we could not protect ourselves, and for this reason Juan Pizarro shoved some of the infantrymen towards the terrace . . . which was low, so that some Spaniards might get up on it and drive the Indians from there. And while he was fighting with these Indians in order to drive them away . . . Juan . . . neglected to cover his head with his shield, and with the many stones that they were throwing one of them hit him on the head and cracked his skull.

Bleeding from what was obviously a serious head injury, Juan nevertheless continued fighting until the Spaniards and their native allies had gained a foothold on top of the first terrace wall. With darkness descending, however, and still pummeled from the two sets of walls above them with a constant avalanche of stones, the Spaniards were gradually forced once again to retreat back down and across the plain, some remounting their horses while others stumbled backward, holding up their shields for protection. Manco's warriors, meanwhile, advanced after them, shouting insults and lifting their tunics to bare their legs while others continued to relentlessly whirl and launch a seemingly inexhaustible supply of stones.

Reaching the relative safety of the knoll, Juan Pizarro now collapsed. Native auxiliaries soon carried the Spanish leader down the steep hillside and back into the city. Mortally wounded, Juan would drift in and out of consciousness for the next few days, while the battle continued to swirl around him. Three days after his assault on Saqsaywaman, the twenty-five-year-old was lucid long enough to dictate his will, which a notary-conquistador duly recorded and then had the dying man scratch his mark upon:

I, Juan Pizarro, citizen of this great city of Cuzco, in the Kingdom of New Castile, son of [Captain] Gonzalo Pizarro [Sr.] and Maria Alonso, [both] deceased (may God rest their souls), being of sick body but of sound mind . . . because I am indisposed and not knowing what our Lord God has in mind for me, I want to make and organize this last will and testament. . . . Firstly, I commend my soul to God, who created and redeemed it with his precious blood and body . . . [and] I order that if God decides to take me from this present life because of the sickness I now have, that my body be buried in the main church [of Suntur Huasi] in this city until such a time as my brothers Hernando Pizarro and Gonzalo Pizarro carry my bones [back] to Spain, to the city of Trujillo, and have them buried there where they see fit. . . . I order that on the day of my death a Requiem Mass be sung, and that a Mass be sung on each of the following nine days. . . .

I [also] order that because I have received [sexual] services from an Indian woman who has given birth to a girl whom I do not recognize as my daughter, [that nevertheless] . . . because of the services of her mother I order that if this girl becomes of marriageable age and weds with the blessing of my brother, Hernando Pizarro, that she will be

given 2,000 ducats for her marriage. [However] if she dies before marrying without heirs . . . it is my desire that those 2,000 ducats be returned to my heirs . . . so that her mother will not inherit them. . . . I
[also] order that . . . my universal heir [will be] . . . and all of my
worldly goods [will go to] my brother, Gonzalo Pizarro. . . . [This will
was] made and approved before the notary public and witnesses . . . in
the said capital of Cuzco on the 16th day of the month of May, in the
year one thousand five hundred and thirty-six of the birth of our Savior,
Jesus Christ.

Two weeks after his injury, Juan Pizarro died, recognizing neither the native woman from whom he had "received services" nor his own mixed-race
daughter, who by his own choice he insisted remain illegitimate. Juan did,
however, pass on his fortune of 200,000 gold ducats to his already fabulously wealthy brother, twenty-one-year-old Gonzalo. Remarkably, Juan
made no mention in his will of the battle that continued to rage around him
in the streets, nor of the possibility that the desperate men who witnessed
his final testament might at any moment be completely wiped out. Despite
his final request, however, Juan's remains would never be returned to Spain.
Juan was the first of the five Pizarro brothers to die as a result of the conquest of Tawantinsuyu and his bones would remain forevermore buried in
Peru.*

With no time to worry about his stricken brother and with a growing legion of wounded men around him, Hernando Pizarro now ordered his
brother Gonzalo to take over command of the assault on Saqsaywaman. The
day after wounding Juan Pizarro, the native infantry within the fortress
counterattacked, carrying the battle away from the fortress walls and out
onto the rocky knoll that Gonzalo and the rest of the cavalry had occupied
since the previous day. "There was such terrible confusion," wrote one eyewitness, "with everyone shouting and they were all tangled up together . . .
[fighting for] the height they [the Spaniards] had won. It looked as if the
whole world was up there fighting with each other."

Receiving constant reports of the situation and realizing how crucial the

---

* Juan Pizarro was later buried in Cuzco's Dominican Monastery of Santo Domingo, built
atop the Qoricancha, the Incas' temple of the sun.

battle of Saqsaywaman was for the outcome of his campaign, Manco Inca ordered that an additional five thousand native troops join the fray. Hernando Pizarro, meanwhile, similarly motivated but with far fewer resources, sent another dozen cavalrymen up from the city to reinforce the embattled men; he did so despite strong complaints from the remaining Spaniards, who by now had fewer than two dozen horsemen with which to defend themselves from the natives' unrelenting attacks. "In the city," one eyewitness wrote, "the Indians waged such a fierce attack that the Spaniards thought themselves a thousand times lost."

All day in Cuzco the fighting continued, again with hundreds of native warriors being slaughtered due to the Spaniards' better armor, horses, and weaponry; nevertheless Manco's warriors continued pressing forward, seemingly undaunted. Piles of dead bodies littered the streets of what had once been a glorious Inca capital but that had now been transformed into a smoking, burned-out shell. Above the city, on the grassy plain before Saqsaywaman, Manco's fresh troops had arrived and now began pressing Gonzalo and his cavalry so much that "the Spaniards were in a very difficult situation with these reinforcements, because the Indians who arrived were fresh and attacked with great determination." Only by redoubling their efforts were the Spaniards able to prevent themselves from being surrounded and annihilated.

That night—exhausted, wounded, and increasingly desperate—the Spaniards were nevertheless ready with a new plan. Realizing that Manco might send even more troops the following day and that their exposed presence above the city only invited greater counterattacks, the Spanish captains had decided to mount a night assault on the fortress. The Spaniards knew full well that Manco's troops would never expect such an attack; they also knew that the natives disliked fighting at night, especially on the night of a new moon, which was due this very night. Thus, despite the day's fierce fighting, the Spaniards had somehow been able to supervise the building of assault ladders, probably constructed by their native auxiliaries. The ladders were similar to those the Spaniards had used on the Iberian peninsula for centuries to assault the castles of the Moors.

Under the cover of darkness, Hernando Pizarro and many of the Spanish soldiers from the city now secretly climbed up the steep hill to join those above. Before them lay the Inca fortress, its gloomy shadows punctuated

here and there by orange campfires on the upper terraces. As quietly as they
could, the Spaniards and their auxiliaries began carrying their assault ladders across the plain, seeking out the darkest sections of the walls against
which to stage their attack. Steel helmets and unsheathed swords glinted
dully as the Spaniards placed the ladders against the walls and then began
creeping upward in the dark.

Pulling themselves onto the top of the first wall, the Spaniards attacked
the first startled sentries before the natives even understood how the armored invaders had so miraculously appeared in their midst. Slicing and
stabbing with their swords, the Spaniards quickly gained the terrace alongside the top of the first wall. Their native auxiliaries, meanwhile, climbed up
after them, pulling the ladders up from behind. Soon, an alert was sounded
and stones began to pelt down, the conquistadors nevertheless throwing
their ladders up against the next giant wall and climbing up, holding their
shields in one hand and their swords in the other.

Caught by surprise, Manco's troops were soon forced to abandon the two
lower terraces but rallied on top of the third. Directly behind rose the complex of buildings and the three towers that loomed overhead in the night.
With only a single wall remaining, the defenders had no other choice than
to make a final defensive stand. According to one of the attacking Spaniards:

> I am able to certify that it . . . [was] the most fearful and cruel war in the
> world, for between the Christians and Moors there is some mercy, and
> those whom they take alive can take some consolation because of the
> ever-present interest in ransoms. But here among these Indians there is
> neither love nor reason, nor fear of God . . . and they kill us as cruelly as
> they can.

With a ferocity born of desperation, the Spaniards swung their swords,
fending off volley after volley of stone missiles with their shields. One man,
an *extremeño* from the town of Badajoz, about seventy miles from Pizarro's
hometown of Trujillo, stood out that night. Hernán Sánchez was one of
twelve cavalrymen Hernando had sent up earlier as reinforcements and was
also one of the first to climb up a ladder set against the third and final wall.
Using his shield to ward off the barrage of stones, Sánchez reached the uppermost level, then threw himself through the window of one of the build-

ings, discovering numerous startled natives inside. Shouting and slashing at them with his sword, Sánchez forced back the natives, who soon began to retreat up a set of stairs that led onto the roof. Like a man who had utterly lost his mind, Sánchez rushed after them onto the roof, howling like a crazed animal, only to find himself at the base of the central, cone-shaped tower. Sánchez now noticed a rope hanging from the top of the tower, which descended to the ground. Fastening his shield to his back, he began pulling himself up, using his feet to push off from the tower wall. Halfway up the tower, native defenders launched a stone from above "as big as a jug" on top of him. Just in time, Sánchez swung forward, causing the stone to glance off his back after smashing against his strapped-on shield. Eventually, Sánchez reached a higher window, leapt into another crowd of warriors, yet somehow still had the wherewithal to shout to his comrades below, encouraging them to continue their attack.

Throughout the long night, the two sides grappled, the Spanish forces on one side pushing against Manco's forces on the other. When dawn broke the next morning, the Spaniards and Manco's troops were still locked together in a desperate embrace, neither side having slept now for a day and a night and with no rest in the offing. Despite the Spaniards' best efforts, however, the native defenders still held the three towers and most of the buildings while the Spaniards and their native auxiliaries held the terraced walls below. Villac Umu, and his general, Paucar Huaman, meanwhile, continued to direct the defenders from somewhere deep within the complex of buildings. Saqsaywaman had one glaring weakness, however: it had no source of water. Further, the piles of stones, darts, and arrows that had once filled its storehouses were now beginning to run low. "They fought hard that day and throughout the night," remembered one eyewitness. "When the following day dawned, the Indians on the inside began to weaken, for they had exhausted their entire store of stones and arrows."

With the situation beginning to deteriorate, Villac Umu and his general decided that there was not enough water and weapons to supply his defenders. Placing a sub-commander in charge—an ethnic Inca noble who wore large earplugs—the high priest ordered the defenders to break through the Spaniards' ranks, thus allowing him and General Paucar Huaman to escape. Making their way to Calca, the two leaders urged Manco to send additional troops, hoping that with a fresh counterattack the Spaniards could be routed and destroyed.

By now, however, the remaining native defenders had retreated to the three towers, with the Inca noble who had been placed in charge striding about on top of the central one. This same *orejón* had no doubt been present less than a month earlier in the town of Lares where he and a host of other nobles had drunk from the golden vases of *chicha* and had pledged themselves to Manco's rebellion. Wearing confiscated Spanish weaponry, the noble presented such a spectacle and fought so ferociously that he guaranteed a place for himself in the otherwise heavily Spanish-centric chronicles. According to Pedro Pizarro:

> [At the top of the highest tower was] an *orejón* so courageous that the same might be written of him as has been written of some Romans. This *orejón* wore an oval shield on one arm and had a club in that hand and a sword in the other and a morión on his head. He had taken these weapons from the Spaniards who had died upon the roads, as well as [from among the] many others that the Indians had in their possession. This *orejón,* then, moved like a lion from one end to the other on top of the highest part of the tower, preventing the Spaniards who wished to climb up it with ladders from doing so, and killing the Indians who surrendered. . . . Whenever one of his men warned him that some Spaniard was climbing up at a certain place, he rushed at him like a lion . . . wielding his sword and shield.

Hernando Pizarro now ordered that the scaling ladders be set against all three of the towers and that his men storm them simultaneously. According to Pedro Pizarro,

> The Indians that this *orejón* had with him had by now all given up and had lost their courage, and it was he alone who was fighting. And Hernando Pizarro ordered those Spaniards who were climbing up not to kill this Indian but to take him alive, swearing that he would not kill him if he had him alive. Then, climbing up one of the towers, the Spaniards reached the top from two or three sides.

According to another eyewitness:

> During this time they hit him with two arrows [yet] he paid as little at-
> tention to them as if they hadn't touched him. And seeing that his peo-
> ple were all weakening and that the Spaniards were everywhere on their
> ladders and each hour were pressing [their advance] more, having noth-
> ing more to fight with, seeing clearly that everything was lost, he threw
> the battle axe he had in his hand [down] at the Christians, and taking
> handfuls of earth he stuffed these in his mouth and rubbed his face with
> such anguish . . . that it can scarcely be described. Not being able to
> stand the sight of the fortress being overcome, and realizing that its loss
> meant his death—due to the promise he had made to [Manco] Inca—he
> covered his head and face with his mantle and threw himself down from
> the tower [to a spot] more than one hundred *estados* below, and thus was
> smashed to pieces. Hernando Pizarro was very disappointed that they
> hadn't taken him alive.

With the native defenders now out of weapons, their heroic commander
dead, and Spaniards clambering into all three towers, the rout soon became
a slaughter. "With his death the remainder of the Indians lost their courage,"
wrote one chronicler, "giving way to Hernando Pizarro and his men who
were [now] able to enter and who put all those inside to the sword." Countless natives, rather than face sure death at the hands of the Spaniards, chose
instead to leap from the high walls and from the towers. Most died on impact. Others, falling on top of the piles of the dead, survived, although
these, too, were soon clubbed or stabbed to death. By the time the last defenders of the fortress were overcome, so many bodies lay strewn about the
area that groups of vultures and majestic black condors soon descended to
the ground to feast upon their flesh. Wrote one of the Spanish attackers,
Alonzo Enríquez de Guzmán:

> We . . . assaulted and captured the fortress, killing 3,000 souls. They
> killed our captain, Juan Pizarro . . . and during the combat in the city
> they killed four Christians, not including more than thirty others who
> they killed on the ranches and farms of the Indian chiefs, while they
> were out collecting their tribute.

As was usual in the lopsided battles between natives and Spaniards, thousands died on the Inca side while the Spaniards suffered relatively few losses. Thus far in Manco's rebellion, in fact, the mortality score had risen to perhaps two to four thousand dead native troops versus roughly thirty-five dead Spaniards, two African slaves, and an unknown number of dead native auxiliaries. That lopsided ratio, however—and indeed nearly three years of almost uninterrupted Spanish victories—was soon about to change.

IO ❖ DEATH IN THE ANDES

"You already know how I prevented you from inflicting harm on those evil people who . . . had entered my realm. . . . [But] what is done is done. . . . From now on beware of them, for . . . they are our worst enemies and we will perpetually be theirs."

MANCO INCA, 1536

"War is just when it is necessary; arms are permissible when there is no hope except in arms."

NICCOLÒ MACHIAVELLI, *THE PRINCE*, 1511

FRANCISCO PIZARRO DID NOT LEARN OF MANCO INCA'S RE-bellion until May 4, 1536, two days before Manco's massive assault on the besieged Spaniards in Cuzco. Alarmed, he dashed off letters to his brother Hernando and to a few other citizens in Cuzco, letting them know that he would send reinforcements as soon as possible. The contents of only one of those letters—which eventually made its way up into the Andes and arrived in Cuzco months later, ripped in pieces and more than likely splattered with blood—has survived. It was sent by Pizarro to Don Alonzo Enríquez de Guzmán, a cavalryman of noble birth, who three weeks later would be in-volved in the desperate storming of Saqsaywaman:

> Magnificent Sir,
>
> Today I arrived in this [City] of the Kings [Lima], after a visit to the cities of San Miguel and [the newly founded city of] Trujillo, with the in-tention of resting after so many hardships and dangers. But before I could

During the Inca rebellion, General Quizo's warriors captured a number
of Spanish survivors and sent them to Manco Inca.

even get off [my horse] they gave me some letters from you and from my brothers through which I was informed of the rebellion of that traitor, the Inca [emperor]. This greatly troubles me on account of the detriment it will cause to the service to the Emperor, our lord, and of the danger that you are in, and of the trouble it will cause me in my old age. I am greatly consoled by your presence there [in Cuzco] and . . . if it is the will of God, we will rescue those of you there. And thus I leave you, praying to our Lord to watch over and to aid your magnificent person.

This 4th of May, 1536

Francisco Pizarro

Pizarro had only founded the City of the Kings—so named because it had been established on the Feast of the Epiphany, also known as the day of the Three Magi Kings—four months earlier. Lying on a flat desert plain, the city was bordered by the Rimac River. Rimac, a *runasimi* word that meant "the Speaker," would later be corrupted into the city's eventual name, Lima. The area Pizarro had chosen had been settled for thousands of years before his arrival and was still littered with scattered adobe pyramids, constructed with millions of bricks so worn by the elements that they resembled natural hills.

Pizarro had been busy distributing *encomiendas* among his Spanish followers in Lima and supervising the construction of buildings around the town square, using the labor of Spaniards, natives, and African slaves. After his brilliant military campaign, beginning with Atahualpa's capture in Cajamarca and ending with the crowning of Manco Inca in Cuzco, Pizarro had done everything in his power to follow up his military victories with the equally important goal of winning the peace. No one was more aware than Pizarro of the necessity of consolidating the Spaniards' grip on the newly won empire, or of how weak that grip actually was.

Even now, four years after his arrival in Tawantinsuyu, Pizarro still had fewer than six hundred Spaniards situated in the central portion of the Inca Empire, an area roughly the size of modern-day Peru, which probably contained more than five million inhabitants. That meant that the Spaniards in Peru were outnumbered by natives in a ratio of nearly 10,000 to 1. Currently, roughly two hundred Spaniards inhabited La Ciudad de los Reyes (The City of the Kings), several dozen lived in Jauja, a small number in San

Miguel and in Trujillo, and 190 were trapped in Cuzco, including two of Pizarro's brothers, Hernando and Gonzalo. Another force of 140 Spaniards, under the leadership of Captain Alonso de Alvarado, was currently beyond Pizarro's reach, mired in the distant cloud forests of northeastern Peru, where they were busy conquering the Chachapoya civilization. Likewise, although Pizarro's former partner, Diego de Almagro, had at his disposal a force of five hundred more Spaniards, these were presently far to the south in what is now Chile and were embroiled in their own desperate struggle for survival.

Pizarro's Captain Sebastián de Benalcázar, meanwhile, commanded two hundred Spaniards far to the north, having conquered what is now Ecuador. But it would take months to convey a message to Benalcázar asking for help, and still more months before any troops could arrive. In reality Pizarro and his Spaniards controlled only tiny pockets of Peru and had relied upon their alliance with Manco Inca to extend that control into the provinces. With the collapse of the Spanish-Inca military alliance, however, Pizarro and his fellow Spaniards were now exposed for what they really were: a relatively tiny group of increasingly desperate foreign invaders. For the time being then, the only troops Pizarro had to send in relief of Cuzco were those with him in the fledgling City of the Kings.

Pizarro was as yet uncertain what precisely had precipitated the rebellion, or how widespread it was, or how many native forces were involved. The cause or causes of Manco's uprising really didn't matter, however. The only important thing was to put an end to it immediately, before the rebellion could spread. If Manco Inca were to seize Cuzco, then not only would Pizarro's brothers and nearly half of his available forces be killed, but the conquest of Peru would have to begin all over again. And this time, the Incas would not be so easily fooled by Spanish promises of goodwill and brotherhood.

Within a week of receiving news of Manco's rebellion, Pizarro had armed and dispatched the first of two relief forces. The initial column consisted of a cavalry contingent of thirty men led by a thirty-three-year-old captain named Juan Morgovejo de Quiñones. Pizarro ordered Morgovejo to head due east along the Inca road that ran from the coast up into the Andes, then to proceed south toward Vilcashuaman, a strategic crossroads that lay a little over a hundred miles to the west of Cuzco, where four Inca roads met. Seizing Vilcashuaman would prevent Inca forces in the north from moving south against Cuzco and would simultaneously prevent Manco's forces from moving north and spreading the rebellion.

After dispatching Morgovejo, Pizarro's next move was to send a second relief force of seventy cavalry, this one led by his relative Gonzalo de Tapia, but by a different route. Tapia's column was to follow the Inca road south on the coast for nearly a hundred miles, then to take a branch heading east that climbed into the Andes. Eventually, the cavalry unit would turn south onto the same main Inca highway, or *capac ñan,* that Morgovejo had taken; it would then ride in relief of the capital.

What neither Pizarro nor his two captains realized, however, was that Manco had already sent a native army north from Cuzco under the command of one of his generals, Quizo Yupanqui. Quizo's orders were to pin down Pizarro's forces in Lima and thus to prevent Pizarro from relieving the besieged mountain capital. That would leave Manco free to deal with "the Spanish problem" in Cuzco as he chose. The two captains of the relief columns, meanwhile, were also completely in the dark about the extent of the Inca rebellion. Neither was aware that they had actually entered enemy territory as soon as they had left Lima. Manco's uprising—like ripples spreading out from the center of a pond—had already progressed from Cuzco south to the Collao near Lake Titicaca and north into central Peru, as far as Jauja. As soon as the two Spanish columns had departed from Lima, therefore, native runners had begun carrying information on their whereabouts to General Quizo, who was kept continually informed of their movements. Undoubtedly, Quizo was also shown clay topographic maps of the area the Spaniards were traveling in. Inca commanders routinely used such models in order to devise their battle plans.

By now, the Spanish forces in Lima, Jauja, and Cuzco were operating in a virtual information blackout, completely unable to communicate with one another. Not only had the Incas succeeded in severing the Spaniards' lines of communication, but they had also been busy redesigning their military tactics. After three and a half years of occupation, Manco's generals knew by now something about the strengths and weaknesses of Spanish military techniques. Attacking Spanish cavalry while on level ground was tantamount to suicide, no matter how many native troops they brought to bear. They also knew that the only successes their troops had thus far enjoyed had been when they had attacked Spaniards in terrain so rough that the superior mobility and speed of the Spaniards' horses had been neutralized. Now, with advance knowledge of two Spanish columns moving slowly between the jagged heights and narrow passes of the Andes and taking into account everything he knew about the invaders, General Quizo carefully made his plans. "[Their strategy] was the following:" wrote the sixteenth-century chronicler Agustín de Zárate, "they would allow the Spaniards to enter a deep, narrow gorge and, seizing the entrance and the exit with a great mass of Indians, they would then hurl down such a quantity of rocks and boulders from the hillsides they would kill them all, almost without having to come to grips with them."

The tactic was one designed by the Incas to harness the jagged contours of the Andes as their ally, while turning that same topography into an enemy of the Spaniards. It was soon to become the central strategy in General Quizo Yupanqui's campaign.

Gonzalo de Tapia's force of seventy men, meanwhile, riding due south from Lima and then eastward up into the Andes, was the first to experience the Incas' new military tactics. Until now, the Spaniards had assumed that mounted cavalry were practically invincible when confronting native armies, no matter how many natives were arrayed against them. Crossing a fifteen-thousand-foot pass, Tapia's column soon came upon the royal Inca road that stretched down along the spine of the Andes from above Quito in what is now Ecuador southward for nearly three thousand miles into Chile. Turning south onto the main highway, the Spaniards next crossed the high, treeless grasslands, or *puna,* of Huaitará, dotted with herds of thickly fleeced alpacas, wisps of quickly moving clouds, and the occasional mountain lion, which the Incas called *puma.** High above the column soared occasional condors, black with white markings and naked yellow heads, whose seven-foot wingspans were nevertheless dwarfed by the immensity of the nearby snow-covered peaks. The relief column next crossed the Pampas River on an Inca bridge, then entered a narrow canyon with high jagged walls, the noise of the river filling the canyon, punctuated only by the clopping of the horses' hooves.

Both the Spaniards and their mounts were tired by now and were feeling

---

* *Puma* is one of many Quechua (or *runasimi*) words that have entered the English language. Others are: condor, guano, gaucho, jerky, Inca, llama, pampa, potato, quinoa, vicuña, and coca.

the effects of the high, thin Andean air, which is alternately warm by day and cold by night. Half drowsing in their saddles and climbing slowly up the canyon toward a pass, the Spaniards were abruptly jolted awake when masses of native warriors suddenly appeared ahead, seemingly out of nowhere. Quizo's troops charged toward the column, launching a volley of sling-driven stones that slammed into the cavalrymen at the front. Caught by surprise, Tapia and his men turned their horses around and raced back down the canyon, only to find that the bridge over the river they had just used had disappeared; native warriors had dismantled it soon after the Spaniards had ridden across.

Surrounded now by sheer canyon walls and with an impassable river behind them, the Spaniards were trapped. As the men shouted to one another, wheeling their horses around and trying to decide what to do, a noise as loud as a cannon suddenly erupted in their midst. A huge boulder had smashed into the ground from above, crushing a number of riders and horses and spraying others with a deadly shrapnel of rocks. Looking up, the Spaniards saw in horror that natives lining the canyon walls were pushing more boulders over the edge and that others were already crashing down. Amid the noise and confusion and the cries of the wounded the Spaniards knew one thing for certain: they had just been caught like rats in a carefully prepared trap.

Two, three, and now four more boulders hit the ground, exploding on impact and taking groups of horses and their riders down with them. Uninjured horses neighed, wounded horses screamed, and the Spaniards shouted hoarsely in the mounting confusion as more boulders continued to crash down upon them. Some riders tried to escape, bolting with their horses either forward or back down the canyon, but these immediately ran into a hail of sling stones and arrows shot by jungle archers. A few slammed their horses into the masses of warriors, slashing at the natives with their swords, but soon a sea of hands surrounded them and pulled the Spaniards from their mounts. Thrown to the ground, the armored invaders immediately disappeared beneath a thicket of copper-, bronze-, and stone-tipped clubs that rose up and then came down again, again and again.

General Quizo more than likely witnessed his carefully designed ambush from a perch high on top of the canyon rim. The general would have watched with satisfaction as wounded Spaniards crawled on the ground, pursued by native troops who used their heavy wooden *porras* to mash in their heads. Other warriors grabbed the now riderless horses by the reins, a few of which reared up on their haunches but were unable to escape. Within less than half an hour a force of seventy Spaniards—only ten fewer than the entire cavalry contingent currently fighting in Cuzco—had been reduced to a few crawling survivors.

While natives busily hacked off the fallen Spaniards' heads, an aide approached the Inca general and presumably showed him a leather bag full of the invaders' strange *quipus*—the magical papers (letters) that were said to have the power of speech. Surveying the carnage below, Quizo now ordered that the few Spaniards who had survived the slaughter be bound and that they—along with five severed Spanish heads and the magic *quipus*—be sent to Manco Inca as a gift from their victory.

General Quizo, meanwhile, had already learned from *chaski* messengers that another Spanish force was in the area and was marching south toward them. This was a detachment of sixty Spanish foot soldiers under a captain named Diego Pizarro who, despite his name, was no relative of the Pizarro brothers. The foot soldiers had marched from the town of Jauja—located about three hundred miles north of Cuzco—in pursuit of Manco's other great general, Tiso, who had been inciting natives in the region to rebel. Quizo's scouts reported that the sixty Spanish soldiers were currently marching south alongside the Mantaro River, toward the Inca town of Huamanga, about midway between Jauja and Cuzco. None of the soldiers was aware of the fact that an entire Spanish cavalry column had just been annihilated nearby.

In another high narrow canyon, similar to the one where Tapia's men had been crushed, Quizo staged his next ambush, just north of Huamanga. There the Inca general caught the entire force of sixty Spaniards by surprise and quite literally crushed them with an avalanche of boulders; Quizo's legions then clubbed the survivors to death.

> The Inca [General Quizo] seized many supplies that these [dead Spaniards] were carrying from Spain, brocades and silks . . . and other rich garments and a lot of wine and food stuffs . . . and swords and

lances which they later used against us and they . . . had more than one hundred horses and had [also] seized much artillery . . . and harque-buses.

Determined to continue his methodical campaign of extermination, General Quizo now marched his army north toward the city of Jauja, which was still inhabited by a community of perhaps several dozen *encomenderos*. Years of military successes and natural arrogance had lulled Jauja's Spanish inhabitants into a false sense of security. Assuming that their force of sixty foot soldiers was still in the area, the *encomenderos* ignored reports by their frightened *yanacona* servants that a large native army was now approaching the city. As the chronicler Martín de Murúa describes:

> [The Spaniards] received news that they [the native warriors] were coming to kill them, but they paid no attention nor did they respect them at all, saying "let these dogs come to where we are waiting for them and we will cut them all to pieces, even if they come with twice the number they [already] have. . . ." And for this reason, they didn't want to take any precautions nor to fortify themselves in a central area, nor to post guards or lookouts, nor to place spies on the road so that they could be warned when the Indians were near.

While the wealthy *encomenderos* ignored the danger, Quizo's troops secretly crept into the valley at night and surrounded the city. At dawn the next morning, the Inca general signaled his forces to attack, catching the Spaniards off guard. Finding themselves surrounded, those Spaniards who could gathered together in the town's center for an Alamo-like last stand; others, caught isolated in their homes, were bludgeoned to death. The battle for Jauja nevertheless lasted from dawn to dusk. Slowly, one by one, the Spaniards were overcome, caught up in the maelstrom of an attack that had been fueled by years of Spanish arrogance and abuse. By nightfall, "the Indians [had] killed everyone, and their horses and their black [African] servants." Only a single Spaniard had managed to escape, leaving the victorious warriors to "enjoy the dead Spaniards' spoils and to cut their bodies into pieces with barbarous cruelty." The lone survivor made his way down out of the Andes and hurried to Lima, where he soon informed a distraught Pizarro of what had happened.

The news of Jauja's loss came too late, however, for Pizarro had already dispatched two additional forces into the Andes to reinforce the city, unaware of the disaster that had befallen his previous column of seventy cavalry or that Jauja had just been overrun. One of the forces Pizarro sent was composed of twenty cavalry and was led by Captain Alonso de Gaete. Their mission was to escort a new Inca emperor—one of Manco's brothers, Cusi-Rimac. Pizarro hoped that by placing a new puppet emperor on the throne he might be able to splinter the Inca elite further, thereby weakening Manco's rebellion. Pizarro had thus conducted a hasty coronation—the third since his assassination of Atahualpa (the first being the short-lived Tupac Huallpa and the second Manco Inca)—and then had dispatched the new puppet emperor to Jauja, along with a Spanish escort and a number of the emperor's native attendants.

Since Jauja was located well north of the rebellion in Cuzco, Pizarro felt that the city would be a secure location where the new emperor could begin gradually to assert his power. Not long after sending this group on its way, however, Pizarro began to worry that the cavalry escort was too small. He therefore ordered an additional thirty foot soldiers, under Captain Francisco de Godoy, to march in support of Captain Gaete and his twenty men. Neither Pizarro nor his two captains knew at the time, of course, that the city where they were headed had just been overrun by General Quizo, that its inhabitants had been slaughtered, or that two forces of seventy and sixty Spaniards respectively had been destroyed almost to the man.

Although Pizarro feared that the new emperor's escort might be vulnerable, he never suspected, however, that Gaete and his men might be attacked by the very natives they were escorting. The puppet emperor, Cusi-Rimac, it turned out, far from being a turncoat against his brother Manco, had apparently been in secret communication with General Quizo's forces for some time. In a canyon somewhere on the way to Jauja, Quizo's army ambushed Gaete's column. Before the Spaniards even realized what was happening, Cusi-Rimac and his followers—the very people whom Gaete and his men had supposedly been protecting—turned on them. The result was another massacre. The combined native forces killed the Spanish captain and eigh-

teen of the twenty Spaniards. Only two escaped—one of them with a fractured leg—riding out of the canyon on a mule.

As the two survivors fled, they soon encountered the thirty Spanish foot
soldiers under Captain Godoy who had been sent to reinforce them. Listening to their story and thoroughly alarmed, Godoy abruptly decided to turn
around, escorting the two survivors back to Lima "with his tail between his
legs, to give Pizarro the bad news." General Quizo, meanwhile, sent Manco
a message about his recent victories, along with gifts of Spanish clothing,
weapons, a number of severed Spanish heads, "and two live Spaniards, one
black man, and four horses." Pizarro's puppet emperor, Cusi-Rimac, meanwhile, traveled southward to join his brother. He would remain Manco's ally
throughout the rebellion.

With three Spanish forces wiped out, only a single, isolated Spanish force
of thirty cavalry now remained in the central Andes. This was the column
that Pizarro had originally sent in relief of Cuzco, led by Captain Juan Morgovejo de Quiñones. General Quizo, however—zeroing in on his goal of
wiping out all Spaniards in the region—soon trapped Morgovejo's men in a
pass and applied to them the same treatment he had applied to the others.
Only a remnant of Morgovejo's force—practically the only survivors of four
separate Spanish columns—made its way back to Lima to report to Pizarro
the additional bad news. In two short months—May and June of 1536—
Spanish military fortunes had plummeted while those of the Incas had dramatically risen. For the first time since the Spaniards had arrived in Peru
four years earlier, an Inca general had successfully eliminated not one but
four Spanish columns, three of which were composed of cavalry. General
Quizo, in fact, had thus far succeeded in eliminating nearly two hundred of
the "invincible" *viracochas*—a number nearly equal to those currently besieged in Cuzco and more than were present at the capture of Atahualpa in
1532.

Only two months earlier, Francisco Pizarro had been in command of
around five hundred Spaniards and had a puppet Inca emperor on the
throne. Now that puppet led a growing native insurgency that had already
wiped out more than a third of Pizarro's forces. Five Spanish captains were
now dead—among them Francisco's own brother Juan. In addition, more
than one hundred horses had been either captured or killed, Jauja had been
sacked and its inhabitants massacred, Cuzco was under siege, and nearly

every Spanish *encomendero* between Cuzco and Lima had been systematically hunted down and slaughtered. Wrote one chronicler:

> The Governor was greatly troubled [after] seeing all of the bad things
> that had happened, because he already had four [sic] dead Captains and
> almost two hundred [dead] men and many horses, and he also knew for
> certain that this city [Cuzco] was either in great danger or was already
> lost, and [if the latter] that his brothers and all of the others in it were
> dead; and for this reason and seeing himself with so few people he was
> very distraught, fearing the loss of this land, for there wasn't a day when
> someone didn't come to tell him that "such and such a chief has re-
> belled," [or] "in such an area so many Christians have died who had
> gone looking for food."

Too late, Pizarro learned that the Incas had figured out a way to destroy
columns of cavalry that only months before appeared invulnerable to attack.
Realizing now that he had just sent more than a hundred cavalrymen to
their deaths, Pizarro was forced to face the unpleasant fact that he had no
more than a hundred Spaniards left with which to defend Lima. In addition,
rumors were swirling in the city almost daily about Inca armies that were on
their way to attack the city, intent on slaughtering all those who lived
here—whether natives, Spaniards, or slaves.

Fearing that his brothers Hernando, Gonzalo, and Juan might be dead, a
now desperate Pizarro sent an emergency appeal to the various Spanish
governors living elsewhere in the Americas. On July 9, 1536, two months
into Manco's rebellion, an uncharacteristically chastened Pizarro wrote a
pleading letter to Pedro de Alvarado, Hernando Cortés's former second-in-
command in Mexico and now the governor of Guatemala:

> Most Magnificent Sir,
>
> . . . The Inca [emperor Manco] . . . has the city of Cuzco besieged,
> and I have heard nothing about the Spaniards in it. . . . The country is
> so badly damaged that no native chief now serves us and they have won
> many victories against us. . . . It is causing me such great sorrow that it is
> consuming my entire life, as well as [the fear of] losing the Governorship.

. . . I beg of you to send me some help, because not only would it be
doing His Majesty a very great service, but it would [also] be doing me a
favor and would save the lives of those . . . who are here [in Lima]. . . .
You can be sure that if we are not rescued then Cuzco will be lost . . . and
then the rest of us will be lost, because we are few and have almost no
weapons and the Indians are fearless. . . . I will not say more except that it
will cost you little to perform this service for our Royal Majesty and [to
grant] the favor that both this realm and myself request. And even if it
costs a lot to help [us] Christians, everyone will be very grateful for it.

   May the Lord grant your magnificent person as prosperous a life as you
desire,

Francisco Pizarro

Pizarro's letters, bearing the news of the massive Inca rebellion, gradually made their way across the Isthmus, into the Caribbean, and on to Spain
itself. There, Emperor Charles V was eventually informed of Manco's revolt.
The unsettling news meant that the king's lucrative 20 percent share of all
the gold and silver that had been streaming out of Peru was, for the moment
at least, ended—like water from a faucet that had suddenly been switched
off. Sending the alarming news both to the Council of the Indies in Santo
Domingo and also to the king, the Spaniard Pascual de Andagoya* wrote
the following from Panama:

   The Lord of Cuzco and of the entire realm has rebelled. The rebellion
   has spread from province to province and suddenly they are all rising up.
   Rebellious chiefs have already arrived forty leagues [140 miles] from
   The City of the Kings. Governor [Pizarro] is asking for help and will be
   given everything possible from here. We will send someone there with
   as much money as will be needed, and we are asking that as many people come as are able, [along with] the greatest amount of artillery, harquebuses, and crossbows.

---

* Pascual de Andagoya was the same explorer who had originally brought back rumors to
  Panama of a wealthy land called *Piru* in 1522, rumors that only Francisco Pizarro followed
  up on.

With Pizarro desperately sending out the equivalent of SOS messages while simultaneously preparing Lima's defenses for the anticipated assault, Manco Inca, meanwhile, was busy celebrating General Quizo's victories at his new headquarters, located about thirty miles northwest of Cuzco. Manco had abandoned his previous headquarters in Calca, which was situated only a dozen miles from the capital, feeling that it was too vulnerable to attack. The rebel emperor had therefore moved another twenty miles further down the Yucay/Vilcanota River, to a fortress-temple complex called Ollantaytambo.* Here the flat-bottomed Yucay Valley, with its terraced hillsides and numerous royal estates, narrowed as the river continued its descent down the eastern side of the Andes toward the Amazon Basin. On the valley's northern side, crowning a rising series of more than a dozen steep agricultural terraces, rose the walled complex of Ollantaytambo, a stronghold that commanded the entrances of both the Yucay Valley and a tributary valley that led up over the Panticalla Pass and then down into the eastern jungles.

After relocating to Ollantaytambo, Manco had assembled his chiefs and captains for an important meeting about their collective failure to hold the fortress of Saqsaywaman. During the three months since Manco had escaped from Cuzco, the young emperor had matured rapidly. Wearing the royal fringe across his forehead and dressed no doubt in a soft vicuña wool tunic, Manco now addressed his audience of native chiefs and military officers:

> [My] sons and brothers,
>
> In past talks . . . you already know how I prevented you from inflicting harm on those evil people who—through the deceit of saying they were the sons of [the creator god] Viracocha and were sent by Him— had entered my realm, which I permitted and for this [reason] helped them, giving them what I had—silver and gold, clothing and corn, llamas and alpacas, men, women, and children and innumerable other things. They seized me, beat me, and mistreated me, without my having merited it, and then they tried to kill me. . . . It has caused me grief that, you being so many and they being so few, they escaped from your

---

* The Yucay/Vilcanota River was called the Willcamayu River by the Incas.

hands. Perhaps Viracocha helped them for you have told me that they were on their knees every night [praying]. . . . For if He did not help them—then how did they escape from your hands, with so many of you? What is done is done. . . . From now on, beware of them for . . . they are our worst enemies and we will perpetually be theirs. I want to strengthen my position in this town and to make a fortress here that no one will be able to penetrate. Do me this favor because one day we may need to make use of it.

While Manco's craftsmen busied themselves reinforcing the fortress's walls, *chaski* runners continued bringing him reports of General Quizo's string of victories to the north. Recalled Titu Cusi:

During this period . . . messengers arrived . . . [with news] of the destruction that had been carried out in . . . Lima and . . . Jauja, where battles had occurred between the Indians and the Spaniards in which the Indians were victorious. And they brought my father many heads of the Spaniards and two live Spaniards and a black man and four horses, which arrived amid great rejoicings for those victories, and my father accepted these [gifts] very honorably and infused everyone [with the desire] to fight with equal vigor.

With full knowledge now that General Quizo had wiped the central Andes clean of the Spanish invaders and had successfully crushed four separate forces of both Spanish foot soldiers and cavalry, and with Pizarro's two brothers virtually powerless in Cuzco and in no danger of being relieved, Manco now sent orders to General Quizo to proceed to Lima to seize the city. Spies in Lima no doubt had already informed Manco that the city was defended by around one hundred Spaniards and eighty horses—roughly half the number of Spaniards presently holding out in Cuzco—and that all the inhabitants—Spaniards and traitorous natives alike—were very much afraid. Once General Quizo had eliminated Pizarro and his forces on the coast, then he and his army could return to the Andes and could help Manco exterminate the remaining Spaniards in Cuzco. Manco could then restore the burned-out capital to its former magnificence and could begin restoring the power, glory, and dominion of his ancestors' empire.

For Hernando and Gonzalo Pizarro and the other nearly 190 Spaniards trapped in Cuzco, meanwhile, their situation was still desperate. Although they had been successful in capturing the fortress of Saqsaywaman, Juan Pizarro and four other Spaniards were now dead, many of them were wounded, food supplies were running low, morale had hit bottom, and—four months after the siege had begun—they still had no word from the outside world. Had Manco's rebellion spread across the Andes and down to the coast? They had no idea. Were Francisco Pizarro and the other Spaniards in the City of the Kings dead? No one knew. But how else could anyone explain why no relief force had arrived? A few thought that Pizarro might be alive, but that any relief force he may have sent had been unable to get through. With no communication and with rumors substituting for news, none of the Spaniards had a clue about what was going on elsewhere in Peru.

After the capture of Saqsaywaman, Hernando had stationed fifty foot soldiers to hold the fortress while he and the rest of his men had continued to hole up in the two buildings on the main square. Daily, however, Manco's forces continued to attack the Spaniards and their native auxiliaries. The once luxurious city now lay sprawled like a ruined corpse across the valley, its roofs crumbled and burned, many of its walls tumbled down, and with sling stones, broken barricades, and assorted rubble strewn across its streets. A number of captains now urged Hernando to assemble a small group of their finest cavalry to try to break out of the city and ride to find help on the coast. There they could learn whether Francisco Pizarro or any other Spaniards were still alive and might gather a relief force that could return to their aid. To stay here and watch both their food supplies and their own numbers dwindle, they argued, would only mean certain death for them all.

Others argued that any cavalry group attempting to break out of the city would only be partaking in a suicide mission. Long before the cavalry had reached the relative safety of the coastal plains, the horsemen would have to travel through passes where they could easily be trapped and slaughtered. If the cavalry unit were lost, that would leave those in Cuzco with fewer horses and with a much weaker force. Either they all broke out of their encirclement together, this second group argued, or they all stayed to fight. To divide their already outnumbered forces would surely result in disaster.

Trapped without hope of relief and knowing that if he could just get word to Lima that his brother Francisco—if still alive—would send them aid, Hernando decided that the escape attempt should proceed. Hernando was unaware, of course, that far larger cavalry forces had recently been annihilated by Quizo's army and that Manco, no doubt, was waiting for just such an opportunity. Seeing no other way out of their impasse, however, Hernando now selected fifteen of his finest riders for a mission that many of them believed would be their last.

Yet the day before the cavalry was to depart, the Incas unexpectedly presented the besieged Spaniards with news from the outside world, in the form of five severed Spanish heads and a large pile of ripped-up letters. According to Alonzo Enríquez de Guzmán:

> One day before the Spaniards were to set out, just after Mass, many Indians on the surrounding hills began to shout . . . and they left five heads of Christians and more than a thousand [ripped-up] letters on the road. The Indians had seized these letters and had killed some Christians whom the Governor had sent to help rescue this city. . . . The Indians had brought these things so that we could see them and know what had happened and so that we would become more discouraged. [But, on the contrary,] this gave us life and rejuvenated us. . . . Because by way of these letters we found out what we wanted to know—that the Governor and his men were alive . . . and we learned about the victory that the emperor [Charles V] had had [against the Moors] in the capture of Tunis. . . . My letters also reached me [in this way] . . . both those from my native land and from Governor [Pizarro].

Convincing Manco to send letters along with the severed heads had apparently been the brainstorm of one of Manco's Spanish prisoners. Somehow this man had been able to dupe the Inca emperor into believing that the Spaniards would be as devastated at the sight of the "useless" [ripped-up] "talking pages" as they would be at the sight of their comrades' severed heads. Even after three years among the Spaniards, it seemed, Manco had no more idea of how writing worked than he had had before the Spaniards' arrival. Pages with incomprehensible squiggles on them continued to make as little sense to the natives of South America as the coded knots of their *quipus* did to the Spaniards. Thus, without even realizing it, Manco had delivered a treasure trove of information—letters, some no doubt covered in blood, taken from the ill-fated Spanish expeditions that had recently been annihilated in the Andes.

Reinvigorated by the knowledge that his brother Francisco was probably still alive, Hernando canceled the attempt to reach the coast and instead decided that perhaps he and the rest of his trapped Spaniards might try to crush the Inca rebellion in one bold move. *Yanacona* spies had informed Hernando that Manco Inca was presently headquartered at a place called Ollantaytambo, some thirty miles northwest of Cuzco. If Hernando could strike directly at the emperor, capturing or killing him, then the trapped Spaniards might be able to break the back of the rebellion. Manco's cousin Pascac, meanwhile, who continued to fight on the side of the Spaniards, could then be placed on the throne. Leaving fifty foot soldiers in control of Saqsaywaman and another forty in the city below, Hernando now led a force of seventy cavalry and thirty foot soldiers, together with Chachapoyan, Cañari, and Inca auxiliaries, out of the city. Hernando's goal was a simple one: to seize or kill the leader of the native rebellion—Manco Inca himself.

Hernando and his men soon fought their way down into the narrow, flat Yucay Valley plain, then began following the Yucay River, fording it five or six times in the process. At each river crossing, Manco's sling throwers hurled rocks from the other side, only to be dispersed with lances and swords once the cavalry swam across. As the valley continued to become more constricted, the Spaniards' native scouts suddenly stopped and pointed. There, on the top of an enormous stone spur jutting out from the valley wall like a buttress, the Spaniards saw for the first time the temple fortress of Ollantaytambo. Remembered Pedro Pizarro, who rode as one of the horsemen:

> When we arrived we found [Ollantay]Tambo so well fortified that it was a horrifying sight, for the place . . . is very strong, with very high terraces and with very large and well fortified stone walls. It has but one entrance that is against a very steep hill. And . . . [on the hill] were many warriors with many boulders, which they had up above in order to hurl them down whenever the Spaniards dared to enter and [attempt to] capture the [fortress] gate.

Dwarfed by the valley's high walls and with tens of thousands of native warriors clustered on the tops of more than a dozen enormous, staggered terraces that led up to the fortress's command center, Hernando's men gathered on the plain below. They soon noticed that, side by side with the usual native warriors, stood what appeared to be legions of bow-and-arrow-wielding natives from the great forests to the east, people their native auxiliaries referred to as the Antis.

Although the Incas had always incorporated Amazonian warriors into their armies, as only those from the jungle knew how to use bows and arrows, the Spaniards were surprised to see that so many of these warriors had suddenly appeared. Unlike the inhabitants of the Andes, many of the Antis painted their faces with dyes; others more than likely had various feathers from tropical birds sprouting from the skin around their noses or mouths, or incorporated into headbands that added bright splashes of color to their long black hair. When the Spaniards rode too close to the fortress's walls, slews of arrows immediately arced into the sky, bearing sharpened bamboo and palm wood points, many of which hit the armored men and their horses. The Antis' aim, Hernando soon discovered, was very, very good.

Thirty miles from Cuzco, in hostile territory and with enemy warriors howling, hurling, and shooting sling stones and arrows down at them, Hernando Pizarro wheeled his horse around and rode over to talk with one of the few gray-haired conquistadors in the group. Wrote one eyewitness:

> Hernando . . . said to an old man whom he was with, "Well, the young men don't dare approach or do anything, so let us old men go try it out [the Indians' defenses]." And he took the old gray-haired man with him and they assaulted the walls until their horses' chests were up against them [the enemy's walls] and, lancing two Indians, it was amazing to see the arrows that rained down upon them as they returned [galloping] and to hear the [Indians'] roar.

While Hernando's qualities of arrogance, greed, and selfishness had made him generally unpopular among the Spaniards, no one had ever accused him of not being brave. Hernando's sudden display of that latter quality, in fact, apparently shamed the other Spaniards so much that now a group of the younger riders spurred their horses and attempted to reach the single stone doorway leading up to the fortress, one that the natives had filled in with stones. The native defenders, however, quickly repulsed the attack, for, as Pedro Pizarro described, they "hurled down so many boulders and fired so many [slingshot] stones and arrows that even had there been many more of us Spaniards than there were, they would have killed us all." During these initial skirmishes, Manco's warriors killed many of the Spaniards' native auxiliaries, wounded several Spaniards, and broke the leg of one of the horses so badly that the horse wandered about, alternately tripping and falling to the ground.

As Hernando's men fell back and regrouped, Manco's warriors now began to descend from the fortress in order to pursue the harried Spaniards. "There is one thing about these Indians," recalled Pedro Pizarro, "that when they are following up a victory they chase after you like demons, and [yet] when they flee they are like wet hens. And since here they were following up a victory, and seeing us in retreat, they pursued us with great determination." The Spaniards found that the Amazonian archers, especially, fought ferociously: "There were among the Incas many . . . [Amazonian natives] who do not know what it means to flee," marveled one Spaniard, "for they continue to fire arrows [even] when they are dying."

Hernando's cavalry continued to circle and skirmish while the Spanish foot soldiers and native auxiliaries tangled with the ever bolder Inca troops. As the two forces grappled with each other, the Spaniards suddenly noticed that the plain they were fighting on had mysteriously begun to flood with water. Manco Inca, it turned out, had devised a secret weapon and had chosen this precise moment to unleash it. Along the nearby Patacancha River, which emptied into the Yucay, Inca engineers had built a series of canals. Manco had now given the signal to open them, flooding the only plain upon which the Spanish horsemen could maneuver. According to one account, Manco Inca himself now emerged, riding a Spanish horse and urging his warriors to attack. Soon, the water had risen so high that it reached the bellies of the Spaniards' horses, paralyzing their ability to attack. According to Pedro Pizarro:

The Indians, without our knowing it, turned the river into the plain where we were, and had we waited longer, we would have all died. Yet when he understood the trick the Indians had played on us and that it was impossible to take this village at that time, Hernando Pizarro ordered us to retreat. And as the night grew darker he sent all the foot soldiers ahead and the baggage with some mounted troops to guard it, and he himself with other troops took the middle, and he ordered his brother, Gonzalo Pizarro, along with a few more of us cavalrymen to bring up the rear, and in this way we retreated.

Through the long, black night the Spaniards carried out a forced retreat, their native auxiliaries helping them to fight off hordes of warriors who continually appeared out of the darkness with no warning, shouting and swinging their mace clubs, then disappearing from the circles of jumping, chaotic light of the Spaniards' torches. Somehow, Hernando and his men managed to struggle across the valley and reach the heights on the opposite side. There they camped for the night in an abandoned Inca village. The next day, tired, wounded, and discouraged, the Spaniards fought their way back to Cuzco, rejoining their embattled countrymen whom they had left behind. Despite their best efforts, their bold military attack had resulted in a number of lost horses and a multitude of wounded men. If anything, the Spaniards' failed campaign and desperate retreat only seemed to have emboldened Manco and his warriors.

Four hundred miles away and roughly eleven thousand feet lower in elevation, Francisco Pizarro anxiously waited for reinforcements from abroad and wondered whether his brothers in Cuzco were still alive. Pizarro was still receiving reports from frightened *yanacona* spies that a massive Inca army was assembling nearby for an attack. This was the same army, his spies no doubt told him—led by a General Quizo—that had wiped out Pizarro's relief forces and had massacred the Spaniards in Jauja. General Quizo, they said, had vowed to destroy every bearded invader on the coast, exactly as he had done in the mountains.

Pizarro had been living in the City of the Kings for the last year and a half. Living with him was his seventeen-year-old Indian mistress, Doña Inés—the daughter of the great Huayna Capac and a sister of Manco Inca—as well as a two-year-old daughter, whom Pizarro doted upon, and a one-year-old son. The city Pizarro had founded, laid out around a traditional Spanish town square, currently consisted of a hodgepodge of recently constructed and in-construction buildings, along with an amalgam of tents, lean-tos, and native dwellings that were inhabited by the servants of the Spaniards and by a recent consignment of African slaves.

Now, because of their recent losses, however, only about a hundred Spaniards were available to defend Los Reyes, or "The Kings," as it was called colloquially. The latter were divided into a force of eighty cavalrymen and twenty foot soldiers. In addition, Pizarro was relying upon at least several thousand native auxiliaries, mostly Chachapoyan, Cañari, and former members of the *yanacona,* or Inca servant class. Rounding out the assemblage were fourteen Spanish women—the only Spanish women in Peru—together with the Spaniards' numerous native mistresses, and a sprinkling of female *morisca* (Islamic) slaves. Constructed upon barren sands, the City of the Kings lay some twelve miles inland from the Pacific Ocean. To the east, northeast and southeast rose a number of dry, steep, and rounded brown hills, the last vestiges of the Andes, which tumbled down from their icy heights and eventually sank beneath the windswept coastal sands.

A general atmosphere of fear and anxiety now gripped the city's inhabitants, given the rumors about the approach of hostile enemy armies, the relatively small number of defenders, and the knowledge that roughly half of the city's Spanish forces had already been wiped out. A giant native rebellion, meanwhile, was rumored to be gathering in the nearby Andes like some catastrophic storm that was slowly headed their way. Spanish-occupied Jauja, Lima's inhabitants knew, no longer existed; its *encomenderos* had been wiped out. Cuzco had possibly suffered the same fate. In addition, nothing had been heard from Diego de Almagro, whose five hundred men had left to explore the Kingdom of New Toledo, as his new realm was called, over a year earlier. They, too, might have been exterminated, for all anyone knew. Nor had any ships with relief forces arrived in response to Pizarro's desperate pleas abroad. Thus far, in fact, Pizarro had not received a single reply.

Finally, late in the Southern Hemisphere's winter, as the omnipresent mist, or *garúa,* clung to Los Reyes like a cold damp cloth, the news that everyone had been dreading now arrived in the form of a lone Spaniard galloping across the plain.

[The conquistador Diego de Agüero] presently arrived, having fled to the [City of the] Kings, [and] who reported that the Indians were up in arms and had tried to set him on fire in their villages. A great army of them was approaching, the news of which deeply terrified the city, all the more so because of how few Spaniards were in it.

Almost immediately, more unwelcome news followed.

> [Auxiliary] Indians from outside of the City of the Kings arrived, complaining that great quantities of Indian warriors were coming down from the mountains to destroy them, killing their women and children. The Governor sent Pedro de Lerma with twenty cavalry in order to find out what was going on and to scout out the area, for [this was happening] not more than three leagues [ten miles] away and on the plain. . . . [Lerma] left that night, and only two leagues [seven miles] from the city he [suddenly] found himself besieged by fifty thousand Indian warriors.

The rumors of an impending attack, the city's inhabitants realized, had indeed been true. Unbeknownst to Lima's defenders, General Quizo had just spent months gathering his forces and raising additional levies of warriors from along the western flanks of the Andes. By now Quizo had plenty of practical experience in combating Spanish troops, both foot soldiers and cavalry. By using the Andes's rugged topography to his advantage, and by collecting accurate intelligence on the disposition and movements of enemy forces, he had been able to destroy previously invincible Spanish cavalry detachments of up to eighty men, with negligible losses of his own. Still, Manco's veteran general clearly knew his own limitations: thus far, neither he nor any other Inca commander had discovered an effective defense against Spanish cavalry on flat ground, no matter how great the numerical superiority of their own forces might be. Quizo's ultimate commander, however—Manco Inca—had yet to learn this lesson.

Months earlier, after hearing the welcome news of his general's unbroken string of victories, Manco had sent Quizo one of his own sisters, "who was very beautiful," to be the general's wife. Manco had also sent Quizo numerous gifts, including high-status royal litters that lent the general even more authority and prestige. In effect, Manco had just promoted his most successful general and was now tied to him through matrimony. The gifts, however, were delivered along with firm instructions: Quizo was to attack Pizarro's coastal city "and destroy it, not leaving a single house standing, and to kill as many Spaniards as he could find." Pizarro himself was to be taken alive, if possible, and was to be brought to Manco as a prisoner. Any natives found helping the Spaniards were to be summarily executed. Once having sacked and destroyed the city, Quizo was to return with his army to Cuzco, where he and Manco would complete the extermination of the remaining Spaniards in Peru.

General Quizo fully realized that the strength and speed of the Spaniards' horses could only be neutralized by steep topography. Horses, it turned out—even more so than men—simply were no good at running up steep hills. As long as his men controlled the heights, Quizo had the advantage. In the case of the Spanish city on the coast, however, which Quizo's scouts had no doubt built small clay models of for him to study, the general quickly saw that his troops would be forced to abandon the protection of the hills and would have to attack the Spaniards on flat terrain. There, they could certainly expect to be attacked by Pizarro's cavalry. As the Inca general studied the clay models and examined the protuberances representing the hills around the city, he undoubtedly realized that Manco's order to attack Pizarro's coastal city was going to be the most difficult challenge of his life.

Meanwhile, Pedro de Lerma, who had found Quizo's advance forces massing some seven miles from the city, decided to attack. Despite suffering numerous casualties, however, Quizo's warriors continued to advance, new ones immediately taking the place of those who had been slain. Quizo's troops eventually killed one Spaniard, wounded a number of others, and then with one well-placed sling stone broke most of the teeth in Captain Lerma's mouth, leaving the captain's face a bloody mess. Lerma broke off the engagement soon afterward and retreated with his troops to Lima.

After a careful examination of the terrain, General Quizo decided to attack Pizarro's city from three sides—north, east, and south. He would then use his overwhelming numbers to overrun the city, similar to Manco's strategy in Cuzco. Dividing his army into three divisions, Quizo ordered a division of Tarama, Atabillo, Huánuco, and Huayla tribes to attack from the north, a second division of Huancas, Angares, Yauyos, and Chauircos to attack from the south, while he himself would lead the third division and

would attack directly from the east. Quizo's forces, like so many Roman legions, now began to take up their positions, making themselves visible to
the city's defenders for the first time as they began emerging from the gray
mist. "The Governor, seeing such a multitude of warriors," wrote one Spanish survivor, "had no doubt whatsoever that our side was completely lost."
Finally, with his legions now waiting for his signal and watching them hoist
their cloth banners aloft, General Quizo gave the command to attack.

Quizo's three forces now began a pincer-like movement toward the city,
advancing across the plain to the sound of the Incas' traditional martial
music of conch shells, clay trumpets, and drums. From above, the divisions
looked like a three-sided clamp that was slowly tightening to crush the city.
Pizarro, meanwhile, had stationed his eighty cavalry within the city, hidden
from sight. When Quizo's divisions finally began arriving at the city's outskirts and the rest of the attacking troops were now well exposed on the
plain, Pizarro gave his own signal to attack.

A group of harquebusiers now suddenly appeared, firing their weapons,
their heavy barrels issuing clouds of smoke and their lead balls ripping into
Quizo's attackers. Next the cavalry charged. With lances and swords drawn
and shouting hoarsely, the Spaniards galloped rapidly toward the attackers'
front lines, smashing into them, then began slashing downward with their
swords and thrusting repeatedly with their spears. The Spaniards' native
auxiliaries, meanwhile, far more numerous than the conquistadors, also
charged out, counterattacking the Inca troops with stone and bronze-tipped
clubs. Fierce fighting broke out, although as usual the warriors' clubs and
sling stones were no match for armored Spaniards with their thousand-
pound horses and their carefully honed, slicing blades of steel. Although
Quizo's troops had succeeded in reaching the outskirts of the city, it was
there that the Inca attack stalled, as the Spanish foot soldiers, cavalry, and
native auxiliaries fought fiercely to prevent Los Reyes from being overrun.

All afternoon the battle raged, with the Spaniards' armored cavalry exact-
ing a deadly and unequal toll on Quizo's troops. Finally, the Inca general ordered his forces to retreat to the hills ringing the city, knowing that the
steep escarpments there would protect them from further cavalry attacks.
Quizo and his own division retired to the tall, brown, sugarloaf-like hill
now called Cerro San Cristóbal, which still rises up over Lima from across

the Rimac River. Quizo's other divisions, meanwhile, seized the hills to the north, south, and west, thus practically encircling the city.

For the next five days Manco's finest general laid siege to Pizarro's City of the Kings, with the Spaniards having to fight fiercely each day to prevent the city from being overrun. By the sixth day, however, General Quizo had reached a turning point. Manco had not ordered his veteran general to lay siege to the city, but to take and destroy it, and to put the Spaniards there to death. The constant, unequal attrition, however, was undoubtedly beginning to demoralize the general's troops. Well aware that Manco's warriors still surrounded Cuzco but had been stalemated there for more than three months, Quizo no doubt felt pressure to finish the job here on the coast and to return and assist his emperor in the battle for the Inca capital. Each day, however, Quizo witnessed from his hilltop position the Spanish cavalry wreak havoc among his attacking warriors, inflicting severe losses. The only chance he had of breaching Pizarro's defenses, Quizo concluded, was to launch one final and overwhelming blow upon the city—but this time he himself would lead the charge.

Calling for an assembly of his captains, Quizo waited patiently for them to arrive. From the heights of Cerro San Cristóbal, the general could look out over the city and could see the Inca roads stretching north, east, and south while to the west lay the dull, metallic blue ocean enveloped in fog. To the east rose the Andes, but only their flanks were now visible due to the constant mist. Gradually, Quizo's captains arrived on their litters, resplendent in their cotton or alpaca tunics, their colorful mantles, and their various ornaments of gold, silver, and copper. Once they had assembled, Manco's general stood and gestured down at the Spanish settlement, announcing gravely that he was "determined to enter the city and take it by force or to die in the attempt. 'I intend to enter the town today and kill all the Spaniards who are in it,'" Quizo said, the golden plugs in his earlobes glinting as he turned. "'Those who accompany me must go with the understanding that if I die, all will die, and if I flee, then all will flee.' The native captains and leaders all agreed to go with him."

Having learned no doubt from his spies that the Spaniards had their own women in the city, Quizo now promised his captains that he would distribute the women to them as gifts, so that the two races could mate and "produce a strong generation of warriors." The general also reminded his captains that if they were successful, then the hated invaders' last toehold on their sacred coast would be smashed, and that Tawantinsuyu, land of the four quarters, would soon be free of the false *viracochas* from across the sea. Later that afternoon, after the captains had returned to their troops and on the sixth day of the siege, General Quizo launched his final assault on Pizarro's City of the Kings. Wrote one chronicler:

> The entire [native] army began to move with a vast array of banners, from which the Spaniards recognized the determination and will they were coming with. The Governor [Pizarro] ordered all the cavalry to form into two squadrons. He placed one squadron under his command in ambush in one street, and . . . the other squadron in another. The enemy was already advancing across the open plain by the river. They were very magnificent men, for all had been hand-picked. The general [Quizo] was advancing in front of them, wielding a lance.

One of the differences between Inca and Spanish methods of warfare was that the Inca general and his field commanders often led the charge. The typically polyglot amalgamation of native troops, apparently, was accustomed to being led and inspired. As long as they could see their commanders riding on their litters beside or ahead of them, the natives fought with determination. If their commanders went down under enemy maces or sling fire, however, then their attack often would falter. The Achilles' heel of Inca warfare, therefore, was the placement of the command center of their assaults often at the very apex of their attacks. Spanish commanders, by contrast, normally directed their battles from a position at the rear. Except in the capture of Atahualpa, for example, Pizarro had always sent others—Diego de Almagro, Hernando de Soto, and other captains—to lead the advance. If something should have happened to them, then Pizarro still would have remained in full control of the invasion. According to one chronicler,

> [General Quizo] crossed both branches of the [Rimac] river in his litter. Seeing that [the enemy warriors] were starting to enter the streets of the city and some of Quizo's men were moving along the tops of the walls, the [Spanish] cavalry charged out and attacked with such great determi-

nation that, since the ground was flat, they routed them instantly. The general [Quizo] was left there, dead, and so were forty commanders and other chiefs alongside him. Although it seemed as if our men had specially selected them, they were killed because they were marching at the head of their men and thus they were the first that the Spaniards smashed into. The Spaniards continued to kill and wound Indians as far as the foot of the hill [of San Cristóbal], at which point they encountered a very strong resistance from a defensive site they had made.

Night began to fall on a battlefield littered with native bodies and with the bloodied and torn litters of the fallen Inca commanders. The next morning, when the Spaniards awakened they found that the entire native army had disappeared as suddenly as it had arrived. Crushed psychologically by the loss of their general and of so many of their leaders, Quizo's troops had retreated to the Andes. Once again, armored Spanish cavalry—given plenty of room to maneuver—had proven to be the decisive factor. That, coupled with Quizo's fatal strategy of placing himself and his commanders in the vanguard, had stopped the Inca assault on Pizarro's coastal city quite literally dead in its tracks.

Three days after Quizo's death, a breathless *chaski* runner arrived at Ollantaytambo to Manco's camp. The emperor sat with a grim face as the *chaski* repeated a message carried by more than sixty different relay runners about the recent disaster on the coast: General Quizo's string of victories had ended; the general to whom Manco had just presented his sister as a wife was dead—and so was a long list of fine Inca commanders; Quizo's army had retreated in disarray back into the mountains, Manco was told. The Spanish city had not been overrun. Francisco Pizarro was still alive, his cavalry intact.

For Manco, the news of Quizo's defeat was devastating. The empire's finest general, upon whom so many of his hopes had been pinned, had been destroyed. Whether Manco realized it or not, however, he himself was responsible for Quizo's death. Encouraged by his general's seeming invincibility, and perhaps also due to sacred omens or to the advice of oracles, Manco had sent his victorious general on a suicide mission. The Inca emperor had apparently ignored the fundamental reason for Quizo's prior successes—the effective use of Andean topography to neutralize the dreaded

Spanish cavalry—and instead had ordered him to attack on a wide-open plain where that same cavalry could not be stopped. Quizo's final, desperate charge calls to mind the much later Pickett's Charge at Gettysburg, the Australian assault on Gallipoli, the Charge of the Light Brigade in the Crimea, or any other number of hopeless military endeavors. No doubt, Quizo himself must have known that he had been ordered to carry out a mission that would very likely result in his death. Yet, under the direct order of his divine emperor, Quizo had had no other choice than to attack.

Inca tradition had further imperiled Quizo's final assault by ensuring that the Inca general would have a front-row seat when the stakes were at their highest, riding on one of the finest litters in the empire at the very point of the attack. Some Spanish accounts stated that General Quizo was ultimately felled by a harquebus bullet, others that he had died from a lance plunged directly into his heart. No matter. The great warrior was dead, and with him died Manco's finest military commander—the only Inca general who had thus far managed to successively defeat the Spaniards. With Quizo's army now in disarray, Manco was no longer in a position to prevent Pizarro's cavalry from riding in relief of Cuzco. Manco was about to receive even worse news, however: a column of four hundred, fully armored Spanish soldiers was on its way back to Peru—and riding at its head was Pizarro's one-eyed ex-partner, Diego de Almagro.

11 ❖ THE RETURN OF THE ONE-EYED CONQUEROR

"And as much friendship and brotherhood of many years as existed between [Pizarro] and Almagro, self-interest severed these, greed clouded his [Pizarro's] mind, and ambition to rule and distribute [*encomiendas*] acted against what would have been more long lasting if they were in poverty and want, not having come upon such a wealthy land as the two of them did—so uneducated that they did not know the letters of the alphabet as such—but there was only envy, deceit, and other unjust ways [between them]."

PEDRO DE CIEZA DE LEÓN,
THE DISCOVERY AND CONQUEST OF PERU, 1554

"The wish to acquire more is admittedly a very natural and common thing; and when men succeed in this they are always praised rather than condemned. But when they lack the ability to do so and yet want to acquire more at all costs, they deserve condemnation for their mistakes."

NICCOLÒ MACHIAVELLI, *THE PRINCE*, 1511

DESPITE THE DEATH OF GENERAL QUIZO, MANCO INCA WAS nevertheless determined to continue his siege of Cuzco, hoping that through a combination of starvation and gradual Spanish attrition that he could eventually overcome Hernando Pizarro's beleaguered men. For four months after Quizo's death, Manco continued to surround the Inca capital, using the converted fortress of nearby Ollantaytambo as his headquarters. Although Manco's forces were ultimately unable to prevent the Spaniards

With the return of Almagro from Chile,
conflicts soon erupted over the control of Peru.

from resupplying themselves with food, they were too strong, however, for Hernando and his trapped men to break out of the city and escape.

Sometime in January or February 1537, roughly nine months into the siege, a *chaski* messenger arrived at Manco's fortress in Ollantaytambo. A large force of Spaniards, the messenger said, roughly four hundred of them and with many horses, had just arrived in the Inca town of Arequipa, a little over two hundred miles to the south. With them rode Manco's brother Paullu on a royal litter, and also Pizarro's old partner, Diego de Almagro. Manco no doubt stared at the messenger, who as a commoner stood with averted eyes to the ground, then looked down at the Yucay Valley, stretching out before him. Suddenly, Manco must have realized, despite all his efforts, the balance of power had abruptly shifted, almost as if there had been another *pachacuti,* or overturning of the world. Diego de Almagro had returned to Peru.

The sixty-one-year-old Almagro had left Cuzco some twenty months earlier, with five hundred Spaniards, twelve thousand native auxiliaries, and hundreds of horses. During nearly two years of savage fighting with local natives and a trek of over three thousand miles, Almagro and his men had crossed over Andean passes so clogged with snow that some Spaniards had pulled their boots off only to discover that their frozen toes had come off. Elsewhere, the Spanish invaders had stacked the numberless dead bodies of their native porters as shelter against the icy wind. The members of Almagro's expedition had endured starvation, constant attacks, and eventually, some two hundred miles to the south of what is now Santiago, Chile, they had run into the fierce Araucanians. The latter not only stopped the Spaniards in their tracks, forcing them to retreat, but would successfully fight off all further attempts to subjugate them for the next two centuries.

To his great disappointment, Almagro had gradually come to realize that the governorship the king had granted him contained none of the riches of Peru. Francisco Pizarro had received by far the wealthiest portion of the Inca Empire, Almagro now knew—and he had received its dregs. Eventually, after a long, debilitating trek north during which many more men and horses died, what was left of the expedition reached the town of Arequipa, in what is now the southern Andes of Peru. At least a hundred Spaniards, innumerable African slaves, and over half of Almagro's horses had died during the expedition. Similarly, most of Almagro's twelve thousand native auxiliaries had either died or else had abandoned the expedition and fled. Their dreams of finding a second Peru full of towns, cities, fertile farms, and rich mines now shattered, Almagro's followers—most of whom had missed out on the distributions of treasure in Cajamarca and Cuzco—were now intent on only one thing: returning to Peru and seizing whatever riches there they could find.

Such was the state of affairs when Almagro first received news that the young Inca emperor Manco Inca had rebelled, that a massive native uprising had occurred, and that several hundred Spaniards were currently trapped in Cuzco, a city that he had personally coveted for years. Paullu, who had accompanied the expedition to Chile, soon sent a messenger to Manco's camp bearing a letter from Almagro. The messenger, presumably, was accompanied by a literate Spaniard and by a native interpreter who could translate Spanish into *runasimi*.

"My well-loved son and brother," Almagro addressed the much younger Manco,

> While I was in Chile . . . they gave me news that the Christians were abusing you, and about the robbery of your property and house, and about the seizure of your beloved wives, which gives me more pain than if they had done that to me, especially because I believe that what they did to you was unjust. And because I appreciate and love you and consider you a true son and brother, as soon as I found out I immediately decided to come with a thousand Christians and seven hundred horses, who are with me now, and with letters and powers from the King, my lord, in order to restore all that they took from you and to punish those responsible for treating you so badly, as their crimes demand.

Almagro had purposely inflated the number of his troops in order to appear more powerful than he actually was, and had also lied about bearing letters regarding Manco's situation from the king. The conquistador continued:

> Because if you rose up or made war, it was caused by their being so wicked that you were unable to tolerate it. And although with your [recent] punishment [of them] you must be satisfied, given that I want to

personally take care of this, in order to send them as prisoners to the
King who will order that they be executed, it seems to me that with my
arrival you should be confident . . . that you will never lack my help
[again]. . . . And even though the troops I have with me are so numerous
and so powerful that they are enough to subjugate a great portion of the
earth, and [even though] I am daily expecting another two thousand
men, I wouldn't think of doing anything without your approval and advice, nor would I ever refuse you the friendship and goodwill that I have
always felt towards you. . . . I can only hope that . . . you will come see
me, if that is possible, [and] you can have complete confidence in me . . .
[for] I give you my word. This will be brief, as I want to know about
your health, which God grants you as you wish.

Almagro quickly followed up his letter by sending two Spanish emissaries to visit with the Inca emperor. Francisco Pizarro, Almagro realized,
was obviously now in a much weaker position in Peru than he had been
only two years earlier. Pizarro's weakness presented an unexpected opportunity for Almagro, who was now intent upon discovering whether the
present turmoil in Peru could be used to his advantage. With the right
diplomatic moves, Almagro reasoned, he might be able to negotiate a truce
with Manco while simultaneously blaming the insurrection on the Pizarros.
Almagro could thus strengthen his own position to win the king's approval
of his right to govern Cuzco. Almagro therefore decided to head north toward the Yucay Valley, where Manco Inca was currently headquartered, instead of riding in relief of the besieged Spaniards, who were as yet unaware
of his return.

Almagro's Spanish emissaries, meanwhile, soon arrived in the Yucay Valley. Everywhere they looked, the two men observed Manco's troops sullenly
watching them, yet allowing them to pass. Eventually, they arrived beneath
the high granite spur upon which Manco's fortress of Ollantaytambo was
situated. Climbing the long flight of stone stairs up to the citadel, they were
greeted there warmly by Manco Inca, who had already received Almagro's
letter. The two emissaries now repeated Almagro's offer: that the governor
was shocked by the unjust treatment Manco had received at the hands of the
Spaniards in Cuzco; that he, Almagro, would make sure that those responsible received the punishment they deserved; and that if Manco would only

end his rebellion, then Almagro would make sure that the king pardoned Manco's attack on the Pizarros and on their followers. In a subsequent letter, the two emissaries reported Manco's response directly to the king.

[Your Sacred Majesty,]

Sent by your Governor [Almagro] in your royal name and given our diplomatic mission, which in effect was to bring [Manco Inca] peacefully [from his rebellion] and to show him the friendship that the Governor [Almagro] had for him and the abuse that it seemed to him that the Christians in Cuzco had done to [Manco] against your Majesty's wishes . . . [we wish to inform you that] the Inca [emperor] received us very well and listened to our message, and responded in the following manner:

"How is it that the great lord from Castile [Spain] orders that they [the Spaniards] seize my wives and take me prisoner with a chain around my neck and that they urinate on me and spit in my face? [How is it that] Gonzalo Pizarro, brother of the elder lord [Francisco Pizarro], stole my wife and has her still? And that Diego Maldonado threatened me [with death] and demanded gold, saying that he, too, was a lord?"

And he [Manco] also complained about Pedro del Barco and Gomez de Macuela, citizens of this city [of Cuzco], and about those who had urinated on him while he was prisoner, which he said were Alonso de Toro and [Gregorio] Setiel and Alonso de Mesa and Pedro Pizarro and [Francisco de] Solares, all citizens [*encomenderos*] of this city. And he also said that they burned his eyebrows with a lit candle. Finally, he concluded, saying "To my father, Almagro, if the message you have sent me is true and you are not lying, then I will come to . . . [you] peacefully . . . and I will stop killing all of these Christians who have done me these wrongs."

. . . May God protect you [the King] and enlarge the [Christian] universe . . .

Your humble vassals,
Pedro de Oñate and
Juan Gómez de Malver

While Manco conferred with Almagro's two emissaries, another messenger now arrived at his camp, this one a native auxiliary from Cuzco and sent by Hernando Pizarro. The Spaniards in Cuzco had finally begun to hear rumors that Diego de Almagro had returned to Peru with a large force of men. Initially, they hadn't believed the rumors, because they had been hearing apocryphal stories of various relief forces for months now, none of which had ever materialized. Recently, however, the Spaniards had woken up one morning to find that the native levies surrounding the city had suddenly been withdrawn. Sending out a reconnaissance party that presumably captured native informants, Hernando soon discovered that Almagro had indeed returned from Chile and was now only a dozen or so miles away to the east, encamped in the town of Urcos. Hernando also learned that instead of coming to their relief, Almagro was engaged in secret negotiations with the Inca emperor.

The majority of the Spaniards in Cuzco were greatly relieved to hear of Almagro's arrival, believing that at last their ordeal had ended. Hernando Pizarro, however, became suspicious once he learned that Almagro had entered into negotiations with Manco rather than traveling directly to Cuzco. Negotiations about what? Hernando no doubt asked. And who had given Almagro the right to negotiate about anything in his brother's kingdom? A naturally distrustful man, Hernando had not forgotten the bitter conflict that his brothers had had with Almagro over the possession of Cuzco while Hernando was in Spain. Anticipating such a conflict, in fact, Hernando had petitioned the king soon after his arrival in Spain, asking the king to extend his brother's original grant to conquer Peru further southward, in an effort to ensure that Cuzco would ultimately be included within his brother's governorship. The king had done so, granting Francisco Pizarro an additional seventy leagues (245 miles) to the south. The king had not, however, stipulated if the measurement of Pizarro's realm was to be conducted in a straight line north and south, or diagonally along the coast. That vagueness, coupled with the difficulty of conducting geographical measurements in sixteenth-century Peru, left Cuzco for the moment in a sort of no-man's-land, with both the Pizarros and Almagro now set to begin a renewed struggle over its control.

Distrusting Almagro's intentions, Hernando quickly wrote a letter to Manco, his first attempt to negotiate with the Inca emperor since Manco had unleashed his rebellion. Hernando informed the emperor that he was willing to forgive and forget all that had happened during the previous year; at the same time, however, he urged Manco not to trust anything that Almagro might tell him. Francisco Pizarro was the king's governor of this area, not Almagro, Hernando insisted, and if Almagro told him anything different, then Almagro was a traitorous liar.

Two different emissaries and three different forces—two Spanish, one Inca—now jockeyed for position at the high fortress citadel of Ollantaytambo. All were competing for the same thing: control over Peru or, in Almagro's case, control of the Cuzco region so that it could be added to his kingdom in the south. For almost a century, Manco's ancestors had ruled the central Andes. Now, however, the young emperor was suddenly confronted with two Spanish forces, both of which were offering to share power with him—if only he were to side with one against the other. But how could he know if either was telling the truth? And how could he know if they weren't secretly working together to destroy both him and his rebellion?

Suspicious of possible duplicity, Manco abruptly asked Almagro's two emissaries to prove their sincerity. If they would chop off the hand of Hernando's native messenger, he said, then that would prove to him that Almagro really hated the Pizarros. In Manco's eyes, the messenger was in any case a traitor, as he had helped Hernando and his men survive the long and bitterly fought battle for Cuzco. Manco's warriors quickly pinned the messenger's arm down while another handed one of the Spaniards a sword. As Manco watched, protected by his elite guards, the Spaniard slowly lifted the sword above the outstretched hand. There it presumably hovered for a moment until the Spaniard brought it down, neatly slicing off four fingers. Apparently satisfied, Manco allowed the two Spanish emissaries to return to Almagro's camp, asking them to arrange a meeting with the governor in the town of Calca, about twenty miles away. Manco meanwhile sent Hernando Pizarro a message that was both blunt and unmistakably clear: the return of the now fingerless native collaborator.

As the two emissaries began riding their horses back up the valley, they soon crossed paths with a third Spaniard, Rui Díaz, who had decided to try to personally negotiate with the Inca ruler. Díaz had been on good terms with Manco prior to departing with Almagro for Chile; he now apparently believed that if he could successfully negotiate a peace accord that would end Manco's rebellion, then he would surely receive an *encomienda* or some other reward in return. Díaz therefore headed directly toward Manco's headquarters. Wrote Pedro Pizarro:

> When Rui Díaz arrived where Manco Inca was, he [Manco] received him very well . . . and he kept him [Díaz] with him for two days. And on the third day Manco asked him a question that, according to what Rui Díaz [later] said, was: "Tell me, Rui Díaz, if I were to give the King a very great treasure, would he withdraw all the Christians from this land?" Rui Díaz replied, "How much would you give?" Rui Díaz said that Manco then had a [large quantity] . . . of corn [kernels] brought out and had it piled on the ground. And from that pile he took one grain, and said: "The Christians have [only] found as much gold and silver as this kernel; by comparison what you have *not* found is as large as this pile from which I took this single kernel." . . . Rui Díaz [then] said to Manco Inca, "Even if all these mountains were made of gold and silver and you were to give them to the King, he would [still] not withdraw the Spaniards from this land." When Manco heard this, he said to him, "Then leave, Rui Díaz, and tell Almagro to go wherever he wants, for my people and I will die if we must in order to finish off the Christians."

Not to be dissuaded from his goal, Díaz did his best to try to convince Manco that he could trust Almagro because Almagro was now an enemy of the Pizarros. If Manco would end his rebellion, Díaz said, then the king would pardon him and Almagro would restore Manco to rule. In an attempt to determine if Díaz was telling the truth, Manco decided to test Díaz's sincerity, just as he had the others. Recently, Manco's troops had captured four of Hernando Pizarro's men, who had been caught while on a reconnaissance mission outside Cuzco. Manco now ordered that all four of the prisoners be brought out; he then asked Díaz to prove Almagro's hatred of the Pizarros by killing them. It was one thing, after all, for a Spaniard to chop off the fingers of a native, but it was quite another for a Spaniard to kill a fellow Spaniard. This Manco had yet to see. Díaz was handed a captured Spanish dagger while the four prisoners stood there, bound with cords, their eyes undoubtedly wide. For a moment, Díaz and the four prisoners looked at one another. Díaz ultimately, however, threw the dagger to the ground, then offered Manco a variety of excuses as to why he couldn't kill the men. Disgusted, Manco ordered a now loudly protesting Díaz to be seized and imprisoned along with the others.

At first interested in exploring whether the possible conflicts between Almagro and the Pizarros might in some way be exploited, Manco finally decided that neither group of Spaniards could be trusted. Now twenty-one years of age, Manco was no longer the inexperienced, seventeen-year-old youth who had met Francisco Pizarro outside Cuzco and to whom Pizarro had promised so many things. Nearly four years of contact with the Spaniards had made it clear to him that not only were these bearded men humans and not gods but, as with any humans, some were worse than others. Manco had hated Juan Pizarro, who had heaped abuse upon him, and he still hated Gonzalo Pizarro for having stolen his wife. On the other hand, Manco had genuine affection for Almagro and had quite liked the charming Hernando de Soto. Manco had even gotten along well with Francisco Pizarro, who, for purely political reasons, had taken pains to treat Manco well. In the end, however, Manco realized that fundamentally the Spanish invaders as a whole couldn't be trusted, since to a man they all seemed to crave what he and his fellow Inca elites possessed: the land, estates, mines, crops, the obedience of the native peasants, the female concubines, the finest dwellings in Cuzco—in sum, the control of all of the rich and varied resources of Tawantinsuyu.

Manco had also apparently received disturbing reports of another large Spanish force, one that had already reached Jauja to the north and was now moving south toward Cuzco. Francisco Pizarro's desperate pleas for help, apparently, had finally borne fruit: one of his captains, Alonso de Alvarado, had cut short his conquest of the Chachapoya natives in the far north of Peru in order to rush back to Lima. Alvarado was now some three hundred miles away, heading south with more than five hundred Spaniards and hundreds of horses.

Having been unable to overcome fewer than two hundred Spaniards with eighty horses in Cuzco after nearly a year of trying and with hundreds of thousands of native troops at his disposal, Manco realized that his plans for raising additional troops with which to overrun Cuzco had abruptly come to an end. Soon, more than a thousand Spaniards and perhaps five hundred horses would be in Cuzco, only thirty miles away. With such a powerful enemy nearby, maintaining his headquarters in Ollantaytambo was obviously no longer an option. Manco was also no doubt unable to forget what Rui Díaz had told him: that even if Manco were somehow able to convert the nearby mountain peaks into gold, and were able to send all of that gold directly to Spain, the Spanish king would still not withdraw these sword-wielding invaders from Tawantinsuyu. Looking out over the majestic valley that his great-grandfather, Pachacuti, had conquered, Manco now undoubt-edly understood at last that the Spaniards were more powerful than he had originally believed. And that, unfortunately, their power seemed only to be increasing.

Soon after learning that Manco had agreed to meet with him, Almagro began moving his force down the Yucay Valley toward Calca, the suggested meeting place. Almagro no doubt expected to witness the typical arrival of an Inca emperor, that is, a standard ceremonial procession replete with dec-orated royal litters, drums, music, thousands of native attendants, and then with Manco Inca, lord of the Incas, carried on the finest litter of them all. In Calca, however, no such procession arrived. Instead, five or six thousand na-tive warriors suddenly appeared on the surrounding hills, then began racing down toward the Spaniards in a full-scale attack. Although Almagro soon launched a counterattack, the fierce assault nevertheless forced his troops out of the city; Almagro and his men were in fact barely able to recross the Yucay River, swollen now from recent rains.

Angry and frustrated with the recent turn of events, Manco now vented his wrath upon the prisoner Rui Díaz, whose refusal to kill Hernando's men had proved, to Manco at least, that he was both a spy and a liar. Wrote the chronicler Cieza de León:

> They treated him very cruelly, like . . . barbarians [and, stripped] naked, they smeared him with their mixtures, and were amused to see how hor-rible and fierce he looked. They made him drink a great quantity of their wine or *chicha,* which they drink themselves, and having tied him to a post they shot a [hard, hand-sized] fruit that we call guavas at him with slings, which bothered him greatly. . . . They then shaved off his beard and cut his hair, wanting to transform him from the good Captain and Spaniard that he was [into a naked Indian].

Both Hernando Pizarro and Diego de Almagro clearly understood Manco's message by this time: that Manco Inca remained at war and that the

Inca rebellion would continue. Although Manco may have briefly enter-tained the notion of negotiating with Almagro in order to return to power in Cuzco, in the end Manco decided that he really had only one choice. As the leader of an insurgency that had already killed hundreds of Spaniards, in-cluding one of Francisco Pizarro's own brothers, for Manco there was no going back. The Pizarros would never forgive him. Besides, Manco had ob-viously also had his fill of playing the puppet king, and of having to con-stantly endure the insults and humiliations of even the lowest-ranking Spaniards.

Diego de Almagro, meanwhile, after failing in his effort to negotiate with the Inca emperor, now shifted his focus to the question of Cuzco. Almagro was by now well aware that—despite nine months of efforts—Manco had been unable to seize the capital. Almagro also knew that Hernando Pizarro, whom Almagro despised, continued to hold the city on behalf of his elder brother. Profoundly disappointed by the king's grant of what he perceived to be an impoverished, largely ungovernable kingdom to the south, Alma-gro now found himself increasingly obsessed with a single idea: to seize Cuzco and the surrounding region as his own. Since Almagro was unaware of the fact that the king had already extended the southern boundary of Pizarro's realm, he believed that there was still a good chance Cuzco actu-ally lay within the northern boundary of his own governorship. Marching his troops to within just a few miles of the Inca capital, Almagro halted his advance and set up camp. The veteran conquistador then dispatched two messengers to

> go to the city of Cuzco and to greet Hernando Pizarro on his behalf and
> to tell him that he had not discovered in the provinces of Chile that
> magnificence [i.e., wealth] that the Indians [in Peru] had told him was
> there . . . [and that he had] received news that the entire kingdom of
> Peru had risen in rebellion and that the Indians were rebelling against
> the service of His Majesty. This news, as well as the arrival of his ap-
> pointment as Governor of the new Kingdom of Toledo, were the rea-
> sons for his return. There was no need to worry, therefore, nor should
> [his arrival] cause any concern, for his [Almagro's] only thought was to
> serve God and the King and to punish the rebellious Indians. . . . In-
> deed, he [Almagro] had felt immense sorrow the moment he had learned

the great hardships that the Governor [Francisco Pizarro] and the rest of the Spaniards had suffered.

Far from feeling "immense sorrow" over the Pizarros' recent hardships, Almagro was masking his true intentions while simultaneously trying to sound out Hernando Pizarro. Hernando, however, was already deeply angered by the fact that Almagro had secretly visited the Yucay Valley, had entered into negotiations with Manco Inca, and was only now bothering to apprise him of his presence. Hernando was in fact certain that, despite Almagro's friendly overture, the one-eyed man's actions spoke far louder than his words. In Hernando's view, Almagro's messengers were merely on a reconnaissance mission in order to collect information on the city's defenses before Almagro tried to capture it. Almagro's statement that he "had not discovered in the provinces of Chile that magnificence that the Indians had told him was there" was no doubt proof enough to Hernando that Almagro had returned from the south empty-handed, and that he was intent on claiming Cuzco as his own. Hernando, however, hadn't just fought for over nine months against nearly impossible odds to meekly surrender the city to Almagro.

A number of Hernando's men were presumably equally suspicious of Almagro's intentions. Most of these were wealthy *encomenderos* who owed their privileged positions directly to Francisco Pizarro. If Almagro did seize the city, then these same men might have the *encomiendas* they had just risked their lives for rescinded, and no doubt transferred to Almagro's followers. They had won their *encomiendas* by force of arms, and by force of arms they would keep them. At one point, a group of them "seized their weapons in great anger and rode their horses out of the city, saying 'Well then! Now that matters have come to a head, Almagro had better not think that he can give our native chiefs away to the men who came with him from Chile!' "

Other Spaniards in the city, however, especially those who had received no *encomiendas,* had mixed feelings. Perhaps Cuzco did lie within Almagro's jurisdiction, after all. If so, then if they sided with Almagro they might be in a better position to receive *encomiendas* of their own. Besides, after being cooped up for nearly a year together under extremely difficult conditions, more than a few of them had developed an extreme dislike for Hernando Pizarro, if they hadn't already felt that way before.

At thirty-six years of age, Hernando Pizarro was still the same tall, heavy, massively built, arrogant, greedy, selfish, and insulting individual that he had been before the siege; that is, he was still the man who wore his position, status, and accomplishments on his sleeve—and who treated almost everyone else as an inferior. The emperor Atahualpa is said to have remarked that he had witnessed no other Spaniard who acted so much like an Inca lord than Hernando Pizarro, for the two shared a similarity of ruling styles in that both displayed open contempt for their subordinates. In the Inca case, such behavior was culturally prescribed—the display of contempt was standard Inca ruling protocol. In Hernando's case, however, such behavior induced a strong negative reaction in many of his fellow Spaniards and thus was a decided defect in his leadership style. For years, Hernando had referred to the illegitimate Almagro as that "circumcised Moor"—one of the worst insults, apparently, that a Spaniard in the sixteenth century could use against a fellow Spaniard. Hernando had also often abused his other contemporaries. It shouldn't be surprising, then, that not only did Diego de Almagro hate Hernando Pizarro, but so, too, did many of Hernando's own men.

Since the recent lifting of Manco's siege, the Spaniards in Cuzco were now no longer holed up in the two buildings on the main square. Many had returned to their original homes in the city, at least those homes that had not been consumed in the great fire. Hernando had already reestablished himself in Huayna Capac's former palace on the eastern side of the main square, known as the Amaru Cancha. Somehow, the palace had miraculously escaped being burned.* Hernando, Gonzalo, and about twenty Spaniards loyal to the Pizarros now set up artillery in the doors of the palace and used it as a redoubt, determined to resist if Almagro tried to seize Cuzco. Although some thought that Hernando's distrust of Almagro was exaggerated, in this case at least, those suspicions turned out to be justified.

On the night of April 18, 1537, at about two in the morning, a heavy cold rain beat down upon the slumbering city. Diego de Almagro, seasoned commander that he was, had chosen this precise moment—when his forces would be least expected—to attack. With cracks of lightning periodically il-

---

* *Amaru Cancha,* in Quechua, means "Snake House"; among the Incas the snake was a symbol of knowledge and learning.

luminating the night, Almagro and his men entered the city and quickly captured the church of Hatun Cancha on the main square, one of the two buildings Hernando's men had taken refuge in during the siege. Other captains now seized the principal streets of the city, deploying more than 280 cavalrymen in the process. Almagro's second-in-command, Rodrigo Orgóñez, meanwhile—the same man who had beaten out Hernando de Soto for that position—led a detachment that surrounded the Amaru Cancha palace, where Hernando and Gonzalo Pizarro and about twenty men were still sleeping, unaware that a political coup was unfolding just beyond their doors.

It wasn't until the Inca capital was already firmly in Almagro's control that Hernando and his men realized that something was amiss. Leaping up, Hernando, Gonzalo, and the rest of the Spaniards grabbed their weapons and began a fierce battle against their attackers, who had seized the small cannons that had been stationed in the doorways and were now trying to force their way inside. Rodrigo Orgóñez, meanwhile, frustrated at not being able to enter, shouted outside in the rain that if Hernando would give himself up then he would be well treated. Hernando, ever disdainful, is said to have retorted "I will not surrender to a [lowly] soldier such as you are!" to which Orgóñez replied, "That he was Captain-General of the Government of New Toledo, and that he [Hernando Pizarro] was only a Lieutenant [Governor] of Cuzco; In any case, Orgóñez was a high-ranking man and Pizarro needn't be so contemptuous [of the thought] of surrendering to him."

With Hernando and his defenders refusing to come out, Orgóñez now ordered that their palace be set on fire. Although the Amaru Cancha was built of high stone walls and possessed two stone towers, part of its roof was covered with a fine, maroon-colored tropical hardwood while the rest was roofed with traditional native thatch. Despite the rain, Almagro's men soon succeeded in setting the thatched roof on fire. Sheets of flame now began to rise up, illuminating in red the faces of many of the besiegers. As the fire spread, smoke began flowing out from beneath the stone lintels of the palace's doors, like a series of black, upside-down waterfalls. Almagro's men, meanwhile, waiting expectantly outside with their swords drawn, were surprised that Hernando and his men made no attempt to surrender. According to Cieza de León,

Hernando Pizarro was determined not to give himself up to Almagro's men, and he told those who were with him that he preferred being burned alive than to obey their commands, and he placed himself in the doorway and defended it in such a way that no one could enter. There was so much smoke that the night was made darker because of it. Orgóñez . . . was not going to allow the men they had trapped to remain alive unless they . . . laid down their arms and gave themselves up. Then suddenly the big beams that supported the roof began to fall, the flames having destroyed the thatch. Seeing that . . . they were about to lose their lives, the Spaniards who were inside begged Hernando Pizarro with great urgency to leave this dangerous place and to surrender to the men of Chile, who after all were Christians. The whole house then began to fall down with a crash and the Spaniards, most of them burned and half suffocated from the smoke . . . rushed out to face the lances of their enemies. . . . As the captains [Hernando and Gonzalo Pizarro] grappled with their enemies, they were seized and treated abominably . . . with blows and other outrages, which was unjust, as they . . . were brothers of Governor don Francisco Pizarro.

Such was the reunion—"with blows and other outrages"—of the two groups of Spaniards who had been separated now for nearly two years, both having desperately fought for their own survival in different parts of the Incas' vast empire. Almagro's men now bound, chained, and imprisoned the two Pizarro brothers along with their twenty supporters. The following day, Almagro had them transferred to the temple of the sun—once the holiest place in the empire, now a makeshift Spanish prison.

While Almagro occupied himself with the capture of Cuzco, Manco Inca, meanwhile, had been gathering an assembly of his chiefs at Ollantaytambo, some thirty miles away. Native spies had informed their emperor about the Spanish struggle over Cuzco and, once the city had been seized, about how most of Hernando's men had gone over to the side of Almagro. Almagro was presently in possession of Cuzco with more than six hundred Spaniards, the spies told Manco, plus perhaps four thousand native auxiliaries. Manco was also well aware that a second Spanish force of nearly five hundred men was fast approaching Cuzco from the north. If either or both groups decided to attack him at Ollantaytambo, this time he would be unable to repel their attack. Looking out over an assembled crowd of expectant chiefs and captains, most of whom had fought alongside him during the last year, and also over the large number of feather-adorned, bow-and-arrow-wielding Antis in attendance, Manco addressed them as follows:

My dearly loved sons and brothers,

I believe those of you who are present here and who have remained with me through all my trials and tribulations don't know why you have been asked to gather here before me. I will tell you shortly. . . . Do not be alarmed by what I am about to tell you, but you know very well that necessity often compels men to do what they don't want to do. For this reason, I feel obligated to please these [bow-and-arrow-wielding] Antis, who for so long have asked me to go and visit them. I will give them this pleasure for a few days. I hope that this [news of my departure] does not cause you grief because that is not my purpose. . . .

You already know very well that I have told you many times besides the present how these bearded people entered my land, under the pretext that they were *viracochas,* which because of their clothes and behavior, so different from ours, both you and even I believed. . . . I brought them to my land and town and I treated them well . . . and I gave them the things that you all know about, for which they treated me in the manner that you have seen. . . .

And realizing these things and many others too numerous to recount, I sent you to surround Cuzco in order to cause them some of the same disaster that they have caused us. And it appears to me that either their God helped them or because I was not present that it did not turn out as we intended, which has given me great sorrow. But as things don't always happen as we want them to, we shouldn't wonder or anguish over it too much, which is why I ask that you not be sad, because in the end it didn't go so badly. . . . For as you know [at the battles of] Lima and Chullcomayo and Jauja we succeeded in some things and that is positive, even though they were not equal to the sorrows that they have inflicted upon us.

It now seems to me that it is time for me to depart for the land of the Antis . . . and that I will be obligated to stay there for some days. . . . I am asking you not to forget what I have told you. . . . Remember how long it has been that my grandfathers and great-grandfathers and I have fed and watched over you, benefiting and governing your families and providing for them as you needed. For this reason all of you have the obligation of not forgetting us for the rest of your lives, both you and your descendants . . . and to show great respect for and to obey my son . . . Titu Cusi Yupanqui, and all the rest of my sons who will follow him. If you do this, it will please me greatly.

The speech was no doubt both a solemn and a poignant one, for, despite Manco's casual mention that he was merely off to visit his fierce Amazon allies "for a few days," its real message was not lost on any of those present. Manco Inca, Son of the Sun, emperor of Tawantinsuyu, was abdicating control of the western, southern, and northern quarters of the empire. He was abdicating control of the coast. He was abdicating control of the majestic, snow-capped Andes—the home of his ancestors and of the Incas' immortal mountain gods. He was abdicating control of Cuzco, his boyhood home and the capital of the empire, despite having fought for nearly a year to recapture it. He was abdicating control of Calca, of Yucay, of Ollantaytambo, and of the entire Yucay Valley. In short, the emperor was abandoning most of the vast empire that he had inherited and that his ancestors had founded. Manco was instead about to take refuge in the small, eastern portion of the empire, in what the Incas called the Antisuyu.

Only in the rugged Antisuyu, Manco felt, could he and his loyal followers find safety from future attacks. Perhaps there, where the Andes sloped down and finally plunged beneath a vast carpet of seemingly endless forests, and where hirsute animals that looked like humans, or *runa,* swung through the trees, could he and his Inca nobles continue to rule. The rest of his subjects, millions upon millions of them, would unfortunately have to submit to the will and depredations of the invaders.

For the audience of native chiefs, it was clear that their own widely scattered towns and villages would soon be heavily affected by Manco's decision. And although many of them likely made their own individual speeches at this historic juncture, Manco's son Titu Cusi recorded only one of them. A noble, wearing a knee-length tunic and with large golden plugs in his ears, replied:

Lord Inca, how can you abandon your children, those who so willingly loved you and desired to serve you and who would give their lives a thousand times over for you if that were required? Which king, what lord, who do you want us [now] to follow? What betrayal, which treason, what evils have we committed that you should now abandon us with neither lord nor king to honor? After all, we have never known another lord or father except for you and Huayna Capac, your father and forefathers. Please, lord, do not leave us helpless like this, or at least make us happy by taking us with you to wherever it is that you are going.

Manco responded to the chiefs by reassuring them that he would soon see them again and that he would also stay in close touch via messengers. Manco warned them, however, not to trust the bearded strangers and not to "believe a word they say because they lie a lot, and have lied in everything they have had to do with me." As the living representative of the divine Inti, or sun god, Manco also warned the assembled crowd that the invaders would probably insist that their own gods be worshipped:

If by chance they make you worship what they worship, which are some painted sheets [the Bible] . . . do not obey. Instead . . . when you cannot resist any longer, go through the motions when you are before them, but on the side don't forget our ceremonies. And if they tell you to destroy your idols [*huacas*], and force you to do so, show them what you must and hide the rest—for that will give me great pleasure.

Having made his decision—and no doubt realizing that the longer he delayed his departure, the more likely it was that he would be attacked—Manco moved quickly to organize his exodus. As his chiefs left to return to their provinces and to take with them the emperor's disturbing message, Manco presided over the final religious ceremonies needed to guarantee his and his followers' safety in the land of the Antis. In the words of the chronicler Cieza de León:

Before leaving they armed themselves and, in a great square near their camp where an idol stood, they prayed to it with much crying, tears, and sighs, begging it not to desert them. And around this idol were others with insignias of the Sun and the Moon, and in the presence of these, which they looked upon as gods, they made sacrifices by killing many animals [llamas and alpacas] on their shrines and altars.

With the ceremonies completed, and with thousands of porters, pack trains of llamas, Anti archers, his elite guard, and his wives and children, Manco gave the signal and the procession began to move. Manco himself rode in a royal litter, no doubt seated on a low throne, or *duho,* and with a canopy overhead. On additional litters rode other Inca elites, as well as the mummified bodies of Manco's father, Huayna Capac, his grandfather Tupac Inca Yupanqui, and his great-grandfather and the creator of the empire, Pachacuti. The mummies' attendants walked beside them, making sure that flies did not annoy these still powerful emperor-gods. Manco didn't dare leave his ancestors behind—nor did he want to risk relocating the capital of his dwindling empire without their guidance and aid. Amid the procession also walked various priests, diviners, astrologers, weavers, stone masons, *quipu* readers, accountants, architects, farmers, herders, and even an oracle— in short, all the people necessary to carry on the functioning of the Inca state. Elsewhere in the procession walked Rui Díaz and five other Spanish prisoners, bound with cords and guarded by native warriors with their mace clubs at the ready.

Slowly the expedition began heading northward, up along the banks of the Patacancha River, a tributary of the Yucay. Eventually, it reached the Panticalla Pass and from there began to descend down the eastern side of the Andes. As the procession gradually disappeared around a bend, behind them lay the broad expanse of the Yucay Valley, its sides checkered with cultivated fields, its lower flanks rimmed with terraces that bore a now abandoned crop of corn. Snow-capped mountains rose in the distance, as the Yucay River, glinting in the sun, continued to roll smoothly down the valley, past the high, now empty fortress of Ollantaytambo, through the tight granite gorge, then on and down, winding its way and gathering speed, as it snaked further and further into the heart of the Antisuyu, the homeland of the Antis.

12 ❖ IN THE REALM
OF THE ANTIS

"This land of the [Antis] . . . is a rugged land with many high peaks and gorges, and for this reason there are many bad passes through which horses cannot travel unless the numerous bad areas are paved over with adobe [and] with an enormous amount of effort. . . . The whole forested [jungle] region . . . is very extensive [and] . . . slopes down towards the northern sea."

PEDRO PIZARRO, *RELACIÓN*, 1571

"Those who dwell on the other side of the land, beyond the summits of the mountains, are like savages who possess but little and have neither houses nor corn. They have immense forests and live almost entirely on fruit from the trees. They have neither places to live nor known settlements [and] there are very great rivers. The land is so useless that it paid all of its tribute to the [Inca] lords in parrot feathers."

PEDRO SANCHO DE LA HOZ, *RELACIÓN*, 1543

AFTER A CLIMB OF PERHAPS FIVE HOURS, MANCO'S PROCES-sion finally crossed the pass of Panticalla, with the snow-capped Apu of Wakay Willka (Mount Veronica) rising brilliantly white on the left. On the other side of the pass they caught their first glimpse of an endless sea of clouds stretching out below them, all the way to the horizon—the fabled land of the Antis. Descending spurs of the Andes, like the flying buttresses of a massive cathedral, extended down from the mountains, gradually sinking until they disappeared into the swirling mists, their upper crests limned

One of Tupac Inca's captains, depicted here shooting a jaguar,
while conquering the Antisuyu.

with a black mane of trees. Manco Inca, riding in a royal litter carried by individuals from the Rucana tribe—the male members of which were trained to bear litters from a young age and hence were famed for their smooth gait—no doubt paused for a moment, looking out over the immense vista before him. Manco knew that his great-grandfather Pachacuti had been the first to enter the Antisuyu, and that his grandfather Tupac Inca had carried out a number of military campaigns in that region as well. Fittingly, he was bringing both of these ancestors with him, each riding in his own litter, dressed in fine vicuña wool cloaks and with their mummified eyes appearing to look out over the same regions they had conquered so many years before.

Before his departure, Manco had also no doubt carefully questioned his *quipucamayocs,* the officials whose specialized profession consisted of memorizing and recounting the royal histories and other information, apparently using the data woven into their *quipu* cords as memory prompts. On multiple occasions, Manco had asked the *quipu* readers about the history of this area, asking them to recall the stories that had been so carefully memorized and then passed on from one generation to the next. The *quipu* readers presumably told Manco that his great-grandfather Pachacuti had conquered the Antisuyu but that at one point Tupac Inca had had to reconquer it. After coming to power, Tupac Inca had called a meeting in Cuzco of all the provincial chiefs from the four quarters of the empire, including those from the Antisuyu. The emperor had then ordered the latter chiefs to pay homage to the Incas' gods and to begin bringing tribute from their forests of hard palm wood, or *chonta,* from which Inca craftsmen could fashion their lances, breast and back plates, and clubs. "The Antis, who did not serve voluntarily, looked upon this demand as a mark of servitude," wrote the chronicler Pedro Sarmiento de Gamboa. "They fled from Cuzco, returned to their country, and raised the land of the Antis in the name of freedom."

In response to the revolt, Tupac Inca angrily gathered a powerful army and led it down the eastern flanks of the Andes, entering the Amazon in the area of what is now southeastern Peru. According to the *quipucamayocs,* although Tupac Inca's soldiers cut trails through the thick forest, they soon became disoriented and were able to locate one another only by climbing tall trees and by looking for the smoke from one another's campfires. Accustomed to the high Andes with its wide sweeping horizons that were punctuated with easily recognizable landmarks, the Incas found the dark, tropical forests claustrophobic and practically impossible to navigate in. Related Sarmiento:

> The forests were very dense and full of evil places, so that they could not force their way through, nor did they know what direction to take in order to reach the settlements of the natives, which were well concealed in the thick vegetation. To find them, the [Inca] explorers climbed up the highest trees and pointed out the places where they could see [campfire] smoke rising. So they worked at building roads through the undergrowth until they lost that [landmark] . . . and found another. In this way the Incas made a road where it seemed impossible to make one.

Despite becoming lost and losing more than half of his men to sickness, Tupac Inca nevertheless persisted. He and his men followed the Tono River, hacking out a trail and eventually conquering four jungle nations: the Manosuyus, the Mañaris, the Chunchos, and the Opataris. Through force of arms, negotiation, and the use of abundant gifts, Tupac Inca was eventually able to form military alliances and trading relationships with these *sacharuna,* or forest people. Unlike the successes they had had with conquering the inhabitants of their other territories, however, the Incas never succeeded in forcing the Antisuyu tribes to pay them tribute. Instead, they simply traded goods (which some chroniclers confused with tribute), exchanging with the often naked warriors their copper and bronze axes and knives, finely woven cloth, and highly prized salt for the Antis's exotic hardwoods, cacao, manioc, bird feathers, jaguar skins, manatee fat, turtle oil (used by the Incas in their lamps), and other forest products.

In order to facilitate such trade, the Incas extended their road system down from the highlands and into the Antisuyu, following the crests of mountain spurs that descended from the Andes. The Incas soon built towns and administrative centers throughout their new province, with typical Inca storage depots, army garrison quarters, plazas, and shrines. To gain further control over the region, the Incas settled key areas of the Antisuyu with *mitmaqcuna*—groups of citizens from elsewhere in the empire whom the Incas relocated as colonists. Grand practitioners of social engineering, the Incas used *mitmaqcuna* extensively throughout their empire. Some *mitmaqcuna* were law-abiding citizens whom the Inca elite relocated to rebellious provinces, in order to calm an area, just as oil calms stormy water. Others consisted of the inhabitants of rebellious areas who were relocated to regions where they were surrounded by groups that had already submitted to Inca rule.

Because they had been uprooted from their homeland, the new settlers were given the equivalent of hardship pay—gifts of cloth, women, narcotic coca leaves (normally reserved for the Inca elites), as well as a temporary exemption from paying labor taxes. Along the warm, forested foothills of the eastern Andes, *mitmaq* colonists planted and harvested coca leaves and cotton, traded with the nearby Antis Indians, and served as a kind of cultural and military buffer along the empire's exposed eastern flank.

It was toward one of the empire's *mitmaq* colonies that Manco Inca and his followers now headed, working their way down through the dripping cloud forest with its orchids, hummingbirds, tree ferns, spectacled bears, and tangled, moss-encrusted vegetation. Following the Lucumayo River, Manco reached the Amaibamba Valley, where he paused to ponder his next step. Eventually, after a period of indecision, Manco crossed the Urubamba River, via the Chuquichaca bridge, and then led his procession up into the Vilcabamba Valley. There he decided to settle at Vitcos, a royal estate and provincial capital, located on a hill at about ten thousand feet in elevation. Vitcos had been founded by his great-grandfather Pachacuti.

Standing on a high outpost overlooking the eastern frontier, where *mitmaq* colonists routinely traded with the Antis Indians in the lower valleys and near the sacred coca plantations and tropical forest, Manco decided that Vitcos would become the new capital of his now truncated empire. Although Vitcos was located only seventy miles from Cuzco, it was nevertheless separated by a very steep and rugged trail, many parts of which Manco had ordered destroyed. Native work crews had carefully crashed down boulders from above or had created barriers of toppled trees, obliterating the trail. The Spaniards were always unpredictable, Manco knew; he could only hope that these defensive measures would keep his most dangerous enemy at bay.

In Cuzco, meanwhile, Diego de Almagro had his own set of problems. After having seized Cuzco and having imprisoned Hernando and Gonzalo

Pizarro, Almagro was now faced with Francisco Pizarro's relief force, five hundred strong, that was quickly approaching the capital from the north. Native scouts had informed both parties of each other's presence, while the relief force's leader, Alonso de Alvarado, soon realized that his order to rescue the Spaniards trapped in Cuzco was no longer relevant. Instead, Alvarado learned that Almagro had seized Cuzco by force, had imprisoned the governor's two brothers, and was openly defying Francisco Pizarro's jurisdiction over southern Peru. The question for Pizarro's captain now was what he should do about that.

Almagro, in the meantime, had already made up his mind to hold Cuzco at all costs and had appointed Rodrigo Orgóñez, his second-in-command, to lead an army in order to prevent Alvarado from reaching the capital. Having spent nearly two years in the southern region of Tawantinsuyu to no avail and now in firm control of Cuzco, Almagro wasn't about to give up the city to an army that owed its allegiance to Pizarro. Almagro had already crossed a personal Rubicon of sorts, after having captured and imprisoned Pizarro's two brothers. From here on, there was no turning back.

Almagro's military commander, Rodrigo Orgóñez, had been with Almagro now for five years. The son of poor Jewish shoemakers who had been forced to convert to Christianity, Orgóñez had fled from his native town of Oropesa in Spain because of a serious brawl he had been involved in. Orgóñez enlisted in the king's army, distinguishing himself for bravery in Spain's Italian Wars: he was, in fact, one of a handful of soldiers who personally captured the French King, Francis I, in the French defeat at Pavia. Returning home a hero, Orgóñez nevertheless found social advancement blocked by the low status of his birth. The young, ambitious ex-soldier, however, soon came up with an ingenious solution to his predicament: shedding his father's last name of Méndez, Orgóñez simply "borrowed" the paternal surname of a local nobleman, Juan Orgóñez. He then did his best to convince the surprised nobleman that the latter was somehow his biological father. Although the elder Orgóñez vehemently denied the connection, Rodrigo "Orgóñez" and his brother, Diego Méndez, soon set sail for the Indies, hoping to improve their fortunes in the New World. With scarcely a copper *maravedi* coin to his name, Rodrigo nevertheless carried with him something potentially far more valuable—his pilfered aristocratic name.

After stints in Panama and Honduras, Orgóñez eventually arrived in Peru with Diego de Almagro in April 1533, missing out in the division of gold and silver at Cajamarca, but participating in the expedition down the Andes and ultimately in the capture of Cuzco and in the division of its spoils. Finding himself suddenly wealthy and one of Cuzco's first *encomenderos,* Orgóñez's ambition, however, had only been whetted by his recent success. An old Spanish proverb says, "He who has more, wants more" *("El que más tiene, más quiere").* Orgóñez not only wanted more, but he now craved the top prize that any conquistador could aspire to: his own governorship. Orgóñez realized, however, that his chances of receiving a governorship and prestigious titles from the king would be greatly improved if he were able to legitimize his paternal last name. From Cuzco, therefore, Orgóñez soon sent the nobleman whose name he had borrowed a rich gift of gold and silver, along with letters that contained an unusual mixture of both braggadocio and pleading:

Sir,

. . . Governor don Diego de Almagro has put me in charge of his naval [resupply] fleet and I am leaving [for Chile] as his Captain General. Not only has he done me this favor . . . treating me as his own son, but he even turned down more than two hundred thousand ducats that Captain Hernando de Soto [had offered] . . . him for the [same position]. . . . And to benefit me even more, he has asked His Majesty to give me a governorship. . . .

What I am asking His Majesty is to give me five hundred leagues [about 1,750 miles] of southern coast that I can govern and be Captain-General of . . . and to grant me the title of Governor . . . and that he do me the favor [of giving me] ten percent of [the profits of] what I conquer, [along] with the title of Marquis, and that he grant me the habit of [the Order of] Santiago. . . .

Sir, what I beg of you is that it be understood by whatever means [necessary] that I am *legitimate* and could thus have the habit of a Knight of Santiago. . . . For the love of God . . . regarding legitimization, you can do this through a lawyer. . . .

Your obedient son,

Rodrigo Orgóñez

Orgóñez's high hopes of finding a governorship somewhere in the south ultimately foundered, however, amidst the frozen passes, dead bodies, and desert wastelands of Chile, as well as under the withering attacks of the southern kingdom's uncooperative inhabitants. Now back in Cuzco, he was determined to seize what he could from the rich Kingdom of New Castile, as Pizarro's governorship was called, and to take back the *encomienda* that he had abandoned two years earlier. Eventually, the man who had once personally captured a French king and who had recently captured and imprisoned two of Francisco Pizarro's brothers now found himself leading an army of 430 men with orders from Almagro to prevent Cuzco from being retaken. Of one thing Orgóñez was certain: he would do whatever was necessary to hold on to the city that he and Almagro had just won by force of arms.

A brilliant military strategist, Orgóñez planned a night attack on Alvarado's forces, hoping that he might thus catch them by surprise. In a nearly bloodless battle that was fought alongside some ten thousand native auxiliaries led by Manco's brother Paullu, Orgóñez soon not only routed his opponent but also succeeded in winning over the majority of Alvarado's troops.

The victorious Orgóñez now returned to Cuzco, urging Almagro to immediately execute the two Pizarro brothers. Orgóñez knew that Hernando Pizarro, especially, was a spiteful man and, if given the chance, would certainly find a way to avenge his present humiliation. Orgóñez also urged Almagro to allow him to attack Lima; there he could seize Francisco Pizarro and, with the remaining Pizarro brothers either captured or killed, the Kingdom of Peru would be theirs. Almagro, however—realizing that if he committed his forces to Lima, Manco Inca might once again attack Cuzco—decided that Orgóñez should first capture or kill the Inca leader, thus removing the threat of an attack. Once Manco had been eliminated, Orgóñez could then lead his army against Pizarro. In the meantime, Almagro said, he wanted to keep Hernando and Gonzalo Pizarro alive—perhaps to use later as bargaining chips.

In mid-July 1537, Rodrigo Orgóñez rode out from Cuzco with three hundred Spanish cavalry and foot soldiers. This time he rode in pursuit of Manco Inca, who, according to native spies, was said to have taken refuge in the land of the Antis. Orgóñez was in fact enthusiastic about the expedition. At the very least, he and his men stood a good chance of seizing plunder, as

Manco was said to have a large quantity of gold and silver in his possession. Orgóñez had also received word that Rui Díaz and a number of other Spaniards Manco held in captivity were still alive. If Orgóñez could capture or kill Manco Inca, could discover a hoard of treasure, and could find the Spanish prisoners and bring them back alive, then he was convinced that both Almagro and the king would reward him handsomely for his efforts.

Orgóñez and his troops now rode down into the Yucay Valley, fording the river and passing by the vacant fortress of Ollantaytambo. Only a year earlier, Manco Inca had repelled repeated attacks here by Hernando Pizarro, had flooded the nearby fields in a brilliant defensive maneuver, and had continued to invest Cuzco with his nearly year-long siege. Now Manco had been forced to abandon the high Andes and was living like a fugitive in the remote Antisuyu. Leading a force nearly twice the size of the one that had captured Manco's brother Atahualpa, Orgóñez turned away from the valley and headed north up toward the Panticalla Pass. Soon, however, the Spaniards found obstructions in their path—large boulders and fallen trees that had clearly been placed there to block their passage. Forced to find alternative routes, the Spaniards relied upon their native auxiliaries from Cuzco, who had been sent by Manco's brother Paullu.

Diego de Almagro, meanwhile—wishing to fracture Inca loyalties and thus to further weaken the native elite—had decided to crown Paullu in Cuzco as the new Inca emperor. Although originally a firm supporter of his brother, Paullu had just spent the previous two years with Almagro in Chile. Without Paullu's constant assistance, in fact, it is unlikely that Almagro and his men ever would have survived the long journey or returned to Peru.

Roughly the same age, Paullu and Manco shared the same father, Huayna Capac, but had different mothers. Paullu's mother, Añas Collque, was the daughter of a non-Inca chief from the province of Huaylas in what is now north-central Peru. By definition, then, Paullu was not of pure royal blood. Manco's mother, by contrast, was Mama-Runtu, a full sister of Huayna Capac; Manco thus held the edge in terms of royal legitimacy. Although Paullu had departed for Chile at Manco's request, he had returned to a burned-out capital city where fewer than two hundred Spaniards and their native auxiliaries had survived an onslaught of some 200,000 of Manco's warriors. Paullu, it seems, didn't need much time to absorb the lesson. When his brother sent him a number of messages from the rebel town of Vitcos for

Paullu to join him there, Paullu rebuffed the invitation. According to the chronicler Cieza de León:

> Every day they sent messengers to Paullu telling him to come and join them, as he had served long enough with the Christians. But Paullu warily replied that he was friends with these men [the Spaniards] who were so courageous that, no matter what they attempted, they always emerged victorious. And, that when there were only two hundred Spaniards in the city of Cuzco, more than two hundred thousand Indians had been assembled to kill them—and the only honor and benefit they got from that was to leave many children fatherless and many women widows. More than fifty thousand men died in the war, according to what he was told. . . . Paullu advised the messengers and other Indians who were going back and forth from his camp not to take up arms against the Spaniards.

Paullu was clearly an opportunist, obviously preferring the life of an emperor in the capital city to the life of a subordinate and fugitive in the Antisuyu. Not surprisingly, his brother was furious; Manco in fact never forgave Paullu for the betrayal. Now, for the second time in a decade, two sons of Huayna Capac simultaneously wore the royal *mascapaicha,* the sacred fringe of the Inca emperor. And, like their own brothers Atahualpa and Huascar before them, both Manco and Paullu each had their group of supporters, thus further weakening allegiances among the Inca elite—precisely as Almagro had planned.

For the moment, however, Manco had other things to worry about: a native runner had just reached him with news that a large Spanish force was making its way down along the Lucumayo River on its way to the Amaibamba Valley, where Manco was visiting. If Manco didn't immediately flee, the messenger said, then the Spaniards would surely capture or kill him. Manco therefore climbed onto his royal litter and was borne across the river over the hanging bridge at Chuquichaca, leaving instructions behind for the town's defense. Not long afterward, Orgóñez and his men arrived and found a legion of native warriors defending the town. According to Cieza de Léon:

Orgóñez, as soon as he was quite close, ordered the crossbow men to shoot many arrows . . . so that the Indians, seeing the damage that was being done to them, might decide that it would be best to abandon the fort. To some extent the Indians proved themselves to be brave and de- termined, defending the area and the fort and launching many darts and stones against the Christians. But the Spaniards wore them out so much that they were compelled to abandon that place, and to save their lives they hurried to use their last resort, which was to flee. The Spaniards wreaked great havoc among them, leaving many of them dead and wounded.

The Spaniards rode after the fleeing Indians with twelve-foot lances, spearing as many as they could. As Manco's warriors and Orgóñez's men fought in the town's streets, a group of bedraggled Spaniards suddenly emerged from one of the buildings and began calling out to their compatri- ots: it was Rui Díaz and the Spanish prisoners who had been captured nearly a year earlier; the latter were practically the only survivors of the var- ious relief forces that General Quizo had exterminated in the Andes.

The next morning, at dawn, Orgóñez and his troops crossed the bridge over the Urubamba River at Chuquichaca, then rode up into the Vilcabamba Valley until they arrived before Vitcos, Manco's new capital. The town sat on a hilltop from which its inhabitants could look over the deep valleys to the east and west and view a series of sacred, eighteen-thousand-to-twenty- thousand-foot peaks to the south. As the Spaniards charged up the hill, pan- demonium broke out as native men, women, and children tried to flee. Instead of slaughtering the inhabitants, however, many of the Spaniards dis- mounted and, with swords drawn, ran into the thatched stone palaces with their trapezoidal doorways; they soon emerged clutching golden vessels, plates, and idols, piles of richly woven *cumpi* cloth—so fine that it felt like silk—along with jewels and other treasures.

As horses whirled about, Spaniards shouted, and terrified native women screamed, Manco Inca was meanwhile fleeing further up the valley and into the mountains. The Inca emperor had escaped with only his principal wife, Cura Ocllo (the same *coya* that Gonzalo Pizarro had stolen but who had somehow managed to escape and rejoin Manco during his rebellion); the two had been in such a hurry, in fact, that they had left their royal litters behind. Instead, twenty of the fastest runners from the Lucana tribe had carried Manco and his wife in relays in their arms, never stopping. Orgóñez, discovering that Manco had fled, quickly sent four of his fastest horsemen after him, then followed a bit later with twenty more cavalry. Despite riding throughout the night, however, Orgóñez found no trace of the renegade emperor. Manco Inca—the rebel ruler of the Incas—had disappeared.

The illusion of security that Vitcos had once seemed to have offered Manco, however, had cost the young emperor dearly. During the looting of the city, Orgóñez had discovered a five-year-old boy, dressed in fine clothing. The boy turned out to be Manco's son, Titu Cusi, and Orgóñez had him seized. In addition to a fortune in gold, silver, fine cloth, and jewels, the Spaniards soon discovered a treasure almost equally as valuable: a large stash of bloodied Spanish clothing and armor. Inca warriors had apparently stripped the clothing from the bodies of the more than 140 dead Spaniards that had been killed in various parts of Peru during the previous year. Imported from distant Spain, the armor and clothes were literally worth a fortune to the isolated Spaniards in Peru. Almagro later distributed the dead men's possessions among his followers, many of whom had worn the same, ragged clothing for years.

As Orgóñez and his troops began marching triumphantly back to Cuzco, they took with them their spoils of gold and silver, Manco's son, a vast herd of llamas, a large number of the province's inhabitants, and even the recovered mummies of Manco's ancestors—whom the Incas continued to revere as gods. Remembered Titu Cusi:

> They herded before them all of the native men and women they could seize, and the [mummified] bodies of my ancestors, whose names were Huayna Kawri, Viracocha Inca, Pachacuti Inca, Topa [Tupac] Inca Yupanqui, and Huayna Capac . . . [along] with many jewels and riches . . . more than 50,000 llamas and alpacas, and these were the best ones chosen from those that were here . . . and they took me and many of my father's other concubines.

Except for the failure to capture Manco Inca, Orgóñez's expedition had been an unqualified success. All the Spaniards in Cuzco, including Almagro and the new puppet king, Paullu Inca, were delighted with its results. The back of the Incas' insurrection had surely been broken, for now Manco—no matter where he had escaped to—barely had any subjects left to rule, let alone to renew his war with. Cuzco, now the unofficial capital of Almagro's Kingdom of New Toledo, was at last secure.

Or was it? Although Almagro was in physical control of the city, with more than eight hundred Spaniards now at his disposal, the Inca capital still suffered from an undefined legal status. The uncertainty was due to the fact that no one had been able to determine whether Cuzco lay within the kingdom granted to Pizarro or the kingdom granted to Almagro. Pizarro, meanwhile—still in Lima yet aware now that Almagro had seized Cuzco and had imprisoned his two brothers—decided that the best course of action would be to try to negotiate with his former partner. Given Almagro's obvious military strength, he had little choice. Pizarro therefore dispatched an old acquaintance—an elderly lawyer by the name of Gaspar de Espinoza—who now traveled to Cuzco with instructions to negotiate with Almagro in order to try to win the release of Pizarro's two brothers.

In Cuzco, however, Almagro immediately began arguing with Espinoza that not only should Cuzco rightfully be his but that the northern boundary of his own governorship should be extended northward to a point just south of Lima. He had, after all, just saved Cuzco and the Spaniards within it from Manco's siege, Almagro said. If he had not returned to Peru then this whole region would still be under the renegade emperor's control.

Despite Almagro's seeming intransigence, Espinoza nevertheless hoped that if he could just negotiate a temporary agreement on a boundary between the two kingdoms—*any* boundary—then at some later date the king's officials could complete their measurements and determine the final boundaries. The main problem, as Espinoza saw it, was whether the two Pizarro brothers would seek revenge if released; if they did, then the current conflict could devolve into an all-out civil war. After listening patiently to Almagro, Espinoza next visited the makeshift Spanish prison located within the temple of the sun. There the aged lawyer found Hernando and Gonzalo Pizarro and, after warmly greeting the two brothers, he turned to Hernando and began to speak, hoping to shed clarity on the present conflict by placing it in a wider perspective:

As I have experience in these parts of the Indies, [I know that] whenever Governors quarrel over differences they lose their property and not only find themselves deprived of what they claim, but most suffer great misfortunes and long periods in prison and even die in them, which is the saddest thing of all. Thus I can promise you that if Governor [Pizarro] does not come to a peaceful agreement with Governor Almagro, without resorting to war . . . then neither will ever be free from great hardships and troubles. For when His Majesty learns of these conflicts, he will be forced to find a solution for this kingdom, which is his, and will send peaceful men to restore order in it, removing those who had previously held office. . . . Once the . . . [king's officials] . . . set foot in a province or in a new kingdom, those who were first to govern will never govern again. . . . I say this because, for my part, now that I have agreed to be a mediator in these negotiations, I wish to arrange a settlement between the Governors so that from now on there will always be peace and conciliation between them, for the success of these negotiations requires nothing less. And I say this, because you [Espinoza said, looking directly at Hernando Pizarro] do not look like the kind of man who, finding himself imprisoned and longing for liberty, is quick to agree to anything, yet who afterwards will remember what he has suffered and . . . will want to avenge his past wrongs . . . [or] who will start the kind of war that the more prudent men who do not want to follow him . . . will nevertheless be unable to stop. Therefore, you should act like someone who desires peace, and not like someone who [only] wants to be freed in order to begin a war.

Hernando Pizarro, his natural arrogance tempered somewhat by his imprisonment, listened to Espinoza carefully and ultimately agreed in principle to negotiate. Elsewhere in the city, however, Almagro's captains—and especially Rodrigo Orgóñez—continued to urge Almagro to execute both Hernando and Gonzalo, insisting that neither of them could be trusted. If the two Pizarro brothers were released, Orgóñez argued, then they would surely return and try to recapture Cuzco. For months, however, the negotiations between Espinoza and Almagro stretched on, during which time Pizarro continued to receive new troops and to build his military force in Lima. During this period, Gonzalo Pizarro somehow managed to escape from prison; the latter made his way to Lima where he rejoined his brother Francisco, whom he had not seen in nearly two years.

The lawyer Espinoza, meanwhile, did his best to persuade Almagro not to precipitate open civil war, which would not only sever Almagro's connections with Francisco Pizarro but would also jeopardize his relationship with the king:

> If all the men who have ever been in this world, and even those who are in it now . . . would give their attention solely to serving God and to guiding their affairs by the light of reason, and would remain satisfied with what is actually theirs and belongs to them, then there would not have been so many wars and so many great battles. But as the human mind has a tendency to always want to command and to dominate, in order to achieve this ambition, not only have many great lords and kings perished, but their souls have also been in danger of being lost. For when it comes to who is to rule, a father will disown his son and a son will cause the death of his father. And those who suffer the most are the miserable countries, which end up wasted and consumed and with most of their people dead, and the buildings in their cities being left in ruins, which is very painful to see. . . . These wars commence for trifling reasons, but afterwards they grow to such an extent that, even though those who were the cause of them wish to end them, they cannot do so. The wars that are to be feared the most and are the cruelest are the civil wars. Rome was never threatened as much by its [foreign] enemies such as Pyrrhus and Hannibal as it was by its own citizens. Nor did any of the wars that the Romans waged during [their] seven hundred years . . . [ever place it in greater danger] than it faced during the civil wars of Sylla and Marius, and of Pompey the Great, and of Julius Caesar. But without . . . such momentous events, many cities in Spain are ruined and are nearly uninhabited because their citizens . . . [are divided into factions], the one against the other.
>
> So now if, in your old age and after having served His Majesty for such a long time, the two of you become the authors of a civil war— what do you think you will gain from it? Because after many deaths on both sides you will be murderers, and then a judge will arrive, by royal order, who will decide your fates. Fly from the thought that it will ever

be said that, during your time, there was a war of Spaniards against Spaniards. You have the means to prevent this in your hands, which is to secure an agreement with Governor [Pizarro]. Don't be deceived by the remarks of immature young men. Nor insist on believing that all of your happiness depends upon being given the district of Mala [below Lima]. Be patient so that [with the pending arrival of] the Bishop of Panama, [and] once the boundaries of the governorships have been determined, each one [of you] will understand what is his and will know the favor His Majesty grants him.

Almagro, now sixty-three years old, was moved by the learned man, whose grasp of history greatly impressed the illiterate old conquistador. Almagro knew nothing of Rome or Caesar or Pompey or of ancient civil wars, but he *did* understand the old lawyer's argument—and was much influenced by it. After years in the saddle and a lifetime of hardship and scrabbling, he had been feeling his age of late and recently had been suffering from a variety of ailments. Realizing that he had had no specific authority to seize Cuzco, nor to have attacked Pizarro's relief force, Almagro began to worry that if he now killed Hernando Pizarro, as some of his captains insisted, he would jeopardize any favor he might still retain with the king. Besides, executing Hernando meant declaring war on his ex-partner; civil war would then be unavoidable.

Eventually, Almagro ordered that Hernando Pizarro be set free, as long as the latter promised he would uphold the peace. Rodrigo Orgóñez—the man who had smoked Hernando out of his Inca palace and who was still angry over Hernando's numerous personal insults—is said to have been mortified by the news. "Raising his head, he [Orgóñez] grabbed his beard with his left hand and made as if to cut his throat with his right one; shouting out 'What a shame, Orgóñez—that because of your friendship with Almagro your throat will be cut!'" Sure enough, within two months further negotiations between Pizarro and Almagro collapsed, war was declared, and Espinoza's long-feared civil war was launched. Orgóñez had been right: the Pizarros were the last people on earth to either forget or forgive.

On Saturday, April 26, 1538, at dawn on the day of St. Lazarus, whom Christ had returned from the dead, amid a swampy area called Las Salinas some two miles west of Cuzco, two European armies faced each other, preparing to do battle. Francisco Pizarro, now sixty years old, had remained in Lima and had placed his thirty-eight-year-old brother, Hernando, in charge of recapturing the Incas' former capital. With the various reinforcements of men and supplies that had arrived in Lima, which had even included a ship sent from Mexico by Cortés, Hernando now commanded a force of more than eight hundred Spaniards and several thousand native auxiliaries.

At least two hundred of Hernando's troops were mounted cavalry, fully armored and wielding lances and swords. These Hernando had divided equally and had positioned on either of his two flanks. Five hundred armored foot soldiers stood in the middle, bearing shields and swords, with the ensigns in the center holding aloft the imperial banners of the various kingdoms of Spain. In the front rows stood a hundred harquebus men, their three-foot guns fully primed and ready to be fired. The guns were currently the vogue in European warfare, as their lead projectiles could penetrate the thickest of armor, thus obviating the need for hand-to-hand combat.

On the other side of the plain, Almagro's forces—five hundred men compared to Hernando's more than eight hundred—waited tensely. These were comprised of some 240 cavalry, roughly 260 foot soldiers, six cannon, and six thousand native warriors bearing mace clubs and slings. The native warriors had been supplied by the newly crowned emperor, Paullu Inca, who, like Manco, now wore the scarlet emperor's fringe and rode in his own royal litter. Almagro had instructed Paullu to position his warriors around the edges of the plain with orders to kill any Spaniard who tried to flee the battle—no matter which side they belonged to. Paullu dutifully transmitted the order to his captains.

Too sick to ride a horse, Almagro had turned his army over to his second-in-command, the marshal Rodrigo Orgóñez, who had hoped in vain to prevent that which was about to unfold. Wrote Cieza de León:

> Governor [Almagro] had come out from Cuzco in [an Inca] litter with his army. And before arriving at Las Salinas he reached a plain where . . . he said to his captains that they would now see how the negotiations had ended up and how he had been rejected and that he would not be coming to do battle if things hadn't broken down [in such a manner],

since war was a disservice to both God and His Majesty. . . . But that they could now see how Hernando Pizarro and his brother, despite so many promises and negotiations, had come looking for them, while those who followed their banners did so because they believed that all the land would be divided up among them. Once they discovered that they had been deceived, [however] they would never dare to start a war again. "Since justice is on your side, fight fiercely so that victory will be yours and so that they will be punished severely."

Hernando, meanwhile, took time to address his own men, many of whom were newly arrived in Peru and who ironically found themselves about to fight not the native insurgency they had been summoned for, but instead their very own countrymen. Nevertheless, the Spaniards on both sides realized that if they were victorious on this day then they would surely be rewarded with lands and spoils. The Kingdom of Peru—each of the assembled combatants understood—was still very much up for grabs.

When he was a few miles away, Hernando Pizarro [halted and], before his captains and his men, made a speech justifying his cause. He said that Almagro had incited the war while he [Hernando] had been in Cuzco striving for justice in the name of the King and that Almagro had imprisoned him and had treated him brutally, as everyone knew. But that, more as a point of honor than because of past injuries, he wanted to punish those who followed Almagro and [who shared in] his blunders, because they had helped him commit his past mistakes. And that now, by order of the Governor [Francisco Pizarro], they had come to regain the city of Cuzco, and to free it from Almagro's oppressive rule. . . . When the war was over, there would be many provinces and discoveries to divide among them, which would be awarded to them and not to any others.

As the two forces readied themselves, Governor Almagro had a seat prepared for himself on a nearby hill, where he could watch the battle unfold. On the adjacent hills, a crowd of native onlookers stood in anticipation of a spectacle they had never before seen: two armies of the bearded invaders, seemingly about to attack each other, in what the natives could only surmise

was the foreigners' version of an Inca-style civil war. According to Cieza de
León:

> As news of the battle that was about to be fought between the "men of
> Chile" and those [supporting Pizarro] . . . spread far and wide, natives
> from many towns came to attend, overjoyed that such a day had arrived
> and believing that some satisfaction might be had for the injuries they
> had suffered from the Spaniards. They stood on the slopes and hills,
> hoping that neither [Spanish] captain would be victorious but that all
> would die and would be killed with their own weapons. . . . The wives
> of the Indian chiefs and the Spaniards' servant girls [concubines] [also]
> came out of the city and went to see those who were going to fight in
> the battle.

According to some, Marshal Orgóñez now rode before his troops, encouraging them, and "boasted a good deal." A veteran of the Italian Wars,
Orgóñez was certain that Hernando would not attack, even though he
wielded superior numbers, as Hernando had to know the kind of carnage
that his troops would suffer. Instead, Orgóñez told his men— walking his
horse before them briskly with his sword drawn and a curved morion helmet on his head—Hernando's troops would surely break away at the last
moment and would attempt to race around their flanks, hoping to reach
Cuzco and seize it, thus avoiding open combat.

On the cold silent plains beyond Cuzco, with the ownership of Peru
hanging in the balance and with Manco's spies watching from the hillsides,
those Spaniards who had them closed their visors, the cavalrymen lifted
their lances, and the rest unsheathed their swords. All now looked to their
commander as, with their banners stirring in the breeze, they waited for the
signal to attack. Hernando Pizarro, his horse snorting, presumably looked
down his lines, then directly at Orgóñez across the plain from him. Not taking his eyes from him, he then raised his sword on high, held it aloft for a
moment, then quickly brought it down.

A hundred harquebus men now pulled their triggers, which brought a
smoldering wick in contact with a line of powder leading directly to their
barrels. The guns exploded, hurling clouds of bluish gray smoke out onto

the plain and projecting lethal lead balls like invisible rockets toward Orgóñez's men. Hernando's crossbowmen, meanwhile, also fired their weapons, launching a volley of metal-tipped arrows at the enemy troops. Behind them, Hernando's army now began advancing across the plain, obeying their orders to carry out a frontal attack.

Orgóñez, stunned that Hernando was attacking instead of attempting to avoid a battle as he had predicted, watched as great clumps of his footmen and many horses and cavalrymen around him suddenly went down, as if their legs had been cut out from under them, some clutching at steel shafts protruding from their armor, others looking down in wonder at small but deadly holes that had miraculously appeared, the lead balls having pierced their armor, expanding, then splattering and ripping up soft organs and flesh.

[The battle then began] and Captain General Rodrigo Orgóñez, seeing that the enemy harquebusiers were gashing his troops, said to one of his captains who commanded fifty cavalrymen "Charge, sir, with your squadron . . . and break up those harquebusiers!" He [the captain] answered . . . "Do you mean for me to be butchered?" Then . . . Orgóñez raised his eyes to heaven . . . and shouted, "Protect me almighty God!" and attacked the enemy single-handedly, a big, powerful man riding a powerful, light gray horse . . . and he speared a foot soldier, [cut open] the head of an harquebusier, and [wounded] another in the thigh, returning to the ranks of his own men in the face of the enemy.

Both armies now smashed into each other, the footmen with swords or pikes, the cavalry with their lances, shouting hoarsely "Santiago!" or "Long live the King!" and then joining together, the sounds of metal clanging, men shouting, horses neighing, then more harquebus explosions, which always startled the natives, and finally the screams of those mortally or gravely wounded filling the air. Decimated by Hernando's fierce harquebus attack and sorely outnumbered, Orgóñez's troops at first struggled to hold their ground. Then, under the full onslaught of their enemies' larger numbers, they slowly began to fall back. Almagro's field commander nevertheless continued to fight fiercely from his horse, attempting to rally his troops by driving his sword under an open visor into one man's mouth, then slashing at another. Spurring his mount forward and shouting for his men to press forward and not to retreat, Orgóñez swiveled and charged just as a volley of harquebus bullets suddenly ripped his horse out from under him, throwing the marshal to the ground.

Regaining his feet, Orgóñez continued to fight, although this time on foot with his sword. Soon, however, six of Hernando's men closed in, attacking the marshal simultaneously. As the men stabbed him repeatedly, Orgóñez finally fell. With shouts of triumph, several of the men now ran their swords completely through the marshal's body until their sword points impaled the stiff soil below. The illiterate son of Jewish cobblers who had stolen a noble pedigree and who had hoped one day to rule his own native kingdom lived just long enough to see his worst prediction come true. Soon, one of the soldiers who had felled him pulled the marshal's beard back and cut his throat, sawing further until he decapitated him. Shoving a sword into the base of Orgóñez's neck, the soldier now lifted the bloodied, bearded head on high for all of the Pizarros' enemies to see. Almagro's troops now broke and began to flee, intent only on saving their lives.

At some point during the melee, Paullu Inca—whose troops had been battling on behalf of Almagro—abruptly switched sides. Paullu had previously drawn the conclusion—perhaps in Chile or perhaps after his return to Cuzco—that the Spaniards were ultimately going to win the battle for Tawantinsuyu against his fellow Incas. It was one thing to side with a group of victorious Spaniards, however; it was quite another to side with a losing one. In the middle of the battle, therefore, as it became obvious that Almagro's men were outnumbered and were going to lose, Paullu suddenly ordered his warriors to begin clubbing Almagro's men to death, instead of Hernando's.

Realizing that the battle was lost and abandoned now by even his own native litter-bearers, Diego de Almagro desperately caught hold of a stray mule and began riding it back toward Cuzco, kicking the animal's sides in order to hurry it along. Undoubtedly, the lawyer Espinoza's warning must have come back to haunt him: "Whenever Governors quarrel over differences they lose their property," the aged lawyer had said, "and not only find themselves deprived of what they claim, but most suffer great misfortunes and long periods of prison—and even die."

Almagro now rode directly to Saqsaywaman, the hilltop fortress that Juan Pizarro had died trying to seize some two years earlier, hoping to avoid being either captured or killed. Climbing up inside one of its three towers, the aged conquistador drew his sword and prepared to make a final stand. Meanwhile, as remnants of Almagro's defeated forces fled back to Cuzco, attempting to recover some of their property and then to escape, Hernando's men chased after them, many of them taking advantage of the present chaos in order to settle old scores. One of those killed was Rui Díaz, who until recently had been a prisoner of Manco Inca and whom Orgóñez had "liberated" just in time for Díaz to fight on Almagro's losing side. Now, just as Almagro's men had stripped Pizarro's supporters of their wealth upon their seizure of Cuzco, Hernando's men began to do the same.

> The soldiers went about looting and argued and came to blows over the spoils. The whole city fell into confusion, the Indian women running about from one place to another, while the victorious Spaniards chased after them. . . . The head of Rodrigo Orgóñez was brought to the city and by order of Hernando Pizarro was hung from a rope.

The Battle of Las Salinas, as it became known, had resulted in a complete rout: 120 of Almagro's men had been killed while on Hernando's side only nine Spaniards had been lost. Amidst the looting, the killing, and the confusion, with wounded from both sides being carried back into the city, a detachment of cavalry now rode out to Saqsaywaman in search of Almagro. With no food or water and realizing that cannons could reduce the Inca tower he had taken refuge in to rubble, Almagro finally decided to give himself up. Soldiers now escorted the short, swarthy governor back down into the city and directly to the Incas' curved temple of the sun. There they placed him in the very same chamber where he himself had imprisoned Hernando Pizarro. As a cold rain began to fall outside, washing maroon-colored bloodstains from the streets and from the distant plain of Las Salinas, the former capital of the Inca Empire once again fell under the control of the Pizarros.

A few days later, Hernando Pizarro went to visit the defeated Almagro—a man he had always competed with for power and had long despised. Despondent now and worried about his fate, Almagro asked Hernando if his old partner, Francisco Pizarro, planned to come to Cuzco, so that the two of them might settle their differences. Hernando—knowing full well that Almagro's fate now lay in his hands—was uncharacteristically kind to the old conquistador; he assured him that his elder brother would more than likely visit and that, even if he were for some reason detained, Almagro could visit the marquis himself in the City of the Kings. Having reassured Almagro, Hernando left. Outside, however, he quietly instructed his notaries to begin judicial proceedings against his brother's former partner—a necessary first step before Almagro could be executed.

For the next few weeks, Hernando reassured Almagro that his brother was sure to visit and he also made sure that his prisoner was well treated. Almagro—believing that the relationship between him and his former partner could somehow be repaired and that Hernando was not nearly as vengeful as he had feared—waited impatiently for the elder Pizarro to arrive. As the days turned into weeks and the weeks into months, the old governor waited in his frigid cell and at night no doubt dreamed—dreamed of his childhood, of the mother who had peered at him from between a partially opened door and had handed him a piece of bread before closing it again, dreamed of how his uncle had once chained him inside a cage. Almagro may even have dreamed of being waited upon as the governor of a suddenly bountiful New Toledo, living a life of luxury in Cuzco, his capital. Two and a half months after the Battle of Las Salinas, however, whatever dreams Almagro may have had collapsed as quickly as one of the mirages he must have glimpsed amidst the endless northern desert of Chile. Recounted one chronicler:

> [Hernando Pizarro] . . . having assembled a great body of armed men in his house . . . entered the prison cell of . . . Governor Don Diego de Almagro . . . [and] notified him of the sentence of death. And when the unfortunate man heard it, he considered it to be an abominable deed, contrary to law, justice, and reason. He was astonished, and replied that he . . . would appeal to the Emperor and King. . . . Hernando . . . responded that he [Almagro] should commend his soul to God because the sentence would be carried out. Then the poor old man fell to his knees and said, "Commander Hernando Pizarro, content yourself with the revenge you have already enjoyed. Be aware that, besides the treason to God and the Emperor that my death will cause, that you are repaying

me poorly, for I was the first rung on the ladder by which you and your brother [Francisco] rose to power. Remember . . . that when you were in my position, and my council members were begging me to cut off your head, I alone spared your life."

Hernando, as disdainful as ever, despised Almagro even more for what appeared to him to be abject groveling. "Stop behaving so despicably," the heavily built man said, turning to leave, "rather die as bravely as you have lived. You are not acting like a knight." Almagro looked after him, then no doubt hung his head, as the door closed firmly behind.

On July 8, 1538, during the month the Incas offered sacrifices to the *huaca* Tocori, the spirit that watches over the irrigation waters of the valley of Cuzco, Don Diego de Almagro gave his last confession to a priest, then dictated his will to a notary who had been brought into his cell. The veteran of hundreds of battles and the executioner of countless natives now set about distributing all the worldly goods he had accumulated since arriving in the New World. In his will, Almagro declared that he possessed hundreds of thousands of castellanos "in gold and silver, gems and pearls, ships and herds." To his only son, eighteen-year-old Diego de Almagro, Jr., whom Almagro had fathered with his Panamanian mistress and who had accompanied him to Chile, Almagro left 13,500 castellanos; to his daughter, Doña Isabella, he left 1,000 castellanos, and asked that she become a nun. "He made a great many other bequests . . . to his servants and to monasteries," wrote one eyewitness. Almagro finished by donating the rest of his property to King Charles, perhaps hoping that in so doing his death might one day be avenged.

The mayor of Cuzco, Antonio de Toraco, now entered Almagro's cell, accompanied by the town crier and the executioner. Still hoping to save his life, Almagro fixed his one bloodshot eye upon the men, trying to use guilt to dissuade them from obeying Hernando's order.

"Gentlemen—doesn't all this land belong to the King? Then why do you want to kill me after I have done His Majesty so many services? Beware, because if you think that His Majesty is [presently] far away, then it will soon seem that his power is quite near. And even if you don't believe that there is a King, then you better well believe that there is a God who watches over everything."

The three men no doubt looked at one another uncomfortably. Then the mayor spoke: there was nothing they could do, he said. It had been ordered that he should die and die he must. The three were simply carrying out orders. Almagro vehemently demanded, however, to speak with Hernando Pizarro one last time, watching with a certain horrified fascination as the executioner prepared the garrote in his presence. This time the mayor agreed, leaving and then returning a short while later with Hernando. Five people now crowded into Almagro's small cell.

"Commander [Pizarro, Almagro said], seeing that you're determined to destroy my body, don't destroy my soul and your honor as well . . . since you say that you're satisfied that I deserve to die [then] send me to be judged by the Emperor. Hand me over to the King or to your brother, the Governor. . . . If you're doing this out of . . . fear that prolonging my life will cause you trouble and danger, then I'll give you any security that you might want. . . . [You know that] I have no more power, since my Second-in-Command, Rodrigo Orgóñez, along with many other officers and men were killed in the battle, and that those who survived are now your prisoners."

Hernando, believing perhaps that with the depositions he had collected against Almagro he would not be held accountable for the governor's death, abruptly told the men to carry out his orders. With Almagro shouting after him, Hernando left the condemned man's cell, heading in the direction of the main square and the Amaru Cancha palace, part of its roof burned yet still his home. As Hernando walked along the square, no doubt looking up briefly at the head of his former enemy, Marshal Orgóñez, caked in dried blood and covered with flies, back in the temple of the sun the executioner was fixing the garrote around Almagro's neck—the same kind of execution that Almagro had once urged his fellow Spaniards to inflict upon the emperor Atahualpa. Almagro—unable to believe that after having helped to conquer the largest native empire ever to have been discovered in the New

World this was how his life was to end—"began to cry out, 'You tyrants! You're stealing the King's land and are killing me for no reason!' "

In the street outside, the muffled shouts were heard for a time and then suddenly ceased. Not long afterward, the town crier emerged from Almagro's prison and, hurrying, was followed by a priest in a long black robe. Both headed up the street lined with cut Inca stones and toward the main square, leaving the rounded contours of the sun temple behind. As they walked, the crier composed in his head the news that he would soon shout out onto Cuzco's streets for one and all to hear: that Don Diego de Almagro—governor of the Kingdom of New Toledo and native of Extremadura—was dead.

13 ❖ VILCABAMBA: GUERRILLA CAPITAL OF THE WORLD

"Being ready to depart [in pursuit of Manco, they] . . . received news that the Inca [emperor] had retreated from there towards . . . the [Antisuyu] . . . which is a very difficult and harsh land to travel in, where horses are worth little, and for which reason from then on the capture of the Inca ceased."

CRISTÓBAL DE MOLINA, *RELACIÓN,* 1553

"In the beginning, the essential task of the guerrilla fighter is to keep himself from being destroyed. . . . When this objective is achieved, [the guerrilla,] having taken up inaccessible positions out of reach of the enemy, or having assembled forces that deter the enemy from attacking, should proceed to the gradual weakening of the enemy. This will be carried out at first at those places nearest the areas of active warfare against the guerrilla band and later will be taken deeper into enemy territory, attacking his communications, later attacking or harassing the bases of operations and the central bases, tormenting him on all sides to the full extent of the guerrilla force's capabilities."

ERNESTO "CHE" GUEVARA, *ON GUERRILLA WARFARE,* 1961

"Counterinsurgency must be initiated as early as possible. An escalating insurgency becomes increasingly difficult to defeat."

U.S. DEPARTMENT OF THE ARMY INTERIM
COUNTERINSURGENCY OPERATIONS FIELD MANUAL, 2004

A native woman in the jungles of Antisuyu,
flanked by a monkey and a macaw.

ALMOST IMMEDIATELY AFTER DIEGO DE ALMAGRO'S EXECU-
tion, news of the governor's death traveled from Cuzco in the direction of
Antisuyu, across the high grassland *puna,* dotted with its blue lakes and
herds of llamas and alpacas, past the mountain peaks with their caps of ice
and snow, then over the eastern rim of the Andes before plunging down
through what the Spaniards called the *ceja de la selva,* or "eyebrow of the forest"—the dense, moist cloud forest that clings to the upper edge of the eastern Andes and is almost perpetually bathed in fog. The news, conveyed by
Manco's spies, continued downward, emerging from beneath the clouds,
zigzagging down the green slopes, then along the tumbling streams and
rivers before plunging into the foothills and finally into the thick rain forest.
Eventually, a lone messenger emerged from beneath the faintly lit canopy
and saw spread out below him a giant, brilliantly lit clearing in the forest,
filled with high-gabled houses and buildings of stone, with tendrils of
smoke filtering through many of the thatched roofs of the houses.

As the messenger ran down the long stone stairway that led into the city,
he also ran past stone conduits carrying water, past flowing fountains, past
noblemen wearing gold earplugs and armbands, and past clusters of brown-
skinned native inhabitants, most of whom wore white cotton tunics, although a few walked about naked with their bodies painted in intricate
designs. In one area of the city a giant granite boulder, or *huaca,* protruded
from the ground, reverenced by all, while a stone temple of the sun, cared
for by the priests, rose up nearby. Further ahead stood a cluster of finely cut
stone buildings, built on three levels. The news from Cuzco had finally arrived at its destination, for this was Manco Inca's palace, his new, Amazon-
ian-based home. It was here, in a provincial town located at 4,900 feet in
elevation, surrounded by high jungle canopy, coca plantations, and chattering troops of monkeys, that Manco Inca had established his new headquarters. This was Vilcabamba, capital of the free Inca state—a province where,
if any Spaniard ventured, he would automatically and without question be
killed.

Although Vilcabamba lay only thirty miles from Manco's previous capital
of Vitcos, his new headquarters was located nearly six thousand feet lower
in elevation and was over one hundred miles from Cuzco. Vitcos—Manco
had painfully learned—had proven too vulnerable to a Spanish attack. Now,
for the first time, Manco had moved his mostly highland followers to a new

and utterly alien realm, migrating thousands of feet further down the flanks of the Andes to where the longest mountain chain on the planet meets the largest rain forest in the world.

The Incas' new capital took its name from the *runasimi* words *huilca,* which means "sacred," and *pampa,* which means "plain" or "valley"; it thus meant "Sacred Plain" or "Sacred Valley." It was here, in a warm, fertile valley lying between two rivers—the Concevidayoc and the Chontabamba—that Manco's grandfather, Tupac Inca, had ordered a typical Inca administrative center to be built; he had soon populated it with transplanted *mitmaqcuna* (colonists) from an ethnic group called the Pilcosuni. Wrote the chronicler Juan de Betanzos:

> As word spread throughout that whole province about how the Inca [Tupac Inca Yupanqui] was conquering it, some of the chiefs of these Indians came in peace to the Inca. When they came out in peace, they gave him parrots, monkeys, and other odd creatures that they call *"perico ligero"* [giant anteaters], which have long snouts and tails and a clumsy walk. They also gave the Inca some feathers, plumage, and some gold dust. . . . This province is a land of gold, and there is gold in it. They also offered the Inca pieces of sweet cane filled with honey, and painted bows and arrows. These people who gave him obedience were given salt, which they valued more than anything that could be given to them. Seeing that these people went naked, as was their custom, they were given tunics and cloaks and made to dress. They wore the clothes that day and in the evening went to their shacks. The next morning they appeared naked, as was their custom, before the Inca [Emperor] and the Inca laughed. . . . In this way the Inca traveled through those woodlands and provinces of the . . . [Antis] conquering those who acted belligerently and treating well those who acted friendly.

In Vilcabamba, the transplanted Pilcosunis and visiting highland masons completing their *mit'a* labor tax soon chopped down the surrounding jungle canopy, cleared away the underbrush, then began erecting a traditional Inca town, complete with rectangular stone houses, storage facilities, a central plaza, fountains, water conduits, and a variety of governmental and religious buildings. Nearby, they cleared and planted coca plantations—the sacred leaf that normally only the Inca royalty were allowed to enjoy. Here, however, in reward to the colonists for the hardship of having to relocate, the *mitmaqcuna* were also allowed to chew the sacred leaves, which contain minute amounts of cocaine and tend to dull both hunger and pain.

Following up on the initial exchange of goods between Tupac Inca's troops and the local tribes, the imported colonists soon set up a frontier trading post that eventually became a link in a far-flung Amazonian trading network that extended deep into the surrounding jungle. Regular pack trains of llamas began arriving from the highlands, bringing Inca goods such as salt, cloth, beads, and bronze and copper axes. These were exchanged for gold, bird feathers, honey, hardwoods, turtle eggs, and other local products that were soon packed securely onto the llamas for their return trip home. Naked and often decorated with distinctive body and face paints, whole families of natives from the various ethnic groups in the area soon began visiting the Inca trading post, bringing their loads of trade items either on their backs or else by canoe. All the while, they looked in wonder at the stone city that had arisen in their midst and at the exotic goods imported from the distant, cold, and treeless land that they had been told existed high above their own.

When Manco Inca arrived on his litter at the Vilcabamba trading post sometime in 1538, he brought with him those of his retinue who had escaped the recent Spanish invasion and sacking of Vitcos. With his sister-queen, Cura Ocllo, and with what was left of his harem, his temple priests, masons, architects, servants, carpenters, healers, royal guards, diviners, farmers, and herders, Manco soon began transforming the rugged frontier town into a makeshift royal city, the capital of a self-sufficient state. True, he had been forced to abandon the highlands, but Manco was nevertheless convinced that here, deep in the Antisuyu, he would be able to maintain Inca sovereignty. Ironically, the Antisuyu had been one of the first provinces his great-grandfather Pachacuti and his grandfather Tupac Inca had conquered. The empire they had created and that had once exploded across the Andes like a supernova, however, had now suddenly fallen back upon itself. It was now up to Pachacuti's twenty-two-year-old heir to try to prevent its collapse.

Manco was not interested in simply maintaining a free Inca state, however. Despite his recent setbacks, he was still determined to continue his struggle to eject the bearded invaders from Tawantinsuyu—or else die in the effort. Although his new headquarters now lay hidden amidst the outer rim of the once vast empire his ancestors had ruled, Manco still maintained lines of communication that snaked out westward from Vilcabamba, climbed up the sheer face of the Andes, and then spread out across the highlands. Manco was also well aware of the fact that, even though his brother Paullu now wore the royal fringe in Cuzco and had assumed Manco's previous role among the Spaniards as a collaborator, many Incas and other highland groups still looked to Manco for leadership, considering him to be the only legitimate Son of the Sun. With a massive native following who still considered him divine and with a new refuge in which he felt secure, Manco believed he was in a position to resume his struggle against those who had usurped his empire.

Manco therefore set about transforming his remote frontier city into a new royal capital, and also created a new command center for his struggle against the Spaniards. Under Manco's guidance, Vilcabamba would soon become the headquarters for native resistance against the arrogant, bearded invaders. From his newly refurbished city, Manco would begin dispatching a stream of messages that would be carried high up into the looming mountains to the south, to the north, and to the west. *Resist,* he told his followers, *the Spaniards are not viracochas but mortals; slaughter them and join me in driving the bearded ones back into the sea.*

A political snapshot of Peru at this time would have revealed that, although Francisco Pizarro had received considerable reinforcements from abroad, the Spaniards still controlled only a handful of cities: Quito, Tumbez, San Miguel, Trujillo, and Cajamarca in the north; Jauja and Lima in the center; and Cuzco in the south. Wide swaths of the rest of the country—especially the countryside outside the cities, the entire southern half of the empire stretching from below Lake Titicaca halfway down into modern-day Chile, and nearly the whole of the eastern quarter, or Antisuyu—lay beyond Spanish control. By 1538, in fact, six years after the capture of Atahualpa, the total population of Spaniards in Peru still amounted to no more than two thousand—roughly one hundred of whom were women—in an empire 2,500 miles long. In addition, most of those Spaniards were concentrated in Cuzco and Lima. The total population of natives in the area now known as

Peru, meanwhile, most of whom lived primarily in the countryside, still numbered at least five million.

A basic rule of modern warfare states that an occupying army should have a ratio of from ten to twenty soldiers per one thousand inhabitants if an army is to adequately control a conquered population. To control the five-million-strong inhabitants of this portion of Tawantinsuyu, therefore, the Spaniards theoretically needed between 50,000 and 100,000 Spanish and/or auxiliary troops. Even with the collaboration of Paullu Inca, Spanish and auxiliary native forces were still greatly outnumbered and, not surprisingly, the Spaniards themselves made few excursions into the countryside. Instead, the Spaniards preferred living in cities, where their own forces remained concentrated, cities that served the same function as military garrisons. It was this basic weakness—the lack of a Spanish presence in the countryside and their concentration in a handful of cities—that Manco Inca was determined to exploit.

When news finally arrived in Vilcabamba of Diego de Almagro's death, therefore, Manco's resolve only stiffened. At one time he had hoped that civil war might break out among the Spaniards and that they would destroy themselves. With Almagro dead, however, Manco no longer had any such illusions; he now knew that he would have to rely on his own resources. In the north, his relative Illa Tupac—one of the high-ranking captains, now a general, who had participated in the rebellion of 1536—still commanded native levies, was still loyal, and remained unconquered. Manco soon sent orders for General Tupac to renew the rebellion and to kill any and all Spaniards in his territory. Not long afterward, Tupac and the various tribes north of the Huánuco area along the upper Marañon River rose in revolt and marched down the Andes toward the coastal city of Trujillo, killing any Spaniards, African slaves, and native auxiliaries they found along the way.

Manco himself now returned to the Andes, traveling to the north of Cuzco, where he personally began to organize groups that would become guerrilla fighters. Eventually, small, mobile groups of warriors began ambushing Spanish *encomenderos,* merchants, and other travelers, all of whom frequented the main Inca highway above Cuzco. According to the chronicler Cieza de León, Manco also incorporated a new tactic into his campaign against the Spaniards—outright terror:

The king, Manco Inca . . . had retired into the mountain fastnesses of the . . . [Antisuyu] with the *orejones* and old military leaders who had made war on the Spaniards. And as . . . the merchants from Lima and other areas carried their goods to Cuzco, the Indians attacked them and, after seizing their goods, they either murdered them or carried some of them away alive. . . . And returning with them on horseback to the . . . [Antisuyu] they tortured those Christians they had taken alive in the presence of their women, revenging themselves for the injuries they had suffered . . . [by] shoving sharp stakes into the lower parts of their bodies until they came out of their mouths. The news of this caused such terror that many Spaniards who had private or even government business to conduct didn't dare go to Cuzco unless they were well armed and had an escort.

While Manco was raiding with his guerrilla forces to the west of Cuzco, Francisco Pizarro, meanwhile, was growing increasingly concerned over reports of the recent disturbances. Pizarro had been in Cuzco since roughly November of 1538, having arrived there some four months after the execution of Diego de Almagro. Informed at first by letter of his former partner's death, Pizarro had no doubt experienced mixed emotions, as his relationship with Almagro had been a complex one. According to Cieza de León,

When he [Pizarro] saw the letters and heard what had taken place, he spent a long time with downcast eyes . . . and appeared to be grief stricken, presently shedding some tears. Whether they were feigned or not only our Lord God knows. Although . . . I have [also] heard it said by some of those who were with the Governor that when he heard this news trumpets were played as a sign of joy.

Whatever emotions Pizarro may have experienced, the destruction of Almagro and his force had allowed Pizarro once again to regain control of Cuzco. Now, however, after receiving reports that Manco Inca had returned to the Andes and was killing Spaniards anew, Pizarro wasted no time; he soon sent a powerful force of more than two hundred Spanish cavalry, under the command of Captain Illán Suárez de Carvajal, to capture or kill the renegade Inca leader whom he himself had crowned.

Suárez soon rode out west from Cuzco along the Inca highway, reaching the town of Andahuaylas, about one hundred miles distant. There, he learned from native spies that Manco was currently northwest of his position, using the nearby hills as a sort of robber's roost from which to stage his guerrilla attacks. Determined to surround the rebel emperor so that he would be unable to escape, Suárez moved his force to the west of Manco's position in order to block any movement in that direction. He then sent a force of thirty men—including seven crossbowmen and five harquebusiers under the command of a Captain Villadiego—to circle around to the east toward the other side. There the Vilcas (Pampas) River served as a natural barricade that would prevent any escape attempt toward the Antisuyu, except over a single bridge. Villadiego and his men were ordered to seize the bridge and to remain there until Suárez had located Manco's position and had begun his attack.

Arriving at the Vilcas River, Villadiego surprised and captured several natives guarding the bridge, whom he tortured into revealing Manco's location. The emperor was in the nearby hilltop town of Oncoy, the prisoners told him—he was attending a festival that had been thrown in his honor. What's more, they said, Manco had with him only eighty warriors—he was thus relatively unprotected. The young Spanish captain—eager to receive both the awards and the glory of being the first to capture the rebel Inca king—decided to ignore his commander's orders and instead to immediately attack. Villadiego thus abandoned the bridge and began leading his men along a trail that led from the bottom of the canyon directly up to the hilltop town above.

The day was hot and the Spaniards were forced to make the steep climb on foot, leading their horses behind them by their reins. Far above, Manco's wife and sister, Cura Ocllo, was the first to see the invaders. She quickly alerted her husband. Manco immediately ordered that the four captured horses they had in their possession be saddled and readied for him and three other Inca nobles, who, like Manco, had learned how to ride. Manco then ordered the women in the town to line up along the hillside, brandishing an assortment of captured Spanish lances, in an effort to fool the Spaniards into thinking that Manco had a much larger force with him. Climbing onto his horse and wheeling about with a long Spanish lance in his hand, Manco now led his three horsemen down the hillside, followed by his warriors on foot.

As Villadiego's men continued struggling up the slope, one of them suddenly shouted a warning, causing the Spaniards to look up and see the silhouettes of what appeared to be numerous warriors on the hilltop above, who now began shouting insults and shaking their lances. The Spaniards were further stunned to see racing down toward them four natives on horseback, carrying lances, with many more warriors racing behind them on foot. Caught by surprise on a steep path and with a sheer drop-off below, the seven crossbowmen raised their weapons to fire as the handful of harquebusiers desperately tried to light the wicks of their guns. As Manco's warriors began hurling down sling stones and darts from above, a few of the harquebuses fired, felling one native, but by then Manco's warriors were among them, smashing the Spaniards with their mace clubs, hurling sling stones, and pressing the Spaniards back down the trail so forcefully that many of the Spaniards and their horses simply tumbled off the slope, the men screaming briefly before hitting the ground far below. Manco and his four-horse cavalry, meanwhile, effectively used their lances to stab and skewer the remaining Spaniards, who presumably had never before been attacked by natives on horseback.

After a fierce struggle, the battle ended in a rout. Captain Villadiego, covered in wounds and with his arm broken by a native battle-axe, had eventually fallen to the ground. The coup de grâce was delivered to him via a flurry of mace clubs. In his eagerness to seize for himself the glory of Manco's capture, the young captain had committed two fatal errors: first, he had allowed himself to be caught by surprise on steep terrain where he and his Spaniards were unable to use their horses; and second, he had allowed Manco's warriors to attack them from the heights above. Of Villadiego's thirty men, twenty-eight were either killed outright or else fell to their deaths. Only two escaped, by running back down to the river, leaping in, and then swimming desperately across. Manco's son Titu Cusi remembered the joy of his father's success:

> And so my father's men, having achieved the victory, gathered the spoils
> from the Spaniards, stripping them naked of everything they could

[and] removing the clothing and weapons that they had. [Then], gathering everything up, they took it to the town of Oncoy above. My father and [his men] . . . rejoiced tremendously and held celebrations and dances for five days in honor of the victory and of the spoils.

Despite his success, Manco no doubt realized that his current military situation was far different from the one he had enjoyed only a few years earlier. No longer did he command the mass levies of troops he had once raised to besiege Cuzco with—the same kinds of vast armies that his forefathers had once used to carve out their empire. Instead, Manco was now reduced to leading smaller groups that, because of their reduced numbers, had to avoid direct confrontations with larger Spanish forces. Nevertheless, Manco's warriors were by now effectively ambushing Spanish supply convoys on the Inca highways, destroying small military contingents, amassing stolen weapons and horses, and then disappearing back into the hills. If the hallmarks of guerrilla warfare are mobility, speed, knowledge of local terrain, peasant support, inflicting frequent ambushes upon the enemy and then disappearing before a larger counterinsurgency force can respond, then Manco Inca had truly transformed himself into an effective guerrilla leader.

Not long after the death of Villadiego and his men, an exasperated Francisco Pizarro led a force of seventy cavalry out from Cuzco in pursuit of the rebel emperor. Although he and his troops scoured the countryside, Pizarro was unable to find the elusive Manco amid the wild, rugged landscape of the interior. Manco's spies, in fact, had warned their emperor of the presence of the cavalry unit; Manco had thus wisely decided to retreat back across the Apurímac River into the Antisuyu, preserving his forces to fight another day. A frustrated Pizarro eventually returned to Cuzco and dictated a letter to King Charles.

Cuzco, the 27th of February, 1539

Sacred Catholic Caesarian Majesty,

. . . Returning by [the Inca] road, I was informed by letters from this city about how Manco Inca has relocated twenty-five leagues [ninety miles] from here and has robbed certain towns and has sent messengers all

across the land telling them to rise up again. . . . Afterwards we provided
men who went to punish him . . . [but], as they have spies . . . he avoids
the open lands and disappears into the forests. When summer arrives, he
will not be able to defend himself against me. . . . I will have him in my
hands, dead or a prisoner.

Manco Inca, meanwhile, had already sent additional messages to his followers in the south of Peru including his high priest, Villac Umu, who was
still holed up in the rugged mountains in the Cuntisuyu quarter of the empire, to the southwest of Cuzco. After receiving Manco's order, Villac Umu
and his forces immediately began attacking Spaniards in the area and encouraging the local natives to rebel. Further to the south, along the altiplano
west of Lake Titicaca, Manco's messages had an equal effect upon the Lu-
paca tribes, which now decided to rise up. In a relatively short period of
time, then, suddenly more than a thousand miles of the Inca heartland, from
just below Cajamarca in the north to the shores of Lake Titicaca in the
south, were once more in the throes of a native rebellion. Frightened Spanish merchants and *encomenderos* now found themselves forced to travel on
the Inca highways in armed convoys for fear of deadly attacks.

Once the Spaniards realized the gravity of the situation, they immediately embarked upon a methodical counterinsurgency campaign, determined to preserve their privileged position at the apex of Peru's newly
reconfigured social pyramid. Hernando and Gonzalo Pizarro now left
Cuzco, leading a large Spanish cavalry force in the company of five thousand native auxiliaries, led by Paullu Inca, against the rebellious Lupacas.
Ferrying horses and men across a portion of Lake Titicaca on rafts, the
Spaniards soon routed the natives, capturing and killing the rebellious Lu-
paca chief and burning his village to the ground.

The Spaniards now began to shift their campaign northward, with Gonzalo Pizarro leading a force of seventy cavalry headed toward the Collao.
After a fierce battle against a confederation of Consora, Pocona, and Chicha
tribes, the Spanish cavalry once again emerged victorious, killing thousands
of natives in the process. An unexpected bonus from that campaign was the
surrender of the Inca general Tiso, the finest general Manco had left.

To put down the rebellion in the Cuntisuyu, to the southwest of Cuzco,
Francisco Pizarro sent another Spanish force, again accompanied by native

auxiliaries, to locate and destroy Villac Umu and his army. Although the campaign would last for eight long months and would wax and wane, in the end the Spaniards succeeded in forcing Villac Umu into surrendering. The same bearded invaders who had profaned the Incas' sacred temples now transported the Inca equivalent of the pope back to Cuzco in chains.

Although Manco's general, Illa Tupac, continued to control a large area in the north near Jauja and would fight on for years, the Spaniards spread their own brand of terror throughout the north by dispatching repeated counterinsurgency forces to the rebellious provinces. In the fertile valley lying before the massive Cordillera Blanca, for example, in the Callejón de Huaylas, some four hundred miles northwest of Cuzco, local natives had killed two *encomenderos*. Lima's town council sent a cavalry force under the command of Captain Francisco de Chávez to exact retribution. Chávez and his cavalry spent three months in the area, raiding native villages, slashing and spearing their inhabitants, torching their houses, and setting fire to their fields.

The marauding Spaniards made no distinction between men, women, and children in their campaign. "The war was so cruel that, fearing they would all be killed, the Indians asked for peace," wrote Cieza de León. Before declaring his counterinsurgency campaign over, however, Chávez—a classic *extremeño* from Pizarro's native town of Trujillo—was said to have slaughtered more than six hundred children under the age of three.

Meanwhile, further to the south, the natives in the area of Huánuco had also responded to Manco's urgings, killing a number of Spaniards; an additional cavalry force was soon dispatched to this region as well. More than one hundred miles south of their destination, however, the cavalry entered the peaceful Inca town of Tarma, which had not rebelled. The Spaniards nevertheless spent seven months there, "eating their corn and sheep [llamas and alpacas], robbing them of all of their gold and silver, taking their wives . . . keeping many Indians chained and making slaves of them and . . . abusing, extorting, and torturing them [the Indian chiefs] so that they would reveal . . . [the whereabouts] of their gold and silver." Clearly, the lines between "conquering," "pacifying," "occupying," "delivering retribution," and "marauding" had become so thin as to be invisible, much to the dismay of Peru's native inhabitants.

In April of 1539, as the counterinsurgency campaign in the north continued, Francisco, Hernando, and Gonzalo Pizarro met in Cuzco in order to discuss their plans for the next steps in the conquest of Peru. Because of the complications caused by Almagro's execution, Francisco thought it best that Hernando return to Spain to exonerate himself. Hernando had too many enemies by now, Francisco believed, who could poison the king's ear and who could thus turn the king against Hernando and the rest of the Pizarro family. If his brother took with him a newly written chronicle of events that featured Hernando as an Indian-fighting hero during the recent siege, and a new load of gold for the king, then Francisco felt that his brother should be able to successfully plead his case to the king.

Gonzalo, by contrast, now twenty-seven years old, thought the plan a poor idea. It would be best for Hernando to remain in Peru, he argued, and if necessary for him to wait here with his lance and sword at the ready. In Spain, Hernando might find himself at the mercy of his enemies—and with none of his family there to help him. Hernando, however, "answered angrily, saying that Gonzalo was a boy and didn't know the King." In any case, Hernando had already made up his mind: he would return to Spain and would meet with the king. Then, once the issue of Almagro's execution had been taken care of, he would petition the king for additional favors.

On the day of his departure, Francisco, Gonzalo, and a small group of conquistadors accompanied Hernando a short way out of town and then dismounted to say goodbye. Hernando embraced both his brothers before taking pains to warn Francisco about the potential danger of Almagro's followers—those who had gone with the now dead governor to Chile, who had fought against the Pizarros, and who had ended up bitter and destitute for their efforts. Wrote Pedro Pizarro:

> Hernando Pizarro, on taking leave of his brother the Marquis, said to him, "[You know] that I'm going to Spain and that, besides God, that we're all depending upon you. I say this because those from Chile are behaving very disrespectfully. If I weren't going away, there would be nothing to fear (and he told the truth because they were very afraid of him). Make friends with them and give something to eat to those who wish it, [but] do not allow [even] ten of those who want nothing to gather together within fifty leagues from wherever you are, for if you . . . [do] they are bound to kill you." . . . Hernando Pizarro said these words

aloud, and we all heard them and, embracing the Marquis, he set off and went away.

Hernando took with him a pack train of gold and silver for the king, letters and requests to the king from Francisco, and a long list of *encomiendas* that Hernando personally wanted for himself and was confident the king would grant him. As they watched their heavyset brother ride off, neither Francisco nor Gonzalo realized that this would be the last time they would ever see Hernando again.

One thing all three brothers had agreed upon before Hernando's departure, however, was that Manco Inca must be exterminated. As long as the rebel emperor remained alive, then Manco would permanently endanger their control of Peru. Thus, soon after Hernando's departure, Gonzalo Pizarro began organizing an expedition, the goal of which was to capture or kill Manco Inca once and for all. Spies had already informed the Pizarros that Manco had relocated to a site called Vilcabamba, hidden somewhere amid the thick lowland forests and protected by bow-and-arrow-wielding Antis. The only remedy for their current predicament, in which a renegade Inca emperor was on the loose, was to track Manco Inca to his jungle redoubt and there, like some noxious pest, to exterminate him.

Thirty-four years younger than Francisco and eleven years younger than Hernando, Gonzalo Pizarro had been only twenty when he had arrived in Peru and had always been overshadowed by his older brothers. Unlike his brother Juan, who had been a year older than him, Gonzalo hadn't become a captain until the siege of Cuzco, and then only perhaps because Juan's death had given him that opportunity. During the siege, however, Gonzalo had distinguished himself as one of the city's best defenders. Tall, black-bearded, and strikingly handsome, Gonzalo was an excellent horseman and an unerring marksman with both the crossbow and the harquebus. He was also fabulously wealthy, for, like his brothers, Gonzalo had received substantial divisions of the gold and silver at Cajamarca and Cuzco.

A classic *extremeño,* possessing many of that region's indelible characteristics—toughness, insularity, suspiciousness of outsiders, and extreme parsimoniousness—Gonzalo was capable of making both good friends and bitter enemies. He was also insatiably ambitious; Gonzalo was keen to have his own governorship and was not shy about letting others know that. An impulsive and profligate womanizer, Gonzalo had stolen Manco's wife, Cura Ocllo. That one action had no doubt helped to spark an Inca rebellion that had thus far cost the life of one of his own brothers as well as the lives of hundreds of his fellow Spaniards.

Whether Gonzalo ever acknowledged his own responsibility in Manco's insurrection is unknown. Gonzalo *did* know, however, that if he were able to capture or exterminate the rebellious Inca emperor, then a governorship might very likely figure in his future. Yet for the time being, it was imperative to pacify *this* realm. "It is believed that, once [the Inca] is surrounded, he cannot fail to be killed or taken prisoner, and then order will be restored to the land," wrote a Spaniard at the time. "But until this is achieved, everything will remain in a state of suspense."

Three hundred Spaniards presently volunteered to accompany Gonzalo, both foot soldiers and cavalry, all of whom were eager to distinguish themselves. Many of the cavalrymen were *encomenderos* and were thus eager to get their hands on Manco; it was the only means they knew of preventing the natives whose tribute they now depended upon from going over to Manco's side. Other volunteers were newly arrived conquistadors—former cobblers, tailors, carpenters, masons, and so on who had arrived in Peru with their own weapons and were eager to improve their fortunes. Gonzalo was well aware of the fact that when Rodrigo Orgóñez had sacked Vitcos and nearly captured Manco Inca two years earlier, his Spaniards had found abundant gold, silver, and some of the most beautiful temple virgins in the land. With any luck, Gonzalo's own expedition might do the same.

As Gonzalo's men prepared for their expedition, Paullu Inca organized a large contingent of native auxiliaries to assist them. This time, however, Paullu himself would accompany the Spaniards. Paullu was now determined to take an active part in the fight against his brother, no doubt in order to protect his continued reign as the *Sapa Inca,* or "Unique Inca"—a position that presently was not unique. Although Paullu knew that Manco had been relegated to the fringes of Tawantinsuyu and was currently living among the Antis barbarians, his brother nevertheless posed a very real danger to him. If Manco were ever to negotiate a truce with the Spaniards and were to return to Cuzco, then Paullu would automatically be deposed as emperor.

Already convinced that the Spaniards were unbeatable, Paullu had been busy experimenting with wearing an assortment of Spanish clothing in the capital—silk stockings, fine cloaks, and a variety of European hats. Paullu had also indicated that he was interested in adopting the Spaniards' religion. Living in an Inca palace and waited upon by a retinue of beautiful concubines, the man who had had virtually no chance of becoming emperor only two years earlier was no doubt loath to give up his luxurious new lifestyle. If he had to kill his own brother to maintain his present position, then kill his brother he would. Besides, Inca tradition dictated that the strongest heir to the throne would ultimately rise to the top. Among the Inca aristocracy, the indubitable message was winner take all.

On a brilliant, sunny day in April 1539, the expedition of three hundred Spaniards and a large force of native auxiliaries set out, followed by llama trains carrying their provisions. As they left the city and began to climb the hill to the north, many of the Spaniards looked back down upon the Inca capital, which, like Paullu's taste in clothes, was gradually being transformed. Ever since Manco had set fire to Cuzco during the siege, most of the city's thatched roofs had disappeared. Now, earth-colored clay tiles crowned the gabled roofs of various buildings, as Spanish workmen grafted some of the architectural features of their own country onto those of the Incas. As the expedition reached the bluff overlooking Cuzco and began riding past the fortress of Saqsaywaman, the sounds of masonry hammers and a church bell could be heard from below—sure evidence that Cuzco was gradually developing a Spanish veneer.

Now, for the second time in two years, a large force of conquistadors headed down the eastern side of the Andes, the Spaniards' horses following the same, stone-paved Inca trail, picking their way carefully to maintain their footing on the often smooth or wet stones. Three royal litters traveled with the expedition, one occupied by Paullu and the other two by Huaspar and Inquill. The latter two were both half-brothers of Manco and Paullu and were full brothers of Manco's wife, Cura Ocllo. Like their brother, Paullu, they had switched their allegiance from Manco to the Spaniards, no doubt based upon their assumption that in the struggle for Tawantinsuyu, Manco Inca would ultimately be the loser.

After three days of travel, the expedition reached the Chuquichaca bridge over the Urubamba River, which Rodrigo Orgóñez and his men had seized on their way to Vitcos two years earlier. The hanging bridge now lay deserted and, unopposed, the Spaniards rode up into the Vilcabamba Valley. Passing the hilltop citadel of Vitcos, which Orgóñez had sacked and which Manco had been forced to abandon, the expedition next headed up to the 12,500-foot Colpacasa Pass. Rugged hills carpeted with thick vegetation now stretched below them into the distance, forming ridge after crumpled ridge. Slowly, the expedition began making its way down the stone-paved trail along the Pampaconas River, past trees festooned with spiky bromeliads and drooping moss, then past waterfalls that would soon become a rushing river.

At one point, clouds choked their descent, the men losing sight of the front and rear ends of the column as the cavalry was suddenly converted into helmeted silhouettes, bathed in a light gray mist. Drops of water like perspiration collected on the Spaniards' armor, coalescing into rivulets that then descended like tiny streams of quicksilver. Finally, after three days of descent from the pass, the vegetation became so thick that the Spaniards were forced to dismount and abandon their horses. Carrying swords, harquebuses, and crossbows at the ready, the Spaniards now followed their native guides single file down into the dark and alien underworld of the Amazon rain forest, or *selva*.

The air by now had become warm and thick as mosquitoes buzzed about, attacking the Spaniards' exposed skin. The men sweated under their armor and cotton clothes while in the distance sounds they had never before heard welled up—deep, lionlike roars that to the Spaniards sounded like the guardians of hell screaming, coupled with strange, haunting trills that wafted through the dripping forest and no doubt sent chills down many of their spines. The men had heard plenty of tales from their native guides of how the Antis natives supposedly ate human flesh and how they would look upon the Spaniards as so many gastronomic delicacies. When another eerie trill erupted, somewhere among the shadowy leaves ahead, the Spaniards no doubt stopped and asked their guides, "Antis?" Pointing up at the tops of giant, soaring trees whose bases stretched for more than twenty feet and had buttresses like giant shark fins, the guides would have replied that these were *"Uru-kusillu-kuna,"* or "spider monkeys." The lionlike roars were from monkeys, too, the guides said, but they used another word for them. The guides were undoubtedly nervous, knowing full well that the enemy was close and that at any time they might be attacked. The question was not if

they would be attacked—but how, where, and when. Wrote the Jesuit priest
Blas Valera:

> Those who live in the . . . [Antisuyu] . . . eat human flesh, they are
> fiercer than tigers, have neither god nor law, nor know what virtue is.
> They have no idols nor likenesses of them. They worship the devil when
> he represents himself in the form of some animal or serpent and speaks
> to them. If they make a prisoner in war . . . and know that he is a ple-
> beian of low rank, they quarter him and give the quarters to their friends
> and servants to eat or to sell in the meat market. But if he is of noble
> rank, the chiefs gather with their wives and children and, like ministers
> of the devil, strip him, tie him alive to a stake, and cut him to pieces with
> flint knives and razors, not so as to dismember him, but to remove the
> meat from the fleshiest parts, the calves, thighs, buttocks, and fleshy
> parts of the arms. Men, women, and children sprinkle themselves with
> the blood and they all devour the flesh very rapidly, without cooking it
> or roasting it thoroughly or even chewing it. They swallow it in mouth-
> fuls so that the wretched victim sees himself eaten alive.

Although cannibalism did exist on parts of the Atlantic coast of Brazil
and some native warriors in Ecuador did shrink one another's heads, the
priest's tales about the Antis Indians were fabricated—fantastic stories told
about a people and an environment so alien to highland Incas and European
Spaniards that they inspired fear and loathing among both. To the
Spaniards listening to such tales, however—and who had now stepped off
the edge of the Andes into a dark and otherworldly realm frequently punctuated by unexpected howls and screams—there was no reason not to accept these apocryphal stories as true. How far this forest stretched, in any
case—and whether it contained rich empires adorned with gold or not—no
one knew. Most of the continent was still terra incognita, after all, a
no-man's-land whose labyrinthine interior could only be imagined. Somewhere ahead might lie new empires and wealth beyond their wildest
dreams—or else deaths so horrible that the Spaniards might be forced to
watch themselves being literally eaten alive. Only God in heaven—or the
devil in hell—really knew.

Walking in single file, the Spaniards eventually arrived at a narrow canyon through which two streams flowed. Crossing over two bridges that had been recently constructed, they now emerged into a clearing that had high bluffs on either side and was filled with the sound of rushing water. Pedro Pizarro later recalled:

> [When] some twenty Spaniards had . . . [crossed the bridge], the Indians who were hidden hurled down . . . many boulders from the mountains above. These boulders are huge stones that they throw from above and which come rolling down with great fury. These boulders carried away three Spaniards, smashing them to bits and knocking them into the river. Those Spaniards who had already gone ahead into the forest found many Indian archers who began to shoot arrows at them and to wound them, and had they not found a narrow path from which they threw themselves into the river, they would have all been killed, for they could not . . . [come to grips with] these Indians who were hidden among the trees.

The Spaniards had obviously blundered into a trap. According to Titu Cusi,

> [My father] had heard from the spies he had stationed on the roads how Gonzalo Pizarro . . . and many others were coming after him and that three of his own brothers were coming with them . . . [And] he [Manco] went there and found I don't know how many Spaniards, because the forest was so thick you couldn't count them . . . [and] he fought with them fiercely on the banks of a river.

The bridges the Spaniards had crossed, it turned out, had recently been built by Manco's warriors in order purposely to divert the Spaniards from the normal trail and to lead them into an area where they could be crushed by falling rocks. The ambush-by-boulder technique was the same that Manco's general Quizo had successfully used in the Andes. Rather than wait until more of the Spaniards had crossed the bridge, however, Manco's warriors had released the boulders too soon, crushing the front of the Spanish column but allowing the rest of the Spaniards to escape by retreating back up the trail.

The ambush nevertheless caused the long Spanish and Inca column to stop dead in its tracks. After fierce fighting throughout the day and with the Spaniards hardly able to see their Antis attackers—so well did the native Amazonians use the forest to hide in—the Spaniards finally retreated. That night, Gonzalo and his men retraced their steps by torchlight back to where they had left their horses, in order to regroup and decide what to do and also because the Spaniards had "many wounded and many who had become unnerved." During the day's fighting, the Spaniards had suffered thirty-six dead.

Demoralized by their recent casualties and by the shadowy Antis who could let loose volleys of arrows yet who could scarcely be seen, the Spaniards sent to Cuzco for reinforcements. Gonzalo Pizarro, meanwhile, hoping to prevent further ambushes before those reinforcements could arrive, now sent Inquill and Huaspar ahead to try to negotiate with their brother. If Manco would lay down his arms, the brothers were presumably told, then he would be pardoned; the Spaniards had also informed the two brothers that they were also prepared to reward Manco with *encomiendas* of his own.

Manco, however, had previously issued a standing order that any natives who collaborated with the Spaniards were to be summarily executed. He was also aware that the Spanish force was large and well armed and that his three half-brothers had led them here. Manco was already furious with Paullu for having rejected his invitation to join him in his rebellion and also for the fact that Paullu had accepted the royal fringe and had allowed himself to be crowned as emperor. When his brothers Inquill and Huaspar arrived at his camp, therefore, Manco was in no mood for either pleasantries or negotiations. According to Titu Cusi,

> My father became so angry that he [Huaspar] had come to see him that the negotiations cost him his life. And [because] my father wanted to kill him due to the anger he had, Cura Ocllo tried to stop him, because she loved him [her brother] so much. [But] my father, not paying attention to her pleas, cut off his head and that of his other brother, Inquill, saying these words: "better that I cut off *their* heads than for them to depart with mine."

Manco's wife—who had already been kidnapped and raped by Gonzalo Pizarro and had somehow escaped, and who was now confronted with the bodies of her two brothers lying on the ground before her, with their severed heads on either side—was devastated by their deaths. Other than Paullu and Manco, these were the last sons of her father, the great Huayna Capac. Now five of her brothers were dead—among them Atahualpa and Huascar—and all had died as a result of the struggle that had ensued due to the death, presumably by European smallpox, of her father. According to Manco's son, Cura Ocllo "was so upset by the death of her brothers that she refused to move ever again from the place where they had been executed."

Manco, however, had little time to worry about his wife's grief. With hundreds of armed Spaniards now only a little more than a dozen miles from his capital and, according to his spies, with more Spanish reinforcements gathering in Cuzco, he had to find a way to destroy his enemies or else make life so difficult for them that they would give up and return to the Andes. All that remained between the Spaniards and his new capital city was a single canyon blocked by a large stone outcropping that formed a natural barricade, blocking the Spaniards' access. Within the canyon high ridges cloaked in dense vegetation rose up on either side. The Incas themselves normally surmounted the barricade with ladders, which they had now of course removed. In addition, Manco had ordered a stone wall to be erected on top of the barricade, leaving small, windowlike openings.

Gonzalo Pizarro soon decided to mount a frontal attack against the barricade, sending a force ahead with orders to seize it. As the Spaniards began attempting to scramble up the stone outcrop and reached the wall, Manco chose this precise moment, however, to reveal his latest military innovation. Loud explosions suddenly erupted and blasts of smoke issued from the perforations in the wall directly before the attackers. Spanish prisoners, apparently, had shown Manco's warriors how to fire his stockpile of captured harquebuses, seized from slain Spaniards. It was for this reason that Manco had left the small openings in the wall atop the barricade. After the stunned Spaniards had retreated and then began to examine the wall carefully, they could see the barrels of harquebuses manufactured in Spain drawing direct beads on them. According to Pedro Pizarro, however, the instructions the warriors had received in the use of gunpowder and reloading were less than ideal:

> At the entrance of this narrow [canyon] . . . [Manco] had made a stone
> wall with some openings in it and through which they shot at us with
> four or five harquebuses that . . . he had taken from Spaniards. And as
> they did not know how to load the harquebuses, they could do us no
> harm, because they left the [lead] ball close to the mouth of the harque-
> bus and so it fell to the ground as it came out.

Nevertheless, after days of skirmishing during which the Spaniards were
unable to breach Manco's barricade, the Spaniards found themselves stalemated. Finally, however, reinforcements from Cuzco arrived and, with a
fresh infusion of troops, Gonzalo now devised an innovative strategy of his
own. Ordering half of his force to conduct a rather halfhearted yet pro-
longed attack against Manco's troops defending the stone barricade, Gonzalo ordered the rest of his men to secretly ascend the back side of the ridge
in an attempt to gain the heights above. As gunshots signaled the barricade
attack, Gonzalo's second group began crawling up through the dense, tangled vegetation, often having to hack their way forward with axes. Eventually, the Spaniards gained the top of the ridge without being noticed. Now,
as the natives focused their efforts on repelling the Spanish attack below,
they suddenly found themselves in the unenviable position of being fired
upon from above with both harquebuses and crossbows. Recalled Pedro
Pizarro:

> Seeing how the Spaniards were coming down from above, the Indians
> came to give Manco Inca news of it at the fort . . . and when he had un-
> derstood three Indians took him by the arms and hurriedly carried him
> over the river . . . which runs close to this fort, and they carried him
> down alongside the river a ways and hid him in the jungle. And the rest
> of the Indians who were there disappeared and fled in many directions,
> taking refuge in the forest.

Frustrated and distraught over his failure to hold the barricade, Manco is
said to have paused on the other side of the river long enough to have
shouted back at his tormentors, "I am Manco Inca! I am *Manco Inca!*" as if to
say "how *dare* you!" One of the Spanish attackers, Mansio Serra de Leguizamón, also remembered Manco shouting across that "he and his Indians had

killed two thousand Spaniards before and after the uprising, and that he intended to kill them all and retain the land that was his and had belonged to his forefathers." Nevertheless, now no longer able to prevent the Spaniards from advancing toward his new capital, Manco turned and fled, assisted by his naked Antis warriors.

Gonzalo and his troops presently followed the stone causeway until they finally reached Vilcabamba, a city that, until now, they had only heard stories about. The Spaniards found the new Inca capital spread out below them in a large forest clearing more than a mile in length; the city, however, appeared deserted, as the frightened inhabitants had fled. As the Spaniards descended the long stone stairway into the city, they were followed by Paullu Inca, wearing the royal fringe and carried in his litter. Smoke still curled up from recently abandoned cooking fires while spider monkey trills sounded in the distance. The excited Spaniards now began ransacking the city, plunging with drawn swords into various buildings and storehouses and emerging with gold and silver plates, goblets, and idols. Several Spanish captains and their native auxiliaries also went in search of the missing emperor, yet found only Manco's wife, Cura Ocllo. Still in shock over the death of her two brothers, the grieving woman apparently had made no attempt to escape.

In July 1539, after two long fruitless months of searching for the rebel emperor, Gonzalo Pizarro gave up and the joint Spanish-Inca expedition began its return journey to Cuzco. They carried with them the spoils of their plunder, their various captives, and with Cura Ocllo, queen of the Incas, bound in cords. Angry no doubt that Manco had once again managed to escape, Gonzalo allowed his fellow Spaniards to brutalize the captured *coya*, the same woman who only a few years earlier Gonzalo had desired so much that in seizing her he had ultimately helped to unleash a deadly native rebellion. According to Titu Cusi, some thirty miles from Vilcabamba, in the village of Pampaconas, Cura Ocllo's captors tried to rape her.

> She refused, defending herself fiercely in any way she could, even resorting to covering her body with filthy and despicable things, so that those who were trying to rape her would be nauseated. She defended herself like this many times during the journey until they reached [Ollantay] Tambo.

While the expedition paused in Ollantaytambo, Francisco Pizarro had meanwhile received a message in Cuzco, supposedly from Manco Inca, that Manco now wanted to negotiate his terms of surrender. Hoping to put an end to the rebellion once and for all, Pizarro hurried to Ollantaytambo, where Cura Ocllo was currently being held, and from there sent Manco a variety of gifts, including a fine pony and an assortment of silk clothes. An African slave and two natives who had been baptized as Christians transported the gifts to the jungle. Instead of accepting Pizarro's gifts, however, Manco had the three envoys and their pony killed, as "the Inca placed no value on the friendship of the Spaniards nor on what they promised him."

Furious at Manco's rebuff and no doubt frustrated that after hundreds of Spanish deaths and three years of warfare that Manco Inca was still on the loose, Pizarro chose to vent his fury on the next best person—the Inca queen. "[As] the Inca [Manco] would not make peace, the greatest pain that could be inflicted upon him was to kill the wife he loved most," wrote Cieza de León. The Spaniards thus brought out Cura Ocllo, daughter of the great Huayna Capac, stripped her of her clothes, then tied her to a stake that had been erected for that purpose. As Pizarro and his captains looked on, native Cañaris—historic enemies of the Incas—now began to beat her, although the Inca queen said not a word. They next readied their bows and, fitting bamboo-pointed arrows onto their corded strings, stretched them back and began firing at her, impaling her limbs. Many of the Spaniards present— hardened conquistadors though they were—were taken aback at this treatment, the torture and murder of an Inca queen. It was, commented one chronicler, an act "completely unworthy of a sane Christian man"; in the words of another, it was punishment for a rebellion that "was not her fault." Nevertheless, the torture continued as Pizarro and his men—all baptized as Christians—continued to watch and made no effort to stop it.

The young queen, impaled with arrows yet still defiant, finally spoke, telling her tormentors bitterly, "You take your anger out on a woman? . . . Hurry up and finish me off, so that you can satisfy all of your desires." It was the only outburst the proud Inca woman made, much to the surprise of those who had gathered to witness the event. Wrote Pedro Pizarro:

In his anger . . . the Marquis ordered that the wife of Manco Inca be killed. Some Cañaris tied her to a stake and then beat her and shot arrows at her until she died. The Spaniards who were present said that this Indian woman never spoke a word nor uttered a single complaint, and in this manner she died from the beating and from the arrows they shot into her. One can only admire a woman who neither complains nor speaks nor makes a single moan from the pain of her wounds while dying!

To further punish Manco, Pizarro now ordered that the dead queen's disfigured body be loaded into a large basket and floated down the Vilcanota River, so that it would eventually be found and retrieved by Manco's men. A few days later, Manco was shown Cura Ocllo's body and was "grief stricken and despondent over the death of his wife. He wept and agonized over her, for he loved her very much, and he returned [with her body], withdrawing towards the site of Vilcabamba."

Pizarro's anger over Manco's rebellion had not yet been sated, however. Returning to Cuzco he soon learned that Villac Umu and some other chiefs, who were now prisoners in the capital, had bitterly denounced the execution of their queen. Pizarro promptly ordered that the high priest and the rest of his chiefs be brought out onto Cuzco's main square, where he had them all burned alive. He next had General Tiso dragged out—Manco's last great general, who had surrendered nine months earlier—and burned him alive as well.

Having stamped out much of Manco's second rebellion through a series of brutally efficient counterinsurgency campaigns, sixty-one-year-old Francisco Pizarro now returned to the coast and to his capital, the City of the Kings, where he soon resumed his duties as *gobernador*. Soon, however, the aging marquis was confronted with a new problem, one every bit as serious as any that had been posed by Manco's rebellion. Rumors were now swirling through the streets of the city that some of its Spanish inhabitants had been secretly meeting together—and were planning on murdering the marquis.

I4 ❖ THE LAST
OF THE PIZARROS

"[The Spanish *encomenderos*] exude an air of success as they go from their card games to their dinners in fine silk clothes. Their money is squandered on these luxuries, as well it may be, since it costs them no work or sweat whatsoever. . . . [They] and their wives have borrowed from the Inca the custom of having themselves conveyed about in litters like the images of saints in procession. These Spaniards are absolute lords without fear of either God or retribution. In their own eyes they are judges over our people, whom they can reserve for their personal service or their pleasure."

FELIPE HUAMÁN POMA DE AYALA, *LETTER TO A KING*, C. 1616

"Et tu, Brute?" ["And (even) you, Brutus?"]

WILLIAM SHAKESPEARE, *JULIUS CAESAR*, C. 1600

IN JUNE OF 1541 FRANCISCO PIZARRO WAS STILL THE SAME unpretentious man of simple interests that he had been when he first arrived in the New World thirty-nine years earlier. Although he had now spent more than two thirds of his life in the Americas, the sixty-three-year-old conquistador still bore the unmistakable stamp of his formative years in rural Extremadura. The son of a distinguished cavalry captain, Pizarro had grown up with his mother—a maid who came from a family of peasants— and her family and not with that of his father's. Francisco's three paternal half-brothers—Hernando, Juan, and Gonzalo—by contrast, although born many years later, had grown up in their father's household, while Hernando,

331

A Spanish *encomendero* being carried in a litter
previously reserved for the Inca elite.

as the eldest among them, had received both a formal education and had inherited his father's estate.

Had Pizarro been a man of lesser ambition, then his future in Spain no doubt would have been circumscribed by the limitations of his family and birth. His normal destiny would have been to perform agricultural work where, occasionally from the fields, the tall, lean man with the thickly callused hands, the thin black beard, and peasant shoes would have looked up in dull envy at the elegantly clothed people riding nearby in carriages or on horseback—people whose pedigrees, accomplishments, and inheritances had rendered unto them not only noble titles and vast estates, but also complete freedom from manual labor. Pizarro *was* ambitious, however, meaning that his own vision of himself and his future did not coincide with the expectations his fellow townsmen had of him. That ambition—coupled with the social stigma of his illegitimacy and perhaps with a subconscious desire as a boy to have grown up in his father's more prestigious house rather than in his mother's home—was undoubtedly the motor that propelled him both across an ocean and a continent. It was also no doubt the driving motivation that ultimately led Pizarro to conquer the largest native empire in the New World.

Unlike his fellow Trujilleño, Rodrigo Orgóñez, who after achieving wealth in Peru had written letters to a local nobleman pleading for him to legitimize his name, Pizarro had in a sense created his own legitimacy through conquest. Orgóñez's craving for a pedigree stemmed from his desire to petition the king to become a Knight of the Order of Santiago—one of Spain's most prestigious titles and one that required legitimate birth on the part of the petitioner. Because of Pizarro's conquest of the wealthy Inca Empire, however, King Charles had overlooked Pizarro's illegitimacy and had made him a knight. Nevertheless, in the sixteenth-century kingdoms of Spain, a well-positioned "gentleman" normally had a full paragraph of titles and descriptive modifiers that preceded his written name. Any inquisitive person had only to scan the paragraph to know precisely where that person fit into society, and the virtues or lack thereof of his pedigree.

By 1541, however, Francisco Pizarro had obtained all the status and prestige that he had ever dreamed of: he was Knight of the Order of Santiago, Governor, Military Commander, and Marquis of His Majesty's Kingdom of New Castile. As governor—a post equivalent to that of a viceroy, or deputy king—Pizarro was in the enviable position of having been personally appointed by the king to represent Spanish power in Peru and to govern the millions of new vassals that the king had acquired by virtue of Pizarro's own sword. If any of Pizarro's enemies were to question his plebeian origins, Pizarro could easily say—as the illegitimate Voltaire would later reply to the inquiries of an insolent French nobleman nearly two centuries later—"I am *beginning* my name—and you are finishing yours."

Despite his titles, his immense wealth, and his power, however, Pizarro's early peasant years nevertheless had left an indelible stamp upon the veteran conquistador's tastes. Although many of the wealthy *encomenderos* to whom he had granted natives had quickly shed their armor and had replaced it with silk stockings, plumed caps, and fine imported European clothes—mimicking the behavior of the nobility in Spain—Pizarro preferred to wear simple clothes with no frills. Wrote the chronicler Agustín de Zárate:

> The Marquis . . . [commonly] wore a high-waisted black cloth coat falling to his ankles, white deerskin shoes, a white hat and a sword with an old-fashioned hilt. And when, on certain festive days, he was persuaded by his servants to wear the sable cloak that the Marquis del Valle [Hernando Cortés] had sent him from New Spain [Mexico], he would take it off after returning from Mass and would . . . [return to wearing ordinary clothes], normally wearing a towel around his neck so that he could wipe the sweat off his face, for . . . [when the country was at peace] he spent most of the day at bowls or *pelota*.*

Not only did Pizarro dress plainly, but in an era when properly bred Spanish noblemen commonly took an interest in horses, hunting, and falconry—the sixteenth-century equivalent of modern-day tennis, golf, and yachting—Pizarro preferred working-class sports and games of chance. Wrote Zárate:

---

* Bowls is a game played outside using heavy metal balls to hit a stationary target and is what the French call *pétanque*. *Pelota* was presumably a sixteenth-century version of jai-alai, a game that is similar to handball but which uses a long wooden device strapped to the arm with which to fling the ball at a higher velocity.

Both captains [Pizarro and Almagro] had great physical endurance and thought nothing of hunger. The Marquis showed this especially in his game playing, for there were few young men who could keep up with him. He was much more inclined to play games of all kinds than the *Adelantado* [Almagro]. So much so that sometimes he would play bowls all day long without caring who he played with, even if it were a sailor or a mill worker. Nor would he allow anyone to go get the bowl for him or to treat him differently as normally his high rank would require.

Rarely could business make him leave the game, especially when he was losing. Only if there were some fresh Indian disturbances—for he was very quick on such occasions and would put on his armor and with his lance and shield would run through the city, heading straight for wherever the trouble was and without waiting for his men, who would only catch up with him later while running as fast as they could.

The man who as a boy had grown up in the poorer part of town not surprisingly preferred plebeian to aristocratic company, spending his time whenever possible among sailors, millers, muleteers, artisans, and other men who worked with their hands. Pizarro spent hours playing cards and gambling with them as well, although, because of his natural stinginess, it was said, "he collected what he won and left unpaid what he lost."

Sometimes, while searching for the governor, Pizarro's contemporaries would find the wealthy marquis in the fields outside Lima, reaping imported European wheat with the natives, "doing what he enjoyed and was his trade." It was an activity that no respectable marquis or any other nobleman in Spain would ever do. As workmen began installing two grinding mills beside Lima's Rimac River, important business meetings and papers sometimes had to be transported along with a notary to the site of the mills, "in whose construction he [Pizarro] spent all his leisure time, urging on the workmen who were building them." Similarly, when the time came for the casting of the first bronze bell of Lima's cathedral, which Pizarro had dedicated to Our Lady of the Immaculate Conception, once again the governor could be found not in his residence relaxing but instead at the forge site personally operating the bellows, sweating profusely, and with his clothes and hands dirty.

While Pizarro busied himself with governing the native empire he had spent all his life striving to obtain, his thirty-eight-year-old brother, Hernando, had meanwhile arrived in Spain in order to defend to the king his execution of the governor Diego de Almagro. One of Almagro's captains, Diego de Alvarado, had arrived before him, however, and had immediately filed charges against Hernando for Almagro's murder. Hernando nevertheless was no doubt counting upon his ability to leverage the shipment of the king's Peruvian treasure to his advantage. Much to his surprise, however, and before even being granted a royal audience, Hernando was arrested and thrown into prison. Soon, other supporters of Almagro returned to Spain and testified against Hernando as well, such as the nobleman Don Alonzo Enríquez de Guzmán. Although the latter had fought alongside Hernando during Manco's nearly year-long siege of Cuzco, the experience had not drawn the two men closer together. In a letter sent to the Royal Council, Enríquez de Guzmán pulled no punches in impugning the large, arrogant man whom he had clearly grown to hate.

> Most powerful Lords,
>
> I, Don Alonzo Enríquez de Guzmán, a knight of the Order of Santiago, a gentleman in the royal palace . . . and citizen of the city of Seville, was appointed executor to the will of Don Diego de Almagro. . . . And, by virtue of that office . . . I accuse Hernando Pizarro of criminal acts, who is currently a prisoner in this court. . . .
>
> The *Adelantado* Don Diego de Almagro, Governor of . . . the Kingdom of New Toledo, in the Indies of the South Sea and in the provinces of Peru, labored in the service of Your Majesty and conquered and settled many kingdoms and provinces in that land, having converted the natives to the service of our Lord God, and to our holy Catholic faith. While he [Almagro] was continuing to work in your royal service in this manner, the aforementioned Hernando Pizarro, moved by envy, hatred, and by an evil disposition . . . as well as by greed and self-interest, drove Manco Inca— king and lord of that land—to rebel against Your Majesty, whom the *Adelantado* [Almagro] had subjugated, reduced to submission, and had induced to submit to the service of God and Your Majesty. . . . King Manco rebelled, and for this reason that kingdom was lost and destroyed

and Your Majesty lost more than four million [pesos] in gold from your rents, [royal] fifths, and royal interests. This was also the reason why the natives killed more than six hundred Spaniards [and that myself and] Hernando Pizarro . . . were besieged in the great city of Cuzco. . . .

Not content with having perpetrated these crimes . . . Hernando Pizarro . . . raised an army and . . . marched against the Governor [Almagro], battling him near the walls of this city of Cuzco, and killing two-hundred-and-twenty-two men. . . . [Then], forgetting the great favor he had received from the Governor, who had released him when he was his prisoner, [Hernando] ignominiously strangled the *Adelantado* Don Diego de Almagro, dishonoring him . . . by saying that he was no *Adelantado* . . . but a castrated Moor. And, in order to increase the insult, he ordered that a black man be his executioner saying, "Don't let this Moor think that I will execute him the way he wanted to execute me, which was to behead me. . . . " He then said, "If . . . the executioner was about to cut off my head with a knife and the gates of Hell were open and . . . [the devil himself was there] ready to receive my soul, I would still do what [I am about to do now]. . . . "

[Hernando Pizarro] unjustly executed [Diego de Almagro] without having the power or authority to do so . . . and for his atrocious and wicked crimes, besides having committed *treason,* he deserves severe civil, military, and capital penalties, which should be carried out against his person and against his possessions as a punishment and example to others.

The accusations—many of them exaggerated and in some cases wholly made up—nevertheless were based upon an inescapable core of truth: Hernando *had* killed Diego de Almagro, despite having been set free by Almagro himself. Thus, even though Hernando had access to the finest legal counsel available in Spain, he would nevertheless spend the next twenty-three years of his life in prison, just outside Madrid. By the time he emerged, at the age of sixty in the year 1561, Hernando was a prematurely aged and partially blind old man. No one who later saw the hunched, white-haired, former conquistador walking down the street with the help of a cane would ever have guessed that this was the same arrogant and boastful man who had once ridden more than a thousand miles among the jagged mountains of Peru, had engaged native armies numbering in the hundreds of thousands, and who had possessed so much wealth, power, and status that he had once believed himself to be virtually untouchable, even by a king. Hernando had clearly overreached and had lost nearly everything in the process. The second eldest of the Pizarro brothers would live another seventeen years, would outlive all four of his brothers, and would eventually die in 1578 at the age of seventy-seven. He would never, however, see any of his brothers nor set foot in Peru again.

While some of Almagro's supporters had returned to Spain in numbers sufficient to turn the king against Hernando, most of the men of Chile—called *Almagristas*—were currently eking out a living in Peru. Spaniards who had only recently arrived in Peru could justify their poverty by saying that they had arrived too late to share in the empire's spoils; those who had supported Almagro, by contrast, could claim no such thing. Most had wasted two years in Chile with Almagro on an expedition that had brought them nothing but hardship and poverty. Later, after the *Almagristas* had successfully seized Cuzco and had reason to believe that they would soon become wealthy *encomenderos* themselves, they were abruptly disabused of this notion by their defeat at the Battle of Las Salinas. Even worse, Diego de Almagro—the leader they had risked their lives for in the expectation of future rewards—was now dead. Only Almagro's son—Diego de Almagro the Younger, whom the elder Almagro had sired with his native mistress from Panama—remained. Yet although the younger Almagro was nineteen years old, he was "so boyish that he personally wasn't mature enough to govern people, nor [to command] a troop."

Clearly, the *Almagristas* had backed the wrong horse. Unable to hold political office and with no employment or other traditional means of support, Almagro's several hundred followers found themselves barely able to scrape together a living. Even worse than their current situation, however, was their realization that their poverty was likely to persist. They had, after all, fought *against* the Pizarros—and the Pizarros were well known for neither forgetting nor forgiving. Spanish Peru was a tiny world, after all; hence, if you had fought against the Pizarros, you might as well have walked about

with the mark of Cain on your forehead. "The citizens [of Lima]," wrote
Pedro de Cieza de León, "were so indifferent that, even though they saw
them dying from hunger, they did not help them with a single thing, nor
did they want . . . to give them any food."

So bitter were the *Almagristas* toward the Pizarros that many didn't even
bother taking their hats off when passing the governor on the street—a
clear and unmistakable insult. Pizarro, in turn, wearing his plain black coat
with his white hat and shoes, behaved as if Almagro's followers didn't exist.
"Poor devils," he was sometimes heard to say, and which he always used in a
pejorative manner, "They've had such bad luck—and now they're destitute,
defeated, and ashamed. Best to leave them alone." For all Pizarro cared, the
men of Chile could rot in hell before he would ever grant them an office or
a favor. Of one fact the *Almagristas* were certain: for as long as Francisco
Pizarro governed Peru, they would remain impoverished with no hope of a
better future.

In June of 1541, nearly three years after the death of Almagro, a group of
Almagristas in Lima made a fateful decision. The only way their fortunes
might improve in Peru, they had decided, was if they removed Francisco
Pizarro from power—and that unequivocally meant killing him. If Pizarro
were dead, then the seemingly inevitable prospect of a lengthy Pizarro dy-
nasty would almost certainly disappear. The king would then be forced to
appoint a new governor and surely, under a new governor, the *Almagristas*
reasoned, they would have a better chance of improving their lot.

Approximately twenty in number, the conspirators chose June 26 as the
date of their assassination attempt: this would be the date of their liberation
from the Pizarros' unjust tyranny, they devoutly believed, and from all their
endless envy and want. Hernando Pizarro had warned Francisco of precisely this danger: "Do not allow [even] ten of . . . [Almagro's followers] to
gather together at one time," he had advised, urging his brother to be generous with them so that they wouldn't cause any trouble in the future. Francisco Pizarro, however, had done precisely the opposite, allowing the
Almagristas to gather as they wished and making no effort whatsoever to
bridge the great divide that separated the two camps.

Because the *Almagristas*' hatred and discontent were difficult to hide, rumors about possible assassination plots had been circulating in Lima for

years. Yet Pizarro had typically paid little heed to them, walking about the city confident in both his own authority and in his physical powers to protect himself. Wrote Cieza de León,

> The Indians were saying that the Marquis' final day was approaching and that he would be killed by those from Chile . . . and some Indian women repeated it to the Spaniards who were their lovers. It is also said that . . . [the conquistador] Garci Díaz heard it from an Indian girl and warned the Marquis about it. Pizarro laughed and said that no attention should be paid to such Indian gossip.

June 26, the day selected for the assassination, was a Sunday. Pizarro would normally leave his house in the morning and walk across the plaza to attend mass. Of great importance to the *Almagristas* was the fact that Pizarro would most likely be unarmed at that time. What the plotters didn't know, however, was that one of their number—a man named Francisco de Herencia—had already divulged the assassination plot the day before, during his confession to a priest. The priest, in turn, had warned Pizarro. Although Pizarro had dismissed the story as mere "Indian gossip," he nevertheless decided not to attend mass the next morning and had asked a priest to come to his house instead. Pizarro decided to go ahead, however, with his typical noonday meal, one that would be prepared for him and for a number of previously invited guests.

The morning of June 26 dawned cold and gray as was normal for this time of year. June is the beginning of the Southern Hemisphere's winter, and Lima in particular is normally blanketed day and night by a fine drizzle of a fog, called a *garua,* that can last up to six months. During the shorter winter days, the sun appears more like a moon over the city, a silver disk that is constantly shifting in opacity as it slowly moves through the cool gray mist. All night long the conspirators waited, nervous and impatient for daylight to begin. By the time a dim gray dawn appeared, the would-be assassins had already finished fastening on their steel breastplates and their coats of mail and had also finished sharpening their knives, daggers, and swords. Later, as the single bronze bell that Pizarro had helped to forge began to reverberate above the cathedral, summoning the town's citizens to gather and consume the blood and flesh of Christ, *Almagrista* spies suddenly arrived at the house of the assassins and breathlessly informed them that Pizarro had not left his house for mass. The governor was said to be ill, the spies said, thus Pizarro would probably remain in his house for the entire day.

The conspirators, quite naturally, immediately suspected that someone had revealed their plot. Now a quick decision had to be made, for if their plan *had* been exposed, then they would surely be apprehended and either imprisoned or killed. Gathered in the house of Diego de Almagro's son, the assassins turned toward the leader of the group, Juan de Herrada, who now offered them a stark choice:

> "Gentlemen . . . if we show determination and are resourceful enough to kill the Marquis, then we will avenge the death of the *Adelantado* [Almagro] and will . . . [receive] the reward that our services to the King in this realm deserve. [But] if we *do not* leave here and carry out our purpose, our heads will be hung from the gallows in the square. It's up to each one of you, however, as to how you want to proceed."

The *Almagristas* agreed that they had but one choice—to carry out the assassination of Pizarro as they had originally planned. Throwing open the door and armed with an assortment of halberds, two crossbows, a harquebus, and a variety of swords, they now swarmed out onto the street and began heading to the central plaza, shouting "Long live the King!" and "Death to Tyrants!" A number of the town's startled inhabitants no doubt watched them as the men burst out onto the plaza and headed directly for Pizarro's home. The latter—a two-story structure with ample rooms for the governor's servants, guards, secretary, majordomo, pages, chamberlains, children, and his native mistress—lay behind two courtyards and fronted the square directly across from the cathedral.

Pizarro, meanwhile, having already heard mass, was presently dining with his half-brother Francisco Martín de Alcántara and with about twenty others in the large dining room upstairs. As the sounds of men shouting began to be heard in the distance, Pizarro's page abruptly burst into the room shouting, "Grab your weapons! Grab your weapons! Because all those men from Chile are coming to murder the Marquis, my lord!" Almost immediately, the guests lurched up from their chairs, unsure about what to do. In the confusion that followed, Pizarro and some of his companions rushed to the stairway that descended to the inner courtyard to see what was going on, just as the mob of *Almagristas* began entering the outer courtyard, brandishing their weapons.

One of Pizarro's pages, who had been working in that area, was the first to encounter the assassins; they stabbed him and left him for dead on the ground. Those of Pizarro's guests who had witnessed the attack now realized that their own lives were in danger and rushed back into the dining hall, showing "great cowardice and fleeing in an abominable way," as Pedro Cieza de León would write more than a dozen years later in his *La Guerra de Chupas*. As the *Almagristas* began ascending the main stairway, shouting for Francisco Pizarro to show himself, Pizarro's lieutenant governor—a man who had recently boasted to Pizarro about how the latter could count upon him in any crisis—climbed through a window, clambered down the balustrade, and then fled through the garden below. Some guests followed suit while others even tried hiding beneath large pieces of furniture.

Pizarro and his brother Francisco Martín, however, along with two of Pizarro's pages and one of his guests, were determined to fight; they quickly rushed into one of the adjoining rooms in order to arm themselves. As the five of them hurried to strap on their breastplates, Pizarro shouted to another guest, Francisco de Chávez, to shut the door to the dining room, in order to prevent the entry of the mob. Chávez, however, apparently hoping to change the minds of the conspirators, walked through the door and left it open behind him. Only two years earlier, Chávez had led a brutal counterinsurgency campaign against rebellious natives in the Callejón de Huaylas, a campaign in which he had allegedly slaughtered some six hundred native children. Now, in deciding to try to speak with the assassins, Chávez had made a fatal error. His last words were reported as being "Don't kill your friends!" before, according to Pedro Pizarro, "they killed him half way up the steps, stabbing him many times with their swords." Chávez's crumpled body soon lay sprawled on the governor's stairs, soaked with blood.

The *Almagristas* had by now reached the dining hall, where they quickly began searching for Pizarro, brandishing their swords and shouting, "Where is the tyrant? Where is he?" Still in the adjoining room, Pizarro was unable to finish fastening on his breastplates and thus was forced to leave them half buckled. He quickly seized a large sword, then turned to face his attackers, along with his two pages, his brother, and the only guest from among the twenty who had chosen not to flee, Gómez de Luna.

A fierce battle now ensued, constrained by the narrow doorway, with fifteen to twenty *Almagristas* on one side and Pizarro and his four companions on the other. Two of the *Almagristas* fell, run through with swords, and now lay clutching at wounds that spurted blood onto the floor. Their fellow conspirators, meanwhile, found themselves unable to breach the doorway, protected as it was by the defenders' five swords. Frustrated by their inability to reach Pizarro, the *Almagristas* now resorted to a desperate measure, shoving one of their own attackers through the doorway as a kind of shield, while the rest pushed forward behind him. Pizarro impaled the man, but in so doing he tied up his sword at precisely the moment that the *Almagristas* pushed their way into the room on either side. As the sharp, slicing twang of sword upon sword filled the air along with the sounds of men's shouts and the scuffling of boots, the attackers finally succeeded in impaling Francisco Martín, Pizarro's brother. Mortally wounded, he now fell to the ground. Pizarro's other three companions soon followed suit, staggered by sword thrusts until, one by one, they crumpled to the floor.

Pizarro now found himself surrounded by a circle of stabbing daggers and swords, receiving wound after wound until he, too, fell heavily to the floor. On his back now and bleeding severely, the governor is said to have used a finger from each hand to make the sign of the cross over his lips, then to have gasped the word "confession," meaning that he wanted time to confess his sins to God. One of the attackers, Juan Rodríguez Barragán, however, is said to have picked up a large vase full of water, to have lifted it high over Pizarro's head, and then to have shouted "You can go to Hell . . . to make your confession!" before bringing the vase down and crushing Pizarro's head. There on the floor, amid a pool of blood and water—in the city he had founded and in the country he had conquered—the sixty-three-year-old conquistador, Francisco Pizarro, expired.

News of Pizarro's death, and of subsequent political events—the arrival in Peru of a representative of the crown, Vaca de Castro; the representative's defeat of Diego de Almagro the Younger's forces at the Battle of Chupas; and the general chaos that descended upon Peru after the deaths of both Almagro and Pizarro—gradually made its way down to Manco Inca in his rebel redoubt of Vilcabamba. Manco had followed the Spaniards' shifting fortunes closely, ever hopeful that his enemies might eventually massacre one another and save himself the trouble. At the Battle of Chupas, in 1542, in fact, a number of Manco's followers had watched as at least twelve hundred Spaniards had done their best to slaughter one another in an effort to determine who would ultimately rule Peru. Once again, however, the followers of Almagro were defeated: more than two hundred died during the fighting and many more were hanged afterward. In the battle's aftermath, as the king's representative hanged the rebel *Almagrista* leaders, chronicler Cieza de León observed that "The ditch beneath the gallows was full of dead bodies. . . . [This gave] considerable pleasure to the natives, although they were amazed when they realized that many of . . . [those killed] had been captains and men holding posts of honor. They took news of all this to their king, Manco Inca."

Not surprisingly, perhaps, within little more than a year after Pizarro's murder, at least fifteen of the roughly twenty *Almagristas* who had murdered the marquis were dead. Two of his assailants had been killed during the attack itself. A dozen others were hanged, quartered, or otherwise killed during or just after the Battle of Chupas. One of the few of Pizarro's assassins to survive was a man named Diego Méndez, a half-brother of Rodrigo Orgóñez, Diego de Almagro's former second-in-command. It was Orgóñez who had almost captured Manco Inca at Vitcos in 1537 and had helped Almagro seize Cuzco from Hernando and Gonzalo Pizarro. A year later, Hernando had defeated and executed Orgóñez outside Cuzco and had displayed the latter's head on the gallows on the main square. It shouldn't have been surprising then that, a little over three years later, Diego Méndez would have been among Pizarro's assassins, bent upon avenging his brother's death.

After the *Almagristas'* latest defeat at the Battle of Chupas, both Diego Méndez and Diego de Almagro the Younger had fled to Cuzco, hoping to escape capture by the royalist forces fighting on behalf of the king. The younger Almagro was nevertheless soon apprehended and was quickly executed, roughly four years after the execution of his father. Diego Méndez, meanwhile, was also captured and charged with having been one of Pizarro's murderers. Méndez, however, somehow managed to escape; he soon fled to the only place where he felt Spanish jurisprudence would be unable to reach him—to Manco Inca's rebel kingdom of Vilcabamba.

Having lived with his followers in Vilcabamba for the last five years, Manco Inca was by now twenty-seven years old. And, despite the Spaniards' successful counterinsurgency campaign against his forces in the Andes, Manco nevertheless continued to train his warriors in insurgency techniques and to stage guerrilla raids on the Spaniards whenever feasible. When Diego Méndez unexpectedly arrived at the outskirts of his small kingdom, therefore, and asked for refuge, Manco's generals not surprisingly wanted to execute him. Manco, however—no doubt having been informed that Méndez was one of those responsible for Francisco Pizarro's murder— instead welcomed the Spanish refugee and offered him sanctuary. The emperor did likewise with six other *Almagristas* who had fled from the highlands and who now sought safety within the Incas' hidden kingdom.

Manco *did* take some precautions regarding his potentially dangerous guests, however; instead of inviting the Spaniards to live in his capital of Vilcabamba, he housed them in Vitcos, about thirty miles away. As Titu Cusi later remembered:

> My father ordered his captains not to harm them [the Spaniards] and to build houses in which they could live. . . . He had them with him for many . . . years, treating them very well and giving them whatever they needed, even ordering his own women to prepare their food and drink. He . . . ate together with them . . . enjoying himself with them as if they were his own brothers.

In return, the renegade Spaniards instructed Manco and his warriors in the finer arts of European warfare, teaching them how to load and fire their captured harquebuses correctly, how to use Spanish weaponry, and how to ride, shoe, and otherwise make use of captured Spanish horses. Pizarro's assassin, Diego Méndez, meanwhile, gradually became Manco's confidant, no doubt informing the emperor about the current conflicts in Spanish Peru, about life and politics in Spain and Europe, and so on. In short, the seven Spanish renegades became advisers to the Incas on all things Spanish, helping Manco to gain a deeper understanding of the nature of his enemies so that he might better be able to defeat them. For their part—exiled in an Inca

kingdom that for all practical purposes was nowhere near Spanish Peru—
the renegades patiently bided their time. The *Almagristas* spent their days
resting, playing games of quoits, and no doubt hoping that one day they
would be able to emerge from their self-imposed exile to rejoin Spanish society.

It took almost two years before political changes in Peru afforded the
Spanish refugees just such an opportunity. In the power vacuum left by the
murder of Pizarro, King Charles had sent his first viceroy—Don Blasco
Núñez Vela—to take over control of the country. A new viceroy was precisely what Pizarro's assassins had hoped for. But more than likely only one
of them—Diego Méndez—had lived to see this happen. Now, deep in the
jungles of the Antisuyu, Méndez and his companions decided that the time
was finally ripe for their next move. Manco's guests had realized that they
were finally in a position to offer something of extreme value to the new
viceroy—the death of Manco Inca. Manco's unconquered kingdom, after
all, still threatened Spanish control of Peru; it also continued to serve as a
lightning rod for native defiance against the Spaniards. Both the viceroy and
the king were therefore quite anxious to put an end to it.

If Méndez and his men could somehow manage to assassinate the rebel
emperor, Méndez believed, he had no doubt that that would end the Inca
rebellion. Méndez and his co-conspirators could then surely win pardons
for themselves and would be able to reintegrate themselves into Spanish
Peru. In fact, if they played their cards right, they might even be rewarded
with *encomiendas* by the grateful new viceroy. The seven renegades made a
decision: just as Méndez had helped to assassinate Francisco Pizarro, now
he and his fellow exiles would likewise assassinate Manco Inca. They would
then escape to Cuzco and would announce Manco's death there as a fait ac-
compli.

In order for Méndez and his coconspirators to carry out their plan, however, they would have to wait until Manco made one of his frequent visits to
Vitcos from his nearby capital. When an unsuspecting Manco finally arrived
with his now fourteen-year-old son, Titu Cusi, the seven renegades quietly
prepared their weapons, readied their horses, and waited.* One of Manco's

---

* After his capture at Vitcos, Titu Cusi had been taken to Cuzco. He later escaped with his
mother.

favorite pastimes was playing horseshoe quoits, a game in which each participant tried to throw a horseshoe so that it touched or encircled a stake driven into the ground. In the hilltop city with sweeping views over the countryside, Manco's son watched as his father began playing quoits with his Spanish guests, having played numerous games with them before. Suddenly, however, just as Manco was about to make a throw, Diego Méndez pulled out a hidden knife and impaled the emperor brutally from behind. Manco's son later recalled:

> My father, feeling himself wounded, tried to defend himself . . . but as he was alone and there were seven of them he finally fell to the ground, covered with wounds, and they left him for dead. I was a small boy and seeing my father treated in this manner I wanted to go there to help him. But they turned angrily towards me and hurled a spear at me . . . that just missed killing me as well. I was terrified and fled into the forest below . . . [and] even though they searched for me they failed to find me.

After repeatedly stabbing their host, Méndez and the other renegades now raced to their horses, leapt upon them, and galloped away. Women screamed while others gathered around the stricken emperor, now covered in blood. Soon, however, Manco's captains sent runners in the direction the Spaniards had gone, in order to alert the countryside as to what had happened and to the fact that those who had attacked their emperor were now trying to escape.

All afternoon the assassins rode in the direction of Cuzco, putting as much distance between themselves and Vitcos as possible. As darkness fell they continued their flight, alternately riding and leading their horses by their reins. In their haste, however, the Spaniards had made a critical error in taking the wrong fork in the trail. By the time daybreak arrived, the fugitives realized that they would probably have to retrace their steps. Exhausted, they decided to rest for a while inside a thatched-roofed building before continuing.

While the Spaniards were sleeping, squadrons of Antis forest archers and native warriors discovered the building and quietly surrounded it. Soon, they set its roof on fire. As flames began to rise up and smoke began to pour

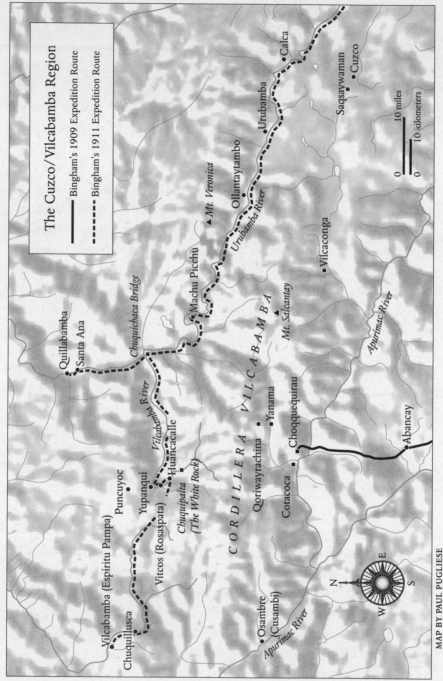

The Cuzco/Vilcabamba Region

Bingham's 1909 Expedition Route
Bingham's 1911 Expedition Route

Calca
Cuzco
Saqsaywaman
Urubamba
Ollantaytambo
▲ Mt. Veronica
Urubamba River
Vilcaconga
Machu Picchu
Chuquichaca Bridge
Quillabamba
Santa Ana
Vilcabamba River
Mt. Salcantay ▲
C O R D I L L E R A   V I L C A B A M B A
Yanama
Qoriwayrachina
Choqquequirau
Apurímac River
Abancay
Cotacoca
Huancacalle
Puncuyoc
Yupanqui
Chuquipalta
(The White Rock)
Vitcos (Rosaspata)
Vilcabamba (Espíritu Pampa)
Chuquillusca
Osambre (Cusambi)
Apurímac River

N
E
S
W

10 miles
10 kilometers
0
0

MAP BY PAUL PUGLIESE

out of the door, one by one, Manco's assassins began to emerge, some desperately running out with their clothes on fire while others attempted to climb up onto their horses and escape. The jungle archers, however, immediately unleashed volleys of arrows at the escaping Spaniards while other natives surrounded their horses and pulled the riders off, spearing and clubbing the men savagely with their *chonta*-wood clubs. "They killed all of them very cruelly and some were even burned," recalled Titu Cusi. Within a short time, native warriors had killed all seven of Manco's assailants, including Pizarro's assassin, Diego Méndez.

The news that Manco's attackers had been captured and killed was quickly sent to Vitcos and was relayed to Manco, who was conscious but lay dying from his wounds. Manco had already designated a successor—his nine-year-old son, Sayri-Tupac Inca. Although native healers no doubt desperately tried to save him, three days after the Spaniards' attack, in the hilltop city of Vitcos high above the western rim of the Amazon, the now twenty-nine-year-old Inca emperor died. The ruler whom Francisco Pizarro had crowned a decade earlier had in the end outlived Pizarro by a mere three years, leaving behind his wives and his three small sons. Manco also left behind a tiny rebel kingdom whose stunned inhabitants now fell into mourning over the loss of their leader. The emperor who had had the force of character and skill to organize the greatest native rebellion ever against Europeans in the New World had ultimately made a single fatal error: Manco had chosen to trust the Spaniards not once but *twice*—and in the process had lost both his empire and his life.

With Manco Inca and three of the five Pizarro brothers now dead—Francisco, Juan, and Francisco Martín—and with Hernando Pizarro currently in prison in Spain, only one surviving member of the Pizarro family remained in Peru, thirty-two-year-old Gonzalo. The youngest of the Pizarro brothers, Gonzalo had been only twenty when he and his brothers had helped to seize Manco's older brother Atahualpa in Cajamarca, twenty-three when he had stolen Manco Inca's wife, and twenty-seven when he had led the expedition that had sacked Vilcabamba.

Strikingly handsome, fabulously wealthy, and an excellent horseman, Gonzalo was also vindictive, impetuous, and possessed of the conviction that other people were either good friends or bitter enemies. Since the death of his three brothers and the imprisonment of the fourth, Gonzalo's tendency to see the world in terms of black and white had no doubt become even more pronounced. Faced now with the unpleasant prospect of having to live under the rule of the king's new viceroy—a man who had taken no part whatsoever in the conquest and who thus had risked nothing—Gonzalo predictably followed the dictates of his own character: with one impulsive decision, Gonzalo now placed the viceroy at the top of his list of enemies and then declared himself the new governor of Peru.

Gonzalo's seizure of power was both an act of impulsiveness and an act of treason. It would soon plunge Peru once again into an all-out civil war. "Is it possible," asked the frustrated viceroy, upon learning of Gonzalo's insurrection, "that the great Emperor our Lord [King Charles], who is feared in all the provinces of Europe, and to whom the Turk, Master of all the East, dare not show himself hostile, should be disobeyed here by a bastard who refuses to comply with his laws?" It was more than possible—indeed it was already a fact. The illiterate, illegitimate Gonzalo Pizarro not only refused to comply with the king's laws; he also repudiated the king's choice of viceroy. Like his elder brother Francisco, however, Gonzalo may have been uneducated but instinctively understood both power and politics. It seemed obvious to him that the king had been attempting through his new viceroy to take over the kingdom that he and his brothers had risked their lives to conquer—and he was determined to prevent that from happening. "Spain's desires . . . [are] well understood despite her dissimulation," Gonzalo wrote caustically to his fellow military commanders who had decided to side with him. "She . . . [wishes] to enjoy what we . . . sweated for, and with clean hands benefit from what we . . . [have given] our blood to obtain. But now that they have revealed their intentions, I promise to show them . . . that we are men who can defend our own."

To an emissary the viceroy had sent to parley with him, Gonzalo revealed an even deeper motivation: his own unequivocal lust for power. "See here, I am to be Governor because we would trust no one else, not even my brother Hernando Pizarro. . . . I don't care a jot for my brother Hernando or my nephews and nieces or the eight thousand pesos I have in Spain. . . . I must die governing! . . . I give this as my reply and there is nothing more to be said about it."

Like a split in a glacier that slowly cracks apart and eventually leaves a gaping chasm, Spanish Peru now became fractured between those who supported the rebel Gonzalo Pizarro and those who supported the king. Almost overnight, Peru became an exceedingly dangerous place for a Spaniard to be living in. Furious with all those who chose either to oppose him or else to remain neutral, Gonzalo began executing any Spaniard who refused to lend him his support. This was despite the fact that many of these men were wealthy *encomenderos* who had fought alongside the Pizarros ever since the capture of Atahualpa. An unsentimental Gonzalo eventually executed some 340 of his fellow compatriots, a number representing more Spaniards than the Incas had managed to kill during all the years of their insurrection.

Despite his impetuous decision, Gonzalo's seizure of absolute power initially went extremely well; he soon gave chase to the king's viceroy, then eventually captured, executed, and decapitated him, placing the viceroy's head on an iron pike for good measure. The crown, however, soon sent another representative to Peru, Pedro de la Gasca, who gradually raised a new army and then proceeded to march in search of the man whom the king now considered a traitor.

On April 9, 1548, on a high, cold, and windswept plain a few miles west of Cuzco called Jaquijahuana, Gonzalo and about 1,500 of his heavily armed followers squared off for battle with a similarly sized royalist force. The striking, black-bearded Pizarro, who had yet to lose a battle against either natives or Spaniards during his sixteen years in Peru, was "very gallant on his powerful chestnut horse, and wore a coat of mail and a rich breast guard with a surtunic of crushed velvet and a golden casque on his head with a gold chin guard," wrote the chronicler Garcilaso de la Vega. The proud owner of various gold and silver mines, of vast *encomiendas,* and the final standard-bearer of the Pizarro family's name, Gonzalo had staked everything on the outcome of this, his most important battle.

The Battle of Jaquijahuana, as it was later called, was ultimately decided, however, not military but politically. At the critical hour most of Gonzalo's men—many of whom had been secretly offered pardons by the king's new representative—deserted and went over to the royalist side. Stubborn, impetuous, and brave, Gonzalo refused to flee, however, even though he knew that if he were captured he was likely to be executed. Instead, once it was obvious that he had been defeated, the veteran conquistador calmly walked his horse over to the royalist forces and surrendered. The following day, "they sentenced him to be beheaded, and ordered that his head should be displayed in a frame that was made for the purpose and hung on the royal gallows of the city of Los Reyes." The thirty-six-year-old Pizarro, who for three and a half years had tasted the power only kings normally enjoyed, looked around for the last time at the country that he had helped conquer, then laid his head quietly against a wooden block. An executioner now lifted a steel axe high, then brought it down, neatly separating the bearded man's head from his body, so that it rolled heavily onto the ground. Later, in his brother's City of the Kings, the head of the most handsome of the Pizarros was

> covered with an iron mesh and above it was placed the notice: "This is the head of the traitor Gonzalo Pizarro, who rebelled in Peru against His Majesty and fought against His royal standard in the Valley of *Jaqui-jahuana.*" Besides this, it was also ordered that all of Gonzalo's goods should be confiscated and that his houses in Cuzco be demolished and be sown with salt, placing a notice with the same inscription on the site. This was done on the same day.

Some sixteen years after arriving in the New World, the last of the four Pizarro brothers to lose his life in Peru was now dead. Together, he and his brothers had beaten the odds by conquering a fabulously wealthy native empire with only the tiniest of military forces. Yet, ultimately, they had unleashed in the process a powerful native rebellion and then their own civil war—and had died amidst the chaos they had created. Yet the Pizarros' taste of wealth and power was short-lived. Francisco Pizarro's reign in Peru, after all, had lasted roughly eight years, a good portion of which had been taken up by Manco Inca's rebellion; Gonzalo, meanwhile, had ruled his brother's kingdom for just three and a half years—a period of constant and bloody turmoil. On the day that Gonzalo Pizarro was executed, in fact, only one of the Pizarro brothers, Hernando, was still alive. And he would remain in prison for another thirteen years. Meanwhile, as the king's men in Cuzco salted the earth surrounding Gonzalo's palace and hung up a placard for all to read—*that here dwelled the traitor and rebel Gonzalo Pizarro*—far to the north, in the tiny rebel kingdom of Vilcabamba, the Incas watched and listened—and patiently bided their time.

15 ❖ THE INCAS' LAST STAND

"Of the gods we believe, and of men we know, that by a necessary law of their nature they rule wherever they can. And it is not as if we were the first to make this law, or to act upon it when made: we found it existing before us, and shall leave it to exist forever after us: all we do is make use of it, knowing that you and everybody else, having the same power as we have, would do the same as we do."

THUCYDIDES, *THE HISTORY OF THE PELOPONNESIAN WAR*, 5TH CENTURY B.C.

IN THE DECADES FOLLOWING THE ASSASSINATION OF MANCO Inca and the execution of Gonzalo Pizarro, Spain's control of the Incas' former empire of Tawantinsuyu gradually increased as a succession of governors, administrators, and other Spaniards continued to pour into the distant colony, so far removed from their homeland. The enterprise of conquest that had been launched by a small, independent group of entrepreneurs—many of whom later became *encomenderos*—had by now been taken over by their mother country, whose tentacles of control continued to multiply, swell, and to wrap themselves around the new resource. In 1532 the Inca Empire, with roughly ten million inhabitants, had been faced with an invasion by a mere 168 Spaniards. Four years later, when Manco Inca rose in revolt, some 1,500 Spaniards were present in different corners of the empire, of whom Manco was able to exterminate less than 15 percent. By the time of Manco's death in 1544, the number of Spaniards had grown to roughly five thousand, and these had imported some two to three thousand African slaves to help with the process of colonization. By 1560, less than twenty years later, the Spanish population had doubled once again to ten thousand while the African

353

The final Inca emperor, Tupac Amaru,
being led out of Vilcabamba in chains.

slave population had doubled to five thousand. Peru, meanwhile, continued to be administered by a viceroy under the supervision of the Spanish crown.

As more and more Spaniards poured into Peru, they continued to construct cities and towns and to supervise the extraction of precious metals, the cultivation of crops, and the collection of tribute. The much larger native population, meanwhile, labored on, having exchanged one master, the Incas, for another, the Christian *viracochas*. The exchange wasn't an equal one, however, as the natives who now paid tribute to the Spaniards had far fewer rights, paid far greater tribute, and received far less than they had while under the control of the Inca elite. In fact, the native inhabitants of Tawantinsuyu now received virtually nothing from their new overlords— the roughly five hundred Spanish *encomenderos* who made up a mere 5 percent of the total Spanish population in Peru. Wrote one observer:

> [It] is true that what they pay in tributes and taxes . . . they endure with great difficulty and hardship. Not only is there nothing left over for them [that would allow them] to rest . . . [but there is also nothing] that allows them to endure times of necessity or illness as we Spaniards have, or to feed and raise their children with. They live in poverty and lack the necessities, and they never finish paying the debts and . . . tributes. We can see that they are wasting away and being consumed very rapidly because of the many aggravations they suffer.

Wrote another:

> They grieve because of the misery and servitude they are in. . . . Even during their festivals they weep . . . and their songs are full of sorrow, because the tributes they pay to the Spaniards have incapacitated them. They have come to believe that for as long as they and their sons and their descendants live they will have to go to work for the Spaniards.

As the natives continued to herd their flocks, to till the land and to work in the mines, they delivered the surplus they produced directly to the new Spanish elite, who in turn used at least a portion of these raw materials to purchase manufactured goods from Spain. The *encomenderos* also used the money derived from their native tribute to purchase more African slaves and to buy products or services from the various Spanish merchants, doctors, lawyers, notaries, and artisans who had followed them into Peru. As under the Incas, the entire colonial superstructure was predicated upon a foundation of endlessly toiling native workers—the control of which was the original motivation for the Spanish conquest of Peru.

Far to the east of the coastal cities with their tall-masted ships now noisily off-loading and on-loading passengers and goods, far beyond the central Andes with their new Spanish colonial towns and their majestic white peaks, and down amidst the remote jungles to the east, the independent Inca kingdom of Vilcabamba continued to carry on. Here, amid the warm, moist forests laced with troops of chattering monkeys, the inhabitants of Vilcabamba continued their traditional practice of worshipping the sun god, or Inti, and his representative on earth, the *Sapa Inca,* or Unique Emperor.

Theirs was a tiny kingdom, to be sure, nothing more than a small collection of tropical valleys, remote mountains, and a handful of towns and cities. Still, within these isolated confines Inca temples continued to be cared for by the *mamaconas,* or "virgins of the sun," traditional festivals continued to be held, astronomical observations made, obeisances given, sacrifices offered, and the life-sized, golden *punchao,* or golden disk of the sun, continued to be removed from its temple every morning and at night laid back to rest. While the original empire of "the four parts united"—the immense Tawantinsuyu—was no longer under the control of a free Inca emperor, the tiny kingdom of Vilcabamba continued to contain within it the blueprint of that much larger Inca state. All that was needed for expansion was that the Andes and coast be wiped clear of the bearded white foreigners and their slaves.

In 1559, some fifteen years after the death of Manco Inca, King Charles died in Spain after a reign of forty years. Now his son, Philip II, was king. Similarly, in 1560, Manco's son Titu Cusi—whose twin names mean "magnanimous" and "fortunate"—was crowned emperor of the Incas. Although Titu Cusi's brother and predecessor, Sayri-Tupac, had inherited the throne after Manco's death, Sayri-Tupac had been only nine years old at the time. Thus Vilcabamba had been ruled by regents for a dozen years. When Sayri-Tupac was finally crowned at the age of twenty-two, however, he made the fateful decision of leaving Vilcabamba and returning to Cuzco, where he had been promised by the Spaniards a number of *encomiendas* and a life of relative ease. By that time Manco's brother Paullu Inca had died of natural causes in Cuzco; thus, for the first time in decades, no longer did two competing Inca emperors wear the royal fringe. Only a year after relocating to Cuzco, however, Sayri-Tupac had fallen ill and had died, possibly having been poisoned by a jealous native chief. The question now was: who would succeed him?

Much to the disappointment of the Spaniards, Titu Cusi inherited the throne, resuming rule over the remote Inca kingdom that the Spaniards thought they had finally stripped of its emperor. Even worse, the new emperor had every reason to hold a grudge against them: the Spaniards had, after all, murdered his father, Manco Inca, and had kidnapped both Titu Cusi and his mother in Vitcos.* For four years, the boy who would eventually become a king had lived in Cuzco, where he no doubt had later seen his captor Diego Orgóñez's head on display. Eventually, Titu Cusi and his mother somehow managed to escape from Cuzco and fled to Vilcabamba. Some years later, Titu Cusi was at his father's side when his father was assassinated; the young prince was only fourteen years old at the time yet would bear on his leg the scars of that attack until the day he died. When Titu Cusi was finally crowned in Vilcabamba in 1560 at the age of thirty, the heads of the seven Spaniards who had murdered his father were still on display in nearby Vitcos, where the assassination had taken place.

A heavyset, emotional man who some observers said bore scars, possibly of smallpox, on his face, Titu Cusi wasted no time in resuming the guerrilla war with the Spaniards that his father had begun but that had lapsed during the time of the regents. Soon, along the Cuzco–Jauja road, and in the area of Huamanga to the northwest of Cuzco, native guerrilla forces once again began launching a series of raids against Spanish travelers and settlements. According to one chronicler, Titu Cusi

> took it upon himself to do as much damage to the Christians as he could; he assaulted the Valley of Yucay and many other places, bringing as many Indians as he could catch back to Vilcabamba and killing people traveling on foot; therefore, there was no safe place in the vicinities

---

* Although Titu Cusi's father was Manco Inca, his mother was not Manco's *coya,* Cura Ocllo, but one of Manco's many concubines.

of Cuzco and Huamanga, nor was it possible to walk without an escort from one place to another.

The new emperor was soon linked as well to deadly rebellions that erupted in what is now Chile and to a plot near Jauja, in central Peru, where the Spaniards discovered a secret native weapons factory that had produced tens of thousands of clubs, battle-axes, and pikes. The weapons, apparently, had been carefully prepared for use against the Spaniards in a planned insurrection. Whether Titu Cusi was actually involved in the Jauja plot, under his rule Vilcabamba once again became a guerrilla sanctuary—the sixteenth-century equivalent of a modern-day state that foments rebellion and exports terror for political ends. The Spaniards, of course, had waged their own campaign of terror and brutality in order to conquer the Inca Empire. Now, a tiny remnant of that empire continued to fight back, resisting the Spanish invasion and the occupation of their land. Eventually, the Spanish government in Peru—receiving increasing reports of attacks—realized that it had no other choice but to neutralize or destroy both Titu Cusi and his Inca kingdom.

Peru's Spanish government soon sent a series of emissaries to the new emperor, offering him rich *encomiendas* if he would only abandon Vilcabamba and relocate to the Yucay Valley near Cuzco. Fully aware of the fact that his kingdom didn't possess enough warriors to repel a serious Spanish invasion, Titu spent years expertly negotiating with the Spaniards, always offering the Spaniards hope that he might at any moment accept their terms, yet inevitably refusing to follow through in the end. In the meantime, he made sure that no Spaniards other than occasional emissaries were allowed into the kingdom.

Finally, in 1569, nine years into Titu Cusi's rule, the hermetically sealed door to Vilcabamba opened just a crack. Due to increasing Spanish threats, Titu Cusi had finally agreed to sign a peace treaty with the Spanish authorities two years earlier. In return for being allowed to rule an independent Vilcabamba without the threat of a Spanish invasion, Titu Cusi had agreed to allow missionaries to enter into his kingdom and had also agreed to end his guerrilla war.

The two friars selected—Marcos García and Diego Ortiz—were aware that no Spaniard was known to have set foot in the capital of Vilcabamba since Gonzalo Pizarro had sacked the city in 1539. Here was a chance to visit the untouched sanctuary of the Incas' religion, where no Christian missionary had yet been able to venture. With any luck, the friars realized, they would soon have the chance to destroy the false idols and the devil worship that they believed constituted the Incas' religion. According to the Spanish priest Bernabé Cobo:

> The Indians of Peru were so idolatrous that they worshiped as Gods almost every kind of thing created. Since they did not have supernatural insights, they fell into the same errors and folly as the other nations of pagans, and for the same reasons both the Peruvians and the other pagans were unable to find the true God. This is because they were immersed in such an abysmal array of vices and sins that they had become unfit and unworthy of receiving the pure light that accompanies a knowledge of their Creator. . . . [The devil] kept them prisoners in harsh bondage, depriving them of the happiness that he himself did not deserve. Upon finding fertile ground in the simplemindedness and ignorance of these barbarians, he reigned over them for many centuries until the power of the Cross started stripping him of his authority and ousting him from this land here as well as from the other regions of this New World.

Because the Incas practiced a religion different from the Spaniards' Christian faith, in other words, by definition they were pagans, and as such were actually believed by the Spaniards to be worshipping a character the Spaniards called *el demonio,* the devil. Now, two humble Spanish missionaries had a golden opportunity to change all that.

The two friars had very distinct personalities. Friar García took a fire-and-brimstone approach to preaching, had a short temper, and was extremely intolerant. Discovering, for example, that the native boys he had begun preaching Christianity to were secretly praying to their other gods as well, the friar "punished them . . . with ten or a dozen lashes," an act that understandably angered the boys' fathers. The latter complained to the emperor and García soon found himself forced to apologize, under threat of being thrown out of the kingdom. On other occasions, horrified by the seemingly bacchanalian festivals and copious drinking associated with Inca religious festivals, the abstemious friar often delivered to groups of drunken native revelers a fiery lesson on the Christian concepts of hell and eternal damnation—then threatened them with both. Nor was Titu Cusi immune to the friar's zealous onslaughts: when Friar García learned that the emperor had more than one wife, "the servant of God castigated him [Titu Cusi] with apostolic zeal." Apparently, the zeal of the apostles not only went unappreciated by the emperor, but greatly annoyed him as well.

Friar Diego Ortiz, by contrast, was much more relaxed in his missionary style and, as a consequence, Titu Cusi is said to have taken an immediate liking to him. Unlike his compatriot, Ortiz was affable and flexible and generally more congenial. Within a short while, two tiny Christian churches began to operate in the Incas' hidden kingdom: Friar García's in the small town of Puquiura and Friar Ortiz's in Huarancalla. Situated roughly eleven miles from each other, the churches were located two to three days' journey from the capital of Vilcabamba, which neither friar had as yet been allowed to enter.

One day, however, Titu Cusi surprised the friars by inviting them to visit what they had long been hoping to see: "I want to take you to Vilcabamba," the emperor told them, "since neither of you have seen that town. Go with me, for I want to entertain you." In early 1570, then, at the height of the rainy season, Titu Cusi, his entourage, and the two friars set out, the emperor carried in his traditional litter and the two friars accompanying him on foot. According to the Augustinian chronicler Antonio de la Calancha, both friars had previously "tried to go to Vilcabamba to preach, because it was the largest town, and in it was the University of the Idolatries, and the witch doctors [who were] masters of the abominations." Neither friar, however, had succeeded in achieving their goal. Now at last, after packing their clothes, Bibles, and crucifixes, they were about to reach the Incas' final religious stronghold—the place where Satan himself must surely dwell.

For the next few days, the friars struggled up and down steep, wet trails, many of them so flooded by rivers that the fathers had to pick their way amid submerged rocks. Wrote Calancha:

Not used to getting their feet wet, they slipped and fell, and there was no one to help them get up. They held one another's hands while the sacrilegious natives laughed aloud at them. . . . The blessed priests walked like this for more than two leagues, praising God and singing Psalms. . . . They reached dry land frozen and covered in mud.

Finally, after following an Inca road alongside a river and then through thick rain forest, the two friars arrived at the outskirts of Vilcabamba. As the two prepared themselves to enter the capital, they received a piece of unsettling news. The emperor had changed his mind, they were informed. Titu Cusi now forbade the two friars from entering the capital; instead he insisted they remain beyond its view. Titu Cusi later explained:

[The friars] have not baptized anyone here [in the city of Vilcabamba] because the things that must be known and understood concerning the law and commandments of God are still very new to the people of this land. [Yet] I will try, little by little, to make sure that they learn.

The chronicler Calancha, however, who did considerable research on the subject, had a different explanation for the emperor's sudden change of mind, believing that Titu Cusi had prevented the friars from entering Vilcabamba simply because he did not wish them to see "the worship, rites and ceremonies that the Inca [emperor] and his captains practiced each day with their witch-doctors." Perhaps anticipating that the friars would react angrily to the city's numerous idols and temples in the Inca capital and perhaps also wishing to avoid a confrontation between the friars and his own priests, Titu Cusi once again declared the Inca capital off limits.

Disappointed, the two missionaries soon trudged back to the village of Puquiura, where Friar García had his church. Frustrated by the emperor's refusal, the friars apparently decided that now was the opportune moment to cleanse their local parishes of the false gods the natives still worshipped. At a place nearby called Chuquipalpa, the friars had been told, there emerged from the ground a giant, light-colored rock that was located next to a spring of water. The Incas worshipped many springs, rocks, hills, caves, and other natural features of their landscape; apparently, they held this site, too, to be sacred, having built a temple of the sun alongside it. According to Calancha, however, the site was obviously devoted to devil worship, for it included a temple of the Sun, and within it a white rock above a spring of water where the Devil appeared. This was worshipped by the idolatrous natives, as it was the principal *mochadero*—the common Indian word for their shrines—in those forests. . . . Inside the white rock, called "Yuracrumi," presided a Devil [who was] captain of a legion of devils. . . . The Devil was extremely cruel, for if they ceased worshipping him for a few days, he killed or injured them, causing great damage and fear.

Convinced that Satan and his minions were purposely blinding the natives from the word of God, the two friars now led some of their congregation to the sacred Inca shrine, uttering prayers and carrying a large cross before them. The friars soon set fire to the complex, doing their best to destroy it and using various solemn incantations with which to banish Lucifer, the fallen archangel, from the area. Their work done, the friars then returned to the village of Puquiura, leaving the smoldering ruins and a group of shocked natives behind.

Word of the friars' blasphemy soon spread throughout the tiny kingdom, however, and the reaction was nearly instantaneous. "The Inca emperor's captains were furious and planned to kill the two friars with their spears, thinking nothing of tearing them to pieces," wrote Calancha. "They arrived at the town [of Puquiura] wanting to give vent to their fury." The two friars, having unleashed a storm of anger, would have immediately lost their lives if it had not been for the intervention of their local congregation. So great was the outrage, in fact, that the emperor Titu Cusi soon arrived, having hurried to the site on his royal litter; he quickly took charge of the situation. The emperor now banished García from the kingdom, no doubt fed up with the friar's messianic fervor. Titu Cusi allowed Friar Ortiz to remain, however, who now meekly returned to his church in Huarancalla.

Although he had escaped unpunished, Ortiz had nevertheless made permanent enemies in Vilcabamba, many of whom would never forgive the friar for the sacrilegious nature of his actions. The displaced residents of Vilcabamba, after all, were well aware of the fact that they had been forced by the Spaniards from their highland empire and had been basically at war with them for the last thirty-four years. Now a Spaniard who was living as a guest in their kingdom had just committed an act equivalent to burning the local church to the ground. It would take considerable skill on Ortiz's part to regain the natives' trust.

During the following year, Titu Cusi did his best to steer his small ship of state safely through the tempestuous waters of post-conquest Peru. The emperor continued to exchange diplomatic letters with the Spanish government in Cuzco, always dangling before them the hope that he might one day abandon Vilcabamba, while Friar Ortiz presumably continued to preach the bearded invaders' religion in Huarancalla. In May of 1571, twenty-six years after Manco's assassination, his now forty-one-year-old son decided to pay a visit to a sacred shrine in Puquiura, located just outside Vitcos, where Manco had been killed. Titu Cusi, in Calancha's description,

remained there all day, mourning the death of his father with pagan rites and shameful superstitions. To conclude the day he started . . . [fencing], which he had learned in the Spanish manner, with his secretary, Martín Pando. He sweated heavily and felt cold. He ended it all by drinking too much wine and chicha, became drunk, and woke up with a pain in his side, a thick tongue (he was very fat) and with a churning stomach. Everything was vomiting, screaming, and drunkenness.

That night, the emperor suddenly began to bleed from his nose and mouth while complaining of severe chest pains. The next morning he was even worse. When two of his assistants gave him a medicinal beverage to try to stop the bleeding, to their horror Titu Cusi stiffened. Then, suddenly, he died.

Grief-stricken and angry at their emperor's abrupt death, a number of natives soon seized upon the notion that Friar Ortiz must have somehow been responsible. Ortiz was a Spaniard, after all, and it had been almost in this same spot that other Spaniards had murdered Titu's father. The bearded friar had also profaned one of their sacred shrines only the year before. Although Ortiz had not been with Titu Cusi when the emperor had become ill, that fact had little significance among a population where illness was often related to witchcraft and where it was known that sorcerers could kill from a distance. Ortiz often ministered to the sick, performing what appeared to be bizarre rituals and speaking in a language or languages (Latin and Spanish) that the natives didn't understand. Ortiz was therefore no doubt considered by the natives to be a sorcerer, or *omo*.

An angry mob soon seized the friar, tying his hands together behind his back so forcefully that they dislocated a bone. Stripping away the friar's clothes, the crowd began shouting that Ortiz had killed the *Sapa Inca;* they then began clubbing and beating him. That night, the natives left the naked and bruised friar outside on the ground in the cold, periodically pouring water on the cords binding his hands in order to ensure that the cords swelled and caused the friar even greater agony.

The next day, Ortiz's captors dragged him to Puquiura, to the church that Friar García had built. Since the two friars had often claimed that their god had the power to restore the dead to the living, the angry natives now demanded that Ortiz raise Titu Cusi from the dead. Freed from his bindings, the naked friar now shuffled slowly into the church, put on some vestments, and then began to say mass, hoping to calm the still angry crowd. Far from Cuzco and thus beyond the help of his countrymen, surrounded by hostile natives and with the dead body of Titu Cusi lying nearby, Friar Ortiz invoked the name of God repeatedly, no doubt in an effort to enlist His aid. The natives, meanwhile, waited impatiently for signs of life from their dead emperor, vowing to kill Ortiz if Titu Cusi didn't stir. When the crowd saw that the friar had finally finished his mass, crossing himself in the name of the Father, the Son, and the *Espíritu Santo,* and seeing that Titu Cusi hadn't moved, they angrily seized the friar again, binding up his arms and demanding to know why Ortiz's god hadn't returned their emperor to the living. "He [Ortiz] responded that the Creator of all things, who was God, could do it," wrote the Mercedarian friar Martín de Murúa, "but that [Titu Cusi] did not come back because it wasn't the will of God—that [God] must not want the Inca [emperor] to return to this world."

The friar's response was clearly not what the natives wanted to hear; the crowd now dragged Ortiz to a large cross that stood outside, bound him to it, and began to flog him. They then forced the hapless friar to swallow a vile concoction of urine mixed with other bitter substances. No doubt worried about the possible repercussions of killing him, however, the mob decided to take Ortiz to Vilcabamba—the city Titu Cusi had never allowed a Spaniard to enter. Lacing a cord through a hole they bored in the flesh behind his jaw, the crowd began dragging the naked friar after them. In Vilcabamba, Titu Cusi's younger brother—Tupac Amaru—would have to decide the friar's fate. For Tupac Amaru was now the new Inca emperor.

If Ortiz's previous journey to Vilcabamba had been a miserable one, his present march was inconceivably worse. It was the rainy season again, thus the exhausted and wounded friar tried to stumble as best he could along the slippery trail on bleeding feet, repeatedly falling to his knees and exclaiming "Oh God!," or wading through water as he was pulled forward by the rope fastened through his skin. For two days the natives dragged the man who they were certain had killed their emperor over the rugged trail, stopping only at night to rest. If ever there were an instance of a Christian being tortured for the sins of others—in this case for the sins of every conquistador who had ever harmed a native in Tawantinsuyu—then this was certainly it. Finally, however, on the third day, in the village of Marcanay, just a few miles from the capital city, the procession stopped; the natives now sent messengers ahead to confer with Tupac Amaru, in order to determine the fate of their prisoner.

Tupac Amaru—whose name means "Royal Serpent"—was at the time around twenty-seven years old. He was both very conservative and religious. He had never agreed with his older brother Titu's policy, for example, of allowing foreign missionaries to enter their kingdom. When informed that the Spaniard who had killed his brother had been brought to nearby Marcanay, Tupac Amaru refused to see him, essentially sealing the friar's fate. The messengers now returned to the village where Ortiz was still enduring attacks from the crowd. Once Tupac Amaru's message had been received, a warrior stepped up and finally put the unlucky friar out of his misery with an Inca axe. As Ortiz's body lay twitching on the ground, it was no doubt clear to all those assembled that neither the teaching of Christianity nor the presence of Spaniards would ever again be allowed into the Kingdom of Vilcabamba.

One hundred miles away and roughly seven thousand feet higher in elevation, the Spaniards in Cuzco were unaware of the recent changes that had occurred in the nearby rebel kingdom—that Titu Cusi had died, that a Spanish friar had been killed, or that another son of Manco Inca had just become emperor. A new Spanish viceroy, Francisco de Toledo, had arrived in Cuzco some three months earlier, after having already spent roughly a year and a half in Peru. At fifty-six years of age, Toledo was a firm, no-nonsense disciplinarian, a man the king had entrusted to reorganize the affairs of his distant colony and to settle the problem of the rebellious natives in Peru.

For the previous half century, Spanish ecclesiastics and philosophers had debated one another over what rights, if any, the natives in the New World should enjoy. Some had argued that Spain had no right to despoil native rulers of their kingdoms and empires and to conquer the inhabitants of the New World. A few had even argued that Spain should *return* the empires they had already conquered to their original rulers or to their heirs. Others felt that the inhabitants of the New World, being pagan, were both morally and intellectually inferior to Europeans and that, like wayward children, they needed to be ruled by Christians. The latter could then not only bestow upon them the word of God, but also the refinements of European civilization.

Viceroy Toledo belonged firmly to this last group. The natives of Peru were inferior peoples, he believed; their destiny was thus to be ruled by a superior civilization—that of the Spaniards—who were entitled by God to organize and dictate the natives' activities for the benefit of all concerned. The inhabitants of Peru should therefore be converted to Christianity, the one true faith, and without question should be forced to give up their idolatrous religious beliefs. Just as important, Toledo felt, was the necessity of neutralizing the influence and power of the natives' previous masters, the Incas, who continued to rule a small kingdom and who still influenced, both morally and spiritually, many of the natives now under Spanish rule. The Incas' independent Kingdom of Vilcabamba, Toledo had concluded, remained a pernicious influence that had caused untold problems in the past. If left unchallenged, it would surely cause many more in the future.

In order to understand the natives' previous rulers better—and thus his enemies—Toledo had begun a series of investigations into the oral history of the Incas soon after his arrival in Peru. Toledo did so by systematically interviewing older natives and the *quipucamayocs*—the native specialists who could still read the Inca *quipus,* the knotted string records. Discovering that the Incas had conquered their vast empire only relatively recently, Toledo concluded that the Inca elite had no more right to rule the various ethnic groups of Peru than did the Spaniards, who had thus been justified in defeating the Incas by force of arms. The only solution to the current "Inca problem," Toledo finally concluded, was to eliminate or neutralize the Incas' remaining monarch—whom the Spaniards still believed to be Titu Cusi.

Such was the state of affairs in July 1571, just a few months after the death of Titu Cusi, when Viceroy Toledo sent an official envoy to Vilcabamba. The envoy soon arrived at the banks of the Apurímac River with a group of native chiefs, then sent four of the chiefs across the river to arrange for permission to enter the kingdom. Although the chiefs dutifully crossed over, all four mysteriously disappeared. Three weeks later, the envoy made a second attempt, this time sending two natives ahead. Only one of the two returned, however, wounded and bleeding, and reported that they had been attacked.

To the Spaniards in Cuzco, a strange and unusual silence seemed to have descended upon the Kingdom of Vilcabamba; messages no longer arrived from the Inca emperor nor were any envoys allowed to enter. An impatient Toledo finally sent a second envoy, his close friend, Atilano de Anaya, this time with a letter that the viceroy had written directly to Titu Cusi:

> If you have faith and devotion to the service of God and to my lord the King as you have said you have [wrote Toledo], show yourself by coming out to meet with them [the envoys] and by listening to what they have to tell you on behalf of my lord, His Majesty the King, and of myself. And if not, we shall certainly be disabused of any illusions and can decide on how to proceed.

Toledo simultaneously sent a letter to King Philip, sounding out the monarch on how he felt about the possibility of launching an unprovoked war on the last independent remnant of the Inca Empire.

> Your Majesty will appreciate that it will be convenient to terminate this affair once and for all in such a way that it has the effect of securing a firm peace or else this debate must be ended by war. One way or the other, a town of Spaniards will be established in the province of Vilcabamba, whose [military] force [on the] frontier will assure peace [there] from now on. . . . Your Majesty should . . . determine whether

war should be waged on him [Titu Cusi] or not . . . [for] if he doesn't
want to come out the cause of the war will be justified.

As the viceroy's letter made its way slowly to Spain, the envoy Anaya arrived at the banks of the Urubamba River, at the hanging bridge of
Chuquichaca, where Gonzalo Pizarro had once battled Manco's defenders.
Spotting native warriors on the other side, Anaya shouted for permission to
come across. The warriors replied that the Spaniard could proceed. But once
he arrived on the other side of the river, they killed him. The Incas had apparently feared that the envoy might learn of Titu Cusi's death and that the
Spaniards would thus learn of their kingdom's weakened condition.

For Viceroy Toledo, Anaya's murder was the proverbial final straw. Not
wishing to wait another eight months for a reply from the king, Toledo
soon began making preparations to invade the Incas' kingdom and to seize
or kill Titu Cusi, intending this time to succeed where two previous Spanish
expeditions had failed. By May of 1572, Toledo had assembled a formidable
army composed of two forces: the first, consisting of 250 armored Spaniards
and some two thousand native auxiliaries, Toledo ordered to enter Vilcabamba via the Chuquichaca bridge and fight its way to the capital. The
second force, which was comprised of some seventy Spaniards, he ordered
to invade Vilcabamba from the opposite direction, across the Apurímac
River, in a sort of pincer movement. Toledo was determined that this time
the Inca emperor would have no chance to escape.

Sometime in early June, the main expeditionary force under the command of General Martín Hurtado de Arbieto crossed the Chuquichaca
bridge and began heading up into the Vilcabamba Valley. Three elderly
conquistadors, now in their sixties, who had fought alongside Francisco
Pizarro, accompanied them as guides: Alonso de Mesa, Hernando Solano,
and Mansio Serra de Leguizamón. The rest of the participants were of a
younger generation, many of them owners of *encomiendas* that had been
handed down to them by their conquistador fathers. All, however, had a
mutual interest in extinguishing the Incas' final remaining stronghold.

Despite a valiant native resistance, the outcome of the campaign was a
foregone conclusion. The invading army was well equipped, well armed,
and determined; it also had the advantage of plentiful cannons, horses, harquebuses, and swords. While the emperor Tupac Amaru's forces dutifully

gave battle, ambushing the Spaniards on the treacherous trails and often delaying their progress, once again the natives found that their wooden maces and clubs and even their bows and arrows were no match for the Spaniards' horses and steel weapons. The only real question for the invaders was: would the Inca emperor escape and, in so doing, live to fight another day?

The Spaniards quickly captured Vitcos, the city that Diego Orgóñez had pillaged and where Manco Inca had almost been captured. They then crossed over the Colpacasa Pass before beginning to head down alongside the Pampaconas River, giving battle to Inca defenders along the way. Finally, on Tuesday, June 24, 1572, just outside the capital of Vilcabamba,

> General Martín Hurtado de Arbieto ordered that all of the men form themselves into companies with their captains and the Indian allies . . . with their generals. . . . [And] with their banners . . . they marched off taking the artillery [with them]. . . . At ten o'clock in the morning they marched into the city of Vilcabamba, everyone on foot, for it is a most rugged and wild country, in no way [suitable] for horses.

The Spaniards found that the hidden capital Gonzalo Pizarro had sacked thirty-three years earlier now lay desolate, smoldering, and empty. In a report the Spanish general later submitted to Viceroy Toledo, Arbieto stated that he and his men "found [Vilcabamba] abandoned [with] around four hundred intact houses and their shrines and idolatries were here just as they had been before this city was captured. We found the houses of the Inca [emperors] burned . . . and all the . . . Indians, warriors as well as peasants, had fled to wherever they could." The chronicler Murúa marveled at how, when the Spaniards arrived,

> The entire town was found to be sacked [so thoroughly] that if the Spaniards and [their auxiliary] Indians had done it, it could not have been worse. . . . All the Indian men and women had fled and had hidden themselves in the jungle, taking everything they could. They torched and burned the rest of the corn and food that was in the . . . storehouses . . . so that when the expedition arrived it was still smoking, and the temple of the Sun, where their principal idol was [located], was burned. [The Incas] had done the same when Gonzalo Pizarro . . . had entered

the city, and the lack of food had forced . . . [Gonzalo's expedition] to return and to leave the country in . . . [the emperor's] power. [The Incas] expected in a similar manner that when the Spaniards presently found no food nor anything else with which to subsist upon, that they would turn back and leave the land and that they would not stay there nor settle it, and for this reason the Indians fled, setting fire to everything that they were unable to carry [away with them].

By now the Spaniards had learned that Titu Cusi was dead, and that a new emperor, Tupac Amaru, had been crowned. But neither the new emperor nor his attendants, nor the temple priests, nor the priestesses, nor anyone else who had inhabited the city could be found. Stone fountains spurted water and streams gurgled nearby as brown and green lizards scrambled across the cut stones of the Incas' deserted palaces. As the Spaniards searched the smoldering city, they also noticed that not all the gabled houses were covered in traditional thatch; instead, a few had rooftops of tile, in imitation of the roofs in Cuzco, which in turn were in imitation of those in Spain. Despite the Incas' sacking of their own capital, Murúa described some of what the Incas had left behind:

The town has, or it would be better to say had, a location half a league [1.75 miles] wide, like the layout of Cuzco, and a long distance in length. In it they used to raise parrots, hens, ducks, local rabbits, turkeys, pheasants, curassows, guans, macaws, and a thousand other kinds of birds of diverse and showy colors and [that are] very beautiful to see. . . . The houses and storage huts are covered in good thatch and there are numerous guavas, pecans, peanuts, lucumas, papayas, pineapples, avocados, and many other cultivated and wild trees. The palace of the Inca [emperor had] different levels, [was] covered in roof tiles, and the whole palace was painted with a great variety of paintings in their manner, which was something well worth seeing. The town had a square large enough for a good number of people, where they used to celebrate and even raced horses. The doors of the palace were made of a very fragrant cedar, which there is a great quantity of in that land, and [some of the] roofs were of the same wood. The Incas barely missed the luxuries, greatness, and sumptuousness of Cuzco in that distant or, better said, exiled land. Because everything they wanted to have from outside [of Vil-cabamba], the Indians brought to them for their contentment and plea-sure—and they enjoyed themselves there.

General Arbieto sent out a number of small, mobile forces in different di-rections, hoping to capture the Inca leaders and especially their new em-peror, Tupac Amaru, who was rumored to be fleeing with his pregnant wife. One unit was formed under the command of a young, ambitious captain, Martín García de Loyola, a man eager to prove himself and who picked a se-lect company of forty men. In a petition he later submitted to the king, Gar-cía de Loyola made clear what had motivated him and many of the other Spaniards to join Arbieto's expedition:

> [When] war was declared by the Viceroy against the Inca [emperor] who was discovered in the province of Vilcabamba working against your Majesty . . . many rewards were offered in your Royal name to those who participated, and in particular an income of a thousand pesos [was promised annually] from [tribute-paying] Indians to the person who captured the Inca.

Whoever captured the Inca emperor, in other words, was to be granted an *encomienda* with enough natives on it to guarantee a lifetime income of one thousand pesos (around ten pounds of gold) per year, a grant that could then be passed on for one additional lifetime to the recipient's son, daughter, or other heir. The stakes on both sides, therefore, couldn't have been any higher: a fortune in gold and an easy retirement for whoever captured the Inca emperor versus the capture and imprisonment or death of the Inca em-peror. The Spaniards also wished to put an end to future native rebellions by driving a stake into the heart of the final pocket of Inca resistance.

The ensuing pursuit through the jungle after the Inca emperor was conse-quently a brutal one. Descending the river Masahuay (probably today's Cosireni and Urubamba Rivers), García de Loyola and his men traveled more than a hundred miles, deep into the region of the Mañari Indians, an ethnic group probably related to today's Campas or Machiguengas. Floating on rafts and led by their native guides, the Spaniards drifted downstream through the primeval wilderness of the upper Amazon. Immense trees in various shades of emerald and green with enormous trunks rose alongside the riverbanks beside them, some with giant crowns full of flowers, others with exotic fruits. Toucans with their disproportionately large and colored beaks occasionally looked down upon the armored men drifting below, cocking their heads sideways for a better view.

As the Spaniards floated downriver, they periodically captured frightened natives on rafts or in canoes and forced their captives to give them information as to the whereabouts of the fleeing Inca emperor. The Spanish bounty hunters soon learned that the emperor "Tupac Amaru was in the Momori Valley, secure [in the belief] that it was not possible to catch him [there] because of the impenetrability of the country and of the rivers." Encouraged by the fact that they were obviously heading in the right direction, García de Loyola and his men now continued on downriver, braving the cataracts and rapids and eventually arriving at Momori. There, the Spaniards were encouraged to learn that they were gradually closing the distance between themselves and the fleeing emperor, as only

> five days previously he [Tupac Amaru] had left that place . . . and had gone by canoe to the [land of the] Pilcosonis, another province further inland. But Tupac Amaru's wife was frightened and depressed because she was within days of giving birth and, because he loved her so much, he himself helped her to bear her burden and waited for her, walking little by little.

Quickening their pace, the Spaniards now began to chase their quarry by both day and night, guided by Mañari Indians and lighting their way late at night with torches. As the orange flames illuminated the strange, eerie black jungle, the Spaniards sometimes froze momentarily as unseen beasts suddenly crashed noisily away. Finally, after a chase that had lasted for more than two hundred miles, the Spaniards eventually glimpsed a small fire flickering ahead through the jungle. Moving cautiously with drawn swords, García de Loyola and his men emerged into a small clearing where they found Tupac Amaru and his pregnant wife huddled beside a campfire. The two royal fugitives no doubt must have looked up bleakly as the bearded men emerged from the darkness, the fire causing the steel of their swords and breastplates to glisten. There, in the middle of the night, deep in the Amazon rain forest, the thirty-five-year-long Spanish campaign to destroy the rebel province of Vilcabamba and to seize its last remaining Inca emperor had finally came to an end.

On September 21, 1572, on what the Spaniards call St. Matthew's Day and in the month the Incas called the *Coya Raymi,* or the "Festival of the Moon," General Arbieto's victorious expedition arrived at the gates of Cuzco. Tupac Amaru and the rest of the Spaniards' high-ranking prisoners marched before the cavalry, tethered by ropes and chains to their Spanish captors. Virtually all the Spanish and native inhabitants of the city turned out to watch the expedition's triumphal return after nearly four months. Arbieto and his men now marched and rode into the city, their native auxiliaries walking alongside together with the Spaniards' numerous black slaves. The victors carried with them their captured treasure, such as the golden *punchao,* or sacred image of the sun, which they had discovered in the forests outside Vilcabamba; they also brought the mummified bodies of Manco Inca and Titu Cusi—the two rebel leaders, now dead, who had caused the Spaniards so much grief with their deadly insurgency campaigns.

As Tupac Amaru and his captains were led away and imprisoned, the conquering Spaniards, by contrast, were treated to celebrations that lasted late into the night. Within a matter of days, the Spaniards quickly tried, convicted, and then executed Tupac Amaru's generals. Their offense, apparently, had been to command the military defense of Vilcabamba against the Spanish invaders. Their real crime, of course, was to have resisted the final Spanish subjugation of Tawantinsuyu. A gathering of Spanish priests who spoke *runasimi,* meanwhile, did their best to convince Tupac Amaru to convert to Christianity, no doubt hoping that the emperor would choose to save himself spiritually, even if it proved impossible to do so physically.

The twenty-nine-year-old emperor, who had done his best to strengthen the Inca religion in Vilcabamba during his brief, sixteen-month reign, eventually agreed to convert. A strong motivation for doing so was no doubt the fact that he had been informed that a trial was being conducted against him, a trial in which his very life hung in the balance. Tupac Amaru was being accused, basically, of having been the ruler of a rebel state that had launched raids upon Spanish-controlled Peru, and also of having allowed heathen religious practices to be tolerated within his kingdom. The raids, of course, had been launched not by Tupac Amaru, but by his older brother Titu Cusi, and by his father, Manco Inca. Both of those emperors had done so only after the Spaniards had attacked and occupied Tawantinsuyu, which, from the Incas' point of view, the Spaniards had no right to rule. The "heathen religious practices" the emperor was accused of were likewise part of the Incas' own native religion, one that they had practiced since time immemorial and long before the arrival of the Spaniards.

Tupac Amaru himself was neither conversant in the Spanish language nor familiar with Spanish jurisprudence, nor did he have any legal counsel to defend him. His trial therefore was the sixteenth-century equivalent of a kangaroo court. Even if the Inca emperor had been supplied with the finest legal representation from Spain, however, and even had such representation argued that the Spaniards had no legal right to invade the Inca Empire, it is unlikely that the results would have been different. The prosecution, no doubt, would have argued that God himself had given the pope the right to assign Tawantinsuyu to the king and queen of Spain, and that the Spaniards were thus simply carrying out God's will. For the Incas of Vilcabamba to resist such a commandment was therefore both blasphemy and treason, and were actions that were obviously contrary to God's will. Besides, even though Tupac Amaru was now converting to Christianity, he had nevertheless been the spiritual leader of a pagan religion, one that had worshipped false idols and that in fact had worshipped Tupac Amaru as a false god himself.

The verdict was thus a foregone conclusion. Neither the Spaniards nor the Incas would ever have allowed an independent, hostile enclave to exist within a territory they had conquered, nor would they have allowed an important resistance figure to inspire disloyalty among their newly conquered citizens. Just as the Romans had destroyed Spartacus, the Spaniards had cleansed from their native country every last vestige of the Moors. The laws of empire building are brutal and dispassionate, and both the Incas and the Spaniards implicitly understood them. No two empires, after all, can exist simultaneously in the same area; the stronger empire will always defeat the weaker, until in the end only a single empire remains.

Not surprisingly then, after only three days of trial, the judge selected by the viceroy condemned Tupac Amaru to death. And although various religious leaders in Cuzco pleaded with the viceroy for the emperor's life to be spared, Toledo insisted that the sentence be immediately carried out. The king's viceroy was determined to remove from Spain's new colony the last vestige of Inca independence and to crush once and for all the possibility of another native rebellion. Tupac Amaru, he therefore insisted, must not be allowed to remain alive.

On September 24, 1572, a phalanx of guards brought the emperor from his prison and led him through the streets to the main square. This was the same square where, thirty-seven years earlier, Francisco Pizarro and his conquistadors had set up camp the day they had first arrived in Cuzco and where once a succession of Inca emperors had held giant religious ceremonies that symbolized their vast power. Now, in the center of the square, a simple scaffold awaited. One chronicler wrote that:

> So many natives attended the death of their King and Lord that those who were present say that it was only possible to push through the streets and squares with the greatest of difficulty. And since there was no room left to stand, the Indians climbed the walls and roofs of the houses. Even the many large hills that can be seen from the city were packed with Indians.

An eyewitness recalled that:

> The open spaces, roofs and windows in the parishes of Carmenca and San Cristóbal were so crowded with spectators that if an orange had been thrown down it could not have reached the ground anywhere, so densely were the people packed.

As crowds of gawking Spaniards, natives, and African slaves watched, Tupac Amaru rode "a street mule draped in black velvet, and he himself was completely covered in mourning." The emperor's hands had been bound together with rope while another rope had been tied around his neck, lest the Inca king should try to escape.

> The Inca was taken from the fortress, through the public streets of the city, with a guard of four hundred Cañari Indians, having their lances in

their hands. . . . He was accompanied by the two monks, one on either side. . . . They went along teaching and saying things of much consolation to the soul, until they reached the scaffold, which was reared on high in the center of the great square, fronting the cathedral. Here they got down, and the Fathers remained with the Inca, comforting his soul with holy preparation.

According to some accounts, just before he arrived at the scaffold, Tupac Amaru's sister, María Cusi Huarcay, suddenly appeared at a window, crying out to him

"Where are you going my brother, Prince and sole King of the four *suyus*?" She tried to move forward [through the crowd but] the ecclesiastics stopped her. . . . [Tupac Amaru] remained very grave and humble [throughout]. The balconies were packed with people, [with Spanish] women and important ladies who, moved by compassion, wept for him, witnessing an unfortunate young man being led away to be killed.

Tupac Amaru now ascended the scaffold, which had been draped in black cloth, aware as he did so that the Spaniards had also murdered both his father, Manco Inca, and his uncle Atahualpa.

As the multitude of Indians who . . . completely filled up [the square] saw that sad and deplorable spectacle [and knowing] that their Lord and Inca was about to die there, they deafened the skies and made them resound with their cries and uproar. . . . [Tupac Amaru's] relatives, who were near him, celebrated that sad tragedy with tears and sobbing.

Standing alongside his executioner—who was an ethnic Cañari and thus an enemy of the Incas—and with a black-robed priest at his side, Tupac Amaru looked out over the vast multitude and slowly raised his right hand. He then "let it fall. With a lordly mind he alone remained calm, and all the noise was followed by a silence so profound that no living soul moved, either among those who were in the square or among those at a distance." Then, when all had become silent and everyone on the square strained to see the last legitimate heir of the four *suyus* and to hear what he might say, Tupac Amaru, the Royal Serpent, addressed the crowd:

> "Lords, you are [gathered] here from all the four suyus. Let it be known that I am a Christian and they have baptized me and I wish to die under the law of God—and I have to die. And that everything that my ancestors the Incas and I have told you up till now—that you should worship the sun god, Punchao, and the shrines, idols, stones, rivers, mountains, and sacred things—is a lie and completely false. When we used to tell you that we were entering [a temple] to speak to the sun, and that it told you to do what we said and that it spoke—this . . . [was] a lie. Because it did not speak rather we did, for it is an object of gold and cannot speak. And my brother Titu Cusi told me that whenever I wished to tell the Indians [to do] something, that I should enter alone into the [sun temple of] Punchao and that no one was to enter with me . . . and that afterwards I should come out and tell the Indians that it had spoken to me, and that it had said whatever I wanted to tell them, because the Indians perform better what they have been commanded to do and . . . [they better obey what] they venerate—and [the god they most venerated] was the [sun god]."
>
> . . . And . . . Tupac Amaru . . . [asked the crowd] to forgive him for having deceived them until now, and to pray to God for him. [And] all of this he said . . . with [great] royal authority and majesty, neither contrived nor artificial but very natural . . . despite his being a prisoner and in this predicament.

After delivering this surprising speech, spoken in *runasimi* so that few Spaniards other than a handful of priests understood it, and which no doubt stunned his native listeners,

> The Inca then received consolation from the Fathers who were at his side and, taking leave of all, he put his head on the block, like a lamb. The executioner then came forward and, taking the hair in his left hand, he severed the head with a knife at one blow, and held it on high for all to see. As the head was severed the bells of the cathedral began to ring, and were followed by those of all the monasteries and parish churches

in the city. The execution caused the greatest sorrow and brought tears to all eyes.

Thus on September 24, 1572, thirty-six years after Manco Inca had launched his great rebellion, the last Inca emperor—Tupac Amaru—lived no more.

16 ❖ THE SEARCH FOR THE "LOST CITY" OF THE INCAS

"Something hidden! Go and find it!
Go and look behind the ranges—
Something lost behind the ranges.
Lost and waiting for you.
Go!"

RUDYARD KIPLING, *THE EXPLORER*, 1898

ON JUNE 8, 1911—339 YEARS AFTER THE EXECUTION OF TUPAC Amaru—a United Fruit Company steamship lay docked in New York City, preparing for departure. As stevedores busily untied the ship's moorings and passengers waved goodbye to the crowd of well-wishers jammed onto the dock, the steamer slowly began motoring out into the harbor in the direction of the Statue of Liberty and out toward the open sea. The ship was bound for Panama, where a transoceanic canal was currently being dug that would not be completed for another three years. At least a handful of the passengers on board intended to cross the Isthmus and then take another steamer bound for Peru. Seagulls cried, whirling over the boat and over the slate-gray water, while on board a thirty-five-year-old assistant professor of Latin American history from Yale University named Hiram Bingham looked out over the water. A tall, extremely thin man with close-cropped brown hair and a gaunt, almost ascetic face, Bingham's goal was to search for the Incas' capital of Vilcabamba—the legendary city that had been lost to history now for more than three hundred years.

From his research, the six-foot-four, 170-pound Bingham already knew that it had taken nearly forty years of warfare and counterinsurgency cam-

379

paigns before the Spaniards had finally been able to extinguish the last rebel capital of the Inca Empire. After the conquest of the Inca Empire, Spain had continued to consolidate its grip on its American possessions, gaining in strength and world power in part because of a steady diet of gold and silver sucked from its new colonies like a bat sucks nectar from a glistening tropical flower. A thick blanket of secrecy had then descended over South America, placed there by the continent's Spanish and Portuguese masters. For more than two centuries, in fact, Spain and Portugal had forbidden any foreign scientists from entering their hard-won possessions, intent on keeping the lands they had conquered to themselves in an effort to prevent the intrusion of European competitors. The fabled capital of Vilcabamba, meanwhile, had gradually become just that: a fable. The story of the reign of the last rebel Inca emperors and of their heroic rebellion had eventually been converted into folk tales that were then passed on orally by the Incas' descendants or else buried in old Spanish chronicles that had soon gathered dust.

It wasn't until the turn of the nineteenth century, during the years 1799 to 1805, that a foreign scientist finally managed to explore South America.* The Prussian Alexander von Humboldt visited the Amazon and the Andes and also traveled to Peru. He was the first to map some of its Inca ruins. Humboldt's writings eventually fueled a resurgence of interest in the history of the Inca Empire and the last Inca kings. The story of a lost, legendary Inca city whose location had disappeared and that thus remained to be discovered seized the imaginations of not a few nineteenth-century explorers. By the time Hiram Bingham set off to search for Vilcabamba in 1911, however, the only ancient ruins that anyone had discovered in the Incas' former province of Vilcabamba were those at a site called Choqquequirau, located about sixty miles west of Cuzco. Some explorers thought that the ruins of Choqque-quirau might be those of Manco Inca's rebel capital. Hiram Bingham and at least one Peruvian historian, however, were convinced they were wrong.

Despite his unsuccessful childhood attempt to flee his Hawaii home, Bingham had never let go of his dreams of adventuring. He had merely postponed them. Bingham, after all, was a great fan of the stories of the nine-teenth-century British novelist Rudyard Kipling, one of whose poems—appropriately enough called "The Explorer"—was Bingham's personal fa-

---

* Humboldt traveled to South America, fittingly enough, on a ship called the *Pizarro*.

vorite. Consumed with a desire to escape his impoverished background and
to make a name for himself in the world—or, as he put it, to "strive for magnificence"—Bingham married an heir to the Tiffany fortune and then
earned a Ph.D. at Yale. Bingham's specialty was modern South American
history, beginning with the wars for independence in the early nineteenth
century when, at long last, the South American colonies finally severed their
ties with Spain. By 1908, however, three years before he would set off for
Vilcabamba, the thirty-three-year-old Bingham was bored with his job as
an assistant professor and frustrated by the fact that he had yet to make his
mark on the world. When Bingham learned that the upcoming 1908 Pan-
American Scientific Congress in Santiago, Chile, was accepting delegates,
he seized the opportunity for adventure. He quickly received a leave of absence from Yale, then traveled to Santiago for the conference. Soon afterward, Bingham made his way by sea and rail to Cuzco, where for the first
time he visited the ancient capital of the Incas. "My previous studies of
South American history had been limited largely to the Spanish Colonial
days," Bingham later wrote, "the wards of independence, and the progress
made by the different republics. Archaeology lay outside my field and I
knew very little about the Incas except the fascinating story told by
[William] Prescott in his famous 'Conquest of Peru.' "

Wandering about Cuzco, gazing in admiration at the remains of Inca
palaces and at the splendor of their intricately cut stones, Bingham was
stunned by the handiwork of an ancient civilization that was unlike any
he had seen. On the hillside overlooking the city, Bingham was further
amazed by the sight of the giant, megalithic fortress of Saqsaywaman,
where more than three centuries earlier Juan Pizarro and thousands of natives had lost their lives while caught up in Manco Inca's rebellion. Bingham wrote:

A little farther up the stream one passes through a massive megalithic
gateway and finds one's self in the presence of the astounding gray-blue
Cyclopean walls of Sacsahuaman. . . . Here, the ancient builders constructed three great terraces, which extend one above another for a third
of a mile across the hill between two deep gulches. The lowest terrace of
the "fortress" is faced with colossal boulders, many of which weigh ten
tons and some weigh more than twenty tons, yet all are fitted together

with the utmost precision. . . . To a superstitious Indian who sees these walls for the first time, they must seem to have been built by gods.

In Cuzco, Bingham soon met the prefect of the nearby province of Apurímac, Juan Núñez, a man who was much impressed by the distinguished North American "doctor," just arrived from an important scientific congress. Only the year before, Núñez had cleared and explored Inca ruins at a site called Choqquequirau. Whether Choqquequirau, which means "the cradle of gold," was the actual name of the ancient site, Núñez didn't know. Thus far, however, it was the only ancient Inca city that had been found in the province of Vilcabamba. The ruins were probably those of Manco Inca's lost city of Vilcabamba, Núñez told Bingham. Would Bingham be interested in accompanying him there, he asked. Bingham recounted:

> The Prefect was particularly anxious that I should visit the ruins and be able to report their importance to the President of Peru. He insisted that as I was a "Doctor" (Ph.D.) and a Government Delegate to a Scientific Congress I must know all about archaeology and could tell him how valuable Choqquequirau was as a site for buried treasure and whether it had been as he believed, Vilcapampa the Old, the Capital of the last four Incas. My protest that he was mistaken in his estimate of my archaeological knowledge was regarded by him merely as evidence of modesty rather than as a true statement of fact. . . .
>
> My efforts to avoid visiting the ruins of Choqquequirau were also laid partly to the very inclement weather and partly to the extreme difficulty of reaching that site. Secretary [of State Elihu] Root had impressed upon us [the U.S. delegates to the scientific congress] the importance of developing international good will by endeavoring in every way to please the officials of the countries we visited. Accordingly, I agreed to the Prefect's proposal, not knowing that it was destined to lead me into a fascinating field. It was my first introduction to prehistoric America.

So it was that in February 1909, Hiram Bingham III, lecturer in modern South American history, found himself accompanying a mule train that was about to penetrate into a quarter of the Inca Empire the Incas had once referred to as the Antisuyu. It would be Bingham's first contact with lost Inca ruins:

> Magnificent precipices guard the ruins on every side and render Choq-quequirau virtually inaccessible to an enemy. . . . At the top of the southern and outer precipice, five thousand eight hundred feet immediately above the Apurímac river, stands a parapet and the walls of two [Inca] buildings without windows. The view from here, both up and down the valley . . . surpasses the possibilities of language for adequate description. . . . Far down the gigantic cañon one catches little glimpses of the Apurímac, a white stream shut in between guardian mountains, so narrowed by the distance that it seems like a mere brooklet. Here and there through the valley are marvelous cataracts, one of which . . . has a clear fall of over one thousand feet. The panorama in every direction is wonderful in variety, contrast, beauty, and grandeur.

The ruins, fortunately, which previously had been overgrown by jungle scrub, had recently been cleared by Núñez. And although Bingham was untrained in either archaeology or in surveying techniques, he had at least brought along with him a Kodak camera and a book that contained the basics of what to do when encountering little known ancient ruins:

> Fortunately I had with me that extremely useful handbook "Hints to Travellers," published by the Royal Geographical Society. In one of the chapters I found out what should be done when one is confronted by a prehistoric site—take careful measurements and plenty of photographs and describe as accurately as possible all finds. On account of the rain, our photographs were not very successful but we took measurements of all the buildings and made a rough map.

One thing Bingham was quick to notice was that the first explorers to visit Choqquequirau had done so more than seventy years earlier. Inside one Inca building, Bingham found a list of their names scratched onto several slabs of rock:

M. Eugene de Sartiges, 1834
Jose Maria Tejada, Marcelino Leon, 1834

Jose Benigno Samanez, Juan Manuel Rivas Plata, Mariana Cisneros,
    1861
Pio Mogrovejo, July 4, 1885

Although Bingham couldn't have known it at the time, his unanticipated visit to these abandoned Inca ruins, located on a nearly inaccessible ridge in a virtually uninhabited corner of Peru, was a turning point in his career. A chance invitation by a Peruvian prefect would soon alter the course of Bingham's life—and of South American archaeological history. For the moment, however, Bingham carefully examined the site, as the prefect wanted to know whether the "esteemed" professor thought these were the ruins of Manco Inca's rebel city or not. Bingham later recorded his impressions:

> The walls . . . [at Choqquequirau] appear to have been built entirely of stone and clay. The construction, compared with that of the Inca palaces in Cuzco, is extremely rude and rough and no two niches or doors are exactly alike. Occasionally the lintels of the doors were made of timber, the builders not having taken the trouble to provide stones wide enough for the purpose.

Elsewhere, Bingham wrote,

> Personally, I did not feel so sure that Choqquequirau was the town of Vilcabamba. The ruins did not seem fine enough for an Inca's residence.

Although an amateur, Bingham was obviously less than impressed by the prefect's ruins. Surely the Inca emperors, Bingham reasoned—even the final, rebel ones—would have lived in finely wrought palaces made in the imperial style that Bingham had so much admired in Cuzco. It therefore seemed unlikely to Bingham that Choqquequirau had ever housed an Inca emperor and hence could be the lost city of Vilcabamba that the prefect hoped it was.

Arriving back in Lima, Bingham soon met a forty-six-year-old Peruvian historian, Carlos Alberto Romero, who agreed with him. Romero showed Bingham two previously unknown sixteenth-century chronicles that had recently been discovered and published. One had been dictated by Manco's son Titu Cusi in 1571 and had lain forgotten for more than three hundred years. The second was a report written by Baltasar de Ocampo, a Spaniard who had participated in the sacking of Vilcabamba in 1572 and who had witnessed the execution of Tupac Amaru shortly thereafter. Both accounts contained descriptions of Manco Inca's capital of Vilcabamba. None of the descriptions seemed to match the physical characteristics Bingham had seen at the ruins of Choqquequirau.

Baltasar de Ocampo's account, for example, made it clear that the way to reach Vilcabamba from Cuzco was "down the valley by Yucay and Ollantay-tampu [Ollantaytambo] to the [hanging] bridge of Chuqui-chaca." The direction, therefore, that an explorer must take to discover the location of Vilcabamba appeared to be parallel to the route followed by the Urubamba River. Once one arrived at the modern Chuquichaca bridge, then one would presumably cross the river and head west. It made no sense to follow this route, Romero said, if one were traveling from Cuzco to Choqquequirau, which lay on the other side of the Vilcabamba mountain range and that could much more easily be reached by crossing the Apurímac River from the west. Thus Choqquequirau could *not* be Vilcabamba, Romero reasoned, contrary to what Prefect Núñez and other explorers had said.

Titu Cusi's narrative also seemed to make it clear, Romero continued, that Manco's original capital of Vitcos had been a stopping-off point on the way to Vilcabamba. Since Choqquequirau could not be Vilcabamba, as it obviously could not be reached by Ocampo's route, it also seemed unlikely that Choqquequirau could be Vitcos for that very same reason. Ocampo's description of Vitcos, in fact, seemed to substantiate this, as the city the Spaniard described seemed to have very little in common with the Choqquequirau ruins:

> The fortress of Pitcos [Vitcos], which is on a very high mountain whence the view commanded a great part of the province of Vilcapampa. Here there was an extensive level space, with very sumptuous and majestic buildings, erected with great skill and art, all the lintels of the doors, as well the principal as the ordinary ones, being of marble, elaborately carved.

Choqquequirau certainly did not lie upon "an extensive level space" but rather was clustered in three sections on a very narrow, jungle-covered ridge. Nor did Choqquequirau contain "sumptuous and majestic buildings,

erected with great skill and art, all the lintels of the doors, as well the principal and ordinary ones, being of marble, elaborately carved." Choqquequirau thus seemed to fit neither the descriptions of Vilcabamba nor of
Vitcos, Romero told Bingham. Both cities therefore remained to be found.
In Romero's opinion, the only way someone was going to find either Vitcos
or Vilcabamba would be to cross the Urubamba River at the Chuquichaca
bridge and then to head up into the Vilcabamba Valley. Somewhere in that
valley Vitcos must be located, Romero said. Manco's capital of Vilcabamba,
then—according to the chronicles—would only be a few days' walk away.

Two years after his meeting with Romero, in June of 1911, Bingham had
organized the Yale Peruvian Expedition and was on a steamer headed out of
New York City on his way back to Peru. If he could discover Manco's fabled
lost city, Bingham knew, then no matter what else he might accomplish in
his life, he would have made his mark upon the world. The man who as a
boy had once dreamed of taking a tramp steamer to mainland America and
one day becoming an explorer, now found himself standing on the deck of
a steamer, bound for South America, on his way to seeking fame and glory
by discovering lost Inca ruins in Peru. Bingham later wrote:

> On the slopes of Choqquequirau [in 1909], the clouds would occasion-
> ally break away and give us tantalizing glimpses of snow-covered
> mountains. There seemed to be an unknown region, "behind the
> ranges," which might contain great possibilities. Our guides could tell us
> nothing about it. Little was to be found in books. Perhaps Manco's cap-
> ital was hidden there.

Accompanying Bingham were six men, including Dr. William Erving—a
medical doctor and Yale classmate of Bingham's who had once paddled a
canoe from Cairo to Khartoum—and thirty-nine-year-old Dr. Harry Foote,
a professor of chemistry at Yale, a personal friend of Bingham's who was officially the expedition's "naturalist."

Shortly after arriving in Lima, Bingham went to visit the Peruvian president, Augusto Leguía, whom he had met during his previous trip in 1909.
Leguía soon gave orders to allow the expedition's baggage to pass unencumbered through customs and assigned a military escort to accompany the
expedition. Bingham also met again with Carlos Romero. Delighted that
Bingham had returned to look for Vitcos and Vilcabamba, Romero gave the

North American additional clues that he had recently uncovered and that might help Bingham in his quest. Romero had recently been examining the work of another Spaniard, Father Antonio de la Calancha, he said, who had written a lengthy chronicle of more than fifteen hundred pages that had been published in 1639.

Poring over Calancha's fourth volume, Romero had come across the story of two Augustinian friars who had entered the Kingdom of Vilcabamba in the late sixteenth century and who had lived and preached there for years. One of the friars, Diego Ortiz, Romero said, had been martyred by the natives at a place called Puquiura, very near the town of Vitcos, after the natives had accused the friar of having killed Titu Cusi, their emperor. According to the chronicle, near Vitcos and Puquiura was a shrine called Chuquipalpa, where a giant white rock was located above a spring of water. Next to it was an Inca temple of the sun. The two friars had burned and destroyed the shrine, Romero said, believing that they were exorcizing the devil. If you can find the great white rock of Chuquipalpa, Romero told Bingham—looking up at the tall North American—then you can be certain that Vitcos must lie nearby. And if you succeed in discovering Vitcos, Romero added, then you will only be a two days' walk away from Manco Inca's lost capital of Vilcabamba.

Bingham thanked Romero, then carefully copied down the various passages of Father Calancha that Romero had pointed out to him. Bingham already had a copy of an article Romero had published two years earlier, "Report on the Ruins of Choqquequirau," in which Romero had argued that previous explorers' assertions that Choqquequirau was the lost city of Vilcabamba were incorrect. Romero had also argued that the city of Vitcos would be found not near Choqquequirau, but on the other side of the Vilcabamba mountain range somewhere in the Vilcabamba River Valley.

With the assorted clues from the sixteenth-century chronicles now safely in his possession, Bingham next visited the Lima Geographical Society, where he purchased several maps of the region he was intent on exploring. One of these was a map separated into folios and made forty-six years earlier by the Italian geographer and scientist Antonio Raimondi, who had visited the Vilcabamba region in 1865. Running his index finger carefully over one of the thick sheets, Bingham noted that in the upper Vilcabamba Valley, on the other side of the mountain range from Choqquequirau, Raimondi had indicated a small village called "Puquira." Could this be the village of Puquiura, where Father Calancha had stated that Friar Diego Ortiz had been martyred? If so, then both the lost city of Vitcos and the great rock shrine over a spring of water at Chuquipalpa had to be nearby.

Taking a ship from Lima to the port of Mollendo, on Peru's southern coast, Bingham and his six expedition members soon boarded a train for the four-day journey up into the Andes, past Lake Titicaca and then on to Cuzco. Once in the capital, the team began to gather mules and provisions and to pack their equipment. Bingham, meanwhile, continued with his research, gathering as much information as he could from anyone who might know of Inca ruins in the Urubamba and Vilcabamba river valleys. Visiting the University of Cuzco, Bingham was surprised to discover that a young American professor was currently rector of the university.* Albert Giesecke, a thirty-one-year-old from Pennsylvania, had settled in Cuzco only a few years earlier. Learning that Bingham was searching for Inca ruins, Giesecke told him about a recent trip that he and a Peruvian congressman, Don Braulio Polo y la Borda, had made on horseback into the Urubamba Valley the previous January, during the rainy season. At a place called Mandor Pampa, Giesecke said, about sixty miles from Cuzco and near a bridge called San Miguel, they had stopped at a small sugarcane farm cultivated by a peasant named Melchor Arteaga. Arteaga had told Giesecke that extensive ruins lay on a ridge high up on a nearby mountain and had suggested that if Giesecke were to return in the dry season, Arteaga would personally guide him there. It was now July, however, the middle of the dry season, and Giesecke had not had the time to return. He was instead happy to pass this information along to Bingham.

As Bingham and his team gradually acclimated themselves to Cuzco's 11,300-foot elevation, Bingham next visited the son of a wealthy planter in the Urubamba Valley, Alberto Duque, whose family kept a home in Cuzco. Bingham later wrote:

> That there were undescribed and unidentified ruins to be found in the
> Urubamba Valley was known to a few people in Cuzco, mostly wealthy
> planters who had large estates in the province of Convencion. One told

* The university is called the Universidad Nacional de San Antonio Abad del Cuzco and was founded in 1692.

us that he went to Santa Ana [a hacienda on the lower Urubamba River] every year and was acquainted with a muleteer who had told him of some interesting ruins near the San Miguel bridge. Knowing the propensity of his countrymen to exaggerate, however, he placed little confidence in the story and, shrugging his shoulders, had crossed the bridge a score of times without taking the trouble to look into the matter. Another, Señor Pancorbo, whose plantation was in the Vilcabamba Valley, said that he had heard vague rumors of ruins in the valley above his plantation, particularly near Pucyura. If his story should prove to be correct, then it was likely that this might be the very Puquiura where Friar Marcos [García] had established the first church in the "province of Vilcapampa." But that was "near" Viticos and near a village called Chuquipalpa, where should be found the ruins of a Temple of the Sun, and in these ruins a "white rock over a spring of water." Yet neither these friendly planters nor the friends among whom they inquired had ever heard of Viticos or a place called Chuquipalpa, or of such an interesting rock; nor had they themselves seen the ruins of which they had heard.

While making a side trip to the nearby Yucay (Vilcanota) Valley to gather more pack mules, Bingham soon met a third informant, the sub-prefect of the town of Urubamba, who told Bingham that unknown Inca ruins existed just a short ways down the Urubamba Valley, near the bridge of San Miguel. The sub-prefect also told Bingham the ruins' name: *Huainapicchu.* According to Bingham, the sub-prefect was

a talkative old fellow who had spent a large part of his life in prospecting for mines in the department of Cuzco [and who] said that he had seen ruins "finer than Choqquequirau" at a place called Huayna Picchu; but he had never been to Choqquequirau. Those who knew him best shrugged their shoulders and did not seem to place much confidence in his word. Too often he had been over-enthusiastic about mines which did not "pan out."

Bingham—a meticulous note taker who even kept a log at his house in Connecticut of guests that visited and for how long—was quick, however, to write down the unfamiliar name in his small, leather-bound notebook:

"Sub-prefect drunk," he wrote in a looping scrawl, then added to that the name "Huainapichu." Bingham wrote next to it "better than Choqq," meaning that the ruins of Huainapicchu were supposedly better than those at Choqquequirau. Huainapichu, the sub-prefect told Bingham, was only eight leagues (twenty-eight miles) further downriver from the town of Urubamba, and was located just beyond a site called Torontoy. None of the names the sub-prefect mentioned, however, seemed to be related to the historical sites that Bingham was searching for: Vitcos, Puquiura, Vilcabamba, or Chuquipalpa, the place with the white rock shrine.

Back in Cuzco, on the eve of his departure, Bingham wrote a hurried letter to his wife:

> Cuzco, July 18, 1911
>
> My Dearly Beloved,
>
> Nearly all the "last things" have been done. It remains to pack my trunk (that stays here), get some sleep, pack my traveling duffel bag, and then start for the interior. . . . We plan to spend about six weeks in the mountains of Vilcabamba. . . . Today I began by trying to solve a puzzle of men, mules, loads, instruments, food, and *arrieros* [mule handlers]. I have twenty mules and one horse, three *arrieros* and six white men. I have two sick mules, sixteen loads and twenty boxes of food.

Bingham had already divided his expedition into three independent teams, each of which would operate under his instructions but which would travel to different areas and would perform different tasks. Team #1 was to head down into the lower Urubamba Valley to the edge of the Amazon Basin and from there was to make a topographic survey up over the Andes Mountains along the 73rd meridian and down to the coast. Team #2 was to travel down the Urubamba River and then up along the Vilcabamba River while making contour maps of both valleys, including the location of local villages and towns. Team #3, meanwhile, which consisted of Bingham and his friend the chemist and expedition naturalist Harry Foote, was to make collections of insects and mosses and to search for Inca ruins. Foote would collect the biological specimens; Bingham would look for ruins.

Soon, the three teams divided up the mules as well as the various wooden boxes of food, measuring and surveying equipment, cameras, film, developing chemicals and photographic paper, insect-collecting flasks, geological hammers, notebooks, medicines, guidebooks, maps, tents, lanterns, altimeters, thermometers, and compasses. Three Peruvian soldiers accompanied the expedition, one for each of the teams, as the president of Peru had promised. The soldier assigned to Bingham's was an army sergeant named Carrasco.

On July 19, 1911, Hiram Bingham and his team finally set out from Cuzco on mule back, traveling up out of the city and then across the divide that separates Cuzco and the Yucay Valley before arriving at the town of Urubamba, where they spent the night. The next day, Bingham traveled another ten miles until they reached Ollantaytambo—the fortress town where Manco Inca had beaten off Hernando and Gonzalo Pizarro's troops in 1536 and had flooded the nearby fields, thus neutralizing the Spaniards' cavalry.

After spending a day investigating and photographing the ruins, Bingham, Foote, the physician Erving, and the Peruvian sergeant Carrasco set out from Ollantaytambo, following the route of the other team members, who had already gone on ahead. Bingham's pack train consisted of two muleteers, two native helpers, and eight mules—four of which were ridden by Bingham and his companions. Not far downstream, the expedition came to a juncture in the road, with 18,975-foot Mount Veronica snow-capped and rising on their right while, across the valley, 20,672-foot Mount Salcantay towered overhead on their left. Before them, snaking along the right side of the Urubamba River as the valley narrowed, ran a relatively new road, blasted and cut into the canyon walls some sixteen years earlier. According to Bingham:

> Before the completion of the river road, about 1895, travelers from Cuzco to the lower Urubamba had a choice of two routes, one by way of the pass of Panticalla . . . and one by way of the pass between Mts. Salcantay and Soray, along the Salcantay River to Huadquina. . . . Both of these routes avoid the highlands between Mt. Salcantay and Mt. Veronica and the lowlands between the villages of Piri and Huadquina. This region was in 1911 undescribed in the geographical literature of south-

ern Peru. We decided not to use either pass, but to go straight down the
Urubamba river road. It led us into a fascinating country.

As the mule train of explorers entered the canyon, the noise of the
Urubamba River gradually grew louder and louder:

> Here the river escapes from the cold plateau by tearing its way through
> gigantic mountains of granite. The road runs through a land of match-
> less charm. . . . In the . . . power of its spell, I know of no place in the
> world which can compare with it. Not only has it great snow peaks
> looming above the clouds more than two miles overhead; gigantic
> precipices of many-colored granite rising sheer for thousands of feet
> above the foaming, glistening, roaring rapids, it has also, in striking con-
> trast, orchids and tree ferns, the delectable beauty of luxurious vegeta-
> tion, and the mysterious witchery of the jungle. One is drawn irresistibly
> onward by ever-recurring surprises through a deep, winding gorge,
> turning and twisting past overhanging cliffs of incredible height. Above
> all there is the fascination of finding here and there under swaying vines,
> or perched on top of a beetling crag, the rugged masonry of a bygone
> race.

Bingham was finally embarking upon what he had dreamed of doing ever
since he was a young boy in Hawaii—leading an expedition into a region of
the world that had been little explored, at least by scientists. As in the title of
an article that he would later write for *National Geographic* magazine, Bingham was becoming ever more immersed "In the Wonderland of Peru."

At the end of their fifth day out from Cuzco, Bingham and his team came
upon the small clearing where Melchor Arteaga cultivated sugarcane. This
was the same peasant who had told Albert Giesecke that high up on a
nearby ridge lay extensive ruins.

> We passed an ill-kept, grass-thatched hut, turned off the road through a
> tiny clearing, and made our camp at the edge of the river Urubamba on
> a sandy beach. Opposite us, beyond the huge granite boulders which in-
> terfered with the progress of the surging stream, was a steep mountain
> clothed with thick jungle. It was an ideal spot for a camp, near the road

and yet secluded. Our actions, however, aroused the suspicions of the owner of the hut, Melchor Arteaga, who leases the lands of Mandor Pampa. He was anxious to know why we did not stay at his hut like respectable travelers. Our *gendarme,* Sergeant Carrasco, reassured him. They had quite a long conversation. When Arteaga learned that we were interested in the architectural remains of the Incas, he said there were some very good ruins in this vicinity—in fact, some excellent ones on top of the opposite mountain, called Huayna Picchu, and also on a ridge called Machu Picchu.

Huayna Picchu, Bingham remembered, was the name the sub-prefect in the town of Urubamba had told him about when Bingham had asked him whether any Inca ruins existed in the nearby Urubamba Valley. Bingham had copied the name down in his notebook along with a note that the ruins there were better than those at Choqquequirau, which lay some thirty miles to the southwest. Now this farmer Arteaga—who wore sandals and spoke with a wad of coca leaves stuffed in his cheek—was essentially saying the same thing. Could Huayna Picchu be the location of Vitcos or Vilcabamba, Bingham wondered. It seemed doubtful. The historian Romero had told him that in order to find either city he had to travel another dozen miles further down the Urubamba River to the Chuquichaca bridge and then to turn left and head up into the Vilcabamba River Valley. Bingham looked up at the massive peak rising up before him, covered in matted, black jungle and silhouetted now against a darkening blue sky. Although it seemed unlikely that any ruins in this area could be those of Vitcos or Vilcabamba, the area was nevertheless still worth taking a look at. Tomorrow, Bingham decided, as he set up one of the two folding canvas cots in the tent he shared with Harry Foote, he would see what, if anything, lay high on the ridgetop above.

The next morning, July 24, the sixth day of their trip,

dawned in a cold drizzle. Arteaga shivered and seemed inclined to stay in his hut. I offered to pay him well if he would show me the ruins. He demurred and said it was too hard a climb for such a wet day. But when he found that I was willing to pay him a sol [a Peruvian silver dollar], three or four times the ordinary wage in this vicinity, he finally agreed to guide us to the ruins. No one supposed that they would be particularly interesting. And no one cared to go with me. Our Naturalist [Foote] said there were "more butterflies near the river!" and he was reasonably certain he could collect some new varieties. Our Surgeon [Erving] said he had to wash his clothes and mend them. Anyhow it was my job to investigate all reports of ruins and try to find the Inca capital.

Contrary to Bingham's account, however, Foote's job was to make collections of insects and mosses, not to look for ruins. The physician, meanwhile, who was in charge of keeping the expedition members healthy, was also working as a physical anthropologist and had been making photographic studies of native physiognomy. He wanted to remain in camp and develop some of the photos that he and other members of the expedition had taken. It was Bingham's self-appointed job, and Bingham's alone, to search for lost Inca ruins. Sitting inside his tent on his cot as a light rain fell, Bingham took out his small notebook. At the top of an unmarked page he wrote down "July 24" and below this, two names: "Maccu Picchu" and "Huaynapichu." These were Bingham's twin objectives for the day.

Around ten o'clock that morning, Bingham and Arteaga, who wore dark pants, a jacket, and a pointed hat, along with Sergeant Carrasco, who wore a dark military uniform with a row of brass buttons and a wide, flat-topped hat, set out upon the dirt road and then began clambering across a makeshift bridge of four slender logs that spanned the Urubamba River. Arteaga and Carrasco each crossed the bridge "native style," walking upright, carrying their shoes, and gripping the flexible logs with their bare feet and toes; they then waited patiently on the other side for the North American *doctor*. Wearing a broad-brimmed hat, khaki trousers, leather boots with knee-high leggings, and a jacket crammed with odds and ends, Bingham didn't trust his balance on the logs. Instead, the esteemed director of the Yale Peruvian Expedition sheepishly crawled after his companions, crossing the unsteady bridge on his hands and knees.

For the next hour and a half, the three men climbed up a steep foot trail that wound up the side of the mountain through cloud forest vegetation, with low clouds ringing the nearby peaks and with the winding, blue-green Urubamba River becoming smaller and smaller below them. When they finally reached the base of a ridgetop that formed a saddle between two peaks, Bingham was surprised to find the ridge already inhabited by three peasant families, who leased their land, it turned out, from Bingham's guide.

> Shortly after noon, just as we were completely exhausted, we reached a little grass-covered hut where several good-natured Indians, pleasantly surprised at our unexpected arrival, welcomed us with dripping gourds full of cool, delicious water. They then set before us a few cooked sweet potatoes. . . . Two pleasant Indian farmers, [Anacleto] Richarte and [Toribio] Alvarez, had recently chosen this eagle's nest for their home. They said they had found plenty of terraces here on which to grow their crops, and they were unusually free from undesirable visitors. . . . Richarte told us that they had been living here four years. It seems probable that, owing to its inaccessibility, the canyon had been unoccupied for several centuries, but with the completion of the new government road, settlers began once more to occupy this region. In time somebody clambered up the precipices and found on these slopes, at an elevation of 9,000 feet [*sic*] above the sea, an abundance of rich soil conveniently situated on artificial terraces, in a fine climate. Here the Indians had finally cleared off and burned over a few terraces and planted crops of maize, sweet and white potatoes, sugar cane, beans, peppers, tree tomatoes, and gooseberries.

From the hut where they were sitting, Bingham could see no signs of Inca ruins, although the view of the surrounding peaks and distant mountains was stupendous. Clouds hid many of the nearby peaks, alternately revealing and then obscuring the sun. Bingham continued:

> Without the slightest expectation of finding anything more interesting than . . . the ruins of two or three houses such as we had encountered at various places on the road between Ollantaytambo and Torontoy, I finally left the cool shade of the pleasant little hut and climbed farther up the ridge and around a slight promontory. Arteaga had "been here once before," and decided to rest and gossip with Richarte and Alvarez in the hut. They sent a small boy with me as a "guide." The Sergeant was in duty bound to follow, but I think he may have been a little curious to see what there was to see. Hardly had we rounded the promontory when

the character of the stonework began to improve. A flight of beautifully constructed [stone] terraces, each two hundred yards long and ten feet high, had been recently rescued from the jungle by the Indians. A veritable forest of large trees which had been growing on them for centuries had been chopped down and partly burned to make a clearing for agricultural purposes. The task had been too great for the two Indians so the tree trunks had been allowed to lie as they fell and only the smaller branches removed. But the ancient soil, carefully put in place by the Incas, was still capable of producing rich crops of maize and potatoes. However, there was nothing to be excited about. Similar flights of well-made terraces are to be seen in the upper Urubamba Valley at Pisac and Ollantaytambo, as well as opposite Torontoy.

Bingham knew very well, however, that at both Pisac and Ollantaytambo not only were there "similar flights" of giant terraces, but that extensive and rather spectacular ruins of perfectly cut stones lay nearby. In addition, near the terraces of Torontoy, Bingham had found "another group of interesting ruins, possibly once the residence of an Inca noble." Bingham had further been told by a number of different sources that there were ruins up here; he must have known, therefore, that significant ruins were probably located nearby.

We scrambled along through the dense undergrowth, climbing over terrace walls and in bamboo thickets where our guide found it easier going than I did. . . . Then the little boy urged us to climb up a steep hill over what seemed to be a flight of stone steps. Surprise followed surprise in bewildering succession. We came to a great stairway of large granite blocks. Then we walked along a path to a clearing where the Indians had planted a small vegetable garden. Suddenly we found ourselves standing in front of the ruins of two of the finest and most interesting buildings in ancient America. Made of beautiful white granite, the walls contained blocks of Cyclopean size, higher than a man. The sight held me spellbound. . . . I could scarcely believe my senses as I examined the larger blocks in the lower course, and estimated that they must weigh from ten to fifteen tons each. Would anyone believe what I had found? Fortunately, in this land where accuracy of reporting what one has seen is not a prevailing characteristic of travelers, I had a good camera and the sun was shining.

For the next five hours, Bingham followed the boy along the ridgetop, examining ruin after ruin. With his Kodak camera and the folding camera tripod he had brought along, Bingham began snapping the first photos of the site that would later become a household name: "Machu Picchu," or "Old Peak." Always meticulous in his habits, Bingham was careful to jot down notes and descriptions of all of his photos:

> Some structures of stone laid in clay. Others nicely squared like Cuzco. Niches nicely made like Ollantaytambo. Cylinders common inside and out. Better fashioned than those at Choq. . . . Views on both sides. Whole place extremely inaccessible.

Similar to his experience at Choqquequirau, Bingham discovered that he was not the first explorer to visit the ruins at Machu Picchu. On the wall of one of the Inca temples, in fact, Bingham soon discovered that a previous visitor had scrawled his name with what looked to be charcoal, along with a date:

> Lizarraga, 1902

Whoever this person Lizarraga was, he had obviously visited the ruins of Machu Picchu nine years earlier. Bingham carefully jotted down the explorer's name, then continued taking notes, snapping photos, and making a rough sketch of the site. At around five in the afternoon, Bingham, Sergeant Carrasco, and Arteaga left the peasant's hut and began making their way back down to the valley floor, moving much more rapidly now as they were aided, not hindered, by gravity. Back in camp, Bingham went inside his tent, then came out and paid Arteaga with a shiny silver sol. As the sun sank and the expedition members prepared for dinner, high above them, beside the ruins of an ancient and unknown Inca city, peasant families cooked pots of stew inside their huts, using dried wood for kindling and letting the smoke percolate through the grass roofs of their homes, much as the Incas who had inhabited this ridgetop had done some four centuries earlier.

Despite his later claims that he had immediately recognized the significance of the ruins at Machu Picchu, Bingham was actually disappointed that the ruins he had just discovered were not the ones he had been searching for. Comparing what he had seen up on the ridgetop of Machu Picchu with the various clues he had culled from the chronicles of Calancha, Ocampo, and Titu Cusi, Bingham found little in common between the ruins he had just visited and the chroniclers' descriptions of Manco Inca's two lost cities.

> When I first saw the remarkable citadel of Machu Picchu perched on a narrow ridge two thousand feet above the river, I wondered if it could be the place to which that old soldier, Baltasar de Ocampo, a member of Captain Garcia's [de Loyola's 1572] expedition, was referring when he said: "The Inca Tupac Amaru was there in the fortress of Pitcos [Vitcos], which is on a very high mountain, whence the view commanded a great part of the province of Vilcapampa. Here there was an extensive level space, with very sumptuous and majestic buildings, erected with great skill and art, all the lintels of the doors, the principal as well as the ordinary ones, being of marble, elaborately carved." Could it be that "Picchu" was the modern variant of "Pitcos"? To be sure, the white granite of which the temples and palaces of Machu Picchu are constructed might easily pass for marble. The difficulty about fitting Ocampo's description to Machu Picchu, however, was that there was no difference between the lintels of the doors and the walls themselves. Furthermore, there is no "white rock over a spring of water" which Calancha says was "near Viticos [Vitcos]." There is no Pucyura in this neighborhood. In fact, the canyon of the Urubamba does not satisfy the geographical requirements of Viticos. Although containing ruins of surpassing interest, Machu Picchu did not represent that last Inca capital for which we were searching. We had not yet found Manco's palace.

The very next day, in fact, Bingham and his team decided to move on, with Bingham intent on continuing the search for Vitcos and for the white rock located over a natural spring. If he could find those two sites, Bingham believed, then he was certain that Vilcabamba must be nearby. As Bingham waited impatiently for his Peruvian assistants to break camp, he ironically had no idea whatsoever that, on only his sixth day out of Cuzco, he had already found the ruins that would forever link his name with one of the most famous lost cities in the world. So slight seemed to be his level of excitement, in fact, that Bingham's friend Harry Foote had written in his diary the day after Bingham's discovery of Machu Picchu "No special things to note."

For the next week, Bingham, Foote, and Carrasco continued their search for Vitcos and for Vilcabamba, paying local guides who claimed they knew the whereabouts of nearby ruins but discovering very little in the process. The three men spent days clambering up the slopes of nearby mountains, yet virtually every time they returned empty-handed. Gradually, the explorers made their way down the Urubamba River as far as the hacienda of Santa Ana, fully aware now that they were on the edge of the upper Amazon Basin. Here, they no doubt saw troops of thickly furred woolly monkeys in the jungle-covered hills, while along the muddy riverbanks they must have encountered abundant tracks of tapirs and peccaries. As vividly colored macaws squawked and flew overhead in flocks and pairs, in a relatively short distance they had traveled from the high, snowy peaks of the Andes all the way down to the Amazon Basin. The Amazon stretched for nearly two thousand miles more, all the way to the Atlantic Ocean. Bingham was certain, however, that somewhere amid the rugged eastern foothills of this massive mountain chain must be hidden the two lost cities he was looking for.

Heading up the Urubamba River again, Bingham and his party eventually came to a bridge that they had passed earlier and that they had learned from the locals was called Chuquichaca. Bingham had immediately recognized that this was one of the ancient place names that he had been seeking, as he knew that the sixteenth-century Spanish captain Baltasar de Ocampo had written "They [the Incas] guarded the bridge of Chuqi-chaca, over the Vilcamayu [Urubamba] River, which is the key to the province of Vilcapampa." Ocampo had also written that the Spanish general Martín Hurtado de Arbieto—who had led the final 1572 campaign that had sacked Vilcabamba and captured Tupac Amaru—had "marched from Cusco down the valley by Yucay and Ollantay-tampu to the bridge of Chuqui-chaca and the province of Vilcapampa."

Encouraged by the fact that they had located "the key to the province" of Vilcabamba, Bingham and his team now began to slowly head up into the Vilcabamba River Valley, one mule step at a time. By now, Bingham had developed a simple yet effective strategy for locating lost Inca ruins: first, he asked the people who lived in the area and who had walked and clambered over most of the surrounding hills and trails. If the locals claimed they knew of nearby ruins, then Bingham offered them a monetary reward if they would take him there. Second, Bingham always sought linguistic help, either from Sergeant Carrasco, who spoke Quechua in addition to Spanish, or from the local officials and landowners, who often spoke both languages as well. Bingham had quickly learned that the locals in the area were often much more fluent in the Incas' ancient Quechua language than in Spanish. To obtain the maximum amount of information, then, Bingham always tried to question his informants in the language they were most fluent in. Now, entering the Vilcabamba Valley, Bingham soon put his strategy to good use.

Our next stop was at Lucma, the home of *Teniente Gobernador* [Evaristo] Mogrovejo. We offered to pay him a *gratificacion* of a *sol,* or Peruvian silver dollar, for every ruin to which he would take us and double that amount if the locality should prove to contain particularly interesting ruins. This aroused all his business instincts. He summoned his *alcaldes* [local mayors] and other well-informed Indians to appear and be interviewed. They told us there were "many ruins" hereabouts! Being a practical man himself, Mogrovejo had never taken any interest in ruins. Now he saw the chance not only to make money out of the ancient sites, but also to gain official favor by carrying out with unexampled vigor the orders of his superior, the sub-prefect of Quillabamba. So he exerted himself to the utmost in our behalf.

Two days later, on August 8, some fifteen days after discovering Machu Picchu, Bingham left with several guides while Harry Foote went off collecting insects.

We . . . forded the Vilcabamba River and soon had an uninterrupted view up the valley to a high truncated hill, its top partly covered with a scrubby growth of trees and bushes, its sides steep and rocky. We were told that the name of the hill was "Rosaspata," a word of modern hybrid origin—*pata* being Quichua for "hill," while *rosas* is the Spanish word for "roses." Mogrovejo said his Indians told him that on the "Hill of

Roses" there were more ruins. We hoped it might be true, especially as we now learned that the village at the foot of the hill, and across the river, was called Puquiura. . . . It was to a Puquiura that Friar Marcos [García] came in 1566 [sic]. If this were his Puquiura, then Vitcos must be nearby, for he and Friar Diego [Ortiz] walked with their famous procession of converts from Puquiura to the "House of the Sun," which was "close to Vitcos."

Following his guides up the hill, Bingham soon discovered an extensive level area on top, and also an ancient square, with the remains of large, ruined, Inca-style buildings flanking it. One building, which Bingham noted was "indeed a residence fit for a royal Inca," was 245 feet long by forty-three feet wide and had thirty trapezoidal doorways perforating it. While the walls of the buildings were not of the classic imperial-style Inca stonework, many of the doorways nevertheless were cut from white blocks of granite and were finished with all of the Incas' finest stoneworking techniques. From this hilltop vantage point, Bingham could look out over the entire Vilcabamba Valley; he couldn't help now but compare the ruins of Rosaspata with how Captain Baltasar de Ocampo had described Vitcos more than three hundred years earlier:

> the fortress of Pitcos [Vitcos], which is on a very high mountain whence the view commanded a great part of the province of Vilcapampa. Here there was an extensive level space, with very sumptuous and majestic buildings, erected with great skill and art, all the lintels of the doors, as well the principal as the ordinary ones, being of marble, elaborately carved.

The ruined city where Bingham stood now was indeed on a very "high mountain," commanded a view of "a great part of the province of Vilcapampa," and contained an "extensive level space," with the remains of large, once majestic buildings. Although the doorways of the ruins at Rosaspata were not made of marble—indeed there was no marble whatsoever to be found in the entire province—they *were* made of finely grained white granite. In addition, because of the roughness of the surrounding walls, the doorways' perfectly cut proportions and finishing clearly stood out. What's more, a village called Puquiura lay nearby—exactly as had been described in the chronicles. All that was needed now to prove that Rosaspata was the site of ancient Vitcos was to find a spring of water nearby, overlain by a giant "white rock" shrine that the chroniclers had called Chuquipalpa. If he could find the Incas' ancient shrine, then that would mean that Rosaspata was indeed Vitcos—the city where Manco Inca's son Titu Cusi had been captured by the Spaniards and where Manco himself later had been murdered by seven Spanish renegades.

Two distinct versions exist as to what happened next. According to Bingham's account, on the following day, August 9, he and the lieutenant governor, Mogrovejo, followed a local guide who led them to a nearby stream. They then followed the stream through thick woods until they came to a clearing where, in its midst, rose a great white rock, completely covered in Inca-style carvings. Bingham excitedly approached the massive rock, which stood about twenty feet high and was some sixty feet in length and thirty feet in breadth. Sure enough, alongside one end of the rock he found a pool of spring water, while flanking it on two sides he found the stone ruins of what certainly could have been an Inca temple of the sun.

Bingham still had with him the carefully copied passages of Father Calancha's account of the Inca shrine at Chuquipalpa:

> Near Vitcos, in a village called Chuquipalpa, was a temple of the Sun, and within it a white rock above a spring of water where the Devil appeared. . . . [And] who gave answers from a white rock . . . and on various occasions he revealed himself. The stone was above a spring of water and they worshipped the water as a divine thing.

Questioning his local guide, Bingham was told that the area was called Chuquipalta—an almost identical match with Calancha's Chuquipalpa.

> It was late on the afternoon of August 9, 1911, when I first saw this remarkable shrine. . . . With the contemporary accounts in our hands and the physical evidence before our eyes we could now be fairly sure that we had located one of Manco's capitals and the residence known to the Spaniards, visited by the [Spanish] missionaries and ambassadors as well as by the [Spanish] refugees who had sought safety here from the fol-

lowers of Pizarro and had unfortunately put Manco to death. While it [Rosaspata] was too near Puquiura to be his "principal capital," Vilca-pampa, it certainly was Vitcos.

Only sixteen days after discovering Machu Picchu, Bingham had now confirmed what he no doubt considered a far more important discovery—he had finally located the lost Inca city of Vitcos.

In the second version of the story, however, it was Bingham's friend Harry Foote who actually discovered the Chuquipalta shrine. According to Foote's journal, the day before Bingham's trip to the shrine Foote had gone off looking for butterflies while Bingham had spent the day investigating the ruins at Rosaspata. Foote later wrote the following entry in his journal about his activities that day:

> I went out collecting and Hi[ram] went to ruins [of Rosaspata] which he [had] located the day before. I spotted a lot of new ones up in a high pastured valley between the mountains. A spring starts at the ruins. There is a fine rock in the ruins which is cut somewhat like the Ro-dadero in Cuzco on one side and curiously cut on the other side.* Very level terraces and heavy stone work separating them beyond. A number of seats cut in the large rock and in others—one in a rock which juts into a room. There were but few species of butterflies and I got all but one or two.

According to Bingham's personal friend and neighbor, then, Foote had inadvertently discovered the Inca shrine of Chuquipalta a day before Bing-ham claimed that *he* had discovered it. Foote no doubt had told Bingham about his discovery, which had surely prompted Bingham to head directly there the next day. In his published accounts, however, Bingham carefully edited Foote out of the story, simplifying the narrative and then rewriting the sequence of events so that he could portray himself as the first scientist to discover the Incas' ancient shrine. Although there is no doubt, of course,

---

* The Rodadero Foote referred to is a rocky knoll across the plain from the fortress of Saqsaywaman. The Incas carved a variety of shapes into the various outcroppings of the Rodadero, including "throne-like" seats similar to those they carved into the great stone of Chuquipalta.

that Bingham was the first scientist in over three hundred years to simultaneously locate and correctly identify the sites of both Vitcos and the shrine of Chuquipalta, Harry Foote was nevertheless the first scientist to locate the Chuquipalta shrine itself. Because Bingham wrote the only popular account of their expedition, however, Foote never received any credit for his part in the discovery.

In any case, no one can contest the fact that, in just over two weeks of hunting for ancient Inca ruins in Peru, Hiram Bingham and his team had already made a series of spectacular discoveries, finding first the ruins of Machu Picchu, then Vitcos, and the shrine of Chuquipalta. Despite his impressive trio of discoveries, however, Bingham was still eager to locate Manco's lost city of Vilcabamba. And, since the chronicles stated that Vilcabamba was only two days' march away from Vitcos, Bingham knew that the ancient city must be close. The question, however, was in what direction? And by what trail? Once again, Bingham used his strategy of pumping information from local informants and offering monetary rewards to anyone who would agree to show him the location of nearby ruins. A week earlier, while still in the lower Urubamba River Valley, Bingham and Foote had stayed with the owner of a hacienda in Santa Ana.

When Don Pedro Duque of Santa Ana was helping us to identify places mentioned in Calancha and Ocampo, the reference to "Vilcabamba Viejo" or Old Vilcapampa, was supposed by two of his informants to point to a place called Conservidayoc. Don Pedro told us that in 1902 López Torres, who had traveled much in the *montaña* looking for rubber trees, reported the discovery there of the ruins of an Inca city.

Elsewhere, Bingham wrote,

They all agreed that "if only Señor López Torres were alive he could have been of great service" to us, as "he had prospected for mines and rubber in those parts more than anyone else, and had once seen some Inca ruins in the forest!"

Thus, several days after discovering Vitcos, Bingham and his team headed further up the valley to the village of San Francisco de la Victoria de Vil-

cabamba, also known as Vilcabamba the New. After the Spaniards had
sacked and plundered Manco's Vilcabamba, Bingham had learned, they had
moved the remaining native population to a new location, higher up in the
Andes and closer to Cuzco. Discovering silver mines nearby, they named the
town Vilcabamba the New, in contrast to Manco's burned and sacked capital, which they now referred to as Vilcabamba the Old. Eventually, as the location of Manco's abandoned capital was gradually forgotten and the city
became overgrown with jungle, all that remained was the town of Vilcabamba the New. Three centuries later, Hiram Bingham found that the latter now consisted of a collection of high-gabled, thatched-roofed houses,
an old ruined church, a school, and a small post office where Bingham was
able to post some mail. Bingham wasted no time in enlisting the aid of the
local governor, Señor Condoré, in order to grill the local inhabitants for
more information.

> On the day following our arrival at the town of Vilcabamba [the New],
> the *Gobernador,* Condoré, taking counsel with his chief assistant, had
> summoned the wisest Indians living in the vicinity, including a very pic-
> turesque old fellow whose name, Quispi Cusi, was strongly reminiscent
> of the days of Titu Cusi. It was explained to him that this was a very
> solemn occasion and that an official inquiry was in progress. He took off
> his hat—but not his knitted cap—and endeavored to the best of his
> ability to answer our questions about the surrounding country. It was he
> who said that the Inca Tupac Amaru once lived at Rosaspata. He had
> never heard of Vitcos or Vilcapampa Viejo, but he admitted that there
> were ruins in the *montaña* [jungle] near the village of Conservidayoc.
> Other Indians were questioned by Condoré. Several had heard of the
> ruins of Conservidayoc, but, apparently, none of them, nor anyone in
> the village had actually seen the ruins or visited their immediate vicinity.
> . . . One of our informants said the Inca city was called Espíritu Pampa,
> or the "Pampa of Ghosts." . . . Although no one at Vilcabamba [the
> New] had seen the ruins, they said that at [the village of] Pampaconas,
> there were Indians who had actually been to Conservidayoc. Accord-
> ingly we decided to go there immediately.

The next day, Bingham, Foote, Sergeant Carrasco, a muleteer, two local
officials, and nine pack animals loaded with food, equipment, and camping

supplies left the old Spanish mining town, located at 11,750 feet, and headed off toward the village of Pampaconas. Bingham hoped that he might find there someone who knew more about where to find Vilcabamba Viejo, Old Vilcabamba, the final refuge of the last four Inca emperors: Manco Inca, Sayri Tupac, Titu Cusi, and Tupac Amaru. After crossing over the 12,500-foot Colpacasa Pass, Bingham and his party began heading down into the adjacent valley. Soon, the trail became a slippery, muddy mess that zigzagged down the slopes. Just before nightfall, they arrived at Pampaconas, which consisted of a scattering of huts set upon a grassy hillside at an elevation of ten thousand feet.

> We were conducted to the dwelling of a stocky, well-built Indian named Guzmán, the most reliable man in the village, who had been selected to be the head of the party of carriers that was to accompany us to Conservidayoc. . . . We carried on a most interesting conversation. . . . He had been to Conservidayoc and had himself actually seen Inca ruins at Espíritu Pampa. At last the mythical "Pampa of Ghosts" began to take on, in our minds, an aspect of reality.

Through sheer persistence and the relentless grilling of informants, Bingham now found himself employing a local guide who claimed to know where the rumored Inca ruins were located, some two to four days ahead. Could these be the ruins of Manco's capital of Vilcabamba? Or would this turn out to be another wild-goose chase? Bingham was determined to find out. Three days later, amid thick, warm jungle at some 4,900 feet in elevation, Bingham, Foote, and the rest of the team arrived at the house of a local planter named Saavedra, who had cleared parts of the surrounding jungle in order to grow bananas, sugarcane, coffee, sweet potatoes, tobacco, peanuts, and manioc.

> It is difficult to describe our feelings as we accepted Saavedra's invitation to make ourselves at home, and sat down to an abundant meal of boiled chicken, rice, and sweet cassava *(manioc.)* Saavedra gave us to understand that we were not only most welcome to anything he had, but that he would do everything to enable us to see the ruins, which were, it seemed, at Espíritu Pampa, some distance farther down the valley, to be

reached only by a hard trail passable for barefooted savages, but scarcely available for us unless we chose to go a good part of the distance on hands and knees.

The next day, Bingham was guided to the tiny village called Espíritu Pampa, consisting of nothing more than a number of huts of a local ethnic group called the Campas—natives who wore long cotton cloaks down to their ankles, had long black hair, and hunted in the forest with bows and arrows. The Incas, Bingham knew, had allied themselves with Antis Indians in the Amazon jungle. Perhaps the Campas were their descendants. In any case, the Campas now guided Bingham's party through dense rain forest until suddenly they halted. There, almost indistinguishable from the surrounding foliage, rose the unmistakable form of a roughly hewn stone wall.

Half an hour's scramble through the jungle brought us to a . . . natural terrace on the banks of a little tributary of the Pampaconas [River]. They called it Eromboni [Pampa]. Here we found several artificial terraces and the rough foundations of a long, rectangular building 192 feet by 24 feet. . . . Near by was a typical Inca fountain with three stone spouts. . . . Hidden behind a curtain of hanging vines and thickets so dense we could not see more than a few feet in any direction, the savages showed us the ruins of a group of Inca stone houses whose walls were still standing in fine condition. . . . The walls were of rough stone laid in adobe. Like some of the Inca buildings at Ollantaytambo, the lintels of the doors were made of three or four narrow uncut ashlars. . . . Below it was a partly enclosed fountain or bathhouse, with a stone spout and a stone-lined basin. The shapes of the houses, their general arrangement, the niches, stone roof-pegs and lintels, all pointed to Inca builders. In the buildings we picked up several fragments of Inca pottery.

Although the buildings appeared to have been constructed by the Incas, their architectural style was nevertheless rough. Most of the walls were made of uncut stones laid in mud and had none of the fine, classic Inca stonework such as Bingham had seen at Machu Picchu or in Cuzco. Giant strangler figs towered above while thick vines coiled and twirled down from the canopy to the ground. The swollen roots of strangler figs had even pierced some of the ruined walls. Spider monkey calls drifted in, causing the Campa natives to occasionally pause and listen, then to point up at the canopy, speaking excitedly to one another in a language that, to Bingham, sounded "like a succession of low grunts, breathings, and gutturals."

As the Campas cleared the vegetation and revealed more stone walls, the metal of their machetes occasionally twanging against the stones, Bingham couldn't help but wonder whether this roughly hewn, difficult-to-find cluster of buildings could actually be the Vilcabamba the Old described in the chronicles. Having begun his expedition in the frigid highlands and now finding himself in a greenhouse-like environment where he was constantly swatting at flies, bees, and mosquitoes, Bingham had his doubts. He found it difficult, in fact, to believe that

> the [Inca] priests and Virgins of the Sun . . . who fled from cold Cuzco with Manco . . . would have cared to live in the hot valley of Espíritu Pampa. The difference in climate is as great as that between Scotland and Egypt. They [the Incas] would not have found in Espíritu Pampa the food which they liked. Furthermore, they could have found the seclusion and safety which they craved just as well in several other parts of the province, particularly at Machu Picchu, together with a cool, bracing climate and food stuffs more nearly resembling those to which they were accustomed. Finally, Calancha says "Vilcabamba the Old" was the "largest city" in the province, a term far more applicable to Machu Picchu . . . than to Espíritu Pampa.

Indeed, after two days of clearing the area, Bingham and his team had found only a few dozen buildings; the jungle, however, was so thick that it was difficult to know unequivocally if these were the only structures around. Still, it was hard for Bingham to imagine—even if there *were* more buildings—that such rough ruins could have ever constituted a major Inca capital or could have housed a succession of Inca emperors. Besides, an additional feature that didn't correspond to the chronicles' descriptions of Vilcabamba was that it had taken Bingham and his team *five days* to travel from Puquiura to Espíritu Pampa, whereas Calancha had stated that the journey from Puquiura to Vilcabamba had taken either "two long days" or three regular ones.

On the other hand, Bingham had found roughly made Spanish roofing tiles on the ground near some of the ruins.

> With one exception everything about the fragments of pottery and the architecture of the houses was unquestionably Inca. This exception was the presence of a dozen or fifteen roughly made Spanish roofing tiles of varying sizes. On account of the small number of them . . . it seemed to me possible that these had been made experimentally by recent Peruvians or possibly early Spanish missionaries, who might have come to this place centuries ago. The Indians could offer no explanation of the mystery. Apparently none of the houses ever had tile roofs, as the number of fragments was not enough to cover more than a few square feet, and nearly all were outside the buildings.

Before their contact with the Spaniards, the Incas had constructed their buildings with typical, high-gabled, thatched roofs; they did not use clay tiles, an idea that was only later imported from Spain. Once the Spaniards had occupied Cuzco and other Inca cities, however, the Spaniards had gradually replaced the Incas' traditional thatched roofs with roofing tiles, which they preferred for keeping out the rain. "Perhaps an Inca who had seen the new red tiled roofs of Cuzco had tried to reproduce them here in the jungle, but without success," Bingham wrote, not believing their presence to be especially significant.

Using interpreters to question the local Campa natives, Bingham repeatedly asked them what name they used to refer to this site. The Campas responded with two names: the first was in Spanish and meant "Plain of Ghosts" while the second was in Quechua, meaning "Sacred Plain." Bingham jotted both down. "Espíritu Pampa or Vilcabamba is the name of the whole place," he wrote in his notebook. Despite the Campas' use of the Inca name Vilcabamba, however, Bingham remained unsure as to the actual identity of the ruins he had found; they would simply have to await further study.

After spending two days at Espíritu Pampa, Bingham began running low on food. He and his team, therefore, soon began the long, slow trek back up into the highlands and eventually back to the United States. Although Bingham would lead two more expeditions to Peru—in 1912, and in 1914—

1915—and during those expeditions would discover more ruins associated with Machu Picchu, he would never again duplicate the amazing series of important discoveries he made during the short, intensely fertile, four-week period between July and August of 1911. In April 1913, *National Geographic* magazine would devote an entire issue to Bingham's discovery of Machu Picchu, thus officially introducing Bingham's lost city to the outside world. The spectacular, photogenic ruins, often smothered in clouds, would soon become South America's most famous landmark and a worldwide icon; their discovery would also make Hiram Bingham famous. Yet although the ruins of Machu Picchu were visually spectacular, Bingham nevertheless struggled to find an explanation for them. As a historian, Bingham was surprised that he was unable to find either Machu Picchu or Huayna Picchu described in the Spanish chronicles.

How could ruins that looked so spectacular, Bingham wondered, not have an equally spectacular history? Bingham, of course, was neither an Inca specialist, nor an archaeologist, nor was he an anthropologist. As Machu Picchu's fame continued to grow, however, so, too, did the pressure upon Bingham to devise a theory to explain the ruins' significance. Eventually—and perhaps partially in response to that pressure—Bingham devised a set of theories that were almost as spectacular as the ruins of Machu Picchu themselves.

Far from being an isolated, little-known citadel located on the edge of the Inca Empire, Bingham claimed, Machu Picchu had actually been the original epicenter of that empire. What Paris was to France and Rome was to Italy, Bingham boldly implied, Machu Picchu was to the Inca Empire. Based upon the flimsiest of evidence, Bingham eventually proposed that the city he had discovered had actually been the first city the Incas had inhabited; thus, according to Bingham, Machu Picchu was the cradle of the entire Inca civilization. Further, based upon what later turned out to be one of his team member's erroneous examination of bones recovered from numerous burials at the site, Bingham theorized that Machu Picchu had been occupied exclusively by female "Virgins of the Sun." After Manco Inca's failed siege of Cuzco, Bingham asserted, Manco had retreated to the ruins of Machu Picchu, the site that, Bingham now believed, was Vilcabamba. Even after Tupac Amaru had been executed, Bingham said, the history of Machu Picchu had still not ended. One of the ironies of Inca history, Bingham explained, was that the citadel that had given birth to the Inca Empire had in the end witnessed that same empire's last breath.

> In its last state it [Machu Picchu] became the home and refuge of the Virgins of the Sun, priestesses of the most humane cult of aboriginal America. Here, concealed in a canyon of remarkable grandeur, protected by art and nature, these consecrated women gradually passed away, leaving no known descendants, nor any records other than the masonry walls and artifacts to be described in another volume. Whoever they were, whatever name be finally assigned to this site by future historians, of this I feel sure—that few romances can ever surpass that of the granite citadel on top of the beetling precipices of Machu Picchu, the crown of Inca Land.

It was a decidedly romantic story and one that Bingham clung to until he died, in 1956, at the age of eighty-one. In the last book Bingham wrote on the subject, *Lost City of the Incas,* published in 1948 when he was seventy-three years old, Bingham staked his worldwide reputation on the fact that Machu Picchu was indeed

> The "Lost City of the Incas," favorite residence of the last Emperors, site of temples and palaces built of white granite in the most inaccessible part of the grand canyon of the Urubamba; a holy sanctuary to which only nobles, priests, and the Virgins of the Sun were admitted. It was once called Vilcapampa but is known today as Machu Picchu.

Such was Hiram Bingham's stature in the archaeological world that few dared question his interpretation of his own discovery, at least during his lifetime. Only a year after Bingham's death, however, in 1957, another American explorer arrived in Peru—an explorer who quickly began to suspect that the great Hiram Bingham had gotten it completely and utterly wrong.

17 ❖ VILCABAMBA
REDISCOVERED

"'Don't think you can just crash around blindly in the jungle and find anything,' he [Savoy] continued. 'You can't. Listen to the campesinos. They know where everything is. Pay attention to their tips and look for old roads. Follow them. They all go somewhere. . . . One thing though: don't trust anyone.' . . . It was the best 30 seconds of advice he could possibly have given us."

VINCENT LEE, RECOUNTING A CONVERSATION
WITH GENE SAVOY, *FORGOTTEN VILCABAMBA*, 2000

"When night was come, the Earth rocked to and fro as if seeking to unite itself with the Light. And the stars fell from heaven in a great shower. And an angel appeared to the Man [Gene Savoy] in his dreams, saying that he should await the signal of God, the cross by which the world was enlightened, at the tomb of the [Christ] Child [Jamil] two days hence."

GENE SAVOY, JUNGLE EXPLORER AND MESSENGER
OF GOD, *JAMIL: THE CHILD CHRIST*, 1976

FIFTY-SIX YEARS AFTER HIRAM BINGHAM'S DISCOVERY OF Machu Picchu, a twenty-nine-year-old American named Gene Savoy arrived in Peru, determined, like Bingham, to discover lost ruins. Six-foot-one, handsome, with an athletic physique, swept-back brown hair, and a certain resemblance to the movie star Errol Flynn, Savoy had recently lost his home, his business, his finances, and his wife. Having hit rock bottom, he had come to Peru to reinvent himself as an explorer.

As unlikely as his decision may have seemed, the truth of the matter was that if you wanted to become an explorer in 1957, Peru was an excellent place to be. Hiram Bingham's final book on his discovery of Machu Picchu, *Lost City of the Incas,* had been published nine years earlier and had become an immediate bestseller. Because of it and of other publications, the ruins of Machu Picchu were now known throughout the world. Bingham himself had returned to Peru in 1948 to help inaugurate the opening of a paved road that allowed an increasing number of tourists to arrive by bus at Machu Picchu.

Meanwhile, in 1947, the Norwegian explorer Thor Heyerdahl had sailed a primitive-style raft, called the *Kon-Tiki,* from Peru to the Marquesas Islands in the South Pacific, hoping to provide evidence that ancient Peruvian cultures could have had contact with islands in the South Seas. Heyerdahl's book about that voyage, *Kon-Tiki,* had also become an immediate bestseller and was published in more than sixty languages. In addition, a documentary Heyerdahl made of the voyage won an Academy Award in 1952 and had been shown in theaters throughout the world. Three years later, in 1955, the American writer-adventurer Victor von Hagen had published *Highway of the Sun,* an account of his exploration of more than 25,000 miles of ancient Inca roads, during which he had discovered many ruins. Two years later, as Gene Savoy stepped off a plane in Lima—Pizarro's former City of the Kings—one thing was certain: a worldwide audience was primed and waiting for more sensational discoveries from Peru. Savoy merely had to find them.

Unlike Hiram Bingham, Savoy possessed no college degrees, having dropped out of the University of Oregon in his sophomore year. Savoy and Bingham did, however, share a marked similarity: both had experienced a spiritual crisis in their youth over whether to forsake the physical pleasures of the world and instead consecrate their lives to God. Perhaps that was not so surprising in the case of Bingham, who, after all, was the product of two generations of Protestant missionaries. Bingham, in fact, while still an undergraduate at Yale had struggled over whether he should become a missionary. "I have been led to consecrate myself anew to the service of my Master," the young Bingham had written to his father. "It is my purpose to save souls for Christ. . . . Oh father, pray for me that I may be kept by the power of the Holy Spirit from all unrighteousness. I do so want to do His will." Six months after receiving his undergraduate degree, however, Bingham had met his future wife. Not long afterward, he switched from wanting to save people's souls to the more worldly pursuit of chasing after fame, status, and fortune by, among other things, exploring for lost ruins in Peru.

Like Bingham, Savoy had experienced a similar religious calling. During his school years, Savoy had developed a strong desire to become a Catholic priest. In college, however, Savoy wrote a paper in one of his religion classes, taking an unusual slant while comparing Christianity with other religions. At least one of his professors labeled Savoy's ideas "heretical." A priest who had befriended the young student suggested that Savoy take some time off from the university. Savoy departed—and never went back.

For much of the next decade, he worked as a journalist and editor for a variety of small newspapers, traveling widely throughout the Pacific Northwest. As he honed his writing skills, Savoy found himself becoming more and more interested in Native American cultures and in local archaeology. Savoy later wrote:

> I was a member of the Oregon Archaeological Society and often joined in on weekend digs where we were overjoyed if we found a few bits of broken bone or a few arrowheads after a hard day's screening. But I grew tired of excavation and took up archaeological photography because it gave me the freedom to roam about, which was more to my nature.

When in 1957 his marriage ended and his finances collapsed, Savoy was forced once again to reevaluate the direction of his life.

> Almost thirty and enflamed with restlessness, an education seemed tame in the light of what I really wanted to do. "Why not strike out and go to Mexico or South America and explore for lost cities as you've always wanted to do?" I asked myself. As a journalist and photographer, perhaps I could write and illustrate articles on a free-lance basis, picking up on the job what had to be learned about archaeology and anthropology.

The more I thought about it, the more intriguing the idea became. I was determined to go.

Savoy eventually ended up in Lima, where he soon lined up freelance work with the *Peruvian Times,* a weekly English-language newspaper. He next founded a club, called the Andean Explorers Club, and appointed himself president and chief explorer. Not long afterward, Savoy met and married Elvira "Dolly" Clarke Cabada, a woman from a powerful and wealthy Peruvian family. In 1960, the couple and their newly born son, Jamil, settled in the small town of Yungay, located in central Peru at the base of the massive Cordillera Blanca, the White Mountains—a particularly impressive stretch of the Andes. Savoy had chosen Yungay because it was near the center of the ancient Chavin civilization, which had flourished some three thousand years earlier, and which intrigued him. A number of decades earlier, a Peruvian archaeologist, Julio C. Tello, had developed the rather unorthodox theory that the Chavin civilization may have originally developed not in the Andes, which was the traditional view, but rather to the east of the Andes, in the jungles of the upper Amazon. It was just the sort of contrarian thinking that fascinated Savoy. Indeed, Tello's theory would influence Savoy's entire career as an explorer.

On January 10, 1962, however, fate dealt Savoy a second blow that once again triggered both a life crisis and an abrupt shift in his thinking. High up on the face of nearby Huascarán Mountain, which at 22,205 feet is Peru's highest peak, a mass of ice and snow suddenly broke loose and created a massive avalanche that crashed down and engulfed the nearby village of Ranrahirca. More than four thousand people were killed. When sickness and disease later broke out among the survivors, Savoy's son—three-year-old Jamil—grew sick and died.

Most parents, of course, are deeply shocked and saddened by the loss of a child. Savoy's grief, however, seemed to trigger a fundamental shift in his perceptions. Despite his aborted college career, Savoy had never lost his interest in theology. Not long after settling in Peru, in fact, Savoy had founded the Andean Mystery Group, a sort of New Age church long before such terminology existed, and of which Savoy became the ordained minister. Now, however, stricken by the sudden death of his son, Savoy began teaching his religious group that his son, Jamil, had actually been a second Christ, and that he—Gene Savoy, who himself had never known his father—was the father of the new Messiah.

In a book he later published in 1976, which he titled *Jamil: The Child Christ*, Savoy informed the world that soon after his son, Jamil, had been born, his infant son had communicated to him—apparently through some nonverbal means—that he was the new Messiah. The tiny infant had also informed Savoy that he was not destined to live long in this world but that Savoy, his father, had been chosen by God to be God's own personal messenger. Savoy wrote that prior to his son's death, Jamil had communicated to him a wealth of detailed information about the spiritual history of humanity, information that Savoy later dutifully wrote down in a series of seven books called *The Prophecies*. Just as Christ had been considered a heretic among the Jews yet had been accepted as the Messiah by his followers, Savoy believed that he, too, was not a heretic but rather God's messenger among the world's Christians. Savoy's years of religious study had obviously reached a sudden and acute apotheosis; at the age of thirty-four, the explorer Gene Savoy was now also in direct communication with God.

Whether consciously or unconsciously, Savoy was reenacting what the founders of hundreds of religions have done since the very first religion appeared on earth. Savoy, after all, was a student of the subject and had always been interested in comparing different faiths. The God of the Old Testament, after all, had "revealed" himself to Moses in the form of a burning bush. Muhammad had likewise told his followers that his new religion, Islam, had been "revealed" to him by an angel. Joseph Smith, the twenty-two-year-old founder of Mormonism, similarly informed the world that in 1827 he had copied the content of the Book of Mormon from golden tablets that an angel had led him to near Palmyra, New York. Gene Savoy was thus well aware of the fact that religions usually begin as cults formed around a charismatic leader, one who offers his or her followers a new way to attain a higher level of spirituality. All the world's great religions had begun as cults that had then gradually transformed into larger sects. As more and more members were gathered and as the new theology was formalized, the sect gradually grew until it ultimately became a church. Savoy's claim that God had contacted him through his dead infant son and had chosen him to be his messenger, Savoy no doubt realized, was at least as valid as any older religious claim. Indeed, Savoy clearly intended to create a new branch of Christianity—offering his departed son as the new church's Messiah and himself as a religious leader who had a direct link to God.

While busy developing his spiritual ideas, Savoy nevertheless continued with his secular research into Peru's ancient cultures. Not surprisingly, Savoy was curious to know more about the history of what were by now Peru's most famous ruins—those of Machu Picchu. Savoy therefore began reading Bingham's account of his 1911 discovery. As skeptical about the accepted truths of ancient Peruvian history as he was about the accepted truths of religion, however, Savoy quickly realized that Bingham's claim that Machu Picchu was Manco Inca's lost city of Vilcabamba was far from proven. In reading Bingham's final popular book on the subject, *Lost City of the Incas,* Savoy was struck by the fact that Bingham had admitted that he had initially been confused about the identities of the two groups of ruins that he had found: one in the cloud forest at 8,000 feet at Machu Picchu and the other at 4,900 feet in the jungles of Espíritu Pampa. "Was this the 'Vilcabamba Viejo' of Father Calancha," Bingham had written about the Espíritu Pampa ruins, "that 'University of the Idolatry where lived the teachers who were wizards and masters of abomination,' the place to which Friar Marcos [García] and Friar Diego [Ortiz] went with so much suffering?"

Or did Machu Picchu deserve that assignation? Savoy was surprised by Bingham's eventual and rather awkward compromise—that there were actually *two* Vilcabambas: the ruins at Espíritu Pampa *and* the ruins at Machu Picchu. Yet although Bingham claimed that some of the last Inca emperors may have temporarily resided at Espíritu Pampa, he nevertheless insisted that Machu Picchu was the "Vilcabamba the Old," or "principal city," that the two friars had tried to enter, and that it was there that Tupac Amaru and his Inca followers had made their final stand. As Bingham wrote in his final book on the subject:

> The ruins of what we now believe was the lost city of Vilcapampa the Old, perched on top of a narrow ridge lying below the peak of Machu Picchu, are called the ruins of Machu Picchu because when we found them no one knew what else to call them. And that name has been accepted and will continue to be used even though no one now disputes that this was the site of ancient Vilcapampa.

Despite Bingham's confident assertion, however, more than a few schol-ars suspected that Bingham might have been wrong. In his book *Highway of the Sun,* Victor von Hagen explained how, in examining a sixteenth-century account describing the journey of a Spanish emissary, Friar Gabriel de Oviedo, to Vilcabamba in 1571, von Hagen observed that in order to ap-proach Vilcabamba the friar had crossed the Urubamba River *downriver* from where Machu Picchu was located, then had headed up into the Vil-cabamba Valley before traveling to "the headwaters of the Pampaconas River where he made contact with the Inca [emperor]." Von Hagen con-cluded, just a year before Bingham's death,

> This could only mean one thing. Machu Picchu was *not,* as Hiram Bing-ham would have it, the fortress of Vilcabamba where thousands of fierce warriors had for years eluded the Spaniard[s] and had organized a new empire. . . . We felt certain that, locked within this montaña [jungle] and accessible, if one could give the time to find it, was Vilcabamba, last cap-ital of the Incas.

Perhaps inspired by von Hagen, and being a skeptic by nature anyway, Savoy soon began to research the source material on Vilcabamba—the orig-inal Spanish chronicles. Like Bingham, Savoy was surprised by the fact that he was unable to find any references in the chronicles to a site called Machu Picchu or Huayna Picchu. Nor did the descriptions of Vilcabamba in the chronicles seem to Savoy to match the characteristics of the ruins at Machu Picchu. The more Savoy read, in fact, the more skeptical he became about Bingham's assertion that Machu Picchu was Manco's Vilcabamba. Savoy later wrote:

> Hiram Bingham, the Yale University professor, started looking for the "Lost City of the Incas," and chanced upon Machu Picchu northwest of Cuzco. He believed this mountain citadel to be . . . Manco's Vil-cabamba. . . . [Yet] Spanish chronicles had placed the central city of Manco in that vigorous land between the Apurímac and Urubamba [Rivers], deep down in the steaming jungles forty to sixty leagues (six to eight days' foot travel) northwest of Cuzco. On this assumption—and the records of reliable writers—I believed that I could expect to find the missing city in that vicinity. . . . If the friars and soldiers placed the city

of Vilcabamba in this valley, then it had to be there. . . . [And while] Bingham . . . did not . . . believe that the Incas would have selected a hot, tropical valley for their last refuge, I decided to take the word of the Spaniards and follow this trail in search of the lost city.

Perhaps there were more ruins at Espíritu Pampa than Bingham had found, Savoy theorized. Bingham may have discovered only a portion of what might still lie buried in thick jungle. Besides, unlike Bingham, who firmly believed that highland Incas wouldn't have felt at ease living in the Amazon, Savoy was a firm believer that the Amazon might actually have given birth to certain highland cultures. In any case, there was really only one way to find out: if Machu Picchu was not Vilcabamba, then clearly there had to be a city larger than Machu Picchu located somewhere else in that same province.

So it was that on the morning of July 2, 1964, thirty-six-year-old Gene Savoy, his twenty-three-year-old Canadian assistant, Douglas Sharon, and an amateur archaeologist from Cuzco, Antonio Santander, boarded a train in Cuzco and headed for Huadquiña, a village that lay some five miles down-stream from Machu Picchu.* More than half a century earlier, Bingham's mule journey down the Urubamba Valley had been greatly facilitated by a road that had recently been carved and blasted into the valley's walls. In the 1920s, a railway had been built in place of the road, which now allowed Savoy and his team to reach in six hours what had previously taken a mule train three long days. Wrote Savoy:

> The Vilcabamba plan was simple enough. Pick up the [Inca] roads and follow them using historical references, including those of Bingham and other explorers who had visited the area off and on over the past seventy years or so. According to the findings, the arrow pointed to a place called Espíritu Pampa, Plain of the Ghosts. I stuck a red flag on the [Andean Explorers] Club map to a remote region less than a hundred nautical air miles northwest of Cuzco.

* Douglas Sharon ultimately went on to earn a Ph.D. in anthropology and is currently the director of the Phoebe Hearst Museum of Anthropology at the University of California, Berkeley. Antonio Santander was in his early sixties at the time and had previously lost an eye while searching for the lost city of Paititi.

In Huadquiña, Savoy and his companions threw their gear onto a truck that took them across the Urubamba River and then headed up into the valley of the Vilcabamba River. Twenty-five minutes later, the road ended; from here on Savoy would have to travel like Bingham, on foot and on mule back.

During the following week, Savoy followed in Bingham's footsteps, revisiting the major Inca sites that Bingham had encountered and examining for himself the ruins and the terrain. Savoy first came to a village called Pucyura, which, like Bingham, Savoy assumed was the site of the Puquiura of the chronicles—the same village where Friar García's church had been and where the emperor Titu Cusi had suddenly died. Next, he visited Rosaspata, which Savoy agreed must be the site of Vitcos, the city where Manco Inca had been assassinated. Savoy then visited the nearby shrine of Chuquipalta (also known as Ñusta Ispana) that Bingham's friend Harry Foote had discovered—the giant "white rock" that rose up beside a natural spring. All of these sites, Savoy concluded, seemed to match what the various Spanish chroniclers had reported for this area.

Five days later, and again following Bingham's lead, Savoy and his team arrived at Espíritu Pampa. When Bingham had arrived here in 1911, a planter named Saavedra had guided him to the ruins. Five decades later, a family named Cobos now farmed the area. Wrote Savoy:

> Our mules negotiate a wide stone Inca road that staircases down the slope into the valley. Overgrown by thick vegetation, it is only partially cleared. A second road drops down from the upper regions. A quarter of an hour later we pull up in front of the Cobos house. It is made of fieldstones cemented with mud and thatched with sugarcane, there being no *paja* [straw] grown in the valley. Two men, later introduced as Benjamin and Flavio, eldest sons of Julio Cobos, step out into the hot mid-morning sun to greet us. I can tell from their faces they have been following us hawkeyed from the moment we first appeared on the promontory. We are invited into the hut, and treated to coffee locally grown on the *chacra* and freshly ground on large stones. I inquire about the Inca road we have been following. Benjamin Cobos informs me that it disappears into the great forest, beyond the coffee fields. I ask if he knows the location of the Eromboni ruins. He explains he and his father were shown these ruins in 1958 by the Machiguengas [natives] who

abandoned Espíritu Pampa several years ago for a new camp farther down the river. My next question animates his black, piercing eyes. "Will you guide me to these ruins?" He mulls over the matter, tosses a glance at his younger, thinner brother. *"Bueno,"* he replies.

That very same day, with the help of the Cobos family, Savoy located and began to clear the ruins that Bingham had been shown some fifty-three years earlier. Whereas Bingham had searched the area for only a few days, however, Savoy was determined to stay for at least several weeks. Savoy had also hired a large number of workers to help him clear away the jungle. Soon, ancient buildings and temple complexes that Bingham had never discovered gradually began to emerge.

The [Inca] road we have been following comes to a halt. Rather than retrace our steps, we decide to keep going in the same direction hoping to pick it up again. I have the men spread out. It is a half hour before we find two groups of buildings. The stonework is of better quality than what we have seen before. It is evident that the cut white limestone blocks had once fit snugly together, although many had now been broken by feeder vines that had wormed their way between the stones and pried them apart. One of the buildings, a rectangular construction with two doorways, guards a green-lit temple; a high elevated bulwark of stone consisting of rooms with niches and fallen door lintels, inner courtyards and enclosures. It must have been very impressive when the Incas lived here. A large huaca [sacred] boulder rests beside one of the walls. It looks as if it may have fallen from the top of the platform wall. A magnificent *matapalo* [strangler fig] tree with a spreading crown some one hundred feet above our heads locks one of the walls in a grip of gnarled roots. Some of the rocks are squeezed out of place by its vice-like grip. Rattan vines hang down from its upper branches, forming a screen through which we must cut our way.

After a week of prying ruin after ruin from the jungle's grip, Savoy gradually began to realize that the ruins he was discovering were not just the few dozen scattered buildings that Bingham had located in 1911 but were actually the remains of a substantial city. As Savoy later wrote:

Bingham had reached the outskirts of this old Inca city. There is no doubt of that. By failing to press on to discover additional ruins he dismissed its importance. This explains why he wrongly assumed Machu Picchu to be the Lost City of Vilcabamba. All he could find on the Eromboni Pampa was the one Inca group, the Spanish Palace, consisting of the road leading into the city, a small watchtower, the fifteen to twenty round houses on the edge of the forest, the bridge, fountain and traces of terraces near the twenty-four-door structure. Our findings show the site to be far more extensive.

Like Bingham, Savoy also discovered clay roofing tiles on the floors of some of the ruined buildings. Unlike his predecessor, however, Savoy immediately grasped their significance.

Who had used these tiles? Unknown in old Peru, roofing tile was introduced by the Spaniards shortly following the conquest. The Incas preferred *ichu* straw. Then I remembered that Manco had taken Spanish prisoners of war. These and the Augustinian friars under Titu Cusi may have passed on the use of this permanent roofing material. The Incas would have been adept at making such tiles; they had worked clay for centuries. The Viceroy had ordered the city of Cuzco tiled in the year 1560, a preventative against fire (Manco had put the old capital to the torch in 1536). From our findings it would appear that the Incas of Vilcabamba learned the art of manufacturing roofing tile and were utilizing it in their modern building; proof that they were experiencing a kind of transition, absorbing Spanish refinements while retaining their own. . . . While he [Bingham] dismissed this find as vague and unimportant, I seized upon it at once. To me it was a key find.

After several weeks of work, Savoy and his crew had partially cleared a site that consisted of hundreds of Inca buildings and stretched for more than five hundred acres. The center of the newly exposed city actually lay some seven hundred yards northeast of the buildings that Bingham had originally found, revealing a jungle metropolis whose existence Bingham had not even suspected.

For the first time I realize what we have found. We are in the heart of an ancient Inca city. Is this Manco's Vilcabamba—the lost city of the Incas? I am certain we are in parts of it. I experience an overwhelming sense of the history the ruins represent. For four hundred years they have remained in the realm of legend. Some even doubted they existed. But I always knew they were there, somewhere, awaiting discovery. To me they were the most important historical remains in Peru. Important because Manco was a glorious hero who gave dignity to Peru when all was lost. Important because so many great names had looked for them. Some would expect to find cyclopean walls covered with sheets of gold, or finely cut stone of the classic Cuzco style. Old Vilcabamba wasn't this at all. She was old and worn. The walls of her buildings were toppled, covered with thick, decaying vegetable matter; their foundations under tons of slide and ooze. She had been put to the torch by the Incas who had built her and ransacked by the Spaniards who were looking for gold. Four centuries of wild jungle had twisted that part which remained. But she had not lost her dignity. One could easily see she had been a great metropolis, a colossus of the jungle. . . . The city represented everything for which the Incas stood. It was a monument to their industry, their struggle with nature, their fight for freedom against overpowering odds. This was immortal Vilcabamba—that legendary city of a thousand history books. If I never succeeded in finding another city it would not matter. Legend had been turned into history.

Bingham, Savoy realized, had made the error of not having spent enough time to investigate the area properly. Hindered by the heavy mantle of jungle and by his own preconceptions, Bingham had discovered only a few scattered clusters of buildings, never realizing that a large, nearly invisible city actually lay stretched out before him, a city many times larger than the citadel he had discovered only three weeks earlier at Machu Picchu. Because the chronicles had made it clear that ancient Vilcabamba was the largest city in the province, however, and because he had found so few buildings at Espíritu Pampa, Bingham decided that Machu Picchu was a better candidate to claim the title of Manco's lost city of Vilcabamba.

Gene Savoy eventually led three expeditions in 1964 and 1965 to the site he now called Vilcabamba the Old, clearing, mapping, and exploring the ruins and the surrounding region. Satisfied that he had discovered and correctly identified the Inca capital that Hiram Bingham had been searching for, Savoy later turned his considerable energies to searching for ruins in the cloud forests of northeastern Peru. There he made a series of discoveries of ancient Chachapoyan cities, vestiges of a cloud forest culture that had once flourished in the region for at least half a millennium before the conquest of the Chachapoyas by the Incas. Later, in 1969—and obviously inspired by Thor Heyerdahl's *Kon-Tiki* voyage—Savoy supervised the construction of a reed raft he called *The Feathered Serpent,* eventually sailing it for two thousand miles, from Peru to Panama. Savoy made the voyage in the hope of providing support for one of his cherished theories, that ancient cultures in Peru, Central America, and Mexico had once had maritime contact.

In 1970, after thirteen years of exploration in Peru, Savoy went through a tumultuous time, divorcing his wife, marrying another Peruvian woman, and leaving Peru with a bitter taste in his mouth. Relocating to Reno, Nevada, Savoy nevertheless reestablished his exploring club, which he now called the Andean Explorers Foundation and Ocean Sailing Club, and also founded his new church, called the International Community of Christ, Church of the Second Advent, a tax-exempt organization. Savoy remained president and chief explorer of his exploring club while also retaining the position of head bishop and official messenger of God of his church. Putting his years of exploration in Peru behind him, Savoy now turned his attention completely to spiritual affairs, writing *Jamil: The Child Christ* and a series of seven religious tomes called *The Prophecies of Jamil.*

As Savoy continued to develop and elaborate upon his new church's doctrines, he began teaching his followers that, among other things, one could obtain immortality by staring directly at the sun, thereby absorbing God as raw energy in its purest form. Just as the Incas and the inhabitants of other ancient agricultural societies had worshipped the sun, Savoy, too, believed the sun to be divine. Savoy wrote in his book *Project X:*

> There can be no doubt that the sun picks up—and responds to—human thoughts, as we suspected. The sun cannot simply be an incandescent ball of nuclear fire—it is a center of consciousness. Man is intimately related to the sun by a sensory makeup not recognized, as yet, by secular science. . . . As man learns to specialize in absorbing solar radiation and

receiving cosmic information, he will automatically become part of the whole. He will transcend his physical being and gain access to cosmic knowledge—stored information far beyond anything that can be learned on this planet. The cumulative effect of all this information from within solar energy will be to give this new breed of man—futuristic man—access to the information locked up in the stars. With this knowledge, death will be overcome, for man will no longer be earthbound, or even individualistic, as we presently know individuality.

The secrets of immortality, Savoy informed his followers, had been revealed to him in the jungles of Peru. Savoy's claim was lent more credibility by the fact that, throughout his forties and fifties, he retained his movie-star good looks and appeared to be years younger than he actually was.

Deeply involved in his new church, Savoy never responded to the various letters he received over the years from people interested in his previous archaeological discoveries in Peru. For the Most Right Reverend Douglas Eugene Savoy, Peru and his life as an explorer there were now officially closed chapters in his past.

Savoy's reluctance to discuss his years of exploration continued, in fact, until one day in 1983 when two of the more persistent of these letter writers suddenly showed up on the doorstep of his home in Reno. The visitors were an American architect and his wife, both of whom had a newly found passion for searching for lost Inca ruins in Peru. The visitors said that after fruitless attempts to contact him, they had decided that they simply had to meet the man they considered to be the most famous living American explorer. Momentarily taken aback, Savoy paused for a moment, then invited the couple into his home for coffee. The visitors were Vincent and Nancy Lee; their sudden appearance on his doorstep would ultimately propel Savoy back to the jungles of Peru, where he would make one of his most controversial discoveries.

Vincent Lee first went to Peru to go mountain climbing. An architect by profession, an ex-Marine, and a mountaineering guide who lived near Jackson Hole, Wyoming, Lee had come across Savoy's 1970 book, *Antisuyo: The Search for the Lost Cities of the Amazon,* in a local library. Although Lee found the story of Manco Inca and Vilcabamba interesting, he was even more intrigued by Savoy's mention of a sheer granite rock, shaped like a giant human head, called Icma Coya—which in Quechua means "Widowed Queen." The giant formation apparently rose out of the southeastern Peruvian jungle, in an area called Vilcabamba, and had yet to be climbed. Inspired by Savoy's account, the six-foot-tall, bearded, blue-eyed, forty-two-year-old and two mountaineering friends made the journey to Peru in 1982 in order to climb the peak. Lee and his companions eventually took the train past Machu Picchu, then climbed onto the back of a truck that took them all the way to Huancacalle, into the heart of the Vilcabamba region. Hiking along the trail to the Pampaconas River, Lee was amazed to find the remains of so many Inca ruins, many of which appeared to have been untouched by the intervening centuries. By the time they arrived at the base of Icma Coya, Lee was hooked. "I couldn't believe all of the ruins that we were finding," Lee recounted. "The whole place looked unexplored. As an architect, I was fascinated by the types of buildings the Incas had left. And I wanted to know why they had built them in such an inaccessible location."

After the successful climb, Lee returned to his home in Wyoming and soon began to read everything he could about the Incas and especially about Manco Inca and his sons, the last of the Inca emperors. Lee also reread Savoy's *Antisuyo,* paying careful attention to Savoy's claim of having discovered the real Vilcabamba, which lay buried in thick jungle not far from where Lee had gone climbing. Although Lee was impressed with Savoy's story, as an architect he was nevertheless disappointed that the only drawing Savoy had published of the ruins was sketchy at best and included few details. The photos Savoy had published in his book were also very poor—partly due to the thick vegetation—and revealed very little.

As Savoy had no archaeological credentials and had provided little solid documentation to substantiate his claims, a number of Inca specialists, Lee soon discovered, had their doubts about whether the ruins at Espíritu Pampa were really what Savoy claimed they were. Where were the detailed site maps of the supposed city, they asked? Where were the various nearby forts and battle sites mentioned in the chronicles? The only way to definitively *prove* that the ruins at Espíritu Pampa were indeed those of Manco Inca's lost capital would be to take the time to carefully map the city and then look for other nearby ruins that were described in the chronicles. Just as Hiram Bingham had confirmed that the ruins of modern-day Rosaspata must be those of ancient Vitcos by discovering the nearby rock shrine of Chuquipalta, only by discovering additional, related sites could anyone definitively prove that the ruins at Espíritu Pampa were really those of Manco's Vilcabamba.

Continuing his research, Lee soon discovered that Gene Savoy was still alive and that he was now the head of a church in Reno. Lee called the church, was given the address of Savoy's house—and then sent a letter there, introducing himself and asking Savoy for information and advice. Eventually, an assistant of Savoy's responded briefly to the letter, but provided none of the information Lee had requested. Lee, however, was not about to give up; he was now not only determined to return and explore the Vilcabamba area but he was just as determined to meet and speak with the mysterious and reclusive Gene Savoy. The only solution, it seemed, was to fly to Reno and try to meet with the fifty-six-year-old explorer. Thus, in November 1983, Lee and his wife, Nancy, eventually found themselves standing in front of Savoy's International Community of Christ in Reno, Nevada. Lee later wrote:

> A visit to his [Savoy's] church confirmed that we had come to the right place, but a somewhat other-worldly woman informed us that Reverend Savoy was "in retreat" and thus not available to receive visitors. Disappointed, we decided to drive across town to the residential area where . . . the explorer lived. There was no missing the house, a large, Frank-Lloyd-Wright affair plunked in the midst of a hilly cluster of conventional suburban homes. In case one couldn't figure out where the neighborhood explorer lived, the double masts of a sizeable sailing ship towered above the fenced-in back yard, apparently beached there during some past oceanic cataclysm. As we drove by the house, a man in jeans and a snap-front, western shirt was out in the driveway, washing his car. I immediately recognized him as Gene Savoy from his picture in *Antisuyo* and stopped. Once we identified ourselves, he hastily invited us in for a cup of coffee.

Savoy, it turned out, still had the slicked-back hair, mustache, and Hollywood good looks that had been evident in the photographs in his books.

Savoy knew of the Lees, he said, from the letter they had sent. He apologized for not having personally answered. The decade he had spent in Peru, Savoy told them, had occurred a long time ago and had not had a very happy ending. In fact, Savoy told the Lees, sipping from a cup and peering at them intently, he had tried to put the entire experience behind him. When the Lees told Savoy of their plans to return to Vilcabamba to do more exploring, Savoy wished them well, but assured them that he himself would never again return to Peru. During the meeting, Lee noted, Savoy sat with his back to a brightly lit window, making it difficult for them to see him clearly.

> He exuded a certain unsettling charisma, but at the same time struck us both as a bit humorless and self-important. . . . Maybe a bit of stand-offishness was to be expected of someone who had literally fathered his own religion, but Nancy and I had both come away from that first meeting feeling awkward and uncomfortable.

Nevertheless, six months later, in May of 1983, the Lees made a short, follow-up trip to visit Savoy, just before heading off to Peru. Savoy was a bit friendlier this time; he seemed to be less suspicious and more relaxed. Savoy surprised the Lees, in fact, by offering them a flag to take along—blue, white, and red and with the words "Andean Explorers Foundation" stenciled onto it. Staring gravely at the Lees, Savoy suggested that his club be the "co-sponsor" of their trip. Although the proposal felt a bit awkward, the Lees were nevertheless flattered. Before they left, Savoy offered them a final bit of advice, advice that had obviously been distilled from more than a dozen years of bushwhacking for lost ruins in Peru:

> "Exploring in South America is serious and sometimes nasty business. . . . Don't think you can just crash around blindly in the jungle and find anything . . . you can't. Listen to the campesinos [the local peasants]. They know where everything is. Pay attention to their tips and look for old [Inca] roads. Follow them. They all go somewhere."

The veteran explorer—discoverer of a host of lost ruins, founder of his own church, and the personal messenger of God—leaned forward toward the Lees, looking at them with his intense brown eyes, and warned them, with the light from the window creating a kind of halo behind him:

"If you're careful and keep a low profile, you'll come out okay. . . . There's supposed to be a beautiful two-story building made of white limestone somewhere up in the Puncuyoc Mountains. If I were going back, that's where I'd go. . . . One thing, though: don't trust anyone."

Lee, his wife, and six companions ultimately did travel to Vilcabamba and spent two months in the area. Although Lee had no experience in archaeology, he was a skilled architect and thus knew how to create detailed site maps. Using nothing more than an altimeter, a compass, a fifty-foot measuring tape, a notebook, and probably one of the first satellite maps anyone had ever taken into the area, Lee and his team began systematically to explore and map the ruins that lay in the Vilcabamba Valley, first at Vitcos and then at the shrine of Chuquipalta. In nearby Huancacalle, Lee made an unexpected discovery: the same Peruvian family that had guided Gene Savoy to the ruins at Espíritu Pampa some twenty years earlier, the Coboses, had relocated to Huancacalle and agreed to guide them to Espíritu Pampa. Soon, Lee and his team began hiking along the old Inca road that led down into the Pampaconas Valley.

On this, his first exploring trip, Lee was surprised that it didn't take long to make a significant discovery of his own. Reading in the Spanish chronicles that in 1572 the Incas had fought a battle with the invading Spaniards at a fort called Huayna Pucará (New Fort)—described as a high, narrow ridge with a stone fort on top—Lee and his companions began searching the area until they found it. On the ridge above the trail, Lee had read, the native warriors under Tupac Amaru had positioned giant boulders in order to roll them down and crush the Spaniards below. Many of those boulders were still there, Lee discovered, still waiting to be pushed downhill, as some four centuries earlier the Spaniards had surprised the Incas by seizing the heights behind them and, under the cover of their harquebus fire, had captured the fort. Lee recalled:

My barometer read 6,500 feet and the air was warm, heavy, and moist. . . . The tropical night closed in with startling suddenness. Reflecting around the fire, we could scarcely believe our luck. There we were, a bunch of neophytes not yet an entire day into the exploration phase of our trip, and we had already found something important, a major ruin that had eluded all our predecessors. Huayna Pucará, the long-lost New Fort, was back on the map.

Although the discovery of Huayna Pucará was exciting in itself, it had an added significance: clearly, the route they were presently following down to the ruins of Espíritu Pampa matched the chroniclers' descriptions of the route the invading Spaniards had taken to Vilcabamba. It was an additional piece of evidence supporting Savoy's claim that the ruins of Espíritu Pampa were those of Vilcabamba. Arriving at the site of the ancient city, which was covered over in jungle again, Lee and his team began carefully to clear and map the area. One piece of information that Lee had—but which Bingham had been unable to use and which Savoy had apparently missed—was a Spanish chronicle that not only provided new descriptive details of Vilcabamba but also contained a crucial piece of evidence. A Mercedarian friar, Martín de Murúa, it turned out, had written in 1590 that the roof of at least one of the buildings in Vilcabamba had been covered not in traditional thatch, but in Spanish roof tiles:

> The town has, or it would be better to say had, a location half a league [1.75 miles] wide, like the layout of Cuzco, and [covering] a long distance in length. In it they used to raise parrots, hens, ducks, local rabbits, turkeys, pheasants, curassows, guans, macaws, and a thousand other kinds of birds. . . . The good disposition of the land and the water with which they irrigated it . . . gave forth to [tropical] pepper orchards in great abundance, coca, sugar cane to make honey and sugar with, manioc, sweet potatoes, and cotton. There are numerous guavas, pecans, peanuts, lucumas, papayas, pineapples, avocados, and many other cultivated and wild trees. The palace of the Inca [emperor] had different levels, [was] covered in roof tiles, and . . . was something well worth seeing.

The Spanish friar's description of macaws and tropical crops, Lee realized, matched perfectly the ruins at 4,900 feet in elevation at Espíritu

Pampa but not at all those at Machu Picchu, at 8,000 feet.* In addition, Lee and his team soon discovered more than four hundred structures at Espíritu Pampa, constituting a city that stretched for more than a mile in length and perhaps a half a mile in width. Lee knew that Machu Picchu, by contrast, was composed of about 150 residential buildings, which covered an area roughly a tenth of a mile long and only a fraction of that in width. Machu Picchu was a *citadel,* not a city. And, even though the ruins looked spectacular, Machu Picchu probably housed fewer than 750 inhabitants, while Vilcabamba had probably housed three or four times that number.

Comparing the two locations, Lee soon realized that the chroniclers' assertions that Vilcabamba was the largest city in the area now made sense: there was indeed no other city of equal size anywhere else in the province, including Machu Picchu. As Savoy had already noted, the roof tiles, too, were a critical find. According to the British historian John Hemming, in fact, the ruined city that first Bingham, then Savoy discovered at Espíritu Pampa was "the only known Inca ruin in the Andes where scorched, Spanish-style roof tiles are found scattered among the remains." As Lee well knew, the Incas had set fire to Vilcabamba before Spanish forces had occupied the city in June 1572, no doubt scorching the roof tiles in the process.

Still, despite his team's discoveries, Lee realized that one of the main obstacles preventing anyone from making sense not only of the ruins of Vilcabamba but also of how those ruins fit into the wider context of the entire Inca province was the simple fact that no one had ever bothered to map the ruins in the area. Lee, the professional architect, was determined to change all that. He later wrote:

> After more than a century of exploration, there still was no accurate map [in 1984] of the province. . . . Yet anyone serious about piecing together the bewildering jigsaw puzzle that was Inca Vilcabamba needed to have all the pieces, or at least all those that were known, laid out on the table.

---

* The friar Martín de Murúa's chronicle was not published in its entirety until 1922 (in Lima), 332 years after it was completed and ten years after Bingham's discovery of Machu Picchu. Although the chronicle was edited by Carlos Romero, the same Peruvian historian who had helped Bingham locate Espíritu Pampa, it was the English historian John Hemming who later drew attention to how Murúa's description of Vilcabamba supported Savoy's identification of Vilcabamba and not Bingham's.

It couldn't be done. Theories abounded, but no one was playing with a full deck. Lying there in the dark, waiting for dawn, I told myself: that, at least, was about to change.

And change it did. Lee knew that the Spaniards had fought the Incas at the site of another Inca fort just prior to their sacking of Vilcabamba. The Incas had called the place Machu Pucará, or "Old Fort." After carefully combing the area, Lee and his team sure enough discovered the second fort just where the chronicles said it should be. Click. Another piece of the Vilcabamba puzzle had fallen neatly into place.

Having retraced the invading Spaniards' presumed route and having rediscovered two lost forts that were located exactly where the sixteenth-century chronicles said they should be, Lee had now gathered additional evidence supporting Savoy's thesis that the ruins of Espíritu Pampa were indeed those of Manco's Vilcabamba. Lee and a friend now decided to break off from the main expedition and go in search of the ruins that Savoy had suggested might exist nearby. "There's supposed to be a beautiful two-story building made of white limestone somewhere up in the Puncuyoc Mountains," Savoy had said. "If I were going back, that's where I'd go." After three days of slogging through steep cloud forest along with two *campesino* guides, Lee and his companions discovered that Savoy had been right. Puncuyoc, it turned out, was a group of surprisingly well-preserved ruins located at an elevation of 12,850 feet. The main ruin was a tall and rather unusual two-story building with associated structures nearby; it was in excellent condition and still stood upright in a gap between two mountain peaks. As Lee later wrote:

Continuing up the final stairway through a dense grove of tangled, moss-covered trees, we arrived at the object of our search and found all our efforts of the past few days repaid several times over. . . . It struck me that our "discovery" of Puncuyoc was exactly the unexpected surprise I had dreamed of. . . . Puncuyoc . . . was a truly magnificent find. Unlike the historic but tumbled ruins we had found along the trail to Vilcabamba the Old, the significance of Puncuyoc seemed to have no known history but was instead a virtually undisturbed relic from the world of the Incas. From my reading, I knew that made it an almost incredible rarity. Better yet, its near-perfect state of preservation (more pristine, in fact, than anything at Machu Picchu) and its complex design made it a veritable laboratory for the study of Incan building techniques. With the expedition all but over, it looked like we had hit the jackpot. Like Bingham, seven decades earlier, we were blessed with unbelievable good luck.

Unbeknownst to Lee at the time, however, the American writer and explorer Victor von Hagen's expedition had actually discovered the ruins of Puncuyoc in 1953 while exploring the Incas' road network. Von Hagen had recounted the discovery in his 1955 book, *Highway of the Sun.* Savoy most likely had either read or remembered von Hagen's account, then had passed along his suggestion to Lee. In any case, after returning to Wyoming, Lee gave Savoy a call, telling him about his "discovery" of Puncuyoc and the two Inca forts—Huayna Pucará and Machu Pucará—and also about the maps and site plans that he planned to create based upon his discoveries. Savoy, Lee said, sounded extremely interested, especially in the ruins of Puncuyoc. The veteran explorer suddenly informed Lee that he had recently decided to update the material in his 1970 book, *Antisuyo,* and would soon publish a new book on the same subject. Lee's recent discoveries, Savoy said, would be perfect to include in his new book. Was Lee interested? And could Lee fly out to Reno when his drawings were done and make a presentation of them to Savoy's Andean Explorers Foundation? Flattered, Lee told Savoy that he would be honored to have his material included in Savoy's book and that he would also be happy to present his new findings.

In the fall of 1984, as snow thickened outside his Wyoming home, Vincent Lee sat in his wood-lined study where, with his field notebooks in hand, he began the process of creating precise maps and three-dimensional reconstructions of the ruins that he had located and taken the measurements of in Peru. For the first time in more than four hundred years—ironically in a studio at the base of the Rocky Mountains—the outlines of ancient cities and settlements in Manco's distant province of Vilcabamba began to emerge, just as remarkably as the outlines of Machu Picchu had once been revealed by Hiram Bingham in the on-site chemical baths he had used to develop his photos. Wrote Lee:

It was a fascinating process. . . . Slowly, as each new bit of information was added, the essence of sites completely unintelligible in the field re-emerged after four hundred years of obscurity. By early November everything we had seen of Inca Vilcabamba was shown on eleven large blue-line print sheets and I put together several hundred of our best slides to augment the drawings.

Lee now felt ready for his presentation to Savoy.

Three months later, Lee stood before a select group that Savoy had assembled in Reno and began showing them his slides of the various ruins. Savoy, Lee said, was keenly interested in Lee's photos and drawings and was increasingly fascinated with his "discovery" of Puncuyoc. After the presentation, Savoy said that if Lee could write up his findings and submit a manuscript to him by June of 1985, then he would include them in his new book. He couldn't pay Lee anything, Savoy said, as there "was no money in it"—but he *would* give Lee fifty copies of the new book to do with as he pleased. Excited at the thought of having his discoveries published, Lee agreed. And, as a gesture of gratitude to the man who in a sense had inspired his own explorations, Lee left Savoy duplicates of all of his recent drawings and maps.

Three months later, while busily working to meet the publishing deadline, Lee received a phone call from Gene Savoy. After an absence of fifteen years, Savoy abruptly told him, he had decided to travel back to Peru—and had just returned from the ruins that Lee had "discovered."

> "[I] Just returned from an expedition to Puncuyoc," he [Savoy] said. "Quite a place!" This, from a man who had only three months earlier assured us he would "never go back" to Peru. It was obvious he had begun planning the expedition before we even left Reno and had the drawings I left behind to show him the way. With the help of the local *campesinos,* he said, he took his family up there for a few days to look around and photograph the ruins. I was stunned! In a matter of seconds, it looked like my mentor had become a competitor, and a formidable one at that.

A few weeks later, Lee had his worst suspicions confirmed. A friend of Lee's in New York City, a documentary filmmaker, had received a form letter written by Gene Savoy that had been sent out to a large number of people, although Lee was not one of them. Gene Savoy, the letter said, had recently returned to Peru after a long absence and had immediately made an exciting "new discovery" of an Inca "Temple of the Sun," set high up in the mountains of Vilcabamba. Savoy was determined to return to the site to do a more thorough exploration, but needed money to help defray the costs. Savoy had thus hit upon an ingenious solution: he had decided to publish a limited edition of 250 copies of *Antisuyo, Search for the Lost Cities of the Amazon* that would be distributed among expedition members and friends at a cost of $250 per book. As an added bonus, Savoy said, the new edition would contain photographs, maps, and architectural renderings of the ruins—all unpublished up to now.

Lee did some quick calculations: 250 books at $250 per copy equaled more than $60,000. "So much for there being no money in it," he later said, shaking his head. Of course there were maps and architectural renderings of the ruins, all unpublished up to now—because Lee had *created* the maps and renderings but had not yet *published* them. Since the book was slated to be published in June 1985—the very month that Savoy had asked Lee to submit his manuscript for inclusion in his "new book"—it appeared to Lee that Savoy had sent him on a "snipe hunt" of sorts, ensuring that Lee couldn't possibly publish his material before Savoy did. Lee later wrote:

> It didn't take Sherlock Holmes to see that the material he had asked me to submit by June 1st would arrive too late to be included in the $250 book. Savoy had gotten all he needed from me back in November, when I had foolishly left my drawings behind. Galvanized into action, I went back to my word processor, double-time. By the end of March, the manuscript was finished and I decided to publish it myself, desktop style, as *Sixpac Manco: Travels Among the Incas*. I was careful to include all the maps and drawings we left with Savoy and I registered the copyright with the Library of Congress. With a certain poetic justice, I sent a copy of the finished product to Savoy on April Fool's day, 1985, with a letter suggesting he let me know if he wanted to use any of its contents in his new book. . . . My only comment [at the end was]: "You've told me from the start that I should 'trust no one'—and I guess you really meant no one."

Savoy never responded—nor was his book on his "new discoveries" in the Vilcabamba area ever published.

Both Gene Savoy and Vincent Lee ultimately helped to gather the evidence that proved for the first time and beyond a shadow of a doubt that the final capital of the Incas—Vilcabamba—had indeed been rediscovered after having been lost to the rest of the world for centuries. Hiram Bingham—despite a lifetime of insisting that Machu Picchu was in fact ancient Vilcabamba—had clearly been wrong. Now that the location of the real Vilcabamba had been discovered, however, the original question inevitably turned itself on its head: for if Machu Picchu was *not* Vilcabamba, then what on earth was Machu Picchu?

EPILOGUE: MACHU PICCHU, VILCABAMBA, AND THE SEARCH FOR THE LOST CITIES OF THE ANDES

❖

"If you take a map of the Vilcabamba area and put a map pin at every major imperial Inca site, then you can see that there's a big hole in the pattern, right along the Apurímac River, downstream from Choqquequirau. There are two Inca roads that lead into that area—and the Incas wouldn't have built them unless they led somewhere. There could be another stone city in there, but who knows? I guess that's one of the reasons why we all keep coming back."

VINCENT LEE, 2005

TO UNDERSTAND HOW VILCABAMBA AND MACHU PICCHU were once intertwined, one has to go back to the decades in which both were constructed: presumably in the mid-fifteenth century.* In the early part of that century, the ethnic group known as the Incas lived within a small kingdom centered around the valley of Cuzco, one of many such small kingdoms in the Andes and on the coast. The Incas told the Spaniards that they were led by an old Inca king named Viracocha Inca. Faced with an approaching army from the powerful kingdom of the Chancas, the Inca ruler

---

* Machu Picchu is believed to have been built between 1450 and 1470. Recent excavations at Vilcabamba indicate that the latter city was also constructed during the fifteenth century.

fled, leaving his adult son, Cusi Yupanqui, behind. The latter quickly took charge, raised an army, and somehow miraculously defeated the invaders. Cusi Yupanqui then deposed his father, arranged for his own coronation, and changed his name to Pachacuti, a Quechua word that means "earth-shaker" or "cataclysm," or "he who turns the world upside down." The name was a prescient one, for Pachacuti would soon revolutionize the entire Andean world.

According to Inca oral history, Pachacuti also had had a profound religious experience when he was young, a sort of epiphany that revealed to him both his divine nature and a vision of a nearly unbounded future. Wrote the Jesuit priest Bernabé Cobo:

> It is said of this Inca [Pachacuti], that before he became king, he went once to visit his father Viracocha, who was . . . five leagues from Cuzco, and as he reached a spring called Susurpuquiu, he saw a crystal tablet fall into it; within this tablet there appeared to him the figure of an Indian dressed in this way: around his head he had a *llauto* like the headdress of the Incas; three brightly shining rays, like those of the sun, sprang from the top of his head; some snakes were coiled around his arms at the shoulder joints . . . and there was a kind of snake that stretched from the top to the bottom of his back. Upon seeing this image, Pachacuti became so terrified that he started to flee, but the image spoke to him from inside the spring, saying to him: "Come here, my child; have no fear, for I am your father the Sun; I know that you will subjugate many nations and take great care to honor me and remember me in your sacrifices"; and, having said these words, the vision disappeared, but the crystal tablet remained in the spring. The Inca took the tablet and kept it; it is said that after this it served him as a mirror in which he saw anything he wanted, and in memory of his vision, when he was king, he had a statue made of the Sun, which was none other than the image he had seen in the crystal, and he built a temple of the Sun called Qoricancha, with the magnificence and richness that it had at the time when the Spaniards came, because before it was a small and humble structure. Moreover, he ordered that solemn temples dedicated to the Sun be built throughout all the lands that he subjugated under his empire, and he endowed them with great incomes, ordering that all his subjects worship and revere the Sun.

Soon after becoming king, Pachacuti wasted no time in remaking the world according to his unique vision, beginning with the city of Cuzco. There, he undertook a major rebuilding campaign, reorganizing the layout of the capital, tearing down old buildings, creating new boulevards, and ordering a host of palaces and temples to be built. All of these were constructed in a new style of stonework that Pachacuti preferred—later referred to as the imperial style—stones cut and fitted together so perfectly that the skill and artistry displayed would eventually become famous as one of the wonders of the New World.

Not satisfied with defeating the Chancas, however, the ambitious young king soon led his army into the nearby Yucay (Vilcanota) Valley, conquering two ethnic groups, the Cuyos and the Tambos. To celebrate these victories, Pachacuti ordered the construction of a royal estate, called Pisac, in the center of the Cuyos' territory; he then ordered that a second royal estate to be built among the conquered Tambos, at a site called Ollantaytambo. The twin estates were unusual, however, in that they were destined to be privately owned by the conqueror himself. It was a model that would soon be copied by succeeding Inca emperors and also by a small number of high-ranking Inca elites. Theirs would be the only privately held lands within the rapidly expanding Inca Empire.

Pachacuti created his new estates with a number of specific purposes in mind, perhaps the most important of which was to support his own family lineage. Each new Inca emperor was supposed to found his own *panaca,* or descent lineage, in essence becoming the patriarch and founder of a new family line. The crops and animal herds raised on Pachacuti's private estates were thus slated to be used to support the members of his royal *panaca.* After his death, the estates would continue to be used and maintained by his descendants.

A second purpose for building the royal estates was to commemorate Pachacuti's recent conquests: when complete, they would serve as monuments that would reflect the new emperor's boldness, initiative, and power. Finally, the estates were also meant to serve as secluded royal retreats— luxury resorts located well away from the capital where the emperor and a select group of relatives and elites could rest, relax, and commune with the local mountain gods.

As with the new palaces and buildings he had ordered built in Cuzco,

Pachacuti was first presumably shown models of his proposed estates in clay, complete with the projected buildings, agricultural terraces, and temples. Once Pachacuti had approved the designs, a legion of the kingdom's finest architects, engineers, stonecutters, and masons went to work. Pachacuti, meanwhile—in his role as commander in chief—continued to expand the Incas' realm, this time pushing northward into the Vilcabamba Valley. Wrote Father Cobo:

> He [Pachacuti] began his conquests with the provinces of Vitcos and Vilcabamba, a very difficult land to subjugate because it is so rough and covered with dense jungle. . . . The Inca [emperor] left Cuzco with the bravest and most carefully chosen men he had; he passed through the Valley of Yucay [Vilcanota] and continued down the river to [Ollantay]Tambo; he came to the Valley of Ambaybamba, and there he got word that it would be impossible to continue ahead, since there was no bridge across the [Urubamba] river; his adversaries had removed the [hanging] bridge of Chuquichaca. . . . But the power of the Inca [Pachacuti] was so great that not only did he make that bridge in the place where it was before but he made many others in places where the river was narrow, and those of Vilcabamba were so astonished and fearful that they confessed that only the power of the Sun's offspring could accomplish those great deeds. Upon finishing the bridges, the Inca [emperor] ordered his men to proceed in a very orderly fashion, so that the enemy would not be able to harm them, and when he arrived at Cocospata, about twenty-five leagues [eighty-seven miles] from Cuzco, ambassadors came to him from the caciques [chiefs] of Vitcos and Vilcabamba. . . . The caciques, in order to please the Inca [emperor] more and gain his good graces, told him that they wanted to give him a mountain filled with fine silver and some rich gold mines. The Inca [Pachacuti] was very pleased with this offer, so he sent some of his men to see if this was true and [to] bring back some samples of gold and silver. They went quickly, and they found that the wealth of the mine was much greater than what had been described to the Inca [emperor], to whom they brought many loads of gold and silver; this made him exceedingly happy. . . . [Pachacuti] left Vilcabamba by the same road he had used to come there, and upon arriving in Cuzco, he ordered that this

expedition and the discovery of the mines be celebrated with public fiestas which lasted for two months.

To commemorate his conquest of the Vilcabamba Valley, Pachacuti ordered that a third royal estate be built, this one very near the Chuquichaca bridge, on a high ridge overlooking what is now called the Urubamba River. The Incas apparently called the new site *Picchu,* meaning "peak." Since the proposed citadel and nearby satellite communities were planned from the start to form part of a luxurious private estate, the entire complex would display some of the finest examples of Inca engineering and art.

The complex of what is now known as the ruins of Machu Picchu, in fact, was carefully planned and designed long before the first white granite block was ever cut and moved into place. The location, first of all, had to be both suitably sacred and spectacular; the site that Pachacuti selected was set high atop a ridge with an almost God-like view over the entire area and of the surrounding *apus,* or sacred peaks. It was essential that the site also contain a source of clean water—a substance sacred in itself—that could be used for drinking, bathing, and for ritual purposes. *Picchu,* in fact, possessed just such a crucial characteristic: on the large peak now known as Machu Picchu, and high above the proposed citadel, Inca engineers located a natural spring. They then designed a gravity-fed water system that would eventually carry water down from the peak to the ridgetop site where it would ultimately pass through sixteen descending ritual fountains.

Portions of the ridgetop were now carefully planed and flattened as workers created foundations of gravel, stones, and even subterranean retaining walls. Archaeologists who have excavated at Machu Picchu have reported that some 60 percent of the architectural engineering associated with the ruins actually lies beneath the ruins. Because of the heavy granite architecture and the region's equally heavy rains, Inca engineers had to be certain that the locations chosen for building had solid foundations capable of withstanding both water and weight. Once the foundation was complete, construction finally began on the citadel itself, with workers cutting stone mainly from a quarry located on the same ridgetop, using a variety of stone and bronze tools. Only once the first stone blocks had been cut did construction begin on the buildings, palaces, and temples of Machu Picchu.

Workers and specialists from around the country now convened on the remote site, all of them supervised by a bevy of architects and engineers. In order to equip the citadel with the latest, state-of-the-art technology, Inca astronomers worked alongside the engineers and stonemasons to fashion observatories that could accurately mark the summer and winter solstices as well as other astronomical events. Workers fulfilling their *mit'a* labor tax, meanwhile, busied themselves constructing roads to and from the royal estate, linking Machu Picchu with the capital, Cuzco, and with other newly built centers, such as Ollantaytambo, Pisac, and, eventually, Vitcos and Vilcabamba. Additional laborers were also put to work constructing large agricultural terraces in order to help provide food for the citadel's future inhabitants as well as for ritual sacrifices. Soon, Inca labor and technology had transformed the steep, jungle-covered slopes into a staggered series of flat terraces that eventually produced fourteen acres of sacred corn.

When Machu Picchu was finally ready for use sometime in the 1450s or 1460s, the first ruler of the newly created Inca Empire, Pachacuti, no doubt arrived there on his royal litter, accompanied by royal guests, a large retinue of servants, and at least part of his harem. The citadel's furnishings, plumbing, food, supplies, servants, and cooks had all been carefully prepared so that the emperor would be able to relax along with his guests. Then, as now, clouds wreathed the surrounding peaks, alternately exposing and obscuring them. Unlike the ruins today, however, the gabled roofs of the buildings were covered with fresh yellow *ichu* thatch while the stones of the citadel were white and freshly cut and glistened in the sun.

Similar to the recent architecture in Cuzco, much of the stonework here had been cut in the imperial style that Pachacuti preferred; some of the buildings, in fact, were constructed with boulders the size of small cars, each cut, fitted perfectly into place, and weighing up to fourteen tons.* The water from the nearby peak of Machu Picchu, meanwhile, descended into the citadel through a stone-lined aqueduct and arrived first at Pachacuti's living quarters, thus allowing the emperor to come into contact with only the purest water available. A stone-cut pool in Pachacuti's dwelling allowed the emperor to bathe in complete privacy while the emperor's residence also had the only water-flushed lavatory at Machu Picchu.

---

* Archaeologists recognize eighteen different types of stone walls and building styles at Machu Picchu, including the imperial style.

As Pachacuti bathed himself in his private bath, the voices of his guests would have floated across the plaza outside along with the distant sounds of metalworkers tending their forges and hammering out gold and silver ornaments, utensils, and jewelry. Strings of llama trains constantly arrived, looking from a condor's perspective like lengths of knotted *quipu* cords; the food and supplies they carried up from the jungle and down from the Andes was carefully unpacked at a station just outside the citadel. Even at this private retreat, *chaski* runners appeared periodically with messages for the emperor and other officials, who in turn sent their commands back to Cuzco and to other parts of the empire. Wherever the emperor went, in fact, his royal court followed. Thus, whenever Pachacuti was in retreat at Machu Picchu, this lofty, isolated citadel temporarily became the power center and locus of the entire Inca world.

Unlike the ruins of Machu Picchu today—which are owned by the Peruvian state and are open to the public, and where tour buses disgorge hundreds of thousands of visitors each year—Machu Picchu in the time of Pachacuti was an exclusive and private affair. The roads here—like the roads elsewhere in the empire—were open only to those individuals traveling on state business. Other than Pachacuti's immediate family, the workers who kept the citadel functioning, and the invited elites who traveled here on canopied litters, often decorated with precious metals and iridescent bird feathers, Machu Picchu was unknown to the rest of the empire's inhabitants. Machu Picchu, quite simply, was Pachacuti's Camp David—a royal resort built by a man who had almost single-handedly transformed a small native kingdom into the largest empire the New World has ever known.

The citadel of Machu Picchu was thus the third and perhaps most important jewel in the crown of architectural monuments that Pachacuti had created, after Pisac and Ollantaytambo. Balmy and warm, the site was no doubt a welcome respite from the often freezing winter weather of the Inca capital and from the high Andes in general. Even after Pachacuti's death and long after the emperor had been ritually embalmed and mummified, Pachacuti's servants no doubt continued bringing their divine emperor to visit Machu Picchu and to visit the other estates he had carved out of the Andes, his sightless eyes seeming to gaze off into the distance as the members of his royal *panaca* continued to enjoy the fruits of their founder's unparalleled conquests and labors.

Since Machu Picchu was Pachacuti's private royal estate, the question remains, however, how it was related to Manco Inca's rebel capital of Vilcabamba. Once again, the answer lies partially within the Incas' oral histories. According to interviews the Spaniards conducted among the Incas in the sixteenth century, Pachacuti is said to have halted his advance after conquering the Vilcabamba Valley. His son, Tupac Inca, however, apparently then extended Inca control down into the Pampaconas Valley and eventually to the area of the future town of Vilcabamba itself.

After Pachacuti's military conquest, the Vilcabamba Valley underwent a set pattern of development that the Incas soon replicated throughout their empire. First, engineers and *quipucamayocs* (accountants) were sent in to assess and catalogue the resources of the new territory. The task of the *quipucamayocs* was to conduct a census of the local population and to enter data onto their knotted string cords about the province's arable lands, native crops, sources of metals (copper, tin, gold, and silver), and other resources. Inca engineers then created clay models of the new area, complete with the location of native settlements, which were taken to Cuzco in order to show to the emperor. Thus informed, Pachacuti and his advisers next decided on how to reorganize the population, where Inca roads should be constructed, and where royal mines and new communities should be established.

Once the overall development plan had been approved, Inca administrators sent *mit'a* laborers to the new province, to build or improve roads into the area and to line the roads with typical Inca *tambos* and storehouses; they then stocked the latter with supplies for the government officials, workers, and for the *mitmaqcuna* colonists who would soon be permanently moved into the area. *Chaski* posts, too, were set up, so that the new province could be connected to the empire's communication system of relay runners. If canals, bridges, agricultural terracing, or towns were needed, Inca administrators then brought in the corresponding architects, stonemasons, and engineers.

As the newly conquered province was being reorganized so that its indigenous people and resources could be smoothly exploited by the Inca elite, construction also began on the new provincial capital. In general, the Incas preferred their provincial capitals to be situated on level areas with good visibility over the surrounding region. In the upper Vilcabamba Valley, Pachacuti himself probably selected a hilltop site located at an elevation of ten thousand feet and that overlooked the fertile valley below. The official town built there became known as Vitcos and eventually contained royal houses, a plaza, an administrative complex, storage facilities, a sun temple, a hilltop fortress, and residential dwellings.

As with most provincial capitals, the various buildings were constructed in the Incas' *pirca* style—rough stones set in adobe—while the royal dwellings contained at least some of the classic, imperial style stonework used in the capital. According to Titu Cusi, both Pachacuti and his son Tupac Inca had houses built in Vitcos, as did Manco's father, Huayna Capac. Although Inca emperors would have remained in Vitcos only for brief visits, each would have appointed an ethnic Inca governor who would have permanently lived in the hilltop capital.*

Sometime after the reconquest of the area by Tupac Inca, Inca administrators selected a site for a frontier outpost and trading center located more than five thousand feet lower down the Andes than Vitcos and about a three days' journey away. They called the site "Vilcabamba," meaning the "sacred plain." Here imported *mit'a* laborers set about hacking down the thick, tropical trees with stone or bronze axes in order to clear the area before building. After designing a plaza and engineering a water delivery system for the settlement, Inca architects then supervised the construction of buildings that were mostly of rough *pirca* construction and had typical, gabled roofs covered in a thatch made from imported *ichu* grass from the highlands. Inca administrators next ordered *mitmaqcuna* colonists to settle the area in order to clear the land and plant coca plantations and also to begin trading goods manufactured in the Andes in exchange for produce and raw materials from the local Amazonian tribes. Local indigenous groups apparently also resided within Vilcabamba, at least temporarily, for the remains of what may have been their cylindrical stone dwellings have been found, lying scattered among the ruins of the city.

When roughly half a century later Manco Inca abandoned Pachacuti's royal estate and makeshift fortress of Ollantaytambo, the twenty-one-year-old emperor ironically sought refuge in one of the very first provinces that his great-grandfather had conquered: the rugged Vilcabamba.

---

* The architect Vincent Lee believes that Vitcos was built as another of Pachacuti's royal estates.

Vilcabamba, then—located some one hundred miles northwest of Cuzco—and *not* Machu Picchu—located a mere fifty miles from the capital—became Manco Inca's capital-in-exile. Surrounded by thick tropical forests, accessible only by steep and difficult trails, and near several rivers upon which Manco could escape, if necessary, Vilcabamba must have seemed to Manco to be an ideal location where he could set about constructing a new capital city and from which he could carry out his guerrilla war. Yet even though Manco eventually built a palace for himself, there was no escaping the fact that his jungle city had originally been designed as an administrative center, not as a royal estate. Of the roughly four hundred buildings that have partially survived, the majority are of rough *pirca* construction—uncut stones laid in clay mortar. Only a limited number were built in the Incas' imperial style. Manco's move to Vilcabamba in 1537, therefore, was a bit as if the president of the United States, circa the 1840s, had suddenly abandoned the White House and had been forced to move his entire administration to a roughly hewn fort located somewhere on the western frontier.

Vilcabamba, therefore, had few of the physical luxuries that Manco's royal ancestors had been accustomed to. Here there were no commanding heights from which to survey the surrounding countryside; the weather was warmer and more humid than the Inca elite normally preferred, and here, too, there was little imperial architecture, such as Pachacuti had ordered to be built at Machu Picchu, Ollantaytambo, Pisac, and in Cuzco. The inhabitants of Vilcabamba, fighting a nearly perpetual guerrilla war with the nearby Spanish invaders, spent most of their energy and resources simply trying to keep their tiny kingdom alive; there was little time or inclination to undertake grandiose architectural projects in a city that, like Cuzco and Vitcos, might at any moment have to be suddenly abandoned.

It is hardly surprising then, that when Hiram Bingham spent a scant few days at Espíritu Pampa in August of 1911, the dozen or so roughly hewn ruins he discovered there made him doubt whether these could have ever formed a part of Vilcabamba—the fabled capital of the last four Inca emperors. Although the location of the ruins seemed to roughly match the descriptions of Vilcabamba in the chronicles, Bingham expected that Manco's city would have had much better architecture. Machu Picchu, Bingham felt—with its more spectacular location and with its abundant imperial architecture—must surely have been the Incas' final capital.

The fact that Machu Picchu was not Vilcabamba, however, but rather one of Pachacuti's royal estates, makes it much more understandable why it was difficult to find any reference to Machu Picchu or Huayna Picchu in the Spanish chronicles. By the time the Spaniards invaded Cuzco in 1534, the citadel at Machu Picchu more than likely had already been largely abandoned. Any members of Pachacuti's royal *panaca* who had been living at Machu Picchu at the time no doubt would have hurried back to Cuzco during the chaos following the Spaniards' arrival. Their servants, meanwhile, who were drawn from throughout the empire, would have also abandoned the royal enclave, either returning with their masters to Cuzco or else departing for their own homes. Like an expensive resort that requires high maintenance yet whose owners no longer have any income, Pachacuti's royal estate was likely abandoned as Inca systems of taxation, labor, and leisure time all simultaneously collapsed.

Stripped by its owners of its sacred metals and with no political or military significance, Machu Picchu would have held little interest for the invading Spaniards. It is unlikely, in fact, that any Spaniard ever visited the site—otherwise its religious temples would no doubt have been destroyed.* Soon, cloud forest vegetation would have obscured the Inca roads into the area and would have overgrown the palaces and buildings. Within probably less than a decade after its abandonment, Pachacuti's finest architectural jewel would have scarcely been visible to anyone traveling far below on the valley floor.

Since the Spaniards tended overwhelmingly to write about what the *Spaniards* were interested in, and omitted almost everything else, it shouldn't be surprising then that both Bingham and Savoy had difficulty finding any references to Machu Picchu in the Spanish chronicles. Eventually, however, modern scholars did find in a few scattered Spanish documents a number of references to a place called "Picho" that more than likely referred to Machu Picchu. A report in 1565, for example, written by a Spanish emissary traveling from Cuzco to Vilcabamba stated, "that night, I slept at the foot of a snowy summit in the abandoned [Inca] town of Condormarca where there

---

* The anthropologist and Inca specialist John H. Rowe believed that a Spaniard named Gabriel Xuárez may have visited Machu Picchu in 1568, for Xuárez had purchased lands near the site. However, no concrete documentation of an actual visit by a European to the site prior to the twentieth century currently exists.

was a bridge in the ancient style that crossed the Vitcos River [that is, the Vilcabamba River] in order to go to [Ollantay]tambo and to Sapamarca and to Picho, which is a peaceful land."

In 1568, four years before the final sacking of Vilcabamba, another Spanish document mentioned a site called "the village of Picho," located in the same area where Machu Picchu is today. Three centuries would elapse, however, before the actual name "Picchu" would surface, this time on a map published in 1865 by the Italian geographer and explorer Antonio Raimondi. The latter included on his map a peak called "Machu Picchu," jutting up alongside the Urubamba River. Ten years later, the French explorer Charles Wiener would travel from Ollantaytambo up over the Panticalla Pass until he arrived at the Urubamba River at the old bridge crossing of Chuquichaca. In a book he published in 1880, Wiener wrote of how locals in Ollantaytambo had told him about "still other [ancient Inca] towns, about *Huaina-Picchu* and about *Matcho-Picchu,* and I decided to make a final excursion towards the east [to look for them], before continuing my route towards the south." Wiener, however, chose to travel downriver from Chuquichaca to the plantation of Santa Ana instead of heading upriver, in the direction of Machu Picchu, as a road along the Urubamba River between Santa Ana and Ollantaytambo would not be built for another fifteen years and the river was not navigable. Wiener did, however, make a detailed map of the Urubamba Valley, on which he included two peaks and marked them with the names Matchopicchu and Huaynapicchu.

Although local Peruvians had told Wiener that there were Inca ruins at this location, the explorer was nevertheless unable to follow up on the leads he had been given. If he had, then no doubt there would be a bronze plaque dedicated to him at the ruins of Machu Picchu today—and few would have ever heard of Hiram Bingham.

Nearly a century after having been led to the ruins that would eventually immortalize his name, however, Hiram Bingham and his discoveries still provoke controversy. Bingham's 1911 visit to Machu Picchu, in fact, continues to prompt a frequently asked question: should Bingham be given the credit for having discovered the most famous archaeological ruins in the

New World? Or should that credit be reserved for those who had obviously discovered Machu Picchu before him?

Three Peruvian families, after all, were already living beside the peak of Machu Picchu and had partially cleared the ruins before Bingham's visit. In addition, the farmer-guide Melchor Arteaga had not only visited the ruins, but apparently had even been leasing the land to the families living there. Bingham, as mentioned, had found the name of an even earlier explorer written on one of the ruin's walls, along with the date of his visit: "Lizarraga 1902." The inscription was that of Agustín Lizarraga, a local muleteer whom Bingham later met. Lizarraga had lived nearby on the valley floor for more than thirty years and obviously felt the ruins of sufficient importance to have written his name in charcoal on one of the walls nine years before the arrival of the tall North American.* The difference, of course, was that Lizarraga had staked his claim of discovery with a bit of charcoal and had no access to national or international publications. At least three other people had told Bingham where to look for the ruins, although none of them had actually visited them, and one of them, Albert Giesecke, even told Bingham to contact a farmer who lived there named Melchor Arteaga, who could lead him to the ruins.

Clearly, then, a number of people in the region knew about the ruins at Machu Picchu and at least some of those had visited or even lived among them. A few of these in turn had passed this information on to Hiram Bingham. Surprisingly, however, after Bingham's discovery of Machu Picchu, Bingham himself made no mention of anyone else's help. In his final book, *Lost City of the Incas,* in fact, Bingham bluntly wrote that "The professors in the University of Cuzco knew nothing of any ruins down the [Urubamba] valley." This was only technically true, of course, if one did not include the rector of that same university.

In a similar fashion, Bingham "forgot" to mention other information that he either brought with him or else had examined prior to his discovery. While Bingham stated that during his 1911 trip that "We had with us the sheets of Antonio Raimondi's great [1865] map which covered the region we proposed to explore," he omitted the fact that Raimondi's map clearly

---

* Lizarraga died in 1912, the year after Bingham's first visit.

had the peak of Machu Picchu written in large type on it and in the correct location. Bingham further claimed that "We did not know until after our return to New Haven [in 1911] that the French explorer Charles Wiener had heard there were ruins in Huayna Picchu and Machu Picchu which he was unable to reach." Only a year earlier, however, in an article published in the *American Anthropologist,* Bingham had obviously carefully examined Wiener's book for he even cited a footnote in it: "Charles Wiener, in his very unreliable but highly interesting *Perou et Bolivie* (Paris 1880)," Bingham wrote, "says ([in a] footnote, p. 294) that Choquequirau has also been visited by another Frenchman. . . . " Whether or not Wiener's book was "unreliable," the map that Wiener included in it—which clearly showed the locations of the Machu Picchu and Huayna Picchu peaks—and the story he related of having been told that there were ruins located there, were anything but unreliable.

By deliberately omitting the substantial help he received from a number of individuals, by downplaying the information he had at his disposal, and even resorting to the use of some fictional techniques, Bingham effectively rewrote the actual history leading up to his famous discovery. Bingham no doubt instinctively understood that it would have been far less interesting and far less dramatic to have related in his books the simple truth: that he had been told in Cuzco where to look and that he even had a map or maps with him that showed him where to look.

Similarly, Bingham the historian was not beyond suppressing other information if such information tended to contradict his own ideas and conclusions. In a scientific monograph he wrote in 1930, for example, he cited a 1565 report by the Spaniard Diego Rodríguez de Figueroa. In the report Figueroa had stated that along the Urubamba River, between Ollantaytambo and the hanging bridge at Chuquichaca, lay a town called "Picho." "This may be a reference to Machu Picchu," Bingham wrote cautiously in a small footnote, [since] "It is the only thing approaching it that we have succeeded in finding anywhere in the early chronicles." Bingham clearly knew, however, that if Machu Picchu in 1565 were indeed called "Picchu" or "Picho"—at the same time that the rebel capital of the Incas was called Vilcabamba—then obviously Machu Picchu was *not* Vilcabamba.

In *Lost City of the Incas,* however—by which time he had staked his reputation on the fact that Machu Picchu was Vilcabamba—Bingham once again quoted Figueroa's 1565 report, but this time he completely omitted the section that referred to "Picho." As the American anthropologist and Inca specialist John Rowe later wrote about the surprising omission, Bingham obviously knew that including it "would have been fatal to his fantasy identification of Machu Picchu with 'Vilcabamba the Old.' "

Despite Hiram Bingham's shortcomings, however, it is also true that in 1911 the ancient Inca citadel of Machu Picchu was unknown except to local people. No scientist or historian—Peruvian or otherwise—had visited the spectacular, ridgetop citadel located just fifty miles from Cuzco. No one had mapped it, no one had photographed it, no one had studied it, nor had anyone published an account of a visit there. For nearly four centuries before the arrival of Hiram Bingham, the ruins of Machu Picchu had been hidden from the rest of the world.

Bingham was not only the first person to inform the world about the existence of Machu Picchu, but he also led three, multidisciplinary scientific teams that mapped, excavated, measured and explored the site and the surrounding area.* Thus, even though Hiram Bingham was certainly not the first visitor since the fall of the Inca Empire to wander about the abandoned ruins of Machu Picchu, he was incontestably the site's first scientific discoverer. Other scientists and explorers had come close—Antonio Raimondi, Charles Wiener, Albert Giesecke—but Bingham had beaten them all. As the writer Anthony Brandt wrote in the introduction to a modern edition of Bingham's 1922 *Inca Land,* "Bingham was an explorer, not an archaeologist; it was not his destiny to understand Machu Picchu, only to find it."

Thirty-seven years after discovering Machu Picchu, Hiram Bingham briefly returned to Peru, in order to attend the inauguration of the first paved road to zigzag up the hill to the ruins from a railway station on the valley floor. As the still gaunt, now gray-haired explorer stood in full view

---

* Bingham sent numerous crates of artifacts excavated at Machu Picchu, estimated by the Peruvian government to contain over five thousand items, to Yale University's Peabody Museum in New Haven, Connecticut, in 1912 and 1916 for their scientific study. Although Bingham did so with the permission of the Peruvian government at the time, the executive decrees agreed to by Bingham and Yale stipulated that the artifacts must be returned to Peru upon Peru's request. Beginning with an official request in 1920, Peru has been trying to secure their return ever since. Many feel that by the one hundredth anniversary of Machu Picchu's rediscovery—in 2011—that these artifacts should be returned to Peru.

of the Incas' sacred peaks, representatives of the Peruvian government christened the new road the Carretera Hiram Bingham ("The Hiram Bingham Highway"). Eight years later, in 1956, at the age of eighty-one, Hiram Bingham passed away. The boy who had longed for "magnificence"—and who had become a lieutenant colonel, a U.S. senator, and had discovered the ruins of Machu Picchu—was buried with full military honors in Arlington National Cemetery. The ancient Inca ruins that Bingham had been fortunate enough to stumble upon one fine July day in 1911, meanwhile, are now visited on average by more than one thousand people per day and overall by more than half a million people a year.

If Hiram Bingham tended to seize the lion's share of the credit for his discoveries and took liberties with or suppressed certain facts in order to enhance his own reputation or to support his theories, the American explorer Gene Savoy tended to venture even further off the path of historical accuracy and to plunge head over heels into his own self-created myths. Even though by the time Savoy ventured into the Vilcabamba area he was able to travel by railway alongside the Urubamba River and then by truck on a road that was being built up into the Vilcabamba Valley, Savoy's description of the Vilcabamba region could have been lifted directly from a Victorian travelogue. As with Bingham's popular books, the familiar theme of the brave white explorer in search of fabled lost ruins in the midst of a hostile jungle is forcefully pounded home in Savoy's 1970 book, *Antisuyo: The Search for the Lost Cities of the Amazon:*

> We are in a tropical country where without medical treatment the slightest infection can spread like wildfire. We will soon be in snake country where the deadly bushmaster, the largest venomous snake in the Americas growing up to twelve feet in length, abounds. The *chimuco,* as it is known, attacks anything on sight. This deadly pit viper is the most feared of all the baneful creatures in the jungle. Then there is the fer-de-lance, the jergon, and many others whose bites spell death. The dangers of tarantulas, scorpions, vampire bats, biting ants and poisonous plants are exaggerated without proper medicines. Fortunately we have many other medical supplies with us. (However, there is nothing in our medi-

cine chest that will handle yellow fever, malaria, leprosy, beriberi, and many other tropical diseases. Nor is there medicine for the bite of a special fly that is believed to cause uta, a malady that eats away the soft tissue of the mouth, nose, and ears.) The water and food is infested with parasites that invade the delicate intestines, liver, and blood. Nevertheless, these are dangers we are prepared to contend with.

Savoy forgot to mention in his account, however, that to prevent yellow fever he needed only a simple vaccination that had been developed in the 1930s, that beriberi is a vitamin deficiency disease, that leprosy was extremely rare and even more difficult to contract, that bushmasters and other snakes do not attack "anything on sight" but only if they are startled or stepped upon, that the chances of being bitten by a tarantula are about a million to one and that, even if a bite did occur, the tarantula's bite is no worse than a bee sting. Despite Savoy's colorful characterization of the Vilcabamba area as a dangerous green hell, the truth was that Savoy and his team stayed comfortably on the Cobos family's plantation, which lay in the midst of the Pampaconas Valley, very near the ruins of Espíritu Pampa.

Similarly, although Savoy gave credit to Bingham for having been the first scientist to visit Espíritu Pampa and for having discovered the Inca ruins there, he nevertheless wanted to make sure that he got the credit for discovering the "real" Vilcabamba—which Savoy flatly stated Bingham had failed to do. Bingham, of course, had suggested at one point that perhaps the ruins at Espíritu Pampa and those at Machu Picchu were *both* known in the sixteenth century as Vilcabamba. It turned out that Bingham was right about the first and wrong about the second: there had never been two Vilcabambas, only one. Savoy could at most claim that he had found more ruins at Vilcabamba than Bingham and that he had correctly identified them.

Like Bingham, Savoy had initially hoped that if he made spectacular discoveries of lost ruins in Peru his exploring career might reach a new level and that he might also win some measure of international fame. Hiram Bingham, however, had gained worldwide recognition because he had discovered Machu Picchu—one of the most photographed and visited archaeological sites in the world. Yet even today, most people have never heard of Vilcabamba or Gene Savoy. Unlike Bingham, Savoy staked everything on becoming an explorer—an odd and tenuous profession at best. Perhaps in order to compensate for his chosen profession's obvious drawbacks—such as how one is supposed to make a living from it—Savoy eventually transformed himself from his self-created image of a great explorer into that of a great religious leader, the father of the new Messiah and the personal messenger of God. Savoy's gradual metamorphosis ironically paralleled the plot of one of Rudyard Kipling's short stories, "The Man Who Would Be King," in which two white explorers fool the locals in a remote, exotic country into believing that the two are gods. In Kipling's tale, the explorers' deceit is eventually exposed and they pay a heavy price for it, one of them losing his head and the other losing both his ill-gotten kingdom and his treasure, escaping with nothing more than his life.

Savoy, by contrast, still continues to preside over the religion he founded in Peru, one that is composed in part of various "secrets" he states that he discovered during his many jungle expeditions. In 1977, Savoy published a book in which he claimed to have discovered the secrets of immortality. For decades, in fact, it appeared to some that Savoy had beaten the aging process altogether. Time, however, eventually did catch up with the maverick explorer and by the year 2004, at the age of seventy-seven, Savoy could no longer ignore his biological clock; he was finally forced to abandon any further expeditions due to poor health. Now Savoy's son Sean, who was raised in his father's religion, continues to lead expeditions into the Chachapoyas region of northern Peru. There he helps to keep his father's discoveries alive by periodically shepherding religious acolytes from Savoy's church to the Peruvian jungle.

A lifelong devotee of the sun, whose energy Savoy allows to enter his body by gazing directly at it, Savoy believes that the sun's energy delays the aging process and restores the body. Meanwhile, Savoy continues to write books while no doubt preparing himself for his final mission—an ecstatic reunion with Inti, the Sun God—that golden, celestial orb the ancient Incas once worshipped and adored.

Exploration for other undiscovered Inca ruins in Peru, meanwhile, continues. Vincent and Nancy Lee, now in their sixties, have returned to the ancient province of Vilcabamba nearly every dry season since their first visit there in 1982. And while Bingham spent roughly four weeks in the Vilcabamba area in 1911 and Gene Savoy spent perhaps three months there in 1964 and 1965, the Lees have spent more than *two years* in that same region during the last few decades—mapping, surveying, and conducting systematic explorations.

Lee has returned a number of times with other specialists to the ruins of Puncuyoc, which he has concluded was a solar observatory that was able to mark both the June solstice and the two equinoxes. Lee believes that Puncuyoc served as the official calendar for the entire Vilcabamba province.

> It was clearly a solar observatory. So all of a sudden now we realize why it was so important, why it was worth building such a beautiful little building in the middle of nowhere and why there is a five-thousand-foot staircase going up there. It was clearly the solar observatory for Vitcos. And I think it was built by Pachacuti. He was the one who built the best buildings at Vitcos, and I think he built Puncuyoc as well. It's a solar observatory—not a sun temple, because the sun temple was at Ñusta Ispanan [Chuquipalta], just up the road from Vitcos. [The archaeoastronomer] Bernard Bell and I are going to do a publication on it because we've found all sorts of new information about Puncuyoc. It's not only an interesting site but it's completely *pristine*—no one has disturbed it in over four hundred years!

While Vincent Lee pursues his investigations of Puncuyoc, other areas of the Vilcabamba region have recently yielded up additional Inca ruins. And, as is usual with discoveries of lost ruins, some of these discoveries have also created their fair share of controversies. Lost Inca cities, after all—like any other highly coveted resource—are in short supply; if you find one that is good enough, fame may lie just around the corner. The competition to find and stake a claim to a lost Inca city, therefore, can be fierce.

In 1999, a fifty-three-year-old British-born writer, guide, and Inca specialist, Peter Frost, was leading a hiking tour in the southern Vilcabamba region, near the ruins of Choqquequirau. One of Frost's clients, Scott Gorsuch, a clinical psychologist from Santa Barbara, California, thought he saw what looked to be ruins on an adjacent ridge in the distance. "We spotted [with binoculars] what appeared to be a sacred platform on one of the peaks," Gorsuch said, "and it seemed to have significance—it caught the sun's first rays in the morning and last ones at night." Frost and his group hiked through brush and reached the ridge, which flanked a 12,746-foot mountain peak called Cerro Victoria that rises up in the southern Vilcabamba Range, about sixty miles northwest of Machu Picchu. There they found various ruins: looted tombs, circular building foundations, and part of what appeared to be an ancient stone aqueduct.

After this initial sighting, Frost passed on the information to Gary Ziegler, a fifty-nine-year-old American explorer, archaeologist, and lifelong Vilcabamba aficionado. As a co-owner of the adventure tourism company Manu Expeditions, Ziegler had employed Frost during the recent trek. According to Ziegler, Gorsuch persuaded him and Frost to write a National Geographic grant proposal.

Eventually, the National Geographic Society (whose first sponsored field expedition was Hiram Bingham's second trip to Machu Picchu in 1912 and which has funded more than eight thousand expeditions since) agreed to provide funds for a research trip to the site, during the dry season of 2001. Frost, Ziegler, and a Peruvian archaeologist, Alfredo Valencia Zegarra, were the co-leaders of the proposed trip. Ultimately, the three put together an expeditionary team that consisted of Peruvian archaeologists, a cartographer, an archaeophysicist, a dozen mule handlers, a helicopter and pilot, and a documentary film team sent along by National Geographic. "I hadn't been involved in anything of that size, ever," Ziegler said. "It was an immense team." It was also the kind of multidisciplinary expedition that Bingham had pioneered in the area some ninety years earlier.

In the Andean winter of 2001, the expedition team finally arrived at remote Cerro Victoria. There, on the mountain's flanks at elevations of between roughly 9,000 and 12,500 feet, they discovered clusters of previously undocumented settlements scattered amidst an area local Quechua speakers called Qoriwayrachina, meaning "where wind was used to refine gold." The team ultimately discovered more than two hundred structures—storehouses, dwellings, Inca roads, a nearly five-mile-long aqueduct, ceremonial platforms, cemeteries, and funeral towers, scattered across an area of over sixteen square miles. The buildings, at least a hundred of which were circular in shape, were badly worn and were built in the Incas' rough pirca-style, unlike the imperial-style architecture of carefully cut stones found at Cuzco and Machu Picchu. As with Bingham's discovery of Machu Picchu, however, while the scattered ruins of Qoriwayrachina may have been previously unknown to science and thus figured on no maps, the area itself was already inhabited by two peasant families who had apparently made use of some of the abandoned stone structures.

Preliminary results indicate that Qoriwayrachina may have been inhabited for more than a thousand years before the Inca Empire, the Incas then presumably expanding into the area after the initial conquests of Pachacuti. Unlike Machu Picchu, which was used as a seasonal resort for the Inca emperor and his royal descent group, Qoriwayrachina during the time of the Incas was more than likely a settlement of non-Inca miners—men who had been imported into the area in order to perform their labor tax by working the nearby silver mines on Cerro Victoria. An Inca road clearly connected the mining community of Qoriwayrachina with Choqquequirau, less than ten miles away, and from there roads connected to Vitcos, Vilcabamba, and Machu Picchu.

The international press, however, soon played up the discovery, sometimes with provocative titles such as "High in Andes, a Place That May Have Been Incas' Last Refuge." The lead paragraph in that story began,

> Every generation or so, explorers of the high Andes of Peru come upon an elaborate sacred place or city that had been unknown to archaeologists studying the Inca civilization. The most impressive still is Machu Picchu, discovered in 1911, and no important "lost city" has come to light since the 1960's [a reference to Savoy's identification of Vilcabamba]. Not, it seems, until now.

Toward the end of the 2001 expedition, however, Frost and Ziegler had a falling out. With the lure of a potential *National Geographic* feature article, the pressure of the film crew, the size of the expedition, and the fact that instead of a single leader, there were three *co-leaders,* perhaps that shouldn't have been surprising. Ziegler decided to depart with a small group in order to do some additional exploring on his own. Ziegler later said:

> One of our wranglers had after our previous trips come back and had cleared a little farm on the trail over to Choqquequirau—he had actu-

ally been down in that canyon. And he said *"Jefe,* I found some walls down there—you ought to go down there and take a look." So I did. That was Froilan Muñoz, one of our wrangler-employees who has worked for us for years.

Less than two miles from the ruins of Qoriwayrachina yet nearly four thousand feet *below* them, on an isolated bench or mesa some one and a half miles long perched above the Yanama River, Muñoz led Ziegler, the English explorer Hugh Thomson, and his team to what was clearly an Inca site. It was an area that had previously been called Cotacoca, a location that they soon discovered was completely cut off from the rest of the world. As Ziegler described it:

> You can't get to it by going down or up the [Yanama] river. The river is about two hundred or three hundred feet below the site and at one time must have been right at the site because there are canals. It's like a time warp—this Lost World just sitting there. And of course it was all covered with this heavy vegetation and because of the heavy impenetrability of the canyon nobody had gotten there.

The Inca site contained more than thirty structures, among them a seventy-five-foot-long Inca-style meeting hall, or *kallanka,* a large walled compound enclosing a central plaza, and numerous rectangular houses as well as circular-shaped structures similar to those found in abundance at Qoriwayrachina and Vilcabamba. According to Ziegler, Cotacoca possibly served as an Inca administrative center and/or as a supply *tambo.* It is located along the main Inca road that once led from the interior of the Vilcabamba province and then crossed the Apurímac River via an immense hanging bridge before heading into the Apurímac region beyond. Ziegler states that:

> I think Cotacoca controlled the access to Choqquequirau and to the upper Apurímac River. Manco's warriors may have used it in the post-conquest period to stage attacks across the Apurímac against the Spaniards. We also finally identified how the Incas got to Choqque-quirau—they went from Cotacoca straight down to the upper Apurímac

and had a hanging bridge there—but before they got there they had a branch up to Choqquequirau.

The following summer, Peter Frost returned to Qoriwayrachina, still working under the auspices of the National Geographic Society, while Ziegler returned with his own exploration team to Cotacoca. In February 2004, *National Geographic* magazine published a feature article on Qoriwayrachina, authored by Frost, in which Frost mentioned Ziegler just once and only in relation to Ziegler having been led by a "local farmer" to another set of ruins nearby. In the various press releases put out by the National Geographic Society about the expeditions to Qoriwayrachina, Gary Ziegler was not mentioned at all.

The fact that two of the leaders of a highly publicized "lost city" expedition had a falling out, of course, no doubt had as much to do with the potential high stakes of discovery as it had to do with anything else. One has only to look at the scramble to gain credit for the discovery of Machu Picchu and Vilcabamba, however, to understand that Frost and Ziegler are in good company. The need to "strive for magnificence" as Bingham put it, to attach one's name to something immortal and permanent seems to be a universal human motivation. Such a need presumably drove Pachacuti to build Machu Picchu in the first place; in doing so, the Inca emperor echoed the same craving for immortality as have other ancient cultures and civilizations.

Manco Inca, unlike Pachacuti and his other royal ancestors, however, had little time to make his architectural mark on history. He had no time to build royal retreats, no time to redesign cities, no time to invent new architectural styles. Manco's capital of Vilcabamba was much like himself—undeveloped in the arts of anything other than as a seat for waging guerrilla warfare and for administering the remnants of a once mighty empire. Although he had been born in a united realm with his father, Huayna Capac, on the throne, Manco was ultimately forced to choose between ruling as a puppet emperor or trying forcibly to eject the Spaniards from his ancestors' lands. Manco, of course, eventually chose the latter. Yet in the end, he was unable to preserve any more than a vestige of the vast empire he had inherited: his capital was sacked, his physical body was burned and destroyed, while the frontier city

he had transformed into a guerrilla capital was ultimately left to be consumed and nearly obliterated by the jungle.

Had Manco succeeded in retaining his independent kingdom and had
his sons arrived at an accommodation with the Spaniards, then the Kingdom of Vilcabamba might even today be represented at the United Nations,
with a Quechua-speaking ambassador and an Inca monarch perhaps still
presiding over the throne. The same tourists who currently visit Machu Picchu, in fact, would then have been able to proceed on to the Amazonian-
based, still inhabited Inca capital, one that no doubt would have displayed
bronze statues of its ancient leader, Manco Inca, perhaps sitting astride a
Spanish horse with a harquebus in one hand and a Spanish sword in the
other. Demonstrations of *quipu* reading, meanwhile, or of the ancient arts of
Inca stonecutting might have been taught, or at least might have been made
available on DVD. Like the Inca Empire, however, which was prematurely
extinguished after an existence of a mere ninety years, Manco's rebel kingdom, too, was ultimately aborted while he and his followers' valiant efforts
came to naught.

Peruvian history since Manco's death, of course, has been a rather sordid
one. The Incas, although an authoritarian monarchy, had succeeded nevertheless during their short reign not only in creating a massive empire, but
perhaps more importantly in guaranteeing all of the empire's millions of inhabitants the basic necessities of life: adequate food, water, and shelter. It
was an achievement that no subsequent government—Spanish or Peruvian—has attained since.

Perhaps partly due to the fact that they lived in a land beset by periodic
earthquakes and destructive El Niños, the ancient Incas once believed that
history unfurled itself in a succession of ages that were separated from one
another by violent upheavals called *pachacutis,* or "overturnings of the
world." Each upheaval was believed to completely reverse the natural order
of things: what had once been upper became lower; what had once been
strong became weak, soft became hard, and so on. A *pachacuti* was believed
to have ushered in the creation of the Inca Empire; it was not a coincidence,
therefore, that the emperor responsible for creating the Inca Empire
adopted that word as his name. Similarly, the Spanish invasion and conquest
were believed to have been the manifestations of another *pachacuti,* ushering
in the "upside-down" world that continues to this day. According to Inca

beliefs, however, previous epochs do not recede into the past; rather they remain dormant in the Inca underworld, awaiting a new *pachacuti* that may one day cause their return. Many inhabitants of the Andes still believe that the next *pachacuti* may as yet usher in the return of the previous Inca world.

Some fourteen million people, meanwhile, still speak the ancient Inca language, Quechua, while many peasants in the Andes still make offerings of *chicha* (corn beer) and coca leaves to the same snow-capped *apus* that their ancient ancestors once worshipped and adored. Tales are still told of the exploits of that small group of people who once possessed a small kingdom in the area of Cuzco and then conquered the entire civilized world, before a *pachacuti* occurred and the immense empire they had wrought suddenly collapsed. Sandal-footed peasants chewing coca leaves, meanwhile, still use many of the roads the Incas built down the eastern side of the Andes into the jungle, some of those roads perhaps linking up with as yet undiscovered and forgotten ruins, as clouds continue to build and dissolve, hummingbirds feed, and the roads, finely laid with so much cut stone, lead off to—well, who knows exactly where?

ACKNOWLEDGMENTS

❖

INEVITABLY, IN A WORK OF THIS SORT, I OWE MANY PEOPLE A great deal of thanks. Years ago, when I worked for a stint as a writer for the *Lima Times,* I met and interviewed the explorer and architect Vincent Lee, who with his wife, Nancy, happened to be passing through Lima after one of their many trips to Vilcabamba. I was relatively new in Peru at the time, was doing graduate work in anthropology, and had only just visited Machu Picchu. It was on a bookshelf in a small *hostal* far below the Inca citadel that I discovered Lee's first book, *Sixpac Manco.* It was my initial glimpse into the world of Vilcabamba, and I was shocked to learn that people were still exploring for and discovering new Inca ruins in the area. Many years later, Vince was kind enough to supply drawings of his detailed reconstructions of Vilcabamba and some of the other nearby ruins for this book. I am proud to call Vince and Nancy friends.

My UK agent, Julian Alexander, never swerved from his initial enthusiasm when I suggested writing an account of the story of Manco Inca and Vilcabamba; it was through his indefatigable efforts and those of my US agent, Sarah Lazin, that this book became a reality. To both of them, I owe a strong debt of gratitude.

I owe many thanks to my editor at Simon & Schuster, Bob Bender, who was also enthusiastic from the very beginning and who always offered great advice and encouragement. During the years that it took to write this book, he was as solid an editor as one could hope for. Thanks also to Ariana Dingman for designing a great book cover, to Fred Chase, the meticulous copy editor, and to Johanna Li, the editorial assistant. To Alan Brooke at Piatkus Books, UK, I am also grateful for his assistance.

During the writing of the book, I relied upon a wide variety of sources and collections. I found the UCLA library system and its excellent Latin American collection to be first rate. I want to thank the staff there, the staff of the map room collection, and also the staffs at libraries in such disparate locations as London; NYC; Washington, DC; and Lima.

A number of specialists were kind enough to take the time from their busy schedules in order to read portions of this book and to offer their insightful comments. Many thanks to Vincent Lee, Dr. Terrence D'Altroy, Dr. Johan Reinhard, Dr. Noble David Savage, Dr. Brian S. Bauer, Dr. Matthew Restall, Dr. Jeremy Mumford, and Dr. Kris Lane. If any errors have remained in the manuscript, I am solely to blame.

I would also like to thank Bart Lewis, who was a great help in many ways, as well as Gary Ziegler, James Gierman, Adriana von Hagen, Sean Savoy, Gene Savoy, Nick Asheshov, Paul Goldrick, Layne MacQuarrie, and Dr. Douglas Sharon, of the Phoebe A. Hearst Museum of Anthropology. Sadhbh Walshe was one of the first to read the entire manuscript at an early stage and made many helpful comments. Finally, I would like to express my love and gratitude to Ciara Byrne, who, more than anyone else, helped to make this book a reality.

NOTES

PREFACE

PAGE

5 *In weighing, cataloguing:* Felipe Huamán Poma de Ayala, *Letter to a King* (New York: Dutton, 1978), 19.

I. THE DISCOVERY

PAGE

10 *"I believe that he got the fancy":* Alfred Bingham, *Explorer of Machu Picchu: Portrait of Hiram Bingham* (Greenwich: Triune, 2000), 37.

11 *"Through Sergeant Carrasco":* Hiram Bingham, *Inca Land* (Boston: Houghton Mifflin, 1922), 317.

12 *"Hardly had we left the hut":* Hiram Bingham, *Lost City of the Incas* (London: Weidenfeld & Nicolson, 2002), 178.

12 *"Suddenly, I found myself":* Ibid., 179.

12 *"I climbed a marvelous great stairway":* Hiram Bingham, *Inca Land,* 321.

13 *"I could scarcely believe":* Hiram Bingham, *Lost City,* 180.

13 *"My dearest love":* Alfred Bingham, *Explorer,* 20.

13 *"The stone is as fine":* Ibid., 25.

14 *"the 'Lost City'":* Hiram Bingham, *Lost City of the Incas* (New York: Duell, Sloan and Pearce, 1948), third photo insert, 2.

2. A FEW HUNDRED WELL-ARMED ENTREPRENEURS

PAGE

15 *"In the last ages of the world":* Seneca, quoted in Henry Kamen, *How Spain Became a World Power, 1492–1763* (New York: HarperCollins, 2003), 46.

20 *I found very many islands:* Cecil Jane (trans.), *The Journal of Christopher Columbus* (New York: Bonanza, 1989) 191–201.

21 *"You have arrived at a good moment":* Bartolomé de Las Casas, *A Short Account of the Destruction of the Indies* (London: Penguin, 1992), xix.

21 *"This news"*: Ibid., xix.

25 *They were cobblers:* James Lockhart, *The Men of Cajamarca* (Austin: University of Texas Press, 1972), 38.

25 *None received:* Rafael Varón Gabai, *Francisco Pizarro and His Brothers* (Norman: University of Oklahoma Press, 1997), 24.

25 *The leaders of most conquest:* Matthew Restall, *Seven Myths of the Spanish Conquest* (Oxford: Oxford University Press, 2003), 35.

25 *By 1524, forty-six-year-old:* The Company of the Levant was signed as a formal contract on March 10, 1526.

26 *"a man of short stature":* Pedro de Cieza de León, *Guerra de las Salinas,* in *Guerras Civiles del Perú,* vol. 1, Chapter 70 (Madrid: Librería de la Viuda de Rico, 1899), 355.

28 *"They were carrying many pieces":* Raúl Porras Barrenechea, *Los Cronistas del Perú* (Lima: Biblioteca Clásicos del Perú, vol. 2, 1986), 55.

29 *"Gentlemen! This line":* Garcilaso de la Vega, *Royal Commentaries of the Incas,* Part 2 (Austin: University of Texas Press, 1966), 651.

30 *Unbeknownst to the Spaniards:* It is also possible that this official was a member of the lower nobility, or *curaca* class.

30 *"where they were from":* Pedro de Cieza de León, *The Discovery and Conquest of Peru* (Durham: Duke University Press, 1998), 108.

31 *"which strangely pleased him":* Ibid.

31 *"all came to see":* Ibid., 109.

32 *"They looked at how the Spaniard":* Pedro de Cieza de León, *Crónica del Perú* (Tercera Parte), Chap. xx (Lima: Universidade Catolica del Perú, 1989), 57.

32 *"saw silver vessels":* Cieza de León, *The Discovery and Conquest of Peru,* 113.

33 *"Be my witnesses":* Ibid., 126.

36 *"As for you, Captain":* Ibid., 136–38.

37 *In Trujillo, Pizarro:* The birth date of Pizarro's maternal half-brother, Francisco Martín de Alcántara, is actually unknown.

3. SUPERNOVA OF THE ANDES

PAGE

38 *"Men do not rest":* Thucydides, *The History of the Peloponnesian War,* quoted in Andrew Schmookler, *The Parable of the Tribes* (Boston: Houghton Mifflin, 1984), 70.

38 *"The Inca [emperor Pachacuti]":* Pedro Sarmiento de Gamboa, *History of the Incas* (Mineola: Dover, 1999), 109.

40 *The empire stitched together:* Much of the information in this paragraph is based upon information from Dr. Terrence D'Altroy, personal communication.

41 *The latter:* Eric Wolf, *Peasants* (Englewood Cliffs: Prentice Hall, 1966), 10.

42 *Over thousands of years:* Luis Guillermo Lumbreras, *De los Orígines de la Civilización en el Perú* (Lima: Peisa, 1988), 51.

42 *According to Inca legend:* For a discussion of the various interpretations of the history of the Inca state, see Brian S. Bauer, *The Development of the Inca State* (Austin: University of Texas Press, 1992), 4.

44 *"turned his attention to the people":* Ibid., 103.

46 *"fell ill":* Juan de Betanzos, *Narrative of the Incas* (Austin: University of Texas Press, 1996), 183.

47 *"but when they arrived":* Miguel Cabello de Balboa, quoted in Noble David Cook, *Born to Die: Disease and New World Conquest, 1492–1650* (Cambridge: Cambridge University Press, 1998), 80.

48 *"It was a dreadful illness":* Francisco López de Gómara, quoted in Cook, *Born to Die,* 66.

48 *Sometime around 1527:* Cook, *Born to Die,* 77.

48 *Where it differed:* D'Altroy, *The Incas,* 106.

49 *Apparently the thinking:* Ibid.

49 *Though Atahualpa:* Ibid., 107.

50 *Atoq was first tortured:* Ibid., 80.

51 *"Huascar was badly":* Betanzos, *Narrative,* 227.

51 *"ordered that each":* Ibid., 244.

53 *"The rest of the lords":* Ibid.

4. WHEN EMPIRES COLLIDE

PAGE

55 *"For ourselves, we shall":* Thucydides, *The History of the Peloponnesian War,* quoted in Andrew Schmookler, *The Parable of the Tribes* (Boston: Houghton Mifflin, 1984), 46.

57 *"rested in the cotton tents":* Francisco López de Xerez, *Verdadera Relación de la Conquista del Perú,* in *Colección de Libros y Documentos Referentes a la Historia del Perú,* First Series, Vol. 5 (Lima: 1917), 41.

58 *"So many tents were visible":* Miguel de Estete, *El Descubrimiento y la Conquista del Perú,* in *Boletín de la Sociedad Ecuatoriana de Estudios Históricos Americanos,* Vol. 1 (Quito: 1918), 321.

59 *"This town":* Xerez, *Verdadera Relación,* 48.

60 *"[The Incas' camp]":* Ibid., 53.

61 *"that great lord Atahualpa":* Estete, *El Descubrimiento,* 321.

61 *Another eyewitness:* Hernando Pizarro, *Carta de Hernando Pizarro a los Oidores de la Audiencia de Santo Domingo,* quoted in Gonzalo Fernández de Oviedo y Valdés,

La Historia General y Natural de las Indias, Book 5, Chapter 15, in *Biblioteca de Autores Españoles (Continuación),* Vol. 121 (Madrid: 1959), 86.

61 *"a very fine scarlet wool":* Pedro Pizarro, *Relación del Descubrimiento y Conquista de los Reinos del Perú,* in *Colección de Documentos Inéditos para la Historia de España.* Vol. 5 (Madrid: 1844), 248.

62 *"Most serene Inca!":* Garcilaso de la Vega, *Royal Commentaries of the Incas,* Part 2 (Austin: University of Texas Press, 1966), 673.

62 *"With regard to the version":* Ibid., 681.

63 *"Atahualpa and his nobles":* Felipe Huamán Poma de Ayala, *Letter to a King* (New York: E. P. Dutton, 1978), 108.

64 *"When I arrived":* Hernando Pizarro, *Carta de Hernando Pizarro,* 85.

64 *"Maizabilica, [a coastal chief]":* Xerez, *Verdadera Relación,* 52.

64 *"of good appearance":* Ibid., 69.

65 *"This punishment filled all":* Ibid., 25.

65 *"[Chief] Maizabilica is a scoundrel":* Ibid., 52.

66 *" A [provincial] chief has refused' ":* Ibid.

67 *"He smiled like a man":* Hernando Pizarro, *Carta de Hernando Pizarro,* 86.

70 *"[We were] very scared":* Estete, *El Descubrimiento,* 322.

70 *"it is certain that everything":* Pedro de Cieza de León, *The Discovery and Conquest of Peru* (Durham: Duke University Press, 1998), 203.

73 *"When his [Atahualpa's] squadrons":* Pedro Pizarro, *Relación,* 227.

74 *"The Governor [Pizarro] and Captain-General":* Xerez, *Verdadera Relación,* 55.

75 *"First came a squadron of Indians":* Ibid., 56.

75 *"Eighty lords carried":* Estete, *El Descubrimiento,* 323.

75 *"Behind him came two other litters":* Xerez, *Verdadera Relación,* 56.

76 *"And indeed the Indians told the truth":* Pedro Pizarro, *Relación,* 227.

78 *"I will not leave this place":* Hernando Pizarro, *Carta de Hernando Pizarro,* 86.

78 *"[In the name of the] high":* Ronald Wright, *Stolen Continents: The Americas Through Indian Eyes Since 1492* (Boston: Houghton Mifflin, 1992), 65.

78 *"And so I request and require":* Ibid., 66.

80 *"With great scorn":* Xerez, *Verdadera Relación,* 57.

81 *"Come out! Come out":* Cristóbal de Mena, in Raúl Porras Barrenechea, *Las Relaciones Primitivas de la Conquista del Perú* (Lima: 1967), 86.

81 *"Didn't you see what happened?":* Estete, *El Descubrimiento,* 323.

82 *"They were so filled with fear":* Juan Ruiz de Arce, *Advertencias que Hizo el Fundador del Vínculo y Mayorazgo a Los Sucesores en Él,* in *Tres Testigos de la Conquista del Perú* (Buenos Aires: 1953), 99.

82 *"The horsemen rode out on top":* Xerez, *Verdadera Relación,* 58.

82 *"The Governor [Pizarro] armed himself":* Ibid., 57.

83   *"Many Indians had their hands cut off"*: Mena, *Las Relaciones,* 87.

83   *"Although [the Spaniards] killed"*: Pedro Pizarro, *Relación,* 229.

84   *"All of them were shouting"*: Pedro Cataño, quoted in José Antonio del Busto Durhurburu, *Una Relación y un Estudio Sobre la Conquista, Revista Histórica,* Vol. 27 (Lima: Instituto Histórico del Perú, 1964), 282.

84   *"[One of the men killed]"*: Xerez, *Verdadera Relación,* 58.

5. A ROOMFUL OF GOLD

PAGE

86   *"'When I had a chief'"*: Francisco López de Xerez, *Verdadera Relación de la Conquista del Perú,* in *Colección de Libros y Documentos Referentes a la Historia del Perú,* First Series, Vol. 5 (Lima: 1917), 59.

86   *"The promise given"*: Niccolò Machiavelli, *Il Principe* [*The Prince*] (Milan: RCS Rizzoli, 1999), 167.

88   *"Don't take it as an insult"*: Xerez, *Verdadera Relación,* 59.

89   *"You should consider it"*: Ibid.

89   *"When I had a chief, the lord"*: Ibid.

89   *"If you were seized"*: Ibid., 60.

90   *"Atahualpa responded that he"*: Ibid.

90   *"The Governor immediately ordered"*: Cristóbal de Mena, in Raúl Porras Barrenechea, *Las Relaciones Primitivas de la Conquista del Perú* (Lima: 1967), 88.

92   *"returned to the camp . . . with"*: Xerez, *Verdadera Relación,* 62.

96   *"The Governor asked him how much"*: Ibid., 68.

96   *"How long will your messengers"*: Ibid., 69.

99   *With four pounds of gold:* Pablo E. Pérez-Mallaína, *Spain's Men of the Sea: Daily Life on the Indies Fleets in the Sixteenth Century* (Baltimore: Johns Hopkins University Press, 1998), 124.

101 *"One can see . . . many"*: Pedro Sancho de la Hoz, *Relación para S.M. de lo Sucedido en la Conquista y Pacificación de Estas Provincias de la Nueva Castilla y de la Calidad de la Tierra,* in *Colección de Libros y Documentos Referentes a la Historia del Perú,* First Series, Vol. 5 (Lima: 1917), 194.

102 *"And thus, [on some days]"*: Xerez, *Verdadera Relación,* 72.

103 *"When the chiefs of this province heard"*: Ibid., 71.

103 *"they came from each province"*: Miguel de Estete, *El Descubrimiento y la Conquista del Perú,* in *Boletín de la Sociedad Ecuatoriana de Estudios Históricos Americanos,* Vol. 1 (Quito: 1918), 325.

103 *"Some of these chiefs were lords"*: Xerez, *Verdadera Relación,* 71.

103 *"behaved towards them"*: Estete, *El Descubrimiento,* 325.

104 *"He delayed somewhat longer"*: Pedro Pizarro, *Relación del Descubrimiento y Conquista de los Reinos del Perú,* in *Colección de Documentos Inéditos para la Historia de España,* Vol. 5 (Madrid: 1844), 248.

104 *"Huascar, after being taken prisoner"*: Felipe Huamán Poma de Ayala, *Letter to a King* (New York: E. P. Dutton, 1978), 110.

106 *Atahualpa soon became proficient:* Ibid.

106 *"After he was a prisoner"*: Xerez, *Verdadera Relación,* 108.

106 *"[The emperor] is the wisest"*: Gaspar de Espinoza, in *Colección de Documentos Inéditos Relativos al Descubrimiento, Conquista, y Organización de las Antiguas Posesiones Españolas de América y Oceanía Sacados de los Archivos del Reino y Muy Especialmente del de Indias,* Vol. 42 (Madrid: 1884), 70.

106 *"The ladies . . . brought him"*: Pedro Pizarro, *Relación,* 249.

107 *" 'those [native] dogs' "*: Ibid., 250.

107 *"I asked him what the trunks"*: Ibid.

109 *Strangers in a strange land:* Francisco Pizarro had actually sent his brother Hernando with twenty cavalry to ride south from Cajamarca on January 5, 1533, prior to the three Spaniards' trip to Cuzco. Hernando had ridden for fifteen days down the Andes before heading to the coast and arriving at Pachacamac, a sacred shrine located just south of modern-day Lima. Hernando and his men, however—unlike the three Spaniards traveling in litters—did not travel further south to Cuzco.

109 *"All the steep mountains"*: Sancho de la Hoz, *Relación,* 190.

110 *"This city is the greatest"*: Municipal Council of Lima, *Libro Primero de Cabildos de Lima,* Part 3 (Lima: 1888), 4.

110 *"[It is] full of the palaces"*: Sancho de la Hoz, *Relación,* 192.

111 *"Upon the hill, which"*: Ibid., 193.

111 *"The most beautiful thing"*: Ibid.

112 *"[And they are] so close together"*: Pedro Pizarro, *Relación,* 275.

112 *"The Spaniards who see them"*: Sancho de la Hoz, *Relación,* 194.

112 *"took possession of that city"*: Xerez, *Verdadera Relación,* 103.

113 *"These buildings were sheathed"*: Mena, *Las Relaciones,* 93.

114 *"To our Indian eyes"*: Huamán Poma de Ayala, *Letter,* 108.

115 *"He didn't like the Christians"*: Mena, *Las Relaciones,* 93.

115 *"The Christians went to the buildings"*: Ibid.

115 *"The greater part of this"*: Xerez, *Verdadera Relación,* 104.

117 *"When Almagro and these men arrived"*: Pedro Pizarro, *Relación,* 244.

117 *"I shall die"*: Ibid.

6. REQUIEM FOR A KING

PAGE

118 *"In 1531 another great villain"*: Bartolomé de Las Casas, *A Short Account of the Destruction of the Indies* (London: Penguin, 1992), 107.

118 *"When they reached the Governor"*: Gonzalo Fernández de Oviedo y Valdés, *Historia General y Natural de las Indias,* in *Biblioteca de Autores Españoles,* Vol. 5 (Madrid: 1959), 122.

118 *"Politics have no relation"*: Niccolò Machiavelli, *The Prince* (New York: Bantam, 1966), 57.

122 *"Almagro . . . did not want"*: Pedro Pizarro, *Relación del Descubrimiento y Conquista de los Reinos del Perú,* in *Colección de Documentos Inéditos para la Historia de España,* Vol. 5 (Madrid: 1844), 245.

124 *"To my sorely missed father"*: James Lockhart, *The Men of Cajamarca: A Social and Biographical Study of the First Conquistadors of Peru* (Austin: University of Texas Press, 1972), 459.

126 *"wept, saying that they"*: Pedro Pizarro, *Relación,* 245.

126 *"this fat man"*: Hernando Pizarro, *Confesión de Hernando Pizarro,* in *Colección de Documentos Inéditos Para la Historia de Chile,* Vol. 5 (Santiago: 1889), 408.

127 *"and that all these men are marching"*: Francisco López de Xerez, *Verdadera Relación de la Conquista del Perú,* in *Colección de Libros y Documentos Referentes a la Historia del Perú,* First Series, Vol. 5 (Lima: 1917), 107.

127 *"What kind of treason is this"*: Ibid., 108.

127 *"Are you joking?"*: Ibid.

127 *"It is true that if any warriors"*: Pedro Cataño, quoted in José Antonio de Busto Duthurburu, *Una Relación y un Estudio Sobre la Conquista,* in *Revista Histórica, Organo del Instituto Histórico del Perú,* Vol. 27 (Lima: 1964), 285.

127 *"[He said] all of this without"*: Xerez, *Verdadera Relación,* 108.

130 *"Insisting vehemently"*: Miguel de Estete, *El Descubrimiento y la Conquista del Perú,* in *Boletín de la Sociedad Ecuatoriana de Estudios Históricos Americanos,* Vol. 1 (Quito: 1918), 328.

130 *"should die by burning"*: Xerez, *Verdadera Relación,* 110.

130 *"Atahualpa wept [openly]"*: Pedro Pizarro, *Relación,* 246.

130 *"If they were going"*: Ibid., 247.

131 *"I saw the Governor weep"*: Ibid.

131 *"When he [Atahualpa] was taken"*: Ibid., 248.

132 *"[He instructed him in]"*: Pedro Sancho de la Hoz, *Relación para S.M. de lo Sucedido en la Conquista y Pacificación de Estas Provincias de la Nueva Castilla y de la Calidad de la Tierra,* in *Colección de Libros y Documentos Referentes a la Historia del Perú,* First Series, Vol. 5 (Lima: 1917), 127.

133 *"Atahualpa said that he was entrusting"*: C. Gangotena y Jirón, *La Descendencia de Atahualpa*, in *Boletín de la Academia Nacional de Historia (Ecuador)*, Vol. 38, No. 91 (Quito: 1958), 118.

133 *"As the sky began turning"*: The actual prayer Friar Valverde said is unknown. Eyewitnesses state that various prayers and credos were uttered during Atahualpa's execution.

134 *"With these last words"*: Sancho de la Hoz, *Relación*, 127.

134 *"He died on Saturday"*: Xerez, *Verdadera Relación*, 111.

135 *"a large felt hat"*: Gonzalo Fernández de Oviedo y Valdés, *Historia General y Natural de las Indias*, in *Biblioteca de Autores Españoles*, Vol. 121, Chapter 22 (Madrid: 1959), 122.

135 *"no native warriors in the"*: Ibid.

136 *"I now see that I"*: Ibid.

136 *"eyes wet with tears"*: Ibid.

7. THE PUPPET KING

PAGE

138 *"For a prince should"*: Niccolò Machiavelli, *The Prince* (New York: Bantam, 1966), 65.

140 *"fleeing constantly from"*: Cristóbal de Molina (of Santiago), *Relación de Muchas Cosas Acaescidas en el Perú*, in *Colección de Libros y Documentos Referentes a la Historia del Perú*, Series 1, Vol. 1 (Lima: 1916), 156.

140 *"[Manco Inca] said to the Governor"*: Pedro Sancho de la Hoz, *Relación para S.M. de lo Sucedido en la Conquista y Pacificación de Estas Provincias de la Nueva Castilla y de la Calidad de la Tierra*, in *Colección de Libros y Documentos Referentes a la Historia del Perú*, First Series, Vol. 5 (Lima: 1917), 167.

142 *"They seemed like* viracochas*"*: Inca Diego de Castro Titu Cusi Yupanqui, *Relación de la Conquista del Perú*, in Carlos Romero, *Colección de Libros y Documentos Referentes a la Historia del Perú*, First Series, Vol. 2 (Lima: 1916), 8.

145 *"in the greatest numbers"*: Miguel de Estete, *El Descubrimiento y la Conquista del Perú*, in *Boletín de la Sociedad Ecuatoriana de Estudios Históricos Americanos*, Vol. 1 (Quito: 1918), 329.

145 *"They killed three of our horses"*: Juan Ruiz de Arce, *Advertencias que Hizo el Fundador del Vínculo y Mayorazgo a Los Sucesores en Él*, in *Tres Testigos de la Conquista del Perú* (Buenos Aires: 1953), 106.

146 *"[The Spaniards] set up their camp"*: Sancho de la Hoz, *Relación*, 169.

146 *"We began marching towards the city"*: Ruiz de Arce, *Advertencias*, 107.

147 *"The Governor and his troops"*: Sancho de la Hoz, *Relación*, 169.

148 *"The Spaniards who have taken"*: Ibid., 201.

148 *"We entered [the city] without"*: Estete, *El Descubrimiento,* 329.

149 *"he was a prudent"*: Sancho de la Hoz, *Relación,* 170.

149 *"Once the fast was over"*: Ibid., 130.

150 *"They then received him"*: Francisco López de Xerez, *Verdadera Relación de la Conquista del Perú,* in *Colección de Libros y Documentos Referentes a la Historia del Perú,* First Series, Vol. 5 (Lima: 1917), 112.

151 *"[They held] huge celebrations"*: Estete, *El Descubrimiento,* 334.

152 *"Once Mass had been said"*: Sancho de la Hoz, *Relación,* 173.

153 *"And so I request and require you"*: Ronald Wright, *Stolen Continents: The Americas Through Indian Eyes Since 1492* (Boston: Houghton Mifflin, 1992), 66.

153 *"sang many songs and gave thanks"*: Estete, *El Descubrimiento,* 334.

153 *"stood up . . . and handed"*: Sancho de la Hoz, *Relación,* 173.

154 *"for himself and [his]"*: Rafael Loredo, *Los Repartos: Bocetos para la Nueva Historia del Perú* (Lima: 1958), 101.

157 *Whatever else may be said:* The anthropologist John Murra believed that the Incas were often given (unwarranted) credit for setting up a welfare system that had most likely existed long before any state governments in the Andes had appeared. Local communities were self-sufficient, Murra argued, and had always been so, and normally always cared for their poor. Nevertheless, various Spanish writers indicated that the vast storehouses of the Incas were indeed tapped for the local population if drought or other emergencies occurred. See John Murra, *The Economic Organization of the Inka State* (Greenwich: Jai, 1980), 121–37.

157 *All male heads:* Terrence N. D'Altroy, *The Incas* (Oxford: Blackwell, 2002), 266.

161 *"His captains told Quisquis"*: Francisco López de Gómara, *Historia General de las Indias,* Vol. 2, Chapter 128 (Madrid: Espasa Calpe, 1932), 46.

161 *"He [Quisquis] threatened"*: Ibid.

161 *"Quisquis heaped scorn upon them"*: Ibid.

161 *"Huaypalcon [one of Quisquis's]"*: Ibid.

162 *"summoned Luyes, a great"*: Marcos de Niza, quoted in Juan de Velasco, in *Biblioteca Ecuatoriana Mínima (Historia del Reino de Quito),* Vol. 2, Book 4, Chapter 6 (Puebla: 1961), 239.

8. PRELUDE TO A REBELLION

PAGE

165 *"As God and my conscience"*: Marcos de Niza, in Bartolomé de Las Casas, *A Short Account of the Destruction of the Indies* (London: Penguin, 1992), 113.

165 *"Men ought either"*: Niccolò Machiavelli, *Il Principe* (Oxford: Clarendon, 1891), 188.

168 *"Juan Pizarro and Gonzalo Pizarro"*: Pedro de Cieza de León, *The Discovery and Conquest of Peru* (Durham: Duke University Press, 1998), 371.

168 *"From then on there were"*: Ibid., 368.

168 *"scandalously emerged"*: Antonio de Herrera Tordesillas, *Historia General de los Hechos de los Castellanos en las Islas y Tierrafirme del Mar Océano,* Vol. 11, Decada 5, Book 7, Chapter 6 (Madrid: 1950), 129.

168 *"Juan Pizarro and Soto"*: Pedro Pizarro, *Relación del Descubrimiento y Conquista de los Reinos del Perú,* in *Colección de Documentos Inéditos para la Historia de España.* Vol. 5 (Madrid: 1844), 285.

168 *"Had the Christians fought"*: Antonio Téllez de Guzmán, in Raúl Porras Barrenechea, *Cartas del Perú,* Carta 140 (Lima: 1959), 205.

169 *"All of them were so frenzied"*: Cieza de León, *The Discovery,* 372.

171 *"a noisy group of them"*: Cristóbal de Molina (of Santiago), *Relación de Muchas Cosas Acaescidas en el Perú,* in *Colección de Libros y Documentos Referentes a la Historia del Perú,* Series 1, Vol. 1 (Lima: 1916), 159.

172 *"fine horseman and"*: Agustín de Zárate, *Historia del Descubrimiento y Conquista del Perú,* in *Biblioteca de Autores Españoles (Continuación),* Vol. 26, Book 5, Chapter 14 (Madrid: 1862), 522.

172 *"he expressed himself well"*: Ibid.

173 *"As the greed of men"*: Inca Diego de Castro Titu Cusi Yupanqui, *Relación de la Conquista del Perú,* in Carlos Romero, *Colección de Libros y Documentos Referentes a la Historia del Perú,* First Series, Vol. 2 (Lima: 1916), 29.

173 *"[who] was the daughter"*: Molina, *Relación,* 163.

174 *"Who gave you the authority"*: Titu Cusi Yupanqui, *Relación,* 50.

175 *"Come on, Mr. Manco Inca"*: Ibid., 54.

175 *"My father, seeing with"*: Ibid.

176 *"When the Spaniards saw her come out"*: Ibid., 55.

176 *"Mr. Manco Inca"*: Ibid.

176 *"Gonzalo Pizarro . . . took my wife"*: Manco Inca, quoted in Porras Barrenechea, *Cartas,* Carta 217, 337.

177 *"Those [natives] who did not"*: Molina, *Relación,* 165.

177 *"They carried off their wives"*: Ibid., 166.

177 *"[They] worked all day"*: Ibid., 171.

178 *"for no woman who was good-looking"*: Ibid., 115.

178 *"was smoldering and this was"*: Ibid., 155.

178 *"We cannot spend our entire"*: Martín de Murúa, *Historia General del Perú* (Madrid: DASTIN, 2001), 222.

179 *"I have sent for you in order"*: Cieza de León, *The Discovery,* 408.

180 *"They keep the daughters"*: Pedro de Cieza de León, *Crónica del Perú* (Tercera Parte), Chap. XC (Lima: Universidad Católica del Perú, 1989), 300.

181 *"[What] justice and reason"*: Ibid.

182 *"Manco Inca . . . sent messengers"*: Murúa, *Historia,* 220.

182 *"wretched, dark, and fearful"*: Cieza de León, *The Discovery,* 409.

182 *"dismounted from his horse"*: Ibid., 410.

183 *"[Manco] feared the enemy"*: Cieza de León, *Crónica del Perú,* Chap. xc, 302.

183 *"Gonzalo Pizarro ordered [his men]"*: Titu Cusi Yupanqui, *Relación,* 45.

183 *"I gave Juan Pizarro 1,300"*: Gonzalo Fernández de Oviedo y Valdés, *Historia General y Natural de las Indias,* in *Biblioteca de Autores Españoles,* Vol. 121, Chapter 7 (Madrid: 1959), 155.

184 *"What have I done to you?"*: Titu Cusi Yupanqui, *Relación,* 30.

184 *"Look, [Manco] Inca"*: Ibid.

185 *"They took and stole"*: Molina, *Relación,* 173.

187 *As a result, King Charles:* Rafael Varón Gabai, *Francisco Pizarro and His Brothers* (Norman: University of Oklahoma Press, 1997), 44.

190 *Hernando—the only Pizarro:* Some sources state that Francisco Pizarro may have served as a soldier in the wars in Italy, sometime before his departure for the New World in 1502, although Pizarro himself never mentioned any military service. See José Antonio del Busto Duthurburu, *Pizarro,* Vol. 1 (Lima: Ediciones Copé, 2000), 58.

191 *"Manco Inca took refuge"*: Pedro Pizarro, *Relación,* 288.

9. THE GREAT REBELLION

PAGE

193 *"The Spaniards in Peru should"*: Felipe Huamán Poma de Ayala, *Letter to a King* (New York: E. P. Dutton, 1978), 141.

193 *"So numerous were the [rebel]"*: Pedro Pizarro, *Relación del Descubrimiento y Conquista de los Reinos del Perú,* in *Colección de Documentos Inéditos para la Historia de España,* Vol. 5 (Madrid: 1844), 289.

193 *"No enterprise is more"*: Niccolò Machiavelli, *The Art of War* (Mineola: Dover Publications, 2006), 161.

196 *"My beloved sons and brothers"*: Inca Diego de Castro Titu Cusi Yupanqui, *Relación de la Conquista del Perú,* in Carlos Romero, *Colección de Libros y Documentos Referentes a la Historia del Perú,* First Series, Vol. 2 (Lima: 1916), 61.

196 *"I am determined to leave"*: *Relación del Sitio del Cuzco,* in *Colección de Libros Españoles Raros o Curiosos,* Vol. 13 (Madrid: 1879), 9.

200 *"When we returned we found"*: Pedro Pizarro, *Relación,* 289.

201 *"greater part [of the infantry]"*: Ibid., 291.

201 *"[they] pulled him off"*: *Relación de los Sucesos del Perú con Motivo de las Luchas de los Pizarros y los Almagros, hasta la Pacificación Realizada por el Licenciado La*

Gasca, in Roberto Levillier, *Los Gobernantes del Perú,* Vol. 2 (Madrid: 1921), 391.

202 *"Coriatao, Cuillas":* Titu Cusi Yupanqui, *Relación,* 65.

204 *"All these rooms":* Pedro Pizarro, *Relation of the Discovery and Conquest of the Kingdoms of Peru,* Vol. 1 (New York: Cortes Society, 1921), 273.

204 *"Over this defensive gear":* Father Bernabé Cobo, in Roland Hamilton (trans.), *Inca Religion and Customs* (Austin: University of Texas Press, 1990), 216.

205 *"Their principal weapon":* Alonzo Enríquez de Guzmán, *Libro de la Vida y Costumbres de Don Alonzo Enríquez de Guzmán,* in *Colección de Documentos Inéditos para la Historia de España,* Vol. 85 (Madrid: 1886), 270.

205 *"There was so much shouting":* Pedro Pizarro, *Relación,* 301.

205 *"baring their legs":* Titu Cusi Yupanqui, *Relación,* 67.

207 *"This [city of] Cuzco adjoins":* Pedro Pizarro, *Relación,* 292.

208 *"There were so many slingshot":* Relación de los Sucesos, 392.

208 *"Hernando Pizarro and his captains assembled":* Pedro Pizarro, *Relación,* 292.

209 *"There happened to be":* Relación del Sitio, 18.

209 *"There was so much smoke":* Cristóbal de Molina (of Santiago), *Relación de Muchas Cosas Acaescidas en el Perú,* in *Colección de Libros y Documentos Referentes a la Historia del Perú,* Series 1, Vol. 1 (Lima: 1916), 175.

210 *"It seemed to them that":* Pedro de Cieza de León, *The Discovery and Conquest of Peru* (Durham: Duke University Press, 1998), 449.

210 *"When these [native warriors] saw":* Garcilaso de la Vega, *Royal Commentaries of the Incas,* Part 2 (Austin: University of Texas Press, 1966), 799.

210 *"The Indians were supporting":* Relación del Sitio, 19.

211 *"As they [the Spaniards] knew":* Titu Cusi Yupanqui, *Relación,* 67.

211 *"On their knees":* Huamán Poma de Ayala, *Letter,* 114.

212 *"Gentlemen":* Relación del Sitio, 22.

212 *"with the men seeing their end":* Relación de los Sucesos, 392.

215 *"They have many offensive":* Enríquez de Guzmán, *Libro de la Vida,* 270.

215 *"The friendly Indians":* Garcilaso de la Vega, *Royal Commentaries,* 804.

217 *"Hernando Pizarro agreed":* Pedro Pizarro, *Relación,* 292.

218 *"On the . . . side":* Pedro Sancho de la Hoz, *Relación para S.M. de lo Sucedido en la Conquista y Pacificación de Estas Provincias de la Nueva Castilla y de la Calidad de la Tierra,* in *Colección de Libros y Documentos Referentes a la Historia del Perú,* First Series, Vol. 5 (Lima: 1917), 193–94.

218 *"emerged from the church":* Titu Cusi Yupanqui, *Relación,* 67.

219 *"We went up through Carmenca":* Pedro Pizarro, *Relación,* 293.

220 *"With at least thirty thousand":* Robert Himmerich y Valencia, "The 1536 Siege of Cuzco: An Analysis of Inca and Spanish Warfare," *Colonial Latin American Historical Review,* Vol. 7, No. 4 (Fall 1998), 393.

221 *"From a terrace"*: Pedro Pizarro, *Relación*, 293.

222 *"I, Juan Pizarro"*: Juan Pizarro, *Testamento de Juan Pizarro*, in *Una Documentación Interesante Sobre la Familia del Conquistador del Perú*, *Revista de Indias*, Año 8, Number 30, October–December (Madrid: 1947), 872–73.

223 *"There was such terrible"*: *Relación del Sitio*, 30.

224 *"In the city,"* one eyewitness: *Relación de los Sucesos*, 394.

224 *"the Spaniards were in a very difficult"*: *Relación del Sitio*, 30.

225 *"I am able to certify"*: Enríquez de Guzmán, *Libro de la Vida*, 271.

226 *"as big as a jug"*: *Relación de los Sucesos*, 395.

226 *"They fought hard that day"*: *Relación del Sitio*, 32.

227 *"[At the top of the highest tower]"*: Pedro Pizarro, *Relación*, 296.

227 *"The Indians that this* orejón*"*: Ibid.

228 *"During this time they hit him"*: *Relación del Sitio*, 32.

228 *"With his death the remainder"*: Ibid., 33.

228 *"We . . . assaulted"*: Enríquez de Guzmán, *Libro de la Vida*, 270.

IO. DEATH IN THE ANDES

PAGE

230 *"You already know how"*: Inca Diego de Castro Titu Cusi Yupanqui, *Relación de la Conquista del Perú*, in Carlos Romero, *Colección de Libros y Documentos Referentes a la Historia del Perú*, First Series, Vol. 2 (Lima: 1916), 72.

230 *"War is just when it is necessary"*: Niccolò Machiavelli, *The Prince* (New York: Bantam, 1966), 88.

230 *"Magnificent Sir"*: Alonzo Enríquez de Guzmán, in *Colección de Documentos Inéditos para la Historia de España*, Vol. 85 (Madrid: 1886), 274.

235 *"[Their strategy] was the following"*: Agustín de Zárate, quoted in John Hemming, *The Conquest of the Incas* (London: Penguin Books, 1970), 206.

235 *The tactic was one*: One of Atahualpa's generals, Quisquis, had used this strategy in 1533, having caught Hernando de Soto's vanguard by surprise at one point and killing six Spaniards and three horses in the process. General Quisquis, however, never succeeded in destroying a large Spanish force.

237 *"The Inca [General Quizo]"*: *Relación de los Sucesos del Perú con Motivo de las Luchas de los Pizarros y los Almagros, Hasta la Pacificación Realizada por el Licenciado La Gasca*, in Roberto Levillier, *Los Gobernantes del Perú*, Vol. 2 (Madrid: 1921), 396.

238 *Determined to continue his methodical*: Many of Jauja's original fifty-three *encomenderos* had relocated to Lima when Pizarro moved the capital there. See Martín de Murúa, *Historia General del Perú* (Madrid: DASTIN, 2001), 219.

238 *"[The Spaniards] received news"*: Ibid., 230.

238 *"the Indians [had] killed"*: Ibid.

238 *"enjoy the dead Spaniards' spoils"*: Ibid.

240 *"with his tail"*: Francisco López de Gómara, *Historia General de las Indias*, Vol. 2, Chapter 128 (Madrid: Espasa Calpe, 1932), 55.

240 *"and two live Spaniards"*: Titu Cusi Yupanqui, *Relación*, 74.

241 *"The Governor was greatly troubled"*: *Relación del Sitio del Cuzco*, in *Colección de Libros Españoles Raros o Curiosos*, Vol. 13 (Madrid: 1879), 76.

241 *"Most Magnificent Sir, . . . The Inca"*: Raúl Porras Barrenechea, *Cartas del Perú*, Carta 143 (Lima: 1959), 216–17.

242 *"The Lord of Cuzco"*: Ibid., 218.

243 *"[My] sons and brothers, In past"*: Titu Cusi Yupanqui, *Relación*, 72.

244 *"During this period . . . messengers"*: Ibid., 74.

246 *"One day before the Spaniards"*: Enríquez de Guzmán, *Libro de la Vida*, 276.

247 *"When we arrived we found"*: Pedro Pizarro, *Relación del Descubrimiento y Conquista de los Reinos del Perú*, in *Colección de Documentos Inéditos para la Historia de España*, Vol. 5 (Madrid: 1844), 306.

248 *"Hernando . . . said to an old man"*: *Relación del Sitio*, 48.

249 *"hurled down so many boulders"*: Pedro Pizarro, *Relación*, 306.

249 *"There is one thing about these Indians"*: Ibid., 307.

249 *"There were among the"*: *Relación de los Sucesos*, 397.

249 *"The Indians, without our knowing"*: Pedro Pizarro, *Relación*, 307.

251 *"[The conquistador Diego de Agüero]"*: López de Gómara, *Historia*, 56.

252 *"[Auxiliary] Indians"*: *Relación del Sitio*, 76.

252 *"who was very beautiful"*: Murúa, *Historia*, 231.

253 *"and destroy it"*: Ibid.

254 *"The Governor, seeing such a multitude"*: *Relación del Sitio*, 77.

255 *"determined to enter the city"*: Ibid., 79.

255 *" 'Those who accompany' "*: Ibid., 80.

255 *"produce a strong"*: Ibid.

256 *"The entire [native] army"*: Ibid.

256 *"[General Quizo] crossed"*: Ibid.

II. THE RETURN OF THE ONE-EYED CONQUEROR

PAGE

259 *"And as much friendship"*: Pedro de Cieza de León, *The Discovery and Conquest of Peru* (Durham: Duke University Press, 1998), 368.

259 *"The wish to acquire more"*: Niccolò Machiavelli, *Il Principe* (Oxford: Clarendon, 1891), 196.

262 *"My well-loved son"*: Gonzalo Fernández de Oviedo y Valdés, *Historia General y*

Natural de las Indias, in *Biblioteca de Autores Españoles,* Vol. 121, Chapter 7 (Madrid: 1959), 151.

262 *"Because if you rose up":* Ibid., 152.

264 *"[Your Sacred Majesty,] Sent":* Pedro de Oñate y Juan Gómez Malaver, *Colección de Documentos Inéditos para la Historia de Chile,* Vol. 5 (Santiago: 1889), 277.

267 *"When Rui Díaz arrived":* Pedro Pizarro, *Relación,* 314.

269 *"They treated him very cruelly":* Pedro de Cieza de León, *Guerra de las Salinas,* in *Guerras Civiles del Perú,* Vol. 1, Chapter 5 (Madrid: Libreria de la Viuda de Rico, 1899), 21.

270 *"go to the city of Cuzco":* Ibid., Chapter 6, 27.

271 *"seized their weapons":* Ibid.

273 *"I will not surrender":* Ibid., Chapter 9, 42.

274 *"Hernando Pizarro was determined":* Ibid., 44.

275 *"My dearly loved sons and brothers, I believe":* Titu Cusi Yupanqui, *Relación,* 76.

277 *"Lord Inca":* Ibid., 78.

277 *"believe a word they say":* Ibid., 79.

277 *"If by chance they make":* Ibid., 80.

277 *"Before leaving they armed":* Cieza de León, *Guerra de Las Salinas,* Chapter 21, 106.

12. IN THE REALM OF THE ANTIS

PAGE

279 *"This land of the [Antis]":* Pedro Pizarro, *Relación del Descubrimiento y Conquista de los Reinos del Perú,* in *Colección de Documentos Inéditos para la Historia de España,* Vol. 5 (Madrid: 1844), 323.

279 *"Those who dwell":* Pedro Sancho de la Hoz, *Relación para S.M. de lo Sucedido en la Conquista y Pacificación de Estas Provincias de la Nueva Castilla y de la Calidad de la Tierra,* in *Colección de Libros y Documentos Referentes a la Historia del Perú,* First Series, Vol. 5 (Lima: 1917), 189.

281 *"The Antis, who did not":* Pedro Sarmiento de Gamboa, *History of the Incas* (Mineola: Dover, 1999), 142.

282 *"The forests were very dense":* Ibid.

285 *"Sir, . . . Governor don Diego":* Raúl Porras Barrenechea, *Cartas del Perú,* Vol. 1, Carta 115 (Lima: 1959), 167 (italics mine).

288 *"Every day they sent messengers":* Pedro de Cieza de León, *Guerra de las Salinas,* in *Guerras Civiles del Perú,* Vol. 1, Chapter 21 (Madrid: Libreria de la Viuda de Rico, 1899), 107.

289 *"Orgóñez, as soon as he":* Ibid., 109.

290 *"They herded before them":* Titu Cusi Yupanqui, *Relación,* 82.

292 *"As I have experience":* Cieza de León, *Guerra de las Salinas,* Chapter 19, 97.

293 *"If all the men who"*: Ibid., Chapter 20, 102.

294 *"Raising his head"*: Ibid., Chapter 48, 266.

295 *"Governor [Almagro] had come"*: Ibid., Chapter 62, 318.

296 *"When he was a few miles"*: Ibid., Chapter 63, 323.

297 *"As news of the battle"*: Ibid., 320.

297 *"boasted a good deal"*: Ibid., Chapter 62, 318.

298 *"[The battle then began]"*: Alonzo Enríquez de Guzmán, *Libro de la Vida y Costumbres de Don Alonzo Enríquez de Guzmán,* in *Coleccion de Documentos ineditos para la Historia de España,* Vol. 85 (Madrid: 1886), 315.

299 *"Whenever Governors quarrel"*: Cieza de León, *Guerra de las Salinas,* Chapter 19, 97.

300 *"The soldiers went about"*: Ibid., Chapter 64, 329.

301 *"[Hernando Pizarro] . . . having assembled"*: Enríquez de Guzmán, in *Libro de la Vida,* 319.

302 *"Stop behaving"*: Ibid., 320.

302 *"in gold and silver"*: Ibid.

302 *"He made a great many"*: Ibid.

302 *" 'Gentlemen—doesn't' "*: Ibid., 321.

303 *" 'Commander [Pizarro, Almagro said], seeing that' "*: Ibid.

304 *"began to cry out"*: Ibid., 322.

13. VILCABAMBA: GUERRILLA CAPITAL OF THE WORLD

PAGE

305 *"Being ready to depart"*: Cristóbal de Molina (of Santiago), *Relación de Muchas Cosas Acaescidas en el Perú,* in *Colección de Libros y Documentos Referentes a la Historia del Perú,* Series 1, Vol. 1 (Lima: 1916), 183.

305 *"In the beginning"*: (Ernesto) "Che" Guevarra, *La Guerra de Guerrillas* (Havana: MINFAR, 1961), 21.

305 *"Counterinsurgency"*: United States Government, *U.S. Department of the Army Interim Counterinsurgency Operations Field Manual* (Washington: 2004), Chapter 3, 3–2.

308 *"As word spread throughout"*: Juan de Betanzos, *Narrative of the Incas* (Austin: University of Texas Press, 1996), 126.

312 *"The king, Manco Inca . . . had retired"*: Pedro de Cieza de León, *Guerra de las Salinas,* in *Guerras Civiles del Perú,* Vol. 1, Chapter 87 (Madrid: Libreria de la Viuda de Rico, 1899), 424.

312 *"When he [Pizarro] saw the letters"*: Ibid., Chapter 186, 419.

314 *"And so my father's men"*: Titu Cusi Yupanqui, *Relación de la Conquista del Perú,* in Carlos Romero, *Colección de Libros y Documentos Referentes a la Historia del Perú,* First Series, Vol. 2 (Lima: 1916), 85.

315 *"Cuzco, the 27th"*: Francisco Pizarro, *Carta de D. Francisco Pizarro a S.M.,* in *Revista de Historia de América,* No. 47 (Mexico: 1959), 154–57.

317 *"The war"*: Pedro de Cieza de León, *Guerra de Chupas,* in *Guerras Civiles del Perú,* Vol. 2, Chapter 17 (Madrid: Libreria de la Viuda de Rico, 1899), 57.

317 *"eating their corn and sheep"*: Municipal Council of Lima, *Libros de Cabildos de Lima,* Second Series, Vol. 1 (Lima: 1935), 280.

318 *If his brother took:* The new chronicle was the *Relación del Sitio del Cuzco y Principio de las Guerras Civiles del Perú Hasta la Muerte de Diego de Almagro,* written in 1539 and whose author is unknown. In *Colección de Libros Españoles Raros o Curiosos,* Vol. 13 (Madrid: 1879), 1–195.

318 *"answered angrily, saying"*: Cieza de León, *Guerra de las Salinas,* Chapter 93, 450.

318 *"Hernando Pizarro, on taking leave"*: Pedro Pizarro, *Relación del Descubrimiento y Conquista de los Reinos del Perú,* in *Colección de Documentos Inéditos para la Historia de España,* Vol. 5 (Madrid: 1844), 340.

320 *"It is believed that, once"*: *Relación del Sitio,* 194.

323 *"Those who live in the . . . [Antisuyu]"*: Blas Valera, quoted in Garcilaso de la Vega, *Royal Commentaries of the Incas,* Part 1 (Austin: University of Texas Press, 1989), 33.

324 *"[When] some twenty Spaniards"*: Pedro Pizarro, *Relación,* 342.

324 *"[My father] had heard"*: Titu Cusi Yupanqui, *Relación,* 88.

325 *"many wounded and many who"*: Pedro Pizarro, *Relación,* 343.

325 *"My father became so angry"*: Titu Cusi Yupanqui, *Relación,* 89. (Italics mine.)

326 *"was so upset by the death"*: Ibid.

327 *"At the entrance of this narrow"*: Pedro Pizarro, *Relación,* 344.

327 *"Seeing how the Spaniards"*: Ibid.

327 *"I am Manco Inca!"*: Titu Cusi Yupanqui, *Relación,* 89 (italics mine).

327 *"he and his Indians had killed"*: Mansio Serra de Leguizamón, *Papeles Varios é Información de Méritos del Marqués Don Francisco Pizarro,* in Roberto Levillier (ed.), *Gobernantes del Perú, Cartas y Papeles, Siglo XVI, Documentos del Archivo de Indias,* Vol. 2 (Madrid: 1921), 146.

328 *"She refused"*: Titu Cusi Yupanqui, *Relación,* 90.

329 *"the Inca placed no value"*: Cieza de León, *Guerra de Chupas,* Chapter 1, 5.

329 *"[As] the Inca [Manco]"*: Ibid., 4.

329 *"completely unworthy"*: Antonio de Herrera Tordesillas, *Historia General de los Hechos de los Castellanos en las Islas y Tierrafirme del Mar Océano,* Vol. 11, Decada 6, Book 7, Chapter 1 (Madrid: 1954), 77.

329 *"was not her fault"*: Martín de Murúa, *Historia General del Perú* (Madrid: DASTIN, 2001), 240.

329 *"You take your anger"*: Titu Cusi Yupanqui, *Relación,* 90.

329 *"In his anger . . . the Marquis"*: Pedro Pizarro, *Relación,* 346.

330 *"grief stricken and despondent"*: Murúa, *Historia,* 240.

14. THE LAST OF THE PIZARROS

PAGE

331 *"[The Spanish* encomenderos*] exude"*: Felipe Huamán Poma de Ayala, *Letter to a King* (New York: E. P. Dutton, 1978), 142.

331 *"Et tu, Brute?" ["And (even) you, Brutus?"]*: Shakespeare, *Julius Caesar,* Act 3, Scene 1.

331 *The son of a:* Not much is known of Francisco Pizarro's youth; it is presumed that he grew up with his mother although it is possible that he spent some time in the house of his paternal grandfather. See José Antonio del Busto Duthurburu, *Pizarro,* Vol. 1 (Lima: Ediciones Copé, 2000), 51.

334 *"I am beginning"*: Jean Orieux, *Voltaire ou la Royauté de L'Esprit* (Paris: Flammarion, 1966), 168. (Italics mine.)

334 *"The Marquis . . . [commonly]"*: Agustín de Zárate, *Historia del Descubrimiento y Conquista del Perú,* in *Biblioteca de Autores Españoles (Continuación),* Vol. 26, Book 4, Chapter 9 (Madrid: 1862), 498.

335 *"Both captains [Pizarro and Almagro]"*: Ibid., 499.

335 *"he collected what he won"*: James Lockhart, *The Men of Cajamarca: A Social and Biographical Study of the First Conquistadors of Peru* (Austin: University of Texas Press, 1972), 148.

335 *"doing what he enjoyed"*: Ibid.

335 *"in whose construction"*: Agustín de Zárate, quoted in Lockhart, *The Men of Cajamarca,* 148.

336 *"Most powerful Lords"*: Alonzo Enríquez de Guzmán, *Libro de la Vida y Costumbres de Don Alonzo Enríquez de Guzmán,* in *Colección de Documentos Inéditos para la Historia de España,* Vol. 85 (Madrid: 1886), 390–95.

338 *"so boyish"*: Pedro de Cieza de León, *Guerra de Chupas,* in *Guerras Civiles del Perú,* Vol. 2, Chapter 29 (Madrid: Libreria de la Viuda de Rico, 1899), 104.

339 *"The citizens [of Lima]"*: Ibid., Chapter 28, 98.

339 *"Poor devils"*: Zárate, *Historia,* 496.

339 *"Do not allow"*: Pedro Pizarro, *Relación del Descubrimiento y Conquista de los Reinos del Perú,* in *Colección de Documentos Inéditos para la Historia de España,* Vol. 5 (Madrid: 1844), 340.

340 *"The Indians were saying"*: Cieza de León, *Guerra de Chupas,* Chapter 28, 99.

341 *" 'Gentlemen . . . if we show' "*: Ibid., 115. (Italics mine.)

341 *"Long live the King!"*: Ibid.

341 *"Grab your weapons!"*: Ibid., 116.

342 *"great cowardice and"*: Ibid.

342 *"Don't kill"*: Pedro Pizarro, *Relación,* 354.

342 *"they killed him half"*: Ibid.

342 *"Where is the tyrant?"*: Cieza de León, *Guerra de Chupas,* Chapter 31, 112.

343 *"You can go to Hell"*: Raúl Porras Barrenechea, quoted in Antonio San Cristóbal Sebastián, *La Ficción del Esqueleto de Pizarro* (Lima: 1986), 30.

344 *"The ditch beneath"*: Cieza de León, *Guerra de Chupas,* Chapter 80, 286.

345 *"My father ordered his captains"*: Titu Cusi Yupanqui, *Relación,* 91.

347 *"My father, feeling"*: Ibid., 92.

349 *"They killed all of them very cruelly"*: Ibid., 95.

350 *"Is it possible"*: Cieza de León, in Clements Robert Markham, *The War of Quito,* Hakluyt Society, Second Series, No. 31 (London: 1913), 82.

350 *"Spain's desires"*: Gonzalo Pizarro, quoted in Sarah de Laredo (ed.), *From Panama to Peru: The Conquest of Peru by the Pizarros, the Rebellion of Gonzalo Pizarro, and the Pacification by La Gasca* (London: Maggs Bros., 1925), 328.

350 *"See here, I am to be Governor"*: Ibid., 416–18.

351 *"very gallant"*: Garcilaso de la Vega, *Royal Commentaries of the Incas,* Part 2 (Austin: University of Texas Press, 1966), 1193.

352 *"they sentenced him"*: Zárate, *Historia,* 569.

352 *"covered with an iron mesh"*: Ibid.

15. THE INCAS' LAST STAND

PAGE

353 *"Of the gods we believe"*: Thucydides, *The History of the Peloponnesian War,* quoted in Andrew Schmookler, *The Parable of the Tribes* (Boston: Houghton Mifflin, 1984), 47.

353 *Four years later:* James Lockhart, *Spanish Peru: 1532–1560* (Madison: University of Wisconsin Press, 1983), 12.

355 *"[It] is true that what"*: Baltasar Ramírez, *Descripción del Reyno del Piru, del Sitio Temple, Provincias, Obispados, y Ciudades, de los Naturales de sus Lenguas y Trage,* in Herman Trimborn, *Quellen zur Kulturgeschichte des Präkolumbischen Amerika* (Stuttgart: 1936), 26.

355 *"They grieve because"*: Hernando de Santillán, *Relación,* in Horacio Urteaga (ed.), *Colección de Libros y Documentos Referentes a la Historia del Perú,* Second Series, Vol. 9 (Lima: 1927), 73.

357 *"took it upon himself"*: Father Bernabé Cobo, in Roland Hamilton (trans.), *History of the Inca Empire* (Austin: University of Texas Press, 1983), 181.

359 *"The Indians of Peru were so idolatrous"*: Father Bernabé Cobo, in Roland Hamilton (trans.), *Inca Religion and Customs* (Austin: University of Texas Press, 1990), 3.

359 *"punished them"*: Antonio de la Calancha, *Crónica Moralizada de Antonio de la*

Calancha, Vol. 5 (Lima: Universidad Nacional Mayor de San Marcos, 1978), 1804.

360 *"the servant of God":* Ibid., 1806.

360 *"I want to take you":* Ibid., 1817.

360 *"tried to go to Vilcabamba":* Ibid.

360 *"Not used to getting":* Ibid., 1818.

361 *"[The friars] have not baptized":* Inca Diego de Castro Titu Cusi Yupanqui, *Relación de la Conquista del Perú,* in Carlos Romero, *Colección de Libros y Documentos Referentes a la Historia del Perú,* First Series, Vol. 2 (Lima: 1916), 107.

361 *"the worship, rites":* Calancha, *Crónica Moralizada,* 1820.

362 *"a temple of the Sun":* Ibid., 1800, 1827.

362 *"The Inca emperor's captains":* Ibid., 1830.

363 *"remained there all day":* Ibid., 1838.

364 *"He [Ortiz] responded":* Martín de Murúa, *Historia General del Perú* (Madrid: DASTIN, 2001), 263.

367 *"If you have faith":* Francisco de Toledo, quoted in Antonio Bautista de Salazar, *Relación Sobre el Período de Gobierno de los Virreyes Don Francisco de Toledo y Don García Hurtado de Mendoza* (1596), in Luis Torres de Mendoza (ed.), *Colección de Documentos Inéditos Relativos al Descubrimiento, Conquista, y Colonización de las Antiguas Posesiones Españolas de América y Oceanía Sacados de los Archivos del Reino y Muy Especialmente de Indias,* Vol. 8 (Madrid: 1867), 267.

367 *"Your Majesty will appreciate":* Francisco de Toledo, in Roberto Levillier, *Los Gobernantes del Perú,* Vol. 4 (Madrid: 1924), 295.

369 *"General Martín":* Murúa, *Historia,* 285.

369 *"found [Vilcabamba]":* Martín Hurtado de Arbieto, *Report to Viceroy Francisco de Toledo,* in Roberto Levillier (ed.), *Don Francisco de Toledo: Supremo Organizador del Perú, Su Vida, Su Obra (1515–1582),* Vol. 1 (Madrid: Espasa Calpe, 1935), 329.

369 *"The entire town was found":* Murúa, *Historia,* 286.

370 *"The town has, or it":* Ibid., 287.

371 *"[When] war was declared":* Martín García de Oñaz y Loyola, *Información de Servicios de Martín García de Oñaz y Loyola,* in Victor Maurtua (ed.), *Juicio de Límites Entre el Perú y Bolivia,* Vol. 7 (Barcelona: 1906), 3.

372 *"Tupac Amaru":* Ibid., 4.

372 *"five days previously":* Ibid., 291.

375 *"So many natives attended":* Antonio de Vega Loaiza, *Historia del Colegio y Universidad de San Ignacio de Loyola de la Ciudad del Cuzco* (1590), quoted in Rubén Vargas Ugarte, *Historia del Perú Virreinato (1551–1600)* (Lima: 1949), 257.

375 *"The open spaces":* Baltasar de Ocampo, in Pedro Sarmiento de Gamboa, *History of the Incas* (Mineola: Dover, 1999), 226.

375 *"a street mule"*: Ibid., 258.

375 *"The Inca was taken from"*: Ibid., 226.

376 *"Where are you going"*: Vega Loaiza, *Historia del Colegio,* quoted in Ugarte, *Historia del Perú Virreinato,* 258.

376 *"The balconies were packed"*: Murúa, *Historia,* 298.

376 *"As the multitude of Indians"*: Ibid.

376 *"let it fall"*: Ocampo, in Sarmiento de Gamboa, *History,* 227.

377 " *'Lords, you are [gathered] here from'* ": Bautista de Salazar, *Relación,* 280.

377 *"The Inca then received consolation"*: Ocampo, in Sarmiento de Gamboa, *History,* 228.

16. THE SEARCH FOR THE "LOST CITY" OF THE INCAS

PAGE

379 *"Something hidden!"*: Rudyard Kipling, "The Explorer," in *Rudyard Kipling's Verse, Inclusive Edition* (Garden City: Doubleday, Page, 1920), 120.

381 *"My previous studies"*: Hiram Bingham, *Lost City of the Incas* (London: Weidenfeld & Nicolson, 2002), 95.

381 *"A little farther up"*: Hiram Bingham, *Inca Land* (Boston: Houghton Mifflin, 1922), 165.

382 *"The Prefect was particularly"*: Hiram Bingham, *Lost City,* 95.

383 *"Magnificent precipices"*: Hiram Bingham, "The Ruins of Choqquequirau," in *American Anthropologist,* New Series, Vol. 12 (1910): 513.

383 *"At the top of the southern"*: Hiram Bingham, *Lost City,* 107.

383 *"Fortunately I had with me"*: Ibid., 106.

383 *M. Eugene de Sartiges:* Ibid., 111.

384 *"The walls . . . [at Choqquequirau]"*: Hiram Bingham, "The Ruins," in *American Anthropologist,* New Series, Vol. 12 (1910), 516.

384 *"Personally, I did"*: Hiram Bingham, "A Search for the Last Inca Capital," *Harper's,* Vol. 125, No. 749 (October 1912): 698.

385 *"down the valley by Yucay"*: Baltasar de Ocampo, *Account of the Province of Vilcapampa and a Narrative of the Inca Tupac Amaru* (1610), in Pedro Sarmiento de Gamboa, *History of the Incas* (Mineola: Dover, 1999), 220.

385 *"The fortress of Pitcos"*: Ibid., 216.

386 *"On the slopes of Choqquequirau"*: Hiram Bingham, *Inca Land,* 2.

388 *Visiting the University of Cuzco:* Albert Giesecke, *The Reminiscences of Albert A. Gieseke* (1962), in *The New York Times Oral History Program: Columbia University Collection,* Part 2, No. 71 (New York: 1963).

388 *"That there were undescribed"*: Hiram Bingham, *Inca Land,* 200.

389 *"a talkative old fellow"*: Ibid., 201.

390 *"Sub-prefect drunk"*: Alfred Bingham, *Portrait of an Explorer* (Greenwich: Triune, 2000), 4.

390 *"My Dearly Beloved"*: Ibid., 150.

391 *"Before the completion"*: Hiram Bingham, *Inca Land,* 208.

392 *"Here the river escapes"*: Hiram Bingham, *Lost City,* 173.

392 *"In the . . . power"*: Hiram Bingham, *Inca Land,* 314.

392 *"We passed an ill-kept"*: Hiram Bingham, Ibid., 215.

393 *"dawned in a cold"*: Hiram Bingham, Ibid., 315.

394 *"And no one cared"*: Hiram Bingham, *Lost City,* 175.

395 *"Shortly after noon"*: Hiram Bingham, *Inca Land,* 317.

395 *"Without the slightest expectation"*: Ibid., 319.

395 *The Sergeant was in duty:* Hiram Bingham, *Lost City,* 178.

395 *Hardly had we rounded:* Hiram Bingham, *Inca Land,* 319.

396 *The task had been too great:* Hiram Bingham, *Lost City,* 178.

396 *"another group of interesting"*: Ibid., 124.

396 *"We scrambled along"*: Ibid., 179.

397 *"Some structures of stone"*: Alfred Bingham, *Explorer,* 13.

397 *Lizarraga 1902:* Ibid., 13.

398 *"When I first saw"*: Hiram Bingham, *Inca Land,* 216.

399 *"No special things"*: Alfred Bingham, "Raiders of the Lost City," *American Heritage,* Vol. 38, No. 5 (July–August 1987): 61.

399 *"They [the Incas] guarded"*: Ocampo, *Account of the Province,* 216.

399 *"marched from Cusco down"*: Ibid., 219.

400 *"Our next stop was"*: Hiram Bingham, *Inca Land,* 235.

400 *"We . . . forded the Vilcabamba"*: Ibid., 237.

401 *We hoped it might be true:* Hiram Bingham, *Lost City,* 132.

401 *"indeed a residence"*: Ibid., 135.

401 *"the fortress of Pitcos"*: Ocampo, *Account of the Province,* 216.

402 *"Near Vitcos, in a village"*: Antonio de la Calancha, *Crónica Moralizada de Antonio de la Calancha,* Vol. 5 (Lima: Universidad Nacional Mayor de San Marcos, 1978), 1800, 1827.

402 *Questioning his:* The area was also known as Ñusta Ispanan, "the place where the Inca Princess urinates." See Vincent Lee, *Forgotten Vilcabamba* (Cortéz: Sixpac Manco, 2000), 142.

402 *"It was late on the afternoon"*: Hiram Bingham, *Lost City,* 137.

403 *"I went out collecting"*: Alfred Bingham, *Explorer,* 186.

404 *"When Don Pedro"*: Hiram Bingham, *Inca Land,* 266.

405 *"On the day following our arrival"*: Hiram Bingham, Ibid., 268.

405 *One of our informants:* Ibid., 269.

405 *Although no one at Vilcabamba:* Hiram Bingham, *Lost City,* 149.

406 *"We were conducted":* Ibid., 274.

406 *"It is difficult to describe":* Ibid., 285.

407 *"Half an hour's scramble":* Ibid., 294.

408 *"like a succession":* Ibid., 290.

408 *"the [Inca] priests":* Ibid., 297.

408 *"two long days":* Calancha, *Crónica Moralizada,* 1796, 1820.

409 *"With one exception":* Hiram Bingham, "The Ruins of Espíritu Pampa," *American Anthropologist,* Vol. 16, No. 2 (April–June 1914): 196.

409 *"Perhaps an Inca":* Hiram Bingham, *Inca Land,* 295.

409 *"Espíritu Pampa or Vilcabamba":* Alfred Bingham, *Explorer,* 196.

411 *"In its last state":* Hiram Bingham, *Inca Land,* 340.

411 *"The 'Lost City of the Incas' ":* Hiram Bingham, *Lost City of the Incas* (New York: Duell, Sloan and Pearce, 1948), third photo insert, 2.

17. VILCABAMBA REDISCOVERED

PAGE

412 *" 'Don't think you can just crash' ":* Vincent Lee, *Forgotten Vilcabamba* (Cortéz: Sixpac Manco, 2000), 52.

412 *"When night was come":* Gene Savoy, *Jamil: The Child Christ* (Reno: International Community of Christ, 1976), 106.

413 *"I have been led":* Alfred M. Bingham, *Explorer of Machu Picchu: Portrait of Hiram Bingham* (Greenwich: Triune, 2000), 40, 43.

414 *"I was a member":* Gene Savoy, *Antisuyo* (New York: Simon & Schuster, 1970), 16.

414 *"Almost thirty":* Ibid.

417 *"Was this the 'Vilcabamba Viejo' ":* Hiram Bingham, *Lost City of the Incas* (London: Weidenfeld & Nicolson, 2002), 159.

417 *"The ruins of what we now":* Ibid., 192.

418 *"the headwaters of the Pampaconas":* Victor von Hagen, *Highway of the Sun* (New York: Duell, Sloan & Pearce, 1955), 106.

418 *"This could only mean":* Ibid., 111.

418 *"Hiram Bingham, the Yale":* Savoy, *Antisuyo,* 55, 71.

419 *"The Vilcabamba plan":* Ibid.

420 *"Our mules negotiate":* Ibid., 94.

421 *"The [Inca] road we have been following":* Ibid., 103.

422 *"Bingham had reached":* Ibid., 106.

422 *"Who had used these tiles?":* Ibid., 97–98.

423 *"For the first time I realize":* Ibid., 105.

426 *"I couldn't believe all of the ruins":* Vincent Lee, interview with author, October
     2005.

427 *"A visit to his [Savoy's]":* Lee, *Forgotten Vilcabamba,* 44.

428 *"He exuded":* Ibid., 206.

428 *" 'Exploring in South' ":* Ibid., 52.

429 *" 'If you're careful' ":* Ibid.

429 *Using nothing more:* It should be mentioned that the Peruvian historian Dr. Ed-
     mundo Guillén explored the Vilcabamba Valley in 1976, a dozen years after
     Savoy's visit, and identified a number of sites mentioned by the invading
     Spaniards on their way to Vilcabamba in 1572. See Edmundo Guillén Guillén,
     La Guerra de Reconquista Inka (Lima: 1994), 206.

429 *"My barometer read":* Lee, *Forgotten Vilcabamba,* 106.

430 *"The town has, or it would":* Martín de Murúa, *Historia General del Perú* (Madrid:
     DASTIN, 2001), 287.

431 *Lee knew that:* Richard L. Burger, *Machu Picchu* (New Haven: Yale University
     Press, 2004), 30.

431 *"the only known Inca ruin":* John Hemming, quoted in Lee, *Forgotten Vilcabamba,* 17.

431 *"After more than a century":* Lee, *Forgotten Vilcabamba,* 144.

432 *"There's supposed":* Gene Savoy, quoted in Lee, *Forgotten Vilcabamba,* 52.

432 *"Continuing up the final stairway":* Ibid., 170–73.

434 *"It was a fascinating":* Ibid., 205.

434 *He couldn't pay:* Ibid., 208.

434 *" '[I] Just returned' ":* Ibid., 215.

435 *"So much for":* Vincent Lee, interview with author, October 2005.

435 *"It didn't take Sherlock":* Lee, *Forgotten Vilcabamba,* 217.

EPILOGUE: MACHU PICCHU, VILCABAMBA,
AND THE SEARCH FOR THE LOST CITIES OF THE ANDES

PAGE

437 *"If you take a map":* Vincent Lee, interview with author, October 2005.

437 *Machu Picchu is believed:* Richard L. Burger, *Machu Picchu* (New Haven: Yale Uni-
     versity Press, 2004), 24.

438 *"It is said of this Inca":* Father Bernabé Cobo, in Roland Hamilton (trans.), *Inca Re-
     ligion and Customs* (Austin: University of Texas Press, 1990), 133.

440 *"He [Pachacuti] began":* Ibid., 135–36.

441 *Archaeologists who have:* Kenneth Wright, *Machu Picchu: A Civil Engineering Marvel*
     (Reston: ASCE, 2000), 59.

441 *Once the foundation:* Ibid., 70, 77.

442 *Archaeologists recognize:* Ibid., 62.

445 *They called the site:* Archaeologists from Peru's Instituto Nacional de Cultura (INC) began a five-year excavation program in 2002 at Espíritu Pampa—the first excavations that have been conducted since the Spaniards sacked the city in 1572. Preliminary results indicate that the city was indeed built by the Incas and most likely in the mid-fifteenth century (personal communication with the INC). The INC has also cleared large portions of the city, allowing visitors for the first time to gain a glimpse of what sixteenth-century Vilcabamba must have been like prior to the city's abandonment.

447 *The anthropologist:* John H. Rowe, "Machu Picchu a la Luz de Documentos de Siglo XVII," *Histórica,* Vol. 14, No. 1 (Lima: 1990): 142.

447 *"that night, I slept":* Ibid., 140.

448 *In 1568:* Ibid., 141.

448 *"still other [ancient Inca]":* Charles Wiener, *Voyage au Perou et Bolivie* (Paris: Librarie Hachette, 1880), 345.

449 *"The professors":* Hiram Bingham, *Lost City of the Incas* (London: Weidenfeld & Nicolson, 2002), 115.

449 *"We had with us":* Ibid.

450 *"Charles Wiener":* Hiram Bingham, "The Ruins of Choqquequirau," in *American Anthropologist,* New Series, Vol. 12 (1910): 523.

450 *"This may be":* Hiram Bingham, *Machu Picchu, A Citadel of the Incas* (New Haven: Yale University Press, 1930), 1.

450 *In* Lost City of the Incas*:* In Bingham's 1930 footnote citation, he had used the original Spanish language version of Figueroa's report, published in its entirety in a 1910 German publication (*Relación del Camino e Viage que D. Rodríguez Hizo Desde la Ciudad del Cuzco a la Tierra de Guerra de Mango Ynga,* in Richard Pietschmann, *Nachrichten der Königlichen Gesellschaft der Wissenchaften zu Göttingen, Philologisch-historische Klasse aus dem Jahre 1910,* Vol. 66, No. 1 [Berlin, 1910]). In Bingham's 1948 book, *Lost City of the Incas,* however, he made use of a bad translation of Figueroa's report created in 1913 by Sir Clements Markham (Clements Markham, *The War of Quito,* Series 2, No. 31 [London: Hakluyt Society, 1913], 175). In Markham's version, he erroneously changed the word "Picho" to "Viticos," thus entirely erasing the reference to "Picho." Nevertheless, Bingham omitted even this garbled version, no doubt aware that he had referred to the missing "Picho" on page one of his 1930 monograph.

451 *"would have been fatal":* John H. Rowe, "Machu Picchu a la Luz de Documentos," 140.

451 *"Bingham was an explorer":* Anthony Brandt, "Introduction," Hiram Bingham, *Inca Land* (Washington, D.C.: National Geographic Society, 2003), xvii.

452 *"We are in a tropical"*: Gene Savoy, *Antisuyo* (New York: Simon & Schuster, 1970), 99.

455 *"It was clearly"*: Vincent Lee, telephone conversation with author, October 20, 2005.

455 *"We spotted"*: D. L. Parsell, "City Occupied by Inca Discovered on Andean Peak in Peru," *National Geographic News,* March 22, 2002.

456 *"I hadn't been"*: Gary Ziegler, telephone conversation with author, October 11, 2005.

457 *"Every generation"*: John Noble Wilford, "High in Andes, a Place That May Have Been Incas' Last Refuge," *New York Times,* March 19, 2002.

457 *"One of our wranglers"*: Gary Ziegler, telephone conversation with author, October 11, 2005.

458 *"You can't get to it"*: Ibid.

458 *"I think Cotacoca"*: Ibid.

460 *It was an achievement:* See Luis Guillermo Lumbreras, *De los Orígines de la Civilización en el Perú* (Lima: Peisa, 1988), 138.

BIBLIOGRAPHY

Early Authors

Bautista de Salazar, Antonio. *Relación sobre el Período de Gobierno de los Virreyes Don Francisco de Toledo y Don García Hurtado de Mendoza* (1596). In Luis Torres de Mendoza (ed.), *Colección de Documentos Inéditos Relativos al Descubrimiento, Conquista, y Colonización de las Antiguas Posesiones Españolas de América y Oceanía Sacados de los Archivos del Reino y muy Especialmente de Indias.* Vol 8. Madrid: 1867.

Betanzos, Juan de. Roland Hamilton (trans.). *Narrative of the Incas.* Austin: University of Texas Press, 1996.

Calancha, Antonio de la. *Crónica Moralizada de Antonio de la Calancha.* Lima: Universidad Nacional Mayor de San Marcos, 1978.

Cieza de León, Pedro de. Alexandra Parma Cook (trans.). *The Discovery and Conquest of Peru.* Durham: Duke University Press, 1998.

———. *Guerra de Chupas.* In *Guerras Civiles del Perú,* Vol. 2. Madrid: Libreria de la Viuda de Rico, 1899.

———. *Guerra de las Salinas.* In *Guerras Civiles del Perú,* Vol. 1. Madrid: Libreria de la Viuda de Rico, 1899.

Cobo, Father Bernabé. Roland Hamilton (trans.). *History of the Inca Empire.* Austin: University of Texas Press, 1979.

———. Roland Hamilton (trans.). *Inca Religion and Customs.* Austin: University of Texas Press, 1990.

Columbus, Christopher. Cecil Jane (trans.). *The Journal of Christopher Columbus.* New York: Bonanza, 1989.

Enríquez de Guzmán, Alonzo. *Libro de la Vida y Costumbres de don Alonzo Enríquez de Guzmán.* In *Colección de Documentos Inéditos para la Historia de España,* Vol. 85. Madrid: 1886.

Estete, Miguel de. *El Descubrimiento y la Conquista del Perú.* In *Boletín de la Sociedad Ecuatoriana de Estudios Históricos Americanos.* Vol. 1. Quito: 1918.

García de Oñaz y Loyola, Martín. "Información de Servicios de Martín García de Oñaz y Loyola." In Victor Maurtua (ed.), *Juicio de Límites Entre el Perú y Bolivia.* Vol. 7. Barcelona: 1906.

Garcilaso de la Vega, El Inca. Harold Livermore (trans.). *Royal Commentaries of the Incas.* Parts 1 and 2. Austin: University of Texas Press, 1966.

Herrera Tordesillas, Antonio de. *Historia General de los Hechos de los Castellanos en las Islas y Tierrafirme del Mar Océano.* Vol. 11, Decada 5, Book 7, Chapter 6. Madrid: 1950.

Hurtado de Arbieto, Martín. *Report to Viceroy Francisco de Toledo.* In Roberto Levillier (ed.), *Don Francisco de Toledo: Supremo Organizador del Perú, Su Vida, Su Obra (1515–1582).* Vol. 1. Madrid: Espasa-Calpe, 1935.

Las Casas, Bartolomé de. Nigel Griffin (trans.). *A Short Account of the Destruction of the Indies.* London: Penguin, 1992.

López de Gómara, Francisco. *Historia General de las Indias.* Madrid: Espasa-Calpe, 1932.

López de Xerez, Francisco. *Verdadera Relación de la Conquista del Perú.* In *Colección de Libros y Documentos Referentes a la Historia del Perú.* First Series, Vol 5. Lima: 1917.

Mena, Cristóbal de. In Raúl Porras Barrenechea, *Las Relaciones Primitivas de la Conquista del Perú.* Lima: 1967.

Molina (of Santiago), Cristóbal de. *Relación de Muchas Cosas Acaescidas en el Perú.* In *Colección de Libros y Documentos Referentes a la Historia del Perú.* Series 1, Vol. 1. Lima: 1916.

Murúa, Martín de. *Historia General del Perú.* Madrid: DASTIN, 2001.

Ocampo, Baltasar de. *Account of the Province of Vilcapampa and a Narrative of the Inca Tupac Amaru* (1610). In Pedro Sarmiento de Gamboa. Clements Markham (trans.). *History of the Incas.* Mineola: Dover, 1999.

Oviedo y Valdés, Gonzalo Fernández de. *Historia General y Natural de las Indias.* In *Biblioteca de Autores Españoles.* Vol. 5. Madrid: 1959.

Pizarro, Pedro. *Relación del Descubrimiento y Conquista de los Reinos del Perú.* In *Colección de Documentos Inéditos para la Historia de España.* Vol 5. Madrid: 1844.

Poma de Ayala, Felipe Huamán. Christopher Dilke (trans.). *Letter to a King.* New York: E. P. Dutton, 1978.

Ramírez, Baltasar. *Descripción del Reyno del Piru, del Sitio Temple, Provincias, Obispados, y Ciudades, de los Naturales de sus Lenguas y Trage* (1597). In Herman Trimborn, *Quellen zur Kulturgeschichte des Präkolumbischen Amerika.* Stuttgart: 1936.

Relación de los Sucesos del Perú con Motivo de las Luchas de los Pizarros y los Almagros, hasta la Pacificación Realizada por el Licenciado La Gasca. In Roberto Levillier, *Los Gobernantes del Perú.* Vol. 2. Madrid: 1921.

Relación del Sitio del Cuzco. In *Colección de Libros Españoles Raros o Curiosos.* Vol. 13. Madrid: 1879.

Rodriguez de Figueroa, Diego. "Relación del camino e viage que D. Rodríguez hizo desde la ciudad del Cuzco a la tierra de guerra de mango ynga" (1565). In Richard Pietschmann, *Nachrichten der Königlichen Gesellschaft der Wissenchaften zu*

Göttingen, Philologisch-historische Klasse aus dem Jahre 1910. Vol. 66, No. 1. Berlin, 1910.

Ruiz de Arce, Juan. *Advertencias que Hizo el Fundador del Vínculo y Mayorazgo a Los Sucesores en él.* In *Tres Testigos de la Conquista del Perú.* Buenos Aires: 1953.

Sancho de la Hoz, Pedro. *Relación para S. M. de lo Sucedido en la Conquista y Pacificación de estas Provincias de la Nueva Castilla y de la Calidad de la Tierra.* In *Colección de Libros y Documentos Referentes a la Historia del Perú.* First Series, Vol. 5. Lima: 1917.

Santillán, Hernando de. *Relación del Origen, Descendencia, Política, y Gobierno de los Incas.* In Horacio Urteaga (ed.), *Colección de Libros y Documentos Referentes a la Historia del Perú.* Second Series, Vol. 9. Lima: 1927.

Sarmiento de Gamboa, Pedro. Clements Markham (trans.). *History of the Incas.* Mineola: Dover, 1999.

Titu Cusi Yupanqui, Inca Diego de Castro. *Relación de la Conquista del Perú.* In Carlos Romero, *Colección de Libros y Documentos Referentes a la Historia del Perú.* First Series, Vol. 2. Lima: 1916.

Zárate, Agustín de. *Historia del Descubrimiento y Conquista del Perú.* In *Biblioteca de Autores Españoles* (Continuación). Vol. 26. Madrid: 1862.

Modern Authors

Bauer, Brian S. *Ancient Cuzco: Heartland of the Inca.* Austin: University of Texas Press, 2004.

Bingham, Alfred M. *Portrait of an Explorer.* Greenwich: Triune Books, 2000.

———. "Raiders of the Lost City," *American Heritage Magazine.* Vol. 38, Issue 5. July/August 1987.

Bingham, Hiram. "Along the Uncharted Pampaconas." *Harper's Magazine.* Vol. 129. 1914.

———. "The Discovery of Machu Picchu." *Harper's Magazine.* Vol. 126. 1913.

———. *Inca Land.* Boston: Houghton Mifflin, 1922.

———. "In the Wonderland of Peru." *National Geographic Magazine.* Vol. 24. No. 4. 1913.

———. *Lost City of the Incas.* London: Weidenfeld & Nicolson, 2002.

———. *Machu Picchu, A Citadel of the Incas.* New Haven: Yale University Press, 1930.

———. "The Ruins of Espiritu Pampa." *American Anthropologist.* Vol. 16. No. 2. 1914.

———. "A Search for the Last Inca Capital." *Harper's Magazine.* Vol. 125. 1912.

———. "Vitcos, the Last Inca Capital." *Proceedings of the American Antiquarian Society.* Vol. 22. 1912.

Burger, Richard L. *Machu Picchu: Unveiling the Mystery of the Incas.* New Haven: Yale University Press, 2004.

Busto Duthurburu, José Antonio del. *Pizarro.* Vols. 1 & 2. Lima: Ediciones Copé, 2000.

Cook, Noble David. *Born to Die: Disease and New World Conquest, 1492–1650*. Cambridge: Cambridge University Press, 1998.

Covey, R. Alan. *How the Incas Built their Heartland: State Formation and the Innovation of Imperial Strategies in the Sacred Valley, Peru.* Ann Arbor: University of Michigan Press, 2006.

D'Altroy, Terrence. *The Incas.* Malden: Blackwell Publishers, 2002.

Diamond, Jared. *Guns, Germs, and Steel: The Fates of Human Societies.* New York: W. W. Norton, 1999.

Frost, Peter. "Lost Outpost of the Inca." *National Geographic Magazine.* Feb. 2004.

Giesecke, Albert. "The Reminiscences of Albert A. Giesecke" (1962). In *The New York Times Oral History Program: Columbia University Collection.* Part 2, No. 71. New York: 1963.

Guillén-Guillén, Edmundo. *La Guerra de Reconquista Inka.* Lima: 1994.

Hemming, John. *The Conquest of the Incas.* New York: Harcourt, 1970.

Himmerich y Valencia, Robert. "The 1536 Siege of Cuzco: An Analysis of Inca and Spanish Warfare," in *Colonial Latin American Historical Review* 7:4. Fall, 1998.

Kamen, Henry. *How Spain Became a World Power, 1492–1763.* New York: HarperCollins, 2003.

Kubler, George. "A Peruvian Chief of State: Manco Inca (1515–1545)." *The Hispanic American Historical Review.* Vol. 24. 1944.

Lee, Vincent. *Forgotten Vilcabamba.* Cortez: Sixpac Manco Publications, 2000.

Lockhart, James. *The Men of Cajamarca: a Social and Biographical Study of the First Conquerors of Peru.* Austin: University of Texas Press, 1972.

———. *Spanish Peru: 1532–1560: A Colonial Society.* Madison: University of Wisconsin Press. 1968.

Lumbreras, Luis Guillermo. *De los Orígines de la Civilización en el Perú.* Lima: Peisa, 1988.

Murra, John V. *The Economic Organization of the Inka State.* In *Research in Economic Anthropology.* Supplement 1. Greewich: Cornell University, 1980.

Pérez-Mallaína, Pablo E. *Spain's Men of the Sea: Daily Life on the Indies Fleets in the Sixteenth Century.* Baltimore: Johns Hopkins University Press, 1998.

Porras Barrenechea, Raúl. *Cartas del Perú.* Lima: 1959.

———. *Los Cronistas del Perú.* Lima: Biblioteca Clásicos del Perú 2, 1986.

Prescott, William Hickling. *History of the Conquest of Peru.* New York: Harper & Brothers, 1847.

Reinhard, Johan. *Machu Picchu: The Sacred Center.* Lima: Nuevas Imágines, 1991.

Restall, Matthew. *Seven Myths of the Spanish Conquest.* Oxford: Oxford University Press, 2003.

Rowe, John H. "Machu Picchu a la Luz de Documentos de Siglo XVII," *Histórica* 14 (1), Lima: 1990.

Savoy, Gene. *Antisuyo*. New York: Simon and Schuster, 1970.

————. *Jamil: the Child Christ*. Reno: The International Community of Christ, 1976.

————. *Project "X": The Search for the Secrets of Immortality*. New York: Bobbs-Merrill, 1977.

Stirling, Stuart. *The Last Conquistador: Mansio Serra de Leguizamón and the Conquest of the Incas*. Phoenix Mill: Sutton Publishing, 1999.

————. *Pizarro: Conqueror of the Inca*. London: Sutton Publishing, 2006.

Thomson, Hugh. *The White Rock: An Exploration of the Inca Heartland*. London: Orion Books, 2001.

Varón Gabai, Rafael. *Francisco Pizarro and His Brothers: The Illusion of Power in Sixteenth-Century Peru*. Norman: University of Oklahoma Press, 1997.

von Hagen, Victor. *Highway of the Sun*. New York: Duell, Sloan & Pearce, 1955.

Wiener, Charles. *Voyage au Perou et Bolivie*. Paris: Librarie Hachette, 1880.

Wolf, Eric. *Peasants*. Englewood Cliffs: Prentice Hall, 1966.

Wright, Kenneth. *Machu Picchu: A Civil Engineering Marvel*. Reston: ASCE Press, 2000.

Wright, Ronald. *Stolen Continents: The Americas Through Indian Eyes Since 1492*. Boston: Houghton Mifflin, 1992.

INDEX

Page numbers in *italics* refer to illustrations and maps.